Life Span Motor Development

FOURTH EDITION

Kathleen M. Haywood, PhD
University of Missouri at St. Louis

Nancy Getchell, PhD
University of Delaware

HUMAN KINETICS

Library of Congress Cataloging-in-Publication Data

Haywood, Kathleen.
 Life span motor development / Kathleen M. Haywood, Nancy Getchell.-- 4th ed.
   p. cm.
 Includes bibliographical references and index.
 ISBN 0-7360-5574-6 (hbk.)
 1. Motor ability in children. 2. Motor ability. I. Getchell, Nancy, 1963- II. Title.
 RJ133.H34 2005
 612.7'6--dc22

                            2004013158

ISBN: 0-7360-5574-6

The Web addresses cited in this text were current as of July 22, 2004, unless otherwise noted.

Acquisitions Editor: Judy Patterson Wright, PhD; **Developmental Editors:** Maggie Schwarzentraub and Anne Rogers; **Assistant Editor:** Amanda M. Eastin; **Copyeditor:** Patricia MacDonald; **Proofreader:** Erin Cler; **Indexer:** Marie Rizzo, **Permission Manager:** Dalene Reeder; **Graphic Designer:** Robert Reuther; **Graphic Artist:** Denise Lowry; **Photo Manager:** Kareema McLendon; **Cover Designer:** Keith Blomberg; **Photographer (cover):** PhotoDisc; **Photographer (interior):** Tom Roberts, except where otherwise noted; photos on pages 16, 17, 18, 75, 85, 138, 140, 165, 198, 286, 325 provided by the authors; **Art Manager:** Kelly Hendren; **Illustrator:** Mic Greenberg; **Printer:** Edwards Brothers

Printed in the United States of America   10 9 8 7 6 5 4 3 2 1

Human Kinetics
Web site: www.HumanKinetics.com

United States: Human Kinetics, P.O. Box 5076, Champaign, IL 61825-5076
800-747-4457
e-mail: humank@hkusa.com

Canada: Human Kinetics, 475 Devonshire Road Unit 100, Windsor, ON N8Y 2L5
800-465-7301 (in Canada only)
e-mail: orders@hkcanada.com

Europe: Human Kinetics, 107 Bradford Road, Stanningley, Leeds LS28 6AT, United Kingdom
+44 (0) 113 255 5665
e-mail: hk@hkeurope.com

Australia: Human Kinetics, 57A Price Avenue, Lower Mitcham, South Australia 5062
08 8277 1555
e-mail: liaw@hkaustralia.com_

New Zealand: Human Kinetics, Division of Sports Distributors NZ Ltd., P.O. Box 300 226 Albany, North Shore City, Auckland
0064 9 448 1207
e-mail: blairc@hknewz.com

In memory of Lolas E. Halverson,
who inspired many in the field of motor development

Contents

PART III **Development of Motor Skills Across the Life Span** **65**

PART VI Interaction of Exercise and Structural Constraints **231**

Preface

Every day, you move. This doesn't happen in a vacuum, though. Every movement you make occurs within your surrounding environment, whether at home, in the gymnasium, or on a ball field. You also move for a purpose—the activities or tasks you perform have specific requirements or rules. The way you move now has changed a great deal from your earliest movements and will keep changing throughout your life. This is the essence of the study of motor development: observing how movements change across the life span, then determining why they change. In this edition, we focus on explanations about why movements change to include the individual, environment, and task, as well as interactions among the three elements. This will provide you with a more complete view of motor development across the life span.

Understanding life span motor development will assist your progress in movement-related fields. You will learn what motor development is as well as the theoretical and historical roots of the field. You will observe the many facets related to development of movement skills such as growth, aging, and perception. In addition, you will discover how different constraints or factors can encourage or discourage different movements—perhaps in ways you hadn't thought about yet!

Who can benefit from reading this text? Many different people who are interested in movement can benefit. Educators at all levels—from early childhood educators to gerontologists—can enhance their teaching by becoming aware of different systems of the body and how these change over time. Those in the health sciences, such as physical and occupational therapists, will find tools that assist them in observing patterns of movement. Those in exercise science will receive guidance from the detailed descriptions and explanations of developmental physical fitness and processes underlying change. However, you don't need extensive experience in movement studies to profit from this text. Because all people go through these developmental changes during their lives, all people can benefit from understanding more about motor development.

FEATURES NEW TO THIS EDITION

New to the fourth edition of *Life Span Motor Development* is the delivery method of the third edition's learning activities that had previously been available under separate cover. Some of these learning activities are now placed at the ends of the text chapters. Others, particularly those involving observation of individuals, are available in the Student Resource section at www.HumanKinetics.com/LifeSpanMotorDevelopment. Some of these lab activities direct you to view specific video segments on the CD-ROM disk that is now included with this text. The video clips allow the written word to come alive in real movement and real opportunities to observe development in individuals of many ages. The text also directs you to specific video segments if you would like to view performers at different developmental levels without doing a lab activity.

We have marked the text in this manner to direct you to the online lab activities and the CD-ROM video clips.

Also in this fourth edition, the text has been streamlined to make it easier to review all of the topics within a semester. Our assumption is that most readers have a general background in prenatal development and genetics and the functioning of the senses from prior study in biology. Hence the third edition discussion of these topics was shortened or dropped for the fourth edition. We also assume that many readers have a basic understanding of the principles of motion and stability, and therefore, we dropped the related chapter for this edition. For those readers who would benefit from a review of those principles and their application to motor development, the third edition chapter "Principles of Motion and Stability" is available on the Web site at www.HumanKinetics.com/LifeSpanMotorDevelopment. We recommend these readers review the chapter before taking up chapter 5 in the fourth edition.

CONTINUING FEATURES

The fourth edition of *Life Span Motor Development* continues several important features of previous editions.

▲ **Real-life experiences.** To remind you that motor development occurs outside of a textbook, we begin each chapter with a real-life experience—something we found in newspapers, magazines, or on the Internet.

▲ **Chapter objectives.** We also include chapter objectives, which list the most important concepts you should learn and understand within the chapter.

▲ **Running glossary.** A running glossary appears in the margins throughout each chapter. The running glossary words are highlighted in the text with a second color. Some terms don't require a margin definition because they are defined sufficiently in the text. Those words are boldfaced to help you locate them.

▲ **Assessment elements.** Most chapters contain an assessment element that will aid you in observing and assessing some aspect of motor development.

▲ **Reflection questions.** We incorporate reflection questions into the chapters, identified by the icon to the left. These questions challenge you to reflect on discussions or apply information to a problem of practice.

▲ **Concept elements.** Concept elements appear periodically throughout the chapter to point out the theme of a discussion amidst chapter details. These elements are identified by the icon to the left.

▲ **Summary and synthesis.** Each chapter ends with a summary and synthesis, which helps you to integrate the different concepts you've learned throughout the chapter into a constraints perspective.

▲ **Discussion questions and learning activities.** In addition to discussion questions at the end of each chapter, we also include one or more learning activities. These activities provide additional opportunities for you to investigate motor development through Internet research or observation.

▲ **National standards.** The fourth edition continues to assist students in meeting national standards. The text and the approach are consistent with the newly revised guidelines for minimum competencies drafted by the Motor Development Academy of the National Association for Sport and Physical Education, American Alliance for Health, Physical Education, Recreation and Dance.

ORGANIZATION

Part I of the text contains two short chapters on fundamental concepts. Chapter 1 defines terms and methods of study in motor development, and chapter 2 briefly introduces theoretical approaches to study. Most important, part I introduces the model around which the entire text is organized: the model of constraints. Part II then takes up physical growth and aging as the significant change in individual structural constraints over the life span.

Part III describes motor development over the life span. The chapters are organized by the type of skill, and the changes in each skill are discussed throughout the life span. The CD-ROM video segments supplement the figure drawings included in these chapters.

The remaining parts focus on additional constraints that influence the movement arising from the interaction of these constraints, emphasizing those that change over the life span. Part IV focuses on sensation and perception as they interact with action; and part V focuses on social, cultural, and psychosocial influences as well as the impact of knowledge on movement. Part VI looks at four important components of physical fitness and how these constrain movement as individuals change over the life span. Many professionals apply adult training principles to children, youths, and older adults without appreciating their unique constraints. These chapters present developmentally appropriate guidelines. For those concerned about the obesity epidemic among children and youth, part VI contains useful information.

The culminating chapter encourages readers to apply what they have learned about changing constraints and their interactions to actual people and situations. We expanded this chapter to provide enhanced opportunities for readers to reflect on all they have learned about motor development over the life span and then to use that knowledge in specific cases.

SUPPLEMENTS AND ANCILLARIES

We continue to make available an instructor guide for the fourth edition of *Life Span Motor Development*. This guide includes fundamental concepts for each of the textbook's parts as well as chapter overviews, classroom activities, background readings, and a test bank with different types of questions. Also, we've included a Microsoft PowerPoint graphics package that may be adapted as desired to suit each instructor's lecture content and style. For a review of these instructor resources, go to www.HumanKinetics.com/LifeSpanMotorDevelopment. Student resources located at the same Web site include the online student labs and the additional biomechanics material ("Principles of Motion and Stability" from the third edition).

USING THE CD-ROM

The CD-ROM included with this text contains more than 130 video clips for assessing developmental levels. The individuals in the video clips on your CD-ROM should be very much like those you might observe in the role of teacher, coach, or therapist. They were not chosen as "special" models for the CD-ROM, and we did not ask them to perform in any special way or look like someone in particular. Also, we tried to film them in realistic settings rather than in a research laboratory. Since they are "real" performers, you might find that some of them do not fit clearly into a developmental level or do not look exactly like the drawings in your text. This is exactly what you find in realistic settings!

Sometimes placing an individual into a developmental level involves watching several times over and making a best judgment. We recall an expert colleague, struggling over whether a child should be placed into developmental level 2 or developmental level 3, saying, "This child is exactly in developmental level 2.5!" (In these cases, it may be best to assign a "plus" or "minus" to the developmental level in question.) Always keep in mind that you can make note of the unique characteristics demonstrated by an individual, even while making your best judgment on where they should be placed in the developmental sequence of movement characteristics.

While we intend for the video clips to show "real" performers, they are indeed video clips and you should feel free to take advantage of this. Watch them in slow motion, stop the action in critical places, or change the rate of speed so that you can see the critical positions and relationships of the limbs and trunk. This is actually the preferred way to categorize performers into developmental levels until you have the experience to do it "live" and in real time!

What Is on the CD?

The clips are organized into two sections: Lab-Specific Videos and Auxiliary Videos.

As you read through the chapters, you will be referred to various lab activities that can be accessed by going to the Student Resource section at www.HumanKinetics.com/LifeSpanMotorDevelopment. The lab instructions will direct you to view video clips that are located in the Lab-Specific Videos on the CD-ROM. Some of these video clips, grouped under Set A: Guided Assessments, include scripts that will guide you through the observation plans (in chapters 6, 7, and 8 of this textbook) to the appropriate category of each developmental sequence. Other video clips are grouped together as Practice Assessments; these clips do not have scripts. You will need to work through the observation plan on your own to categorize the developmental sequence for each individual. Your instructor may assign these clips for tests, homework assignments, or in conjunction with a lab activity. Instructors will find our categorizations of the developmental sequences for Lab-Specific Videos in the instructor guide.

In addition to referencing a specific lab activity, the text occasionally directs you to view video segments in the Auxiliary Videos section on the CD-ROM; these video clips are useful for those who would like to view performers at different developmental levels without doing a lab activity.

Getting Started

To begin, follow the getting started procedures included in the CD-ROM Instructions on the last page of this textbook. Using the CD-ROM does not require a password or access code; simply insert the *Life Span Motor Development* CD-ROM. Once the program is started, click the Begin button from the title screen.

You can choose between Lab-Specific videos and Auxiliary videos. Remember that the videos grouped under Set A: Guided Assessments in the Lab-Specific videos include scripts at the bottom of the screen. These scripts will guide you in assessing the developmental levels of the performers in the video clips. You may have to scroll down to see the scripts; the CD-ROM Instructions page at the back of this book as well as the Help section on the CD-ROM itself has instructions for changing the resolution of your computer monitor so that you can see more of the screen.

The CD-ROM Instructions page (and the Help section on the CD-ROM) also include information on navigating from clip to clip and using the video player.

Acknowledgments

The *Life Span Motor Development* project began in 1983. Each edition and each addition to what has now become an instructional package reflects the contributions of many. We would like to acknowledge all of those contributions here. Any undertaking this ambitious could only be completed with the help and support of those contributing their unique expertise and talents. Certainly this fourth edition builds on the previous editions, and contributions anywhere along the way have made this work what it is today.

First, we would like to extend our appreciation to those who appeared in photographs: Jennifer, Douglas, and Michael Imergoot; Laura, Christina, and Matthew Haywood; Anna Tramelli; Cathy Lewis; Jules Mommaerts; and Connor Miller.

Next, we would like to acknowledge friends who took some of the photographs: Brian Speicher, Dr. William Long, Rosa Angulo-Barroso, PhD, and Susan Miller, PhD. Mary Ann Roberton, PhD, Ann VanSant, PhD, John Haubenstricker, PhD, B.D. Ulrich, PhD, and Jill Whitall, PhD, contributed film tracings from which some of the art was drawn. Additional thanks to Mary Ann Roberton for supplying a great picture of Hal in action.

The content of *Life Span Motor Development* touches many subdisciplines and specialty areas of study. Our thanks are extended to John Strupel, MD, Elizabeth Sweeney, BSN, Bruce Clark, PhD, Jane Clark, PhD, Maureen Weiss, PhD, Kathleen Williams, PhD, Ann VanSant, and Mary Ann Roberton who were all kind enough to read sections of the text or contribute information.

Ann Wagner and Cynthia Haywood Kerkemeyer helped by keyboarding and checking parts of the earlier editions, and Lynn Imergoot, Linda Gagen, Patricia Hanna, and Cathy Lewis were kind enough to help with the index of an earlier edition.

We especially thank our many colleagues in motor development who have made helpful suggestions along the way. Their dedication to helping students of motor development appreciate this area of study is always an inspiration. Last but not least, we appreciate the patience and dedication of our team at Human Kinetics. In particular, we would like to thank Maggie Schwarzentraub for keeping us on track through the vast amount of details on the fourth edition, and Judy Wright, who has helped nurture *Life Span Motor Development* since the first edition.

Credits

Figure 1.6 Reprinted, by permission, from A. Maclaren (Ed.), 1967, *Advances in reproductive physiology,* Vol. 2 (London: Elek Books).

Figure 2.4 Adapted, by permission, from E. Thelen, B.D., Ulrich, and J. L. Jensen, 1989, The developmental origins of locomotion. In *Development of posture and gait across the life span,* edited by M.H. Woolacott and A. Shumway-Cook (Columbia, SC: University of South Carolina Press), 28.

Table 3.1 Adapted, by permission, from P.S. Timiras, 1972, *Developmental physiology and aging* (New York; Macmillan), 63–64.

Figure 3.3 Reprinted, by permission, from P. Rhodes, 1969, *Reproductive physiology for medical students* (London: J. & A. Churchill Ltd.), 191.

Figure 3.4, a and b Data from the National Center for Health Statistics in collaboration with the National Center for Chronic Disease Prevention and Health Promotion 2000. Adapted from www.cdc.gov/nchs/about/major/nhanes/growthcharts.clinical_charts.htm.

Figure 3.5, a and b Data from the National Center for Health Statistics in collaboration with the National Center for Chronic Disease Prevention and Health Promotion 2000. Adapted from www.cdc.gov/nchs/about/major/nhanes/growthcharts.clinical_charts.htm.

Figure 3.6 Reprinted, by permission, from J.M. Tanner, R.H. Whitehouse, and M. Takaishi, 1966, "Standards from birth to maturity for height, weight, height velocity, and weight velocity: British children, 1965–1," *Archives of Disease in Childhood* 41: 454–471.

Figure 3.7 Adapted, by permission, from P.S. Timiras, 1972, *Developmental physiology and aging* (New York: Macmillan), 284.

Figure 3.8, a through c Reprinted, by permission, from A. Maclaren (Ed.), 1967, *Advances in reproductive physiology,* Vol. 2 (London: Elek Books).

Figure 3.10 Reprinted, by permission, from W.W. Spirduso, 1995, *Physical dimensions of aging* (Champaign, IL: Human Kinetics), 59. Adapted, by permission, from A.R. Frisancho, 1990, *Anthropometric standards for the assessment of growth and nutritional status* (Ann Arbor: University of Michigan Press), 27.

Figure 3.11 Reprinted, by permission, from J.F. Aloia, 1989, *Osteoporosis* (Champaign, IL: Human Kinetics).

Figure 3.12 Reprinted, by permission, from W.W. Spirduso, 1995, *Physical dimensions of aging* (Champaign, IL: Human Kinetics), 59. Adapted, by permission, from A.R. Frisancho, 1990, *Anthropometric standards for the assessment of growth and nutritional status* (Ann Arbor: University of Michigan Press), 27.

Figure 4.1 Used by permission of Carolina Biological Supply Company.

Figure 4.3 Reprinted from J.J. Pritchard, 1979, *Bones,* 2nd ed. (Burlington, NC: Carolina Biology Reader Series). Used by permission of Carolina Biological Supply Company.

Figure 4.4 Reprinted, by permission, from S.I. Pyle, 1971, *A radiographic standard of reference for the growing hand and wrist* (Chicago: Year Book Medical), 53, 73. Copyright Bolton-Brush Growth Study – B.H. Broadbent D.D.S.

Figure 4.5 Reprinted, by permission, from P.A. Houglum, 2001, *Therapeutic exercise for athletic injuries* (Champaign, IL: Human Kinetics), 168.

Figure 4.7 Reprinted, by permission, from National Strength and Conditioning Association, 2000, *Essentials of strength training and conditioning* (Champaign, IL: Human Kinetics), 116.

Figure 4.8 From R.M. Malina and C. Bouchard, 1988, Subcutaneous fat distribution during growth. In *Fat distribution during growth and later health outcomes,* edited by C. Bouchard and F.E. Johnston (New York: Liss), 70. Copyright © 1988 by Alan R. Liss, Inc. Reprinted by permission of Wiley-Liss, a division of John Wiley and Sons, Inc.

Figure 4.9 Reprinted, by permission, from National Strength and Conditioning Association, 2000, *Essentials of strength training and conditioning* (Champaign, IL: Human Kinetics), 93.

Figure 4.10 Reprinted, by permission, from J.H. Wilmore and D.L. Costill, 1999, *Physiology of sport and exercise,* 2nd ed. (Champaign, IL: Human Kinetics), 55.

Figure 4.11 Adapted, by permission, from S.J. Shultz, P.A. Houglum, and D.H. Perrin, 2000, *Assessment of athletic injuries* (Champaign, IL: Human Kinetics), 347.

Figure 4.12 Reprinted, by permission, from J.H. Wilmore and D.L. Costill, 1999, *Physiology of sport and exercise,* 2nd ed. (Champaign, IL: Human Kinetics), 67.

Figure 5.5 From B.I. Bertenthal, J.L. Rose, and D.L. Bai, 1997, "Perception-action coupling in the development of visual control of posture," *Journal of Experimental Psychology: Human Perception and Performance* 23: 1631–1634, fig. 1. Copyright © by the American Psychological Association. Reprinted with permission.

Tables 6.2 and 6.3 Reprinted, by permission, from R.L. Wickstrom, 1983, *Fundamental motor patterns,* 3rd ed. (Philadelphia: Lea & Febiger) 68.

Table 6.4 Adapted, by permission, from V. Seefeldt, S. Reuschlein and P. Vogel, 1972, "Sequencing motor skills within the physical education curriculum." Paper presented to the annual conference of the American Association for Health, Physical Education and Recreation.

Table 6.5 Adapted, by permission, from J.E. Clark and S.J. Phillips, 1985, A developmental sequence of the standing long jump. In *Motor development: Current selected research* Vol. 1, edited by J.E. Clark and J.H. Humphrey (Princeton Book), 76-77. Copyright 1985 by Princeton Book Company, Publishers.

Table 6.6 Reprinted, by permission, from M.A. Roberton and L.E. Halverson, 1984, *Developing children—Their changing movement* (Philadelphia: Lea & Febiger), 56, 63.

Figure 6.2, a and c Drawn from film tracings taken in the Motor Development and Child Study Laboratory, University of Wisconsin–Madison and now available from the Motor Development Film Collection, Kinesiology Division, Bowling Green State University.

Figure 6.2b Adapted from R.L. Wickstrom, 1983, *Fundamental motor patterns,* 3rd ed. (Philadelphia: Lea & Febiger), 29. By permission of M.A. Roberton.

Figure 6.4a Drawn from film tracings taken in the Motor Development and Child Study Laboratory, University of Wisconsin–Madison and now available from the Motor Development Film Collection, Kinesiology Division, Bowling Green State University.

Figure 6.4b Redrawn from R.L. Wickstrom, 1983, *Fundamental motor patterns,* 3rd ed. (Philadelphia: Lea & Febiger). By permission of M.A. Roberton.

Figure 6.5 Adapted from R.L. Wickstrom, 1983, *Fundamental motor patterns,* 3rd ed. (Philadelphia: Lea & Febiger), 29.

Figure 6.6 Adapted from R.L. Wickstrom, 1983, *Fundamental motor patterns,* 3rd ed. (Philadelphia: Lea & Febiger), 74. By permission of M.A. Roberton.

Figure 6.7 Drawn from film tracings taken in the Motor Development and Child Study Laboratory, University of Wisconsin–Madison and now available from the Motor Development Film Collection, Kinesiology Division, Bowling Green State University.

Figure 6.9 Adapted, from R.L. Wickstrom, 1983, *Fundamental motor patterns,* 3rd ed. (Philadelphia: Lea & Febiger), 77. By permission of M.A. Roberton.

Figure 6.11 through 6.14 Drawn from film tracings taken in the Motor Development and Child Study Laboratory, University of Wisconsin–Madison and now available from the Motor Development Film Collection, Kinesiology Division, Bowling Green State University.

Figure 6.15 Reprinted, by permission, from L. Halverson and K. Williams, 1985, "Developmental sequences for hopping over distance: A prelongitudinal screening," *Research Quarterly for Exercise and Sport* 56: 38.

Figure 6.16, a and b Adapted from J.E. Clark and J. Whitall, 1989, Changing patterns of locomotion: From walking to skipping. In *Development of posture and gait across the life span,* edited by M.H. Woollacott and A. Shumway-Cook (Columbia, SC: University of South Carolina Press), 132.

Figure 6.17 Adapted from J.E. Clark and J. Whitall, 1989, Changing patterns of locomotion: From walking to skipping. In *Development of posture and gait across the life span,* edited by M.H. Woollacott and A. Shumway-Cook (Columbia, SC: University of South Carolina Press), 132.

Figures 7.1 through 7.14 Drawn from film tracings taken in the Motor Development and Child Study Laboratory, University of Wisconsin–Madison and now available from the Motor Development Film Collection, Kinesiology Division, Bowling Green State University.

Tables 7.1and 7.2 Reprinted, by permission, from M.A. Roberton and L.E. Halverson, 1984, *Developing children—Their changing movement* (Philadelphia: Lea & Febiger), 103, 106–107, 118, 123.

Table 7.4 The preparatory trunk action and the parenthetical information in Step 3 of Racket Action are reprinted, by permission, from J.A. Messick, 1991, "Prelongitudinal screening of hypothesized developmental sequences for the overhead tennis serve in experienced tennis player 9–19 years of age," *Research Quarterly for Exercise and Sport* 62: 249–256. The remaining components are reprinted, by permission, from S. Langendorfer, 1987, Prelongitudinal screening of overarm striking development performed under two environmental condition. In *Advances in motor development research,* Vol. 1, edited by J.E. Clark and J.H. Humphrey (New York: AMS Press), 26.

Figure in chapter 7 (pp. 116-117) Line art drawn from film tracings taken in the Motor Development and Child Study Laboratory, University of Wisconsin–Madison and now available from the Motor Development Film Collection, Kinesiology Division, Bowling Green State University.

Table 8.1 Reprinted with permission from *Research Quarterly for Exercise and Sport,* Vol. 62, pp. 249–256, Copyright 1991 by the American Alliance for Health, Physical Education, Recreation and Dance, 1900 Association Drive, Reston, VA 20191.

Figure 8.1 Reprinted, by permission, from H.M. Halverson, 1931, "An experimental study of prehension in infants by means of systematic cinema records," *Genetic Psychology Monographs* 10: 212–215, a publication of the Helen Dwight Reid Educational Foundation.

Figure 8.3 Reprinted, by permission, from L. Hay, 1990, Developmental changes in eye–hand coordination behaviors: Preprogramming versus feedback control. In *Development of eye–hand coordination across the life span,* edited by C. Bard, M. Fleury, and L. Hay (Columbia, SC: University of South Carolina Press), 235.

Figure 8.5 Drawn from film tracings taken in the Motor Development and Child Study Laboratory, University of Wisconsin–Madison and now available from the Motor Development Film Collection, Kinesiology Division, Bowling Green State University.

Figure 8.7 From P. McLeod and Z. Dienes, 1996, "Do fielders know where to go to catch the ball or only how to get there?" *Journal of Experimental Psychology: Human Perception and Performance* 22: 541. Copyright © 1996 by the American Psychological Association. Adapted with permission.

Figure 8.8 From "Intercepting moving objects during self-motion," *Journal of Motor Behavior* 31: 57 (1999) by M. Lenoir et al. Adapted with permission of the Helen Dwight Reid Educational Foundation. Published by Heldref Publications, 1319 Eighteenth St., NW, Washington, DC 20036-1892. Copyright © 1999.

Figure 9.1 Reprinted from G.H. Sage, 1984, *Motor learning and control: A neuropsychological approach* (Dubuque, IA: Brown), 111. Reproduced with permission of The McGraw-Hill Companies.

Figure 9.4 From *Perception: The world transformed* by Lloyd Kaufman, copyright 1979 by Oxford University Press. Used by permission of Oxford University Press, Inc.

Figure 9.5 Selected material from the Figure-Ground Perception Test of the Sensory Integration and Praxis Tests copyright © 1972 by Western Psychological Services. Reprinted by permission of the publisher, Western Psychological Services, 12031 Wilshire Boulevard, Los Angeles, California, 90025, U.S.A. Not to be reprinted in whole or in part for any additional purpose without the expressed, written permission of the publisher. All rights reserved.

Figure 9.6 From "Studies in perceptual development: II. Part-whole perception," by D. Elkind, R.R. Koegler, and E. Go, 1964, *Child Development,* 35, p. 84. Reprinted with permission.

Figure 9.7 Reprinted, by permission, from R. L. Gregory, 1972, *Eye and brain,* 2nd ed. (New York: World University Library, McGraw-Hill), 151.

Figure 9.10 Reprinted, by permission, from *A Primer of Infant Development* by T.G.R. Bower, 1977 (San Francisco: W.H. Freeman). Copyright 1977.

Figure 10.1 From R. Held and A. Hein, 1963, "Movement-produced stimulation in the development of visually guided behavior," *Journal of Comparative and Physiological Psychology* 56: 872–876, fig. 1. Copyright © 1963 by the American Psychological Association. Reprinted with permission.

Figure 10.2 Reprinted, by permission, from R. Kermoian and J.J. Campos, 1988, "Locomotor experience: A facilitator of spatial cognitive development," *Child Development* 59: 911. © The Society for Research in Child Development, Inc.

Figure 12.4 Reprinted, by permission, from J.L. Duda and M.K. Tappe, 1989, Personal investment in exercise among adults: The examination of age and gender-related differences in motivational orientation. In *Aging and motor behavior,* edited by A.C. Ostrow (Dubuque, IA: Benchmark Press), 246, 248.

Figure 12.5 Reprinted, by permission, from J.L. Duda and M.K. Tappe, 1989, Personal investment in exercise among adults: The examination of age and gender-related differences in motivational orientation. In *Aging and motor behavior,* edited by A.C. Ostrow (Dubuque, IA: Benchmark Press), 246, 248.

Figure 13.4 Reprinted, by permission, from R.E. Dustman, R.O. Ruhling, E.M. Russell, D.E. Shearer, H.W. Bonekat, J.W. Shigeoka, J.S. Woods, and D.C. Bradford, 1989, Aerobic exercise training and improved neuropsychological function of older individuals. In *Aging and motor behavior,* edited by A.C. Ostrow (Indianapolis: Benchmark Press), 75.

Figure 14.1, a and b Reprinted, by permission, R.M. Malina and C. Bouchard, 1991, *Growth, maturation, and physical activity* (Champaign, IL: Human Kinetics), 222.

Figure 14.2, a and b Reprinted, by permission, from O. Bar-Or, 1983, *Pediatric sports medicine for the practitioner* (New York: Springer), 4, 5.

Figure 14.4, a and b Adapted, by permission, from R. J. Shephard, 1982, *Physical activity and growth* (Chicago: Year Book Medical), 70.

Figure 14.5 Redrawn from B.J. Sharkey, 1990, *Physiology of fitness,* 3rd ed. (Champaign, IL: Human Kinetics), 282.

Figure 14.6, a and b Reprinted, by permission, from B.A. Stamford, 1986, Exercise and the elderly. In *Exercise and sport sciences reviews,* Vol. 16, edited by K.B. Pandolf (New York: Macmillan), 344. Reproduced with permission of The McGraw-Hill Companies. Data plotted are from (a) Dehn and Bruce 1972; (b) Dill et al. 1967; (c) Hollman 1965, all cited in Dehn and Bruce 1972; and (d) Dehn and Bruce 1972.

Figure 14.7 Reprinted, by permission, from L.D. Zwiren, 1989, "Anaerobic and aerobic capacities of children," *Pediatric Exercise Science* 1: 40.

Figure 14.8 Reprinted, by permission, from W.W. Spirduso, 1995, *Physical dimensions of aging* (Champaign, IL: Human Kinetics), 108.

Figures 15.1 and 15.2 Adapted, by permission, from R.J. Shepard, 1982, *Physical activity and growth* (Chicago: Year Book Medical), 80, 104.

Figure 15.3 Reprinted from A. Aniansson, M. Hedberg, G.B. Henning, and G. Grimby, 1986, "Muscle morphology, enzymatic activity, and muscle strength in elderly men: A follow-up study," *Muscle & Nerve* 9: 588. Copyright © 1986 by John Wiley & Sons. Reprinted by permission of John Wiley & Sons, Inc.

Figures 15.5 and 15.6 Reprinted, by permission, from R.M. Malina and C. Bouchard, 1991, *Growth, maturation, and physical activity* (Champaign, IL: Human Kinetics), 385, 386.

Figure 15.7 Adapted with permission from *Research Quarterly for Exercise and Sport,* 39: 30–32, copyright 1950 by the American Alliance for Health, Physical Education, Recreation and Dance, 1900 Assoiation Drive, Reston, VA 20191.

Figure 15.9 Reprinted, by permission, from J. Simons, G.P. Beunen, R. Renso, A.L.M. Claessens, B. Vanreusel, and J.A.V. Lefevre, 1990, *Growth and fitness of flemish girls* (Champaign, IL: Human Kinetics), 118.

Figure 16.2 From J. Parizkova, 1977, *Body fat and physical fitness* (The Hague, The Netherlands: Martinus Nijhoff B.V.). Copyright © 1977 by Kluwer Academic Publishers. Reprinted with kind permission from Kluwer Academic Publishers.

Figure 16.3 From J. Parizkova, 1977, *Body fat and physical fitness* (The Hague, The Netherlands: Martinus Nijhoff B.V.), 130. Copyright © 1977 by Kluwer Academic Publishers. Reprinted with kind permission from Kluwer Academic Publishers.

Figures 17.2 and 17.3 Reprinted, by permission, from J. Herkowitz, 1978, Developmental task analysis: The design of movement experiences and evaluation of motor development status. In *Motor development,* edited by M.V. Ridenour (Princeton, NJ: Princeton Book), 141, 149.

Figure B.1 Reprinted by permission from G.A. Bray, 1992, "Pathophysiology of obesity," *American Journal of Clinical Nutrition* 55 (2 Suppl), 4885-4995.

Figure B.2, a and b Adapted from www.cdc.gov/nchs/about/major/nhanes/growthcharts/clinical_charts.htm. Developed by the National Center for Health Statistics in collaboration with the National Center for Chronic Disease Prevention and Health Promotion (2000).

Figure C.1, a and b Reprinted from www.cdc.gov/nchs/about/major/nhanes/growthcharts/clinical_charts.htm. Developed by the National Center for Health Statistics in collaboration with the National Center for Chronic Disease Prevention and Health Promotion (2000).

PART I

Introduction to Motor Development

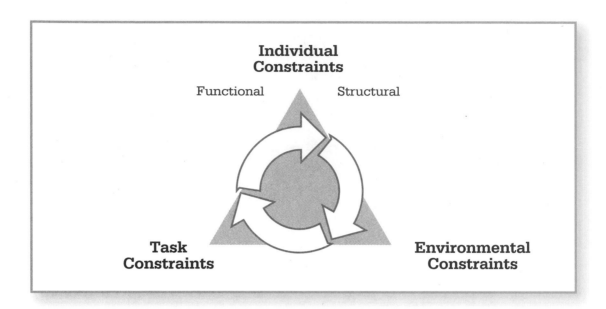

You probably have experienced joining a club or organization and going to a meeting knowing few other members and little about the bylaws and procedures of the organization. In your first few meetings you faced the task of getting to know members' names and something about each of them. You also tried to learn how the organization worked, how it determined its tasks or activities, and how it carried out those tasks.

Your early readings in motor development serve much the same function. You must learn basic terms so that you can read about motor development and converse with others about this field of study. You must learn the scope of the field and how it goes about researching the developmental aspects of motor behavior. It benefits you to learn how information is pictured or presented within the field of study. All of these topics represent the goal of chapter 1.

You also need to know the various perspectives that professionals in the field of motor development have adopted to view motor behavior and interpret studies of that behavior. Often, what is known within a discipline of study is a function of the perspective adopted by those studying in the field. This is the goal of chapter 2.

Most important, part I introduces you to a model that will be used to guide your study of motor development. The model is pictured here. Chapter 1 describes its various parts and what it depicts. This model will give you a way of organizing new pieces of information. Moreover, it will give you a means to analyze and think about issues and problems in motor development. It will be useful not only in the short term of your study of motor development but also in the long term as you move into a professional position or interact with family and friends regarding their motor skills.

Suggested Reading

Clark, J.E., & Whitall, J. (1989). What is motor development? The lessons of history. *Quest, 41,* 183–202.

Thelen, E. (1995). Motor development: A new synthesis. *American Psychologist, 50,* 79–95.

Thelen, E., & Ulrich, B. (1991). Hidden skills. *Monographs of the Society for Research in Child Development, 56,* Serial No. 233.

VanSant, A.F. (1989). A life span concept of motor development. *Quest, 41,* 224–234.

Fundamental Concepts

chapter 1

EXTRA!!! The Times EXTRA!!!

MOTOR DEVELOPMENT NEWS HOUR

Imagine that a TV network wants to start a weekly prime-time news hour on motor development. What types of story segments would you see? Here might be the promotion lines for some interesting stories:

Girls On Boys' Teams Stirs Controversy
A debate over girls playing on boys' wrestling teams and whether boys' "physiological advantages" place the girls at risk of injury

Education Helps Prevent Falls in Older People
A review of a study in which physical therapists taught adults over age 70 how to avoid falls

Gauging Use of Drugs, Alcohol in Pregnancy
A report on drug and alcohol use by mothers and the effect on their babies both before and after birth, including abnormal physical development and developmental delays

School Board Proposes Dropping Physical Education
Board members suggest physical education costs more than it's worth because some children are born athletes and some are not

As these story segments indicate, motor development covers a broad range of topics related to the physical self and to movement abilities (figure 1.1). Also, it concerns individuals of any age, from birth across the entire life span to old age. Movement abilities of interest could be those used in sport and dance, or they could be the everyday movements allowing people to walk to the grocery store or type on keyboards. Individuals of interest could be healthy, young, old, living with disabilities, or in rehabilitation.

Who would watch our fictitious motor development program? These topics affect everyone to some extent. All of us want our children to grow up healthy and able to reach their full potential, for adults to work and play as they desire, and for retirees to enjoy a quality life. We all have a developmental perspective. Many professionals would watch. Educators, especially physical and early childhood educators, are interested in developmentally appropriate practices. Therapists want to know the factors that affect movement abilities. Engineers and designers want to make appropriately sized and arranged living spaces, control panels, work equipment, sport equipment, and transportation vehicles. Health care providers want to promote movement and exercise as a means to a healthy lifestyle. Clearly, motor development interests many people for many reasons.

The range of topics, issues, and concerns related to motor development would draw quite an audience. Indeed, even though we rarely see a television program devoted solely to motor development (although Discovery Health airs a program dedicated to infancy and early development), many of the stories on radio, on television, in newspapers, and in magazines are related to physical growth and aging and motor development. Whether for sport, dance, or everyday tasks, we value our ability to move and interact with our environment throughout our entire lives.

Figure 1.1 Do boys' physiological advantages place girls at risk of injury in wrestling?
© Associated Press

 ## *Chapter Objectives*

This chapter will

▲ define motor development,

▲ distinguish developmental issues from other issues,

▲ describe some of the basic tools used by researchers in motor development, and

▲ introduce a model to guide our discussion of motor development.

DEFINING MOTOR DEVELOPMENT

Our imaginary television program's story segments have probably given you a rough idea of what motor development is. Let's now be more exact and give the field some boundaries, much as a television producer would do in order to decide which story segments are appropriate for the motor development program and which are not.

Development has several defining characteristics. First, development is a continuous process of change in functional capacity. Think of functional capacity as the capability to exist—live, move, work—within the real world. This is a cumulative process. Living organisms are always developing, but the amount of change may be more noticeable, or less noticeable, at various points in the life span.

Second, development is related to (but not dependent on) age. As age advances, development proceeds. However, development can be faster or slower at different times, and rates of development can differ among individuals of the same age. Individuals do not necessarily advance in age and advance in development at the same rate.

Third, development is sequential change. One step leads to the next step in an orderly and irreversible fashion. This change is the result of interactions within the individual and interactions between the individual and the environment. All individuals of a species undergo predictable patterns of development, but the result of development is always a group of unique individuals.

Individuals function in a variety of arenas, including physical, social, cognitive, and psychological. Hence, we use terms such as **cognitive development** or **social development** to address the process of change in particular arenas. Social scientists often specialize in the study of one aspect of development.

We use the term motor development to refer to the development of movement abilities. Those who study motor development study developmental change in movement behavior and the factors underlying those changes. This includes both the process of change and the resultant movement outcome. Not all change in movement is development. For example, if a tennis teacher elicits a change in a student's forehand stroke by changing the student's grip on the racket, we do not call the change motor development. Rather, we use the term motor learning for movement changes that are relatively permanent but related to experience rather than age. We use the term **motor behavior** when we prefer not to distinguish between motor learning and motor development, or when we want to include both.

Motor control refers to the nervous system's control of the muscles to permit skilled and coordinated movements. In recent years, researchers in motor development and in motor control have found much in common. Understanding how the nervous system and movement abilities change with age informs our knowledge of motor control, and so we now see much overlap in motor development and control research.

Undoubtedly, you have heard the term *development* paired with *growth*, as in "growth and development." **Physical growth** is a quantitative increase in size or magnitude. Living organisms experience a period of growth in physical size. For humans this growth period starts with conception and ends in late adolescence or the early 20s. Changes in the size of tissues after the physical growth period (e.g., an increase in muscle mass with resistance training) are described with other terms. The phrase *growth and development* thus includes change in both size and functional capacity.

The term *maturation* also is paired with the term *growth*, but it is not the same as development. **Maturation** connotes progress toward physical maturity, the state of optimal functional integration of an individual's body systems and the ability to reproduce. Development continues long after physical maturity is reached.

Physiological change does not stop at the end of the physical growth period. Rather, it can occur throughout life. Physical change tends to be slower after the growth period but nevertheless remains prominent. The term aging can be used in a broad sense to refer to the process of growing older regardless of chronological age, or the changes that occur with the passage of time that lead to a loss of adaptability or function and eventually to death (Spirduso, 1995).

The physiological processes of growth and aging fall on a continuum of life span development. Although some motor development students might be more interested in one portion of the continuum than another, motor development as a field still concerns

Motor development is the sequential, continuous age-related process whereby movement behavior changes.

Motor learning refers to the relatively permanent gains in motor skill capability associated with practice or experience (Schmidt & Lee, 1999).

Motor control is the study of the neural, physical, and behavioral aspects of movement (Schmidt & Lee, 1999).

Physical growth is an increase in size or body mass resulting from an increase in complete, already formed body parts (Timiras, 1972).

Physical or physiological maturation is a qualitative advance in biological makeup and may refer to cell, organ, or system advancement in biochemical composition rather than to size alone (Teeple, 1978).

Aging is the process occurring with the passage of time, leading to loss of adaptability or full function and eventually to death (Spirduso, 1995).

? Scan a daily newspaper for stories related to motor development. What criteria did you use to determine whether a story fit this topic?

change in movement across the life span. Understanding what drives change in one part of the life span often helps us understand change in another part of the life span. That process of examining change is part of adopting a developmental perspective.

A MODEL FOR STUDYING MOTOR DEVELOPMENT

It is useful to have a model or plan for studying the change in movement that occurs over the life span. A model helps us include all the relevant factors in our observation of motor behavior. This is particularly true as we think about the complexity of motor skills and how our skills change over the life span. For this textbook, we adopted a model associated with a contemporary theoretical approach known as the ecological perspective (see chapter 2). We find that this model helps us make sense of developmental changes by providing a framework for observing change. We believe this model—Newell's constraints model—will help you better understand motor development across the life span.

Newell's Model

Karl Newell (1986) suggested that movements arise from the interactions of the organism, the environment in which the movement occurs, and the task to be undertaken. If any of these three factors change, the resultant movement changes. We can picture the three factors as points on a triangle with a circle of arrows representing their interaction (figure 1.2). Because we are concerned only with human movement here, we use the term *individual* instead of *organism*. In short, to understand movement, we must consider the relationships between or among the characteristics of the individual mover, his surroundings, and the purpose or reasons for his moving. From the interaction of all these characteristics, specific movements emerge.

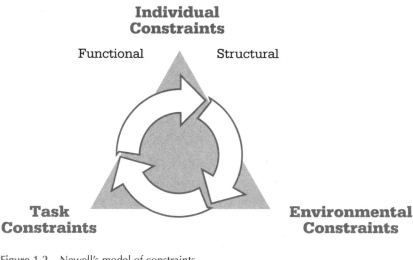

Individual Constraints

Functional   Structural

Task Constraints

Environmental Constraints

Figure 1.2 Newell's model of constraints.

Picture the different ways an individual can walk: a toddler taking her first steps, a child walking in deep sand, an adult moving across an icy patch, and an older adult trying to catch a bus. These examples illustrate that changing one of the factors often results in a change in the interaction with one or both of the other factors; hence, a different way of walking arises from the interaction. For example, being barefoot or in rubber-soled shoes might not make a difference in your walking across a dry tile floor. Your walk might change notably if the floor is wet and slippery. The *interaction* of individual, task, and environment changes the movement.

Why is Newell's model so helpful in studying motor development? Because the individual is always undergoing age-related changes. This constantly changes the interaction with environment and task and subsequently changes the way individuals move. In other words, constraints not only affect each other but can also be affected and change based on their interactions. If the environment or the task, or both, also changes, the interaction is changed to an even greater extent. Newell's model reflects the dynamic, constantly changing interactions in motor development.

Newell calls the three factors we placed on the points of our triangle **constraints.** A constraint is somewhat like a restraint—it *limits or discourages*, in this case, movement—but at the same time it *permits or encourages* other movements. It's important not to consider constraints as negative or bad. Constraints simply provide channels from which movements most easily emerge. A riverbed acts as a constraint. It restrains the river water from flowing anywhere and everywhere, but it also channels it to follow a specific path. Movement constraints are characteristics that shape movement. They restrain and channel movement to a particular time and place in space; that is, they give movement a particular form.

Individual constraints, the top point on our triangle, are a person's own unique physical and mental characteristics. For example, height, limb length, strength, and motivation can all influence the way individuals move. Consider the swimmer with a disability in figure 1.3. The disability constrains, but does not prevent, this individual's ability to swim; it simply modifies the form with which the swimmer performs his strokes. Individual constraints are either structural or functional.

▲ **Structural constraints** are slow to change but obviously do change with growth and aging. Examples include height, weight, muscle mass, and leg length. As we discuss these changes throughout the text, we will see how structural factors constrain movement.

▲ **Functional constraints** can change in a short time. Examples include motivation, memory, and attentional focus. You might be motivated to run several miles in cool weather but not in hot, humid weather. This functional constraint shapes your movement to running, walking, or even sitting.

For many professionals, it is important to know whether the student's or client's movement is being shaped by structural or functional constraints. This provides information regarding how much a movement could change in a short time and if a change in an environmental or task constraint would be in order to modify the resultant movements. For example, knowing that young volleyball players cannot block a ball at the net because they are not yet at their adult height would lead a youth sport organizer to change the task by using a lower net height.

Environmental constraints exist outside the body, as a property of the world around us. They are global, not task specific, and can be physical or sociocultural. Physical environmental constraints are characteristics of the environment, such as temperature, amount of light, humidity, gravity, and the surfaces of floors and walls (figure 1.4). Notice that in the earlier example, the functional constraint of motivation actually interacted with environmental constraints, in this case temperature and humidity, to constrain movement.

Figure 1.3 This swimmer's disabled limb is a structural constraint that gives rise to a different swimming movement from that of someone without a disabled limb.

A **constraint** is a characteristic of the individual, environment, or task that either facilitates or restricts movements.

Individual constraints are a person's or organism's own unique physical and mental characteristics.

Structural constraints are individual constraints related to the body's structure.

Functional constraints are individual constraints related to behavioral function.

Environmental constraints are constraints related to the world around us.

Our sociocultural environment can be a strong force in encouraging or discouraging behaviors, including movement behaviors. A most obvious example is how the change of sociocultural environment in Western society has changed the involvement of girls and women in sport over the past three decades. In the 1950s, society did not expect girls to participate in sport. As a result girls were channeled away from sport.

Task constraints are also external to the body. They are the goals, rules, and equipment we use. For example, using a strung racket rather than a wood paddle changes the game played on an enclosed (racquetball) court. Notice that our youth sport organizer mentioned previously, by lowering net height, used the interaction of a structural individual constraint (body

Figure 1.4 A hot and humid environment can constrain the movements of this runner.

Task constraints are goals undertaken within rules and choices of equipment.

height) and a task constraint to allow a certain movement (blocking) to emerge in the game played by our young volleyball players. Examine figure 1.5. You can probably imagine many of the task constraints in this situation. The kicker must pass the ball to a teammate, while protecting the ball from a defender.

Throughout this discussion of motor development we demonstrate how changing individual, environmental, and task constraints shapes the movement that arises from their interaction. Newell's model will guide us in identifying the developmental factors affecting movements, help us create developmentally appropriate tasks and environments, and help us understand individual movers as different from group norms or averages.

Figure 1.5 This soccer player's task is to dribble or pass so that his team maintains control of the ball.

Changing Views on the Role of Constraints

It is important to recognize that in the history of motor development research, certain researchers and practitioners focused primarily on individual factors to the exclusion of others. For example, in the 1940s it was assumed that an individual constraint, specifically the structural constraint of the nervous system alone, shaped movement in infants and children (see chapter 2). Later, in the 1960s, developmentalists commonly believed that environmental and task more than individual constraints shaped movement. Only recently have motor developmentalists focused on all three types of constraints simultaneously.

Obviously, when one or two types of constraints are deemphasized, so is the rich effect of the three constraints interacting to shape movement. This limits the resulting view of the emerging movement. In our survey of motor development we identify the effects of these various viewpoints on the importance of the three constraints. Sometimes what we know about an aspect of motor development is influenced by the perspective of the researcher who studied that behavior. It is much like seeing the color of a flower change as we try on sunglasses with different colored lenses. We might "color" our conclusions about motor development as we emphasize one type of constraint and deemphasize other types.

Newell's model is more global than most models previously used in the study of motor development. We can better account for the complexity of age-related change in movement with this model through the interactions of individual, environment, and task. Keep the model in mind throughout our survey of motor development.

? Knowing how height and body size change with growth, how would you adapt the game of basketball (especially the **task** through the equipment used) so that movements (shooting, dribbling, passing) remain nearly the same during the growth years?

HOW DO WE KNOW IT IS CHANGE?

We've established that age-related change is fundamental in the study of motor development and the developmental perspective. Developmentalists are focused on change. How do we know, though, that a change is age-related and not a fluctuation of behavior or a product of our measuring instrument? One way to determine developmental change is to carefully observe individuals' movements, then describe differences between people or observation times.

You can gain some experience in observing movement by downloading Lab 1.1 Observation As a Tool of Inquiry from the Student Resources section at www.HumanKinetics.com/LifeSpanMotorDevelopment.

In addition, behavioral scientists use statistical techniques that can identify significant change. We sometimes discuss these in the context of a research study. For now, let's focus on the straightforward technique of picturing change by graphing an aspect of development over time. We can then see whether a trend is *emerging*.

Picturing Change

When we picture age-related measurements by graphing, we traditionally put time or age on the horizontal axis. It can be measured in days, weeks, months, years, or decades, depending on our frame of reference. A measurement of interest in infancy might be plotted in days or weeks, but a measurement of interest over the life span may be plotted in years or decades.

The measurement is plotted on the vertical axis. Usually we arrange the measurements so that "more" or "faster" or "more advanced" is higher on the scale. A typical graph of the measurement of growth in childhood would look like figure 1.6. It is common to take a measurement periodically and plot its value at a given chronological age. We assume that change has occurred consistently in the time between our measurements, so we often connect our data points to make a line. When we graph change using a developmental perspective, we should not make the assumption that "more" is always "better." Individuals move in a variety of ways that are qualitatively different. Some ways of moving may result in longer throws or faster runs, but that does not imply that children who do not move this way are in error or are wrong. It simply means that these children move at a different or lower developmental level.

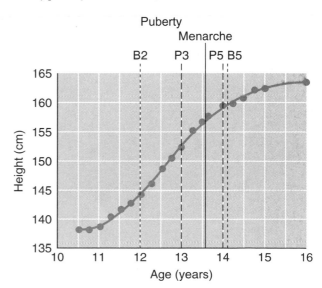

Figure 1.6 A typical graphical representation of growth in childhood.

Reprinted from Maclaren 1967.

Can You Tell It's Developmental? A Litmus Test

Armed with definitions of motor development and motor learning, you still might find it difficult to distinguish whether a particular behavior is a matter of learning or development. Mary Ann Roberton (1988, p. 130) suggests that the answers to three questions help us distinguish developmental issues and topics:

1. Are we interested in what behavior is like now and why the behavior is the way it is?

2. Are we interested in what behavior was like before our present observation, and why?

3. Are we interested in how the present behavior is going to change in the future, and why?

Students of motor learning and motor development answer "Yes" to the first question, but only developmentalists answer "Yes" to the second and third questions. Motor learning specialists are concerned with making changes that bring about a relatively permanent change in behavior within a short time. Motor developmentalists focus on a longer time during which a sequence of changes occurs. Developmentalists might introduce a change in a task or environment to make either or both age-appropriate, but developmentalists realize that the task or environment will have to change again and again as individuals age and change.

Researching Developmental Change

A **longitudinal research study** is a study in which the same individual or group is observed performing the same tasks or behaviors repetitively, over a long time.

A **cross-sectional research study** is a study in which developmental change is implied by observing individuals or groups of varying ages at one point in time.

In the study of development, we ideally watch an individual or group actually change with age for the entire length of the period we are interested in. This is termed a **longitudinal research study.** The difficulty here comes when our frame of reference is years or decades. For example, a teacher may be interested in the changes in locomotor skills across childhood. We can see that individual researchers might be able to do only a few such studies in their lifetimes. This would not inform us about motor development very quickly!

Researchers have several ways of learning more in a shorter time. One of these techniques is termed **cross-sectional research study.** In a cross-sectional study, researchers select individuals or groups at chosen points within the age span of interest. For example, researchers interested in change during adolescence would measure a group of 13-year-olds, a group of 15-year-olds, a group of 17-year-olds, and so on. When the measurements of each group are plotted, we assume that any observed change reflects the same change we would observe in a single group over the whole time period. The advantage of this method is that researchers can study development in a short time. The disadvantage is that we never really observe change; we merely infer it from age group differences. If something else is responsible for the age group differences, we could be fooled into thinking the differences were caused by developmental change.

Consider the example of tricycles. At one time, all tricycles were metal and shaped so that the seat was relatively high off the ground. Children under 3 years of age had difficulty just getting on the tricycle. Then someone invented the Big Wheel tricycle with the large front wheel and the seat only inches off the ground. Toddlers can easily sit on this vehicle.

Let's pretend that a researcher did a cross-sectional study on coordination of the cycling motion of the legs in toddlers 1.5, 2.0, 2.5, and 3.0 years of age. The study was done just 1 year after the Big Wheel tricycle came on the market. The researcher observed that toddlers 2.5 and 3.0 years of age could coordinate this movement and concluded that approximately 2.5 years was the age toddlers could coordinate the cycling movement of the legs. However, what if the researcher had done the study a year earlier, before any of the children would have been on a Big Wheel? The researcher might have observed that none of the children could coordinate the cycling movement since none would have been able to ride the high-seat tricycle. The researcher would then have concluded that this coordination developed after the age of 3.0 years.

The invention of the Big Wheel gave a **cohort,** or mini-generation, of toddlers earlier practice in coordinating the cycling movement. Older cohorts could not practice the movement until they were big enough to get up on the higher tricycle. So, one cohort had an experience that another did not. Such a cohort difference can fool researchers in a cross-sectional study because researchers would associate performance differences among age groups with age alone and not factors such as exposure to new inventions.

However, researchers cleverly devised a way to identify cohort influences, while at the same time conduct developmental research in less time than required by a longitudinal study. They do it by combining longitudinal and cross-sectional studies. In effect, they conduct several small longitudinal studies with subjects at different ages of the period of interest. For example, in the first year they would measure three groups of children, one at 4 years of age, one at 6 years of age, and one at 8 years of age. Notice that if the researchers stopped here, they would have a cross-sectional study. Instead, a year later they measure all the children again. This time they are 5, 7, and 9 years of age. They do the same thing another year later when the children are 6, 8, and 10. So, they have done three small longitudinal studies: one cohort that was the original 4-year-olds at 4, 5, and 6; one cohort that was the original 6-year-olds at 6, 7, and 8; and one cohort that was the original 7-year-olds at 7, 8, and 9.

Information is available about ages 4 through 9, but only 2 years were needed to obtain the information. What about the possibility of cohort differences? Note that the mini-longitudinal studies cover overlapping ages. Two groups were tested at age 6, and two groups were tested at ages 7 and 8. If performance of the different cohorts is the same at a given age, then it is likely that cohort differences are not present. If the cohorts perform differently at the same age, cohort influences might well be present. This type of design is called a **mixed-longitudinal,** or **sequential, research study.**

New students of motor development can tell whether a research study is developmental or not by considering the design of the study. The study is developmental if the design is longitudinal, cross-sectional, or sequential (figure 1.7). Research studies that focus on one age group at one point in time are not developmental.

To gain experience graphing and interpreting developmental data, download Lab 1.2 Graphing Developmental Data from the Student Resources section at www.HumanKinetics.com/LifeSpanMotorDevelopment.

> A **cohort** is a group whose members share a common characteristic, such as age or experience.

> A **mixed-longitudinal,** or **sequential, research study** is a study in which several age groups are observed repetitively over a shorter time span, permitting observation of an age span that is longer than the observation period.

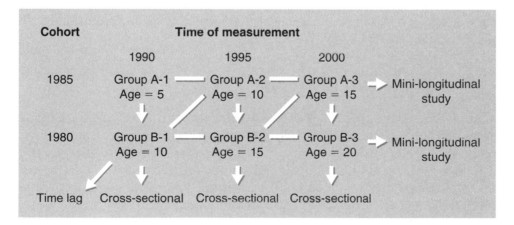

Figure 1.7 A model of sequential research design. Note that each row is a short longitudinal study and that each column is a small cross-sectional study. The time-lag component of sequential research design, shown by the diagonal lines, allows comparison of groups from different cohorts but at the same chronological age, thus identifying any cohort differences. Ages 5 to 20 can be studied in 10 years—1990 to 2000.

A DEVELOPMENTAL PARADOX: UNIVERSALITY VERSUS VARIABILITY

A paradox in development centers on the universality of development as opposed to individual differences (Thelen & Ulrich, 1991). Individuals in a species show great similarity in their development in that they go through many of the same (stereotypical) changes. You have heard reference to "stages of development." Stages, of course, describe the emergence of universal behaviors. Those who anticipate working with individuals in a particular age range often are interested in the behaviors typical of those in that range.

However, individual differences in development exist. Any individual we might observe is more likely to be above or below average, or to achieve a milestone earlier or later than average, than to be exactly average. In addition, children can arrive at the same point in development by very different pathways (Siegler & Jenkins, 1989). All individuals, even identical twins, have different experiences. Those who work with any group of individuals supposedly at the same stage of development are usually amazed by the variability within the group.

Developmentalists, educators, parents, and health professionals must consider an individual's behavior in the context of both universal behaviors and individual differences. It is also important to recognize when others are using a perspective that focuses on the universality of behavior and when they are focusing on variability in behavior. Systematic and controlled observation, in other words *research*, helps us distinguish between those behaviors that tend to be universal and those behaviors that reflect human variability. Research also helps us identify the role of our environment and experience in creating variability of behavior.

As much as possible, the ideas presented in this text are based on research studies. The information comes from an objective source. Keep in mind that this is not the same as saying that any one or two research studies provide us with all the answers we need. Individual research studies do not always rule out all the other possible explanations for the results—to do that, additional research might be required.

Deriving the principles and theories from research that can guide educational and health care practice is a *process*. Although practitioners are sometimes frustrated to see that researchers are only in the middle of the process, it is better to recognize that this is the case than to take all research results as the final word. Our goal here is not only to use available research information to make insightful conclusions and decisions about the motor development of individuals but also to learn how to obtain and analyze further research information as it becomes available.

? Think of generalizations we tend to make about people, such as "tall people are thin," and think of at least one person you know who is an exception to this "rule." What is the consequence of expecting a student or patient to follow a generalization?

 ## Summary and Synthesis

Now that we understand the developmental perspective, it is easy to see why our new prime-time program on developmental topics would be of interest to many viewers. At the present moment, each of us is a product of "what we were like before," and each of us will change to become something different in the future. We are all developing!

Many professions involve relationships with people at critical points of the life span, points when the change taking place influences life thereafter. This is especially true in regard to the physical being and physical skills. So, your knowledge of motor development will help you and those around you through life. If you choose a profession such as teacher, coach, or therapist it will help you help others by providing developmentally appropriate activities.

Your study of motor development will be easier if you equip yourself with a few basic tools. A framework or model to which to relate new information is the most important. We use Newell's model of constraints throughout this text. Another important tool is knowledge of how research in motor development is designed. That way, you can understand how researchers address development issues.

Another important tool, which we have not yet discussed, is knowledge of the various perspectives developmentalists adopt as they approach their research. Because the same problem can be approached from many perspectives, it is valuable to know which approach is taken. In the next chapter, we explore these approaches and discuss the theoretical roots of motor development.

 ## Discussion Questions

1. What is the fundamental developmental perspective that separates the study of motor development from other subdisciplines of the movement sciences?

2. What is the difference between physical growth and physiological maturation?

3. Think of your favorite physical activity, exercise, or sport. Describe some of the individual (both structural and functional), environmental, and task constraints of this activity.

4. Why might a person planning a career teaching children study older adults?

5. What are the differences between longitudinal research studies and cross-sectional research studies? What characteristics of each are used in sequential, or mixed-longitudinal, research studies?

6. What is a developmental perspective? What does "developmentally appropriate" mean?

 ## Learning Activities

Searching the Internet for Information on Motor Development

The Internet can be an incredible resource for any practitioner. Many organizations and advertisers provide information that anyone with a computer can access. It is important to keep in mind that there are few regulations on the Internet; anyone can make almost any claim (whether it is based on research, opinion, or something else). You, as an informed consumer, must examine Web sites carefully and determine the usefulness and accuracy of their information, just as you would with library research. In this learning activity, you will explore the Internet and try to determine the theoretical assumptions and underpinnings of various Web sites.

1. Using any Internet browser you choose, enter the term *motor development* on the search engine (e.g., Yahoo, Google). How many hits are there? Do any of the Web sites surprise you?

2. Find a Web site that sells motor development products. What is the product and what is its purpose? Why is it developmental, according to the advertiser? Based on what you've learned, is it *really* developmental?

3. Pick three different types of Web sites (e.g., academic, sales, medical) related to infancy and motor development (perform a new Internet search). Try to pick some that seem different or interesting. If you were a parent searching for information, what could you learn from these Web sites?

Theoretical Perspectives in Motor Development

chapter 2

Changing Interpretations of Constraints

IS IT A MIRACLE? NO! IT'S DEVELOPMENTAL CHANGE!

Imagine that you visit your older sister, who has just had a baby. You see the baby as a newborn, and he seems uncoordinated and weak. He either randomly moves or responds to touch or other stimuli reflexively. After 9 months, you visit your nephew again. What a change! He sits up on his own, reaches for toys, and has started to crawl. He can even stand when you hold him. He begins to coordinate his actions so that he can move purposefully. Now, let's say you visit one more time, 9 months later. Your nephew is no longer an infant but a full-fledged toddler. Your nephew now can walk—rather rapidly when he wants to—and has no problem with reaching and grasping. He is beginning to respond to language, particularly with the word "No." He seems so very different from the newborn you met a mere 18 months before!

A natural question you may have about this real-life experience is, "What has happened during the past year and a half that resulted in these changes?" In other words, how can you (or anyone else) explain the changes seen across development (figure 2.1)? There appear to be similarities in the development of different people (universality, described in chapter 1)—how do we organize and understand these changes so that we can explain them and predict future development? Certain facts exist; how can we make sense of them? To do this, we must look at the different theoretical perspectives in motor development. Theories provide a systematic way to look at and explain developmental change.

Theories of motor development have their roots in other disciplines, such as experimental and developmental psychology, embryology, and biology. Contemporary research in motor development often uses an ecological perspective to describe, explain, and predict change. To interpret developmental "facts," it is important to understand the different theoretical perspectives from which the facts emerge. Knowing these theoretical perspectives will help us understand the explanations and interpret when several explanations conflict.

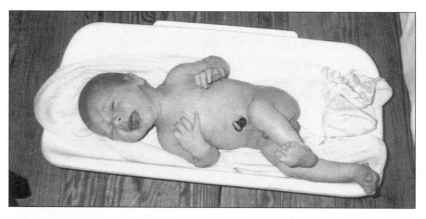

a

b

c

Figure 2.1 Observe the rapid developmental changes that occur in the first 2 years of life: *(a)* A newborn seems to have little ability to perform goal-directed movements; *(b)* at 9 months, the same infant can sit alone, reach, and move toward an object; *(c)* 9 months later and no longer an infant, the 18-month-old toddler moves with relative ease in his environment.

Photos courtesy of Susan L. Miller.

Chapter Objectives

This chapter will

▲ describe the theories currently used to study motor development,

▲ illustrate how different theories explain changes in motor behavior, and

▲ describe the history of the field of motor development.

MATURATIONAL PERSPECTIVE

In a nutshell, the maturational perspective explains developmental change as a function of maturational processes (in particular, through the central nervous system) that control or dictate motor development. According to the assumptions of this theory, motor development is an internal or innate process driven by a biological or genetic time clock. The environment may speed or slow the process of change, but it cannot change one's biologically determined course.

 Maturationists believe that genetics and heredity are primarily responsible for motor development and that the environment has little effect.

The maturational perspective became popular during the 1930s, led by Arnold Gesell (Gesell, 1928, 1954; Salkind, 1981). Gesell believed that the biological and evolutionary history of humans determined their orderly and invariable sequence of development (i.e., each stage of development corresponds with a stage of evolution). The rate at which a person passes through that developmental sequence, however, can be different for each individual. He explained maturation as a process controlled by internal (genetic) factors rather than external (environmental) factors. Gesell believed that environmental factors would only temporarily affect motor development since hereditary factors were ultimately in control of development.

Using identical twins as subjects, Gesell and his associates introduced the co-twin control strategy to developmental research (figure 2.2). What better way to test the different effects of environment and heredity than to look at twins? In this strategy, one twin receives a specific training (the experimental treatment) while the other receives no special training (the control treatment). Thus, the control develops naturally, as any child would without special training. In this manner, he examined the effects of the environment on development.

After a certain period of time, the twins were measured and compared with previously determined developmental criteria to see if the enhanced experience affected the "experimental" child in any way. Co-twin research provided significant contributions to the study of motor development. In particular, these studies allowed developmentalists to begin identifying the sequence of skill development, noting variations in the rate of skill onset.

In addition to describing the course of motor development, many maturationists were interested in the processes underlying development. Myrtle McGraw (1943), for example, associated changes in motor behavior with development of the nervous system. She considered maturation of the central nervous system to be the trigger for the appearance of new skills. McGraw was also

Figure 2.2 Using twins in studies allowed researchers like Gesell and McGraw to "control" genetics while manipulating the environment.

interested in learning, but those who followed in the study of development generally overlooked this aspect of her work (Clark & Whitall, 1989a). Use of the maturational perspective as a research tool in motor development began to wane by the 1950s. However, the influence of this theory is still felt to this day. For example, the focus on maturation as the primary developmental process led researchers and laypersons alike to assume that basic motor skills will automatically materialize. Hence, even today many researchers, teachers, and practitioners feel it is unnecessary to facilitate development of basic skills. In addition, the maturationists' emphasis on the nervous system as the *one* system triggering behavioral advancement evolved to almost single-minded emphasis on that system—to the point that no other system was believed to have much significance. The cardiovascular, skeletal, endocrine, or even muscular systems were not deemed of primary importance to motor development. By the mid-1940s, developmental psychologists began to change the focus of their research, and their interest in motor development waned. At this point, physical educators took up the study of motor development, influenced by the maturational perspective. From this time to 1970, people studied motor development by describing movement and identifying age group norms (Clark & Whitall, 1989a). During this period, motor developmentalists from the physical education discipline focused their attention on school-age children. Researchers still used the maturational perspective; their task was therefore to identify the naturally occurring sequence of changes.

> 💡 People have interpreted the maturationist perspective to mean that motor skills will automatically emerge, regardless of differing environments. This has influenced many teaching, parenting, and research concepts during the 20th and into the 21st centuries.

Normative Descriptive Period

Anna Espenschade, Ruth Glassow, and G. Lawrence Rarick led a normative description movement during this era. In the 1950s, education became concerned with standardized tests and norms. Consistent with this concern, motor developmentalists began to describe children's average performance in terms of quantitative scores on motor performance tests. For example, they described the average running speed and jumping and throwing distance of children at specific ages. Although motor developmentalists were influenced by the maturational perspective, they focused on the *products* (scores, outcomes) of development rather than the developmental *processes* that led to these quantitative scores.

Biomechanical Descriptive Period

Ruth Glassow led another descriptive movement during this era. Glassow made careful biomechanical descriptions of the movement patterns children used in performing fundamental skills such as jumping. Lolas Halverson (figure 2.3) and others continued these biomechanical descriptions with longitudinal observations of children. As a result, the developmentalists were able to identify the course of sequential improvement through which children moved in attaining biomechanically efficient movement patterns. The knowledge obtained from the normative and biomechanical descriptive periods was valuable in that it provided educators with information on age-related changes in motor development. Because description prevailed as the primary tool of these researchers during this time, motor development became labeled as descriptive. Interest in the

Figure 2.3 Lolas Halverson paved the way for contemporary research in motor development.

processes underlying age-related changes, which had been so meticulously recorded prior to this period of history, seemed to disappear.

Information Processing Perspective

A different theoretical approach focuses on behavioral or environmental causes of development (e.g., Bandura's social learning [Bandura 1986] and Skinner's behaviorism, among others). The perspective most often associated with motor behavior and development is called **information processing.** According to this perspective, the brain acts like a computer, inputting information, processing it, and outputting movement. The process of motor learning and development, then, is described in terms of computer-like operations that occur as a result of some external or environmental input.

This theoretical perspective appeared around 1970 and became the dominant perspective among experimental psychologists, developmental psychologists, and motor learning scientists specializing in physical education during the 1970s and 1980s (Schmidt & Wrisberg, 2000; Schmidt & Lee, 1999). This perspective emphasized concepts such as the formation of stimulus–response bonds, feedback, and knowledge of results (for more detailed information, see Schmidt & Wrisberg, 2000; Pick, 1989). Although some motor developmentalists continued with the product-oriented work of the normative and biological descriptive era, others adopted the information processing perspective. Researchers studied many aspects of performance, such as attention, memory, and effects of feedback, across age levels (Thomas, 1984; French & Thomas, 1987). Motor learning researchers and experimental psychologists tended to study the perceptual-cognitive mechanism in young adults first. Then, developmentalists studied children and older adults, comparing them with the young adults. In this way, they could identify the processes that control movement and change with development (Clark & Whitall, 1989a). Today, the information processing perspective is still a viable approach to the study of motor development.

Within the framework of information processing, some developmentalists continued to study perceptual-motor development in children. This work began in the 1960s with proposals that linked learning disabilities to children's delayed perceptual-motor development. Early research focused on this link; by the 1970s, researchers had turned their attention to the development of sensory and perceptual abilities, adopting information processing research strategies (Clark & Whitall, 1989a). Therefore, much of what we know about perceptual-motor development resulted from researchers within an information processing and mechanistic theoretical standpoint.

ECOLOGICAL PERSPECTIVE

A new perspective on development appeared during the 1980s and has become increasingly dominant as the theoretical perspective used by motor development researchers today. This approach is broadly termed the **ecological perspective** because it stresses the interrelationships between the individual, the environment, and the task. Does this sound familiar? It should—it's the perspective adopted by this text! We adopted this perspective because we feel it best describes, explains, and predicts motor development. According to the ecological perspective, you must consider the interaction of all elements (body type, motivation, temperature, ball size) to understand the emergence of a motor skill (kicking) (Roberton, 1989). Although one element or system may be more important or may cast a larger influence at any given time, all systems play a role in the resultant movement. This point makes the ecological perspective very appealing—at any given moment, how you move is not related to just your body or your environment but to the complex interplay of many internal and external factors.

The ecological perspective takes into account many different systems that exist both within the body (e.g., cardiovascular, muscular) and outside the body (e.g., ecosystem, social, cultural) when observing the development of motor skills across the life span.

The ecological perspective has two branches, one concerned with motor control and coordination (dynamic systems) and the other with perception (perception–action). The two branches are linked by several fundamental assumptions that differ notably from the maturational and information processing perspectives. In contrast to the maturational perspective, the ecological perspective considers motor development to be the development of multiple systems rather than only one (the central nervous system, or CNS). Because these different systems change throughout your life, motor development is considered a life span process. In information processing theory, an "executive" function is thought to decide all action, based on calculations of perceptual information resulting in hundreds of commands to control the individual muscles. The ecological perspective maintains that a central executive would be overwhelmed by this task, and in addition, this is a very inefficient way to move. Rather, perception of the environment is direct, and muscles self-assemble into groups, reducing the number of decisions required of the higher brain centers (Konczak, 1990). Let's look more closely at each branch of the ecological perspective.

Dynamic Systems Approach

One branch of the ecological systems perspective is called the **dynamic systems approach.** In the early 1980s, Peter Kugler, Scott Kelso, and Michael Turvey (1980, 1982) and others introduced this approach as an alternative to existing motor control and coordination theories. Following the writings of Soviet physiologist Nikolai Bernstein, they suggested that the very organization of physical and chemical systems constrains behavior. Think about it: Your body can move in many different ways. However, because of the structure of your hip joint and legs (your skeletal system), you, as an adult, tend to walk (as opposed to crawl, scoot, or squirm) as a primary mode of transportation. The structural organization of your body encourages—constrains—you to walk. In other words, your body's structure removes some of the movement choices your CNS might have to make (i.e., among crawling, scooting, squirming, or walking). It's not that you cannot perform these movements; it's just that because of your body structure, you are more "attracted" to walking.

Unlike the maturational and information processing perspectives, the dynamic systems approach suggests that coordinated behavior is "softly assembled" rather than "hard wired." This means the interacting systems within your body act together as a functional unit to enable you to walk when you need to. By *not* having a hard-wired plan, you have greater flexibility in walking, which allows you to adapt your walk to many different situations. This process is called spontaneous self-organization of body systems. As we stated in chapter 1, movement emerges from the interaction between constraints (individual, environmental, task).

The resultant behavior emerges or self-organizes from these interrelationships. If you change any one of these, the emergent movement may change (Clark, 1995). This is the concept of constraints within the dynamic systems approach.

An important motor development concept to come from the dynamic systems approach is the notion of **rate limiters,** or **controllers.** The body's systems do not develop at the same rate. Some might mature quickly, others more slowly. Consider the hypothetical example graphed in figure 2.4. The development of four hypothetical systems is pictured in each of the small graphs numbered 1 to 4. As time passes, the development of system 1 remains at a constant value. System 2 plateaus, advances in a large step, and then plateaus again. System 3 advances gradually and more continuously, whereas system 4 alternately advances and plateaus in a steplike fashion. The exhibited behavior, represented in the large graph, is the product of all the individual systems.

An individual might begin to perform a new skill, such as walking, only when the slowest of the necessary systems for that skill reaches a certain point. Any such system or set of

---

? Imagine a human infant is born in a space station on the moon. Predict the types of movements you would see during the first 2 years of life; in particular, how would you expect the infant to get around?

One of the fundamental principles or assumptions of the dynamic systems approach is that movements and motor behaviors self-organize or emerge from the interactions between the individual environment and tasks within a context.

A rate limiter, or controller, is a system within an individual that holds back or slows the emergence of a motor skill.

systems is known as a rate limiter, or controller, for that skill because that system's development controls the individual's rate of development at that time. Suppose that system 4 in figure 2.4 is the muscular system. Perhaps an infant's muscular strength must reach a certain level before the legs are strong enough to support the infant's weight on one leg to walk. Hence, *muscular strength* would be a rate limiter, or controller, for walking.

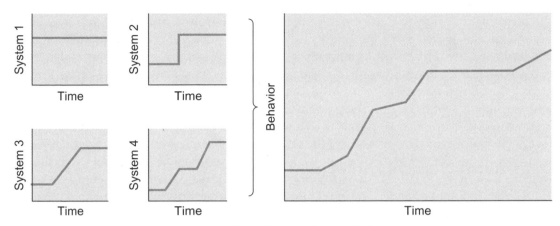

Figure 2.4 Here, four developing systems are depicted as contributing to behavior within an environmental context and for some particular task. The horizontal axis is time, and the vertical axis represents several parallel components or systems developing in different ways.

Adapted from Thelen, Ulrich, and Jensen 1989.

These tenets of the dynamic systems approach differ significantly from those of the maturational perspective. Maturationists tended to focus on the central nervous system as the only system relevant to development and the only rate controller. The dynamic systems approach focuses on many systems and acknowledges that different systems might be rate controllers for different skills (Thelen, 1998).

Another feature of the dynamic systems approach is that it allows for the study of development across the life span. The concept of a system acting as a rate limiter, or controller, for a movement behavior applies into older adulthood as well. The maturational perspective does not address aging since the predetermined endpoint of motor development is maturation, which occurs within the first several decades of life. In contrast, the dynamic systems approach accounts for changes in older adults as well as advancement in youths. When one or more of an individual's systems decline to a critical point, a change in behavior might occur. This system is a rate controller; it is the first to decline to some critical point, and it triggers the reorganization of a movement to a less efficient pattern. For example, if an individual's shoulder joint deteriorates as a result of arthritis and loses flexibility, at some point that individual might have to use a different overhand throwing motion or even throw underhand. The dynamic systems approach is very appropriate for explaining developmental changes because changes do not necessarily occur in all systems over the entire span of older adulthood. Disease or injury might strike one system, or systems might be differentially affected by lifestyle. An active older adult who maintains a regular and balanced exercise program might experience fewer declines in many of the systems than a sedentary peer might.

? In your experience, what have been significant rate limiters in your motor behavior? How have these changed at different times in your life?

Perception–Action Approach

The second branch of the ecological perspective is the **perception–action approach.** J.J. Gibson proposed this model in his writings during the 1960s and 1970s (1966, 1979), but

When a person looks at an object, he directly perceives the function that the object will allow, based on both his body and the object's size, shape, texture, and so forth. This is called an **affordance.**

Body scaling involves using a particular individual's body proportions (an internal reference system) when making movement decisions (picking equipment, selecting a gait pattern).

The concept of body scaling means that an object, although it has an absolute size and shape, has a function relative to the size and shape of the person using it. An activity may become easier or more difficult if the equipment size is changed relative to a person's body dimensions.

? What activities would a 10-speed bicycle afford for an infant, an adult, a paraplegic, or a chimpanzee?

those who study movement have only recently adopted this approach. Gibson proposed that a close interrelationship exists between the perceptual system and the motor system, emphasizing that these systems evolved together in animals and humans. In this approach, we cannot study perception independent of movement if our findings are to be *ecologically valid*—that is, applicable to real-world movement behavior. Likewise, the development of perception and the development of movement must be studied together. In addition, we cannot study the individual while ignoring the surrounding environment. Gibson used the term **affordance** to describe the function an environmental object provides to an individual; this is related to the size and shape of the object and the individual within a particular setting. For example, a horizontal surface affords a human a place to sit, but a vertical surface does not. A squirrel can rest on a vertical tree trunk, so a vertical surface affords a squirrel a resting place. A baseball bat affords an adult, but not an infant, the opportunity to swing. Hence, the relationship between individual and environment is so intertwined that one's characteristics define objects' meanings. This implies that people assess environmental properties in relation to themselves, not according to an objective standard (Konczak, 1990). For example, an individual perceiving whether he or she can walk up a flight of stairs with alternate footsteps considers not just the height of each stair alone but the height of each stair in relation to the climber's body size. Obviously, a comfortable step height for an adult is not the same as that for a toddler. The use of intrinsic (relative to body size) rather than extrinsic dimensions is termed **body scaling.**

The implications of these ideas for motor development are that affordances change as individuals change, resulting in new movement patterns. Growth in size or enhanced movement capabilities might allow actions not previously afforded. When an infant first faces stairs, her perception of their function is not likely to be "climbable" because of her small size and lack of strength. As a toddler, though, she grows to a size that makes climbing stairs with alternate footsteps easy. Scaling environmental objects to one's body size permits actions that are otherwise impossible. Body scaling also applies to other age periods. For example, steps that are an appropriate height for most adults might be too high for an older adult with arthritis to climb comfortably with alternate footsteps. A wall-mounted telephone might be at a comfortable height for most adults, but it may be a frustrating inch too high for someone in a wheelchair. At any age, achievement of a movement goal relates to the individual, who is a certain shape and size, and to environmental objects, which afford certain movements to that individual.

Gibson also rejected the notion of a CNS executive that performs almost limitless calculations on stimulus information to determine the speed and direction of both the person and the moving objects. The information processing perspective holds that such calculations are used to anticipate future positions so that we can reach up to catch a thrown ball, for example. Instead, according to Gibson, individuals perceive their environment directly by constantly moving their eyes, heads, and bodies. This activity creates an optic flow field that provides both space and time information. For example, the image of a baseball approaching a batter not only indicates the ball's location but also expands on the eye's retina. The batter uses this rate of image expansion to time his swing—that is, the rate of expansion gives the batter's central nervous system direct information about when the ball will be in range. Likewise, the expansion rate of an oncoming car's image on a driver's retina yields the "time to collision." From Gibson's perspective, an individual can perceive this time to collision directly and does not need to perform a complicated calculation of speeds and distances to predict where and when collisions and interceptions will occur.

The ecological perspective has been taking hold in motor development research throughout the past two decades. Developmentalists are asking different types of questions, such as, "How does an infant's context affect her motor behavior?" (Adolph, 1997;

Adolph, Vereijken, & Shrout, 2003). Concurrently, they have developed new types of research studies, such as examining the relationship between infant reflexes and adult movements (Thelen & Ulrich, 1991). The ecological perspective encourages professionals to view developing individuals in a very different way than before. As a result, these perspectives will excite and challenge students in the field. In many sections of this text, we examine the maturation and dynamic systems approaches on a particular issue and highlight the differences between these perspectives.

 ## *Summary and Synthesis*

Chapter 2 reviews the history and different theoretical viewpoints specific to motor development—the maturational, information processing, and ecological perspectives. The maturation perspective emphasizes biological development, specifically maturation of the central nervous system. The information processing perspective sees the environment as the main force driving motor development. Ecological theorists stress the interaction between all body systems and the inseparable nature of the individual, environment, and task.

Diametrically opposed perspectives cannot be merged, but students of motor development are free to view behavior from different perspectives. It is important to remember that these theoretical viewpoints often focus only on specific aspects of development; that is, developmentalists with a particular perspective tend to study certain behaviors or age spans. Maturationists focus on infancy, whereas descriptive developmentalists focus on late childhood and adolescence. Information processing theorists search for age differences, whereas those studying from an ecological perspective observe transitions from one skill to another (e.g., from crawling to walking).

 ## *Discussion Questions*

1. Who are the key researchers in the field of motor development from the 1920s until today?
2. How can a teacher or therapist use the concept of body scaling to help individuals develop different motor skills?
3. Why should physical educators be interested in affordances?

 ## *Learning Activities*

Body Scaling to Design Sports Equipment

You have been hired by Schmidt's Tennis Supplies to design a line of "body scaled" tennis rackets. They would like their product line to be distinguishable from others on the market. You must prepare an initial report, discussing important aspects of the new rackets, such as the available product lines from other companies and how your rackets will differ from theirs. Develop this report, answering the following questions as a guide.

1. What are the important individual constraints to consider when body scaling tennis rackets?
2. How have other companies body scaled their rackets? Upon what individual constraint or constraints do they scale?
3. What are novel ways to scale Schmidt's new rackets? What have other companies overlooked?

Hunting for Rate Limiters in Everyday Situations

Physical educators, physical therapists, parents, and many others want to encourage proficient motor skills in those with whom they interact. One important consideration for improving motor skill performance is this: What is "holding back" or limiting the rate at which an individual acquires a skill? In this exercise, you will attempt to determine the key rate limiter for a particular skill, given the constraints described.

1. An 11-month-old infant can pull himself upright on the furniture, can "cruise" the length of the couch if he keeps one hand in contact, and can push a toy shopping cart down the hall. However, when placed standing in the center of the room, he does not walk but gets down on all fours and crawls. What is his primary rate limiter for walking?

2. A stroke patient has control over her limbs and has little difficulty walking. She can lift a pencil and write lists and letters. She can comb her hair and brush her teeth. She experiences problems, however, when she tries to lift cans and jars overhead onto the shelves. What is her primary rate limiter for reaching?

3. A 5-year-old can easily walk, run, jump, and hop. She plays games with other children on the playground and is very attentive in physical education class. Where she has problems with locomotion is in her ability to gallop and skip. She cannot seem to master the asymmetrical rhythms of these skills. What is her primary rate limiter for galloping and skipping?

PART II

Physical Growth and Aging

© Human Kinetics

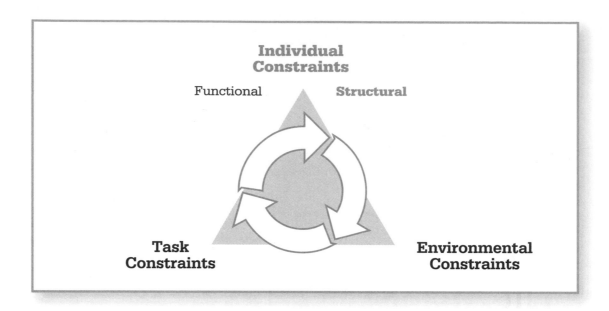

One reason the model of constraints is so useful to those studying motor development is that it shows how physical growth and aging change individuals' interactions with the environment and with the task in order to change the movement arising from a particular movement setting. The change in individual structural constraints through growth in particular is very dramatic. This is evident on a whole-body level as well as on a system level. That is, the whole body changes in size and proportion, and the body systems, such as the skeletal system, the muscular system, and the endocrine system, also change. The changes are more subtle in aging, but nonetheless, they are present.

Chapter 3 considers the typical pattern of growth and aging of the body as a whole. It emphasizes body size and proportion as well as maturity. Chapter 4 examines five different body systems and how they change over the life span. These are the five systems most related to the performance of motor skills. The role of these whole-body and system changes in the age-related change in skill performance is so great that it makes little sense to attempt a study of the course of motor development without a thorough knowledge of physical growth and aging.

Suggested Reading

Lohman, T.G., Roche, A.F., & Martorell, R. (Eds.). (1988). *Anthropometric standardization reference manual*. Champaign, IL: Human Kinetics.

Malina, R.M., Bouchard, C., & Bar-Or, O. (2004). *Growth, maturation, and physical activity* (2nd ed.). Champaign, IL: Human Kinetics.

Nilsson, L. (1990). *A child is born*. New York: Delacorte Press/Seymour Lawrence.

Spirduso, W.W. (1995). *Physical dimensions of aging*. Champaign, IL: Human Kinetics.

Physical Growth, Maturation, and Aging

Changing Individual Constraints Across the Life Span

chapter 3

EXTRA!!! The Times EXTRA!!!

FRESHMAN STANDS TALL, CARRIES BIG DREAMS

Read the headline in *USA Today* (September, 1994). It seems that a high school freshman was already receiving recruiting letters from major college athletic programs to play football and basketball, all because of his size. This freshman was over 6 ft, 6 in. tall; weighed 277 lb; and wore a size 14 shoe. His neighbor, also a freshman, was 5 ft, 5 in. tall and weighed 120 lb!

Physical growth and aging are fascinating. Humans, as members of a species, experience many common steps and processes in growth and aging. The adolescent growth spurt is an example. Genetic factors drive a very orderly and sequenced pattern of growth and aging, so in many respects we know what to expect.

On the other hand, individuals have their own unique potential and their own timing. When we observe a group of preadolescents of the same chronological age, we find a huge range of sizes. In addition, a variety of extrinsic factors influence growth and aging. Nutrition and disease are just two examples.

Genetic and extrinsic factors combine to influence physical growth and aging. We can identify patterns and relationships in the growth and aging of humans (universality), but we are reminded over and over again of the individual differences (variability). It is important for us to know both the expected pattern and the range of variation.

You might wonder why motor developmentalists have any interest at all in physical growth and aging. Recall our triangular model, which pictures the interaction of individual, environmental, and task constraints, and think back to one of the reasons we gave for the usefulness of this model to developmentalists. As individuals grow and age (in other words, as the individual constraints related to the body's structure change), the interactions between the three types of constraints must change, giving rise to different movements. If our goal is to make the same movements possible over a long range of the life span, then we would need to constantly change the environment or the task to accommodate the changing physical constraints. For example, if we want players of a variety of ages to be able to dunk a basketball, we would have to adjust the task by changing the basket height as the height of the players or their jumping ability changed. We need to be constantly alert to changing the environment and task in order to help each individual achieve a desired movement.

Understanding the patterns and variations of growth and aging is fundamental to helping individuals develop their motor skills. A goal of educators and health care providers is to make motor tasks developmentally appropriate—achievable by those at any age and with any set of abilities or disabilities. This would be impossible without a knowledge of physical growth and aging.

An understanding of growth and aging begins with the study of prenatal growth and development, even for those who anticipate working with those past infancy. The talents and limitations each individual brings to a task often are influenced by the course of prenatal growth and development. So, we will begin a review of the growing and aging processes with prenatal development. This brief discussion highlights how very sensitive individuals are to extrinsic influences, even in the relatively protective womb.

? Recall your adolescent growth spurt. Did you spurt sooner or later than most of your friends? Did this have any effects on your relationships with others? On your performance in games or sports? Can you think of classmates who grew sooner or later than others? How did the other children react to them?

 ## *Chapter Objectives*

This chapter will

▲ describe the course of body growth and aging over the life span,

▲ review the role of genes in the course of early physical growth and development,

▲ review the influence of extrinsic factors on growth and development and the increasing role of extrinsic factors as individuals proceed through the life span,

▲ identify typical patterns of growth while recognizing individual differences in the timing of growth, and

▲ distinguish between growth and maturation.

PRENATAL DEVELOPMENT

The growth process begins the instant an ovum (egg) and spermatozoon fuse in fertilization. Early development is astonishingly precise, carried out under the control of genes. Genes, then, determine the normal aspects of development and inherited abnormal development. At the same time, the growing embryo, and later the fetus, is very sensitive to extrinsic factors. These include the environment in which the fetus is growing—the amniotic sac in the uterus—and the nutrients delivered to the fetus via the mother's circulation and the placenta. So even in the womb, individual genetic factors and extrinsic factors interact in the fetus's development. Some extrinsic factors, such as abnormal external pressure applied to the mother's abdomen or the presence of certain viruses and drugs in the mother's bloodstream, are detrimental to the fetus. Other factors, such as delivery of all the proper nutrients, enhance the fetus's growth.

 Both genetic and extrinsic factors influence normal and abnormal embryonic and fetal growth.

Prenatal growth is divided into two phases: embryonic growth, from conception to 8 weeks, and fetal growth, from 8 weeks to birth. Let's consider the key features of each phase.

Embryonic Development

Development begins with the fusion of two sex cells, an ovum from the female and a spermatozoon from the male. The genes direct the continuous development of the embryo in a precise and predictable pattern.

The number of cells increases and the cells also **differentiate** to form specific tissues and organs. This process occurs in a predictable time line, summarized in table 3.1. The limbs are roughly formed and the heartbeat begins at 4 weeks. The eyes, ears, nose, mouth, fingers, and toes are formed at approximately 8 weeks. By this time the human form also has taken shape (see figure 3.1).

Differentiation is the process wherein cells become specialized, forming specific tissues and organs.

TABLE 3.1 Landmarks in Embryonic and Fetal Growth

Age (wk)	Length	Weight	Appearance	Internal development
3	3 mm		Head, tail folds formed	Optic vesicles, head recognizable
4	4 mm	0.4 g	Limb rudiments formed	Heartbeat begins; organs recognizable
8	3.5 cm	2 g	Eyes, ears, nose, mouth, digits formed	Sensory organs developing; some bone ossification beginning
12	11.5 cm	19 g	Sex externally recognizable; head very large for body	Brain configuration nearly complete; blood forming in bone marrow
16	19 cm	100 g	Motor activity; scalp hair present; trunk size gaining on head size	Heart muscle developed; sense organs formed
20	22 cm	300 g	Legs have grown appreciably	Myelination of spinal cord begins
24	32 cm	600 g	Respiratory-like movements begin	Cerebral cortex layers formed
28	36 cm	1,100 g	Increasing fat tissue development	Retina layered and light-receptive
32	41 cm	1,800 g	Weight increasing more than length	Taste sense operative
36	46 cm	2,200 g	Body more rounded	Ossification begins in distal femur
40	52 cm	3,200 g	Skin smooth and pink; at least moderate head hair	Proximal tibia begins ossification; myelination of brain begins; pulmonary branching 2/3 complete

Adapted from Timiras 1972.

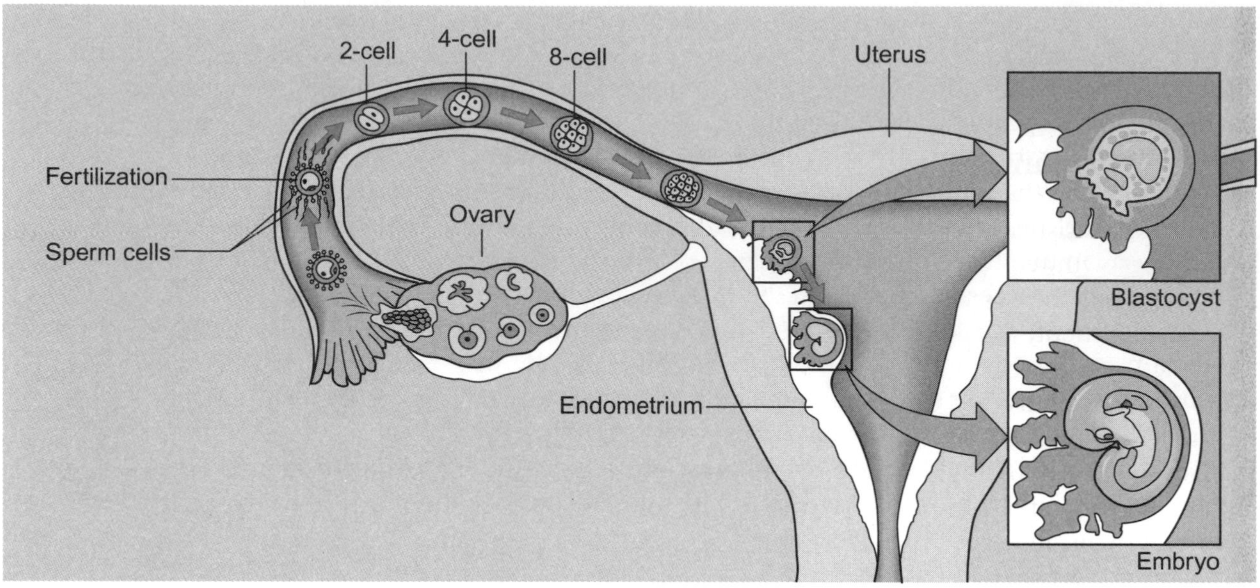

Figure 3.1 As the embryo moves through the oviduct, its cells divide and multiply. By the time it implants on the lining of the uterus, it is several hundred cells in size. It is embedded in nutrient cells that nourish it. Implantation in the uterus is facilitated by protuberances of sugar molecules on the surface of the blastocyst.

Fetal Development

The fetal stage, from 8 weeks to birth, is characterized by further growth and cell differentiation of the fetus, leading to functional capacity. This continued growth of the organs and tissues occurs in two ways: by **hyperplasia** and by **hypertrophy.** If you examine the landmarks of growth carefully, you will also see that growth tends to proceed in two directions. One direction is **cephalocaudal,** meaning that the head and facial structures grow fastest, then the upper body, followed by the relatively slow-growing lower body. At the same time, growth is **proximodistal** in direction, meaning the trunk tends to advance, then the nearest parts of the limbs, and finally the distal parts of the limbs (figure 3.2). Body weight increases and the body tissues grow steadily, with the rate of growth increasing at about 5 months and continuing at that rapid rate until birth.

Although cells differentiate during growth to perform a specialized function, some cells have an amazing quality termed **plasticity,** the capability to take on a new function. If some of the cells in a system are injured, for example, the remaining cells might be stimulated to perform the role the damaged cells

Hyperplasia is an increase in the absolute number of cells.

Hypertrophy is an increase in the relative size of an individual cell.

Cephalocaudal is the direction of growth beginning at the head and extending toward the lower body.

Proximodistal is the direction of growth proceeding from the body toward the extremities.

Plasticity is modifiability or malleability; in regard to growth, it is the ability of tissues to subsume functions otherwise carried out by other tissues.

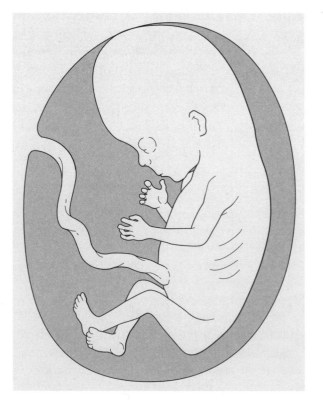

Figure 3.2 A fetus at 3 months.

ordinarily carry out. The cells of the central nervous system have a high degree of plasticity, and their structure, chemistry, and function can be modified pre- and postnatally (Timiras, 1972).

Fetal Nourishment

Many characteristics of the fetal environment have the potential to affect growth, either positively or negatively. The nourishment system is the extrinsic factor that has the most impact on fetal development; thus it is helpful to know how the fetus is nourished.

The fetus is nourished by the diffusion of oxygen and nutrients between fetal blood and maternal blood in the placenta (figure 3.3). Carbon dioxide and excretory byproducts also are exchanged and carried away in the mother's blood.

The growing fetus needs energy, nutrients, and oxygen. If these are in short supply, mother and fetus compete for limited resources, possibly compromising the needs of the fetus. Obviously, maternal health status plays a role in prenatal development.

A woman living in better conditions, with an adequate and safe food supply and a protective, clean environment, who receives early prenatal health care is more likely than a woman living in poorer conditions to meet the needs of the fetus. She is also more likely to be at lower risk for illnesses and infections that might compromise the needs of the fetus and would result in low-birth-weight infants. Consequently, women at lower socioeconomic levels typically give birth to lighter infants than do women from higher socioeconomic levels. This is significant because low-birth-weight infants are at greater risk of disease, infection, and death in the weeks after birth than are normal-weight infants.

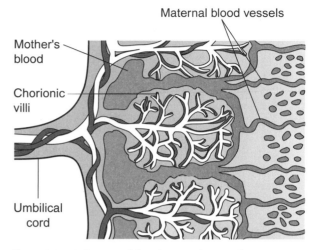

Figure 3.3 A diagram of the placenta showing the two circulations, mother and fetus, which come close enough to each other that substances diffuse from one to the other, but the bloodstreams never mingle.

Reprinted from Rhodes 1969.

? Where in the world today would we find pregnant women with poor health status? Would we find them only in poor third world countries with more primitive living conditions than we have in industrialized societies?

Abnormal Prenatal Development

Abnormal growth may arise from either genetic or extrinsic factors. Genetic abnormalities are inherited and may be immediately apparent or may remain undetected until well into postnatal growth. A host of extrinsic factors can also negatively affect the fetus. A few examples include drugs and chemicals in the mother's bloodstream, viruses in the mother's bloodstream, and excessive pressure applied to the mother's abdomen. Let's consider some examples of **congenital defects** in more detail.

Congenital defects are anomalies present at birth, regardless of whether their causes are genetic or extrinsic.

Genetic Causes of Abnormal Prenatal Development

An individual may inherit genetic abnormalities as dominant or recessive (including sex-linked) disorders. Dominant disorders result when one parent passes on a defective gene. Recessive disorders occur in children who inherit a defective gene from each parent.

Genetic abnormalities can also result from a new mutation, the alteration or deletion of a gene during formation of the egg or sperm cell. Researchers suspect irradiation and certain hazardous environmental chemicals of causing genetic mutations, and the potential for genetic damage to sex cells increases with advancing maternal age (Nyhan, 1990). Mutations can also occur spontaneously, without cause.

Both new mutations and inherited disorders can result in single or multiple malformations of an organ, limb, or body region; deformations of a body part; or disruptions in development resulting from the breakdown of normal tissue. Many of these abnormalities

Congenital disorders arising from extrinsic factors can affect the potential for postnatal growth and development. When medical professionals and parents are aware of negative influences, they can manage these influences to minimize the risk to the fetus.

A **teratogen** is any drug or chemical agent that causes abnormal development in a fetus upon exposure.

are obvious at birth, but some do not appear until later. Genetic abnormalities vary considerably in appearance and severity.

Extrinsic Causes of Abnormal Prenatal Development

Our earlier discussion of fetal nourishment revealed how dependent the fetus is on the mother for the oxygen and nutrients it needs. Unfortunately, the fetal nourishment system can also deliver harmful substances to the fetus. In addition, a variety of factors can potentially affect the fetus's physical environment and thereby its growth and development.

Teratogens   In addition to oxygen and nutrients necessary for fetal life and growth, other substances can diffuse across the placenta. Among these are viruses, drugs, and chemicals. Sometimes, either too much or too little of the necessary vitamins, nutrients, and hormones is delivered to the fetus through the placenta. Some of these substances can also act as malformation-producing agents, or **teratogens.** The specific effect a teratogen has on the fetus depends on the stage of fetal development when the substance is introduced as well as the amount of the substance.

There are critical periods, periods of particular vulnerability to change, for the growth and development of tissues and organs. For example, the rubella virus is harmful if the embryo is exposed to it during the first 4 weeks of pregnancy. The earlier the infection, the more serious the resulting abnormalities. Very early exposure can result in miscarriage.

Some malformation-producing or growth-retarding conditions arise because a nutrient is delivered to the embryo or fetus through the placenta in an insufficient amount. Other abnormal conditions arise if too much of a substance is present. Still other congenital defects result from the mere presence of a harmful substance in the maternal blood. Whether the fetus is exposed depends on the size of the substance. For example, small virus particles present in maternal blood can cross the placenta and harm the fetus. Drugs with molecular weights under 1,000 cross the placenta easily, whereas those with molecular weights over 1,000 do not. Parents can maximize fetal growth and development by avoiding substances that might be teratogenic. Mothers can maintain a diet that supplies adequate but not excessive nutrients. Otherwise, the fetus might develop a specific malformation or be generally retarded in growth and small for age at birth. It is important to recognize that these conditions, including low birth weight, can affect postnatal growth and development.

Other Prenatal Extrinsic Factors   Malformation, retarded growth, or life-threatening conditions can also result from external factors affecting the fetus's environment. Examples include

▲   external or internal pressure on the infant, including pressure from another fetus in utero;

▲   extreme internal environmental temperature, as when the mother suffers from high fever or hypothermia;

▲   exposure to X rays or gamma rays;

▲   changes in atmospheric pressure, especially those leading to *hypoxia* (oxygen deficiency) in the fetus; and

▲   environmental pollutants.

The precise effects of these factors also depend on the fetus's stage of development. Like teratogens, external factors have the potential to affect present and future growth and development.

Prenatal Development Summary

Prenatal development is under genetic and extrinsic influences. The genes direct an orderly and precise course of development, but extrinsic factors can influence the process either positively or negatively. Many of these extrinsic factors exert their influence through the fetal nourishment system. A fetus that receives appropriate levels of oxygen and nutrients has the best chance of reaching its full genetic potential, including its potential for skill performance.

Prenatal abnormalities can arise from genetic and extrinsic influence. Some abnormal conditions are a product of *both* genetic inheritance and the environment; that is, a tendency for a disease might be inherited, and subsequently the disease will appear only under certain environmental conditions (Timiras, 1972). We should view physical growth and development, then, as a continuous process that begins at conception. Individuals are, in part, products of the factors that affected their prenatal growth and development. Hence, the individual structural constraints that educators and therapists consider when planning activities for individuals reflect the course of prenatal development. The process of postnatal development is the continuation of prenatal development.

POSTNATAL DEVELOPMENT

Is an 11-year-old capable of long-distance runs? How about a 60-year-old? We know that no one answer applies to all 11-year-olds or all 60-year-olds because we have acknowledged the coexistence of universality and specificity in development. Educators and therapists benefit from knowing the universal pattern of postnatal growth and physiological maturation and the typical pattern of aging in adults. Yet, we work with individuals who have their own timing and potential for growth. So, we must be able to evaluate an individual's status and potential to help him or her set reasonable personal goals. We must be able to compare an individual with the average and adjust expectations for performance accordingly.

Overall Growth

Overall body growth after birth is a continuation of prenatal growth. The growth pattern is predictable and consistent but not linear, no matter which measure of overall growth we choose to study. For example, look at the growth curves for height and weight in figure 3.4, a and b, and figure 3.5, a and b. They are characterized by rapid growth after birth, followed by gradual but steady growth during childhood, rapid growth during early adolescence, and then a leveling off. Thus, the curves are roughly S-shaped. We call this pattern of overall body growth a **sigmoid curve** after the Greek letter for *s*.

Although a normal growth curve is always sigmoid, the timing of a particular individual's spurts and steady growth periods is likely to vary from the average. The slope of the curve can also vary from the average. For example, one girl might begin her adolescent growth spurt at 8 years, whereas another might begin hers at 10. The second girl might grow more rapidly than the first (have a steeper growth curve). Note on the growth charts that the range of variation, the gap between the 3rd and 97th percentiles, widens with age, especially for weight (Malina & Bouchard, 1991). This is another example of universality and specificity in development. The sigmoid pattern of a graph of overall growth is universal, but the timing and steepness of segments of the curve are specific to the individual.

Postnatal growth proceeds in a precise and orderly pattern; but individual variability, especially in the timing of landmark events, is increasingly obvious as individuals move through infancy, childhood, preadolescence, and adolescence.

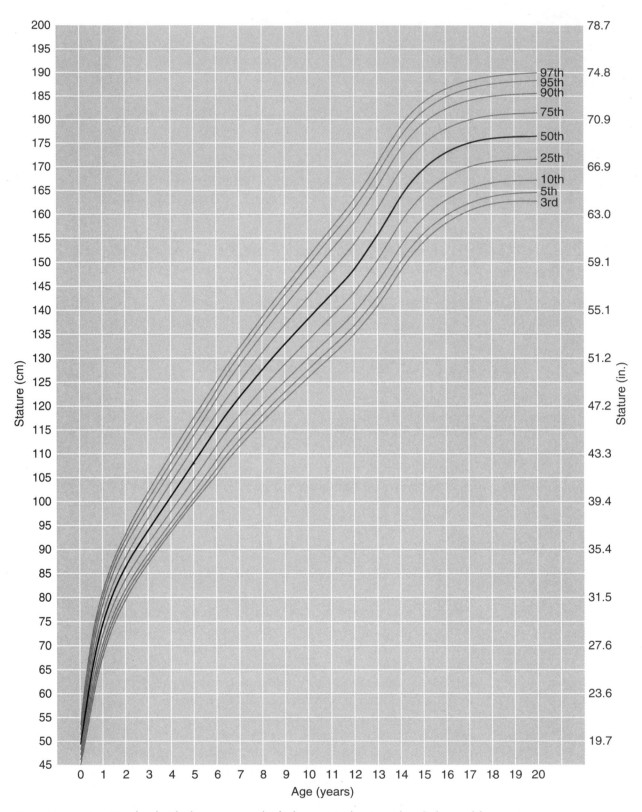

Figure 3.4a Stature (standing height) by age percentiles for boys. Note the sigmoid, or S-shape, of the curves.

Data from the National Center for Health Statistics in collaboration with the National Center for Chronic Disease Prevention and Health Promotion 2000. Adapted from www.cdc.gov/nchs/about/major/nhanes/growthcharts/clinical_charts.htm.

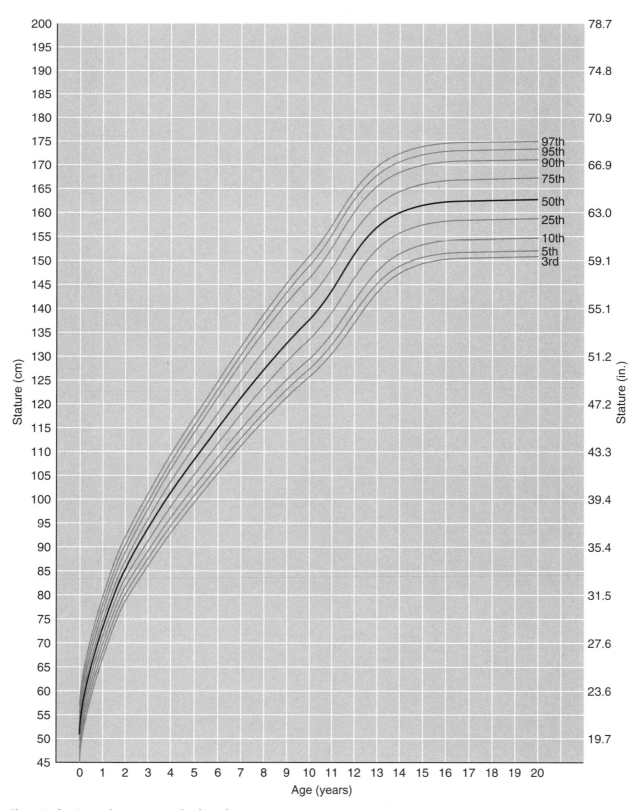

Figure 3.4b Stature by age percentiles for girls.

Data from the National Center for Health Statistics in collaboration with the National Center for Chronic Disease Prevention and Health Promotion 2000. Adapted from www.cdc.gov/nchs/about/major/nhanes/growthcharts/clinical_charts.htm.

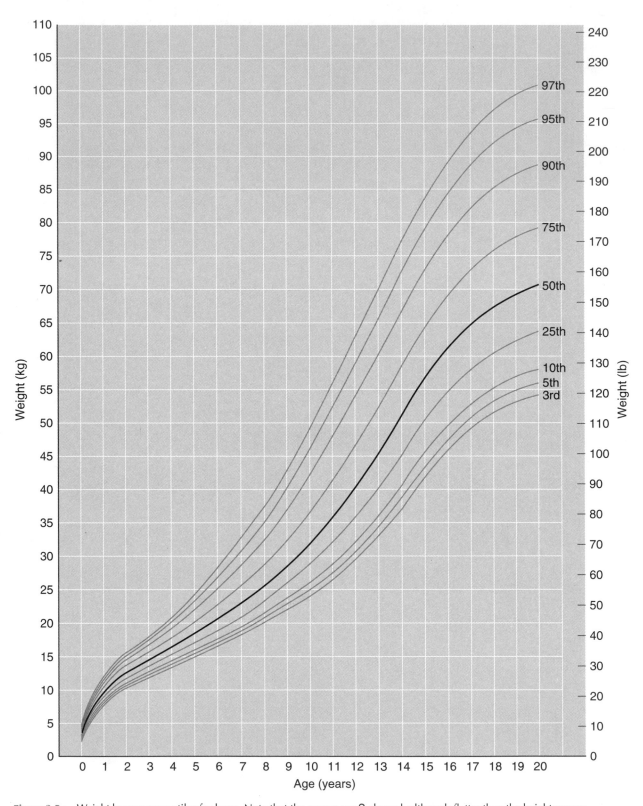

Figure 3.5a Weight by age percentiles for boys. Note that the curves are S-shaped, although flatter than the height curves.

Data from the National Center for Health Statistics in collaboration with the National Center for Chronic Disease Prevention and Health Promotion 2000. Adapted from www.cdc.gov/nchs/about/major/nhanes/growthcharts/clinical_charts.htm.

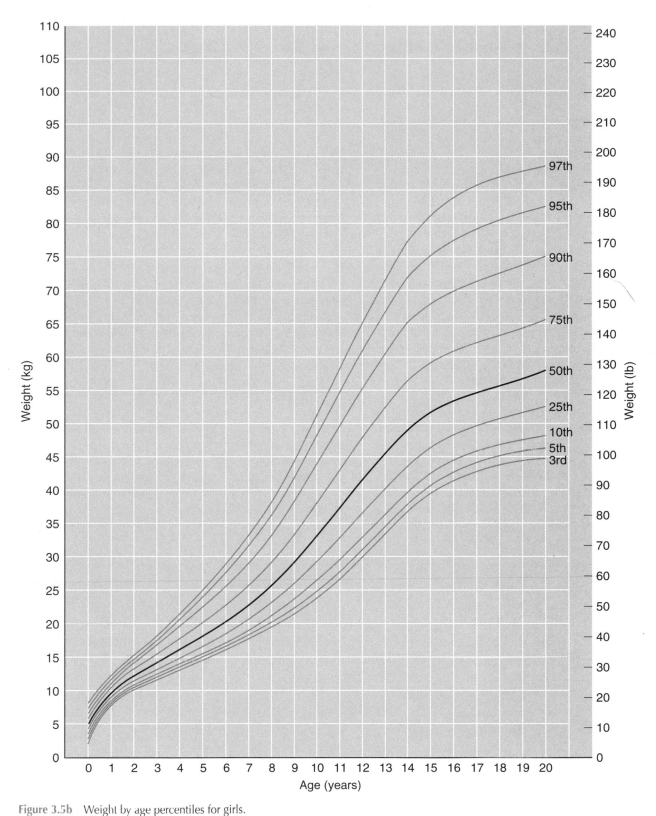

Figure 3.5b Weight by age percentiles for girls.

Data from the National Center for Health Statistics in collaboration with the National Center for Chronic Disease Prevention and Health Promotion 2000. Adapted from www.cdc.gov/nchs/about/major/nhanes/growthcharts/clinical_charts.htm.

Assessing the Extent and Rate of Growth

In chapter 1 we acknowledged that we often picture growth and development through graphs. This practice is common in describing physical growth. We often see measurements of height, weight, or length plotted against advancing age. These plots are called **distance curves** because they convey the extent of growth. Figures 3.4 and 3.5 are examples. If we want to know the distance growth has progressed at a certain age, we merely read the value opposite that age. For example, from a height curve we can determine how tall an individual was at any age, using the plot of an individual person, or what the average height for a group was at any age, if group averages are plotted.

If the line plotted is going up with age, we know that growth is taking place, provided the axes of the graph are arranged from low (at the origin) to high. We expect growth measurements to increase with age during the growth period. In adulthood, measurements might go up or down as extrinsic factors influence the measurement. A good example of this is body weight. If the slope of a distance curve is gradual, the change is moderate for that age period. If the slope is steep, the change is rapid for that age period. So, the slope of a distance curve can indicate changes in the *rate* of growth.

The rate of growth can be more dramatically illustrated on graphs of growth rate, or speed. These are called **velocity curves.** Velocity curves are plotted by first selecting small age spans, such as the time between the 8th and 9th birthdays, the 9th and 10th birthdays, and the 11th and 12th birthdays, and so on. Then, for each of these short age spans, we find the change in growth as indicated by the distance curve. For example, we might check a distance curve for height and see that the increase in height between the 8th and 9th birthdays is 5 cm. We would then plot

a point at 5 cm per year and 8.5 years (representing the midpoint of the age span during which the growth was 5 cm). By doing this for a number of age spans and connecting our points with a smooth curve, we produce a velocity curve.

Velocity curves look very different from distance curves. They often have sections where the graphed line is decreasing, indicating that the rate of growth is slowing. They also have peaks (i.e., points at which the rate of growth changes from faster to slower). Humans have a peak velocity in their overall growth measurements during early adolescence (termed peak height velocity, peak weight velocity, and so on). This is the age at which growth is the fastest for this age period. During the downslope of the peak, growth slows, although it may still be quite rapid. For example, a typical peak height velocity for girls is 8 cm per year, as shown in figure 3.6. It typically occurs around 12 years of age. Immediately before this age the velocity of growth in height speeds up and increases from 5 to 6 to 7 to 8 cm per year. After this age, growth slows, from 8 to 7 to 6 cm per year, and so on. Yet all through the age span of 10.5 to 13 years of age, there is a fairly rapid increase in height (6–8 cm per year).

In reading a velocity curve we must keep in mind that we are reading a rate of growth for a short age span, not the extent of growth. We can say how tall an individual girl is from her distance curve for height but not from her velocity curve. On the other hand, we can easily determine the age at which she was growing the fastest from her velocity curve.

Readers who have studied calculus will recognize that a velocity curve is the first derivative of a distance curve. The second derivative would provide an acceleration curve, indicating the ages at which growth is accelerating or decelerating.

To better appreciate velocity curves and what they represent, download Lab 3.1 Graphing a Velocity Curve from the Student Resources section at www.HumanKinetics.com/LifeSpanMotorDevelopment.

Gender

Gender is a major factor in the timing as well as the extent of growth. Gender differences are minimal in early childhood, with boys being very slightly taller and heavier. Throughout childhood, though, girls tend to mature at a faster rate than boys so that at any given age, girls as a group are biologically more mature than boys. Important gender differences in growth and development are especially pronounced at adolescence. Girls begin their adolescent growth spurt when they are about 9 years old (often termed the **age at takeoff** because the rate of growth begins to increase), whereas boys begin theirs at about 11. Note that these ages are group averages. About two-thirds of all adolescents will initiate their growth spurt during the year before or the year after these averages, meaning that approximately one-third will initiate it even earlier or later.

Age at takeoff is the age at which the rate of growth begins to increase.

Height

Height follows the sigmoid pattern of growth: a rapid increase in infancy, tapering off to steady growth in childhood, with another rapid increase during the adolescent growth spurt, followed by a tapering off until the end of the growth period. An individual's height can be compared with group norms. Often this comparison is made using a family of height curves plotted against age. The individual curves represent various percentiles, usually the 3rd, 5th, 10th, 25th, 50th, 75th, 90th, 95th, and 97th percentiles (e.g., figures 3.4a and 3.4b). This allows us to approximate at what percentile an individual falls for height at a specific age or over time, as well as whether he or she maintains position in the group or changes. For example, we might find an individual who remains in the 40th percentile for most of the growth period or another individual who begins the adolescent growth spurt early and goes from the 60th percentile at age 8 to the 90th percentile at age 10.

Children tend to maintain their relative percentile positions in comparison to group norms after they are 2 or 3 years old; that is, a 3-year-old child in the 75th percentile for height is most likely to be around the 75th percentile throughout childhood. A large fluctuation in relative position could indicate that some extrinsic factor is influencing growth (Martorell, Malina, Castillo, Mendoza, & Pawson, 1988), and medical examination is warranted.

In addition to the extent of growth, it is interesting to examine the rate, or velocity, of growth (i.e., when individuals are growing rapidly or slowly). When the rate of growth is plotted, we can then find the age at which one is growing the fastest (**peak velocity**) or the age at which one changes from slow growth to rapid growth (age at takeoff), or vice versa (see Assessing the Extent and Rate of Growth).

On the average, girls reach peak height velocity during the adolescent growth spurt at 11.5 to 12.0 years (figure 3.6). Their growth in height then tapers off at approximately age 14, with notable increases in height ending around age 16. Boys reach their peak height velocity at 13.5 to 14.0 years; this velocity is somewhat faster than that of girls— approximately 9 cm per year for boys compared with 8 cm per year for girls (Beunen & Malina, 1988). Boys' growth tapers off at 17 years, with notable increases ending by age 18. Note that males have about 2 more years of growth than females, amounting to 10 to 13 cm of height. This longer growth period accounts for much of the average absolute height difference between adult men and women.

Late maturers have a longer growth period than early maturers and consequently tend to be taller.

Weight

Growth in weight also follows the sigmoid pattern of growth: a rapid increase in infancy, moderate increase in childhood, a spurt in early adolescence, then a steady increase that tapers off at the end of the growth period. Weight, however, is very susceptible to extrinsic factors and can reflect variations in the amount of muscle with exercise as well as variations in the amount of fat tissue with diet and exercise. Disease can also influence body weight.

Peak weight velocity during the adolescent growth spurt follows peak

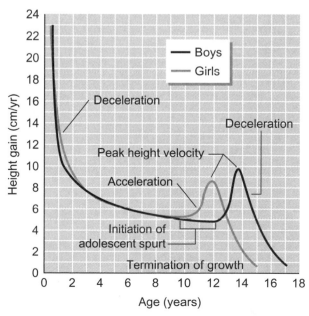

Figure 3.6   Velocity curves for height of British boys and girls in the 1960s. Note the age at takeoff of the growth spurt in height and the peak height velocity. These ages and the peak height velocities are slightly different for this sample from the population averages discussed in the text, but the shape of the velocity curves is the same.

Reprinted from Tanner, Whitehouse, and Takaishi 1966.

height velocity in adolescents by 2.5 to 5.0 months in boys and 3.5 to 10.5 months in girls. The growth of various segment lengths and breadths sometimes reaches peak velocity before the individual reaches peak height velocity and sometimes reaches it after, but all reach their peak before or at peak weight velocity (Beunen, Malina, Renson, & Van Gerven, 1988). This is the factual basis for the commonly observed pattern of individuals growing "up" first, then filling "out."

Relative Growth

Although the body as a whole consistently follows the sigmoid growth pattern, specific body parts, tissues, and organs have differential rates of growth. In other words, each part of the growing individual has its own precise and orderly growth rate. These differential growth rates can result in notable changes in the body's appearance as a whole. Observe how the proportions illustrated in figure 3.7 change dramatically throughout life. Body proportions at birth reflect the cephalocaudal (head to toe) and proximodistal (near to far) directions of prenatal growth. Therefore, a newborn's form is quite different from that of an adult. The head is one-fourth of the total height at birth but only one-eighth of adult height. The legs are about three-eighths of the height at birth but almost half of adult height.

For a newborn to achieve adult proportions, some body parts must grow faster than others during postnatal growth. For example, the legs grow faster than the trunk and head in infancy and childhood, and they undergo a growth spurt early in adolescence. Growth in height results mostly from an increase in trunk length during late adolescence and early adulthood. Boys and girls have similar proportions in childhood, but by the time they are adults, relative growth of some body areas brings about noticeable differences between the sexes. In girls, shoulder and hip breadth increase at about the same rate, so their shoulder-to-hip ratio is fairly stable during growth. Boys undergo a substantial increase in shoulder breadth during their growth spurt, so their ratio changes as they move into adolescence.

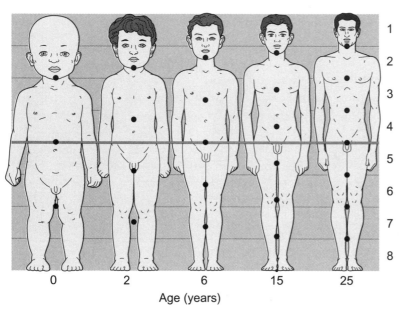

Figure 3.7 Postnatal body proportion changes.
Redrawn from Timiras 1972.

💡 Postnatal growth patterns differ among body parts and body systems.

Teachers, personal trainers, physical therapists, researchers, and many other professionals take anthropometric measurements. These measurements must be taken with great precision if they are to be used for comparisons with norms or measurements taken at a later date.

💻 You can practice taking some of the major anthropometric measurements by downloading Lab 3.2 Taking Growth Measures from the Student Resources section at www.HumanKinetics.com/LifeSpanMotorDevelopment.

Body form might have implications for skill performance in early childhood. For example, even if 5-month-old infants were neurologically ready to coordinate and control the walking pattern, it is unlikely that they could balance their top-heavy bodies on such thin, short legs and small feet. Varying limb lengths and weights can affect balance, momentum, and potential speed in various movements. Recall Newell's model. Changing individual structural constraints related to body form and proportion could certainly interact with task and environment to produce different movements.

Measuring Height, Lengths, and Breadths

Frequent measurement of children's growth and comparisons of the values with averages at a given age can help detect abnormal growth. Medical or environmental factors influencing abnormal growth can then be identified and moderated or corrected. Of course, such growth measurements reflect the individual's genetic potential for height and body build (which often correspond to the parents' height and build) as well as the individual's personal growth timing. Therefore, in screening growth measurements, children and teens who measure above the 90th or below the 10th percentile for their age, especially those whose parents are not exceptionally tall or short, respectively, should be referred to medical personnel for examination (Lowrey, 1986).

For growth screenings to be meaningful, measurements must be done accurately, and they must use the same measurement techniques used to establish group norms or averages. Descriptions of standard techniques are widely available (Lohman, Roche, & Martorell, 1988, is one example of a standardization manual). You should refer to these standards if you decide to conduct a screening program. A detailed description of standard techniques is beyond the scope of this text, but let's briefly consider the various measurements used to assess physical growth and body size.

The measurements used to assess growth and size are known as **anthropometric** measures, and they include height, weight, segment length, body breadth, and circumferences. The measurements are sometimes used in ratios to illustrate a particular aspect of size. Standing height is the most common growth measure, but sitting height is an interesting measurement to observe during the growth period. Standing height minus sitting height yields a functional measure of leg length. Infants have relatively long trunks and short legs, so the proportion of standing height to leg length changes over the growth period to reach the typical adult proportion.

Various other segment lengths, such as that of the upper arm and the thigh, can be measured, as can the breadth of the body at specified locations. Typically, length and breadth measurements are taken where skeletal landmarks can be located so that the measurement reflects skeletal structure and not soft tissues such as fat and muscle that can change with diet and exercise. The most common breadth measures are taken at the shoulders and the hips, and often the shoulder width is divided by the hip width to form a ratio. This shoulder-to-hip ratio is also interesting to observe over the growth period because it undergoes dramatic change in boys during the adolescent growth spurt as they reach the typical male body build of broad shoulders and narrow hips.

Circumference measurements can be taken at numerous locations and often represent soft tissue—fat and muscle—as well as bone structure. We expect circumference measurements to increase with growth in size, but a circumference measurement by itself cannot provide information about the amount of fat tissue versus lean body tissue. Pediatricians closely monitor head circumference in infants and toddlers. An abnormally large measurement is associated with hydroencephalus, excess cerebrospinal fluid that could cause brain damage.

Body weight is another common measure of growth and body size. Growth in weight reflects the increase in lean body tissues, which is genetically driven, and the increase in adipose, or fat, tissues, which can be readily influenced by extrinsic factors such as exercise and nutrition. Body weight can be apportioned into lean body mass and fat tissue mass by one of several means described later in this text. The resulting measurement typically is expressed as "percent fat."

An interesting ratio is one that divides body weight by the standing height squared. This ratio is called the body mass index (BMI). BMI is a useful ratio for measuring obesity, especially in adults. The normal range for BMI is 18.5 to 24.9, with obesity defined as a BMI over 30.0.

Many methods exist for measuring physical growth and body size. Each measurement yields a specific type of information. Particularly in combination, they can provide a great deal of information about the course of growth in size. This information can be used by medical professionals to enable individuals to reach their growth potential or to maintain good health after the growth period. The information can also be used to help children and youths understand the changes their bodies undergo, especially during the adolescent growth spurt.

Specific tissues and organs also grow differentially. Although their prenatal growth tends to follow the increase in body weight, the postnatal growth of some tissues and systems follows unique patterns. The brain, for example, achieves more than 80% of its adult weight by the time the individual reaches age 4. Because various tissues of the body grow differentially after birth, our knowledge of individual structural constraints is made more complete by study of the individual body systems. Growth, development, and aging of each of the relevant body systems will be discussed in chapter 4.

Anthropometry is the study of the measurement of the human physical form.

Physiological Maturation

Tissues of the growing body can advance without necessarily increasing in size. The biochemical composition of cells, organs, and systems can advance qualitatively. This is termed

Physiological maturation is the developmental process leading to a state of full function.

Secondary sex characteristics are aspects of form or structure appropriate to males or females, often used to assess physiological maturity in adolescents.

physiological maturation. Chronological age, growth in body size, and physiological maturation are related to one another in that as children and youths get older, they tend to grow in size and mature. However, these dimensions can proceed with their own timing. For example, two children of the same age can be dramatically different in maturation status, one being an early maturer and one being a late maturer. Or, two children of the same size can be different ages; they could be at similar levels of maturation or very different levels of maturation. Thus it is difficult to infer maturity from age alone, from size alone, or even from age and size considered together. An individual child can appear to be small and slight of build but may actually be relatively mature for his or her chronological age.

Appearance of the **secondary sex characteristics** during the adolescent growth spurt is a function of maturation. The secondary sex characteristics appear at a younger age in girls and boys who are early maturers and at an older age in those who are late maturers. As noted previously, girls as a group mature at a more rapid rate than boys. They enter their adolescent growth spurt sooner, and their secondary sex characteristics appear sooner. The breasts enlarge; pubic hair appears; and menarche, the first menstrual cycle, occurs. Regardless of the exact chronological age when a girl begins her growth spurt, menarche typically follows the peak height velocity by 11 to 12 months (figure 3.8). The average age of menarche therefore is 12.5 to 13.0 years. In boys, the testes and scrotum grow in size, and pubic hair appears. Boys have no landmark comparable to girls' menarche for puberty; the production of viable sperm is a gradual process.

Maturation status is relevant as a structural constraint influencing movement. Individuals who are more mature are likely to be stronger and more coordinated than those who are less mature, even at the same chronological age. Parents, educators, and therapists must consider maturation status when designing activities and therapies for youth and when setting performance goals. It is tempting to infer movement performance potential from size alone or age alone, but in fact maturation status is a powerful predictor of performance potential.

? Imagine that you are coaching a girls' basketball team. All of your players are 11 and 12 years of age. What should you expect the variation in growth and maturation to be? What would be the effect on skill performance?

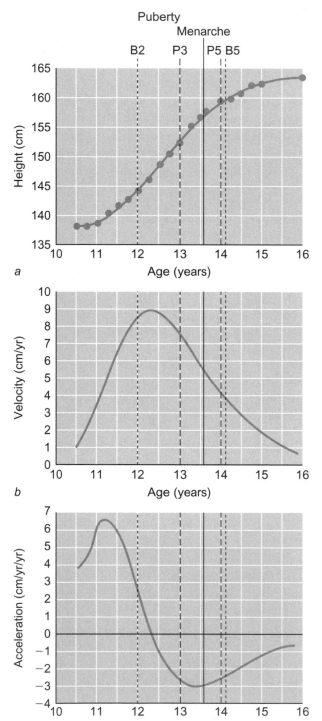

Figure 3.8 *(a)* Height attained (distance), *(b)* height velocity, and *(c)* height acceleration curves for a girl at adolescence. Note menarche comes after peak height velocity. B2 marks beginning of breast development; B5, adult form. P3 marks intermediate stage of pubic hair development; P5, adult form.

Reprinted from Maclaren 1967.

Extrinsic Influences on Postnatal Growth

As noted earlier, extrinsic factors can have a great influence on prenatal growth even within the relatively protective environment of the womb. It is no surprise, then, that after birth extrinsic factors have an increased influence on growth and development. Genetics controls the timing and rate of an individual's growth and maturation, but extrinsic factors can also have a great impact, especially those influencing body metabolism. During periods of rapid growth, just after birth and in early adolescence, growth is particularly sensitive to alteration by environmental factors.

The phenomenon of **catch-up growth** illustrates the susceptibility of overall body growth to extrinsic influence. A child might experience catch-up growth after suffering a period of severe malnutrition or a bout with a severe disorder such as chronic renal failure. During such a period, body growth is retarded. After the diet is improved or the child recovers from the disorder (i.e., a positive environment for growth is restored), growth rate increases until the child approaches or catches up to what otherwise would have been the extent of growth during that period (Prader, Tanner, & von Harnack, 1963) (figure 3.9). Whether the child recovers some or all of the growth depends on the timing, duration, and severity of the negative environmental condition.

Extrinsic factors continue to play a larger role as individuals proceed through adulthood, leading to great variability among individuals in older adulthood.

Catch-up growth is relatively rapid physical growth of the body to recover some or all of retarded growth during a period of negative extrinsic influence once the negative influence is removed.

Early maturers are likely to demonstrate better athletic performance than their late-maturing counterparts. If parents or coaches overlook this and expect these early maturers to maintain their performance edge into adulthood, what could be the repercussions when the late maturers catch up?

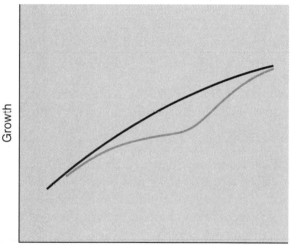

Growth

Time

Figure 3.9 A hypothetical illustration of catch-up growth. The black line represents the course of normal growth as it might have been. The blue line represents the actual growth as influenced by a negative extrinsic factor. As the factor has its influences, growth slows, but with removal of the negative factor, growth speeds up to catch up to the level that otherwise would have been reached. How close actual growth comes to catching the line representing normal growth depends on the time of occurrence and the length of time the factor has its influence, as well as its severity.

Assessment of Physiological Maturation

Maturation can be assessed directly or indirectly. A direct measurement would be ideal, but the direct measures of maturation are not always easy to obtain or applicable to the entire growth period. For example, dental eruption, the appearance of new teeth, indicates maturation status but is restricted to two age spans: between approximately 6 months and 3 years, when the deciduous (baby) teeth first appear, and between approximately 6 and 13 years, when the permanent teeth appear. The appearances of baby and permanent teeth follow a typical order. For early maturers, teeth appear at a younger age than for late maturers.

The appearance of the secondary sex characteristics can be used to assess maturation. Tanner (Marshall & Tanner, 1969, 1970;

Tanner, 1975) devised a system of assessment that separately places boys and girls into one of five stages based on breast, pubic hair, and genitalia development. Stage 1 is the immature, prepubertal state and stage 5 is the fully sexually mature state. The average individual moves through these stages in approximately 4 years, so even with several years of variation in the timing of maturation, this assessment can only be used for about 6 years of the growth period. In addition, there are many individual exceptions to the course of progression. Ratings for axillary hair, voice change, and facial hair aren't precise enough for assessing maturation, although these are obvious characteristics of ongoing maturation.

A relatively precise assessment of maturation can be obtained from skeletal maturation. By comparing an X ray of skeletal

(continued)

(continued)

maturation to a set of standards, developmentalists can assign individuals a skeletal age. Early maturers have an older skeletal age than chronological age, and late maturers have a younger skeletal age than chronological age. This maturation assessment is described in more detail in chapter 4.

Given the disadvantages of the direct assessments of maturation, many educators and therapists infer maturation status by comparing a set of growth measurements with group norms. That is, if a girl is in the 75th percentile for height, the 70th percentile for weight, the 80th percentile for shoulder breadth, and so on, we could infer that she is an early maturer. Of course, we could be fooled if her genetic potential was to be a large individual. She might be average in maturation status, just larger for her age than average because she has inherited the genetic potential to be large in size. We must always keep in mind the limitations of inferring maturation from growth measurements, yet we still might find it useful to do an inference when considering the movement performance potential of an individual child or youth.

Adulthood and Aging

Growth ends for humans in the late teens or early 20s, but the status and size of the body attained during the growth years are not necessarily maintained in adulthood. Some measures of body size can change in adulthood. These changes reflect the aging of tissues but probably reflect to a greater extent the influence of extrinsic factors. For example, a lack of weight-bearing exercise and calcium in the diet could contribute to osteoporosis and a resulting decrease in height. Over the life span, the range of extrinsic factors that might or might not influence an individual and the timing of their influence are extremely variable. Naturally, then, we expect to see more and more individual variability in changes of body size as we move through the life span.

Men and women grow slightly in height into their 20s. Trunk length may even increase very slightly into the mid-40s. Aside from these small increases, height is stable through adulthood. It is common for an individual's stature to decrease slightly in older adulthood (figure 3.10). Some of this decrease results from the compression and flattening of the body's connective tissues, especially the cartilage pads between the vertebrae in the spinal column. The result is a compression of the spinal column and a decrease in trunk length. The bones also lose density as a result of progressive modifications in the protein matrix of the skeleton (Timiras, 1972). This breakdown is more severe in persons with osteoporosis and can result in the collapse of one or more vertebrae. If this occurs, the loss of stature is pronounced (figure 3.11). Heightened awareness in recent years of the devastating effects of osteoporosis on well-being has led to more interest in the prevention and treatment of osteoporosis. In the future, this could lead to less pronounced loss of height in older adulthood.

Figure 3.10 Body height in adulthood.
Reprinted from Spirduso 1995; adapted from Frisancho 1990.

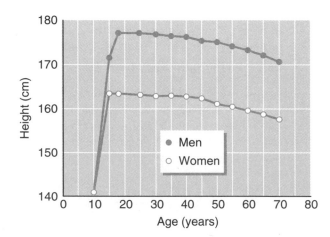

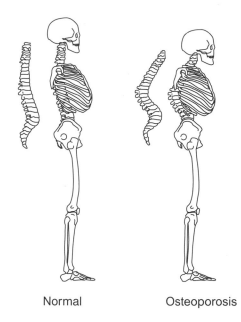

Normal   Osteoporosis

Figure 3.11 Loss of height in those with osteoporosis can be pronounced. Compression fractures of the vertebrae lead to kyphosis (dowager's hump) and pressure on the viscera, causing abdominal distension.

Reprinted from Aloia 1989.

 For additional experience taking anthropometric measurements on older adults, download Lab 3.3 Anthropometric Measurement of an Older Adult from the Student Resources section at www.HumanKinetics.com/LifeSpanMotorDevelopment.

Adults typically start gaining weight in their early 20s (figure 3.12). This is related to changes in lifestyle. Young adults who begin careers and families commonly take less time to exercise and prepare healthy meals. In contrast, adults who exercise regularly and eat wisely often maintain their weight or even gain muscle and lose fat. Older adults sometimes lose weight, probably as a result of inactivity and a consequent loss of muscle tissue. Loss of appetite accompanying lifestyle changes can also be a factor. Again, active older adults are not as likely to lose muscle weight.

Summary and Synthesis

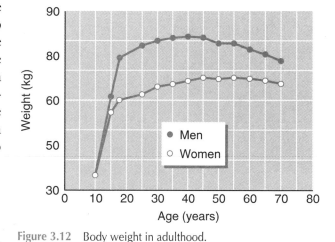

Figure 3.12 Body weight in adulthood.

Reprinted from Spirduso 1995; adapted from Frisancho 1990.

Knowledge of the process of overall postnatal growth provides parents, educators, and therapists with the information they need to see how changing structural constraints affect the movement that arises from individual, task, and environmental constraints. Whole-body growth proceeds in a characteristic pattern known as the sigmoid pattern, but the rate of maturation varies between the sexes and among individuals. Knowing the normal process and the normal variability among individuals helps professionals detect abnormal or retarded growth in individuals.

As individuals move through their growing years and then through their adult years, extrinsic factors contribute more and more to the variability we see among individuals. Because extrinsic factors usually can be manipulated (i.e., accentuated, minimized, or removed), everyone has an interest in knowing what factors have an effect and how they act on individuals.

The individual structural constraints that affect movement often do so at a system level rather than at a whole-body level. For example, muscle growth influences available strength for executing skills. Our understanding of the role of changing structural constraints requires a look at the development of those body systems involved in movement over the life span. This is our task in the next chapter.

 ## Discussion Questions

1. Discuss the differences between measurements of growth and direct measurements of maturation. What does each measure? What are examples of each?

2. What is the difference between a distance curve and a velocity curve? What does each type of curve tell you about growth? Why are peaks in the velocity curves of interest?

3. What areas of a fetus's body advance first? In what directions does growth proceed?

4. Describe how teratogens reach a fetus. What are some of the factors that determine the effect a teratogen has on a fetus?

5. Describe the gender differences in the course of overall growth from infancy to adulthood. Include the average ages for entering the adolescent growth spurt, peak height velocity, puberty, and the tapering off of growth in height.

6. What body measurements can change in older adulthood? How do they change?

7. Imagine someone who gradually gains 20 pounds between the ages of 20 and 40 years. What could have caused the change? What are the repercussions of this additional weight?

 ## Learning Activities

Secular Trends

A **secular trend** is a change in a landmark of development over successive generations, usually by influence of extrinsic factors. Some researchers have hypothesized that currently there are secular trends toward earlier maturity, taller standing heights, and greater body weights. Conduct an Internet search to locate information on these possible secular trends. Classify your information as objective research conducted on a large number of participants, anecdotal information about a single case, or opinion. Taken all together, do you find credible evidence that a secular trend exists for any of these three landmarks of development?

Development and Aging of Body Systems

The Systems Act As Individual Constraints

chapter 4

HOW TO BUILD A BABY'S BRAIN

STUDIES SHOW TALKING WITH INFANTS SHAPES BASIS OF ABILITY TO THINK

HOW BREAST MILK PROTECTS NEWBORNS

GRANDPARENT DEVELOPMENT AND INFLUENCE

These are all titles of recent articles in popular publications such as the *New York Times*, *Newsweek*, and *Scientific American*. There is great interest in doing anything and everything that might improve the quality of life at any point in the life span. In particular, articles sell that help parents give their children an edge, that tout remedies for the symptoms of aging, that promise quick results. How do we know whether ideas have merit?

Notice that most of the aforementioned influences on growth and development operate at the system level. In other words, they promote neurological development, bone growth, and so on. These systems act as the individual's structural constraints. So, the fundamental questions are how do the body systems normally develop; what can influence this development and when; and for those of us interested in motor development, what influence does all of this have on movement?

We already acknowledged that postnatal growth, development, and aging are a product of genetic and extrinsic influences. Obviously this hints that we might indeed manipulate extrinsic factors to influence development, but again, the influence is likely to be on one of the body's systems. To fully understand how the interaction of the changing, developing individual with the task and with the environment gives rise to movement, we must answer these fundamental questions at the system level. We must understand how growth and aging of the systems typically proceed and the range of variation in system development among individuals, how and when the systems might be influenced, and what the impact on movement might be. We start our discussion of the systems with the skeletal system and continue with the other major systems. Our discussion of these systems' impacts on movement continues throughout this text.

 Chapter Objectives

This chapter will

- ▲ identify developmental changes in the skeletal, muscular, adipose, endocrine, and nervous systems over the life span,

- ▲ note the interaction of the systems during development and aging,

- ▲ discuss the periods when rapid change in the systems makes them particularly sensitive to external influences, and

- ▲ identify a trend of increasing influence of external factors and decreasing influence of genetic factors as individuals proceed through the life span.

DEVELOPMENT OF THE SKELETAL SYSTEM

The skeletal system defines an individual's structure. It is not a hard and static structure. Rather, the skeleton is living tissue. It undergoes considerable change over the life span and reflects the influence of both genetic and external factors.

Early Development of the Skeletal System

Early in embryonic life the skeletal system exists as a "cartilage model" of the bones. At the fetal age of 2 months, **primary ossification centers** appear in the midportions of the long bones, such as the humerus (upper arm) and femur (thigh), and begin to form bone cells (figure 4.1). The bone shafts ossify outward in both directions from these primary centers until the entire shafts are ossified at birth. At birth, about 400 ossification centers exist. Another 400 appear after birth.

Postnatal bone growth in length occurs at a **secondary ossification center** at the end of the shaft, termed the **epiphyseal plate,** growth plate, or **pressure epiphysis** (figure 4.2). The epiphyseal plate has many cellular layers (figure 4.3) where cartilage cells are formed, grow, align, and finally erode to leave new bone in place. Bone is thus laid down at the epiphyseal plates. These cells and the process of laying down new bone depend on nourishment through the blood supply, shown as the capillary invasion zone

The **primary ossification centers** are areas in the midportion of the shafts of long bones where bone cells are formed so that the cartilage model bones of the fetal skeleton begin ossifying, from the center outward, to form bone shafts.

The **secondary ossification centers,** or **epiphyseal plates,** are the areas near the ends of long bones where new bone cells are formed and deposited so that the bones grow in length. Active secondary ossification centers are indicated on X rays by a line (an area not opaque) that is a layer of cartilage cells. Such an area is also called a **pressure epiphysis,** especially if it is at the end of a weight-bearing bone.

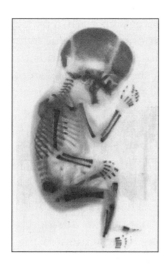

Figure 4.1 A human fetal skeleton at about 18 weeks. Dark areas indicate the ossified portions of the developing skeleton. Spaces between dark areas are occupied by cartilage models.

Provided by Carolina Biological Supply Company.

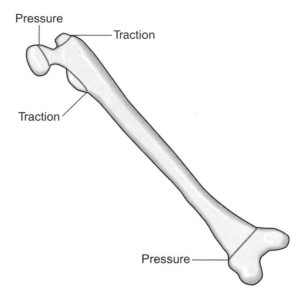

Figure 4.2 Pressure epiphyses are located at the ends of long bones, such as the femur (thigh bone) pictured here. Epiphyses also occur at muscle tendon attachment sites, called traction epiphyses.

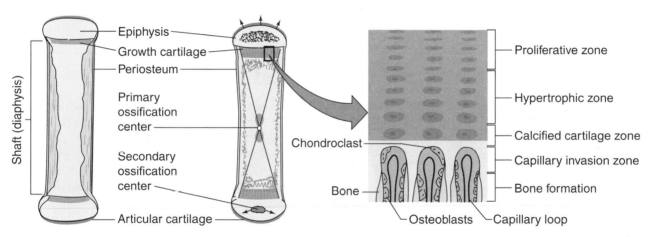

Figure 4.3 Development of a long bone in childhood. The epiphyseal growth plate, between the epiphysis and shaft, is enlarged on the right to show the zones in which new cells ossify.

Reprinted from Pritchard 1979.

in the figure. Small round bones, such as those in the wrist, simply ossify from the center outward.

Growth at the ossification centers ceases at different times in various bones. At the epiphyseal plates, the cartilage zone eventually disappears, and the shaft, or diaphysis, of the bone fuses with the epiphysis. Once the epiphyseal plates of a long bone fuse, the length of the bone is fixed. Almost all epiphyseal plates are closed by age 18 or 19.

Recall that girls as a group mature faster than boys. It is no surprise, then, that the various ossification centers appear at younger chronological ages in girls than in boys. Likewise, the epiphyseal plates close at younger chronological ages in girls than in boys. For example, the epiphysis at the head of the humerus closes in girls at 15.5 years but in boys at 18.1 years, on average (Hansman, 1962). Individuals, of course, have their own unique timing, so a group of children at the same chronological age could easily vary in skeletal age by 3 years or more.

Appositional bone growth is bone growth by addition of new layers on previously formed layers so that a bone grows in girth.

💡 Because linear growth is almost completely the result of skeletal growth, measures of stature reflect the linear growth of bone.

❓ Broken bones are not uncommon for children. Breaks in a bone shaft usually heal quickly and completely. What might be the repercussion, however, of a break at an epiphyseal plate?

While the long bones are growing in length, they also increase in girth, a process called **appositional bone growth.** This is achieved by the addition of new tissue layers under the periosteum, a very thin outer covering of the bone, much like a tree adds to its girth under its bark. The shaft of a long bone is narrower than the ends. Therefore, the bone must be reshaped as it grows in length through a resorption process in the metaphyseal region between the diaphysis (shaft) and epiphysis (figure 4.3).

🖥 **If you are interested in learning more about the process of establishing skeletal age, download Lab 4.1 Estimating Skeletal Age from the Student Resources section at www.HumanKinetics.com/LifeSpanMotorDevelopment.**

Epiphyses also occur at muscle tendon attachment sites, where they are called traction epiphyses. You might have heard of a familiar condition that occurs during the growth period in some youths—Osgood-Schlatter disease. This is an irritation of the traction epiphysis at the tibial tuberosity where the patellar tendon attaches to the shin bone below the knee. Pediatricians usually have youths with this condition refrain from vigorous, especially weight-bearing and jumping, activities to prevent further irritation of the site. Injuries to both traction and pressure epiphyses can influence growth status.

🖥 **To explore the significance of various sport injuries to children and youths, download Lab 4.2 Exploring Skeletal Injuries in Youth Sport from the Student Resources section at www.HumanKinetics.com/LifeSpanMotorDevelopment.**

Assessment of Skeletal Age

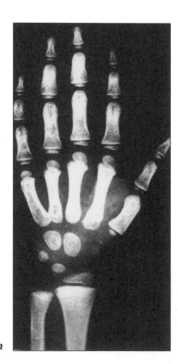
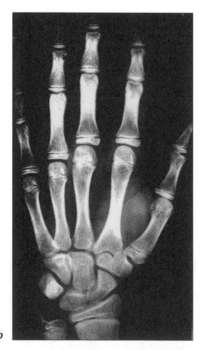

The growth status of the bones can be used as an assessment system by comparing an individual's status of development with an atlas or standard, a publication that pictures skeletal development at many levels. These levels are assigned a skeletal age. The most common bones used for this purpose are the hand and wrist bones (figure 4.4). So, from an individual's X ray of the hand and wrist, one could determine skeletal age by finding the picture in the atlas closest to the individual's X ray. For example, a boy might have a skeletal age of 8.5 years. If his chronological age is under 8.5 we would know he is an early maturer; if it is over 8.5 we would know he is a late maturer. Skeletal age easily can be a year ahead or behind chronological age, so we see how much variation there can be in maturation status even among those born on the same day. An obvious disadvantage to this method of assessing skeletal age is the necessity of an X ray, which is expensive and exposes the child to radiation.

Figure 4.4 Hand and wrist X rays are often used for assessment of skeletal age. The numerous hand and wrist bones provide multiple sites for comparison of a child's X ray with the numerous standard X rays found in an assessment atlas. Here are two X rays from an atlas. *(a)* The standard for boys 48 months old and girls 37 months old. *(b)* The standard for boys 156 months old and girls 128 months old. Note how much more ossification (hardening) has occurred in the small wrist bones and the larger ossified area at the epiphyseal plates of the hand bones and the forearm bones.

Reprinted from Pyle 1971.

Aging of the Skeletal System

Bone undergoes remodeling throughout the life span. Old bone is replaced by new bone. In youth, new bone is formed faster than older bone is resorbed, allowing for growth. In adulthood, though, bone formation begins to slow and eventually can't keep pace with resorption. The result is a loss of bone tissue, starting as early as the mid-20s and averaging about 1% of bone mass per year (Smith, Sempos, & Purvis, 1981).

Bone composition also changes over the life span. Children have essentially equal amounts of inorganic and organic components in their bone tissue, but older adults have seven times more inorganic material, making the bone more brittle and subject to microfracture (Astrand & Rodahl, 1986; Exton-Smith, 1985).

The skeletal structure itself changes little in young adulthood. Many older adults suffer from a major bone mineral disorder, osteoporosis, which is characterized by a loss of bone mass and, consequently, bone strength. The loss can be as great as 2 to 3% of bone mass per year (Parfitt & Kleerkoper, 1984). The bone becomes abnormally porous through the enlargement of the canals or the formation of spaces in the bone. This condition increases the risk of fractures, especially at the hip, and adds to the difficulty of fracture repair (Timiras, 1972). Microfractures of the vertebrae in the spine are another consequence of osteoporosis. Eventually vertebrae may even collapse, resulting in a dramatic change of skeletal structure (figure 3.11 on p. 45). The rib cage collapses forward, the lower edge resting on the pelvis, so the posture becomes stooped, and standing height is notably reduced.

Bone loss with aging is related to changes in certain hormone levels, dietary deficiencies, and decreased exercise. In postmenopausal women, decreased levels of estrogen are implicated because estrogen hormones stimulate osteoblastic activity. This might account for the higher incidence of osteoporosis in older adult women than in men. Prolonged deficiency of calcium in the diet is a major factor in osteoporosis, along with a shortage of vitamins and minerals. Cumming (1990) demonstrated the importance of dietary calcium by finding that women in early menopause who took a calcium supplement lost less than half the bone mass of women who took no supplement. Exercise probably has an effect on the maintenance of bone by increasing bone formation, whereas calcium and estrogen supplementation lower bone resorption (Franck, Beuker, & Gurk, 1991; Heaney, 1986). When a person engages in physical activity, the mechanical forces applied to the bones help maintain bone thickness and density. In fact, significant increases in bone mass are seen when older adults initiate exercise programs (Dalsky, 1989; Smith, 1982).

It is likely that these extrinsic factors—hormone level, diet, and exercise—work in combination to influence bone loss and that we do not fully understand how they interact. However, it is clear that strategies are available to minimize the loss of bone tissue in adulthood. Widespread attention to the factors that can be manipulated, such as diet and exercise, and to early detection and treatment of osteoporosis changes the outlook for many in regard to maintaining bone tissue over their life span.

DEVELOPMENT OF THE MUSCULAR SYSTEM

Whereas the skeletal system provides the body's structure, the muscular system allows its movement. More than 200 muscles permit a vast number of movements and positions for the human body. Like the skeletal system, the muscular system changes over the life span, under the influence of genetic and external factors.

Early Development of the Muscular System

Muscle fibers (cells) grow during prenatal life by hyperplasia, an increase in the number of muscle cells, and by hypertrophy, an increase in muscle cell size. At birth, muscle mass

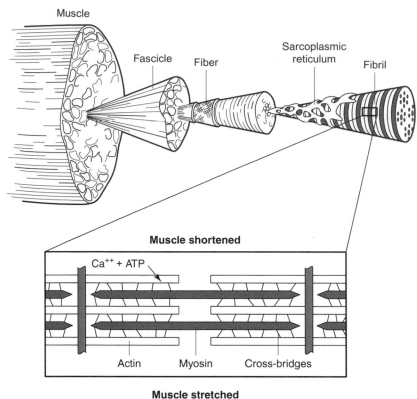

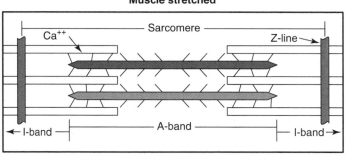

Figure 4.5 Muscle structure. The sarcomeres, or contractile units, compose muscle cells (myofibrils), which in turn make up a muscle fiber. Bundles of fibers compose the muscle.

Reprinted from Houglum 2001.

accounts for 23 to 25% of body weight. Hyperplasia continues for a short time after birth, but thereafter muscle growth occurs predominantly by hypertrophy (Malina, 1978). The sigmoid pattern of growth in weight reflects the growth of muscle tissue.

Muscle growth occurs in two dimensions, diameter and length. Muscle fiber diameter increases with growth, although the extent of increase in diameter is related to the intensity of activity to which the muscle is subjected during growth. Naturally, muscles must increase in length as the skeleton grows, and this occurs by the addition of sarcomeres (contractile units; figure 4.5) at the muscle–tendon junction as well as by the lengthening of the sarcomeres (Malina & Bouchard, 1991).

Gender differences in muscle mass are minimal during childhood, with muscle mass constituting a slightly greater proportion of body weight in boys. During and after adolescence, however, gender differences are marked. Muscle mass increases rapidly in boys up to about age 17 and ultimately accounts for 54% of men's body weight. In sharp contrast, girls add muscle mass only until age 13, on the average, and muscle mass makes up only 45% of women's body weight (Malina, 1978). The large gender differences in muscle mass involve upper body musculature more than leg musculature. For example, the rate of growth in arm musculature is nearly twice as high for males as for females, but the difference in calf muscle growth is relatively small. These gender differences in the addition of muscle mass are related to hormonal influences, which we will discuss later in this chapter.

Muscle Fiber Type

Adult muscle consists of three main types of fibers: type I (**slow-twitch**) fibers, which are suited to endurance activities; and types IIa and IIb (**fast-twitch**) fibers, which are suited to intense short-duration activities (figure 4.6). At birth, 15 to 20% of the muscle fibers have yet to differentiate into type I, type IIa, or type IIb fibers (Baldwin, 1984; Colling-Saltin, 1980). This has led to speculation that an infant's early activities might influence the ultimate proportion of the three types of fibers, but this issue remains unresolved.

A **twitch** is a brief period of contraction of a muscle fiber (cell) followed by relaxation. Muscles can be classified as **slow twitch** or **fast twitch,** with slow-twitch muscles having a slower contraction–relaxation cycle and greater endurance than fast-twitch muscles.

The proportion of type I fibers is fixed by 1 year of age. The percentage of type IIa fibers compared with type IIb fibers is greater in adults than in children, implying that this proportion is not fixed during childhood, but it is difficult for researchers to measure the number of type IIb fibers accurately. Proportions also vary greatly among individuals (Malina & Bouchard, 1991), so the shift in proportion could reflect the makeup of groups tested by researchers. Questions about the alteration of fiber type proportions must await further research on the biochemical factors involved in muscle development (Baldwin, 1984).

Motor Units

We can also categorize **motor units** as either fast twitch or slow twitch by their speed of contraction and relaxation. Many human muscles are composed of both fast- and slow-twitch motor units. At birth, these mixed-composition muscles are composed predominantly of fast-twitch units. During the first 2 years of postnatal life, some units become slow twitch (Malina & Bouchard, 1991). This transition also leads to speculation that the ultimate proportions can be influenced during early development, but far more research is needed before we can consider this suggestion seriously.

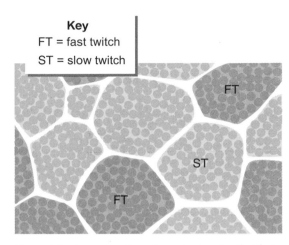

Key
FT = fast twitch
ST = slow twitch

Figure 4.6 A cross section of muscle showing that fast-twitch (FT) and slow-twitch (ST) fibers are intermingled.

A **motor unit** is all of the muscle fibers that are innervated by a single motor neuron (nerve cell).

Aging of the Muscular System

Body composition begins changing in young adulthood, with the proportion of lean body weight decreasing. This reflects not so much a loss of muscle but an increase in fat weight. Only 10% of skeletal muscle mass is lost on average between the mid-20s and age 50. Changes in diet and physical activity level are probably responsible for this shift.

Beginning around age 50, though, individuals begin to lose muscle mass at a greater rate. The extent of loss varies greatly, with those individuals who maintain a good diet and participate in resistance exercise losing far less muscle than others lose, but on average an additional 30% of muscle mass is lost by age 80. By very old age, sedentary individuals with poor nutrition can lose as much as 50% of the muscle mass they possessed in young adulthood.

The number and the diameter (size) of muscle fibers appear to decrease (Green, 1986; Lexell, Henriksson-Larsen, Wimblad, & Sjostrom, 1983). The loss in number of fibers is small before the 50s, only about 5% of the adult number (Arabadjis, Heffner, & Pendergast, 1990), but is more rapid thereafter, approximately 35% (Lexell, Taylor, & Sjostrom, 1988). There is still debate whether the loss in muscle mass is of all three types of muscle fibers or whether type II fibers undergo a greater loss than type I fibers (Green, 1986).

? Are there any psychological, social, or cultural factors that could explain gender differences in muscle mass? Consider various points in the life span.

Cardiac Muscle

The heart is muscle tissue, too. Like skeletal muscle, it grows by hyperplasia and hypertrophy. The right ventricle (lower chamber) is larger than the left ventricle at birth, but the left ventricle catches up after birth by growing more rapidly than the right so that the heart soon reaches adult proportions (figure 4.7). The heart generally follows the sigmoid pattern of whole-body growth, including a growth spurt in adolescence such that the ratio of heart volume to body weight remains approximately the same throughout growth.

Early in the 20th century some researchers thought that the large blood vessels around the heart developed more slowly than the heart itself. This implied that children who engaged in vigorous activity might be at risk. Later, it was shown that this myth had

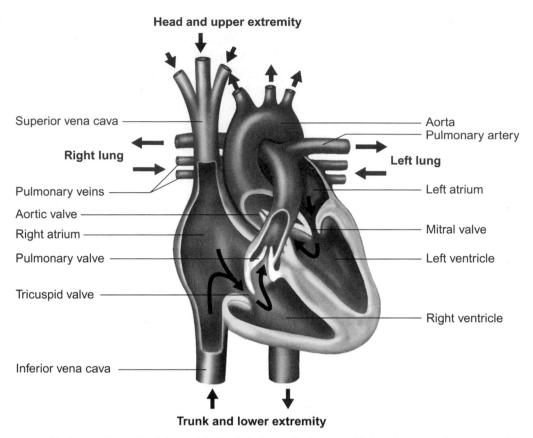

Head and upper extremity

Superior vena cava

Aorta
Pulmonary artery

Right lung

Pulmonary veins

Left lung

Aortic valve

Left atrium

Right atrium

Mitral valve

Pulmonary valve

Left ventricle

Tricuspid valve

Right ventricle

Inferior vena cava

Trunk and lower extremity

Figure 4.7   The human heart. The left ventricle is relatively smaller in size at birth and must catch up in growth in the early postnatal weeks.

Reprinted from National Strength and Conditioning Association 2000.

resulted from a misinterpretation of measurements taken in the late 1800s; in fact, blood vessel growth is proportional to that of the heart (Karpovich, 1937, 1991).

In old age, the heart's ability to adapt to an increased workload declines. This might relate in part to degeneration of the heart muscle, a decrease in elasticity, and changes in the fibers of the heart valves (Klausner & Schwartz, 1985; Shephard, 1981). The major blood vessels also lose elasticity (Fleg, 1986). Most changes in the heart muscles of individuals, however, are related to changes in lifestyle and resulting pathology rather than aging of the cardiac muscle fibers.

> It has been difficult for researchers to distinguish the changes that are an inevitable result of age from those that reflect the average older adult's lack of fitness or poor diet.

DEVELOPMENT OF THE ADIPOSE SYSTEM

A common misconception about adipose (fat) tissue is that its presence in any amount is undesirable. In reality, adipose tissue plays a vital role in energy storage, insulation, and protection.

Early Development of the Adipose System

The amount of adipose tissue increases in early life. It first appears in the fetus at 3.5 months and increases rapidly during the last 2 prenatal months. Despite this late prenatal increase, adipose tissue accounts for only 0.5 kg (1.1 lb) of body weight at birth. After a rapid increase of fat during the first 6 postnatal months, fat mass increases gradually until age 8 in both boys and girls. In boys, adipose tissue continues to gradually increase through adolescence, but girls experience a more dramatic increase. As a result, adult women have more fat weight than adult men, with averages of 14 kg (31 lb) and 10 kg (22 lb), respectively. Fat weight during growth increases by both hyperplasia and hypertrophy, but cell size does not increase significantly until puberty.

Individual fatness varies widely during infancy and early childhood. A fat baby will not necessarily become a fat child. After 7 to 8 years of age, though, it is more likely that individuals maintain their relative fatness. An overweight 8-year-old has a high risk of becoming an overweight adult.

Fat Distribution

The distribution of fat in the body changes during growth. During childhood, internal fat (fat around the viscera) increases faster than subcutaneous fat, which actually decreases until age 6 or 7. Boys and girls then show an increase in subcutaneous fat until they are 12 or 13. This increase in subcutaneous fat continues in girls, but boys typically lose subcutaneous fat in midadolescence. Adolescent boys also tend to add more subcutaneous fat to their trunks than to their limbs, whereas girls have increased subcutaneous fat at both sites. Note in figure 4.8 that skinfold measurements for boys' extremities (top blue line) actually decrease, except during the growth spurt. Trunk skinfolds tend to hold steady but also increase during the growth spurt. Girls' skinfold measurements (black lines) increase steadily for both trunk and limbs, especially after age 7. Girls usually add more subcutaneous fat to their legs than to their arms.

There is much we don't know about adipose tissue development and obesity. Researchers are currently examining many topics, including maternal weight gain during pregnancy, early infant feeding, and genetic factors. Of particular interest are the two periods when the number of adipose cells increases: during the first 6 postnatal months and around puberty. Increases in cell number are significant because once they are formed, adipose cells persist, even with malnutrition; that is, the cells may be "empty" of fat, but they still exist. Therefore these two periods may be critical in the control of obesity.

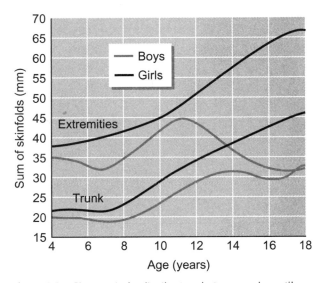

Figure 4.8 Changes in fat distribution during growth are illustrated by plotting the sum of five trunk skinfold measurements and five extremity skinfold measurements. Note the increase in both in girls, contrasting with a decrease in extremity subcutaneous fat in boys during adolescence.

Reprinted from Malina and Bouchard 1988.

? What are the life span implications of individuals adding too much fat during the periods of increase in fat tissue?

Adipose Tissue in Older Adults

Both sexes tend to gain fat weight during the adult years, reflecting changes in nutrition and activity level. The average woman gains 11.8 kg (26 lb) and the average man gains 8.2 kg (18 lb) between 20 and 50 years of age (Hellmich, 1999). Total body weight begins to decline after age 50, but this reflects loss of bone and muscle because body fat actually continues to increase.

Body fat redistributes with aging. In men, subcutaneous fat on the limbs decreases, while subcutaneous fat on the trunk and internal fat around the organs increase (Schwartz et al., 1990; Borkan, Hunts, Gerzof, Robbins, & Silbert, 1983). In women, subcutaneous fat tends to be stable after age 45 years, but internal body fat continues to increase.

It is difficult to identify the typical pattern of adipose tissue gain or loss in older adults. Because obese individuals have a higher mortality rate, either lighter individuals survive to be included in studies of older adults, whereas obese individuals do not, or thinner adults are more eager to participate in research studies. It appears that an increase in fat weight with aging is not inevitable; for example, lumberjacks in Norway who have a very active lifestyle as a result of their profession, persons from undernourished parts of the world, and master athletes do not demonstrate such gains (Shephard, 1978b; Skrobak-Kaczynski & Andersen, 1975). Typically, though, most older adults add some fat weight as they age, with active older adults adding less than their sedentary peers.

DEVELOPMENT OF THE ENDOCRINE SYSTEM

Hormones are chemical substances secreted into body fluids by a gland. The substances have a specific effect on the activities of target cells, tissues, or organs.

The cells of a living being must be precisely regulated for their content and temperature as well as the concentration of hydrogen ions in the cell. The nervous system and the endocrine system are the control systems regulating the cells of the body. The endocrine system controls specific cellular functions through chemical substances called **hormones.**

Early Development of the Endocrine System

Hormones play an important role in regulating growth and maturation. Regulation of growth, however, is a complex and delicate interaction of hormones, genes, nutrients, and environmental factors. This discussion highlights only the major features of endocrine growth regulation.

Although many hormones are involved in the regulation of growth and maturation, three major types of hormones are discussed here:

1. Pituitary growth hormone (GH)
2. The thyroid hormones (thyroxine, triiodothyronine, thyrocalcitonin)
3. Two gonadal hormones (androgen, estrogen)

Either an excess or a deficiency of these hormones may disturb the normal process of growth and development. Although different in their chemical structure, all three promote growth in the same way: they stimulate protein anabolism (constructive metabolism), resulting in the retention of substances needed to build tissues. Each hormone plays a unique role in growth at a unique time (Timiras, 1972).

The endocrine system acts in concert with the neurological system. Hormones secreted by the hypothalamus in the brain regulate the pituitary gland, which, in turn, regulates the adrenal gland, thyroid gland, and release of the sex hormones.

Growth Hormone

Growth hormone (GH) influences growth during childhood and adolescence by stimulating protein anabolism so that new tissue can be built. Under the control of the central nervous system, GH is secreted by the anterior pituitary gland (figure 4.9). Growth hormone enhances the mobilization of stored fat while conserving carbohydrates. The body needs this hormone for normal growth after birth. A deficiency or absence of GH results in growth abnormalities and in some cases the cessation of linear growth.

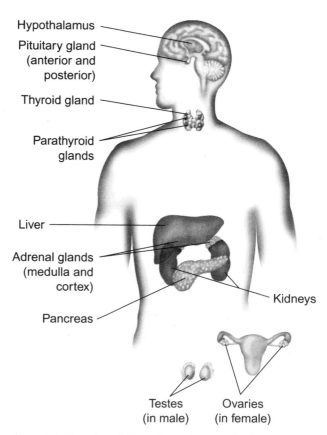

Hypothalamus
Pituitary gland (anterior and posterior)
Thyroid gland
Parathyroid glands
Liver
Adrenal glands (medulla and cortex)
Pancreas
Kidneys
Testes (in male)
Ovaries (in female)

Figure 4.9 Location of the various endocrine glands.
Reprinted from National Strength and Conditioning Association 2000.

Thyroid Hormones

The thyroid hormones are secreted by the thyroid gland, located in the anterior neck region. Thyroxine and triiodothyronine influence whole-body growth after birth, but they also influence the development of certain tissues by increasing oxygen consumption in these tissues. The thyroid gland also secretes thyrocalcitonin, which plays a role in skeletal growth. It decreases circulating calcium by inhibiting bone resorption and by promoting calcium deposition in the bones.

The level of thyroid-stimulating hormone (TSH) secreted by the pituitary gland regulates secretion of the thyroid hormones secreted by the thyroid gland. TSH excretion is, in turn, increased by a releasing factor found in the brain's hypothalamus. Thus, two systems appear to be acting in concert: a pituitary–thyroid system and a nervous system–thyroid system. You can see that the endocrine system is delicately balanced. In fact, a GH–thyroid relationship also exists because thyroxine must be present for GH to be effective.

Gonadal Hormones

The gonadal hormones affect growth and sexual maturation, particularly during adolescence, by stimulating development of the secondary sex characteristics and the sex organs. The androgens, specifically testosterone from the testes and androgens from the cortex of the adrenal glands, hasten fusion of the epiphyseal growth plates in the bones. Thus, these hormones promote skeletal maturation (fusion) at the expense of linear growth; this explains why early maturers tend to be shorter in stature than later maturers.

Androgens also play a role in the adolescent growth spurt of muscle mass by increasing nitrogen retention and protein synthesis. This spurt is more significant in young men than in young women because men secrete both testosterone and adrenal androgens, whereas women produce only the adrenal androgens. In women, the ovaries and the adrenal cortex secrete estrogens. Increased estrogen secretion during adolescence, as with androgens, speeds epiphyseal closure, but estrogen also promotes fat accumulation, primarily in the breasts and hips. Androstenedione, one of the adrenal androgens, is converted to estrogen in males, and dehydroepiandrosterone, another adrenal androgen, is converted to testosterone in females. As a result, men and women have both estrogen and testosterone but in very different proportions.

Insulin

The hormones we have discussed up to this point all play a major and direct role in growth and development. Another familiar hormone, insulin, has an indirect role in growth. Produced in the pancreas, insulin is vital to carbohydrate metabolism, stimulating the transportation of glucose and amino acids through membranes. Its presence also is necessary for the full functioning of GH. A deficiency of insulin can also decrease protein synthesis. This is detrimental at any time in life but especially during growth.

Aging of the Endocrine System

In adults, hormones play a role in three areas that relate to physical activity:

1. Regulation of cardiovascular performance
2. Mobilization of fuel
3. Synthesis of new protein (Shephard, 1978b)

Information about age-related hormonal changes is limited, but we are aware of several features of hormonal function in aging. Basal levels of GH seem to be stable throughout life, but during exercise, older adults can have a more pronounced increase in GH levels

? Teenage boys sometimes take steroid supplements so that they add muscle mass and look older. Increased secretion of androgen (a steroid) at puberty, though, hastens fusion at the epiphyseal plates. What unintended effect might these supplements have on growing boys?

than younger exercisers. This increase may be an attempt by the body's metabolism to conserve glycogen (the form in which the body stores glucose, a sugar) and reduce protein breakdown through the release of stored fat.

Thyroid function also declines with aging, and thyroid disorders become more prevalent in older adults. A long-term increase in thyroid hormone levels can be related to congestive heart failure. It is therefore important for older adults to be screened for hyperthyroidism. On the other hand, insufficiency of thyroid hormone, or hypothyroidism, is associated with acceleration of aging systems.

Gonadal hormone levels decrease with age. Although we need more information about the side effects of replacement therapy, gonadal hormone replacement therapy appears to counteract many of the effects of aging. Prescribing androgen supplements has been successful in countering muscle wasting and osteoporosis.

Older adults maintain the younger adult secretion levels of insulin, but the incidence of type 2 diabetes (non-insulin-dependent diabetes mellitus, which is caused by insulin deficiency) increases markedly with age. It is possible that older adults do not utilize insulin as effectively as younger adults to promote glycogen storage, thus retarding the mobilization of fuel for exercise.

Proponents of the gradual imbalance theory of aging hold that the neurological system (brain), endocrine system, and immune system begin to fail with advancing age. They also age at different rates, creating imbalances and making it difficult for the aging body to respond to environmental challenges. Although further research on this topic is needed, it is clear that the endocrine system plays a role in aging.

DEVELOPMENT OF THE NERVOUS SYSTEM

No one system is as much the essence of an individual as the nervous system. We need only observe an individual with severe brain injury to know this. The nervous system controls movement and speech. It is the site of thinking, analysis, and memory, and its development is important to social, cognitive, and motor development.

Early Development of the Nervous System

Much of neurological development occurs very early in the life span. The course of neurological development is a prime example of the interplay of genetic and extrinsic factors. Genes direct the development of the nervous system structures and its main circuits. The trillions of finer connections between nervous system cells, however, are greatly influenced by extrinsic factors. Let's consider neurological development in more detail, including the role of extrinsic factors in its development.

Prenatal Growth of the Nervous System

Neurons are the cells of the nervous system that receive and transmit information.

In general, the formation of immature **neurons,** their differentiation into a general type, and their migration to a final position in the nervous system occur prenatally. Neurons proliferate in the prenatal period at an astonishing rate of 4,000 per second. As many as 100 billion are formed. During the third and fourth prenatal months, almost all the neurons that the individual human brain will ever have are formed. Neurons contain a cell body, which carries out functions to keep the cell alive; dendrites, which receive impulses from other neurons; and an axon, which transmits impulses to other structures (figure 4.10).

The new neurons also travel to a final destination during the prenatal period. Some form the brain stem, which controls heartbeat and breathing; some the cerebellum, which

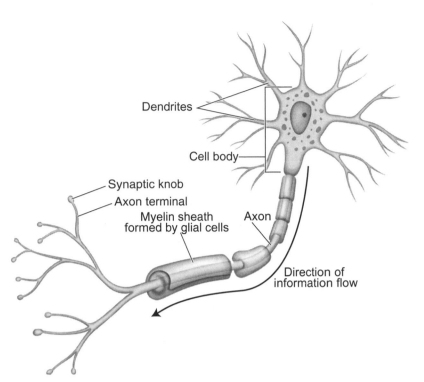

Figure 4.10 The structure of a nerve cell, or neuron. Note that there can be multiple dendrites to carry nerve impulses to the cell body, but only one axon emerges to carry an impulse to other neurons, glands, or muscle. The axon can branch extensively, though.

Reprinted from Wilmore and Costill 1999.

controls posture; and some the cerebral cortex, where perception and thought take place. Generally, neurons are in their final location by the sixth prenatal month.

Once the neurons are in place, they grow an axon. The axon carries an electrical signal to another neuron, a gland, an organ, or muscle. These neuron-to-neuron connections form the brain's circuits. Under genetic control, a neuron's growing axon follows a chemical trail to its general destination.

Late in the prenatal period and early in postnatal life, the neurons fire electrical impulses that strengthen some of the connections among neurons to form circuits. The firing is somewhat automatic prenatally, but stimuli from the senses trigger the firings postnatally. Greenough and colleagues (Comery, Shah, & Greenough, 1995; Comery, Stamoudis, Irwin, & Greenough, 1996; Greenough et al., 1993; Wallace, Kilman, Withers, & Greenough, 1992) found that rats raised with much stimulation grew significantly more **synapses** than those raised without stimuli. The same pattern likely holds for humans. The first postnatal year is one of prolific synaptic formation. Each neuron can establish 1,000 to 100,000 connections.

Postnatal Growth of the Nervous System

At birth the brain is about 25% of its adult weight. Brain growth increases rapidly after birth and reaches 80% of adult weight by age 4. Then it enters a period of steady growth through adolescence. This rapid early growth reflects an increase in the size of the neurons, further branching to form synapses, and an increase in **glia** and **myelin.**

This early, rapid growth makes neurological development very susceptible to extrinsic factors. Poor nutrition, for example, could stunt the growth of the brain, a deficit that might never be recovered. As another example, injury to the left side of the **cerebral cortex** (figure 4.11) early in life leads to deficits in language ability (Witelson, 1987).

A **synapse** is a connection between two neurons, the connection being made by the release of chemicals called neurotransmitters from an axon. These neurotransmitters permeate the cell wall at the dendrite, or cell body, of a receiving neuron to trigger an electrical impulse.

Glia are the cells of the nervous system that support and nourish the neurons. **Myelin** is an insulating sheath around the axons.

The **cerebral cortex** is the wrinkled surface of the brain containing millions of neurons and regulating many human functions and behaviors.

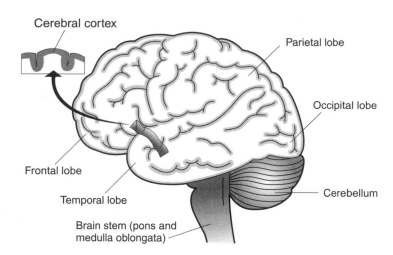

Figure 4.11 The cerebrum and cerebellum of the brain, with a cross section of the cerebral cortex.

Adapted from Shultz, Houglum, and Perrin 2000.

Brain Structures

The spinal cord and lower brain structures are more advanced at birth than the higher brain structures. Lower brain centers involved in vital tasks, such as respiration and food intake, are relatively mature. Lower brain centers also mediate many reflexes and reactions. These automatic movement responses dominate the fetus's and newborn's movements. This also indicates that lower brain centers are relatively more advanced than higher brain centers at this time.

For many years, researchers have interpreted the onset of goal-directed movements in infants as evidence that higher brain centers are maturing. The cortex is involved in purposeful, goal-directed movement. The first clear evidence of successful intentional movement (reaching) occurs at 4 to 5 postnatal months (Bushnell, 1982; McDonnell, 1979). Hence, early researchers assumed that this behavior signaled the functioning of the cortex at about 4 months of age, even though the cerebral hemispheres are formed at birth. More recently, researchers have used positron emission tomography (PET) scans to study the infant brain. The scans show little activity in the frontal cortex at 5 days of age, increased activity at 11 weeks, and adult levels at 7 to 8 months (Chugani & Phelps, 1986). Obviously the process whereby the frontal cortex becomes functional is a gradual one. Specialization of areas of the cortex actually continues well into adulthood.

The development of myelin in the nervous system contributes to speedy conduction of nerve impulses. Myelin cells, composed mostly of fat, wrap themselves around the outgoing neuron cell process, or axon (figure 4.10). Myelinated axons can fire nerve impulses at higher frequencies for longer periods than those not myelinated (Kuffler, Nicholls, & Martin, 1984).

Axons that are as yet unmyelinated in the newborn are probably functional, but **myelination** improves the speed and frequency of firing. The function of the nervous system in movements requiring or benefiting from speedy conduction of nerve impulses, such as a series of rapid movements or postural responses, might be related to the myelination process during development. The importance of myelin is evident in multiple sclerosis, a disease that strikes young adults and breaks down the myelin sheath, resulting in tremor, loss of coordination, and possibly paralysis.

The spinal cord is relatively small and short at birth. A cross-sectional view of the spinal cord, as in figure 4.12, shows a central horn-shaped area of gray matter and a surrounding area of white matter. This central area contains tightly packed neuron cell bodies. Note the roots that lie just outside the cord; they contain the axons of the cord's neurons, and in the case of the sensory roots, nerve cell bodies as well. Fibers from the dorsal and ventral roots merge to form the peripheral (spinal) nerves outside the cord. A

Myelination is the process whereby the axons of the neural cells are insulated when Schwann cells form and wrap themselves around the axon.

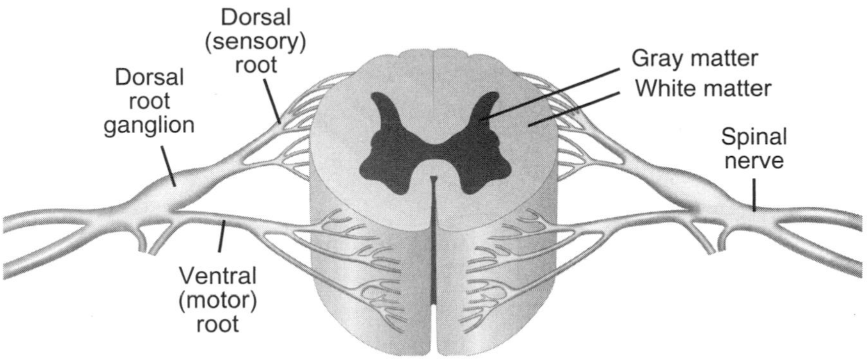

Figure 4.12 A cross section of the spinal cord.
Reprinted from Wilmore and Costill 1999.

marked increase in the myelination of these peripheral nerves occurs 2 to 3 weeks after birth, and this process continues through the second or third year of life.

Two major motor nerve pathways, or **nerve tracts,** carry impulses from the brain down the spinal cord to various parts of the body. One pathway, the **extrapyramidal tract,** is probably involved in delivering the commands for both the random and the postural movements made by the infant in the first days after birth. The other, the **pyramidal tract,** myelinates after birth. It is functioning by 4 to 5 months and controls the muscles for finger movements.

The myelination pattern that the spinal cord and nerve pathways undergo might have implications for motor development. Myelination proceeds in two directions in the cord: first in the cervical portion, followed by the progressively lower portions; and then in the motor (ventral) horns, followed by the sensory (dorsal) horns. The direction of myelination tends to be away from the brain in the motor tracts. In contrast, the direction of myelination is toward the brain in sensory tracts, occurring first in the tactile and olfactory pathways, then in the visual pathways, and finally in the auditory pathways. Sensory pathways mature slightly faster than motor pathways, except in the motor roots and cerebral hemispheres. Higher-level functioning might be possible only when the neurons involved in a behavior are myelinated, allowing faster and more frequent conduction of nerve signals.

Nerve tracts are major neurological pathways. There are two major motor tracts, the extrapyramidal and the pyramidal.

Aging of the Nervous System

As an individual ages, there is a loss or decline in neurons, dendrites, synapses, neurotransmitters, and myelin. The number of glial cells increases, but overall brain weight decreases. In addition to these physiological changes, motor responses to stimuli slow down, although the effect is not nearly so pronounced among older adults who remain physically active and in good health.

Several theories have been advanced to explain how physiological changes result in slowing of responses. One of these theories is the neural network model. In this model, the nervous system is seen as a neural network of links and nodes. To respond to a stimulus, a signal begins at the input end of the individual's nervous system and travels through the network to the output end. With aging, links in the network are thought to break at random so that the neural signal must detour, increasing the time before the response is made. With advancing age, more links break and the processing time for a signal gets longer and longer (Cerella, 1990). Obviously, the loss of neurons, dendrites, and synapses and the decline in neurotransmitters are all physiological changes that would result in broken links within the neural network.

The repercussions of age-related changes in the nervous system are widespread. Slowing of responses can affect movements in recreational activities as well as activities of daily living. Response slowing also affects the performance of cognitive tasks. As in young people, extrinsic factors play a role in nervous system changes. One of the most important is exercise.

 ## Summary and Synthesis

A major theme in this discussion of body systems is that the systems do not develop and age independently of one another. Rather, they develop in concert, one system often stimulating change in another. For example, growth of the long bones may stimulate the muscles to grow in length. In addition, the neurological system directs secretion of the pituitary hormones, which have their own effects (e.g., falling estrogen levels affect bone strength in older women). Thus, a system can have its own timing or pattern of development but still interact with other systems in the bigger picture of the individual's development. Even when we want to focus on the development or aging of one body system, we should do so in the context of the other systems changing as well.

In addition, there are periods when change in a system is more rapid. These are often called sensitive periods because we expect extrinsic factors to be more influential at times of greater change than times of gradual change. Of course, the extrinsic influence could be positive, facilitating growth or slowing aging, or it could be negative, slowing growth or accelerating aging. Insufficient nutrition in the months after birth can have a limiting and lasting effect on development of the nervous system. In contrast, adults who consume a diet rich in calcium can forestall loss of bone density. We benefit from knowing the course of growth and aging in the individual systems because we then can identify the points in the life span that are most susceptible to extrinsic influence, for better or for worse.

Last, extrinsic factors can influence development at any point in the life span but have more influence in development as individuals move through the life span. Genes are influential throughout the life span, but they have their greatest influence in transforming a tiny embryo of a few cells to a complex individual, all in less than 20 years. Extrinsic factors can affect a fetus, but the fetus is protected in the womb from many extrinsic factors. After birth, though, numerous extrinsic factors can influence many aspects of development, at the cell, system, or organism level. These extrinsic factors can have transient or long-lasting effects. For example, resistance exercise promotes muscle strength, but when an individual stops exercising, the muscles begin losing strength. On the other hand, an active lifestyle in preadolescence may promote bone density that has a lifelong benefit.

The structural constraints influencing movement can operate at the system level. So, when we consider how the changing individual interacts with the task and environment to give rise to movement, it will most often be in the context of change in a system. We now know more about changes in the systems that make up an individual's structure. Of course, other characteristics of the individual change with growth and aging. Vision, hearing, and self-confidence are just a few examples. Our knowledge of change in structural constraints, however, allows us to consider the course of motor development.

The model of constraints offers a deeper understanding of motor development than simply a description of the interaction of changing individual, task, and environmental factors. It can also explain why certain movements can arise when they do. This is so because often a particular structural constraint shapes movement at a particular point in the life span. For example, consider a 4-month-old who can hold his head up but can't sit or stand on his own. Why not? We might suggest that the infant needs to undergo an improvement in balance, an increase in trunk muscle strength, an increase in leg muscle strength, an increase in bone density, an increase in leg length to offset the large size of the upper body, or other changes. Which system is the limiting one? The balance system? The muscle system? The skeletal system? That is, which system is the rate limiter, the system limiting the rate of development?

We have come a long way in knowing more about some of the structural changes that accompany growth and aging. We can better predict how specific changes might influence movement, and because we know more about the course of physical development, we can better predict when structural changes might change the movement. We also know more about when an individual is subject to greater or lesser influence from extrinsic factors. This can inform us about changes in extrinsic factors that could bring about changes in movement. Part III will consider the course of motor development as this individual, changing in structure over the life span, interacts with the task to be done and the surrounding environment.

 ## Discussion Questions

1. What is the epiphyseal growth plate? What is the difference between a pressure epiphysis and a traction epiphysis? Why would an injury to the growth plate in a young child be of concern?

2. What is osteoporosis? Whom does it affect, and what are the repercussions for health and participation in activities?

3. Discuss gender differences in the growth of muscle tissue. How does the growth of cardiac muscle compare with that of skeletal muscle?

4. How does the distribution of fat change over the growth period? How does the amount and distribution of fat change in adulthood?

5. What are the major types of hormones involved in growth? How does each affect growth?

6. What contributes to the rapid gains in brain weight during the first year after birth? What part of the brain is most advanced at birth?

7. Choose one extrinsic factor and describe how it might influence the growth of various systems.

8. Design a research study that would tell us if increasing fat weight during adulthood is inevitable or a consequence of extrinsic factors.

9. A few service organizations and agencies focus on eliminating starvation among children in poor countries. Given our description of neurological development, what repercussions would result from ignoring the problem of starvation among the world's children?

 ## Learning Activities

System Changes in Older Adults

Throughout our discussion we described the average or typical course of aging for each system. It is interesting to consider how an individual person either matched or varied from the typical. Locate an adult 60 years of age or older who is willing to discuss what he or she remembers about changes in their skeletal structure, their muscle tissues, and their adipose tissues. You might ask about osteoporosis screenings, changes in body weight during middle and older adulthood, and changes in fat versus muscle weight as they changed body shape. Write a short paper summarizing your conversation, indicating what matched and what varied from the norm described in the text.

Human Growth Hormone

Human growth hormone or GH (or a releasing factor that stimulates GH secretion) is available for sale on the Internet. Yet, the use of GH is banned by many sport governing bodies, and some of these are preparing to test athletes for use of GH as a supplement. Research the use of GH in order to answer the following questions:

1. Why would athletes want to use GH? What effect does it have in individuals who have reached maturity? How does it have these effects?

2. Are there known risks of using GH supplements? If yes, explain your findings.

3. Even if there has been little research on the long-term effects of using GH as a supplement, what are some of the suspected risks of long-term GH supplementation?

Development of Motor Skills Across the Life Span

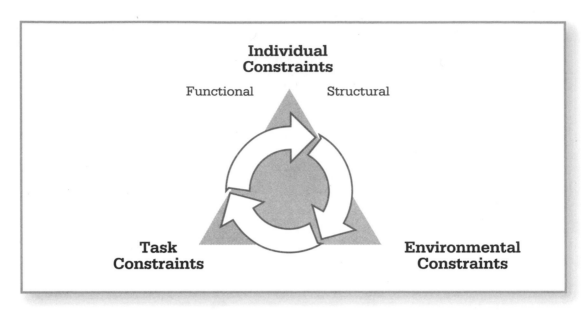

Part III examines motor development over the life span. That is, it discusses the changes in skill performance observed from birth to older adulthood as well as identifies the individual, environmental, or task constraints that might bring about these changes. Chapter 5 discusses early motor development. The acquisition of motor skills is so rapid in the first year of life, and so varied in scope, that the chapter covers all of the changes from birth to approximately 1 year of age.

In chapter 6, changes in locomotor skills are discussed from approximately 1 year of age through the life span. These skills include the most commonly used locomotor patterns, walking and running, as well as skills used in play and sports contexts, such as jumping, hopping, and galloping. Ballistics skills, such as throwing, striking, and kicking, are discussed in chapter 7; manipulative skills, both fine motor skills such as reaching and grasping and gross motor skills such as catching, are covered in chapter 8.

Suggested Reading

Adolph, K.E. (1997). Learning in the development of infant locomotion. *Monographs of the Society for Research in Child Development, 62,* Serial No. 251.

Carr, G. (1997). *Mechanics of sport.* Champaign, IL: Human Kinetics.

Clark, J. (1994). Motor development. In V.S. Ramachandran (Ed.), *Encyclopedia of human behavior* (Vol. 3) (pp. 245-255). New York: Academic Press.

Jeannerod, M. (1996). Reaching and grasping: Parallel specification of visuomotor channels. In H. Heuer & S.W. Keele (Eds.), *Handbook of perception and action. Vol. 2: Motor skills.* London: Academic Press.

McGraw, M.B. (1939). Later development of children specially trained during infancy. *Child Development, 10,* 1–19.

Ridenour, M.V. (1978). Programs to optimize infant motor development. In M.V. Ridenour (Ed.), *Motor development: Issues and applications* (pp. 39–61). Princeton, NJ: Princeton Book Company.

Roberton, M.A., & Halverson, L.E. (1984). *Developing children: Their changing movement.* Philadelphia: Lea & Febiger.

Savelsbergh, G.J.P., & Whiting, H.T.A. (1996). Catching: A motor learning and developmental perspective. In H. Heuer & S.W. Keele (Eds.), *Handbook of perception and action. Vol. 2: Motor skills.* London: Academic Press.

Thelen, E., & Ulrich, B. (1991). Hidden skills. *Monographs of the Society for Research in Child Development, 56,* Serial No. 223.

Wickstrom, R.L. (1983). *Fundamental motor patterns* (3rd ed.). Philadelphia: Lea & Febiger.

Early Motor Development

Fundamental Individual Constraints

GROUNDBREAKING BABY RESEARCH

"Esther Thelen's research on how babies' brains and bodies interact has led her to submerge tots in tanks of warm water and place them on tiny treadmills."

Advancing Indiana, January 2004

RESEARCHERS LOOK AT BRAIN AND BEHAVIOR DEVELOPMENT IN INFANTS

Taking two steps forward sometimes requires a step back when it comes to babies' motor development, according to ongoing research at Purdue University. "These findings indicate that as a baby learns a new skill, such as walking, the brain appears to reorganize itself, resulting in a temporary developmental step backward," says Daniela Corbetta (director of Purdue's Infant Motor Development Laboratory).

Purdue News, August 2000

In the past few years, researchers have taken a careful look at the relationship between movements that infants make and their developing minds. It appears as though this link is much stronger than originally believed. In other words, it is becoming clear that to understand cognitive development in infancy, you need to understand motor development and, eventually, determine the interactions and transactions between them. This chapter provides you with information about the motor behaviors exhibited by infants, which is the first step toward understanding how motor development is related to cognitive and perceptual development during infancy. There are some important practical reasons for knowing about infant motor development as well. In typically developing infants, many movements occur with a fairly predictable order and timing. In fact, it is essential to learn about and understand typical development so that it is apparent when there is deviance—either progression or regression—from the typical pattern.

In terms of motor development, most newborn infants exhibit spontaneous and reflexive movements. As infants move toward becoming toddlers, they begin to attain motor milestones. These gross movements slowly become more refined throughout infancy and early childhood. In addition, infants gain the ability to lift their heads, sit up, and eventually stand with minimal support. In the past, parents and educators alike have thought of this process as maturation. In other words, maturation of the central nervous system was the sole individual constraint to guide early motor behavior. This notion was discussed in chapter 2, and comes from the maturational perspective. However, current research from an ecological perspective suggests that the interplay of many systems (cognitive, perceptual, motor) leads to the movement adaptations seen in infancy. Therefore, this chapter presents the concept that many different constraints in addition to maturation encourage or discourage early motor behavior.

 Chapter Objectives

This chapter will

- ▲ describe different types of movements that occur in infancy,
- ▲ list different infantile reflexes and postural reactions,
- ▲ explain the relationship between infants' early and later movements,
- ▲ describe motor milestones,
- ▲ explain how early movements are shaped by a variety of constraints, and
- ▲ examine postural development and balance in infancy.

HOW DO INFANTS MOVE?

If you watch newborns, you will notice that some of their movements seem to be undirected and without purpose. For example, infants often kick their legs while lying on their backs. These spontaneous movements appear without any apparent stimulation. At other times, infants will move in a specific way every time they are touched in a certain place. Who can resist an infant "holding your hand": grabbing your finger when you touch her palm? An infant is born with a variety of different reflexes that seem to slowly disappear as she ages, and she appears to move with discrete, purposeless actions that have little to do with future voluntary movements. However, there is more to infant motor behavior than meets the eye. Those seemingly random infant movements have an important relationship with intentional movements that occur later in life. After the first few months of life, the infant will begin to attain motor milestones. These motor milestones are particular movement skills that eventually lead to locomotion, reaching, and upright posture.

Newborn movements have been classified into two general categories: random, or spontaneous, movements and infantile reflexes (Clark, 1995). These two types of movements are very different from each other.

Spontaneous Movements

People give much attention to the study of infantile reflexes; however, reflexes represent only a small portion of early motor behavior. How else do newborns move? If not eating or sleeping, newborns most likely will squirm, thrust their legs or arms, stretch their fingers and toes, or make other **spontaneous movements.** Pediatricians, parents, and others believed these movements were without any particular purpose or had no relationship to the future movements the child will someday choose to make. These spontaneous movements seem very different from walking or reaching. However, this may not be the case.

Spontaneous movements are infants' movements that occur without any apparent stimulation.

Supine Kicking and Walking

If a child is laid on his back (the supine position), he will likely spontaneously thrust his legs. This is called supine kicking. Thelen and her colleagues decided to study the nature of supine kicking in infancy (Thelen, 1985, 1995; Thelen & Fisher, 1983; Thelen, Ridley-Johnson, & Fisher, 1983). They analyzed the position and timing of leg segments in these kicks as well as muscular activity in the leg muscles. They discovered some surprising results. The supine kicking was not random but rhythmical, and the kicks had a coordinated pattern. The ankle, knee, and hip joints moved cooperatively with each other, not independently from one another. It seems amazing that these supine kicks during infancy have a coordinated pattern. What is more remarkable is that the coordination of these kicks resembles the positioning and timing of an adult walking step (figure 5.1). The pattern of muscle use in infant supine kicking is also coordinated. Sometimes an infant kicks only one leg, but at other times, an infant will kick both legs alternately, just as an adult alternates legs in walking. Even premature infants perform coordinated supine kicks (Piek & Gasson, 1999; Geerdink, Hopkins, Beek, & Heriza, 1996; Heriza, 1986).

? What might account for some of the differences in infant kicking and adult walking? Think in terms of individual, environmental, and task constraints.

An infant's supine kicks are similar to an adult's walking steps, but they are not identical. Infants' timing is more variable from kick to kick, and they tend to move the joints in unison rather than in sequence. Infants also tend to activate both the muscles for flexing the limb (flexors) and for extending the limb (extensors). This is called cocontraction. In contrast, adults move by alternating flexor and extensor muscles. However, by the end of their first year, infants begin to move the hip, knee, and ankle sequentially rather than in tight unison. Both alternating and synchronous (both legs in unison) kicks are evident after 6 months, indicating that infants are developing more ways to coordinate the two limbs (Thelen, 1985, 1995; Thelen & Fisher, 1983; Thelen et al., 1983).

Spontaneous Arm Movements

Besides supine kicking, infants also move their arms. Newborns' spontaneous arm movements also show well-coordinated extension of the elbow, wrist, and finger joints. In other words, the fingers do not extend independently, or one at a time, but in unison with the hand, wrist, and elbow (just as with the kick). Arm movements are not as rhythmical and repetitious as leg kicks, though (Thelen, 1981; Thelen, Kelso, & Fogel, 1987). As with the kick, early arm thrusts are not identical to adult reaching movements. It takes infants several months to begin opening their fingers independently of the other joints in anticipation of grasping objects, as adults do (Trevarthan, 1984; von Hofsten, 1982, 1984). In addition, these spontaneous movements appear to be influenced by environmental constraints, as Kawai, Savelsbergh, and Wimmers (1999) found when they placed newborn infants in four different environmental conditions and discovered differences in frequency and activity of spontaneous arm movements.

Infants' movements, although not always goal-directed or goal achieving, can be coordinated. The coordination patterns may resemble patterns seen in adults.

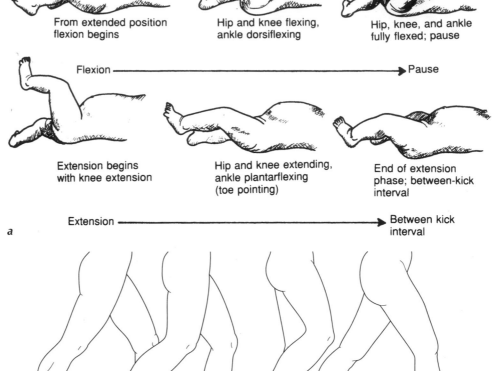

From extended position
flexion begins

Hip and knee flexing,
ankle dorsiflexing

Hip, knee, and ankle
fully flexed; pause

Flexion ——————————————→ Pause

Extension begins
with knee extension

Hip and knee extending,
ankle plantarflexing
(toe pointing)

End of extension
phase; between-kick
interval

Extension ——————————————→ Between kick
interval

a

Right leg: ——————→ Flexion ——————————→ Extension/beginning
b extension   of support

Figure 5.1 Kicking. *(a)* Infant kick. *(b)* Adult step.

What do the previous paragraphs suggest? First, newborns may be weak and unable to produce intentional, precise goal-directed movements, but even at a young age they exhibit coordination within limbs or pairs of limbs (Piek, Gasson, Barrett, & Case, 2002). Second, these coordination patterns resemble the coordination patterns we see in later voluntary movement. This suggests some relationship between random and voluntary movement. Perhaps spontaneous movements could be part of the fundamental building blocks of voluntary, functional movement (Jensen, Thelen, Ulrich, Schneider, & Zernicke, 1995).

Infantile Reflexes

An **infantile reflex** is an involuntary, stereotypical movement response to a specific stimulus that is seen only during infancy.

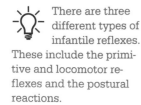
There are three different types of infantile reflexes. These include the primitive and locomotor reflexes and the postural reactions.

Reflexive movements are often visible in young infants. Unlike random movements, reflexes are involuntary movements that an individual makes in response to specific stimuli. Sometimes these responses occur only when the body is in a specific position. An infant does not have to think about making reflexive movements; reflexes occur automatically. Some reflexes, such as eye blinking, occur throughout the life span, but others are present only during infancy **(infantile reflexes).** We can categorize those seen during infancy into three types of movements: primitive reflexes, postural reactions, and locomotor reflexes (table 5.1). We will define each of these categories and then discuss their purpose.

TABLE 5.1 Infantile Reflexes

Reflex/reaction	Starting position (if important)	Stimulus	Response	Time	Warning signs
Primitive reflexes					
Asymmetrical tonic neck	Supine	Turn head to one side	Same-side arm and leg extend	Prenatal to 4 mo	Persistence after 6 mo
Symmetrical tonic neck	Supported sitting	Extend head and neck; flex head and neck	Arms extend, legs flex; arms flex, legs extend	6 mo to 7 mo	
Doll-eye		Flex head	Eyes look up	Prenatal to 2 wk	Persistence after first days of life
Palmar grasping		Touch palm with finger or object	Hand closes tightly around object	Prenatal to 4 mo	Persistence after 1 yr; asymmetrical reflex
Moro	Supine	Shake head, as by tapping pillow	Arms and legs extend, fingers spread; then arms and legs flex	Prenatal to 3 mo	Presence after 6 mo; asymmetrical reflex
Sucking		Touch face above or below lips	Sucking motion begins	B to 3 mo	
Babinski		Stroke sole of foot from heel to toes	Toes extend	B to 4 mo	Persistence after 6 mo
Searching or rooting		Touch cheek with smooth object	Head turns to side stimulated	B to 1 yr	Absence of reflex; persistence after 1 yr
Palmar-mandibular (Babkin)		Apply pressure to both palms	Mouth opens; eyes close; head flexes	1 to 3 mo	
Plantar grasping		Stroke ball of foot	Toes contract around object stroking foot	B to 12 mo	
Startle	Supine	Tap abdomen or startle infant	Arms and legs flex	7 to 12 mo	
Postural reactions					
Derotative righting	Supine	Turn legs and pelvis to other side	Trunk and head follow rotation	From 4 mo	
	Supine	Turn head sideways	Body follows head in rotation	From 4 mo	
Labyrinthine righting	Supported upright	Tilt infant	Head moves to stay upright	2 to 12 mo	
Pull-up	Sitting upright, held by 1 or 2 hands	Tip infant backward or forward	Arms flex	3 to 12 mo	
Parachute	Held upright	Lower infant toward ground rapidly	Legs extend	From 4 mo	
	Held upright	Tilt forward	Arms extend	From 7 mo	
	Held upright	Tilt sideways	Arms extend	From 6 mo	
	Held upright	Tilt backward	Arms extend	From 9 mo	
Locomotor reflexes					
Crawling	Prone	Apply pressure to sole of one foot or both feet alternately	Crawling pattern in arms and legs	B to 4 mo	
Stepping	Held upright	Place infant on flat surface	Walking pattern in legs	B to 5 mo	
Swimming	Prone	Place infant in or over water	Swimming movement of arms and legs	11 d to 5 mo	

B = birth

Primitive Reflexes: Around From the Beginning

When a newborn infant grasps an object placed in her hand, she does this automatically and without conscious thought. This is an example of a primitive reflex, an involuntary response to specific stimulation. Lower brain centers often mediate these primitive reflexes (Peiper, 1963). Generally, newborns exhibit strong reflexes at birth—these tend to lose their strength until they disappear around the fourth month. How can you tell primitive reflexes from spontaneous movements?

> ▲ Reflexes are responses to specific external stimuli, whereas spontaneous movements do not result from any apparent external stimuli.

> ▲ Reflexive movements are specific and often localized, whereas spontaneous movements tend to be nonspecific and generalized.

> ▲ The same stimulus will elicit a specific reflex over and over again (McGraw, 1943).

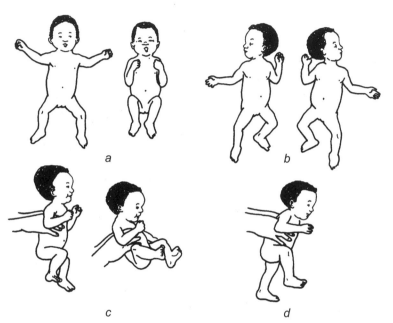

Figure 5.2 Selected reflexes. *(a)* Moro reflex. Arms extend then flex. *(b)* Asymmetrical tonic neck reflex. Note the "fencer's" position, which is one way to identify and describe this reflex. *(c)* Labyrinthine righting reflex. The infant rights the head when tipped backward. *(d)* Stepping reflex.

Figure 5.2 shows examples of several different reflexes.

Postural Reactions: Moving Upright in the World

As their name implies, postural reactions, or gravity reflexes, help the infant automatically maintain posture in a changing environment (Peiper, 1963). Some of these responses keep the head upright, thereby keeping the breathing passages open. Others help the infant roll over and eventually attain a vertical position. Postural reactions generally appear after the infant is 2 months old. For example, an infant can roll over only after derotative righting appears after 4 months of age. By late in the first year or early in the second year of life, these isolated reactions requiring specific postures and stimuli drop out of the infant's repertoire of movements. However, these reflexes don't literally disappear. Children and adults react to being thrown off balance with specific muscle responses intended to bring the body back to balance. If you have recently tried in-line skating or snowboarding for the first time, you probably know this. As you start to fall, you automatically extend your arms. This automatic response results in many broken wrists—and unbroken skulls.

Locomotor Reflexes: Moving in Place

For a while in the 1980s, infant swim classes were all the rage. In these classes, parents placed their newborns in the water and the infants could actually swim! Precocious newborns? Perhaps, but more likely the infants were exhibiting the swim reflex. The swim reflex, like other locomotor reflexes, gets its name because it appears similar and related to a voluntary movement (swimming). The locomotor reflexes appear much earlier than the corresponding voluntary behaviors and typically disappear months before the infant attempts the voluntary locomotor skill. There are three such locomotor reflexes: stepping, swimming, and crawling.

Appearance and Disappearance of Reflexes

In typically developing infants, infantile reflexes gradually show less of a specific response with time; eventually, you can no longer stimulate these reflexes. In fact, the primitive reflexes may start to weaken or become modified after about 2 weeks (Clark, 1995). In fact, infants learn to adapt their reflexes even after 2 weeks in order to modify the movement outcome (e.g., faster sucking leads to faster supply of milk). Those who work with infants sometimes use the pattern of reflex appearance and disappearance to assess an individual infant's development. If the reflexes appear and disappear at an age close to the average, they consider the infant's development typical. Deviation from the typical pattern and execution of the response may signal a problem. There are two ways an individual may deviate from typical:

▲ Exhibiting a reflex when the individual should not

▲ Not exhibiting a reflex when the individual should

A reflex that persists well after the average age of disappearance may indicate a pathological cerebral condition (Peiper, 1963). A nonexistent or very weak response on one side of the body compared with the other also could reflect a pathological condition.

In the popular television program *ER*, the doctors often check an incoming patient by running a probe along the bottom of the patient's foot. This is a real technique, called the Babinski test (see table 5.1 for a description of the Babinski reflex). The Babinski test is used to check for neurological problems in patients with head injuries. A positive Babinski sign indicates that the Babinski reflex has "returned"—and that the patient most likely has an injury to the central nervous system.

Be careful when attempting to assess the neurological status of an infant (Bartlett, 1997). Remember that each individual develops as a result of interacting individual, environmental, and task constraints. This means one infant may continue exhibiting reflexes after another of the same age has stopped. Most infants are ahead of or behind the average ages. In addition, it is difficult to establish the exact time a reflex disappears. Only when the reflex persists for several months past the average might it constitute a warning sign of a pathological condition. You should be aware that reflexive responses are very sensitive to environmental conditions. If you change an infant's body position or provide her with a different stimulus than those in table 5.1, you won't get a response. It is easy for an untrained person to overlook some aspect of the environment and thus fail to elicit a response; as a result, he or she may incorrectly conclude that a pathological condition exists. Therefore, trained professionals should be consulted for such assessments.

Parents, teachers, and others outside of the medical profession should bring infants in question to trained personnel for assessment.

WHY DO INFANTS MOVE? THE PURPOSE OF REFLEXES

Ask any mother and she will tell you that infant movements start well before birth! In fact, several reflexes appear as soon as 2 to 3 months in utero. But why are infants born with reflexes? Some, like the rooting reflex, seem to have an obvious purpose: to help an infant survive. Others, such as the asymmetrical tonic neck reflex (ATNR) or swimming reflex, seem to have no clear relevance to the infant at birth. Perhaps some reflexes are important before birth. Researchers have explained the role of reflexes in three general ways: structural, functional, and applied.

The structural explanation views reflexes as a byproduct of the human neurological system. That is, some theorists believe that reflexes merely reflect the structure of the nervous system—in other words, the way humans are "wired." A functional explanation suggests that reflexes exist to help the infant survive—to eat, breathe, and grasp (Clark, 1995). Milani-Comparetti (1981; Milani-Comparetti & Gidoni, 1967) suggests that the fetus uses reflexes to position itself for birth, then to assist in the birthing process. Both the structural and functional explanations consider reflexes at birth but do not suggest

? Look at table 5.1 again. How do you see each reflex fitting into a role (structural, functional, applied)?

anything about their purpose past birth. Applied theories examine the role of reflexes in future volitional movements. Once again, we see some very different ideas based on the theoretical viewpoints of the researchers. Others take the view that reflexive movements lead to coordinated limb movements (Peiper, 1963), giving the infant the opportunity to practice coordinated movements before the higher brain centers are ready to mediate such actions.

Relationship of Reflexes to Voluntary Movement

Ideas on the relationship between reflexes and later movement have changed dramatically over the past 50 years as a result of some unique experiments. Early researchers such as McGraw (1943) believed infants could not move voluntarily until reflexes had been inhibited by the CNS, a theory termed motor interference. As time went on, researchers began to question the idea of motor interference. A relatively simple experiment by Zelazo and associates challenged the notion that reflexes and voluntary movements were not related (Zelazo, Zelazo, & Kolb, 1972a, 1972b). They elicited the stepping reflex daily in a small number of infants during their first 8 weeks. This daily practice actually increased the stepping reflex in these infants and also resulted in the earlier onset of voluntary walking in the trained infants compared with infants who did not practice the reflex. The investigators concluded that the involuntary walking reflex could be transformed into voluntary walking (see also Zelazo, 1983). They proposed that the disappearance of the reflex was due to disuse, that the period of reflex inhibition before onset of the voluntary skill was unnecessary, and that the systematic stimulation of a locomotor reflex could enhance infants' acquisition of voluntary locomotion.

Ester Thelen (1983, 1995; Thelen & Ulrich, 1991) also questioned whether reflexes had to be inhibited before voluntary movement could occur. With her colleagues, she proposed that other constraints, rather than strictly maturation, may be related to the stepping reflex's disappearance. Thelen examined the changing individual constraints during early childhood and noticed that infants have a dramatic increase in leg weight, primarily from fat, during the first 2 months of life. With that great increase in leg weight without a corresponding increase in muscle strength, she reasoned, the stepping reflex may disappear because the infant has insufficient strength to lift the now-heavier legs.

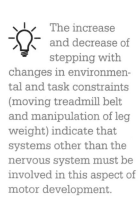

The increase and decrease of stepping with changes in environmental and task constraints (moving treadmill belt and manipulation of leg weight) indicate that systems other than the nervous system must be involved in this aspect of motor development.

To test this, Thelen and her associates took a group of 4- to 6-week-old infants who were still reflex kicking and added small weights, equal to the amount of weight gain the infants were to experience, to their ankles. The amount of reflex stepping decreased, suggesting that the "weight gain" concept might be a viable explanation for the disappearing reflex. However, studies of these very young infants showed only half the picture. Thelen had to demonstrate that reflex stepping still existed in older infants if she accounted for the constraint of strength. To do this, she took older infants (who no longer reflex stepped) and submerged them to their chests in a small tank of water. The water had the effect of buoying the legs (simulating an increase in strength), and these infants began to step with greater frequency. This result is similar to that of Zelazo's, whose training may have made the infants' legs strong enough to step despite weight gain. Finally, Thelen (1985; Thelen & Ulrich, 1991; Vereijken & Thelen, 1997) found that infants at 7 months who did not reflexively step did step when held over the moving belt of a motorized treadmill. The sum total of these studies suggests that several different individual constraints (rather than simply maturation) play a strong role in movement patterns during infancy. These studies have inspired several other infant research studies that utilized treadmills. Figure 5.3 illustrates the ongoing research that uses treadmills to elicit stepping in infants with Down syndrome.

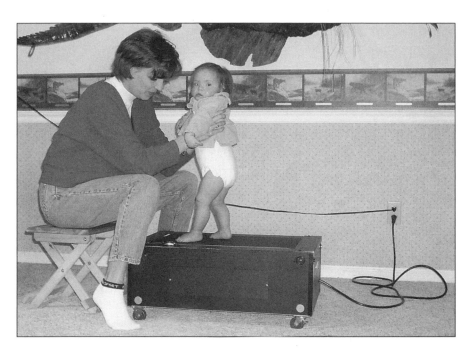

MOTOR MILESTONES: THE PATHWAY TO VOLUNTARY MOVEMENTS

Compare the movements of a newborn with those of the same child 12 months later. Somehow, those spontaneous and reflexive movements give way to complex, coordinated, purposeful activities such as walking, reaching, and grasping. What happens to the infant in those intervening months? Clearly, the infant does not suddenly acquire a complex skill; rather, she must learn how to coordinate and control the many interacting parts of her body. She must attain certain fundamental skills that lead to skilled performance. We call these fundamental skills **motor milestones** (figure 5.4). Each motor milestone is a landmark or turning point in an individual's motor development. Think of them this way: to walk, you must be able to stand; to stand, you must be able to hold your trunk upright; to hold your trunk upright, you must be able to hold your head erect. Each skill has a preceding milestone associated with it. Individual infants vary in the time they reach a motor milestone, but they acquire these different rudimentary skills in a relatively consistent sequence. Table 5.2 shows the timing and sequence of selected motor milestones.

A **motor milestone** is a fundamental motor skill whose attainment is associated with the acquisition of later voluntary movements. The order in which an infant attains these milestones is relatively consistent, although the timing differs among individuals.

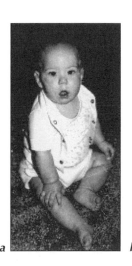

Figure 5.4 Some of the motor milestone skills: *(a)* sitting alone steadily, *(b)* standing up by furniture, *(c)* creeping, *(d)* rolling from back to front.

TABLE 5.2 Selected Motor Milestones

Average age (mo)	Age range (mo)	Milestone (Bayley Scales of Infant Development)	Milestone (Shirley Sequence)
0.1		Lifts head when held at shoulder	
0.1		Lateral head movements	
0.8	0.3–3.0	Retains red ring	
0.8	0.3–2.0	Arm thrusts in play	
0.8	0.3–2.0	Leg thrusts in play	Chin up
1.6	0.7–4.0	Head erect and steady	
1.8	0.7–5.0	Turns from side to back	
2.0			Chest up
2.3	1.0–5.0	Sits with slight support	
4.0			Sits with support
4.4	2.0–7.0	Turns from back to side	
4.9	4.0–8.0	Partial thumb opposition	
5.0			Sits on lap; grasps object
5.3	4.0–8.0	Sits alone momentarily	
5.4	4.0–8.0	Unilateral reaching	
5.7	4.0–8.0	Rotates wrist	
6.0			Sits in chair; grasps dangling object
6.4	4.0–10.0	Rolls from back to front	
6.6	5.0–9.0	Sits alone steadily	
6.9	5.0–9.0	Complete thumb opposition	
7.0			Sits alone
7.1	5.0–11.0	Prewalking progression	
7.4	6.0–10.0	Partial finger prehension	
8.0			Stands with help
8.1	5.0–12.0	Pulls to standing	
8.6	6.0–12.0	Stands up by furniture	
8.8	6.0–12.0	Stepping movements	
9.0			Stands holding furniture
9.6	7.0–12.0	Walks with help	
10.0			Creeps
11.0	9.0–16.0	Stands alone	Walks when led
11.7	9.0–17.0	Walks alone	
12.0			Pulls to stand
14.0			Stands alone
14.6	11.0–20.0	Walks backward	
15.0			Walks alone
16.1	12.0–23.0	Walks up stairs with help	
16.4	13.0–23.0	Walks down stairs with help	
23.4	17.0–30.0+	Jumps off floor, both feet	
24.8	19.0–30.0+	Jumps from bottom step	

Bayley (1935), Shirley (1963), and other researchers observed infants and determined a sequence of motor milestones as well as the average ages at which the infants achieved them. This progressive pattern of skill acquisition can be related to predictable changes in individual constraints that occur in typically developing infants. These include

- ▲ maturation of the central nervous system,
- ▲ development of muscular strength and endurance,
- ▲ development of posture and balance, and
- ▲ improvement of sensory processing.

Constraints and the Attainment of Motor Milestones

Remember that individual constraints can act as rate limiters, or controllers. That is, for an infant to exhibit a certain skill, he needs to develop a certain system to a particular level. For example, an infant must have sufficient strength in his neck and shoulders to lift his head while lying on his belly. Because different systems advance earlier in some infants than in others, the rate of appearance of the motor milestones varies. Experience and environmental constraints also play a role in individual variability (Adolph, Vereijken, & Denny, 1998). Culturally defined parental handling practices can alter the rate at which an infant attains motor milestones (Clark, 1995). For example, an infant born to a new mother may experience "first child syndrome." This is not actually a disease but a cultural phenomenon in the United States: first-time mothers avoid putting the infants on their stomachs for a long time and hold their infants for long periods. These periods of prolonged holding result in delayed onset of certain motor milestones such as crawling; the infant does not have the opportunity to strengthen his neck muscles when lying prone. Once again, we see that motor development arises from the interaction of individual, environment, and task.

Recent research suggests that the attainment of certain milestones themselves can act as rate limiters for other skills. Corbetta and Bojczyk (2002) looked at the reaching and nonreaching movements and hand preferences of nine infants from the age of 3 weeks until the time at which they could walk independently. The most striking finding was that when the infants attained certain motor milestones such as sitting, crawling, or walking, they changed their hand preference and even reverted back to an earlier form of reaching (with two hands). In the attainment of walking, the change back to two-hand reaching is likely the result of the infants' balance acting as a rate limiter; these types of reaches are less likely to compromise the infants' newfound ability to walk. The fluctuation in hand preference provides more evidence to suggest that many interacting constraints act in the development of motor skills.

Norm-Referenced Versus Criterion-Referenced Scales

It is obviously necessary and beneficial to assess individual children and groups of children. Assessment can help professionals identify children who need special attention, chart individual and group progress, choose appropriate educational tasks, and so on. Professionals must recognize, though, that testing instruments have specific purposes and are best used when the purpose matches a particular need. For example, we can broadly classify testing instruments as *norm-referenced* or *criterion-referenced*.

The purpose of *norm-referenced scales* is to compare an individual or group with previously established norms. This comparison indicates where a person falls within a group of like individuals matched on relevant factors, such as age, gender, and race. The value of norm-referenced scales in identifying slowly

(continued)

(continued)

developing children is obvious. On the other hand, such scales give professionals no information about the nature or cause of a delay or about what educational experiences to prescribe to facilitate future development.

Criterion-referenced scales are designed to indicate where a child falls on a continuum of skills that we know are acquired in sequence. The developmentalist administers the criterion-referenced scale periodically, comparing individuals with their own previous performances rather than with a population norm. Often, criterion-referenced scales indicate what skills the individual has mastered and what skills are just emerging. Educators can prescribe education and practice activities based on those emerging skills, guaranteeing that the educational task is developmentally appropriate for the individual.

Most of the scales developed for infants are the norm-referenced type. Typically, more expertise is needed to administer a criterion-referenced scale than a norm-referenced scale. The Bayley Scales of Infant Development, discussed in this chapter, are norm-referenced (Bayley, 1969). The complete Bayley Scales consist of a mental scale (163 items), a motor scale

(81 items), and a behavior record for social and attentional behaviors. Those using these scales can compare infants and toddlers from 2 months to 2.5 years with mental and motor norms.

Another well-known norm-referenced scale is the Denver Developmental Screening Test (Frankenburg & Dodds, 1967). This test can be used from birth to 6 years of age and assesses four areas:

1. Gross motor performance (31 items)
2. Fine motor performance (30 items)
3. Language development (21 items)
4. Personal-social skills (22 items)

A third well-known norm-referenced scale is the Gesell Developmental Schedules (Gesell & Amatruda, 1949). All these instruments are well standardized, but their motor scales are less reliable and valid than is desirable. In this sense they are useful but limited in the information they provide about motor development.

Motor Milestones As an Indicator of Atypical Neurological Development

? What are some of the different types of delays you might see in the attainment of motor milestones, and why might they occur? Don't limit yourself to disease or disorders.

Because of their sequential nature, motor milestones may provide clues for trained professionals, such as doctors and physical therapists, to an infant's neurological health. In a study of 173 high-risk preterm infants, Allen and Alexander (1994) evaluated six motor milestones on sequential visits to screen for cerebral palsy. They found that they could predict cerebral palsy accurately when looking for a 37.5% delay on all six motor milestones on subsequent evaluations. This finding underscores two important points. First, the milestone sequence is fairly predictable in typically developing infants. Second, although variability exists in the acquisition of milestones, if an infant is substantially delayed in several milestones, this may indicate some developmental problem. Of course, it's always best to check with a professional before assuming that an infant has such a problem.

For experience in assessing the motor milestones of infants, download Lab 5.1 Assessing the Motor Milestones from the Student Resources section at www.HumanKinetics.com/LifeSpanMotorDevelopment. In addition, you can gain experience in assessing toddler behavior by downloading Lab 5.2 Assessing Toddler Motor Behavior.

DEVELOPMENT OF POSTURAL CONTROL AND BALANCE IN INFANCY

Many of the motor milestones of the first year of life involve the attainment of certain postures, of which sitting and standing are the most obvious examples. Once infants can maintain a posture, they are balancing. Developmentalists have been interested in whether postural control and balance make up the rate-limiting system in the onset of these milestone skills. They have also been interested in whether infants rely on the same cues for balance that adults do.

There is some evidence that newborns make postural adjustments of the head in response to a visual display of optical flow, or the change in optic patterns while one moves (Jouen, 1990; Jouen, Lepecq, Gapenne, & Bertenthal, 2000). This might indicate that the perception of optical flow is not the rate-controlling factor but, rather, making appropriate postural responses is. Researchers have used the "moving room" technique to study this (figure 5.5). Pope (1984) held infants in a seated position on a stationary platform and observed their muscular responses through electromyograph recordings when the walls and ceiling of the small room surrounding them were moved. The effect was to provide visual information that made it seem as if the body, not the room, were moving, while kinesthetic information from the vestibular and somatosensory receptors indicated the body was not moving. Thus, the visual information and the kinesthetic information were in conflict. The 2-month-olds reacted to the visual information rather than the kinesthetic information. That is, they responded as if their bodies were swaying, and they activated muscle to regain their starting posture.

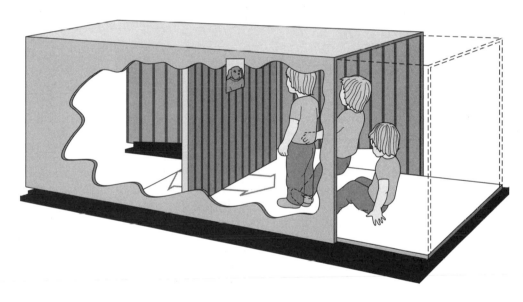

Figure 5.5 A moving room. In this drawing, the small room is moved toward the child, and the child falls backward. This response would occur if the child perceived the optical flow produced by the room movement as forward sway rather than as room movement.

From B.I. Bertenthal, J.L. Rose, and D.L. Bai, 1997, "Perception-action coupling in the development of visual control of posture," Journal of Experimental Psychology: Human Perception and Performance 23: 1631–1634, fig. 1. Copyright © by the American Psychological Association. Reprinted with permission.

Bertenthal, Rose, and Bai (1997) observed 5-, 7-, 9-, and 13-month-olds sitting in a moving room when the room moved at two different speeds. This age span includes infants who could and could not sit alone. The investigators found that all the infants, even those not yet capable of sitting alone, responded to room movement (they "believed" the visual information more than the kinesthetic information), and their action was linked to the movement speed. They also observed that infants improved their responses with sitting experience. Postural responses were made sooner, more accurately, and more consistently with experience.

When infants who have just begun standing are placed in a moving room, they often sway, stagger, or fall—unlike adults, who can keep their balance (Bertenthal & Bai, 1989; Butterworth & Hicks, 1977; Lee & Aronson, 1974; Woollacott & Sveistrup, 1994). Newly standing children take longer than adults to use their postural muscles when thrown off balance and sway more before attaining stability (Forssberg & Nashner, 1982). The moving room effect diminishes in children after their first year of standing.

It seems, then, that visual perception of self-motion is not the rate-controlling factor in infant posture and balance. Rather, the rate-controlling factor may be a coupling of the sensory information to the appropriate motor response. The refinement of this coupling occurs for every task, such as sitting and standing. This is consistent with research on the neurological system, suggesting that vision must be linked to specific motor response loci (Goodale, 1988; Milner & Goodale, 1995). Once refined, these perception–action couplings provide very sensitive and rapid adjustments to the environment.

Barela, Jeka, and Clark (1999) observed touch control in infants as they reached four important stages: pulling to stand, standing alone, onset of walking, and 1.5 months of walking experience. As the infants acquired standing experience, the force they applied to a nearby contact surface and their body sway decreased. At the three earlier stages (pulling to stand, standing alone, and walking onset), the infants responded to body sway by applying force to the surface. After the infants gained walking experience, they used the touch information to control posture rather than simply react to sway. Somatosensory information certainly plays an important role in posture and balance. Infant research on posture and balance has established the important role of perceptual information from the various systems in actions that maintain our posture and balance. More research is needed on how these various sources of information are integrated to maintain posture and balance.

 ## *Summary and Synthesis*

A newborn infant moves in a variety of ways. She may kick her legs and wave her arms in a seemingly random fashion; we call these spontaneous movements. She may respond to a touch with a specific movement pattern; these responses are called infantile reflexes. During the first year, she will begin to lift her head and sit alone. These skills, which appear in a fairly well-defined sequence, are called motor milestones. She will sit, crawl, and stand, all of which demand postural control. In a typically developing infant, these motor behaviors come forward in a relatively predictable sequence and time frame. Differences among infants in sequence and timing do exist, however, and they shouldn't be viewed as an indication of neurological difficulties without consulting a professional. The difference may simply indicate that for this particular infant, the interactions between individual, environmental, and task constraints encourage motor behaviors in a unique way.

What do the movements we see during infancy tell us about the infant herself? Developmentalists still debate the purpose of reflexes and spontaneous movements. However, several things are becoming clear. First, these movement patterns are not random but coordinated (if not purposeful). Second, early movement patterns play some role in future movement. Perhaps these movements are the foundations of future movements. In any case, we cannot separate early movements from later skills. The infant's experiences coupled with her physical characteristics, the environment, parental handling, and other constraints acting within the context of her infancy all interact in the development of movement skill.

 ## *Discussion Questions*

1. For four of the infantile reflexes listed in table 5.1, describe a survival function or purpose each reflex might have.
2. If an infant does not attain all motor milestones, what does this suggest about interacting constraints?
3. Describe how both task and environmental constraints can have a profound effect on the emergence of motor skills.
4. On what perceptual system do young infants seem to rely for balance information?

Learning Activities

Identifying Constraints During Infancy and Toddlerhood

The attainment of a milestone indicates a unique interaction of various constraints that allows the particular behavior to emerge. For each infant, the rate at which motor milestones appear (and to a certain extent, the type of milestone) for one infant can differ from that for other infants. This indicates that particular constraints may act as rate limiters, or controllers, for a given infant. When a critical value of that rate limiter is at last reached, the infant will achieve the motor milestone or skill.

On your CD-ROM are video clips of several infants at different points in infancy and toddlerhood. The clips are not in a particular order. You will watch the clips and then determine developmental order and different constraints.

1. Put the video clips in order of attainment—that is, which skill was most likely attained first, second, and so on?

2. For each video clip, list which constraints are most likely to encourage this skill.

3. For each video clip, list which constraints are most likely to act as rate limiters in the attainment of future skills.

4. Discuss the role of constraints in the attainment of motor skills. Explain why the milestones were attained in a particular order and how constraints change throughout infancy and toddlerhood.

Development of Human Locomotion

chapter 6

RECORD-SETTING ATHLETE—
ONLY 86!—GETS BETTER WITH AGE!

To say the U.S. masters track and field superstar Albert Morrow started running a little late in the game is an understatement. He leapt his first hurdle 17 years ago—when he was 69.

Morrow competes in the 85–90 age group and holds two indoor world records: 60 meters (11.10 seconds) and 200 (39.14). He'll compete in the 100, 200, 80 hurdles, javelin, and discus in the World Masters Track & Field Championships at Gateshead, England, July 29–Aug. 8. Seven thousand athletes are expected.

Morrow plans to keep hurdling until he's 100, when he will "reassess the situation."

"He's always been on the go," Morrow's granddaughter, Deanna Hutcheson, 31, says. "He pretty well proves you're only as old as you think you are."

—Highlights from an article in USA Today, May 26, 1999

People interested in motor development often focus on early acquisition of locomotor skills. Our introduction demonstrates, however, that locomotion is a lifelong movement activity. Changes occur in walking, running, galloping, and other motor skills as individual, environmental, and task constraints change. This chapter examines different locomotor skills across the life span—how these skills systematically change and how individual constraints act as rate controllers.

Locomotion is defined as the act or capability of moving from place to place (*American Heritage Dictionary,* 2000). Moving around, getting from here to there: locomotion is something we do each day without much thought at all. However, this seemingly simplistic definition may hide the fact that moving from place to place is a complex activity that involves many interacting systems and constraints. The study of locomotion falls within many fields, from medicine to psychology, and includes many movements, from squirming to swimming. Across the life span, individuals use many different methods of locomotion. Of course, the type of locomotion they use depends on interacting constraints. During the childhood years, height, weight, and lengths change dramatically; these may act as rate controllers. During much of the life span, other types of constraints such as motivation or even the perceived gender association of a skill (e.g., "skipping is for girls") may encourage or discourage behavior. As one approaches old age, structural constraints such as physical characteristics may return as important rate controllers. However, functional constraints such as fear of falling or loss of balance capability may act just as strongly to discourage locomotion, as can environmental constraints such as weather changes (e.g., snow and ice). So, we must examine many changing constraints to understand locomotion across the life span.

Locomotion is the act of moving from place to place.

Chapter Objectives

This chapter will

▲ define the concept of locomotion in humans,

▲ describe the different types of locomotion,

▲ discuss the development of specific locomotor patterns, and

▲ explain the different individual constraints that affect development of locomotor patterns.

THE FIRST VOLUNTARY LOCOMOTOR EFFORTS: CREEPING AND CRAWLING

What does it take for an infant to move from one place to another for the first time? Certain motor milestones must be achieved, such as lifting the head in the prone position. The infant must also have enough strength to support and move himself and must uncouple his limbs, which have primarily moved simultaneously. In addition to these individual constraints, the environment must allow for infant locomotion. The infant must evaluate the environment to see how well it matches his individual constraints. Adolph (1997) suggests the environment must afford several things to the infant:

> The surface must provide a continuous path to support the body, must be large enough to allow passage as the body moves forward, must be sturdy enough to support body weight, and must be firm enough, flat enough, and have sufficient friction to maintain balance as weight shifts from limb to limb. (p. 6)

Certain systems act as rate limiters, or controllers, that hold an infant back from the initiation of locomotion. Once critical levels of these systems are reached, an infant can begin to move. The first types of locomotion infants exhibit are usually **creeping** (moving on hands and knees) (figure 6.1) and **crawling** (moving on hands and stomach, combat crawl). The following progression of skills leads to creeping and crawling:

1. Crawling with the chest and stomach on the floor
2. Low creeping with the stomach off the floor but the legs working together (symmetrically)
3. Rocking back and forth in the high creep position
4. Creeping with the legs and arms working alternately

Although not typically seen, another form of quadrupedal gait exists in infants: walking on hands and feet. Burton (1999) reviewed the work of Hrdlicka, who published a book in 1931 called *Children Who Run on All Fours*, and interpreted Hrdlicka's work using a dynamic systems approach. He concluded that the emergence of this gait pattern resulted from infrequently occurring interactions between different constraints. First, environmental constraints related to crawling surface may make knee support uncomfortable (e.g., gravel, asphalt); thus the infant changes to feet support. Next, the reinforcement or response of the parent or caregiver may encourage further use of this gait. Finally, average or above average strength and health of the infant must interact with these environmental factors to allow the hands-and-feet gait pattern to appear. Because these factors (and perhaps others that haven't been explored) often do not exist and interact to encourage the hands-and-feet gait pattern, we hardly ever see "running on all fours" in infants.

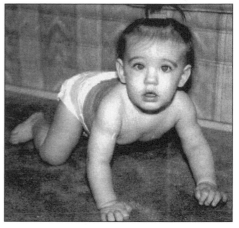

Figure 6.1 Infant creeping. Balance and strength must be sufficient for infants to support themselves, first on three limbs and eventually on one arm and the opposite leg in creeping.

Creeping and crawling occur when all four limbs are in contact with the supporting surface. In crawling, the infant's chest and stomach also touch the surface. In creeping, only the hands and knees touch the surface.

? What sort of rate controllers might exist that could keep a crawling infant from creeping?

Walking is defined by a 50% phasing relationship between the legs, as well as a period of double support (when both feet are on the ground), followed by single support.

 After infancy, most humans move from place to place using upright bipedal locomotion. A particular pattern of locomotion is called a "gait." Upright bipedal gait patterns include walking, running, galloping, skipping, and hopping.

WALKING ACROSS THE LIFE SPAN

Typically, a developing human can look forward to a long career as a walker. It's easy to assume that once people can walk, they won't change their walking technique much over the life span. Just like other motor behaviors, however, people continually change the way they walk as different constraints change. What remains the same across one's lifetime is the underlying timing of **walking,** which is 50% phasing between the legs (Clark, Whitall, & Phillips, 1988). In other words, individuals alternate their legs so that the left leg is halfway through its motion as the right leg begins its own. Also, there is a period of double support, when both feet contact the ground, followed by single support. These are the relative timing relationships (coordination) that appear early in life, and they don't seem to change much (Clark, 1995). However, as an individual's body or the environment changes, the absolute timing (i.e., slower or faster) and placement (i.e., step height or length) can change substantially.

First Steps: Characteristics of Early Walking

Most people—especially parents—know what a toddler's first solo steps look like. In fact, different researchers have studied and described these first steps (Adolph, Vereijken, & Shrout, 2003; Burnett & Johnson, 1971; Clark et al., 1988; Sutherland, Olshen, Cooper, & Woo, 1980). At first, each step tends to be independent of the next. The toddler takes short steps with little leg and hip extension. She steps with flat feet and points her toes outward. The infant spreads her feet wide apart when planted to improve her lateral balance. She doesn't use any trunk rotation. The toddler holds her arms up in high guard; that is, her hands and arms are carried high in a bent position. All of the characteristics in early walking lead to improved balance for the new walker (figure 6.2, a and b). As the child continues to develop, her arms will drop to about waist level (middle guard) and later to an extended position at the sides (low guard) (figure 6.2c), but they still will not swing. When children begin to use the arm swing, it frequently is unequal and irregular; both hands might swing forward together (Roberton, 1978b, 1984).

Figure 6.2 *(a)* A beginning walker. Note the short stride and high-guard arm position. *(b)* To maintain balance beginning walkers often plant the feet wide apart with the toes out. *(c)* Rather than swing the arms in time with the legs, beginning walkers often hold their arms in high-, middle-, or low-guard position.

Parts a and c are drawn from film tracing taken in the Motor Development and Child Study Laboratory, University of Wisconsin–Madison and now available from the Motor Development Film Collection, Kinesiology Division, Bowling Green State University; part b is redrawn from Wickstrom 1983.

Observing Motor Skill Performance

An instructor of motor skills must be able to critically observe children's skill patterns. The instructor needs to give students feedback, provide further practice experiences, and formally assess their skills. The observation process requires a disciplined, systematic focus on the critical features of a skill pattern rather than on the outcome, or product, of a skill. The observer must learn observation techniques and practice them like any other skill before they can become automatic.

Barrett (1979) has provided a guide for improving the observation skills of instructors and coaches based on three principles:

1. Analysis
2. Planning
3. Positioning

To analyze developmental movement, the observer first must know the developmental sequences of the skill, including the critical features that characterize a given developmental step and the mechanical principles involved in proficient performance.

Observers must organize and plan their observations to prevent their attention from wandering once activity begins. They may find it helpful to have written observation guidelines, many of which can be based on the developmental sequences suggested by researchers. However, one can design suitable observation guidelines by simply listing the critical features of the skill to be watched. It might also be a good idea for observers to watch a given feature of a skill many times (two tries, three tries, or more).

The third principle is positioning. Many new observers rivet themselves to one location and attempt to watch everything from there. Some critical features of motor skills can be seen only from the side; others are best seen from the front or back. It is important, then, for the observer to move about and to watch the performer from several angles.

The process of motor skill observation demands focused attention: new observers must plan ahead, know the critical features of the skill to be watched, position themselves properly, and practice observing.

You can see the key features that distinguish developmental levels by simply watching skill performance, but often there is a need to conduct a more formal assessment. Teachers, therapists, or researchers typically need to record an individual's development level so that progress can be tracked, activities designed, or comparisons made. Several tools are needed to conduct a more formal assessment:

- A description of the movements and positions characteristic of each step in a developmental sequence
- A plan for observing movement so that an individual can be quickly and accurately placed into a developmental step or level
- A recording sheet so that the developmental step can be quickly recorded for future use

These tools are provided for many of the fundamental motor skills discussed in the next several chapters. A Developmental Sequence table lists the developmental steps accompanied by a

(continued)

description of the movements or positions characteristic of that developmental step. These are organized by a body component, such as the legs or arms, or by a phase of the skill, such as the backswing. An observation plan follows. For each component, the observation plan directs you, in the form of a question, to watch for one specific movement or position at a time. By indicating what you observe you move through the observation plan until you arrive at the performer's developmental level. Finally, a record sheet is provided in the corresponding lab in the Student Resources section at www.HumanKinetics.com/LifeSpanMotorDevelopment so that you can record the developmental level for each component and for each person observed.

Rate Controllers in Early Walking

Infants have the ability to move their legs in an alternating pattern from birth onward. Yet, they cannot walk for at least 7 months after birth. Clearly, several individual constraints must develop to certain critical levels before the infant can support and move his own weight. His legs must be able to move alternately. The infant must have enough strength to support himself on a single limb. He must also balance on one leg while transferring his weight to his other foot. These suggest specific rate-controlling factors. Thelen, Ulrich, and Jensen (1989) suggest that infants must have muscle strength in the trunk and extensor muscles to allow them to maintain an upright posture on a small base of support. In addition, they must develop balance or an erect posture, or body position, to the point that they can compensate for the shift of weight from one leg to the other (Adolph et al., 2003; Clark et al., 1988; Clark & Phillips, 1993).

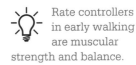 Rate controllers in early walking are muscular strength and balance.

? What environmental or task constraints might limit the rate at which infant walking develops?

Proficient Walking Patterns

Part of becoming a proficient walker involves taking advantage of biomechanical principles. For example, new walkers optimize balance by widening their stance, which increases their base of support. However, sometimes stability is not desirable, especially because it comes at the expense of mobility. Once an infant's balance improves, he must decrease his base of support to become more mobile. Many of the characteristics of proficient walking relate to exploiting biomechanical principles as body dimensions change. Consider these characteristics of proficient walking:

▲ Absolute stride length increases, reflecting greater application of force and greater leg extension at push-off. Also, as children grow, increased leg length contributes to a longer stride.

▲ Planting the foot flatly on the ground changes to a heel-then-forefoot pattern, which results from an increased range of motion.

▲ The individual reduces out-toeing and narrows the base of support laterally to keep the forces exerted in the forward–backward plane.

▲ The skilled walker adopts the **double knee-lock** pattern to assist the full range of leg motion. In this pattern, the knee extends at heel strike, flexes slightly as the body weight moves forward over the supporting leg, then extends once more at foot push-off. Because the knee extends twice in one step cycle, we call this pattern a double knee-lock.

▲ The pelvis rotates to allow the full range of leg motion and oppositional movement of the upper and lower body segments.

▲ Balance improves and forward trunk inclination is reduced.

▲ The skilled walker coordinates oppositional arm swing (with the arms extending at the sides) with the movement of the legs. This is consistent with the principle of action and reaction; that is, the opposite arm and leg move forward and back in unison. The arm swing must become relaxed and move from the shoulders with a slight accompanying movement at the elbow.

Developmental Changes in Walking During Early Childhood

Children usually achieve developmental changes in walking early; by age 4 most children have the essential ingredients of an advanced walk (Sutherland, 1997). Adolph and her colleagues provide an excellent overview of the development of infant walking in their 2003 paper aptly titled "What Changes in Infant Walking and Why." Children exhibit pelvic rotation at an average age of 13.8 months, knee flexion at midsupport at 16.3 months, foot contact within a trunk-width base of support at 17.0 months, synchronous arm swing at 18.0 months, and heel-then-forefoot strike at 18.5 months (Burnett & Johnson, 1971). The length of time that one foot supports body weight while the other swings forward increases, especially from 1.0 years to 2.5 years (Sutherland et al., 1980).

Stride length increases through midadolescence partly because of the fuller range of motion at the hips, knees, and ankles and partly because of the increase in leg length resulting from growth. The velocity of the walk increases, especially between 1.0 and 3.5 years of age (Sutherland et al., 1980). The rhythm and coordination of a child's walk improve observably until age 5 or so, but beyond this age, pattern improvements are subtle and probably not detectable to the novice observer.

Developmental Changes in Walking During Older Adulthood

Figure 6.3 Walking patterns in adulthood tend to change as a result of changing individual constraints.
© DigitalVisionOnline

We do not wish to imply that no development occurs between early childhood and older adulthood. However, the changes that do occur happen on an individual basis. That is, we cannot make generalizations about any specific developmental trends in walking in the late teens or early 20s; this is partly the result of a lack of research in this area. If an individual changes his or her walking pattern, the change may result from exercise, injury, or change in body weight. Unlike developmental changes in early childhood, we cannot predict changes in middle adulthood (figure 6.3). As individuals enter older age, they will again tend to change in a more predictable way.

A number of research studies have focused on walking patterns in adults over 60 years old. Murray and her coworkers (Murray, Drought, & Kory, 1964; Murray, Kory, Clarkson, & Sepic, 1966; Murray, Kory, & Sepic, 1970) conducted a series of studies on gait patterns in older men and women. They measured the linear and rotary displacements and the velocity of the limbs during walking. They found that the older men walked in a pattern similar to that of younger men but with these differences:

▲ Step length of the older men was approximately 3 cm shorter.

▲ Older men toed out approximately 3 degrees more than younger men.

▲ Older men had a reduced degree of ankle extension.

▲ Pelvic rotation was diminished in older men.

Older women also showed greater out-toeing, shorter stride length, and less pelvic rotation than younger women.

Another common finding is that older adults walk more slowly than younger adults (Drillis, 1961; Gabel, Johnston, & Crowinshield, 1979; Molen, 1973). Schwanda (1978) confirmed the finding of a shorter stride length among older men and further demonstrated that most other aspects of the walking pattern (stride rate, swing time of the recovering leg, time of support, and vertical displacement of center of gravity) remain similar to those of middle-aged men.

You may recall that new walkers also had greater out-toeing and a shorter stride length to assist in balance; could this be the reason older adults have the same? That possibility exists because balance can be affected by the aging process. On the other hand, researchers have associated some of these changes with differences in walking speed. When younger adults walk slowly, they too shorten their strides and decrease joint rotation (Craik, 1989; Winter, 1983). In an interesting study, Gabell and Nayak (1984) observed walking in a group of 32 older adults, 66 to 84 years old, who were selected from a group of 1,187. The researchers repeatedly screened members of the large group for various types of pathologies in order to select the small healthy group. They found no significant differences between walking patterns of the 32 older adults and those of younger adults. Thus, some of the changes in older adults' movement patterns might be related to diseases and injuries in the various body tissues, especially those that result in loss of muscle strength. Even so, these and other studies (Adrian, 1982) indicate that the changes in older adults' walking patterns are minor.

Rate Controllers in Later Walking

Any of the changes associated with the aging process can act as rate controllers in the task of walking. Structural constraints may result from osteoarthritis in the joints or from a decline in muscle mass. However, as noted previously, older adults do not necessarily change their gait in a drastic way. A disease state must progress to a critical level before it will discourage all walking. More often, older adults modify their gait to accommodate pain or changes in balance. Functional constraints, such as balance and fear, can also affect walking patterns. Often, two types of individual constraints interact, the sum of which acts as a rate controller. If older adults fall, they may develop a fear of falling. That fear of falling results in a gait designed to assist with balance (wide base of support, short step length). If this is combined with pain from osteoarthritis, older adults may be less inclined to walk distances. Unfortunately, a decrease in walking (and other physical activities) leads to a decrease in muscle mass and flexibility, which in turn affects walking patterns. What results is a sequence of events that eventually discourages walking—a sequence that can be altered if one or several individual constraints are actively manipulated.

Rate controllers in walking during older adulthood may be caused by factors such as disuse and fear of falling and therefore may be altered and improved.

RUNNING ACROSS THE LIFE SPAN

Picture this scenario: You leave your house late in the morning and must rush to catch the 8:00 A.M. bus. As you approach the bus stop, you notice the bus begin to leave the curb. What do you do? This is not a trick question; of course you run to catch the bus. Humans often run when they need to get from one place to another quickly. **Running** is a more advanced motor skill than walking, but the two motor patterns have many similar features. For example, in both patterns an individual's legs move symmetrically but in an alternating pattern with each other. Walking and running also have distinct differences. Walking has a period of double support when both feet are in contact with the ground.

Running, like walking, has a 50% phasing relationship between the legs. Unlike walking, there is a period of flight, when neither foot is in contact with the ground.

This never occurs in running; in fact, running has a flight phase, during which neither foot is on the ground.

Children typically start to run about 6 to 7 months after they begin to walk (Clark & Whitall, 1989b; Whitall & Getchell, 1995). Remember, for a gait to be considered a run, it must include a flight phase. That means that an infant's earliest attempts to run are actually fast walks. Infants running for the first time may exhibit some of the characteristics of an early walk, even though the infant no longer uses these characteristics in her walk (Burnett & Johnson, 1971). When first learning to run, the child may adopt a wide base of support, a flat-footed landing, leg extension at midsupport, and the high-guard arm position. This regression probably reflects an attempt by the child to simplify the task (e.g., by eliminating the arm swing) until she acquires more experience. As the child practices the running stride and gets used to its balance demands, she will put the swing back into the movement pattern.

Characteristics of Early Running

Imagine toddlers attempting to run for the first time. All prior attempts at upright locomotion involved at least one limb on the ground at all times. Now, they must propel themselves into the air with one leg and then catch themselves with the other. For a toddler, this feat takes tremendous strength and balance.

Early characteristics of running reflect the changes in speed (task constraint) between walking and running (see table 6.1 for the developmental sequence). Some of these characteristics are pictured in figure 6.4. Notice the leg action. You see a brief period of flight, but the legs still have a limited range of motion. The rear leg does not extend fully as the child pushes off the ground. As the swinging leg comes forward, the recovering thigh moves with enough acceleration that the knee bends but not with enough acceleration to carry the thigh to a level parallel with the ground at the end of the leg swing. Therefore, the range of motion is limited, and the stride length is short.

Next, examine the arm swing, and note the opposition of the arms to the legs. The arms swing to accompany the trunk's rotation rather than drive forward and back as they would

TABLE 6.1   **Hypothesized Developmental Sequence for Running**

	Leg action
Step 1	Minimal flight. The running step is short and flat-footed. On the recovery swing forward, the leg is rather stiff.
Step 2	Crossover swing. The stride is long, and the recovery leg knee flexes to at least a right angle. The leg action, though, has lateral movements wherein the legs swing out and in during the recovery.
Step 3	Direct projection. The stride is long, and the recovery leg tucks to swing forward. The legs project directly backward on takeoff and swing directly forward for the touchdown.
	Arm action
Step 1	High or middle guard. The arms are both held up at waist to shoulder level and move very little as the legs stride forward and back.
Step 2	Bilateral arm swing. The arms swing but they are coupled, moving forward and backward together.
Step 3	Opposition, oblique. The arms drive forward in the opposition pattern, moving forward and backward with the opposite leg, so that one arm is moving forward while the other is moving backward. The arms, though, swing across the chest or out to the side, in a plane oblique to the plane of movement.
Step 4	Opposition, sagittal. The arms swing forward and back in the opposition pattern and stay nearly in the sagittal (or forward-backward) plane of movement.

in a skilled sprinter. The elbows extend when they swing back, which is unnecessary movement; the arms swing out slightly to the side, wasting energy. Beginning runners sometimes swing their arms horizontally, across the body rather than forward and back; this is probably to aid their unsteady balance.

Figure 6.4b portrays some characteristics of early running that one can observe from the rear. As the child swings the recovering thigh forward, it inefficiently rotates to the side rather than move straight forward. The arm swings to the side, away from the body, probably to assist with balance, but again, this movement pattern wastes energy that could be directed toward running forward.

Figure 6.4 A beginning runner. *(a)* The legs have a limited range of motion. The arms extend at the elbows and swing slightly to the side rather than drive forward and back. *(b)* The thigh and arms swing out rather than forward and back.

Part a is drawn from film tracing taken in the Motor Development and Child Study Laboratory, University of Wisconsin–Madison and now available from the Motor Development Film Collection, Kinesiology Division, Bowling Green State University; part b is redrawn from Wickstrom 1983.

Rate Controllers in Early Running

To understand the rate controllers in early running, we must review similarities and differences between walking and running. First of all, the coordination patterns are quite similar; both have a 50% phasing relationship between the legs. Therefore, coordination is not likely to be a rate limiter for running. However, running requires a flight phase. To propel themselves in the air, toddlers must have sufficient strength in each leg to lift themselves off the ground. Clearly, strength is a very important rate limiter in running (Clark & Whitall, 1989b). Also, once in the air, infants must catch themselves on the other leg and then balance on that leg while shifting their weight forward. So, balance is another important rate limiter for running.

Proficient Running

Like walking, proficient running requires an effective use of biomechanical principles. When running, you must optimize movement forms that allow you to move quickly, even at the expense of balance. Keeping this in mind, we can identify the developmental changes beginning runners make to optimize their performance, as pictured in figure 6.5, as follows:

▲ Stride length increases, indicating that the runner is applying greater force. As greater force is used, several characteristics of mature running emerge: the rear leg is fully extended at push-off; the heel is tucked close to the buttocks and the thigh swings forward with greater acceleration; and before foot strike, the thigh has come parallel to the ground. When the recovery leg is swung forward in a tuck position, the runner's effort is conserved.

▲ The runner eliminates lateral leg movements so that forces are kept in the forward–backward plane.

▲ For extended running, each foot strikes the ground heel first, then forefoot, or it strikes the ground in an approximately flat pattern.

▲ The runner eliminates out-toeing and narrows the base of support.

? Most elite sprinters look very similar— their form is almost identical. However, the form of marathon runners differs greatly among individuals. Can you speculate on why sprinters are similar and distance runners are different in form?

Figure 6.5 An advanced runner. Note the full range of leg motion.
Redrawn from Wickstrom 1983.

▲ The runner's support leg flexes at the knee as the body's weight comes over the leg.

▲ Trunk rotation increases to allow for a longer stride and better arm–leg opposition. The trunk leans slightly forward.

▲ The arms swing forward and back, with the elbows approaching right angles, and move in opposition to the legs.

Developmental Changes in Early Running

As children grow, these qualitative changes in running pattern, together with increased body size and strength and improved coordination, typically result in improved quantitative measures of running speed and time in flight. Such changes have been well documented in several University of Wisconsin studies of children between ages 1.5 and 10 years (Beck, 1966; Clouse, 1959; Dittmer, 1962) and in other studies (Branta, Haubenstricker, & Seefeldt, 1984; Roberton, 1984). Therefore, we can expect improvement in the process and product of running performances as children grow. Improvements in the product of running performance—increased speed, for example—certainly may continue through adolescence. However, not every individual achieves all of the improvements in running pattern during childhood. Most teenagers continue to refine their running form, and it is not uncommon to observe inefficient characteristics in adults' running, especially out-toeing, lateral leg movements, and limited stride. Perhaps these reflect skeletal and muscular imbalances in individual runners. Thus, age alone does not guarantee perfect running form; adolescents and adults may have inefficient running patterns.

Developmental Changes in Later Running

Some research exists on the developmental changes we see as people age. Nelson (1981) studied the walking and running patterns of older women (ages 58 to 80). She asked the participants in her study to walk normally, walk as fast as possible, jog, and run as fast as possible. Average speed, stride length, and stride frequency all tended to increase over this sequence, but individuals varied greatly in how they changed from walking to jogging. The older women generally increased their walking speed by lengthening their stride, but they increased their running speed by increasing stride frequency, as do young women.

A major difference between younger and older women was found in the pattern used for fast running:

▲ Older women did not tuck their recovering leg as completely.

▲ Older women had a shorter stride length.

▲ Older women took fewer strides than younger women.

The absolute speeds of jogging and running also differed between the age groups. Older women jogged more slowly (1.85 vs. 3.93 m/s) and ran more slowly (2.60 vs. 6.69 m/s) than a group of 20-year-old women (Nelson, 1981).

Rate Controllers in Later Running

Many of the rate controllers mentioned for later walking exist for running. However, because running requires a greater generation of force and a greater ability to balance, considerably smaller changes in these constraints may lead to the disappearance of this skill. Further, one may have the ability to run but not the desire or the opportunity. In other words, an older adult may only run to escape a burning house. However, as more and more seniors discover that maintaining fitness levels can postpone changes associated with aging, more and more opportunities for running exist. The Senior Olympics have expanded greatly in the past decade; many states have statewide games, and the Huntsman World Senior Games are held in Utah each year. The running events range from the 100 m dash to the half-marathon and even the triathlon. Runners' age categories range from 50 to 85 or 90-plus for men and women. Still, participants in the Senior Olympics represent a small portion of the population over 50. In fact, it is still newsworthy when an older adult participates in athletics.

? Not all of the constraints that discourage running in older adults are structural. Try to think of at least two other constraints in each of the different constraint categories.

Assessment of Running: Observation Plan

Assessing motor skills using developmental sequences can seem like a daunting task to a novice observer. Fortunately, by using an observation plan such as the one for running (pp. 93-94), the task becomes much simpler. Basically, the observation plan allows you to make quick judgments on the development level of a particular runner by completing a flow chart of quick "yes" or "no" checkpoints. By observing a runner and making decisions on movements, you can establish developmental levels very efficiently and effectively.

To gain experience in assessing the developmental level of runners through photos, video clips, and direct observation, download Lab 6.1 Assessing the Developmental Levels of Runners from the Student Resources section at www.HumanKinetics.com/LifeSpanMotorDevelopment.

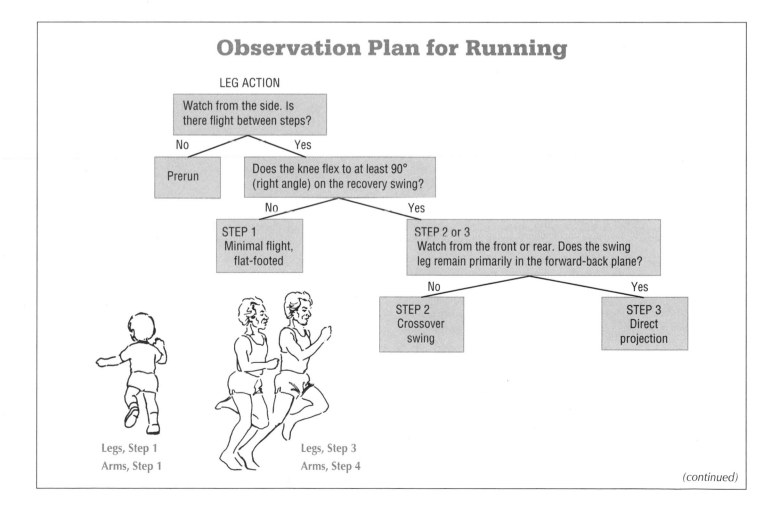

Observation Plan for Running

LEG ACTION

Watch from the side. Is there flight between steps?

No → Prerun

Yes → Does the knee flex to at least 90° (right angle) on the recovery swing?

No → STEP 1 Minimal flight, flat-footed

Yes → STEP 2 or 3 Watch from the front or rear. Does the swing leg remain primarily in the forward-back plane?

No → STEP 2 Crossover swing

Yes → STEP 3 Direct projection

Legs, Step 1
Arms, Step 1

Legs, Step 3
Arms, Step 4

(continued)

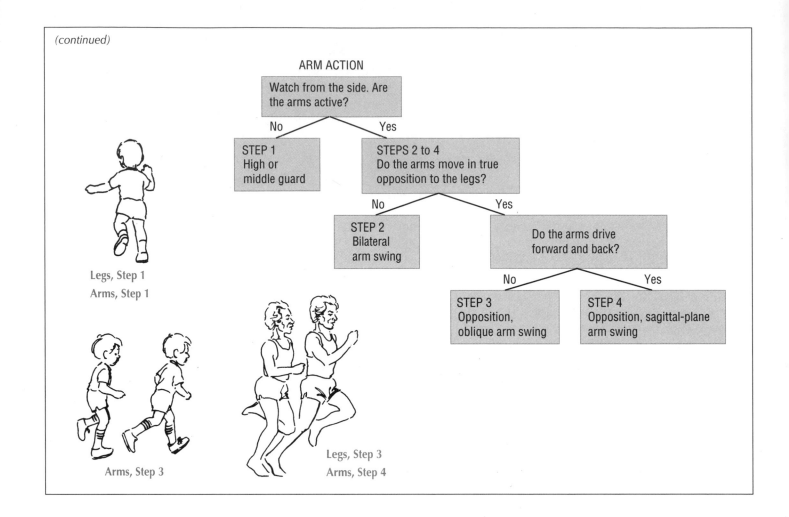

(continued)

ARM ACTION

Watch from the side. Are the arms active?

No — STEP 1 High or middle guard

Yes — STEPS 2 to 4 Do the arms move in true opposition to the legs?

No — STEP 2 Bilateral arm swing

Yes — Do the arms drive forward and back?

No — STEP 3 Opposition, oblique arm swing

Yes — STEP 4 Opposition, sagittal-plane arm swing

Legs, Step 1
Arms, Step 1

Arms, Step 3

Legs, Step 3
Arms, Step 4

OTHER LOCOMOTOR SKILLS

Most other locomotor skills have not received the amount of empirical attention that walking and running have. However, many different researchers, teachers, and therapists have observed these skills, and we can gain many insights from their observations. In many cases, observers have focused on changes occurring in childhood. The skills we discuss are jumping, hopping, galloping, sliding, and skipping; we, too, focus primarily on the childhood years.

Jumping

Typically, children attempt jumping tasks at a young age, often achieving the simplest forms before age 2. In **jumping,** individuals propel their bodies from a surface with either one or both feet and land with both feet (table 6.2). Children also acquire specialized forms of jumping during childhood, such as hopping and leaping. **Hopping** requires taking off and landing on the same leg, often repeatedly. **Leaping** is a run with a projection forward from one foot to a landing on the other (increased flight time). Table 6.2 outlines several examples of jumping, hopping, and leaping. Let's first look at jumping.

Characteristics of Early Jumping

We can gauge developmental changes in jumping in various ways:

Jumping occurs when individuals propel themselves off the ground with one or both feet, then land on both feet.

Hopping occurs when individuals propel themselves with one foot, then land on the same foot.

Leaping occurs when individuals propel themselves on one foot and land on the other foot.

▲ The age at which a child can perform certain kinds of jumps (age norms)

▲ The distance or height of a jump

▲ The jumping form or pattern

Early developmentalists determined age norms for preschool children's jumping achievements (Wickstrom, 1983). These norms appear in table 6.3. The table indicates that children learn to step down off a higher surface from one foot to the other before jumping off the floor with both feet. Children then learn to jump down from progressively greater heights onto both feet. Later, they master forward jumps, jumps over objects, and hopping a few times on one foot. By school age, children usually can perform all of these jumps.

Because of a secular trend, the exact ages at which children today can perform the various jumps might be younger than those in table 6.3, but the order in which they acquire those skills still applies. Developmentalists frequently use product assessments—that is, they measure the horizontal or vertical distance jumped—to assess jumping skill after the children have refined the movement process. We focus here on the movement pattern because the measurement of distance jumped is rather self-explanatory and straightforward.

TABLE 6.2 Types of Jumps Arranged by Progressive Difficulty

Jump down from one foot to the other foot.

Jump up from two feet to two feet.

Jump down from one foot to two feet.

Jump down from two feet to two feet.

Run and jump forward from one foot to the other.

Jump forward from two feet to two feet.

Run and jump forward from one foot to two feet.

Jump over object from two feet to two feet.

Jump from one foot to same foot rhythmically.

Reprinted from Wickstrom 1983.

TABLE 6.3 Jumping Achievements of Young Children

Achievement	Motor age (mo)	Source
Jump from 12 in. height; one foot	24	M & W
Jump off floor; both feet	28	B
Jump from 18 in. height; one foot	31	M & W
Jump from chair 26 cm high; both feet	32	B
Jump from 8 in. height; both feet	33	M & W
Jump from 12 in. height; both feet	34	M & W
Jump from 18 in. height; both feet	37	M & W
Jump from 30 cm height; both feet	37.1	B
Jump forward 10 to 35 cm from 30 cm height; both feet	37.3	B
Hop on two feet 1 to 3 times	38	M & W
Jump over rope 20 cm high; both feet	41.5	B
Hop on one foot 1 to 3 times	43	B

Reprinted from Wickstrom 1983. Compiled from information in studies by Bayley (1935) (B) and McCaskill and Wellman (1938) (M & W).

Basic skill development in children is a gradual process of refining skills. Oftentimes, this process includes a qualitative change in the skill, such as taking a step forward when throwing. Authors have described development of a particular skill through successive steps, or developmental sequences, based on qualitative changes in critical features of the skill. Two types of developmental sequences exist. The whole-body approach describes all characteristic positions of various body components within a step (table 6.4). The component approach follows each separate body component through whatever number of steps accounts for the qualitative changes observed over time (table 6.5).

TABLE 6.4 Developmental Sequence of the Standing Long Jump for the Whole Body

Step 1	Vertical component of force may be greater than horizontal; resulting jump is then upward rather than forward. Arms move backward, acting as brakes to stop the momentum of the trunk as the legs extend in front of the center of mass.
Step 2	The arms move in an anterior–posterior direction during the preparatory phase but move sideward (winging action) during the in-flight phase. The knees and hips flex and extend more fully than in step 1. The angle of takeoff is still markedly above 45°. The landing is made with the center of gravity above the base of support, with the thighs perpendicular to the surface rather than parallel as in the reaching position of step 4.
Step 3	The arms swing backward and then forward during the preparatory phase. The knees and hips flex fully before takeoff. On takeoff the arms extend and move forward but do not exceed the height of the head. The knee extension may be complete, but the takeoff angle is still greater than 45°. On landing, the thigh is still less than parallel to the surface, and the center of gravity is near the base of support when viewed from the frontal plane.
Step 4	The arms extend vigorously forward and upward on takeoff, reaching full extension above the head at liftoff. The hips and knees are extended fully, with the takeoff angle at 45° or less. In preparation for landing the arms are brought downward and the legs are thrust forward until the thighs are parallel to the surface. The center of gravity is far behind the base of support on foot contact, but at the moment of contact the knees are flexed and the arms are thrust forward to maintain the momentum to carry the center of gravity beyond the feet.

Note: Degrees are measured from horizontal.

Adapted from Seefeldt, Reuschlein, and Vogel 1972.

TABLE 6.5 Developmental Sequence of the Standing Long Jump Takeoff for Body Components

	Leg action
Step 1	One-foot takeoff. From the beginning position the jumper steps out with one foot. There usually is little preparatory leg flexion.
Step 2	Knee extension first. The jumper begins to extend the knee joints before the heels come off the ground, resulting in a jump that is too vertical to achieve maximum horizontal distance.
Step 3	Simultaneous extension. The jumper extends the knees at the same time the heels come off the ground.
Step 4	Heels up first. The jump begins with the heels coming off the ground, then the knees extend; the jumper appears to start the takeoff by tipping forward.
	Arm action
Step 1	No action. The arms are stationary. After takeoff they may "wing" (shoulder girdle retracts).
Step 2	Arms swing forward. The arms swing forward at the shoulder from a starting position at the sides. The arms also might swing out to the side (abduct at the shoulder).
Step 3	Arms extend, then partially flex. The arms extend back together during leg flexion, then swing forward together at takeoff. Arm swing never reaches a position overhead.
Step 4	Arms extend, then fully flex. The arms extend back together during leg flexion, then swing forward to a position overhead.

Adapted from Clark and Phillips 1985.

Several published developmental sequences help us examine the developmental changes that occur in jumping movement patterns. Such sequences identify the steps children achieve in making the transition from inefficient to proficient movement patterns. The advancements reflect the children's adoption of movements that take advantage of the principles of motion. We can see improvements in the vertical and the horizontal (standing long) jump, but the developmental sequences researchers have suggested thus far are based on the standing long jump (Clark & Phillips, 1985; Roberton, 1978b, 1984; tables 6.4 and 6.5).

We first identify some of the characteristics of beginning jumpers in both the vertical jump and the standing long jump. Most young jumpers begin by executing a vertical jump, even if they intend to jump horizontally. Look at the beginning jumpers in figures 6.6, 6.7, and 6.8. A vertical jump is shown in figure 6.6 and a horizontal jump in figures 6.7 and 6.8. Note that in all three jumps the preparatory crouch is slight and the legs are not fully extended at liftoff. In fact, the vertical jumper in figure 6.6 tucks the legs to leave the ground rather than extend them at takeoff to project the body up. In this example, the head is no higher at the peak of the jump than at takeoff.

Another characteristic of beginning jumpers is that they do not use a two-foot (symmetrical) takeoff or landing, as shown in figure 6.6, even when they intend to do so. A one-foot takeoff, or step-out, is the lowest level of leg action in the developmental sequence of the standing long jump takeoff. The legs may also be asymmetrical during flight. To improve this leg action, the jumper needs to (1) make a symmetrical two-foot takeoff, flight, and landing and (2) fully extend the ankles, knees, and hips at takeoff, following a deep preparatory crouch. The knees and hips flex together in the flight phase of the standing long jump, following a full and forceful extension of the legs at takeoff.

To jump a long distance, the skilled performer leans the trunk forward at least 30 degrees from the vertical. By age 3, children can change their trunk angle at takeoff to make either a vertical or a horizontal jump (Clark, Phillips, & Petersen, 1989). However, beginning jumpers often keep the trunk too erect during a horizontal jump. When a skilled jumper leans the trunk forward to facilitate jumping for distance, the heels usually come

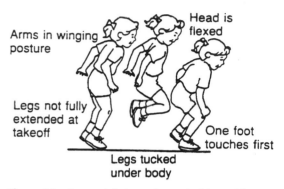

Figure 6.6 Sequential views of a vertical jump. The form here is inefficient. The legs are tucked up under the body rather than fully extended to project the body off the ground. Notice that one foot touches down first. The arms do not assist the jump. The jumper holds them in the winging posture.

Redrawn from Wickstrom 1983.

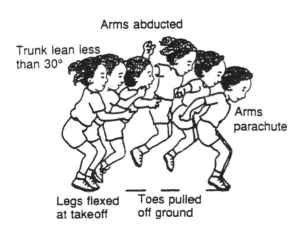

Figure 6.7 A beginning long jumper. As the jumper's weight shifts forward, the toes are pulled off the floor to "catch" the body at landing. The trunk lean at takeoff is less than 30 degrees from the vertical. The arms are used at takeoff but are in an abducted position, laterally rotate in flight, and "parachute" for the landing.

Drawn from film tracing taken in the Motor Development and Child Study Laboratory, University of Wisconsin–Madison and now available from the Motor Development Film Collection, Kinesiology Division, Bowling Green State University.

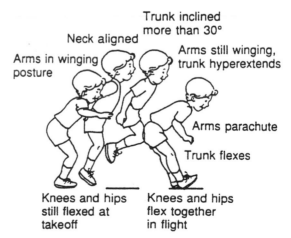

Figure 6.8 A beginning jumper. The leg action is in step 3 (table 6.5) at takeoff because the knees extend at the same time the heels leave the ground. The knees and hips flex together during flight, and the knees then extend before landing. The trunk is somewhat erect at takeoff. The trunk hyperextends in flight, then flexes for landing. The arms wing at takeoff, step 1, before parachuting for the landing.

off the ground before the knees start to extend (Clark & Phillips, 1985). Skilled jumpers appear to tip forward at the start of the takeoff. The leg action wherein "heels up" begins the takeoff is the most advanced step in the developmental sequence for the leg action of the horizontal jump.

Lack of coordinated arm action also characterizes beginning vertical and horizontal jumpers. Rather than use their arms to assist the jumping action, they may use their arms asymmetrically, hold them stationary at the side, or keep them in a high-guard position as a precaution against falling. Arms may *wing* (extend backward) ineffectively during flight (figure 6.6) or *parachute* (extend down and out to the side) during landing (figure 6.7). To achieve a proficient jump, the jumper must use the arms symmetrically to lead the jump from a preparatory extended position to an overhead swing. The developmental sequence for the arm action of the standing long jump progresses from no arm action to limited arm swing; to extension, then partial flexion; and to extension, then complete arm swing overhead.

Proficient Jumping

Through these developmental changes, performers can develop a proficient jumping pattern, as shown in figures 6.9 and 6.10. To execute proficient jumps, they

▲ get into a preparatory crouch that will stretch the muscles and allow the legs to apply maximal force as they fully extend at the moment of liftoff;

▲ take off for a horizontal jump with the heels coming off the ground and both feet leaving the ground at the same time; and

▲ extend the arms backward, then initiate the takeoff with a vigorous arm swing forward to a position overhead.

One arm swings down as other reaches up

Arm swing begins the jump

Trunk is straight during crouch

Preparatory crouch

Full leg extension

Figure 6.9 An advanced vertical jump for the purpose of reaching high. From a preparatory crouch, this basketball player swings his arms forward and up to lead the jump. The hips, knees, and ankles extend completely at takeoff. Near the peak of the jump, one hand continues up while the other comes down, tilting the shoulder girdle to assist the high reach. Note that the trunk tends to remain upright throughout.

Redrawn from Wickstrom 1983.

In jumping for height, proficient jumpers do the following:

▲ Direct force downward and extend the body throughout flight. If they are to strike an object or touch something overhead, the dominant arm reaches up and the opposite arm swings down. The person jumping gains height through a lateral tilt of the shoulders.

▲ Keep the trunk relatively upright throughout the jump.

▲ Flex the ankles, knees, and hips on touchdown to allow the force of landing to be absorbed.

In jumping for distance, proficient jumpers do the following:

▲ Direct force down and back by beginning the takeoff with the heels leaving the ground before the knees extend. The trunk appears to tip forward.

▲ Flex the knees during flight, then bring the thighs forward to a position parallel with the ground.

▲ Swing the lower legs forward for a two-foot landing.

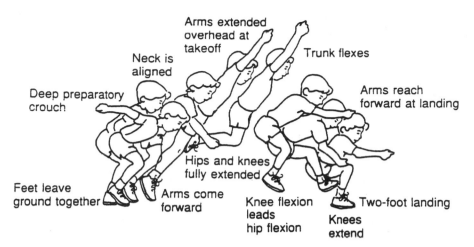

Figure 6.10 An advanced long jump. The feet leave the ground together and touch down together. The legs fully extend at takeoff, beginning with heels up. The knees then flex in flight, followed by hip flexion and finally knee extension to reach forward for landing. The trunk is inclined more than 30 degrees at takeoff, and the jumper maintains this lean in flight until the trunk flexes for landing. The arms lead the jump and reach overhead at takeoff. They then lower to reach forward at landing.

▲ Let the trunk come forward in reaction to the thigh flexing, putting the body in a jackknife position.

▲ Flex the ankles and knees when the heels touch the ground to absorb the momentum of the body over distance as the body continues to move forward.

Developmental Changes in Jumping

With practice, children can eventually make refinements in jumping pattern as described. Continuous growth in body size and strength also contributes to quantitative improvements in how far children can jump. During the elementary school years, children average increases of 3 to 5 in. a year in the horizontal distance they can jump and approximately 2 in. a year in vertical height jumped (DeOreo & Keogh, 1980). Qualitative improvements in jumping vary among children. For example, Clark and Phillips (1985) observed that fewer than 30% of the 3- to 7-year-olds they filmed had the same level of leg and arm action. Most had more advanced leg action than arm action, but some had more advanced arm than leg action. If one component was more advanced than the other, it was usually by only one step, but some children were two steps more advanced in one component than the other. Thus, we see many different movement patterns among developing children.

You can observe jumpers at different developmental levels by viewing video clips on your CD-ROM. Select Auxiliary Videos, then Skill Videos Not Used in Labs, then Standing Long Jump.

The differences between a vertical jump and a standing long jump involve position and movement speed. For example, in the standing long jump, the hips are more flexed than in the vertical jump as the jumper makes the transition from the preparatory crouch to the takeoff. The hips extend faster in the standing long jump, whereas the knees and ankles extend faster in the vertical jump. Other characteristics of jumping remain stable across developmental steps and type of jump. Clark et al. (1989) found that 3-, 5-, 7-, and 9-year-olds and adults all used the same pattern of leg coordination. In addition, all used that same pattern for both standing long jumps and vertical jumps. Specifically, the timing of hip, knee, and ankle joint extension at takeoff was similar in all groups. Perhaps this reflects the mechanics involved in propelling the body's mass off the ground. The neuromuscular system must use a leg coordination pattern that gets the body off the ground, but limb positions and movement speeds change as the jumper is better able to optimize jumping distance or adapt the jump to a specific task, such as shooting the basketball jump shot.

It is clear that all persons do not master jumping in childhood or even in adolescence. Zimmerman (1956) found many inefficient jumping characteristics in college women, including limited arm swing and incomplete leg extension at takeoff. For children and teens to receive assistance from their instructors in perfecting an advanced jumping pattern, instructors must be able to critically observe and analyze jumping performance.

Use the observation plan provided here (p. 101) to assess the developmental level of the standing long jump takeoff.

To gain experience in assessing the developmental levels of jumpers, download Lab 6.2 Assessing the Developmental Levels of Long Jumpers from the Student Resources section at www.HumanKinetics.com/LifeSpanMotorDevelopment.

Rate Controllers in Jumping

For children to perform a two-foot jump, they must be able to develop enough force to bring their bodies into the air from a still position. Unlike in walking and running, they cannot take advantage of a "fall and catch" motion but must project their entire bodies into the air.

Hopping

Adults rarely use hopping to move around, yet to become a skillful mover, an individual should develop hopping skills during childhood. To hop, especially repeatedly, one must project and absorb body weight with just one limb and maintain balance on the small base of support that one foot provides. Complex sport and dance skills often incorporate these movement abilities.

Characteristics of Early Hopping

Children may move through the levels of arm action and leg action at different rates. Look at the two early hoppers shown in figures 6.11 and 6.12. The leg action of the hopper in figure 6.11 is ineffective as a force producer. The child momentarily lifts the support leg from the floor by flexing it rather than project the body up by leg extension, and the swing leg is inactive. The arms are also inactive; the child's leg and arm actions fall into the first developmental step (see table 6.6 for the developmental sequence). The hopper in figure 6.12 has achieved some leg extension; this child is in step 2 of leg action but still uses the first step of arm action.

Proficient Hopping

To become proficient hoppers, children need to make the following improvements:

▲ The swing leg must lead the hip.

▲ The support leg must extend fully.

▲ The arms must move in opposition to the legs.

▲ The support leg must flex at landing to absorb the force of the landing and to prepare for extension at the next takeoff.

The hopper in figure 6.13 has made one of these improvements by moving the arm opposite the swing leg in opposition, but the other arm does not move in a consistent way. The

Observation Plan for the Standing Long Jump Takeoff

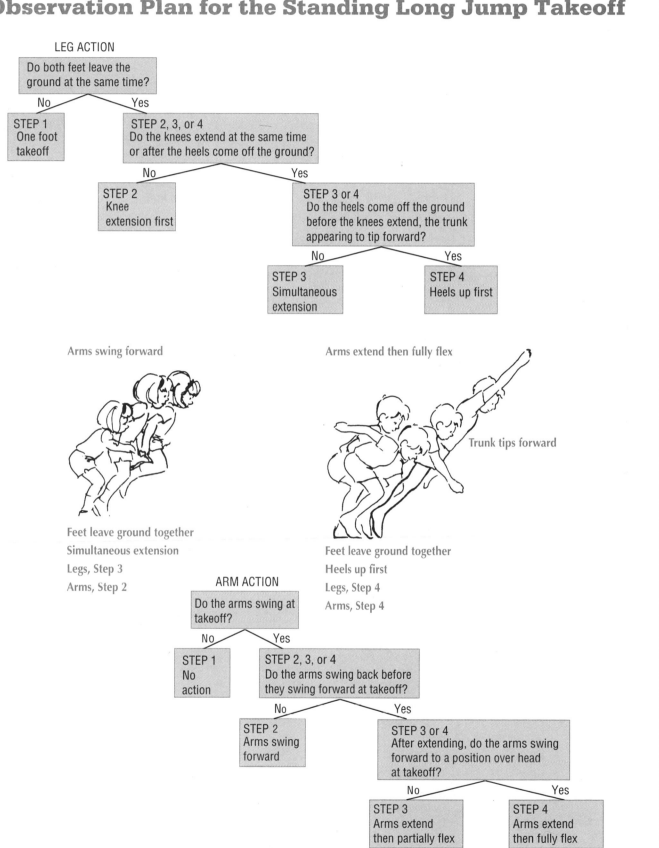

LEG ACTION

Do both feet leave the ground at the same time?

No → STEP 1
One foot takeoff

Yes → STEP 2, 3, or 4
Do the knees extend at the same time or after the heels come off the ground?

No → STEP 2
Knee extension first

Yes → STEP 3 or 4
Do the heels come off the ground before the knees extend, the trunk appearing to tip forward?

No → STEP 3
Simultaneous extension

Yes → STEP 4
Heels up first

Arms swing forward

Arms extend then fully flex

Trunk tips forward

Feet leave ground together
Simultaneous extension
Legs, Step 3
Arms, Step 2

Feet leave ground together
Heels up first
Legs, Step 4
Arms, Step 4

ARM ACTION

Do the arms swing at takeoff?

No → STEP 1
No action

Yes → STEP 2, 3, or 4
Do the arms swing back before they swing forward at takeoff?

No → STEP 2
Arms swing forward

Yes → STEP 3 or 4
After extending, do the arms swing forward to a position over head at takeoff?

No → STEP 3
Arms extend then partially flex

Yes → STEP 4
Arms extend then fully flex

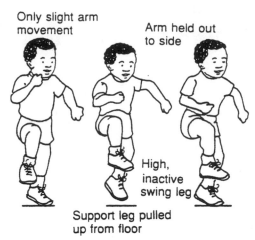

Only slight arm movement

Arm held out to side

High, inactive swing leg

Support leg pulled up from floor

Figure 6.11 An early hopping attempt exhibiting step 1 leg action and step 1 arm action. The support leg is pulled off the floor to produce only momentary flight. The arms are high and are not working in opposition.

Drawn from film tracing taken in the Motor Development and Child Study Laboratory, University of Wisconsin–Madison and now available from the Motor Development Film Collection, Kinesiology Division, Bowling Green State University.

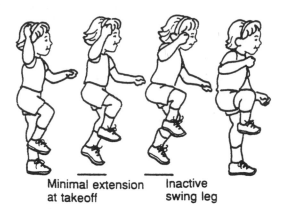

Minimal extension at takeoff

Inactive swing leg

Figure 6.12 This girl uses some leg extension to leave the ground, but her swing leg is still inactive. She is in step 2 of the developmental levels of leg action.

Drawn from film tracing taken in the Motor Development and Child Study Laboratory, University of Wisconsin–Madison and now available from the Motor Development Film Collection, Kinesiology Division, Bowling Green State University.

TABLE 6.6 Developmental Sequence for Hopping

	Leg action
Step 1	Momentary flight. The support knee and hip quickly flex, pulling (instead of projecting) the foot from the floor. The flight is momentary. Only one or two hops can be achieved. The swing leg is lifted high and held in an inactive position to the side or in front of the body.
Step 2	Fall and catch; swing leg inactive. Body lean forward allows minimal knee and ankle extension to help the body "fall" forward of the support foot and then quickly catch itself again. The swing leg is inactive. Repeat hops are now possible.
Step 3	Projected takeoff; swing leg assists. Perceptible pretakeoff extension occurs in the hip, knee, and ankle in the support leg. There is little or no delay in changing from knee and ankle flexion on landing to extension before takeoff. The swing leg now pumps up and down to assist in projection. The range of the swing is insufficient to carry it behind the support leg when viewed from the side.
Step 4	Projection delay; swing leg leads. The weight of the child on landing is now smoothly transferred along the foot to the ball before the knee and ankle extend to takeoff. The support leg nearly reaches full extension on the takeoff. The swing leg now leads the upward-forward movement of the takeoff phase while the support leg is still rotating over the ball of the foot. The range of the pumping action in the swing leg increases so that it passes behind the support leg when viewed from the side.
	Arm action
Step 1	Bilateral inactive. The arms are held bilaterally, usually high and out to the side, although other positions behind or in front of the body may occur. Any arm action is usually slight and not consistent.
Step 2	Bilateral reactive. Arms swing upward briefly, then are medially rotated at the shoulder in a winging movement before takeoff. It appears that this movement is in reaction to loss of balance.
Step 3	Bilateral assist. The arms pump up and down together, usually in front of the line of the trunk. Any downward and backward motion of the arms occurs after takeoff. The arms may move parallel to each other or be held at different levels as they move up and down.
Step 4	Semi-opposition. The arm on the side opposite the swing leg swings forward with that leg and back as the leg moves down. The position of the other arm is variable, often staying in front of the body or to the side.
Step 5	Opposing assist. The arm opposite the swing leg moves forward and upward in synchrony with the forward and upward movement of that leg. The other arm moves in the direction opposite to the action of the swing leg. The range of movement in the arm action may be minimal unless the task requires speed or distance.

Note: This sequence has been partially validated by Halverson and Williams (1985).

Reprinted from Roberton and Halverson 1984.

Arm opposite swing leg comes forward with that leg

Range of swing leg is larger | Takeoff leg is extending | Swing leg pumps up and down

Figure 6.13 A more advanced hop: step 3 in the developmental sequence of leg action, step 4 in arm action. The swing leg leads the hop. Although the range of the swing leg is larger, it could still increase even more.

Drawn from film tracing taken in the Motor Development and Child Study Laboratory, University of Wisconsin–Madison and now available from the Motor Development Film Collection, Kinesiology Division, Bowling Green State University.

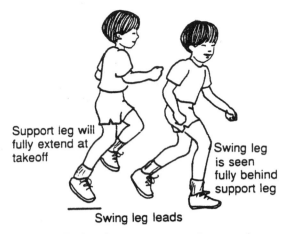

Support leg will fully extend at takeoff

Swing leg is seen fully behind support leg

Swing leg leads

Figure 6.14 This boy demonstrates step 4 leg action because the range of the swing is sufficient to carry the swing leg completely behind the support leg. Both arms move in opposition to the legs.

Drawn from film tracing taken in the Motor Development and Child Study Laboratory, University of Wisconsin–Madison and now available from the Motor Development Film Collection, Kinesiology Division, Bowling Green State University.

advanced hopper in figure 6.14 assists the hop with both arms moving in opposition to the legs. The hopper in figure 6.13 extends the support leg at takeoff, reflecting good force application, and uses the swing leg, but not vigorously. The hopper in figure 6.14 has made this improvement—the swing leg leads the takeoff, allowing the momentum of several body parts to be chained together, then swings back behind the support leg to lead the next takeoff.

Developmental Changes in Hopping

Few children under age 3 can hop repeatedly (Bayley, 1969; McCaskill & Wellman, 1938). Developmentalists often cite the preschool years as the time children become proficient hoppers (Gutteridge, 1939; Sinclair, 1973; Williams, 1983). Yet Halverson and Williams (1985) found that more than half of a group of 63 children (3-, 4-, and 5-year-olds) were at step 2 in the arm and leg action. They observed few attempts that they could classify at the advanced levels, and hopping on the nonpreferred leg was developmentally behind hopping on the preferred leg. Figure 6.15 shows that many more children were at the lowest developmental step when hopping on their nonpreferred legs than when hopping on their preferred legs. Few children were beyond step 2 when hopping on either leg. If the children in this study are representative of this age group, hopping continues to develop well past the age of 5.

You can observe hoppers at different developmental levels by viewing video clips on your CD-ROM. Select Auxiliary Videos, then Skill Videos Not Used in Labs, then Hopping.

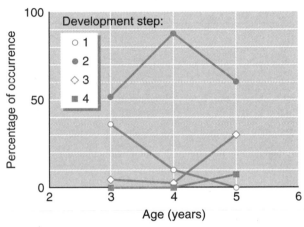

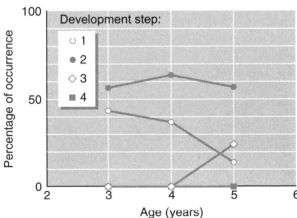

Figure 6.15 The developmental level of leg action in 3-, 4-, and 5-year-old hoppers on their preferred legs (top) and nonpreferred legs (bottom). Note that more children were at step 1 when hopping on their nonpreferred legs than when hopping on their preferred legs. Only at age 5 were any notable portion of the children at step 3.

Reprinted from Halverson and Williams 1985.

? Part of the rehabilitation process for some injuries to the lower limbs includes hopping on the injured leg (generally later in the rehabilitation process). If adults do not hop regularly, why is hopping so important in rehabilitation? Consider this in terms of constraints.

Why do children advance from one developmental level of hopping to another? Several researchers attempted to answer this question by examining the force and stiffness of landing in hopping (Getchell & Roberton, 1989; Roberton & Halverson, 1988). Note that in step 2 the hopper lands flat-footed and holds the swing leg still. By step 3 the hopper uses a softer landing (more leg flexion to cushion the landing, followed by extension to the next takeoff) and swings the nonhopping leg. The researchers confirmed that the force of landing in a step 2 hop rises sharply on landing, whereas in a step 3 hop, it rises gradually. To achieve a soft landing, the neuromuscular system probably prepares ahead of time (ahead of the landing) to moderate the force of landing by allowing the leg to "give" (flex). Perhaps, then, once children achieve a step 2 hop, their ability to project the body higher and to travel faster, and perhaps their increasing body weight, increases the force of the landing. Once that force reaches a critical value that could cause a damaging, jarring landing, the neuromuscular system changes children's hopping movements to allow a softer, more cushioned landing. Hence, children advance to the next developmental level.

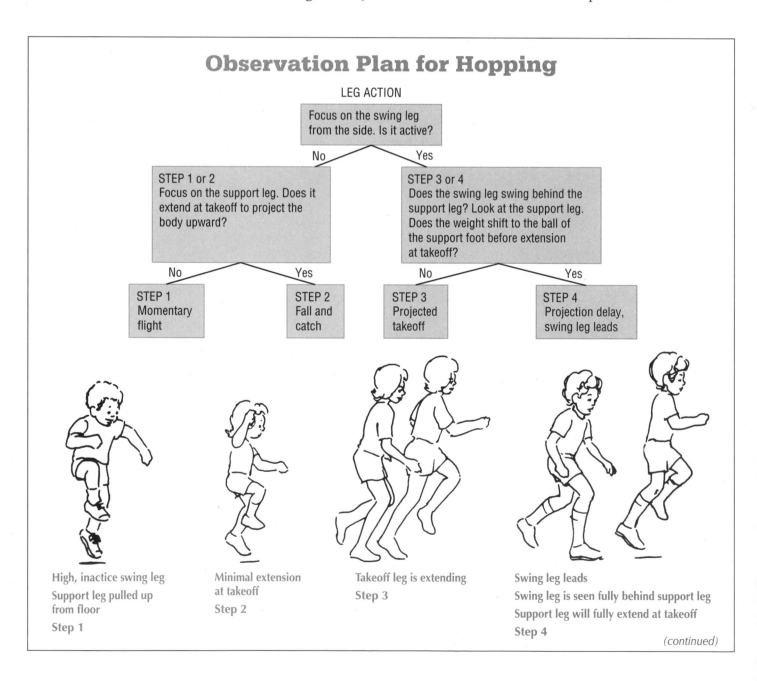

Observation Plan for Hopping

LEG ACTION

Focus on the swing leg from the side. Is it active?

No → **STEP 1 or 2** Focus on the support leg. Does it extend at takeoff to project the body upward?

Yes → **STEP 3 or 4** Does the swing leg swing behind the support leg? Look at the support leg. Does the weight shift to the ball of the support foot before extension at takeoff?

No → **STEP 1** Momentary flight

Yes → **STEP 2** Fall and catch

No → **STEP 3** Projected takeoff

Yes → **STEP 4** Projection delay, swing leg leads

High, inactice swing leg
Support leg pulled up from floor
Step 1

Minimal extension at takeoff
Step 2

Takeoff leg is extending
Step 3

Swing leg leads
Swing leg is seen fully behind support leg
Support leg will fully extend at takeoff
Step 4

(continued)

(continued)

ARM ACTION

Move to watch the arms from the side and the front. Is arm action bilateral or opposing?

Bilateral / Opposing

STEP 1, 2, or 3
Are the arms noticeably active?

STEP 4 or 5
Do both arms move in opposition to the legs or just one?

No / Yes

One / Both

STEP 1
Bilateral inactive

STEP 2
Do the arms pump up and down or wing?

STEP 3
Semiopposition

STEP 4
Opposing assist

Wing / Pump

STEP 2
Bilateral reactive

STEP 3
Bilateral assist

Only slight arm movement

Arm held out to side

Arm opposite swing leg comes forward with that leg

Step 1

Step 4

An Integrated Approach to Understanding Hopping

If we dig deeper into understanding the change in developmental levels in the hop, we reveal the remarkable interaction of individual constraints within the body. Let's consider a child who hops with step 2 action. The swing leg is held in front; therefore it simply reacts to rather than contributes to the hop. For a lightweight child who needs to produce little force to move, a stationary swing leg does not prevent hopping. The child produces force, primarily downward, from the stance leg. As the child grows, she adds body weight and size. Projecting force downward from the stance leg no longer suffices for a hop; she adds swing leg movement to add additional force. The movement of the swing leg provides force that helps push the body down and back. The ground responds by pushing the body up and forward, and the child hops into the air. However, what goes up must come down—and the child returns to earth with a greater amount of force (due to her increased weight and the height of the hop) than in a step 2 hop. To break the fall, the child must "give" to land softly. So, the changes in the swing leg in step 3 are complemented by changes in the stance leg, both of which lead to a higher, safer hop.

Observing Hopping Patterns

As with the other locomotor skills, a novice observer must practice hopping assessment. Halverson (1983; see also Roberton & Halverson, 1984) suggests a systematic pattern of observation that focuses on the body parts one at a time. As a novice observer, you should observe leg action from the side. Initially, pay attention to the swing leg. Is it active? If so, does it move up and down or swing past the support leg? Next, observe the support leg. Does it extend at takeoff? Does it flex on landing and extend during the next hop? Look at arm action from the side and the front. Watch first to see whether the arm movement is bilateral or opposing. If it is bilateral, you can then categorize arm movement as inactive, reactive, or backward in direction. If arm movement is opposing, note whether one or both arms move synchronously with the legs. Use the observation plan provided here (pp. 104-105) to assess the developmental levels of hoppers.

To gain experience in assessing the developmental levels of hoppers, download Lab 6.3 Assessing the Developmental Levels of Hoppers from the Student Resources section at www.HumanKinetics.com/LifeSpanMotorDevelopment.

Rate Controllers in Hopping

Hopping likely depends on the postural system's ability to balance the body on one limb for a succession of hops. Also, the individual must be able to generate enough force to lift the body with one limb, recover, and quickly generate enough force again to hop repeatedly. Running also requires projection and weight acceptance on one limb; however, in running, legs alternate and are able to regain energy as they swing in a flexed position. In the hop, the leg stays extended—thus hopping requires more effort than running. Therefore, the ability to generate force can act as a rate controller.

Galloping, Sliding, and Skipping

? Try to consider situations or contexts in which locomotor skills other than walking and running are socially acceptable. Do not limit yourself to sport and dance applications.

Galloping, sliding, and **skipping** all involve the fundamental movements of stepping, hopping, or leaping. Galloping and sliding, both asymmetric gaits, consist of a step on one foot, then a leap-step on the other foot (Roberton & Halverson, 1984; Whitall, 1988b). The same leg always leads with the step. The difference between galloping and sliding is the direction of movement. In galloping, the individual moves forward; in sliding, the movement is sideways. Skipping is a step and a hop on the same foot, with alternating feet: step-hop on the right foot, step-hop on the left foot, step-hop on the right foot, and so on. The movement is usually forward (figure 6.16, a and b).

Characteristics of Early Skill Patterns

Children's early attempts at these skills are usually arrhythmic and stiff, as shown in figure 6.17. The arms are rarely involved in projecting the body off the floor. Children might hold their arms stiffly in the high-guard position or out to the side to aid their balance. Their stride or step length is short, and they land flat-footed. Little trunk rotation is used, and they exaggerate vertical lift. In early galloping attempts, a child's trailing leg may land ahead of the lead leg.

Proficient Skill Patterns

In contrast, children proficient at galloping, sliding, and skipping are rhythmical and relaxed, as seen in figure 6.18. Proficiency in these skills includes the following characteristics:

▲ The arms are no longer needed for balance.

▲ In skipping, arms swing rhythmically in opposition to the legs and provide momentum.

▲ The child can use the arms for another purpose during galloping and sliding, such as clapping.

▲ Heel-forefoot or forefoot landings prevail.

▲ The knees "give" on landing, remaining flexed while they support the body's weight, and then extend at takeoff, especially when the child is traveling quickly.

Figure 6.16 *(a)* Galloping is a step on the lead leg and a leap-step on the trailing leg. *(b)* Skipping is a step, then a hop on one foot and a step, then a hop on the other foot, alternately continuing.

Redrawn from Clark and Whitall 1989.

Figure 6.17 A beginning galloper. The arms are held stiffly, the stride length is short, and vertical movement is exaggerated.

Redrawn from Clark and Whitall 1989.

Figure 6.18 An advanced galloper. The arms move in opposition to the legs. Movements are rhythmic and landings are not flat-footed.

Developmental Changes

Galloping is the first of these three bipedal patterns to emerge. It develops after the child has firmly established the running pattern (around age 2) and usually before hopping (at age 3 or 4). Galloping is the first asymmetrical locomotor pattern a child learns. As noted earlier, walking and running have 50% phasing—the legs make the same movement, but the cycle of one leg is halfway behind the cycle of the other. Galloping is uneven. The steps take longer than the leap-steps. Gallopers, regardless of age, tend to use one of two timing patterns: the step takes either approximately twice as long as the leap-step (a 66 to 33% phasing) or three times as long (a 75 to 25% phasing) (Clark & Whitall, 1989b; Whitall, 1988b). Children master sliding next, but in both galloping and sliding, they develop the ability to lead with the nondominant leg much later than with the dominant leg.

Skipping is usually the last of the locomotor patterns to emerge, usually between 4 and 7 years of age. A little more than half of 5-year-olds demonstrate early skipping (Branta et al., 1984). At first, a child might perform a unilateral step-hop—that is, a skip with the dominant leg and just a running step with the other leg. When the child begins to skip with both legs, occasional breaks with a step or gallop interjected are common (Gutteridge, 1939; Wickstrom, 1987).

Though no one has validated developmental steps for skipping, several changes are obvious. A beginning skipper uses a high hop and knee lift. The skip appears jerky. Perhaps this reflects the need for much effort to project the body off the ground for the hop. Eventually, the child partially extends the leg on the hop and uses a lower but smoother knee lift, making the skip smoother and more rhythmic. Perhaps greater leg strength allows the child to get the body off the ground with only partial leg extension.

Several changes in arm action occur. Beginners use the arms inconsistently, often swinging one or both arms up to the side. Then skippers begin to use the arms bilaterally, swinging them sometimes forward and back in circles, sometimes forward and down. Skilled skippers can use their arms in opposition to their legs (Wickstrom, 1987).

It is easy to speculate about why skipping is the last fundamental locomotor skill that children develop. The coordination between the legs is symmetrical, but within each leg, the pattern of movement is asymmetrical. Girls typically perform these locomotor skills at an earlier age than boys, perhaps reflecting their slight edge in biological maturity for chronological age, imitation of other girls, or possibly encouragement from family and friends.

Observing Galloping, Sliding, and Skipping Patterns

While observing galloping, first take a side view and note where the trailing foot lands in relation to the lead foot. The extent of vertical lift is also clearly visible from the side. Arms can be viewed from any angle. In proficient galloping, the trailing foot lands alongside or behind the lead foot; the flight pattern is low; and the arms are free to swing rhythmically, to clap, or to engage in another activity. Note whether a child can lead with the dominant leg only or with either leg.

Sliding is best observed from the front. Focus on the knees to see if they are stiff, as in early sliding, or relaxed so that the child's steps have the spring characteristic of proficient sliding. Note whether the arms are in an inefficient guard position or are relaxed and free to be used for another task. As with galloping, you should see if a child can slide to the dominant side only or to both sides.

When watching skipping, observe whether the child skips with one leg and runs with the other or skips with both. If the child skips with both legs, look at the height of the hop and the knee lift from the side. Lower height and knee lifts characterize a more proficient, smoother skip. Finally, watch the arm pattern to see if it is bilateral or, in a more proficient skipper, in opposition to the leg movement.

Rate Controllers for Galloping, Sliding, and Skipping

Galloping generally follows running in the development of motor skills. What rate controllers exist for galloping? To gallop, individuals must uncouple their legs from the 50% phasing they use when walking and running. This requires timing changes. At the same time, the two legs are performing different tasks (step vs. leap-step); therefore, they require different amounts of force (Clark & Whitall, 1989b). To slide, individuals must also turn to one side. The neuromuscular system may limit the rate at which these two requirements of galloping and sliding occur.

The emergence of skipping does not appear to be limited by generation of force for the hop because children hop before they skip. Nor is balance a probable rate limiter because it is more difficult to balance while hopping than while skipping. As mentioned earlier, however, skipping is the most complex fundamental locomotor pattern. Skipping might not appear until the individual's neuromuscular system can coordinate the two limbs as they alternately perform asymmetric tasks.

 Summary and Synthesis

Transporting ourselves from here to there is an important part of human life. We consider locomotion as one of the first signs of an infant's independence. Infants may creep, crawl, or move on hands and feet as their initial means of getting around. Not long after, infants develop the ability to walk, the most basic form of upright bipedal locomotion. Walking involves alternating leg motion, with a period of single foot support following a period of double foot support. Next, toddlers run. Running is similar to walking, with alternating foot strikes, but has a period of flight rather than double support. Children then develop the ability to jump, gallop, hop, slide, and skip. All of these more complex locomotor patterns have different constraints that will affect the timing and sequence in which they emerge. We can trace the changes in these motor skills throughout individual life spans as the form of the movements change with the changing constraints of adolescence, adulthood, and older adulthood.

From crawling through skipping, children acquire fundamental locomotor skills as their bodies and the world around them change. Many different individual constraints act as rate limiters to these emerging skills. After individuals acquire these skills, the form of the skills changes as the child becomes more proficient at them. If you look across locomotor skills, you can see patterns of changes that are similar. For example, in all of the locomotor skills, individuals narrow their base of support to increase mobility and widen it (as in infancy and older adulthood) to increase stability. The developmental changes described in this chapter can be used to generally estimate individuals' developmental status. Of course, the developmental sequences provide specific characteristics of these changes.

It is perhaps not surprising that researchers tend to focus on childhood when studying locomotor skills. Children not only acquire the skills rather quickly, but they also use the skills regularly, which is not the case for most adults. Try to remember the last time you galloped. If you can, you will probably remember that you galloped for some purpose, such as performing a dance. Adults generally do not use the entire range of fundamental locomotor patterns, at least not in the United States. What constrains these patterns from emerging? Farley (1997) describes the energetic inefficiency of human skipping; because skipping is "slow, jolting and tiring," it makes an unlikely candidate for adult locomotion. In addition, sociocultural attitudes suggest that these motor skills are not appropriate for adults. The question still remains: do adults and older adults hop, gallop, jump, slide, and skip the same way that children do?

Discussion Questions

1. Describe the different constraints that may act as rate controllers for specific loco-motor activities.

2. How can a teacher or therapist manipulate task constraints to help a child acquire the skill of galloping?

3. What are some of the other ways that humans can move from place to place (without equipment)? Why are these locomotor forms rarely used?

4. What movement characteristics might you see in an older adult who is galloping? Why?

 ## Learning Activities

Comparing Preferred and Nonpreferred Hopping Legs

What individual constraints could be involved in determining the developmental level of hopping?

1. Observe three different people (try to observe at least one child). Ask them to hop on their preferred legs (i.e., on which foot do they naturally choose to hop?). Assess their developmental levels using the observation plan provided in the chapter.

2. Now, ask them to hop on their opposite, or nonpreferred, legs. What happens to their developmental levels?

3. Particularly in children, there will be a difference of one developmental level between their preferred and nonpreferred legs. Try to come up with a list of reasons why these differences might exist.

Development of Ballistic Skills

chapter 7

EXTRA!!! The Times EXTRA!!!

DODO'S DYNASTY, TENNIS' GRANDE DAME CLOSES IN ON 300 TITLES

Read the cover of a recent *USTA Magazine* (April 1999, pp. 11–13) featuring Dorothy Cheney. At 82 years of age, Dodo Cheney was practicing for her 300th U.S. Tennis Association championship. She won her first tennis tournament at age 10 and won the Australian Open as a young adult. She began playing senior tennis when she turned 40 and now competes in the 75-and-over and 80-and-over divisions. Dodo Cheney is proof that ballistic skills can be executed over the life span.

Ballistic skills are those in which a person applies force to an object in order to project it. The ballistic skills of throwing, kicking, and striking have similar developmental patterns because the mechanical principles involved in projecting objects are basically the same. The ballistic skill that researchers have studied most is the overhand throw for distance. Much of the discussion on throwing also applies to kicking and striking, which we examine later in this chapter.

 ### *Chapter Objectives*

This chapter will

▲ identify developmental changes in throwing, kicking, punting, and striking movements,

▲ compare and contrast the characteristics of early performers across the various ballistic skills, and

▲ note similar characteristics of proficient performance of ballistic skills.

OVERARM THROWING

Throwing takes many forms. The two-hand underhand throw (windup between the legs) and one-hand underhand throw are common in young children. There is also a sidearm throw and a two-hand overarm throw. The type of throw people use, especially children, often depends on task constraints, especially the size of the ball. Our focus, though, is on the one-hand overarm throw. It is the most common type of throw in sport games and has been studied more widely than other types. Many of the mechanical principles involved in the overarm throw also apply to other types of throws.

Researchers often make product assessments to gauge throwing skill development. That is, they measure the end product, or result, of the throwing movement, such as the accuracy, distance, or ball velocity. However, product measures have several drawbacks. Researchers often must change an accuracy assessment task when working with children of different ages. Young children need a short distance over which to throw to reach the target. However, a short distance makes the task too easy for older children, who might all achieve perfect scores, so researchers must increase the distance or decrease the target size for older groups. Also, scores on throws for distance often reflect factors such as body size and strength in addition to throwing skill. Two children may have equal throwing skills but quite different distance scores because one child is bigger and stronger. Finally, measuring ball velocity at release requires specialized equipment that may not be readily available. Thus, we could argue that product scores are not as useful to teachers, parents, and coaches as knowing how a child throws. Let's now turn our attention to the quality of the throwing pattern.

Characteristics of Early Overarm Throwing

It is helpful to contrast children's early attempts to throw with an advanced overarm throw. Young children's throwing patterns, especially those of children under 3 years, tend to be restricted to arm action alone (Marques-Bruna & Grimshaw, 1997). The child depicted in figure 7.1 does not step into the throw or use much trunk action. This child merely positions the upper arm, often with the elbow up or forward, and executes the throw by elbow extension alone. Figure 7.2 shows more movement but little gain in mechanical efficiency. Obviously, these children demonstrate minimal throwing skill.

 In very young children, throwing consists of arm action alone.

Figure 7.1 A beginning thrower simply brings the hand back with the elbow up and throws by extending the elbow without taking a step.

Drawn from film tracing taken in the Motor Development and Child Study Laboratory, University of Wisconsin–Madison and now available from the Motor Development Film Collection, Kinesiology Division, Bowling Green State University.

Figure 7.2 A beginning thrower. Note the trunk flexion, rather than rotation, with the throw.

Drawn from film tracing taken in the Motor Development and Child Study Laboratory, University of Wisconsin–Madison and now available from the Motor Development Film Collection, Kinesiology Division, Bowling Green State University.

Proficient Overarm Throwing

By studying the characteristics of a proficient throw, we can identify the limitations in early throwing attempts. Thus, an advanced, forceful throw for distance has the following movement patterns:

▲ The weight shifts to the back foot; the trunk rotates back; and the arm makes a circular, downward **backswing** for a windup.

▲ The leg opposite the throwing arm steps forward to increase the distance over which the thrower applies force to the ball and to allow full trunk rotation.

▲ The trunk rotates forward to add force to the throw. To produce maximal force, trunk rotation is differentiated, resulting in a movement that looks like the body "opens up."

▲ The trunk bends laterally, away from the side of the throwing arm.

▲ The upper arm forms a right angle with the trunk and comes forward just as (or slightly after) the shoulders rotate to a front-facing position. This means that from the side, you can see the upper arm within the outline of the trunk.

▲ The thrower holds the elbow at a right angle during the forward swing, extending the arm when the shoulders reach the front-facing position. Extending the arm just before release lengthens the radius of the throwing arc.

▲ The forearm lags behind the trunk and upper arm during the forward swing. While the upper trunk is rotating forward, the forearm and hand appear to be stationary or to move down or back. The forearm lags until the upper trunk and shoulders actually rotate in the direction of the throw (the front-facing position).

▲ The follow-through dissipates the force of the throw over distance. The greater portion of wrist flexion comes during follow-through, after the thrower releases the ball.

▲ Dissipating force after release allows maximal speed of movement while the ball is in the hand.

▲ The thrower carries out the movements of the body segments sequentially, progressively adding the contributions of each part to the force of the throw. Generally, the sequence is as follows:

1. Step forward and pelvic rotation
2. Upper spine rotation and upper arm swing

The **backswing** is the backward, or take-away, movement to put the arm, leg, or racket in a position to move ballistically forward to project an object.

3. Upper arm inward rotation and elbow extension
4. Release
5. Follow-through

Developmental Changes in Overarm Throwing

Now that we have discussed the characteristics of an advanced, forceful throw, we can examine how an individual progresses through the developmental steps from initial throwing attempts to advanced throwing skill. Several developmental sequences of overarm throwing have been proposed, beginning with a sequence outlined by Wild in 1938 and including that of Seefeldt, Reuschlein, and Vogel in 1972. Then, Roberton proposed a developmental sequence for the overarm throw using the body component approach. Two of the component sequences, arm action and trunk action, are **validated developmental sequences** (Roberton, 1977, 1978a; Roberton & DiRocco, 1981; Roberton & Langendorfer, 1980). In fact, Roberton and Konczak (2001) determined that changes in developmental sequences actually accounted for more than half the change in velocity in 39 children studied over 7 years. Carefully studying the developmental overarm throw sequence outlined in table 7.1 will help you compare these steps with the different characteristics of early throwers depicted in figures 7.1 and 7.2 and the more advanced throwers in figures 7.3 through 7.6.

Validated developmental sequences are sequences of advances in the performance of a skill that have been determined by longitudinal study and shown to fall in the same fixed order for all individuals.

? What factors could increase the likelihood of a developing child reaching the advanced steps in each component of throwing?

TABLE 7.1 Developmental Sequence for Throwing

Trunk action in throwing and striking for force	
Step 1	No trunk action or forward–backward movements. Only the arm is active in force production. Sometimes the forward thrust of the arm pulls the trunk into a passive left rotation (assuming a right-handed throw), but no twist-up precedes that action. If trunk action occurs, it accompanies the forward thrust of the arm by flexing forward at the hips. Preparatory extension sometimes precedes forward hip flexion.
Step 2	Upper trunk rotation or total trunk "block" rotation. The spine and pelvis rotate away from the intended line of flight and then simultaneously begin forward rotation, acting as a unit, or "block." Occasionally, only the upper spine twists away, then toward the direction of force. The pelvis, then, remains fixed, facing the line of flight, or joins the rotary movement after forward spinal rotation has begun.
Step 3	Differentiated rotation. The pelvis precedes the upper spine in initiating forward rotation. The child twists away from the intended line of ball flight and then begins forward rotation with the pelvis while the upper spine is still twisting away.
Backswing, humerus, and forearm action in the overarm throw for force *Preparatory arm backswing component*	
Step 1	No backswing. The ball in the hand moves directly forward to release from the arm's original position when the hand first grasped the ball.
Step 2	Elbow and humeral flexion. The ball moves away from the intended line of flight to a position behind or alongside the head by upward flexion of the humerus and concomitant elbow flexion.
Step 3	Circular, upward backswing. The ball moves away from the intended line of flight to a position behind the head via a circular overhead movement with elbow extended, or an oblique swing back, or a vertical lift from the hip.
Step 4	Circular, downward backswing. The ball moves away from the intended line of flight to a position behind the head via a circular down-and-back motion, which carries the hand below the waist.

(continued)

	Humerus (upper arm) action component during forward swing
Step 1	Humerus oblique. The upper arm moves forward to ball release in a plane that intersects the trunk obliquely above or below the horizontal line of the shoulders. Occasionally, during the backswing, the upper arm is placed at a right angle to the trunk, with the elbow pointing toward the target. It maintains this fixed position during the throw.
Step 2	Humerus aligned but independent. The upper arm moves forward to ball release in a plane horizontally aligned with the shoulder, forming a right angle between humerus and trunk. By the time the shoulders (upper spine) reach front-facing, the upper arm and elbow have moved independently ahead of the outline of the body (as seen from the side) via horizontal adduction at the shoulder.
Step 3	Humerus lags. The upper arm moves forward to ball release horizontally aligned, but at the moment the shoulders (upper spine) reach front-facing, the upper arm remains within the outline of the body (as seen from the side). No horizontal adduction of the upper arm occurs before front-facing.
	Forearm action component during forward swing
Step 1	No forearm lag. The forearm and ball move steadily forward to ball release throughout the throwing action.
Step 2	Forearm lag. The forearm and ball appear to lag (i.e., to remain stationary behind the child or to move downward or backward in relation to the child). The lagging forearm reaches its farthest point back, deepest point down, or last stationary point before the shoulders (upper spine) reach front-facing.
Step 3	Delayed forearm lag. The lagging forearm delays reaching its final point of lag until the moment of front-facing.
	Foot action component in forceful throwing and striking
Step 1	No step. The child throws from the initial foot position.
Step 2	Homolateral step. The child steps with the foot on the same side as the throwing hand.
Step 3	Short contralateral step. The child steps with the foot on the opposite side of the throwing hand.
Step 4	Long contralateral step. The child steps with the opposite foot a distance of over half the child's standing height.

Note: Validation studies support the trunk sequence (Roberton, 1977; Roberton, 1978a; Roberton & Langendorfer, 1980; Langendorfer, 1982; Roberton & DiRocco, 1981). Validation studies support the arm sequences for the overarm throw (Halverson, Roberton, & Langendorfer, 1982; Roberton, 1977; Roberton, 1978a; Roberton & Langendorfer, 1980; Roberton & DiRocco, 1981), with the exception of the preparatory arm backswing sequence, which was hypothesized by Roberton (1984) from the work of Langendorfer (1980). Langendorfer (1982) believes the humerus and forearm components are appropriate for overarm striking. The foot action sequence was hypothesized by Roberton (1984) from the work of Leme and Shambes (1978); Seefeldt, Reuschlein, and Vogel (1972); and Wild (1937).

Reprinted from Roberton and Halverson 1984.

Just as with locomotor skills, you can more easily assess the developmental sequences of throwing using an observation plan (pp. 116-117).

To gain experience in assessing the developmental levels of throwers, download Lab 7.1 Assessing the Developmental Levels of Throwers from the Student Resources section at www.HumanKinetics.com/LifeSpanMotorDevelopment.

Begin the comparison by focusing on the trunk action component. In the first step of the developmental sequence, you do not see trunk action or forward–backward movements before the thrower releases the ball (figures 7.1 and 7.2). In the second step, the thrower proceeds to a **block rotation** of the trunk. Block rotation occurs between the third and fourth positions in figure 7.4. Distance throwers typically flex the trunk laterally (figure 7.5). Often, you can see the most advanced trunk action, differentiated rotation, in pictures of baseball pitchers. In figure 7.6, the pitcher has started to rotate the lower trunk toward

Block rotation of the trunk is forward rotation of the lower and upper trunk as a unit.

Observation Plan for Throwing

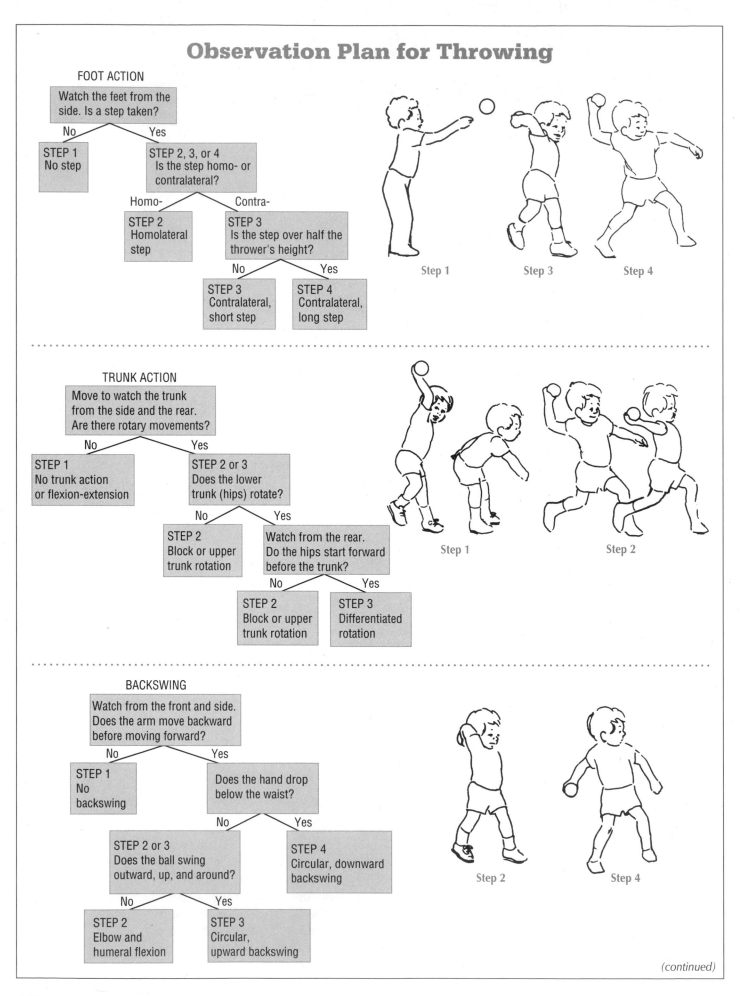

FOOT ACTION

Watch the feet from the side. Is a step taken?

- No → STEP 1 / No step
- Yes → STEP 2, 3, or 4 / Is the step homo- or contralateral?
  - Homo- → STEP 2 / Homolateral step
  - Contra- → STEP 3 / Is the step over half the thrower's height?
    - No → STEP 3 / Contralateral, short step
    - Yes → STEP 4 / Contralateral, long step

Step 1   Step 3   Step 4

TRUNK ACTION

Move to watch the trunk from the side and the rear. Are there rotary movements?

- No → STEP 1 / No trunk action or flexion-extension
- Yes → STEP 2 or 3 / Does the lower trunk (hips) rotate?
  - No → STEP 2 / Block or upper trunk rotation
  - Yes → Watch from the rear. Do the hips start forward before the trunk?
    - No → STEP 2 / Block or upper trunk rotation
    - Yes → STEP 3 / Differentiated rotation

Step 1   Step 2

BACKSWING

Watch from the front and side. Does the arm move backward before moving forward?

- No → STEP 1 / No backswing
- Yes → Does the hand drop below the waist?
  - No → STEP 2 or 3 / Does the ball swing outward, up, and around?
    - No → STEP 2 / Elbow and humeral flexion
    - Yes → STEP 3 / Circular, upward backswing
  - Yes → STEP 4 / Circular, downward backswing

Step 2   Step 4

(continued)

116

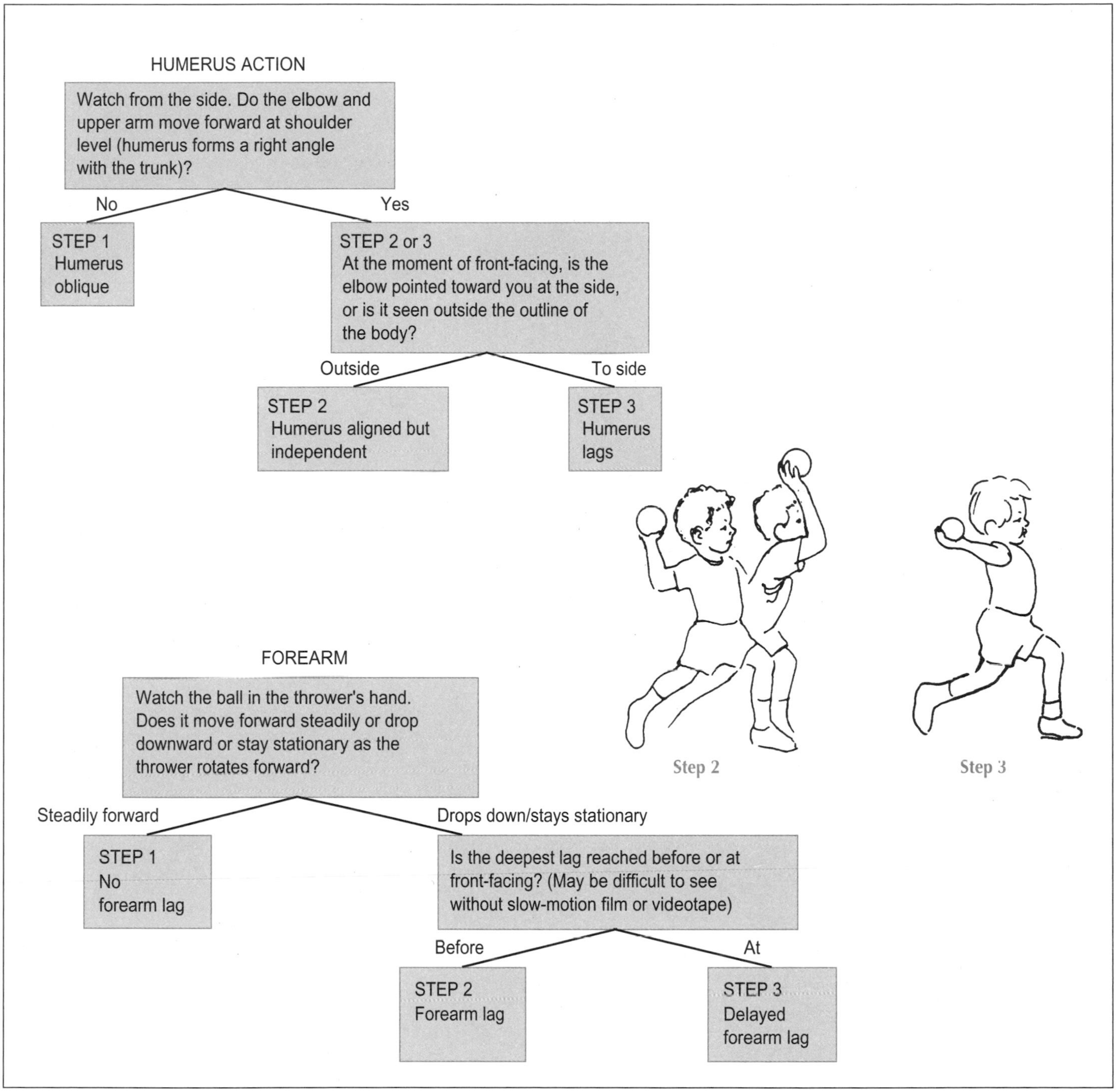

HUMERUS ACTION

Watch from the side. Do the elbow and upper arm move forward at shoulder level (humerus forms a right angle with the trunk)?

No — Yes

STEP 1
Humerus oblique

STEP 2 or 3
At the moment of front-facing, is the elbow pointed toward you at the side, or is it seen outside the outline of the body?

Outside — To side

STEP 2
Humerus aligned but independent

STEP 3
Humerus lags

Step 2

Step 3

FOREARM

Watch the ball in the thrower's hand. Does it move forward steadily or drop downward or stay stationary as the thrower rotates forward?

Steadily forward — Drops down/stays stationary

STEP 1
No forearm lag

Is the deepest lag reached before or at front-facing? (May be difficult to see without slow-motion film or videotape)

Before — At

STEP 2
Forearm lag

STEP 3
Delayed forearm lag

the direction of the throw while the upper trunk is still twisting back in preparation to throw. Different parts of the trunk start rotating forward at different times.

To analyze the complexity of arm movements in throwing, first study the preparatory backswing, then the upper arm (humerus) motions, and finally the forearm motions. An unskilled thrower often does not use a backswing (figure 7.1). At the next step in the developmental sequence, a thrower flexes the shoulder and elbow in preparation for elbow extension, as in figure 7.2. A more advanced preparation is to use an upward backswing, but the most desirable backswing for a throw for distance is circular and downward. The thrower pictured in figure 7.4 is using this pattern.

Figure 7.3 A thrower with stage 2 arm action. The forearm reaches its farthest point back before the shoulders rotate to front-facing, but the humerus then swings forward before the shoulders; the elbow is consequently visible outside the body outline. Note the right angle between the humerus and trunk.

Drawn from film tracing taken in the Motor Development and Child Study Laboratory, University of Wisconsin–Madison and now available from the Motor Development Film Collection, Kinesiology Division, Bowling Green State University.

Figure 7.4 A relatively advanced thrower. Arm, leg, and preparatory action are characteristic of the most advanced step, but the trunk action is characteristic of stage 2, or block rotation, rather than differentiated rotation.

Drawn from film tracing taken in the Motor Development and Child Study Laboratory, University of Wisconsin–Madison and now available from the Motor Development Film Collection, Kinesiology Division, Bowling Green State University.

In **differentiated trunk rotation**, the lower trunk (hip section) rotates forward while the upper trunk (shoulder section) is rotating backward, still preparing to rotate forward.

Figure 7.5 From the rear you can see that this advanced thrower flexes the trunk laterally away from the ball at release.

Drawn from film tracing taken in the Motor Development and Child Study Laboratory, University of Wisconsin–Madison and now available from the Motor Development Film Collection, Kinesiology Division, Bowling Green State University.

Figure 7.6 This still drawing of a baseball pitcher captures the forward movement of the hips while the upper trunk is still back. This is called **differentiated trunk rotation** because the hips and upper trunk rotate at different times.

Drawn from film tracing taken in the Motor Development and Child Study Laboratory, University of Wisconsin–Madison and now available from the Motor Development Film Collection, Kinesiology Division, Bowling Green State University.

As an unskilled thrower begins to swing the upper arm forward to throw, he or she often swings it at an angle oblique to the line of the shoulders—that is, with the elbow pointed up or down. A desirable advancement is to align the upper arm horizontally with the shoulders, forming a right angle with the trunk, as seen in figure 7.3. Even so, the upper arm may move ahead of the trunk's outline. This movement results in a loss of some of the momentum the thrower gains from moving the body parts sequentially for a forceful throw. In the most advanced pattern, the upper arm lags behind so that when the thrower reaches a front-facing position, you can see the elbow from the side within the outline of the trunk, as in figure 7.4.

It is also desirable for the forearm to lag behind. The thrower in figure 7.3 has some forearm lag, but the deepest lag comes before rather than at the front-facing position. The thrower in figure 7.4 demonstrates the advanced pattern of delayed forearm lag.

Most unskilled throwers throw without taking a step, like the child in figure 7.1. When a child learns to take the step, he or she often does so with the homolateral leg, the leg on the same side of the body as the throwing arm. This reduces the extent of trunk rotation and the range of motion needed for a forceful throw. When the child acquires the advanced pattern of a contralateral step, he or she may initially take a short step, as in figure 7.2. A long step (more than half the thrower's height) is desirable.

The body component analysis of overarm throwing demonstrates that individuals do not achieve the same developmental step for all body components at the same time. For example, the thrower in figure 7.2 is in step 1 of trunk, humerus, and forearm action but in step 3 of foot action. The thrower in figure 7.4 is in step 3 of humerus, forearm, and foot action but in step 2 of trunk action. Children the same age may be at various levels of the body component sequences, so they look different from one another as they advance through the developmental sequence.

However, not every possible combination of steps within the components is observed. Langendorfer and Roberton (2002) considered the trunk, humerus, and forearm components. They observed just 14 of the possible 27 combinations of developmental steps for these three components. It is likely that structural constraints limit the movements some body sections can make while other body sections are moving in a particular way. When you observe throwing, then, you will tend to see certain common combinations and probably not see others at all. Langendorfer and Roberton (2002) also studied the common combinations of steps within components as children develop. They found a tendency for children to change from no trunk rotation to trunk rotation before the upper arm and forearm advanced to intermediate levels. The shift of the humerus to an advanced level occurred after both the upper arm and forearm advanced to the intermediate level. Mechanical constraints and neurological development are likely responsible for these trends. That is, they are likely to be rate controllers in the development of throwing.

It is desirable for all individuals to move through the various developmental steps during childhood to achieve an advanced throwing pattern that they can use in a number of different physical activities, such as softball, football, and team handball. In fact, several authors noted that children can develop a skillful throwing pattern by age 6 (DeOreo & Keogh, 1980; McClenaghan & Gallahue, 1978; Zaichkowsky, Zaichkowsky, & Martinek, 1980). At least two studies present contradictory results. Halverson, Roberton, and Langendorfer (1982) filmed a group of 39 children in kindergarten and first, second, and seventh grades and classified them according to Roberton's developmental sequence. Their analysis of upper arm action demonstrated that most of the younger boys were already at step 2 of humerus action, and by the seventh grade, more than 80% of boys had achieved the most advanced level (step 3). In contrast, approximately 70% of the girls were still in step 1 of humerus action when initially filmed. By the seventh grade, only 29% of the girls had reached step 3.

This trend was also apparent for forearm action. Almost 70% of the boys demonstrated step 2 forearm action when initially filmed. Some were still at this level by the seventh grade, but considerably more, 41%, had reached step 3. More than 70% of the girls began in step 1, and the majority, 71%, was only at the second level in the seventh grade. Gender differences in developmental throwing progress were even more apparent for trunk action. Almost all the boys started in step 2, and 46% advanced to step 3 by the seventh grade. Similarly, almost 90% of the girls were in step 2 in kindergarten, but by the seventh grade, all the girls remained in step 2, none having advanced to step 3.

Letting distal body sections lag behind more proximal ones allows momentum to be transferred and distal sections to increase speed, providing the movements are well timed.

Another study (Leme & Shambes, 1978) focused on throwing patterns in adult women. The 18 women were selected because they had very low throwing velocities. All demonstrated inefficient throwing patterns, including block rotation, lack of a step forward with the throw, and lack of upper arm lag. Although these women were unique because of their low throwing velocities, the study certainly demonstrates that not all adults achieve an advanced throwing pattern. Perhaps these women lacked practice opportunities or good instruction in childhood. Together, these two studies suggest that progress through the developmental levels is not automatic and may not ever be completed.

Observing Overarm Throwing Patterns

Overarm throwing is complex and difficult to observe in detail. The best procedure is to focus on a small number of components, or even a single component, at any one time. Some characteristics are best observed from the front or back:

▲ Trunk to upper arm angle

▲ Elbow angle

▲ Lateral trunk bend

Others are best observed from the throwing side:

▲ The step

▲ Trunk rotation

▲ Upper arm and forearm lag

Videotaping is particularly valuable in helping you learn to observe the overarm throw.

You can observe throwers at different developmental levels by viewing video clips on your CD-ROM. Select Auxiliary Videos, then Skill Videos Not Used in Labs, then Overarm Throw.

Throwing in Adulthood

As we have seen, throwing is a complex skill that requires the coordination of many body segments. To execute a maximum throw, the thrower must move many joints through a full range of motion with precise timing. This makes throwing an interesting skill to study in older adults. For example, we can ask if older adults coordinate their movements for throwing just as young adults do or if they use different movement patterns. If they use the same patterns, we can ask if older adults control those movements as young adults do or whether they vary the extent or speed of movements compared with young adults.

Let's begin with observations of older adults that tell us what movement patterns older adults use. Williams, Haywood, and VanSant (1990, 1991) used the developmental steps in table 7.1 to categorize active older adult men and women between the ages of 63 and 78. Although the developmental steps were identified to monitor change in children and youths, they can be used to describe the movement patterns used by throwers of any age.

The older adults were active in a university-sponsored program but did not practice throwing or participate in activities with overarm movement patterns. The investigators found their throwing movements to be only moderately advanced on the developmental sequences. Most older throwers took a short contralateral step (step 3) and were categorized at step 1 or 2 of humerus action and step 1 or 2 of forearm action. Almost all used block rotation of the trunk (step 2). Gender differences existed similar to those in children; that is, men generally had better form. However, qualitative throwing status also related to childhood and young adult experiences. Those who had participated in sports with overarm movement patterns at younger ages had better throwing form.

The ball velocities the older adults generated also were moderate; they were similar to velocities generated by 8- to 9-year-olds. The men averaged 54.4 ft/s (16.6 m/s), and the women averaged 39.1 ft/s (11.9 m/s). Hence, the older adults also confirmed the gender differences in velocity noted in youths.

Because actions during the backswing in ballistic skills generally are related to ball velocity, Haywood, Williams, and VanSant (1991) closely examined the backswing used by older adults. The older adults who used a circular, downward backswing threw faster than those using an upward (therefore shorter) backswing. Many older adults used backswing movement patterns that seemed different from those that children use. For example, many started the circular, downward backswing (step 4) but did not continue the circle. Instead, they bent the elbow to bring the ball up behind the head. A possible reason for this could be a change in the musculoskeletal system, such as decreased shoulder flexibility or a loss of fast-twitch muscle fibers. Possibly the throwers could not continue arm movement at the shoulder joint, or would experience pain in doing so, and reorganized the movement.

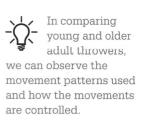 In comparing young and older adult throwers, we can observe the movement patterns used and how the movements are controlled.

The older adults in these studies were not observed when they were young adults, so we do not know if any or all of them reached the highest developmental level in all the body components when they were younger. We can only hypothesize that their moderate status as older adults reflects at least some change from the movement patterns of their youth.

A commonly held notion of skill performance in older adulthood is one of consistent decline with advancing age. To observe throwing with advancing age, Williams and colleagues (Williams, Haywood, & VanSant, 1998) observed eight older adults over 7 years. One individual was in her 60s, but most were in their late 70s. In contrast to what many would predict, throwing movements were relatively consistent over the years. Participants were placed in the same sequential step in 80% of the possible observations of body components over all the years. In those cases where individuals changed, the change was often, but not always, a decline. Increased variability was associated with change; that is, of the five throws observed in each of the years, a change in category was associated with varying movement patterns within the set of five throws. Williams and colleagues also observed small changes over the years that did not necessarily result in a change in developmental step. These small changes included decreased range of motion and slower movement speeds. This longitudinal observation shows that throwing performance in older adulthood is relatively stable. Small changes are more typical of performance than large declines.

It's clear that older adults coordinate their throwing movements as do young adults of moderate throwing skill. Few older adults are observed to use the same movement patterns as the most advanced young adults, but this could reflect the limited number of observations of older adults as well as the constraints imposed by rate-controlling systems. The change observed over time in older adulthood is most likely to be change in the control of movements, especially a slowing of speed or a decrease in range of motion.

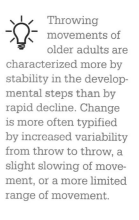 Throwing movements of older adults are characterized more by stability in the developmental steps than by rapid decline. Change is more often typified by increased variability from throw to throw, a slight slowing of movement, or a more limited range of movement.

Though we need more research and more longitudinal observation of older adults, the model of constraints can guide our study of older adult performance. One or more body systems might regress, causing a slowing or limitation of movement, then reach a critical point at which the movement pattern must change. For example, advancing arthritis in the shoulder joint could result in the musculoskeletal system acting as a rate controller for throwing movements. Some movement patterns might be unique to older adulthood because declines in the various body systems that occur with aging might not be exactly the opposite of the advances that occur with physical growth. Others might well be the same movement patterns seen in children and youths as they advance through the developmental sequence.

Throwing for Accuracy

The developmental sequences constructed for overarm throwing specifically address a throw for distance rather than for accuracy. The model of constraints would lead us to predict that changing the task characteristics from throwing for distance to throwing for accuracy results in a change in the movement pattern. Langendorfer (1990) demonstrated this to be the case. He had young adults and 9- to 10-year-olds throw for distance and accuracy. The accuracy task was to hit an 8-foot circular target at a distance of 10 m (adults) or 6 m (children). Male throwers were categorized at significantly lower developmental steps when throwing for accuracy than for distance. Female throwers tended toward lower steps but were not significantly different in the two task conditions. Langendorfer felt that the distance for the accuracy throw for females actually resulted in a forceful task condition. This suggests then that under true accuracy conditions throwers use movement patterns different from those for distance conditions.

Williams, Haywood, and VanSant (1993, 1996) replicated Langendorfer's study with older adults, asking them to throw for distance and for accuracy to a target 10 m away. Throwing velocity in the two task conditions was also measured. The throwers used a slower velocity in the accuracy condition. As a group, the older adults changed little from one condition to the other, but most individuals adapted their movements in at least one body component. As with Langendorfer's female throwers, the older adults likely found the 10 m distance of the accuracy throws to require relatively more force than young men would perceive was necessary. An accuracy condition at a shorter distance might have elicited more differences in the movements used.

Of course, in sports and games, throws are rarely for distance without some accuracy constraint or for accuracy without the need for force. What this research demonstrates is that different movement patterns arise for different task constraints, even for the same person in the same environment. When we compare movement patterns, either by using developmental categories or some other description of a movement pattern, we must recognize that the comparisons are only valid when the task constraints are identical. Even then, the person–task interaction influences the movement. For example, a strong individual could throw a given distance without the need for a step of the contralateral foot, while a weaker individual needs a step to reach that same distance. Parents, coaches, teachers, and recreational leaders must keep this in mind when comparing throwers.

🖳 To observe changes in movement patterns by switching a task constraint from the goal of force to the goal of accuracy, download Lab 7.4 Comparing Throws for Force With Throws for Accuracy from the Student Resources section at www.HumanKinetics.com/LifeSpanMotorDevelopment.

KICKING

Like throwing, kicking projects an object; but unlike in throwing, the individual strikes the object. Children obviously must have the perceptual abilities and eye–foot coordination necessary to execute a **kick** and consistently make contact with the ball. Teachers and parents can simplify the task for young children by challenging them to kick a stationary ball.

If the developmental sequences for forceful throwing are used to describe a short throw for accuracy, even the most proficient throwers might not use the most advanced movement patterns.

? Think of throwing as it is required in three or four sports and games. Do these games emphasize distance, accuracy, or a combination of both? In which of these conditions would it be appropriate to use the developmental sequences with the perspective that the most proficient throwers would place in the upper steps?

A **kick** is a ballistic strike from the foot.

Characteristics of Early Kicking

As with throwing, unskilled kickers tend to use a single action rather than a sequence of actions. As you can see in figure 7.7, there is no step forward with the nonkicking leg, and the kicking leg merely pushes forward at the ball. The knee of the kicking leg may be bent at contact, and an unskilled kicker may even retract the leg immediately after contacting the ball. The trunk does not rotate, and the child holds the arms stationary at the sides. The child in figure 7.8 demonstrates more advanced kicking skill by stepping forward with the nonkicking foot, thus putting the kicking leg in a cocked position.

Just as young children throw with arm action alone, young kickers use only leg action.

Figure 7.7 A beginning kicker simply pushes the leg forward.

Drawn from film tracing taken in the Motor Development and Child Study Laboratory, University of Wisconsin–Madison and now available from the Motor Development Film Collection, Kinesiology Division, Bowling Green State University.

Figure 7.8 This kicker has made some improvements compared with the beginning kicker. He steps forward, putting the leg in a cocked position, but the leg swing is still minimal. The knee is bent at contact, and some of the momentum of the kick is lost.

Drawn from film tracing taken in the Motor Development and Child Study Laboratory, University of Wisconsin–Madison and now available from the Motor Development Film Collection, Kinesiology Division, Bowling Green State University.

Proficient Kicking

Compare the characteristics of early kicking with the critical features of advanced kicking shown in figure 7.9. The advanced kicker does the following:

▲ Starts with a preparatory windup. The kicker achieves this position, with the trunk rotated back and the kicking leg cocked, by leaping or running up to the ball. As a natural consequence of the running stride, the trunk is rotated back, and the knee of the kicking leg is flexed just after the push-off of the rear leg. Hence, the kicker is able to apply maximal force over the greatest distance. Running up to the ball also contributes momentum to the kick.

▲ Uses sequential movements of the kicking leg. The thigh rotates forward, then the lower leg extends (knee straightens) just before contact with the ball to increase the radius of the arc through which the kicking leg travels. The straightened leg continues forward after contact to dissipate the force of the kick in the follow-through.

Figure 7.9 An advanced kicker. Note the full range of leg motion, trunk rotation, and arm opposition.

Drawn from film tracing taken in the Motor Development and Child Study Laboratory, University of Wisconsin–Madison and now available from the Motor Development Film Collection, Kinesiology Division, Bowling Green State University.

▲ Swings the kicking leg through a full range of motion at the hip.

▲ Uses trunk rotation to maximize the range of motion. As a result of complete leg swing, the kicker compensates by leaning back at contact.

▲ Uses the arms in opposition to the legs as a reaction to trunk and leg motion.

Developmental Changes in Kicking

The study of kicking development in children has not been as extensive as educators would like. Although we know the overall changes children must undergo to perform an advanced kick, the qualitative changes that each body part makes are not well documented. Haubenstricker, Seefeldt, and Branta (1983) found that only 10% of the 7.5- to 9.0-year-old children they studied exhibited advanced kicking form. So we have reason to speculate that, as with throwing, children do not automatically achieve proficient kicking.

You can observe kickers at different developmental levels by viewing video clips on your CD-ROM. Select Auxiliary Videos, then Skill Videos Not Used in Labs, then Kicking.

Observing Kicking Patterns

To give children adequate instruction in kicking, it is especially important to observe individual children. From the side, a teacher or coach can look for

- ▲ placement of the support foot,
- ▲ range of motion and precontact extension in the kicking leg,
- ▲ range of trunk motion, and
- ▲ arm opposition.

Let's now turn to the development of punting—a special form of kicking for which researchers have hypothesized a developmental sequence.

PUNTING

A **punt** is a form of kicking where an object is dropped from the individual's hands prior to impact with the foot.

Punting is a ballistic skill that is mechanically similar to kicking, yet punting tends to be more difficult for children to learn. To **punt,** a child drops the ball from the hands and must time the leg swing to the dropping ball.

Characteristics of Early Punting

A beginning punter tends to toss the ball up rather than drop it and will often release the ball after the support leg contacts the ground, if the child even takes a step at all. The arms drop to the sides. The child might rigidly extend the kicking-leg knee or bend it at a right angle, as in figure 7.10. The child typically holds the foot at a right angle to the leg so that the ball contacts the toes rather than the instep, resulting in an errant punt.

Figure 7.10 A beginning punter takes only a short step and flexes the kicking-leg knee 90 degrees at contact (step 1). The ball is dropped from waist height (step 3), but the arms drop to the sides at contact (step 1).

Drawn from film tracing taken in the Motor Development and Child Study Laboratory, University of Wisconsin–Madison and now available from the Motor Development Film Collection, Kinesiology Division, Bowling Green State University.

Arms drop to sides

Kicking knee flexed at contact

Short step

Proficient Punting

To execute a sound punt, as shown in figure 7.11, a child must

- ▲ extend the arms forward with the ball in hand before dropping it as the final leg stride is taken,

- ▲ move the arms to the side after releasing the ball, then move into an arm opposition pattern,

- ▲ leap onto the supporting leg and swing the punting leg vigorously up to contact the ball such that the body leaves the ground with a hop of the supporting leg, and

- ▲ keep the kicking-leg knee nearly straight and the toes pointed at time of contact.

Figure 7.11 An advanced punter. The last step is a leap, the ankle is extended (plantarflexed) at ball contact, and the punt is completed with a hop on the support leg (step 3). The ball is dropped early from chest height (step 4), and the arms abduct and move in opposition to the legs (step 3).

Drawn from film tracing taken in the Motor Development and Child Study Laboratory, University of Wisconsin–Madison and now available from the Motor Development Film Collection, Kinesiology Division, Bowling Green State University.

Developmental Changes in Punting

Roberton (1978b, 1984) hypothesized a developmental sequence for punting (table 7.2). Arm action is divided into two sequences, one for the ball-release phase and one for the ball-contact phase. The ball-release sequence outlines progress, from tossing the ball up to begin the punt to dropping the ball late to timing the drop appropriately. The ball-contact sequence shows that the arms make a transition, from nonuse to bilateral movement to the arm opposition pattern that characteristically accompanies forceful lower trunk rotation.

The leg action sequence reflects a developmental transition, from a short step of the nonkicking leg to a long step and finally to a leap. At contact, the ankle of the kicking leg changes from a flexed to an extended position.

Observing Punting Patterns

Observing a punter from the side offers you a view of the ball drop, the arm position, and the foot position. (See the observation plan for punting on p. 127.) You can clearly see the degree of foot extension at ball contact from this position.

TABLE 7.2 **Developmental Sequence for Punting**

	Arm action: ball-release phase
Step 1	Upward toss. Hands are on the sides of the ball. The ball is tossed upward from both hands after the support foot has landed (if a step was taken).
Step 2	Late drop from chest height. Hands are on the sides of the ball. The ball is dropped from chest height after the support foot has landed (if a step was taken).
Step 3	Late drop from waist height. Hands are on the sides of the ball. The ball is lifted upward and forward from waist level. It is released at the same time as or just prior to the landing of the support foot.
Step 4	Early drop from chest height. One hand is rotated to the side and under the ball. The other hand is rotated to the side and top of the ball. The hands carry the ball on a forward and upward path during the approach. It is released at chest level as the final approach stride begins.
	Arm action: ball-contact phase
Step 1	Arms drop. Arms drop bilaterally from ball release to a position on each side of the hips at ball contact.
Step 2	Arms abduct. Arms bilaterally abduct after ball release. The arm on the side of the kicking leg may pull back as that leg swings forward.
Step 3	Arm opposition. After ball release, the arms bilaterally abduct during flight. At contact the arm opposite the kicking leg has swung forward with that leg. The arm on the side of the kicking leg remains abducted and to the rear.
	Leg action: ball-contact phase
Step 1	No step or short step; ankle flexed. No step or one short step is taken. The kicking leg swings forward from a position parallel or slightly behind the support foot. The knee may be totally extended by contact or, more frequently, still flexed 90°, with contact above or below the knee joint. The thigh is still moving upward at contact. The ankle tends to be (dorsi-) flexed.
Step 2	Long step; ankle extension. Several steps may be taken. The last step onto the support leg is a long stride. The thigh of the kicking leg has slowed or stopped forward motion at contact. The ankle is extended (plantarflexed). The knee has 20 to 30° of extension still possible by contact.
Step 3	Leap and hop. The child may take several steps, but the last is actually a leap onto the support foot. After contact, the momentum of the kicking leg pulls the child off the ground in a hop.

Note: This sequence was hypothesized by Roberton (1984) and has not been validated.

Reprinted from Roberton and Halverson 1984.

To gain experience in assessing the developmental levels of punters, download Lab 7.3 Assessing the Developmental Levels of Punters from the Student Resources section at www.HumanKinetics.com/LifeSpanMotorDevelopment.

SIDEARM STRIKING

Sidearm striking is a form of striking where the arm remains at or below shoulder level. One example of sidearm striking is a person swinging a baseball bat.

Although many sports and physical activities incorporate striking, research data on the development of striking is sparse. Striking encompasses numerous skills. It can be done with various body parts, such as the hands or feet. People can also use a variety of implements in various orientations, such as swinging a bat sidearm, a racket overhand, or a golf club underhand. In our discussion, we focus on one-hand **sidearm striking** with an implement and one-hand overarm striking with an implement.

Of the basic skills we've discussed so far, striking involves the most difficult perceptual judgment. Success in meeting a moving object is limited in early childhood; therefore, it is difficult to assess striking of a moving object in young children. For this reason, teach-

Observation Plan for Punting

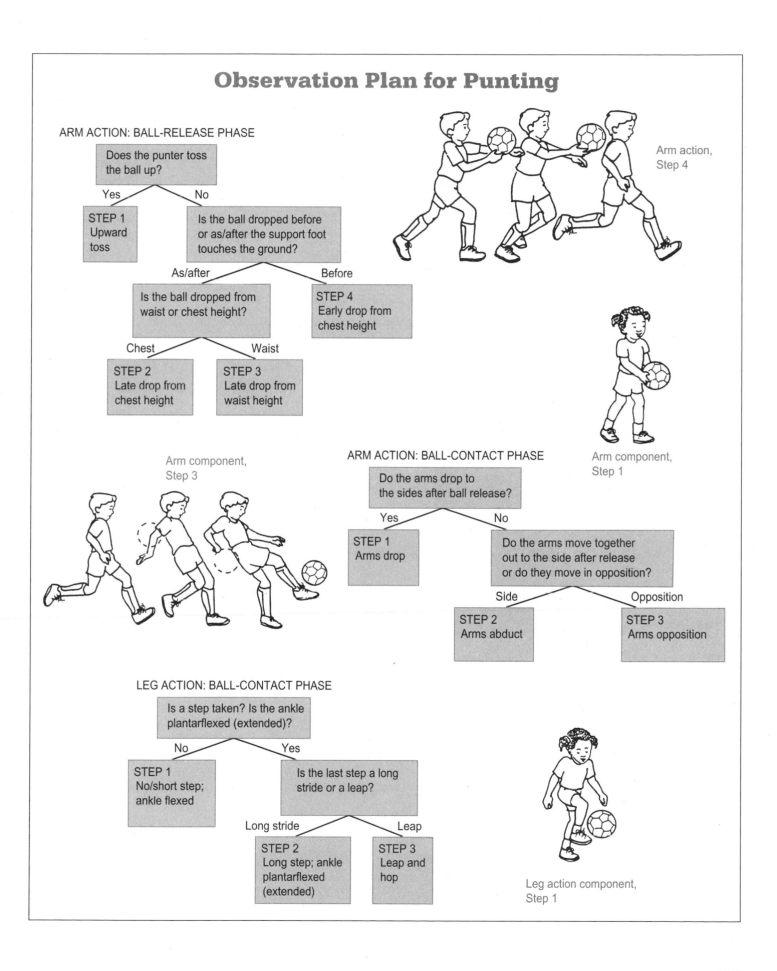

ARM ACTION: BALL-RELEASE PHASE

Does the punter toss the ball up?

Yes → **STEP 1** Upward toss

No → Is the ball dropped before or as/after the support foot touches the ground?

As/after → Is the ball dropped from waist or chest height?

Chest → **STEP 2** Late drop from chest height

Waist → **STEP 3** Late drop from waist height

Before → **STEP 4** Early drop from chest height

Arm action, Step 4

Arm component, Step 1

Arm component, Step 3

ARM ACTION: BALL-CONTACT PHASE

Do the arms drop to the sides after ball release?

Yes → **STEP 1** Arms drop

No → Do the arms move together out to the side after release or do they move in opposition?

Side → **STEP 2** Arms abduct

Opposition → **STEP 3** Arms opposition

LEG ACTION: BALL-CONTACT PHASE

Is a step taken? Is the ankle plantarflexed (extended)?

No → **STEP 1** No/short step; ankle flexed

Yes → Is the last step a long stride or a leap?

Long stride → **STEP 2** Long step; ankle plantarflexed (extended)

Leap → **STEP 3** Leap and hop

Leg action component, Step 1

TABLE 7.3 Developmental Sequence for Sidearm Striking

Racket action component	
Step 1	Chop. The racket is swung in the vertical plane.
Step 2	Arm swing only. The racket swings ahead of the trunk.
Step 3	Racket lag. The racket lags behind trunk rotation but goes ahead of the trunk at front-facing.
Step 4	Delayed racket lag. The racket is still lagging behind the trunk at front-facing.
Foot, trunk, and upper arm action component	
See the foot, trunk, and upper arm sections in table 7.1.	

Figure 7.12 This young girl executes a striking task with arm action only. She faces the ball and swings down rather than sideways.

Drawn from film tracing taken in the Motor Development and Child Study Laboratory, University of Wisconsin–Madison and now available from the Motor Development Film Collection, Kinesiology Division, Bowling Green State University.

ers often adapt striking tasks for young children by making the ball stationary. Researchers often base the developmental sequences on striking a stationary ball so that they can describe the changes in young children's movement patterns.

We can apply the mechanical principles and developmental aspects of one-hand striking of a stationary object to other types of striking tasks. Keep this in mind as we examine the development of the striking pattern. Table 7.3 shows the developmental sequence of the sidearm strike.

Characteristics of Early Sidearm Striking

A child's first attempts to strike sidearm often look like unskilled attempts to throw overhand. The child chops at the oncoming ball by extending at the elbow, using little leg and trunk action. As in figure 7.12, the child often faces the oncoming ball.

Proficient Sidearm Striking

An advanced sidearm strike incorporates many of the characteristics of an advanced overarm throw. Such characteristics include the following:

▲ Stepping into the hit, thus applying linear force to the strike. The step should be a distance more than half the individual's standing height (Roberton, 1978b, 1984). The preparatory stance should be sideways to allow for this step and the sidearm swing.

▲ Using differentiated trunk rotation to permit a larger swing and to contribute more force through rotary movement.

▲ Swinging through a full range of motion to apply the greatest force possible.

▲ Swinging in a roughly horizontal plane and extending the arms just before contact.

▲ Linking or chaining the movements together to produce the greatest force possible. The sequence is backswing and step forward, pelvic rotation, spinal rotation and swing, arm extension, contact, and follow-through.

Developmental Changes in Sidearm Striking

Researchers have not validated a completed developmental sequence for sidearm striking, but we can apply the sequences for foot and trunk action in the overarm throw to striking. (See the observation plan for sidearm striking on p. 129.) In addition, we know some of the qualitative changes individuals make in the arm action for sidearm striking. The arm action for sidearm striking is distinct from that for overarm and underarm (as in the golf swing) striking, but all three forms share many of the same mechanical principles. We discuss sidearm striking first, but keep in mind that many of the qualitative changes in the arm action for sidearm striking and the mechanical principles involved apply to overarm striking as well.

The first obvious change in sidearm striking from the technique shown in figure 7.12 occurs when a striker stands sideways to the ball. By transferring the weight to the rear foot, taking a step forward, and transferring the weight forward at contact, a striker is able to improve striking skills. The child in figure 7.13 turns sideways but has not yet learned to step into the strike.

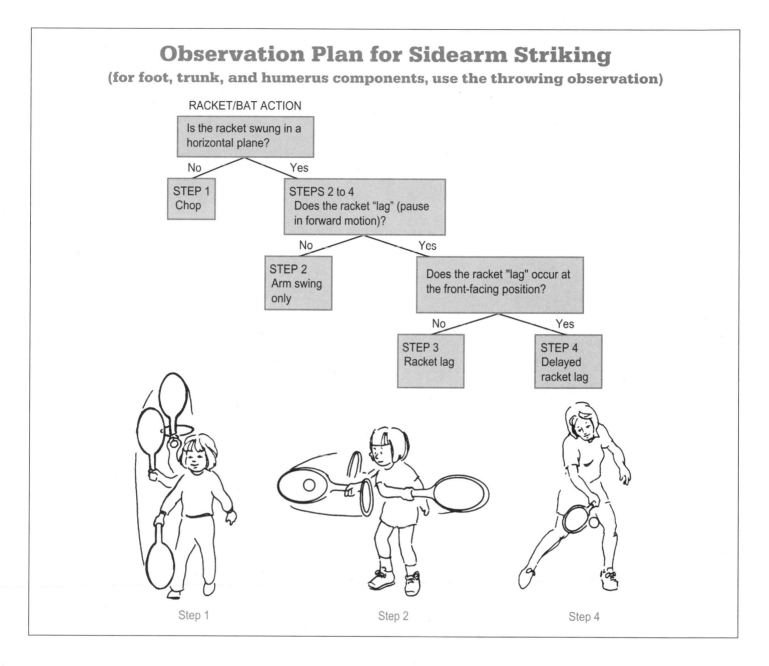

Observation Plan for Sidearm Striking
(for foot, trunk, and humerus components, use the throwing observation)

RACKET/BAT ACTION

Is the racket swung in a horizontal plane?

No → STEP 1 Chop

Yes → STEPS 2 to 4 Does the racket "lag" (pause in forward motion)?

No → STEP 2 Arm swing only

Yes → Does the racket "lag" occur at the front-facing position?

No → STEP 3 Racket lag

Yes → STEP 4 Delayed racket lag

Step 1   Step 2   Step 4

A second beneficial change is the use of trunk rotation. Individuals first use block rotation before advancing to differentiated (hip, then shoulder) rotation, a developmental sequence similar to that in throwing. A skilled striker who uses differentiated rotation appears in figure 7.14.

Strikers also progressively change the plane of their swing from the vertical chop seen in figure 7.12 to an oblique plane and finally to a horizontal plane, as seen in figure 7.13. They eventually obtain a longer swing by holding their elbows away from their sides and extending their arms just before contact. A beginning striker frequently holds a racket or paddle with a power grip, where the handle is held in the palm like a club (figure 7.15, a and b; Napier, 1956). With this grip the striker tends to keep the elbow flexed during the swing and

Figure 7.13 This girl has made improvements compared with the beginning striker. She stands sideways and executes a sidearm strike but does not involve the lower body.

Figure 7.14 An advanced striker. The swing arm moves through a full range of motion. The striker steps into the swing and uses differentiated trunk rotation.

Drawn from film tracing taken in the Motor Development and Child Study Laboratory, University of Wisconsin–Madison and now available from the Motor Development Film Collection, Kinesiology Division, Bowling Green State University.

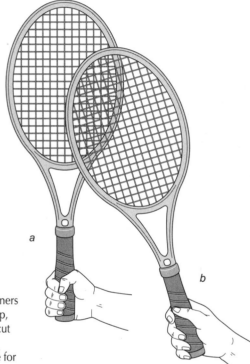

Figure 7.15 *(a)* Beginners often use a "power" grip, causing them to undercut the ball. *(b)* A "shake-hands" grip is desirable for sidearm striking.

to supinate the forearm, thus undercutting the ball. Although children tend to use the power grip with any striking implement, they most often adopt it when given implements that are too big and heavy for them. Educators can promote use of the proper "shake-hands" grip by giving children striking implements that are an appropriate size and weight (Roberton & Halverson, 1984)—that is, by scaling the size and weight of the implement to the size and strength of the child.

Observing Sidearm Striking Patterns

As with many of the skills we've looked at thus far, studying a child's swing from more than one location yields the most information. From the "pitching" position you can observe the direction of the step, the plane of the swing, and arm extension. From the side, you can check the step, the trunk rotation, and the extent of the swing.

To gain experience in assessing the developmental levels of strikers, download Lab 7.2 Assessing the Developmental Levels of Strikers from the Student Resources section at www.HumanKinetics.com/LifeSpanMotorDevelopment.

OVERARM STRIKING

Overarm striking is a form of striking where the arm travels above the shoulder level. One example of overarm striking is a person swinging a racket in a tennis serve.

One can execute **overarm striking** without an implement, such as in the overarm volleyball serve, or with an implement, such as in the tennis serve. We will focus on overarm striking with an implement.

Characteristics of Early Overarm Striking

A beginning striker demonstrates limited pelvic and spinal movement, swings with a collapsed elbow, and swings the arm and racket forward in unison, as in figure 7.16. The collapsed elbow leads to a low point of contact between the racket and the ball. The movement pattern of early overarm striking, then, is similar to that of early overarm throwing and early sidearm striking.

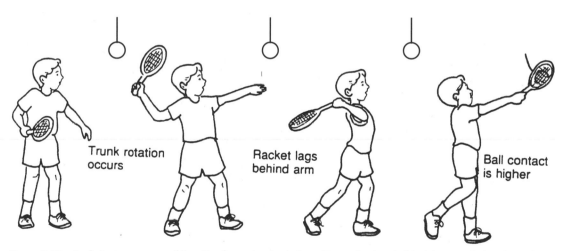

Figure 7.16 Beginning overarm striking. Trunk movement is minimal. The elbow is collapsed, the arm and racket move together, and contact point is low.

Proficient Overarm Striking

A person who is skilled at overarm striking, as depicted in figure 7.17,

▲ rotates both the pelvis and the spine more than 90 degrees,

▲ holds the elbow at an angle between 90 and 119 degrees at the start of forward movement, and

▲ lets the racket lag behind the arm during the forward swing.

Figure 7.17 Proficient overarm striking. Trunk rotation is obvious. The racket lags behind the arm during the swing.

Racket lag is consistent with the open kinetic chain principle, where force is generated by a correctly timed sequence of movements. The humerus and forearm lag is an example of an open kinetic chain: the humerus lags behind trunk rotation, the forearm lags behind the humerus, and the racket lags behind the forearm to create the chain of sequential movements.

Developmental Changes in Overarm Striking

Langendorfer (1987) and Messick (1991) proposed developmental sequences for overarm striking. Both based these sequences on cross-sectional studies and have not validated them with longitudinal research.

TABLE 7.4 Developmental Sequence for Overarm Striking

Preparatory phase: trunk action	
Step 1	No trunk action or flexion/extension of the trunk
Step 2	Minimal trunk rotation (<180°)
Step 3	Total trunk rotation (>180°)

Ball-contact phase: elbow action	
Step 1	Angle is 20° or less, or greater than 120°
Step 2	Angle is 21 to 89°
Step 3	Angle is 90 to 119°

Ball-contact phase: spinal range of motion	
Step 1	Spine (at shoulders) rotates through less than 45°
Step 2	Spine rotates between 45 and 89°
Step 3	Spine rotates more than 90°

Ball-contact phase: pelvic range of motion	
Step 1	Pelvis (below the waist) rotates through less than 45°
Step 2	Pelvis rotates between 45 and 89°
Step 3	Pelvis rotates more than 90°

Ball-contact phase: racket action	
Step 1	No racket lag
Step 2	Racket lag
Step 3	Delayed racket lag (and upward extension)

The preparatory trunk action and the parenthetical information in step 3 of racket action are reprinted from Messick 1991. The remaining components are reprinted from Langendorfer 1987.

Overarm striking is similar to overarm throwing and sidearm striking, but it has unique features, too. Langendorfer identified eight component sequences from a study of children 1 to 10 years old. The trunk, humerus, forearm, and leg sequences are similar to those for overarm throwing (table 7.1). Sequences unique to overarm striking include pelvic range of motion, spinal range of motion, elbow angle, and racket action (table 7.4). Messick observed 9- to 19-year-olds executing tennis serves. She identified elbow angle and racket sequences similar to those Langendorfer identified except that extending the forearm and racket up to contact the ball was characteristic of the tennis serves. She also noted a developmental sequence of preparatory trunk action in tennis overarm striking. This appears in table 7.4.

Neither Langendorfer nor Messick found the developmental sequences for foot action in throwing to apply to overarm striking, although they observed age differences in weight shifting—older performers shifted their weight more than younger ones. Perhaps overarm striking requires a different sequence that has not yet been identified. This may be especially true in the context of tennis, where the rules specify that the server must not step on or over the baseline before striking the ball.

Observing Overarm Striking Patterns

Observation of overarm striking is similar to that of sidearm striking. You might prefer, though, to watch from behind rather than from the "pitching" position, in addition to watching from the side.

Older Adult Striking

As active middle-aged and older adults such as Dodo Cheney make sport news, we know that ballistic skills can be lifetime skills. The research on active adults performing ballistic skills is limited but likely will increase as larger numbers of seniors maintain an active lifestyle with sports that require ballistic skills. It is not surprising that tennis and golf are two of the contexts for older adult research since both sports have a large senior following and both have established senior programs.

The tempo and rhythm of a short iron shot in golf have been compared in younger (19–25 years) and older (60–69 years) males, all experienced golfers (Jagacinski, Greenberg, & Liao, 1997). This task, of course, emphasizes accuracy more than distance. As a group, the older golfers had a slightly faster tempo, or overall speed of the shot. Differences in rhythm also existed. Older golfers reached peak force earlier in the swing, whereas younger players reached it just before impact. Also, older golfers had larger force changes in later phases of the swing. This might indicate that the older golfers exert relatively more force to execute this short iron shot than younger golfers. In terms of accuracy, 3 of 12 older golfers made less than 10% of their shots, but the remainder were as accurate as the younger golfers. Increased variability in accuracy among members of the older

? What might be the rate controllers that would cause older adults to reorganize their striking movement patterns? Would these differ for those who remain active in a "striking" sport compared with those who are sedentary?

group was found, then, with many older golfers showing no decrement. We should keep in mind that the strength and flexibility demands of this task were relatively low. Losses of strength and flexibility with advancing age would not have constrained the older golfers compared with younger ones.

Haywood and Williams (1995) observed older adult tennis players as they executed an overarm serve. These older adults played tennis an average of 2.7 times per week. They were divided into a younger group (from 62 up to 68 years old) and an older group (over 68 up to 81 years old). The developmental steps described earlier for preparatory trunk action, elbow action, and forearm/racket action were used to categorize the servers for movement pattern used. Ball impact velocity was also measured. The younger and older servers did not differ in any of these measures, nor did men and women servers differ. Most used moderate-level trunk and forearm/racket movements, but the older group was somewhat more advanced in elbow action. So, the investigators found little evidence of significant decline for a population continuing to use a striking skill.

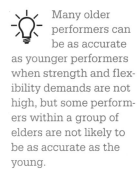

Many older performers can be as accurate as younger performers when strength and flexibility demands are not high, but some performers within a group of elders are not likely to be as accurate as the young.

The investigators measured static shoulder flexibility in the senior tennis players to determine if a decline of flexibility might act as a rate controller for overarm striking movements; however, there was no difference in flexibility between the two age groups.

Of course, as with the older throwers described earlier, these tennis players were not observed longitudinally, and we do not know if they ever used more advanced movement patterns. Two of the servers, one man and one woman, were placed into the highest developmental category of each body component observed; both servers were former tennis teaching professionals. This investigation therefore suggests that well-practiced movement patterns tend to be maintained over the older adult years and perhaps even from younger years.

Well-practiced movement patterns might be well maintained over the life span.

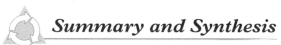

Summary and Synthesis

Proficient performance in the ballistic skills exhibits movements that obey mechanical principles for maximizing force and speed. As children and youth improve their performance of ballistic skills, we see changes that are more and more consistent with those mechanical principles. Examples include a forward step that transfers momentum into the direction of the throw or strike; rotary motions of the trunk, usually sequenced as lower trunk followed by upper trunk for arm throws and strikes; and sequential movement of the projecting limb to allow distal body components and striking implements to lag behind larger and more proximal body components such that momentum is transferred and speed is increased. We know that transition to the most efficient movement patterns is not automatic. Some adults continue to use movement patterns that produce moderate results when maximal ones are desired. Since little life span observation of striking performance is available, it is difficult to know the amount of decline in the throwing and striking performance of older adults. Active older adults, however, appear to maintain movement patterns fairly well, especially when the patterns are well practiced.

Task conditions and the interaction between the person and the task are important in what movement patterns emerge in performance. In assessing how youth are progressing or if seniors are declining, along with the rate controllers possibly influencing those changes, we must acknowledge the particular task conditions for the movement observed. An individual throwing a short distance for accuracy would not necessarily need to use the movements characteristic of the most advanced level in each body component.

Discussion Questions

1. What distinguishes kicking from punting?
2. Identify four of the major qualitative changes in the development of each of the following ballistic skills: throwing, punting, overarm striking.
3. What qualitative developmental changes are common to throwing and overarm striking?

 ## *Learning Activities*

Overarm Throwing: Changes in Form Related to Changes in Throwing Arm

What individual constraints could be involved in determining the developmental level of overarm throwing for force?

1. Observe three different people (try to observe at least one child). Ask them to throw with their preferred arms (i.e., with which arm do they naturally choose to throw?). Assess their developmental levels using the observation plan provided in the chapter.
2. Now, ask them to throw with their opposite, or nonpreferred, arms. What happens to their developmental levels?
3. Even more so than with hopping, there will be a difference of at least one developmental level between their preferred and nonpreferred throwing arms. Try to come up with a list of reasons why these differences might exist.

Development of Manipulative Skills

chapter

8

EXTRA!!! The Times EXTRA!!!

HANDFULS OF HAPPINESS

The story of the first hand transplant in the United States made headline news (Handfuls of Happiness, 2000). Matthew Scott, a left-hander, lost his left hand in a firecracker accident 13 years earlier. He received the transplant from a cadaver in a 15-hour operation. A year and a half after the operation Scott was able to sense temperature, pressure, and pain in his new hand; turn pages; tie shoelaces; and throw a baseball. Those of us who have had an arm or wrist in a cast can probably begin to imagine what it would be like to attempt certain tasks or sports without one or both of our hands. Our hands allow us to perform a wide range of skills, from handling small, delicate objects to steering large ships. With practice we can move our hands and fingers quickly over a keyboard or build a piece of beautiful furniture. Our manipulative skills certainly set us apart from other living creatures.

As with any other movement, we expect limb movements to arise from the interaction of individual, task, and environmental constraints. Consider the example of lifting a heavy crystal bowl from a table and whether an individual should use one hand or two to pick it up. The environment plays a role because gravity acts on the object. Crystal is heavier than plain glass. The task is a factor in several ways. Consider the shape of the bowl. Does the shape and the weight, the environment and task interacting, afford lifting the bowl with one hand, or does it require two? Now consider the person's strength. Does this individual structural constraint interact with task and environment to afford lifting with one hand or two?

With growth and aging, many individual structural constraints change. The length and size of the limbs change with growth, as does strength. When we age, conditions such as arthritis can make manipulative skills difficult or even painful. Thus, just as with other types of skills, the performance of manipulative skills changes with growth and aging.

 ## Chapter Objectives

This chapter will

- ▲ document a transition in infancy from the use of power grips to pick up objects to the use of precision grips,
- ▲ demonstrate how the size of an object, relative to the size of the hand, can influence the grip used to pick up an object,
- ▲ examine the role of vision in reaching for objects,
- ▲ identify developmental changes in catching, and
- ▲ consider how catchers are able to intercept objects.

GRASPING AND REACHING

Prehension is the grasping of an object, usually with the hand or hands.

When a skilled adult wants to obtain a small object, the arm reaches forward, then the hand grasps the object. The reach and grasp form a smooth movement unit. To simplify our study of the development of reaching and grasping in infancy, however, we'll consider grasping, or **prehension,** first.

Grasping

In 1931, H.M. Halverson published a classic description of grasping development, the 10 phases of which are summarized in figure 8.1. Halverson filmed infants between 16 and 52 weeks of age grasping a 1 in. cube. In early grasping, the infant squeezes an object against the palm without the thumb providing opposition. Eventually, the infant uses the thumb in opposition but still holds the object against the palm. These types of grips are collectively called power grips. Halverson observed that after about 9 months of age, infants began to hold objects between the thumb and one or more fingers. These are called precision grips. Thus, the first year is characterized by a transition from power grips to precision grips.

Hohlstein (1982) later replicated Halverson's study, but in addition to the 1 in. cube used in the original study, she provided objects of different size and shape. The transition from power to precision grips still was evident, but shape and size of the object influenced the specific type of grasp used.

Through Halverson's early work, developmentalists viewed prehension as a behavior acquired in steps. Maturationists of Halverson's era viewed these age-related changes in the same vein as motor milestones. Each progression to a new stage was linked to neuromotor maturation. Maturation of the motor cortex probably is a factor in prehension. However, the finding that shape and size of the object to be grasped influence the grip used suggests that the individual, the environment, and the task interact in prehension movements. Halverson studied only one set of environment and task characteristics. More variety of movement grips is observed with changing environment and task characteristics in the early months of life.

For example, Newell, Scully, McDonald, and Baillargeon (1989) watched 4- to 8-month-old infants grasp a cube and three cups of different diameters. They found that infants used five types of grips 95% of the time. The grip seemed to depend on the size and shape of the object. They even observed precision grips with the smallest cup at a younger age than Halverson observed. Since we can observe this precision grip at so young an age, it's clear that the neuromotor system must be mature enough in this age span to control the precision grip. Clearly, neuromotor maturation is not the only structural constraint involved in grasping.

Newell, Scully, Tenenbaum, and Hardiman (1989) suggested, based on observations of older children, that the grip used to obtain any particular object depends on the relationship between hand size and object size. This is the notion that the movement selected by individuals is related to their size compared with an object's size, or that movements are **body scaled.** Butterworth, Verweij, and Hopkins (1997) decided to test this idea. They had infants between 6 and 20 months of age pick up cubes and spheres of different sizes. They confirmed Halverson's general trend from power to precision grips. By early in the second year, precision grips predominated. Younger infants tended to use more fingers to grasp the objects than older infants did. Object *size* greatly influenced the grip selected, with *shape* having somewhat less influence on the grip. Butterworth and colleagues observed all but Halverson's inferior-forefinger grasp in the youngest infants, 6 to 8 months of age, so infants use a greater variety of grips than we would assume from Halverson's work. Thus, neuromotor development for grasping movements must be more advanced than those in Halverson's day thought.

It so happened that the boys in Butterworth and colleagues' study had longer hands than the girls had. The hypothesis of Newell et al. predicted that these boys and girls would use different grips. This was not the case. Thus, the influence of object size on grip used

After infancy, visual information and body size appear to constrain the shape of the hands in grasping and the number of hands used to grasp a particular object.

Body scaling is adapting characteristics of the task or environment to the overall body size or size of a body component such that a body-scaled ratio is used to choose an action.

Type of grasp	Weeks of age
No contact	16
Contact only	20
Primitive squeeze	20
Squeeze grasp	24
Hand grasp	28
Palm grasp	28
Superior-palm grasp	32
Inferior-forefinger grasp	36
Forefinger grasp	52
Superior-forefinger grasp	52

Figure 8.1 A developmental grasping progression.
Reprinted from Halverson 1931.

supports the idea that the ratio between hand size and object size is important, but the lack of a difference between the boys and girls does not. More research is needed before we know if infants actually use body scaling in selecting a grip. Still, this work affirms that interactions between the infant, the environment, and the task are important even in early grasping and that changes in movement patterns related to changing structural constraints occur even in infancy.

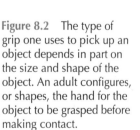 To observe the types of grips an infant uses to grasp objects of varying shape and size, download Lab 8.1 Observing Grasping Development from the Student Resources section at www.HumanKinetics.com/LifeSpanMotorDevelopment.

? Think about making and eating your breakfast in the morning. How many objects do you grip, and how does the configuration of your hand change for each one?

Is body scaling used at older ages? Do older children and adults use the ratio of hand size to object size in selecting a grip? Newell, Scully, Tenenbaum, and Hardiman (1989) observed 3- to 5-year-olds and adults. They found that a relatively constant ratio of hand size to object size determined when individuals chose to use two hands to pick up an object instead of one no matter what their age. Thus, the ratio was consistent even though the adults had larger hands. The same has been found true in children 5, 7, and 9 years of age (van der Kamp, Savelsbergh, & Davis, 1998). The interaction of the individual's structural constraints with environmental and task constraints, then, gives rise to either a one-hand or a two-hand grasp.

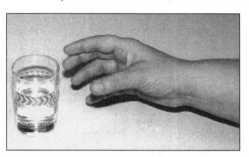

a

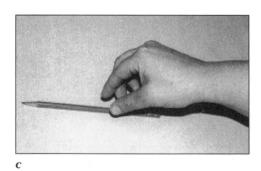

b

Vision plays a role in this type of task. From a young age on, we select the grip appropriate for the size, weight, and shape of the object to be obtained (figure 8.2). Butterworth et al. observed that infants often knocked an object before actually grasping it. In contrast, adults configure, or shape, their hands for a particular object *before* making contact with it. Adults also make a decision about whether to reach for an object with one hand or two *before* making contact with it. That is, visual information is used in preparation for the grasp. During childhood, individuals acquire the experience with objects needed to precisely configure the hand. Kuhtz-Buschbeck et al. (1998) noted that 6- and 7-year-olds were more dependent than adults on visual feedback during the reach to shape their hand for the grasp. Similarly, Pryde, Roy, and Campbell (1998) observed 9- and 10-year-olds slowing down more than adults at the end of a reach, presumably taking more time to use visual information for grasping the object.

Figure 8.2 The type of grip one uses to pick up an object depends in part on the size and shape of the object. An adult configures, or shapes, the hand for the object to be grasped before making contact.

c

? Have you ever heard anyone pick up an object then say, "This is heavier than it looks"? What does this tell you about the role of vision in grasping?

If indeed body scaling determines grip selection starting in childhood, grasping quickly becomes a well-practiced skill, with growing hand size and arm length taken into account in the body-scaled ratio. Grasping need not be relearned with increases in growth. Thus, we might expect it to be a very stable skill over the life span. Only conditions such as arthritis or a loss of strength in old age would influence hand configuration. Indeed Carnahan, Vandervoort, and Swanson (1998) found that young adults (average age 26 years) and older adults (average age 70 years) accurately adapted the opening of the hand to grasp moving objects of different size. Of course, most manipulative tasks are not just a matter of grasping an object but rather of bringing the hand to an object so that it can be grasped. We now examine the development of reaching over the life span.

Reaching

Reaching development is characterized by three phases over the first year:

- ▲ Prereaching (birth to 4 months)
- ▲ Visually guided reaching (4 to 8 months)
- ▲ Visually elicited reaching (9-plus months; Bushnell, 1985)

Prereaching

Contradictory hypotheses about eye–hand coordination in newborns have prompted research on **prereaching** (see Whitall, 1988a, for a review). The traditional viewpoint is that in newborns, reaching is limited to excited thrashing of the limbs and reflexive movements (White, Castle, & Held, 1964). But Bower and his colleagues (Bower, 1972, 1977; Bower, Broughton, & Moore, 1970a, 1970b, 1970c) contend that newborns demonstrate eye–hand coordination. They observed newborns reaching toward objects and making grasping motions, although actual contact with the objects was sporadic. Moving objects trigger prereaching better than stationary ones, and infants prereach more often when they fix their gaze on an object (von Hofsten, 1982).

> **Prereaching** is an extension movement elicited by an object but typically not accurate enough to contact the object.

The controversy over the degree of eye–hand coordination in newborns is fueled by researchers who failed to replicate Bower's results (Dodwell, Muir, & DiFranco, 1976; Ruff & Halton, 1978). A variable that influences results is the infant's posture. The researchers observing prereaching movements typically support the infant in an upright sitting position with the arms free to move. Typically, prereaching occurs only when an infant's trunk is supported, thus affording arm extension. The abilities to move the head to direct gaze and to hold the head up, typically developing around 3 months of age, undoubtedly also facilitate prereaching (Bertenthal & von Hofsten, 1998). Thus, posture might be a constraint for prereaching.

Even if some degree of eye–hand coordination is present in newborns, important differences still exist between prereaching and the reaching that older children demonstrate:

- ▲ Newborns do not use visual information to guide their hands to objects.
- ▲ Infants do not correct their movement midcourse, as older children do.
- ▲ Newborns also do not shape, or configure, their hands to correspond to the shape and size of the object toward which they reach.
- ▲ Infants who prereach rarely contact the target object (Bushnell, 1985).

Visually Guided Reaching

Success in reaching for and grasping objects increases greatly when an infant reaches approximately 4 months of age. Between 4 and 7 months, infants increasingly use vision to guide their hands to an object, typically making several corrections in their reach on their way to contact (von

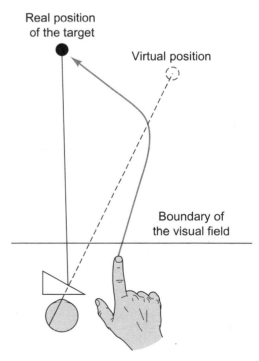

Figure 8.3 An infant's reliance on visual guidance in reaching is demonstrated in a displaced vision task. Prisms placed in front of the eyes shift the apparent location of an object from its real position. An individual relying on visual guidance begins to adapt the hand position as the hand comes into sight after initially moving toward the object's apparent or virtual position.

Reprinted from Hay 1990.

Hofsten, 1979). Infants at this age adapt their reach when their view of an object is distorted by prisms that displace the apparent location of the object (McDonnell, 1975), and their reaching is disrupted when they are not allowed to see their hands (Lasky, 1977). As shown in figure 8.3, placing a prism over a person's eyes causes the apparent or virtual position of an object to shift. An adult would reach directly at the virtual location of the object and end up grasping thin air. An infant, however, would adjust the position of the hand as it came into view, using the apparent location of the hand and the apparent location of the object to close the gap between the two. An infant therefore uses vision to guide the hand to the object. In addition, starting at about 4 months of age, infants shape their hands according to the shape, location, and orientation of the object they are reaching for. **Visually guided reaching** predominates around 7 months of age then gives way to a more thrusting, ballistic type of reach that is **visually elicited.**

Visually Elicited Reaching

Toward the end of the first year, the initial part of an infant's reach becomes so accurate that he or she needs to make few if any corrections (McDonnell, 1979). Presumably, complete and fast arm movements result from the initial information of an object's position rather than the slower method of comparing arm and object position (McDonnell, 1979). The infant no longer needs to see the hand to complete a successful reach (Bushnell, 1982)—that is, less attention to the hand is required (Bushnell, 1985). Further improvements in prehension appear by the end of the first year. The infant shapes the hand very early in the reach, and the shape is more likely to be appropriate for the object.

Hand–Mouth Movements

Another type of arm movement brings the hand, with or without an object, to the mouth. Between 3 and 4 months, infants become more consistent at bringing the hand to the mouth rather than other parts of the face. At 5 months they begin to open the mouth in anticipation of the hand's arrival (Lew & Butterworth, 1997). The role of vision in these movements has not been studied yet, nor has the relationship between hand–mouth movements and reaches for objects in the same infants.

Bimanual Reaching and Manipulation

Infants exhibit bimanual reaching during the first year but cannot perform complementary activities with two hands until the second year.

The reaches we've discussed thus far are unimanual, or one-arm, reaches. Infants also acquire bimanual reaching and grasping (Corbetta & Mounoud, 1990; Fagard, 1990). Skilled performers know to grasp objects that are too large for one hand with two hands, and they can use one hand to complement the other. For example, they might use one hand to hold a container and the other to open the lid.

Figure 8.4 Obtaining large objects necessitates bimanual reaching. In young infants, one hand might reach the object before the other. Infants older than 7 months reach either unimanually or bimanually, depending on the object's characteristics.

Newborns' random arm movements are asymmetrical (Cobb, Goodwin, & Saelens, 1966). The first bilateral movements are extending and raising the arms, observed at approximately 2 months of age (White et al., 1964). Within a few months, infants can clasp their hands at the body midline. At approximately 4.5 months, infants often reach for objects with both arms (Fagard, 1990). Reaches begun with two hands usually result in one hand reaching and grasping the object first so that after 5 months bimanual reaching declines (Ramsay & Willis, 1984). After 7 months, infants select a unimanual or a bimanual reach depending on their position and the size, weight, and shape of the object they wish to grasp (Fagard, 1990; figure 8.4.) Bimanual reaches at this age are simultaneous in time and space.

Both hands start for the object at the same time and arrive at the object at the same time (Goldfield & Michel, 1986a).

After 8 months, infants start to dissociate simultaneous arm activity so they can manipulate an object cooperatively with both hands (Goldfield & Michel, 1986b; Ruff, 1984). Late in the first year, infants learn to hold two objects, one in each hand, and often bang them together (Ramsay, 1985). By 12 months, they can pull things apart and insert one object into another. Soon infants can reach for two objects with different arms simultaneously. Not until the end of the second year can infants perform complementary activities with the hands, such as holding a lid open with one hand while withdrawing an object with the other (Bruner, 1970).

The Role of Posture

Postural control is important in reaching. Consider that as adults we often lean forward or twist as we reach for an object. Infants typically sit independently around 6 to 7 months. Before this, their trunks must be supported for them to achieve a successful reach. Reaching improves when infants are able to maintain postural control (Bertenthal & von Hofsten, 1998). Even at 4 months of age, infants adjust their posture as they reach, and improvements in these adjustments during the first year continue to facilitate reaching (Van der Fits & Hadders-Algra, 1998).

The learning activity at the end of this chapter provides an opportunity to observe an infant and the type of grasp the infant uses to pick up various objects.

Manual Performance in Adulthood

The ability to reach and grasp remains an important motor skill throughout the life span. Many careers involve manipulation, and in older adults the ability to perform some activities of daily living, such as bathing and dressing, meal preparation, and making a phone call, can dictate whether the individual is able to live independently. We discussed earlier some of the changes in individual constraints that accompany aging. It is easy to see that some of these might play a significant factor in the performance of large motor activities, but would they also affect manipulative skills? Would fine motor skills be better maintained over the life span than large motor skills? Let's consider some of the research on manipulation in adulthood.

Kauranen and Vanharanta (1996) conducted a cross-sectional study of men and women between 21 and 70 years of age. A test battery was administered that included reaction time, movement speed, tapping speed, and coordination of the hands and feet. Scores declined on all of the hand measures after age 50. The reaction, movement, and tapping times slowed and coordination scores declined.

What about manual performance at older ages? Hughes et al. (1997) observed older adults with an average age of 78 over a 6-year time span. Every 2 years these adults completed the Timed Manual Performance Test and a grip strength measure. The Timed Manual Performance Test consists of 22 different manipulative tests, 17 from the Williams board tests of manual ability and 5 from Jebsen's test of hand skills. Each subject's score was the total time in seconds needed to complete the test. Generally, more individuals at older ages went over the time threshold on the performance test. Grip strength declined with advancing age as well. Loss of strength and upper joint impairment resulting from musculoskeletal disease were associated with declining manual performance. In reaching for objects, older adults slow down more than young adults at the end of the reach, presumably to make more corrections in their trajectory (Roy, Winchester, Weir, & Black, 1993).

Contreras-Vidal, Teulings, and Stelmach (1998) observed young (20s) and older (60s and 70s) adults in handwriting movements. Handwriting movements, of course, do not demand speed of movement, and the accuracy requirements are not great. Compared with the young, the older adults could control force well but did not coordinate their finger and wrist movements as well.

Loss of speed in movement with aging is a common finding for large and fine motor movements. Additionally, these studies indicate that movements might not be as finely coordinated with advancing age. We can see, however, that disuse and disease are every bit as important in the loss of manipulative skills as in locomotor or ballistic skills. Greater loss can be expected among those who curtail manipulative activities as they age, contributing in turn to a loss of strength that might further hurt performance. In fact, compensatory strategies are adopted among those who continue activities over the life span. An example is that of older transcription typists who type out documents from shorthand notes. It seems that older, experienced typists enlarge their preview span to give themselves more time to respond (Salthouse, 1984).

It is obvious that the interaction of individual, task, and environmental constraints is as important in fine, manipulative motor skills as it is in large motor skills. Over the age span, changing individual constraints in turn change the interaction with environmental and task constraints to change movement.

Rapid Aiming Movements

In some complex motor skills, participants make rapid aiming movements. Such arm movements involve an initiation and acceleration phase from the start of the movement to the point when peak velocity of the arm movement is reached, then a deceleration and termination phase from peak velocity to the end of the movement.

Young adults tend to make this movement symmetrically; that is, the acceleration and deceleration phases are equal. In contrast, older adults tend to have a longer deceleration phase, especially when the aiming movement needs to be very accurate (Vercruyssen, 1997). Older adults do not begin the movement as forcefully or travel as far in the acceleration phase, so they need more adjustments in the final phase.

Rapid aiming movements are involved in tasks requiring monitoring and manipulation of complex displays such as cockpits. In critical tasks, many such movements can be required in sequence, and any slowing effects can accumulate. Age differences, then, might not be important in single, simple, or self-paced arm movements but may be critical when many sequential movements are needed in a short time. The interaction of individual and task constraints is evident in this type of skill. Practice is important to older adults. They can compensate for some slowing when they know the location of buttons or levers very well.

FUNDAMENTAL MANIPULATIVE SKILLS

Several manipulative skills are basic to sport performance. In these skills, a performer must gain possession or control of an object. The most common manipulative skill is catching. Fielding in hockey also allows a player to control the ball or puck such that it remains in the player's control and doesn't bounce or roll away, but these skills of course involve use of an implement. Of these reception skills, we know the most about the development of catching.

Catching

Baseball trivia buffs never tire of recounting great outfield catches. Perhaps the greatest was Willie Mays' over-the-shoulder catch in the 1954 World Series. The score was tied

---

Some aspects of older adults' reaches slow down, putting them at a disadvantage in making sequential movements, but accuracy of manipulation is stable, especially on well-known tasks.

2–2, with two runners on base and no outs. Vic Wertz hit a long drive to right center field. Mays turned and ran full speed, his back to home plate. Just a few feet from the wall he was able to stretch his arms and catch the ball. If he hadn't, the ball probably would have cleared the fence for a home run. The Cleveland Indians weren't able to score that inning, and the New York Giants went on to win the game and eventually the world championship.

The goal of catching is to retain possession of the object you catch. It is better to catch an object in the hands than to trap it against the body or opposite arm because if the object is caught in the hands, the catcher can quickly manipulate it—usually by throwing it. A child's initial catching attempts involve little force absorption. The young child pictured in figure 8.5 has positioned his hands and arms rigidly. Instead of catching the ball in his hands, he traps it against his chest. It is common to see children turn away and close their eyes in anticipation of the ball's arrival. The next section discusses characteristics of proficient catching and then examines how children typically develop proficient catching.

Figure 8.5 This young boy holds his arms and hands rigidly rather than "giving" with the ball to gradually absorb its force.

Drawn from film tracings taken in the Motor Development and Child Study Laboratory, University of Wisconsin–Madison and now available from the Motor Development Film Collection, Kinesiology Division, Bowling Green State University.

Proficient Catching

In moving from novice to proficient catching skills, as shown in figure 8.6, a child must

▲ learn to catch with the hands and "give" with the ball, thus gradually absorbing the ball's force;

▲ master the ability to move to the left or the right, forward or back, to intercept the ball; and

▲ point the fingers up when catching a high ball and down when catching a low one.

Developmental Changes in Catching

It is more difficult to identify developmental sequences for catching skills than for most locomotor or ballistic skills because the sequence is specific to the conditions under which the individual performs the skill. Many factors are variable in catching: the ball's size, shape (e.g., a round basketball vs. a football), speed, trajectory, arrival point, and so on. Haubenstricker, Branta, and Seefeldt (1983) conducted a preliminary validation of a developmental sequence for arm action in

Figure 8.6 Proficient catching. The ball is caught with the hands, and the hands and arms "give" with the ball.

two-hand catching. They used progressively smaller balls as children demonstrated better skill. The sequence, originally outlined by Seefeldt, Reuschlein, & Vogel (1972), is summarized in table 8.1. At 8 years of age, most of the boys and almost half of the girls tested were at the highest level of arm action. Virtually all of the children had passed through steps 1 and 2 by this time. Slightly higher percentages of boys than girls performed at higher levels at any given age, but overall this group demonstrated well-developed arm action by age 8. Table 8.1 also suggests the key observation points that can help you place performers at a developmental level.

Strohmeyer, Williams, and Schaub-George (1991) proposed developmental sequences for the hands and body in catching a small ball (table 8.1). A unique feature of this work is that it is based on catching balls thrown directly to the catcher as well as balls thrown high or to the side of the catcher. These sequences suggest that as catchers improve they

▲ are better able to move their bodies in response to the oncoming ball,

▲ catch the ball in their hands, and

▲ adjust their hands to the anticipated location of the catch.

TABLE 8.1 Developmental Sequence for Two-Hand Catching

	Arm action
Step 1	Little response. Arms extend forward, but there is little movement to adapt to ball flight; ball usually trapped against chest.
Step 2	Hugging. Arms are extended sideways to encircle (hug) the ball; ball is trapped against chest.
Step 3	Scooping. Arms are extended forward again but move under (scoop) the object; ball is trapped against chest.
Step 4	Arms "give." Arms extend to meet object with the hands; arms and body "give"; ball is caught in hands.
	Hand action
Step 1	Palms up. The palms of the hands face up. (Rolling balls elicit a palms-down trapping action.)
Step 2	Palms in. The palms of the hands face each other.
Step 3	Palms adjusted. The palms of the hands are adjusted to the flight and size of the oncoming object. Thumbs or little fingers are placed close together, depending on the height of the flight path.
	Body action
Step 1	No adjustment. No adjustment of the body occurs in response to the ball's flight path.
Step 2	Awkward adjustment. The arms and trunk begin to move in relation to the ball's flight path, but the head remains erect, creating an awkward movement to the ball. The catcher seems to be fighting to remain balanced.
Step 3	Proper adjustment. The feet, trunk, and arms all move to adjust to the path of the oncoming ball.

The arm action component is adapted from Haubenstricker, Branta, and Seefeldt 1983, which is based on Seefeldt, Reuschlein, and Vogel 1972. The hand and body action components are reprinted from Strohmeyer, Williams, and Schaub-George 1991.

The investigators tested their sequences on a cross section of children between 5 and 12 years old. All of the children over 8 years old made some adjustment in body position to the oncoming ball, and 11- to 12-year-olds successfully adjusted their body positions about 80% of the time. In contrast, this older group could properly adjust their hand positions to the ball only 40% of the time if the ball was thrown directly to them and less than 10% of the time if it was thrown to various positions around them.

Of course, catching, like striking, involves anticipation of where a ball can be intercepted as well as ability to complete the movements that position the hands at that location. As we would expect, children better predict the ball flight as they get older, especially when the viewing time (path of the ball) is short (Lefebvre & Reid, 1998). We discuss the anticipatory aspects of manipulative skills in more detail in the next section of the chapter.

Observing Catching Patterns

Catching can be observed from the front, allowing you to toss the ball, or from the side. It is easy to assess the product in catching tasks. One can simply record a percentage of balls successfully caught, noting the task constraints. Important constraints include the size and type of ball used, the throwing distance, and the trajectory of the ball.

Parents, teachers, and coaches, though, often want to know about the movement process used in catching. The observation plan for catching on p. 145 provides a suggested developmental sequence that indicates which step the catcher demonstrates for each body component. For example, if you observe a child who extends her arms, palms up, and scoops a large ball thrown to her, trapping it against her chest, all without moving her feet, the developmental levels would be step 3 for arm action, step 1 for hand action, and step 1 for body action.

Observation Plan for Catching

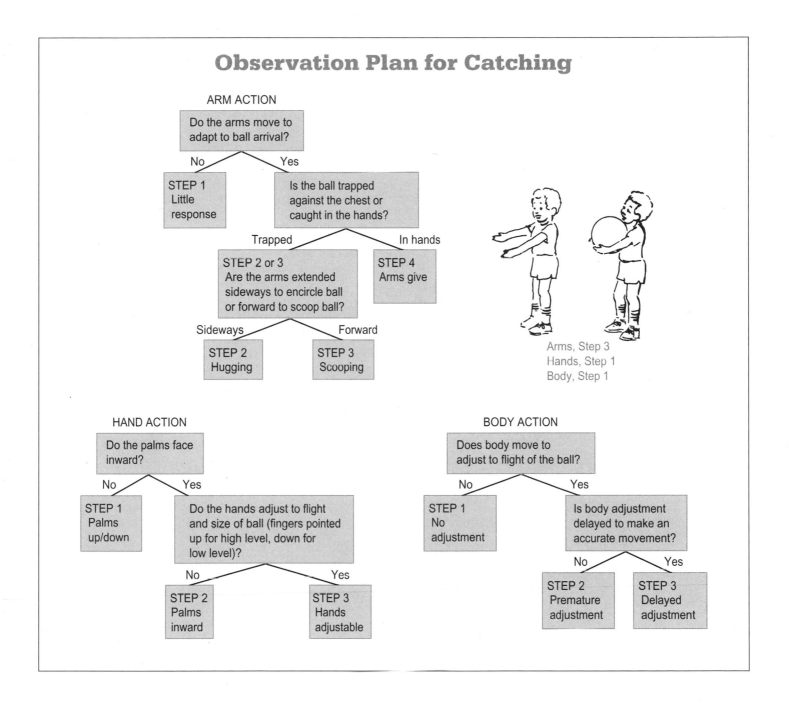

ARM ACTION

Do the arms move to adapt to ball arrival?

No → STEP 1 Little response

Yes → Is the ball trapped against the chest or caught in the hands?

Trapped → STEP 2 or 3 Are the arms extended sideways to encircle ball or forward to scoop ball?

In hands → STEP 4 Arms give

Sideways → STEP 2 Hugging

Forward → STEP 3 Scooping

Arms, Step 3
Hands, Step 1
Body, Step 1

HAND ACTION

Do the palms face inward?

No → STEP 1 Palms up/down

Yes → Do the hands adjust to flight and size of ball (fingers pointed up for high level, down for low level)?

No → STEP 2 Palms inward

Yes → STEP 3 Hands adjustable

BODY ACTION

Does body move to adjust to flight of the ball?

No → STEP 1 No adjustment

Yes → Is body adjustment delayed to make an accurate movement?

No → STEP 2 Premature adjustment

Yes → STEP 3 Delayed adjustment

To gain experience in assessing the developmental level of catchers, download Lab 8.2 Assessing the Developmental Levels of Catchers from the Student Resources section at www.HumanKinetics.com/LifeSpanMotorDevelopment.

ANTICIPATION

It is clear that many manipulative tasks and interception skills involve anticipation. The ball or other moving object can approach at different speeds from different directions along different trajectories and may be of differing sizes and shapes. To be successful, performers must initiate movements well ahead of the time of interception so that the body and hands (or implement, such as a hockey stick) can be in the proper position

Coincidence-anticipation tasks are motor skills in which one anticipates the completion of a movement to coincide with the arrival of a moving object.

when the object arrives. In fact, the manipulative component of reception skills (e.g., positioning and closing the hands on the ball) is often perfected before the ability to be in the right place at the right time.

Some developmentalists have researched this aspect of reception skills through **coincidence-anticipation** tasks. Through coincidence-anticipation tasks it is easy to vary task characteristics and observe the effect on performance. Variations in task characteristics influence not only the product of performance—a hit or catch versus a miss—but also the process, or movement pattern, used in the task. For example, children who are capable of catching *small* balls in their hands may choose to scoop very *large* balls with their arms, perhaps as a surer means of retaining them (Victors, 1961). Thus, a task can be defined as requiring a simpler or more complex movement response, and the characteristics of the ball can vary to further constrain the movement. An example of the latter is the position of a fielder in baseball. A fielder could be positioned along the trajectory of the ball to be caught and need only move three steps forward to catch it. Or, a fielder could be positioned some distance from the trajectory of the ball and be required to move forward and to the side to catch it.

It is important that we consider the task constraints for interception skills. Various task constraints interact with individual and environmental constraints, resulting in more or less difficult tasks. Let's consider some of the task constraints in coincidence-anticipation tasks.

Several researchers have found that coincidence-anticipation performance improves throughout childhood and adolescence (Bard, Fleury, Carriere, & Bellec, 1981; Dorfman, 1977; Dunham, 1977; Haywood, 1977, 1980; Lefebvre & Reid, 1998; Stadulis, 1971; Thomas, Gallagher, & Purvis, 1981). However, the exact pattern of improvement with advancing age depends on task constraints:

▲ Young children are less accurate as the movement required of them gets more complex (Bard et al., 1981; Haywood, 1977). So, response complexity is one task characteristic that influences how well children perform on interception tasks.

▲ Children's accuracy decreases if the interception point is farther away. For example, McConnell and Wade (1990) found that the number of successful catches and the efficiency of the movement pattern used decreased if children 6 to 11 years old had to move 2 feet instead of 1 foot, left or right, to catch.

▲ Young children are more successful at intercepting large balls than small ones (Isaacs, 1980; McCaskill & Wellman, 1938; Payne, 1982; Payne & Koslow, 1981).

▲ A high trajectory also makes interception more difficult for young children because the ball changes location in both horizontal and vertical directions (DuRandt, 1985).

▲ Some ball color and background combinations influence young children's performance. Morris (1976) determined that 7-year-olds could better catch blue balls moving against a white background than white balls against a white background. The effect of color diminished with advancing age.

? Identify the many ways pitchers and servers in various sports change the pitch or serve to make interception of the ball more difficult. In contrast, how do we throw to small children when we want to increase the likelihood that they will catch or strike a ball?

▲ The speed of the moving object affects coincidence-anticipation accuracy but not in a clear pattern. A faster speed makes interception more difficult, especially when the object's flight is short. But researchers often note that children are inaccurate with slow velocities because they respond too early (Bard et al., 1981; Haywood, 1977; Haywood, Greenwald, & Lewis, 1981; Isaacs, 1983; Wade, 1980). Perhaps children prepare for the fastest speed an object might travel and then have difficulty delaying their responses if the speed is slow (Bard, Fleury, & Gagnon, 1990). Also, the preceding speeds might influence young children more than they do older performers. If the previous moving object came quickly, young children judge the next object to be moving faster than it really is

(Haywood et al., 1981). Educators should be aware, then, that when they vary the speed of an object in an interception task greatly from one repetition to the next, children can have difficulty adjusting their responses. This is particularly true if the object's flight is short or the response required is complex.

What underlies these age-related trends in coincidence anticipation? Remember that earlier studies of these skills took an information processing perspective. That is, performers were thought to receive visual and kinesthetic information and perform "calculations" on that data, much like a computer, to project the future location of the moving object to intercept it.

The perception–action perspective, in contrast, considers all information in the environment—no calculations necessary. Meaningful information in the environment specifies the action or movement possibilities of that environment and for specific events. This relationship is called an **affordance.** For catching, two important characteristics of the person–environment system concern constant patterns of change, called **invariants,** and the expanding **optic array.** The optic array refers to the visual picture falling on our retinas as we approach an object or a moving object approaches us. That picture expands in size on the retinas with approach and constricts with retreat.

From the perception–action perspective, it is possible that we use the rate of expansion of this image on our retinas to know when arrival or collision will occur (Lyons, Fontaine, & Elliott, 1997). Insects that intercept prey and birds that fold their wings back before diving into water demonstrate perfect timing in these interceptions. It is more likely that they perceive aspects of the environment directly than that they perform complex calculations to predict arrival times.

Researchers recently have taken the perception–action perspective to study catching through various patterns of change, or invariants. McLeod and Dienes (1993, 1996), for example, demonstrated that catchers could intercept an approaching ball by keeping a ratio, based on the angle of gaze, at or near zero. (For those with a mathematical background, the ratio is the second derivative of the tangent of the angle of gaze.) If the ratio is positive in value, the ball will land behind the catcher, but if it is negative in value, it will land in front. By keeping the ratio near zero, the catcher knows whether to move forward or backward and how quickly to move (figure 8.7).

Oudejans and colleagues (Michaels & Oudejans, 1992; Oudejans, Michaels, Bakker, & Dolne, 1996) similarly demonstrated that catchers could keep the vertical optical

An **affordance** is an action or behavior provided or permitted an actor by the places, objects, and events in an environment, often related to the relative sizes of the actor and the objects.

Invariance is stability in the kinematic values of a set of movements (i.e., keeping patterns in the environment constant).

An **optic array** is the light waves reverberating from surfaces in the environment, the stimulus for visual perception; when there is movement of environmental objects or of the viewer in the environment, the optic array expands when the movement is "toward" and constricts when the movement is "away."

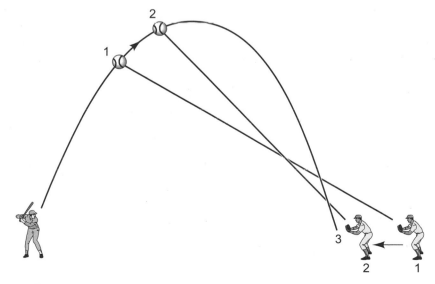

Figure 8.7 The catcher might intercept the approaching ball by keeping a ratio, based on the angle of gaze, at or near zero. When the ball and catcher are in position 1, this ratio is a negative number. The catcher must move forward to bring the ratio closer to zero. At position 2 it is closer to zero but still not zero. The catcher continues to move until the ratio is zero and both the catcher and the ball arrive at position 3.

From P. McLeod and Z. Dienes, 1996, "Do fielders know where to go to catch the ball or only how to get there?" *Journal of Experimental Psychology: Human Perception and Performance* 22: 541. Copyright © 1996 by the American Psychological Association. Adapted with permission.

acceleration of the ball close to zero. Compared with McLeod and Dienes' focus on angle of gaze, this approach focuses on the acceleration of the ball in the vertical plane as the catcher views the ball. Similarly, however, this value tells the catcher whether to move forward or backward.

Of course, many catches require sideways movement. A strategy proposed for this condition is keeping the lateral position of the ball constant with respect to the catcher. This is called the constant bearing angle strategy (Lenoir, Musch, Janssens, Thiery, & Uyttenhove, 1999). Thus, to successfully arrive in position to catch a fly ball, a catcher need not make predictions regarding the point at which the object is aimed, its distance from the start, or its velocity. As the catcher moves, keeping a constant relationship with the ball takes the catcher to the right place, provided the catcher can travel fast enough (figure 8.8). In fact, catchers are observed to adjust their velocities as they move to intercept balls rather than to move at a constant velocity. This implies that they are using an invariant relationship rather than a calculated prediction of the landing point (Lenoir et al., 1999). Thus, interception skills might be undertaken more by movement within the environment to keep certain patterns invariant rather than by anticipation of a coincidence point.

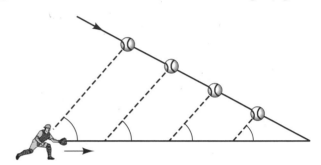

Figure 8.8 A catcher moves to the side to intercept a ball by keeping the bearing angle formed by the dashed line constant.
Redrawn from Lenoir et al. 1999.

Those who adopt the perception–action approach believe catchers are able to intercept fast-moving balls by keeping certain relationships between themselves and objects or spaces in the environment invariant as they move to intercept.

What task characteristics constrain the movement required to intercept a moving object to make the goal easier or more difficult to achieve?

How Do Children Learn to Arrive at the Right Place?

From an information processing viewpoint, children must learn to make more precise calculations to become proficient catchers. Errors made in early attempts become informative feedback that can be used to refine the calculation process. From a perception–action viewpoint, children need to subconsciously discover an invariant. When they begin catching by standing still, for example, McLeod and Dienes' ratio is zero for balls that land in their arms and something else for balls that do not land in their arms. With sufficient exposure children discover the relationship between the ratio and the "catchability" of a ball and eventually use the relationship when they begin moving for a ball.

A role of parents, teachers, and coaches, from the perception–action perspective, is to help children discover the various sources of perceptual information that constrain movement in interception tasks. This is done by manipulating informational constraints during the exploratory process of practice. Bennett, Button, Kingsbury, & Davids (1999) recently demonstrated that 9- and 10-year-olds asked to practice one-hand catching with a restricted view of the ball later benefited when learning a catching task under new conditions. Thus, highlighting the useful sources of information by varying task constraints during practice can be helpful.

Some attempts to improve anticipatory sport skills in novice adults with training have been ineffective (Wood & Abernethy, 1997). Abernethy, Wood, and Parks (1999) suggest that training must be sport specific (environment and task specific) and focus on the factors known to limit novice performance. They demonstrated that novice adults can benefit from such training; the novice adults performed a laboratory task similarly to experts after training. Identification of the perceptual information that constrains movement is important. This suggests that whether the individual is a child or a novice adult, manipulating constraints to help the performer identify the important information in the environment subconsciously facilitates the movements that result in success. More information, however, is needed about the relative merits of simple exploratory practice and instruction.

Catching in Older Adulthood

Little information about older adult catching is available through research. We might suspect that experienced older adults "know" the invariant patterns that provide information about intercepting balls. The factors that might change, however, would be the quickness with which movement is initiated, the maximum speed that could be achieved in moving to the ball, and the extent of reach if "catchability" of a given ball were at the boundary or limit for an individual's speed in moving. All of these might contribute to an older adult being unable to catch as many balls as a younger adult can.

Coincidence-anticipation research provides some information about the anticipatory aspects of skills such as catching. Older adults are somewhat less accurate and more variable in their performance than younger performers, the differences being greater when the moving object moves faster and the older adults are sedentary rather than active (Haywood, 1980, 1982; Wiegand & Ramella, 1983). Wiegand and Ramella (1983) observed that older adults improved with practice at the same rate as younger adults. Over a 7-year period, from an average age of 66.9 years to an average age of 73.5 years, active adults actually demonstrated improvement in performance on a coincidence-anticipation task (Haywood, 1989). Thus, repetition of such skills probably is important for maintaining skill. The task constraints on the movement response in the coincidence-anticipation tasks, however, were minimal. When task constraints are such that larger, more complex movements are required, especially moving over distance in a short time, a higher number of older adults might be less successful at these tasks given their individual constraints.

Driving and Piloting

Although only a portion of older adults participate in sports involving interception, a large number drive automobiles. In fact, the issue of whether an older adult should continue driving is often an emotional one because driving represents independence and freedom for many older adults. Driving is a complex perceptual-motor skill involving manipulation. Skillful driving depends on vision (and sometimes audition), attentional focus, experience, speed, and coordination, all under occasionally stressful conditions.

Older adults have more difficulty than younger adults in dividing their attention and performing two tasks at once in driving situations (Brouwer, Waterink, Van Wolffelaar, & Rothengartter, 1991; Ponds, Brouwer, & Van Wolffelaar, 1988). Older adults also take longer to plan movements and are slower in executing movements, especially when speedy movement is needed (Goggin & Stelmach, 1990; Olson & Sivak, 1986). Goggin and Keller (1996) examined whether aging differentially affects the sensory-cognitive or motor functions in driving. They had older adult drivers take a written test about a videotape of 15 driving situations. The older drivers also made actual driving responses to the same videotaped situations on a driving simulator. Goggin and Keller reasoned that if older adults had difficulty only on the written test, aging likely affected sensory-cognitive functions, but if they had difficulty only with the simulator responses, aging likely affected motor functions. The adults actually performed less well on the written test and better on the simulator. Thus, sensory-cognitive factors such as attention and decision making might be more significant factors in poor performance of driving-related motor skills.

The effects of aging on airplane piloting performance have also been studied (see Morrow & Leirer, 1997, for a review). Mandatory retirement ages for commercial pilots are also an emotional issue for those involved. Like driving, piloting is affected more as task complexity increases. Perceptual aspects of piloting, attention, and working memory are particularly affected by aging. Expertise on familiar tasks, however, offsets aging effects, and highly practiced skills are well maintained.

Applying the model of constraints, we can see that more constraints on the task add to complexity, and when individual constraints change with aging, the interaction of constraints can quickly cause the difficulty of driving and piloting tasks to reach a critical point. As mentioned earlier in regard to rapid aiming tasks, experience with a set of environmental and task constraints allows older adults to compensate for slowing of manipulative movements. Thus, continued practice with tasks, whether sport or driving tasks, is important for maintaining skill. Eventually, however, decrements in sensory-cognitive systems as well as in speed of movement lead to a loss of skill.

Summary and Synthesis

Manipulative skills set humans apart from other species. Whether in executing sport skills or in tasks of everyday living, people need to reach, grasp, and maneuver objects. Infants become skilled at reaching and grasping early in life, during the first year, although using the two hands in complementary ways comes a little later. Children also seem more reliant on vision than do adults for many reaching and grasping tasks.

Children can become accomplished catchers by 11 or 12 years of age, but in all catching tasks at any age, the farther the catcher must travel, the more difficult the catch. Aging probably affects a catcher's ability to get to a ball more than the ability to know where to be to catch the ball. Changing structural constraints influence the speed with which manipulative and locomotor movements can be initiated and completed. When tasks demand great speed, older adults are disadvantaged compared with younger adults.

Children need practice to learn, even if subconsciously, the information available in the environment that is important for catching success. Adults need practice to maintain their skills, especially in demanding conditions. Thus, at any age, a person's skill in challenging manipulative tasks often reflects experience and practice at dealing with the individual, task, and environmental constraints of the task.

The development of manipulative skills certainly emphasizes the importance of task and environmental constraints to performance. The perception–action perspective in particular holds that the environment provides individuals with much of the information they need to intercept objects. Thus, manipulative skills such as catching do not improve just because individual constraints change. The changing interaction of individual constraints with task and environmental constraints is an important aspect of the development of manipulative skills. This interaction is equally important in the maintenance of manipulative skills in older adulthood.

Discussion Questions

1. How does the size of an object affect the grip an infant uses? How might this influence where an infant falls on Halverson's prehension sequence?

2. What are the three types of reaching used by infants? Define each and indicate when it predominates.

3. Does manipulative skill change in older adulthood? If so, how does it change and how can older adults adapt to these changes?

4. What are the major developmental trends we see in children as they become increasingly proficient in catching?

5. When balls do not come directly to the catcher, what situations (environmental and task constraints) make catching success difficult for children? For adults?

6. Explain, from the information processing perspective and the perception–action perspective, how children learn to go to the proper place to catch a ball not traveling directly toward them.

7. Identify various sport implements that accommodate participants with differing hand sizes.

8. Think about the term "coincidence anticipation." Explain why someone who prefers the perception–action approach might consider this to be a misnomer for interception skills.

 ## *Learning Activities*

Investigating Infant Reaching

Place an infant between 6 and 12 months of age sitting upright in front of a table or tray. One at a time, place three small objects that vary in size, weight, and shape (but are still small enough for an infant to pick up with one hand) in front of the infant. Note the type of grip the infant uses, consulting figure 8.1. Repeat this process to see if the infant uses the same grip on the same object. Be careful not to let the infant put small objects in his or her mouth! Prepare a report on the different grips you observed for the various objects, especially distinguishing power and precision grips. Include whether or how the grips changed as the weight or shape of the object changed.

PART IV

Perceptual-Motor Development

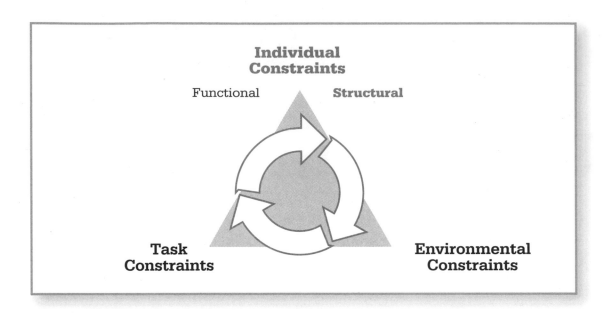

The changes in perception that infants and toddlers undergo are dramatic during this portion of the life span. Infants learn, for example, the names and locations of their body parts and the relationships between objects, such as "in front of" or "behind." Moreover, these changes play a large part in the cognitive and physical skills infants and toddlers can undertake. There is no doubt that the perceptual systems, as individual structural constraints, interact with the task and environment to give rise to movement. In fact, we will see that the interactions between the perceptual systems and the environment are very rich.

The study of perception and its relationship to movement, or action, has been as controversial as any aspect of motor development, if not more so. Certainly, professionals have adopted varying perspectives on the role of perception in motor development. Perhaps even more controversial, though, was the movement to promote perceptual-motor tests as a means to identify children with learning disabilities, and motor activity programs as a means to remediate these disabilities. We begin our discussion by reviewing the age-related changes in sensation and perception within the vision, kinesthetic, and audition systems.

Suggested Reading

Dent-Read, C., & Zukow-Goldring, P. (Eds.). (1997). *Evolving explanations of development: Ecological approaches to organism–environment systems.* Washington, DC: American Psychological Association.

Gottlieb, G., & Krasnegor, N.A. (Eds.). (1985). *Measurement of audition and vision in the first year of postnatal life: A methodological overview.* Norwood, NJ: Ablex.

Kellman, P.J., & Arterberry, M.E. (1998). *The cradle of knowledge: Development of perception in infancy.* Cambridge, MA: Bradford Book, MIT Press.

Konczak, J. (1990). Toward an ecological theory of motor development: The relevance of the Gibsonian approach to vision for motor development research. In J.E. Clark & J.H. Humphrey (Eds.), *Advances in motor development research* (Vol. 3, pp. 201–224). New York: AMS Press.

Sensory-Perceptual Development

chapter

9

FILM SICKENS MOVIE PATRONS

A few years ago, a movie about three film students was released. After it had been open only a short time, newspapers ran stories about movie patrons who experienced motion sickness while watching the film. The director used the technique of showing footage supposedly shot by the students with handheld cameras. The result was an unsteady, jittery effect. Why did some viewers experience motion sickness? Our balance is controlled by vision, sensory receptors in the inner ear, and sensory receptors in the joints. When watching a bouncy film on a big screen, signals from vision contradict the other two systems. This contradiction caused the motion sickness. Later, when viewers watched the movie on their home televisions, motion sickness was unlikely. In a theater the screen occupies 75 to 80% of our visual field, but on a television the screen occupies a smaller portion and makes the contradiction unlikely.

The scenario on the previous page is one example of the influence of our sensory-perceptual systems on our behavior. In many ways almost every motor act can be considered a perceptual-motor skill. Human movement is based on information about the environment and one's position or location within it. For example, a softball infielder sees the location of the pitch, the batter striking the ball, and the ball bouncing on the ground; hears the hit and perhaps sees a runner on the base path; and feels the position of her body and arms. The infielder uses this information to decide where and when she can intercept the ball, where to move, and how to position her body. It might seem that not all movements are so dependent on sensing and perceiving the environment. Yet even an experienced platform diver, blindfolded and wearing earplugs, must feel how gravity pulls his body and know where his trunk and limbs are relative to one another to execute his dive.

As the motion sickness effect of a movie demonstrates, sensory information and perceptual information are highly integrated. We typically experience events in multiple sensory systems. We are uncomfortable if the information from one sense contradicts the information from another—we stagger, fall, or feel sick. If we are denied information from one sense, we can compensate by attending to information from another, but we might not be as accurate in our perceptions. Moreover, our sensory-perceptual selves and the environment are interactive systems. We do not simply receive information from the environment but act to obtain information. For example, we turn our ears toward a sound or reach to feel the texture of a surface. Thus, we must keep in mind the highly integrative nature of **sensation, perception,** and movement even as we discuss individual systems or types of perceptual discrimination.

Individuals with normally functioning sensory receptors can attach different meanings to the very same stimulus, and the same individual can even interpret a single stimulus in different ways. You might remember seeing in a general psychology class some visual displays that have this effect. Remember the one that can be seen as two facial profiles or as a vase (figure 9.1)? Thus, perception is the process whereby we attach meaning to sensory stimuli. How individuals interpret sensory stimuli is the fascinating topic of perceptual development. For individuals to move or act in an environment, they must perceive that environment. In fact, some views of perception and action see them as so interactive as to be inseparable. The environment influences what movements are possible or efficient; moving through the environment informs us about the nature of the environment and our interactions with it. No study of motor development is complete without the study of the relationship between perception and action.

The sensory-perceptual systems, of course, are individual structural constraints to movement and other activities such as reading. Earlier chapters discussed the development of many of the structural systems, such as the skeletal and muscular systems. This chapter discusses the development of visual, auditory, and kinesthetic sensation and perception.

Sensation is the neural activity triggered by a stimulus that activates a sensory receptor and results in sensory nerve impulses traveling the sensory nerve pathways to the brain.

Perception is a multistage process that takes place in the brain and includes selecting, processing, organizing, and integrating information received from the senses.

Figure 9.1 This drawing can be seen as two facing facial profiles or as a vase.

Reprinted from G.H. Sage, 1984, *Motor learning and control: A neuropsychological approach* (Dubuque, IA: Brown), 111. Reproduced with permission of The McGraw-Hill Companies.

 Chapter Objectives

This chapter will

▲ review developmental changes in the vision, audition, and kinesthetic systems,

▲ discuss changes in visual, auditory, and kinesthetic sensation with aging,

▲ trace the development of visual perception, in particular perception of space, objects, and motion,

▲ provide an overview of the development of kinesthetic perception, especially perception of tactile location, the body, limb movements, spatial orientation, and direction,

▲ describe the development of auditory perception, and

▲ study the process whereby environmental objects and events perceived in different modalities are perceived as the same object or event.

VISUAL DEVELOPMENT

Vision plays a major role in most skill performance. To understand this role better, we need to examine age-related changes in visual sensation and visual perception (figure 9.2).

Visual Sensation

Several aspects of vision determine how clearly one can see objects. Here, we will confine our discussion to visual **acuity.** During the first month of life, the visual system provides the infant with functionally useful but unrefined vision at a level approximately 5% of eventual adult acuity, or 20/400 on the Snellen scale of visual acuity (20/20 is desirable) (figure 9.3). The newborn's resolution of detail is such that she can differentiate facial features from a distance of 20 in.; beyond this, she probably cannot see objects clearly (Kellman & Arterberry, 1998).

At about 6 months of age, as infants' motor systems are ready to begin self-propelled locomotion, their visual systems perceive adequate detail to assist them in the task. From the ecological perspective, vision is another system that must develop to an adequate level to facilitate locomotion.

Visual sensation continues to improve during childhood. Five-year-olds have visual acuity of about 20/30, and by age 10 children without a visual anomaly score at the desired level of 20/20. It is likely that visual experience is necessary for the development of vision, since deprivation of vision during development is known to induce refractive errors in animals (Atkinson & Braddick, 1981).

As a person ages, changes in the visual system occur naturally, and some conditions and diseases become more prevalent, especially in older adults. These changes may affect the quality of the visual information that reaches the central nervous system and may have implications for the performance of skills as well as tasks of everyday living.

For example, the condition termed **presbyopia** (from *presbys* for "old man" and *ops* for "eye") becomes clinically significant at around age 40. It affects the ability to see nearby images clearly. The resting diameter of the pupil also decreases with aging, reducing retinal illuminance (the amount of light reaching the retina) in a 60-year-old to one-third that in a young adult. The lens yellows with age, further reducing the amount of illuminance reaching the eye and making glare a problem for older adults.

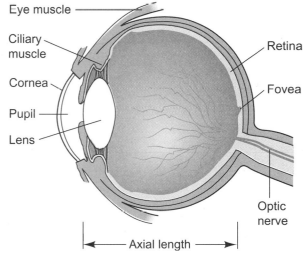

Eye muscle

Ciliary muscle

Cornea

Pupil

Lens

Retina

Fovea

Optic nerve

Axial length

Figure 9.2 The human eye. An axial length that is too short or too long results in farsightedness or nearsightedness, respectively. An imperfect curvature of the cornea also causes blurred vision, a condition known as astigmatism.

Acuity is sharpness of sight.

? How does the need for visual sensitivity change over the first year of life? What is responsible for this changing need?

 Vision reaches adult levels around 10 years of age, but any refractive errors resulting from imperfections in the axial length of the eye can be corrected with glasses or contacts.

Presbyopia is the gradual loss of accommodation power to focus on near objects. It accompanies advancing age.

Some visual disturbances more prevalent in older adults include

▲ cataracts,

▲ glaucoma, and

▲ **age-related maculopathy.**

People who work with children or older adults can look for certain signs that may indicate a visual problem. These include

▲ a lack of coordination in eye–hand tasks,

▲ squinting,

▲ under- or overreaching for objects, and

▲ unusual head movements to align one's gaze with a particular object.

Activity leaders should make sure activity areas are well lit but without glare, and they should encourage performers to wear any corrective lenses prescribed for them (Haywood & Trick, 1990). Because vision provides so much of the perceptual information that people need to perform skills successfully, efforts to enhance the visual information that the central nervous system receives should also enhance visual perception and thus skill performance. An excellent way to remind ourselves of how much we rely on sensory information is to artificially limit our sensory information. The learning activity "Limited Sensation" at the end of this chapter suggests ways to do this.

> **Age-related maculopathy** is a disease that affects the central area of the retina that provides detailed vision.

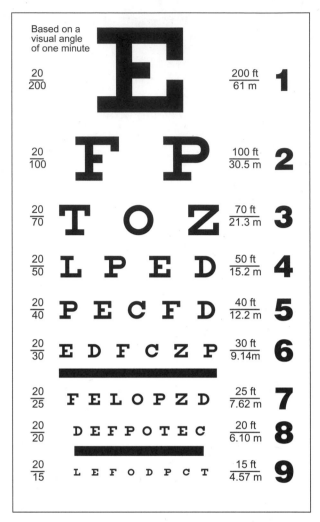

Figure 9.3 A Snellen chart. Sharpness of sight is measured by whether observers can distinguish letters that differ only by whether a small gap is filled, such as *F* and *P,* or *C* and *O.* Children must know letters to be measured in this manner. Alternate methods are available for testing infants and toddlers.

Visual Perception

People depend heavily on visual perception in the performance of most skills. The development of visual perception is a topic for texts in and of itself, so only major aspects of visual perception are highlighted here.

Perception of Space

One of the fundamental perceptions is that of three-dimensional space. Almost all movements—reaching and grasping, locomotion, and complex skills such as automobile driving and piloting a plane—depend on a perception of three-dimensional space. Visual sensations are received by sensory receptors in the retina in approximately a two-dimensional format. How do people interpret the world in three dimensions?

To perceive space in three dimensions, individuals must perceive depth and distance. The visual system has numerous sources of information about distance and **depth**

perception. One source is **retinal disparity.** Because an individual's two eyes are in different locations, each eye sees the visual field from a slightly different angle (figure 9.4). The information needed to judge depth results from a comparison of the two slightly different pictures. Depth perception is aided by good visual acuity because a sharper picture from each eye provides more information for the comparison.

Viewers have other sources of information about depth. By moving the head or moving through space, they receive depth cues from **motion parallax.** Objects in space change locations on our retinas, and nearer objects overlap more distant objects as the head moves. Gibson (1966) suggested that this transformation of the optical array, which he called **optic flow,** provides much information about the three-dimensional nature of our environment. Some researchers even feel that properties of this transformation guide locomotion, control posture, and anticipate contact with objects and surfaces (Johansson, von Hofsten, & Jansson, 1980; Warren & Wertheim, 1990; Crowell & Banks, 1993).

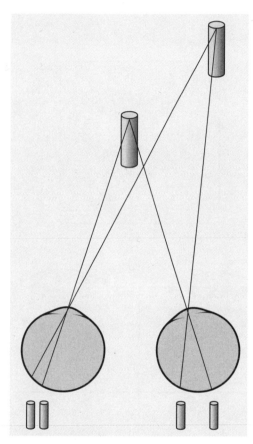

Figure 9.4 Retinal disparity. Images on the left retina are closer together than the images on the right retina. The observer sees the two rods in depth.

From PERCEPTION: THE WORLD TRANSFORMED by Lloyd Kaufman, copyright 1979 by Oxford University Press. Used by permission of Oxford University Press, Inc.

Viewers with experience in the world also use an assumption of physical equality to judge depth. That is, when two like objects can be expected to have the same size but project different relative sizes on the retina, we assume the object with the larger retinal size is closer to us. Similarly, if we look down a roadway, we assume it is the same width across even though the curbs appear to get closer to one another (the curbs form converging lines).

Infants have functional vision and, therefore, the mechanics for retinal disparity and motion parallax as sources of depth perception. From about 1 month of age on, infants blink more often when shown a display that appears to be approaching than when shown a display that does not (Nanez & Yonas, 1994), demonstrating that they perceive the object is moving toward them, not merely increasing in size. In the well-known visual cliff experiments of Walk and Gibson (1961; Gibson & Walk, 1960; Walk, 1969), infants between 6 and 14 months of age, placed on one side of an apparent drop-off (a piece of glass over the drop-off prevented it from being a real cliff), stopped at the edge even though their mothers beckoned them from the other side. These studies demonstrate that even young infants have some level of depth perception. Yet, children may err in judging depth until near-adult levels are reached in early adolescence (Williams, 1968).

Behavioral experiments on depth perception are consistent with work on maturation of the visual cortex of the cerebrum. At birth, the cells in layer four of the cortex receive neural input from both eyes. By 6 months of age, these neural inputs separate into alternating columns receiving input from the right and left eyes, respectively (Held, 1985, 1988; Hickey & Peduzzi, 1987). Disparity information would depend on knowing which

Depth perception is a person's judgment of the distance from self to an object or place in space.

Retinal disparity is the difference in the images received by the two eyes as a result of their different locations.

Motion parallax is the change in optical location for objects at different distances during viewer motion.

Optic flow is change in the pattern of optical texture, a transformation of the optic array, as a viewer moves forward or backward in a stable environment.

 Cues about depth and distance in our environment are often derived from the two eyes being in different locations or from movement of the head.

eye is sending what information, so this aspect of neurological maturation might well be crucial in the onset of depth perception through retinal disparity.

More older adults than younger adults fail depth perception tests, but thresholds for distinguishing depth change little if at all (Yekta, Pickwell, & Jenkins, 1989; Wright & Wormald, 1992). Higher failure rates probably reflect an increase with advancing age in the number of viewers with visual problems. While perception of space is an important aspect of visual perception, our environment also includes objects. It is equally important to perceive objects, the relationship of objects to oneself and to others, and the attributes of those objects.

Perception of Objects

Among the important attributes of objects are size, shape, and motion. The concept of an "object" is relative. An airplane pilot might consider a runway to be an object, whereas a person standing on the runway considers it a surface. With growth, what infants initially perceive as a surface might become an object. For example, the floor of a playpen is a surface to an infant, while the playpen is an object to an adult, who can fold it and carry it away. Adults use a variety of diverse information sources in perceiving objects (Kellman & Arterberry, 1998). For example, it is likely that we detect edges (discontinuities in the visual display) and decide whether or not they are object boundaries. If we see a person standing in front of a car, we assume the nearer object, in this case the person, has a boundary, while the car continues behind the person. We do not think the car stops at one edge of the person and then starts again at the other edge. Depth and motion cues help in these perceptions.

The perception of edges and boundaries helps us extract an object or figure from the background environment (figure 9.5). You might recall doing puzzle pages of embedded figures. In these pages, an artist embeds familiar objects such as a ball or candy cane in a line drawing. The type of perception that allows us to find the embedded objects is **figure-and-ground perception.** The perception of edges and boundaries also helps us distinguish whole objects from parts of an object, called **whole-and-part perception.** For example, if you are driving down the street and see half a bicycle tire protruding from a row of parked cars and a child's head above it, you are not puzzled.

Figure-and-ground perception is the ability to see an object of interest as distinct from the background.

Whole-and-part perception is the ability to discriminate parts of a picture or an object from the whole, yet integrate the parts into the whole, perceiving them simultaneously.

a

b

Figure 9.5 A test plate from the Figure-Ground Perception Test of the Southern California Sensory Integration Test. A child must identify which of the six objects in *(b)* are present, or embedded, in picture *(a)*.

You immediately perceive that a child on a bicycle is pulling into your path, and you slow down.

We know little of infant perception of edges and boundaries. Some research indicates that infants rely more on depth and motion cues than edges to perceive objects (Granrud et al., 1984; von Hofsten & Spelke, 1985). Children improve in figure-and-ground perception tasks between 4 and 6 years of age (Williams, 1983) and again between 6 and 8 years (Temple, Williams, & Bateman, 1979).

Very young children have difficulty integrating objects that form a whole. For example, you might recall seeing sculptures composed of familiar objects, such as a stick man constructed from nuts and bolts. Pictures of this nature are used to assess whole-and-part perception (figure 9.6). Children under 9 years of age typically report seeing only the man, only the nuts and bolts, or both but at different times. After 9, most children can integrate parts and the whole into the total picture (Elkind, 1975; Elkind, Koegler, & Go, 1964). Realize, though, that adult levels of sensitivity to object perception cues far exceed what is necessary to perceive objects in typical environments (Kellman & Arterberry, 1998). So, infants may still perceive objects fairly well, even though not at adult levels.

? What environmental conditions would make the perception of objects more difficult than usual?

Figure 9.6 The drawing used by Elkind, Koegler, and Go to study whole-and-part perception. Very young children typically report seeing the pieces or the whole object but do not say they see the whole object made up of familiar pieces, such as a bicycle made from pieces of candy.

Reprinted from Elkind, Koegler, and Go 1964.

The perception of distances influences our perception of objects in the environment and their properties. We must perceive that an object has constant size even though it might vary in distance from us (figure 9.7). Slater, Mattock, and Brown (1990) showed that newborns have **size constancy.** They demonstrated first that infants look more at objects with a larger projection size on the retina. Then they familiarized the infants with cubes (large and small) whose size remained constant but whose distance from the infants was varied. When a familiar object with constant size was shown to the infants along with

Size constancy is the perception of actual object size despite the size of its image as projected on our retina.

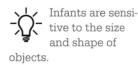

Figure 9.7   Size constancy. The image of an object halves in size with each doubling of the distance of the object from the eye, but the object does not appear to shrink. We assume the object is constant in size and is changing distance from us rather than changing in size and remaining at a constant distance.
Reprinted from Gregory 1972.

an object of novel size (at distances to make both projected sizes equal), they looked more at the novel-sized object, indicating they detected the difference in size.

Evidence of newborn sensitivity to shape or form, that is, **shape constancy,** has also been found through the **habituation** method (see Assessment of Infant Perception). **Face perception** is a particular type of form perception. In fact, 4-day-old infants already spend longer time looking at their mothers' faces than at a female stranger's (Bushnell, Sai, & Mullin, 1989; Bushnell, 1998). They probably use the outer contour of faces to perceive patches of light and dark as faces. It is important that viewers either attend to or ignore the **spatial orientation** of objects, depending on whether this is relevant to the task at hand. In some cases, it is important to recognize that two objects are identical even if one is tipped to one side, upside down, or rotated. In other situations, an object's or symbol's differing orientation is critical to its meaning. Such is the case with letters such as *d* and *b*.

Children seem better able to attend to spatial orientation of an object than to ignore it (Gibson, 1966; Pick, 1979). Three- and 4-year-olds can learn directional extremes such as high and low, over and under, and front and back, but they often call intermediate orientations the same as the nearest extreme. By age 8, most children have learned to differentiate obliques (various angles) and diagonals (45 degrees) but may still confuse left and right (Naus & Shillman, 1976; Williams, 1973).

Shape constancy is the perception of actual object shape despite its orientation to a viewer.

Habituation is the state of having adapted to a stimulus.

Spatial orientation is the orientation or position of objects as they are located in space or as a two-dimensional drawing.

Infants are sensitive to the size and shape of objects.

Assessment of Infant Perception

Infants are not able to describe what they perceive. Researchers must devise other ways to discover what infants perceive, through observation of their actions and responses. One of the clever ways this is done is through **preferential looking.** Infants tend to look at objects or events that are new, surprising, or different from those they are familiar with. Similarly, the attention of an infant tends to wander away from objects and events to which they are exposed continuously or repeatedly. In the latter case, we say the infant has habituated to the object or event.

To determine what infants perceive with this method, researchers first expose an infant to an object or event, typically for a length of time or a number of presentations. When the infant habituates to this stimulus and becomes so used to it that the infant's attention wanders elsewhere, the researcher presents another object or event that is different along some dimension. For example, the researcher changes the size of the object if she is interested in perception of size, or the shape if she is interested in perception of shape. The infant attends to the new stimulus if he perceives it as different. The infant shows little interest if the object is perceived to be the same as the familiar one. Obviously, the researcher could vary the amount of change to see how much difference the infant perceives.

(continued)

Researchers also habituate an infant to an object and then present it along with a novel object. Usually, one object is placed on the infant's right and the other on the left. The researcher, positioned directly in front of the infant, records the amount of time the infant looks at each object. The infant presumably prefers the object that is novel, if indeed the infant perceives a difference, hence the term preferential looking. If much more time is spent looking at the novel object, the researcher concludes that the infant perceives the new object as different from the familiar one. If there is no difference in looking time, the researcher concludes that the difference is not perceived. To learn more about this method, see Bornstein, 1985.

Perception of Motion

Motion perception is of particular interest in the study of motor development. We know that there are dedicated neurological mechanisms for detecting motion. Individual cortical cells fire according to the direction, location, and speed of an object on the retina, and the medial temporal area of the visual cortex is dedicated to processing motion signals (Kellman & Arterberry, 1998). Therefore, it is not surprising that infants perceive motion.

Early in infancy, however, infants lack adult sensitivity to motion. *Direction* of motion is not well perceived until 8 weeks of age (Wattam-Bell, 1996a, 1996b). Thresholds for detecting *velocity* are higher in newborns than in adults; however, by 6 weeks of age only extremely slow velocities of nearby objects are difficult for the infant to perceive (Aslin & Shea, 1990; von Hofsten, Kellman, & Putaansuu, 1992). Older adults have difficulty perceiving motion at the **detection thresholds** (Elliott, Whitaker, & Thompson, 1989; Kline, Culham, Bartel, & Lynk, 1994). It is not clear whether this has practical significance in real-world conditions; further research is needed.

This discussion of visual perception has been necessarily brief. Overall, however, the evidence discussed here indicates that basic visual perceptions provide even infants with a great deal of information about the environment. As a child grows, perception at thresholds of detection improves to adult levels. However, perception at thresholds will most likely show decrements in older adulthood. Far more information is needed on what significance performance at thresholds has for daily tasks in the real world.

Preferential looking is a research technique in which two stimuli are presented to a subject, who turns to look toward the preferred stimulus.

Infants perceive motion, but direction and velocity are better perceived with advancing age.

A **detection threshold** is the point on a continuum wherein the energy level is just sufficient for one to register the presence of a stimulus.

KINESTHETIC DEVELOPMENT

The kinesthetic system might be described as the system that gives us "body sense." It is certainly vital to our ability to position ourselves and move in our environment. We need only recall walking through a "haunted" house at a fair or circus, where our visual system and our kinesthetic system are given conflicting information, to know that is true.

Kinesthetic Sensation

The kinesthetic, or proprioceptive, system is important to skill performance because it yields information about

▲ the relative position of the body parts to each other,
▲ the position of the body in space,
▲ the body's movements, and
▲ the nature of objects the body comes in contact with.

Unlike the visual system, which relies on the eyes as sensory receptors, kinesthetic information comes from various types of receptors throughout the body called **proprioceptors** (table 9.1). Those proprioceptors located in the muscles, at

TABLE 9.1 Kinesthetic Receptors and Their Locations

Kinesthetic receptor	Location
Muscle spindles	Muscles
Golgi tendon organs	Muscle–tendon junctions
Joint receptors	Joint capsule and ligaments
Spray-type Ruffini endings	
Golgi-type receptors	
Modified Pacinian corpuscles	
Vestibular semicircular canals	Inner ear
Cutaneous receptors	Skin and underlying tissues

Proprioceptor is the collective name of the various kinesthetic receptors located in the periphery of the body; the two types of proprioceptors are the somatosensors and the vestibular apparatus.

Somatosensors are the receptors located under the skin, in the muscles, at muscle–tendon junctions, and in joint capsules and ligaments.

The **vestibular apparatus** houses the receptors located in the inner ear.

the muscle–tendon junctions, in joint capsules and ligaments, and under the skin are called **somatosensors,** and those located in the inner ear are called the **vestibular apparatus** (figure 9.8).

Many infantile reflexes are stimulated through kinesthetic receptors. Therefore, the onset of a reflex indicates that the kinesthetic receptor involved is functioning. The first prenatal reflex that can be elicited is opposite-side neck flexion through tactile stimulation around the mouth at just 7.5 weeks after conception.

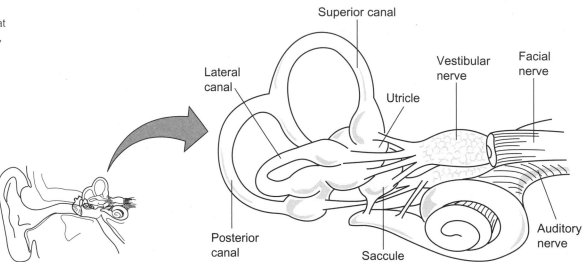

Figure 9.8 Structures of the inner ear. Sensory receptors are located in the utricle and saccule.

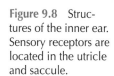 Infants, of course, do not understand the words spoken to them. What are some of the ways parents use touch to communicate with their infants?

Researchers have used tactile stimulation to other body parts to determine that cutaneous receptor development proceeds in an oral, genital–anal, palmar, and plantar (sole of foot) sequence. This developmental sequence follows the cephalocaudal and proximodistal growth directions we discussed in chapter 3.

At birth, infants clearly respond to touch. They can also identify the location of touches, especially in the region of the mouth and the face (Kisilevsky, Stach, & Muir, 1991). We know, too, that the vestibular apparatus is anatomically complete at approximately 9 to 12 weeks of prenatal life, but its functional status before birth is unclear. The labyrinthine righting reflex appears around the second postnatal month (Timiras, 1972), so we know it is functioning by this age. Therefore, the system for kinesthetic sensation is functional in early life.

Although anecdotal information on age-related changes in kinesthetic sensation is available, little research data is available (Boff, Kaufman, & Thomas, 1986). Indications are that absolute thresholds increase and at least some older adults experience decreased sensitivity (Kenshalo, 1977). Far more objective research is needed on the aging of kinesthetic receptors.

Tactile Localization

Tactile localization is the ability to identify without sight the exact spot on the body that has been touched.

As noted earlier, newborns feel touches. Beyond feeling a touch, though, an individual must know where on the body a touch occurs and the nature of that touch; this knowledge is termed **tactile localization.** Making fine discriminations of where one has been touched, sight unseen, and whether the touch is one point or two in close proximity is an ability that develops in childhood. Four-year-olds are less accurate than 6- to 8- year-olds in locating a touch on the hands and forearms. Performance on this type of task does not improve significantly between ages 6 and 8 (Ayres, 1972; Temple et al., 1979). Based on this limited data, then, the perception of tactile localization on the hands and arms seems to be relatively mature around age 5.

Threshold discrimination—detecting the smallest gap between two points that touch the skin—varies in different areas of the body (figure 9.9). Unfortunately, we do not know if these judgments also vary with age (Van Duyne, 1973; Williams, 1983). Ayres (1966), however, reported that only half of a group of 5-year-olds could consistently discriminate a touch on different fingers, though average performance improved through 7.5 years of age (the oldest age tested).

Recognizing unseen objects and their characteristics by feeling them with the hands is the kinesthetic perception parallel to the visual perception of objects. In infants, such manipulation is often more accidental than purposeful. Yet by age 4 the average child can handle objects purposefully, and by age 5 a child can explore the objects' major features. Manual exploration becomes systematic, that is, it follows a plan, at about age 6 (Van Duyne, 1973), and in the next 2 years, haptic (cutaneous) memory and object recognition also improve (Northman & Black, 1976). Research by Temple et al. (1979) indicates that children also increase their speed of tactile recognition during this time.

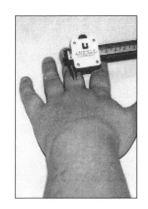

Children improve in their ability to locate touches, but little is known about threshold discriminations for touch.

Figure 9.9 Tactile point perception includes accurate judgment of the number of simultaneous touches on the skin. As two points get closer and closer, it is difficult to discriminate between a single touch and two touches.

Perception of the Body (Body Awareness)

To carry out everyday activities as well as to perform complex skills, it is necessary to have a sense of the body, its various parts, and its dimensions. One aspect of **body awareness** is the identification of body parts. As children get older, more of them can label the major body parts correctly (DeOreo & Williams, 1980), and they can name more detailed body parts (Cratty, 1979). The rate at which an individual child learns body part labels is largely a function of the amount of time parents or other adults spend practicing with the child. Probably two-thirds of 6-year-olds can identify the major body parts, and mistakes are rare in all normally developing children after age 9.

Children also need a sense of the body's spatial dimensions, such as up and down. They usually master the up–down dimension first, followed by front–back, and finally side. A high percentage of 2.5- to 3-year-olds can place an object in front of or behind their bodies, but more of them have difficulty placing an object in front of or behind something else. By about age 4, most children can do the latter task as well as place an object to the side of something (Kuczaj & Maratsos, 1975).

Laterality Although children typically master up–down and front–back awareness before age 3, they develop an understanding that the body has two distinct sides, or **laterality,** at approximately 4 to 5 years of age (Hecaen & de Ajuriaguerra, 1964). The child comes to realize that even though his two hands, two legs, and so on are the same size and shape, he can position them differently and move them independently. Eventually, the child is able to discriminate right and left sides—that is, to label or identify these dimensions.

An age-related improvement in the ability to make right–left discriminations occurs between ages 4 or 5 and age 10, with most children responding almost perfectly by age 10 (Ayres, 1969; Swanson & Benton, 1955; Williams, 1973). However, children can be taught to label right and left at younger ages, too, even as young as 5 (Hecaen & de Ajuriaguerra, 1964). Young children also have difficulty executing a task when a limb must cross the midline of the body, such as writing on a chalkboard from left to right. This ability improves between ages 4 and 10, but some 10-year-olds still have difficulty with such tasks (Ayres, 1969; Williams, 1973).

Body awareness is the recognition, identification, and differentiation of the location, movement, and interrelationships of body parts and joints; also, a person's awareness of the spatial orientation and perceived location of the body in the environment.

? In what sports and daily activities is body awareness particularly important?

Laterality is the awareness that one's body has two distinct sides that can move independently; a component of body awareness.

Lateral dominance is the consistent preference for use of one eye, ear, hand, or foot instead of the other, although the preference for different anatomical units is not always on the same side.

Lateral Dominance   Interest in **lateral dominance,** especially hand dominance, dates back to Aristotle. Over the centuries, some have favored a nativist view of dominance, suggesting that lateral dominance is inborn, especially after Broca's studies suggested asymmetries between the right and left halves of the brain. Broca was a French surgeon who first reported in 1861 that individuals with loss of language abilities had lesions in a specific area on only one side of the brain. This first suggested that an entire function, in this case speech, might be controlled by only one side of the brain. Today we know that "Broca's area" is not the only site in the brain involved in speech.

Other behavioral scientists have favored a nurturist perspective, holding that preference for writing and tool use can be changed by training. In recent years, the study of lateral dominance has been tied to the study of language development. This has hindered rather than helped our understanding of handedness (see Hopkins & Ronnqvist, 1998, for a discussion).

Asymmetries in hand use have been widely observed in infants. Infants younger than 3 months of age grasp objects longer, make a fist longer, and are more active with one hand than the other (Hawn & Harris, 1983; Michel & Goodwin, 1979; Michel & Harkins, 1986). These asymmetries are not consistently predictive of adult hand dominance (Michel, 1983, 1988), but a link may exist between early asymmetries and later hand dominance because the asymmetries tend to follow orientation. Infants who prefer to turn their heads to the right seem to prefer reaching with their right hands, and vice versa. These self-generating experiences may facilitate eye–hand coordination of one hand more than the other (Bushnell, 1985; Michel, 1988).

? What daily activities have tasks structured to favor right-handers over left-handers?

When infants begin to reach after 3 months, they also demonstrate a hand preference (Hawn & Harris, 1983). Unimanual manipulation appears at approximately 5 months, and by 7 months infants show a preference for manipulating with a particular hand (Ramsay, 1980; table 9.2). Approximately 1 month after bimanual manipulation first appears, a hand preference is evident, even as both hands hold an object (Ramsay, Campos, & Fenson, 1979). Infants typically prefer the same hand in unimanual and bimanual handling; that is, they use either the right or left hand in both types of manipulation (Ramsay, 1980). Although these early preferences might change, usually the hand that emerges as preferred in early childhood, most often by age 4, remains the dominant hand in youth and adulthood (Sinclair, 1971). It is important to remember that in certain environmental situations children might find it convenient to use their nonpreferred limbs (Connolly & Elliot, 1972). By adulthood, individuals typically use their dominant limbs even if it is more awkward to do so.

TABLE 9.2 **Infant Hand Preferences**

Nature of hand preference	Approximate age
Fisting and longer grasps	Before 3 mo
Unimanual reaching	After 3 mo
Unimanual manipulation	7 mo
Bimanual manipulation	Within 1 mo of emergence of unimanual manipulation
Hand dominance	By 4 yr

In addition to hand preferences, we come to favor one of our eyes, ears, and feet over the other. If the favored are all on one side of the body, the dominance is termed pure; otherwise, it is mixed. Some developmentalists have suggested that pure dominance is preferable, the implication being that one side of the brain is clearly dominant. For example, Doman and Delacato proposed a popular perceptual-motor theory in the 1960s (Delacato, 1966). The theory held that pure dominance is necessary for proper neurological organization. Those with mixed dominance could anticipate problems in perceptual-motor performance, reading, speech, and other cognitive abilities. Research has never shown this to be the case. Studies have failed to show any real cognitive advantage for individuals with more lateralized brains (Kinsbourne, 1988, 1997).

Although some researchers have suggested that pure dominance is necessary for proper neurological organization, no objective evidence indicates that it is advantageous to have a more lateralized brain.

Limb Movements

You can assess a child's perception of the extent of movement at a joint by asking the child to accurately reproduce a limb movement or to relocate a limb position without looking. Children improve in this task between ages 5 and 8, with little improvement noted after age 8 (Ayres, 1972; Williams, 1983).

Spatial Orientation

Kinesthetic spatial orientation involves perception of the body's location and orientation in space independent of vision. Temple et al. (1979) tested this perception by asking children to walk a straight line while blindfolded and then measuring their deviation from the straight path. Performance improved between 6 and 8 years of age, 8-year-olds being the oldest age group included in the study. Because these were the only children tested, investigations of spatial orientation over a wider age range are necessary.

Direction

Directionality is often linked to laterality, an awareness of the body's two distinct sides. Children with a poor sense of laterality typically also have poor directionality. Although this relationship seems intuitively logical, deficiencies in laterality are not known to cause deficiencies in directionality (Kephart, 1964).

Individuals obtain information for directional judgments through vision, so these judgments rely on integration of visual and kinesthetic information. Long and Looft (1972) suggested that children improve their sense of directionality between ages 6 and 12. By age 8, children typically can use body references to indicate direction. They are able to say correctly both, "The ball is on my right," and, "The ball is to the right of the bat." At age 9, children can change the latter statement to, "The ball is to the left of the bat," when they walk around to the opposite side of the objects. They can identify right and left for a person opposite them. Improvements in directional references such as these continue through age 12. Long and Looft noted that some refinement of directionality must take place in adolescence because many 12-year-olds are unable to transpose left and right from a new perspective, such as when looking in a mirror.

> **Directionality** is the ability to project the body's spatial dimensions into surrounding space and to grasp spatial concepts about the movements or locations of objects in the environment.

Kinesthetic Changes With Aging

We know very little about how aging affects the kinesthetic receptors themselves, but researchers have identified age-related changes in kinesthetic perception. Some, but not all, older adults lose cutaneous sensitivity, vibratory sensitivity, and sensitivity to temperature and pain (Kenshalo, 1977). Older adults experience some impairment in judging the direction and amount of passive lower limb movements (in which someone else positions the limb) (Laidlaw & Hamilton, 1937). However, they remain fairly accurate in judging muscle tension produced by differing weights (Landahl & Birren, 1959).

AUDITORY DEVELOPMENT

Although it is not as important to skill performance as vision or kinesthesis, auditory information is still valuable for accurate performance. People often use sounds as critical cues to initiate or time their movements.

Auditory Sensation

The external ear, the middle ear, and the cochlea of the inner ear are involved in hearing. The inner ear develops first and is close to adult form by the third prenatal month. By midfetal life, the external ear and middle ear are formed (Timiras, 1972). Fetuses reportedly respond to loud sounds, but perhaps this response is actually to tactile stimuli, that is, vibrations (Kidd & Kidd, 1966).

A newborn's hearing is imperfect partly because of the gelatinous tissue filling the inner ear. The **absolute threshold** is about 60 decibels higher for a newborn than an adult. So, a newborn can detect only an average speaking voice when an adult can detect a whisper (Kellman & Arterberry, 1998). Newborns also do not discriminate changes in the intensity of sounds (**differential threshold**) or in sound frequencies as well as adults can.

The gelatinous material in the inner ear is reabsorbed during the first postnatal week so that hearing improves rapidly (Timiras, 1972; Hecox, 1975). By 3 months, infants hear low-frequency sounds (500–1,000 Hz) very well but do not hear high-frequency sounds (4,000 Hz) quite as well. Because human speech generally is under 5,000 Hz, this level of hearing permits the infant to sense speech; the infant can hear low- to mid-pitched voices better than high-pitched voices. By 6 months infants have hearing similar to that of adults, including hearing of high-frequency sounds (Spetner & Olsho, 1990).

More older adults than younger adults suffer from **presbycusis** (from *presbys* for "old man" and *okousis* for "hearing"), but the source of this loss varies among individuals. Some hearing loss might result from physiological degeneration. However, hearing loss often results from lifelong exposure to environmental noise (Timiras, 1972).

The absolute threshold for hearing pure tones and speech increases in older adults, meaning that sounds must be louder for older adults to hear them. Differential thresholds also increase for pitch and speech discrimination (Corso, 1977). As a person ages, the ability to hear high-frequency sounds is particularly affected. One result is that older adults cannot hear certain consonant sounds well; they might report that they hear someone talking but cannot understand the message. Older adults are also at a distinct disadvantage in adverse listening situations, such as attempting to listen to one person in a room crowded with talking people (Stine, Wingfield, & Poone, 1989).

Auditory Perception

It is easy to overlook the amount of information we get from sound. We can determine the location of an event by sound, whether something or someone is leaving or approaching, who or what made a sound, and even the material from which an object is made. Although we think of vision and kinesthesis as more important to skill performance, auditory perception gives us much information about the environment in which we move. The aspects of auditory perception we discuss here are

▲ location,
▲ differences in similar sounds,
▲ patterns, and
▲ auditory figure and ground.

Notice that several of these are parallel to types of visual and kinesthetic perception.

Location

We locate a sound by determining its direction and distance from us (figure 9.10). Newborns turn in the direction of a sound and rapidly improve in their ability to locate sound during the first year. The minimum audible angle 6- and 7-month-olds can detect is in the range of 12 to 19 degrees (Ashmead, Clifton, & Perris, 1987; Morrongiello, 1988b), compared with 1 to 2 degrees in adults. Infants determine the direction of nearby sounds better than distant sounds, but there is continuous improvement such that by age 3 chil-

Absolute threshold is the minimal detectable sound a hearer can sense at least half of the time a signal is sounded.

Differential threshold is the closest two sounds can be yet still allow the hearer to distinguish them at least 75% of the time.

Presbycusis is a loss of hearing sensitivity.

? What activities in their daily living routine can present difficulties for seniors with presbycusis?

? What are some tasks of daily living that involve localizing sound?

dren can determine the direction of even distant sounds (Dekaban, 1970).

It is more difficult to determine how well infants perceive the distance of a sound. Clifton, Perris, and Bullinger (1991) found that 7-month-olds reached for an object that was the source of a sound significantly more often when it was within reach than when it was out of reach. It seems that from birth, individuals have some sense of the location of sounds in the environment and rapidly improve in determining both the direction and distance of sounds.

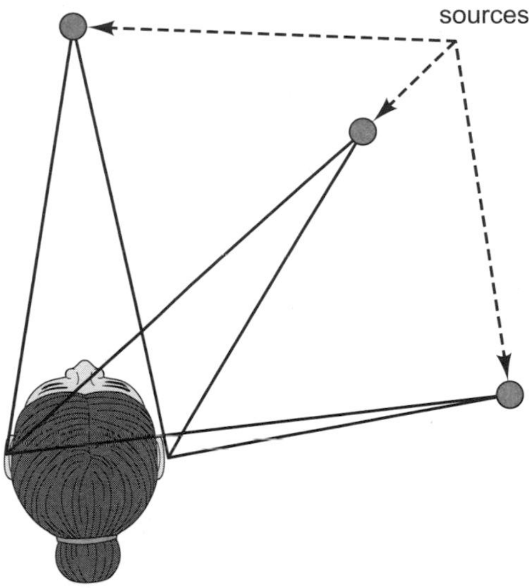

Older adults with presbycusis show a notable decrement in the ability to localize sound (Nordlund, 1964). This is not surprising because localization depends on accurate auditory sensations related to the time at which sounds arrive at the two ears and the intensity differences in sound. In fact, older adults who demonstrate good speech discrimination abilities also show normal sound localization, whereas those with poor speech discrimination show poor sound localization (Hausler, Colburn, & Marr, 1983).

Sound sources

Figure 9.10 Sound localization. The more a sound deviates from the straight-ahead position, the greater the time difference in the arrival of the sound at each ear.

Reprinted, by permission, from *A Primer of Infant Development* by T.G.R. Bower, 1977 (San Francisco: W.H. Freeman). Copyright 1977.

 Auditory acuity is not as good in infants as in adults; but since infants cannot reach distant objects or events on their own, their hearing is sufficient for their needs.

Differences

The perception of sound differences by children is often studied through discrimination tasks. For example, children are asked to distinguish two sounds similar in pitch, loudness, or speech sound, such as *d* and *t*, or *b* and *p*. Infants as young as 1 to 4 months can discriminate among basic speech sounds, such as *p*, *b*, and *m* (Doty, 1974), but children between 3 and 5 years old experience increasing accuracy in recognizing differences in sounds (DiSimoni, 1975). Temple et al. (1979) found a further improvement in auditory discrimination between 6 and 8 years, as did Birch (1976) between 7 and 10 years, with an auditory matching task. A similar trend apparently exists for discrimination of pitch (Kidd & Kidd, 1966). In general, it appears that by 8 to 10 years of age, children have greatly improved their ability to detect differences in similar sounds, but they continue to refine their auditory discrimination skills until they are at least 13.

If we could set aside age-related changes in pure-tone sensitivity, the deficits in speech recognition among older adults would be minimal (Helfer, 1992; Lutman, 1991; van Rooij & Plomp, 1992). Therefore, age deficits in speech perception are largely a function of decline in pure-tone sensitivity. Interestingly, older adults often make better use of context cues to help their recognition of speech than young adults do (Craig, Kim, Rhyner, & Chirillo, 1993; Holtzman, Familant, Deptula, & Hoyer, 1986).

Patterns

For speech and music to be more than just noises, individuals must perceive relationships among sounds. Of course, we perceive patterns in other senses. Visual pattern perception has long interested developmentalists, but only recently has auditory pattern perception received attention.

Auditory patterns are nonrandom, temporally (time) ordered sound sequences. Three properties of sound give rise to auditory patterns:

1. Time
2. Intensity
3. Frequency (Morrongiello, 1988a)

Speech and music have a temporal pattern, an intensity (loudness or softness) pattern, and a frequency (high pitch or low pitch) pattern simultaneously. Developmentalists usually study one characteristic at a time.

Infants as young as 2 to 3 months old react to changes in the temporal pattern of a tone sequence, showing that they perceive temporal patterns (Demany, McKenzie, & Vurpillot, 1977). Young infants, however, perceive only pattern changes involving the number of groups of tones (e.g., changing nine tones from three groups of three to two groups, one of five and one of four) (Morrongiello, 1984). At 12 months infants can perceive changes in the number of groups and the number of tones in each group (figure 9.11). Thus, by the end of the first year, infants can perceive sound on the basis of temporal pattern, which is probably a prerequisite for language development.

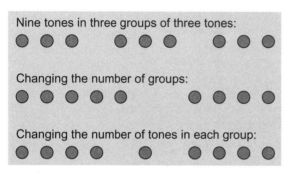

Figure 9.11 Auditory stimulus patterns presented to infants. Young infants can detect a change in the number of groups from what is familiar to them, but not until they are 12 months old can they detect changes in both the number of groups and the number of tones in a group. Time between tones in a group was 0.2 s and time between groups was 0.6 s.

Based on Morrongiello 1988a.

Infants between 5 and 11 months can discriminate intensity changes for vowels in a syllable (Bull, Eilers, & Oller, 1984), but we know little else about infants' intensity perception. Infants younger than 6 months can discriminate frequency relationships in a simple, short sequence. Not until the end of their first year, though, can infants perceive frequency relationships among the tones in a long, complex sequence (Morrongiello, 1986; Trehub, Bull, & Thorpe, 1984). The same is true of speech patterns. Children between 4 and 6 years of age can discriminate the frequency features of six-tone melodies played at normal speed (Morrongiello, Trehub, Thorpe, & Capodilupo, 1985). Infants progress rapidly in auditory pattern perception during their first year. These advances probably are prerequisites to language development. Preschool children make further progress in perceiving patterns in increasingly longer and more complex contexts.

What systems might limit the development of auditory pattern perception? Obviously, the auditory system must be developed. As mentioned earlier, auditory sensation is quite mature within days of birth. The sensory cortex of the brain, however, is still maturing rapidly over the first few years of life. With continuing development it probably permits conceptualization of patterns and of the identity of transformed patterns (Morrongiello, 1988a)—for example, the same rhythmic pattern played at different tempos. Cognition also must advance because to perceive patterns an individual must be able to remember and process information, especially long and complex sequences.

In addition, the environment in which infants develop might "tune" the developing auditory system to recognize certain features of language and music. In this way, we might learn to prefer the perceptual patterns prevalent in our native language and the music of our culture (Morrongiello, 1988a).

Auditory Figure and Ground

Often a person must attend to certain sounds while ignoring other irrelevant sounds in the background (figure and ground). For example, try listening to someone talk to you on the telephone (figure sounds) while your stereo is playing and several people in your room are talking (background sounds). Young infants can detect sounds amid ambient noise (Morrongiello & Clifton, 1984), but some children have more difficulty than others in separating auditory figures from the background. We would benefit from more research on the processes underlying these differences.

Older adults commonly report difficulty hearing in background noise (see Tun & Wingfield, 1993, for a review). It is possible that this reflects changes in the sensory system or parts of the neurological system related to hearing. It is also possible that this

? Why do driver training instructors emphasize playing an automobile radio or stereo at moderate levels?

reflects changes in attention mechanisms—that is, older adults might have more difficulty attending to a particular sound source amidst other sounds.

As noted previously, development of auditory perception is rapid. Not long after birth, infants can already perceive the location of and differences in sounds. An individual's ability to make fine discriminations improves in childhood. Perceptions of auditory events in the environment in adulthood are likely disturbed only when age-related changes in sensation affect detection of sounds.

Sensation, Perception, and Perceptual-Motor Development Summary

It is clear that some aspects of visual, kinesthetic, and auditory perception exist in infancy. Developmental trends continue throughout childhood, especially in the finer discriminations. By the time children are 8 to 12 years old, aspects of their visual perception have developed to near-adult levels. Kinesthetic perception typically develops to near-adult levels by about age 8, somewhat earlier than visual perception, although this generalization is based on limited research.

Young children can perceive the location of sound, and by age 10 they perform at near-adult levels on many auditory discrimination tasks. Refinement of auditory skills continues through the early teens. Some aspects of auditory perception have not been studied in children. In general, however, children between the ages of 8 and 12 approach adult levels of performance on many perceptual tasks, with only small refinements in perceptual skills yet to be made. Assessments of perceptual-motor development have been designed; educators and therapists sometimes screen young children for deficits in perceptual-motor development.

To observe the progress of a child in acquiring perceptual-motor skills, download Lab 9.1 Testing Perceptual-Motor Development from the Student Resources section at www.HumanKinetics.com/LifeSpanMotorDevelopment.

Some aspects of perceptual development are not well documented; further research is needed. In addition, little is known about what causes changes in perceptual processes as people age, but it is known that decremental changes in the sensory systems reduce the quality of the sensory information reaching the central nervous system, potentially affecting perception.

The perceptual systems do not operate in isolation of one another. To complete this discussion of perceptual development, the following section explores the issue of how information perceived in one sense, or modality, is related to that perceived in other modalities.

INTERMODAL PERCEPTION

Events occur in the environment and are often sensed and, therefore, perceived in different modalities, or senses. If while we are trying to open a jar, it slips from our hands, we feel it slipping, we see it falling, we hear it hit the floor and break, and we might even smell the released contents. This event can be perceived through vision, kinesthesis, and audition. Developmentalists have considered perception through different modalities from two very different perspectives. From the first, or integrational, perspective, the energy reaching the different senses is of different forms—light, sound, temperature, and so on. Each sensory system yields a unique sensation. The task of a developing infant would then be to learn how to integrate the separate systems, that is, to learn how those unique sensations are related to one another.

The second, or unified, perspective sees the senses as united in bringing information about events, but through different modalities. The perceptual systems extract patterns; many patterns are similar across the modalities. For example, events occur at a point in time, so the temporal properties of an event are not unique to any one modality. In a sense, these patterns are **amodal invariants.** We see a drummer strike a drum and we hear the drum's sound, but we also perceive the rhythmic pattern that existed across vision and audition. The central task of development would be to learn about events in the world with the information coming through various sensory systems (Kellman & Arterberry, 1998). Research in neurophysiology during the 1980s and 1990s lends some support to this unified perspective of intermodal perception. This research has identified areas of the brain containing neurons that receive input from different modalities (Stein, Meredith, & Wallace, 1994). This calls into question views of separateness among the sensory-perceptual systems.

The unified perspective is more consistent with the ecological perspective of perception and action. The integration perspective is more consistent with an information processing perspective. Earlier chapters acknowledged that much of the research on perception has been done from the information processing perspective. Keep this in mind as we review research in the following areas of intermodal perception:

▲ Auditory-visual

▲ Visual-kinesthetic

▲ Auditory-kinesthetic

▲ Spatial-temporal

Auditory-Visual Intermodal Perception

Newborn infants have been observed to move their eyes in the direction of a sound. Morrongiello, Fenwick, Hillier, and Chance (1994) played a 20 s recording of a rattle to newborns. They placed the loudspeaker at varying angles from the infant's midline. The farther the speaker from the midline, the farther the newborns turned their heads. The investigators also shifted the sound from one loudspeaker to another on some trials. The infants correspondingly adjusted their heads. Although this is a rudimentary response, it appears that even newborns seek to match their visual fixation to the spatial origin of a sound.

More challenging auditory-visual perceptions show a developmental trend in childhood. Goodnow (1971b) tapped out a sequence [* ***] and then asked children to write the sequence, using dots and spaces to picture where the taps occurred. She also reversed the auditory-visual (A-V) task by asking children to tap out a pictured sequence (V-A). Children around age 5 did not perform the A-V sequence as well as children at age 7. A trend toward improved performance on the V-A was also found in children between ages 6.9 and 8.5 years. The result of this and similar studies indicates that visual and auditory intermodal perception improves between ages 5 and 12 (Williams, 1983). Young children find A-V tasks more difficult than V-A tasks, but this difference diminishes after age 7 (Rudel & Teuber, 1971).

Visual-Kinesthetic Intermodal Perception

Visual-kinesthetic perception is the coordination between seen and felt properties of objects. Because infants do not reach for and manipulate objects before 4 to 5 months of age, the study of visual-kinesthetic (V-K) perception at young ages centers on mouthing of objects. Meltzoff and Borton (1979) found that 1-month-olds looked longer at the

Amodal invariants are patterns in space or time that do not differ across the sensory-perceptual modalities.

One view emphasizes the development of infants' abilities to integrate separate perceptual systems. The other emphasizes the perception of patterns about an environment unified across the systems.

Newborns link visual and auditory events, and children improve in finer visual-auditory intermodal discriminations.

type of pacifier that they had mouthed but had not seen, either one that was a cube with nubs or one that was a smooth sphere. At some level, then, infants relate oral and visual information.

Visual-kinesthetic perception involving manipulation of objects has been explored at later stages of infancy. Research study outcomes have been variable. Goodnow (1971a) studied visual and kinesthetic integration in children. She presented five shapes (Greek and Russian letters) by either sight or feel to three age groups (5.0- to 5.5-year-olds, 5.6- to 6.8-year-olds, and 9.0- to 10.0-year-olds). She then presented these five shapes along with five new ones, again by sight or feel, and challenged the children to identify the familiar shapes. Four presentation patterns were possible:

1. Visual presentation–visual recognition (V-V)
2. Kinesthetic presentation–kinesthetic recognition (K-K)
3. Visual presentation–kinesthetic recognition (V-K)
4. Kinesthetic presentation–visual recognition (K-V)

Goodnow found that children, especially the youngest ones, had more difficulty in the K-K pattern than in the V-V pattern. This performance discrepancy narrowed in the older age groups. The K-V task proved more difficult for the children than the V-K task. Goodnow noted that the scores of the youngest group in the kinesthetic conditions were extremely variable. This study and others, using similar tasks and different age groups, lead us to the conclusion that there is a developmental trend in visual-kinesthetic intermodal perception during childhood. When the kinesthetic task involves active manipulation of an object, 5-year-olds can recognize the shapes relatively well, but slight improvement continues until age 8. If passive movements are involved, performance is not as advanced, and improvements continue through age 11 (Williams, 1983).

Children have more difficulty in intermodal perception if their initial exposure is through the kinesthetic system.

Auditory-Kinesthetic Intermodal Perception

The amount of research conducted on auditory-kinesthetic integration is small compared with the amount involving vision. Temple et al. (1979) included the Witeba Test of Auditory-Tactile Integration in a test battery administered to 6- and 8-year-olds. In this test, an experimenter twice tells a child the name of an object or shape. The child then feels a number of objects or shapes, attempting to select the one that matches the auditory label. The investigators found that 8-year-olds performed this task much better than 6-year-olds.

This experimental method is based on children understanding the label given to the object or shape. Possibly, this age difference resulted from younger children's misunderstanding or not remembering the auditory label in addition to, or instead of, their auditory-kinesthetic intermodal perception. With this limitation in mind, we can conclude that auditory-kinesthetic integration improves in childhood.

Spatial-Temporal Intermodal Perception

Recall that we earlier discussed amodal invariants. Space and time are examples of the patterns that might be invariant across modalities. For example, in Goodnow's experiment, when children viewed the dot pattern, they were dealing with a spatial stimulus, the arrangement of dots in space. When they listened to an auditory pattern, they were attending to a temporal (time) stimulus. They were perceiving, then, a pattern that crossed space and time as well as vision and audition.

Sterritt, Martin, and Rudnick (1971) devised nine tasks that varied the number of perceptual integrations to be made as well as the type of integration, including spatial-temporal characteristics—for example, a child must integrate a short pause between two tones (temporal) with a short space between two dots (spatial). They presented the nine tasks to 6-year-olds. The easiest task for the children was the V-V spatial (intramodality) task. Children had some difficulty with those tasks requiring them to integrate visual-spatial stimuli and visual- or auditory-temporal stimuli. They had more difficulty integrating two temporal patterns, whether the task was intra- or intermodal. While progressing in intermodal perception, then, children also improve their ability to integrate spatial and temporal stimuli as well as to integrate two sets of temporal stimuli.

 Temporal patterns are more difficult for children than spatial patterns to integrate.

Difficult or subtle aspects of intermodal perception might continue to develop during adolescence. Intermodal perception most likely is stable in adulthood and older adulthood. Any decrements are probably a function of changes in the sensory-perceptual systems, changes that affect the amount of information available. For example, if cataracts cause a viewer to miss seeing the details of an object, the visual information for an integration may not be available. On the other hand, older adults might be able to use their experience as a compensatory mechanism, with information from one modality being used to compensate for information not available in another because of age-related change in the sensory or neurological systems. Certainly, more research on this topic is needed.

Intermodal Development Summary

Intermodal coordination begins at birth, but there appears to be a developmental trend in childhood and adolescence on tasks that involve matching and subtle aspects of integration. The accuracy of children's performance is related to the order of presentation. That is, presenting the visual pattern or object first yields better performance than auditory-first presentation. Also, children first master spatial-spatial integration tasks, followed by mixed spatial and temporal tasks, and finally temporal-temporal tasks.

To observe children matching objects through perceived vision and kinesthesis, download Lab 9.2 Development of Intermodal Perception from the Student Resources section at www.HumanKinetics.com/LifeSpanMotorDevelopment.

Summary and Synthesis

The visual, kinesthetic, and auditory systems function at birth and continue to improve throughout infancy and childhood. The level of function in infancy appears adequate for the learning tasks facing infants, and the rate of improvement seems consistent with the learning tasks facing toddlers. By late childhood the senses function at levels similar to those of adults. Detecting stimuli, though, is not the same as knowing what the stimuli mean—sensation is not the same as perception. In the following chapter we consider the advancement of perception and perceptual-motor behavior.

With aging there is change in the sensory systems, although we know more about the changes in vision than those in kinesthesis or audition. Decrements tend to vary widely among older adults. Compensation for some of these losses is possible. For example, seniors can wear eyeglasses or hearing aids. Conditions that accentuate differences are also helpful to older adults. Examples include the provision of good lighting and the reduction of background noise. Of course, a decrement in sensation can mean difficulty in perception, so just as with the early portion of the life span, it is important to study age-related change in perception.

Traditionally, much of the study of perceptual and perceptual-motor development has focused on the changing capacity of each individual system regardless of the environment. Even study of how the perceptual systems put together information received by each system about the same object or event assumed integration was a step that followed perceptual processing. More ecological views of perception have been around for some time, but the difficulty of studying a perceptual system and the environment as an eco-system has limited the data available to inform this perspective.

The model of constraints we are using throughout our discussion of motor development stresses interactions. Thus, the ecological viewpoint is a better fit with our model of constraints. If we extend the ecological viewpoint a step further, "perceptual" and "motor" or "perception–action" become inseparable. Each continually informs the other so that there is a continuous interaction of perceiving the world and moving in it. As the final part of this discussion of perceptual-motor development, the following chapter explores perception–action from this viewpoint.

Discussion Questions

1. Discuss the changes in visual sensation that occur during infancy and then during childhood.

2. Describe how humans perceive depth in the space around them.

3. Describe the various aspects of visual object perception.

4. Discuss the changes in kinesthetic sensation that occur during infancy and then during childhood.

5. Discuss the various aspects of kinesthetic perception and at what age each likely reaches near-adult levels.

6. Discuss the changes in auditory sensation that occur during infancy and then during childhood.

7. Describe the various aspects of auditory perception and what information about the sound source each provides.

8. Describe the changes that occur in the visual, kinesthetic, and auditory receptors in older adulthood.

9. Describe the typical method for studying intermodal perception.

10. What are amodal invariants?

Learning Activities

Limited Sensation

We can gain an appreciation of the information that comes to us through our sensory-perceptual systems by artificially limiting that information. Working with a partner, try these activities:

▲ Play catch in an old pair of sunglasses with one lens taped over.

▲ Walk the hallway blindfolded (with your partner guiding you for safety).

▲ Facing away from your partner, carry on a conversation while wearing a pair of earplugs as your partner slowly increases the distance between the two of you.

Afterward, discuss what tasks were difficult or impossible and what the implications would be for daily living in attending a university, driving a car, and playing intramural sports.

Perception and Action in Development

chapter 10

SHOULD YOU REDSHIRT YOUR KINDERGARTENER?

Read a promotion for a television segment of the *Today Show*. The term *redshirt* was borrowed from a practice in athletics in which college freshmen are held out of athletic participation for a year to give them additional time to grow and mature. The practice has been particularly popular in sports such as football. The television segment examined the practice of parents delaying the start of children in kindergarten for a year, especially if they were among the younger children to start in a given year. Parents have always been concerned about the readiness of their children to start school. They want their children to reach a maturity level that will enable them to have success in school once they start rather than risk their being behind the majority of their classmates.

This concern of parents has encouraged some individuals to offer special programs, claiming that participation in the programs develops the perceptual skills necessary for classroom success. Certainly, success in the classroom depends on a level of perceptual development. At times, the readiness programs promoted to parents have emphasized perceptual-motor development. So far, this text has emphasized the sensory and perceptual systems used in motor skills. But, might movement actually play a significant role in the development of sensory-perceptual systems? Are the two, perception and movement, more tightly coupled than our discussion has thus far acknowledged? Certainly there are those who believe so, although a variety of views exist on the exact nature of the relationship.

This chapter discusses the interrelationship between perception and movement actions. It begins with the notion that movement has a role in, and perhaps is even necessary for, perceptual development. This is followed by an examination of an aspect of everyday life in which perception and action are linked—maintenance of posture and balance.

 Chapter Objectives

This chapter will

- ▲ review the various historical perspectives on the role of action in perceptual development,

- ▲ survey the contemporary views on perceptual-motor programs and the linkages among the cognitive, perceptual, and motor systems,

- ▲ examine the differences in perception between infants with and without experience in self-produced locomotion, and

- ▲ study the interaction between perception and action in maintaining balance after infancy.

THE ROLE OF ACTION IN PERCEPTION

Developmentalists have long suspected that movement is extremely important to the development of perception. That is, they suspect movement through the environment is vital to the coupling of perceptions and purposeful movements in the environment. The exact role of motor activity in the development of perception is difficult for researchers to study. The ideal experiment on this topic, of course, would be to deprive some individuals of movement and compare them with others who were allowed to move through the environment. Since this isn't possible, our information must come from animal studies and other research situations in which movement experiences vary through naturally occurring circumstances.

Historical Views

The exact nature of the perception–action link, especially in the early years, is so elusive that it has spawned controversies among developmentalists. Around the 1960s a number of individuals proposed perceptual-motor theories, screening tools, and remedial programs. Many of these developmentalists were interested in perceptual-motor activity because they realized that perceptual development was as important to the development of cognition as to the development of skilled movement. For example, individuals must perceive the difference in spatial orientation between a circle and a line when they are arranged to form the letter *d* and when they are arranged to form the letter *b*. If an individual can't perceive this difference, reading is difficult. So, some earlier developmentalists saw perception as a precursor to both movement and cognition and proposed that children with learning disabilities had perceptual development deficits. Further, they hypothesized that deficits could be remediated by perceptual-motor activity programs. By practicing to improve perceptual-motor responses, children would overcome perceptual deficiencies, and cognitive activities reliant on perception would benefit as much as motor activities.

Among the more popular theories in the mid-20th century were the neurological organization theory of Delacato (1959, 1966); the physiological optics program of Getman (1952, 1963); the visual perception tests and program of Frostig, Lefever, and Whittlesey (1966); the sensory-integration tests of Ayres (1972); the movigenics theory of Barsch (1965); and the perceptual-motor theory of Kephart (1971). Early on there appeared to be support for these theories and programs. Children placed in the remedial programs showed improved classroom performance. The evaluations of these programs, though, were often flawed because they did not account for other factors that could contribute to improvement, such as the increased attention children received in the remedial programs. Eventually sufficient information from well-designed evaluations failed to show improvements in readiness skills, intelligence, classroom achievement, or language from participation in a perceptual-motor program (Goodman & Hamill, 1973). Perceptual-motor programs did help in the development of motor skills.

Piaget (1952) also recognized the importance of movement. He proposed that reality is constructed by relating action to sensory information in well-defined developmental stages during infancy, childhood, and adolescence. For Piaget, neither perception nor action is well organized in infancy.

Contemporary Views

Today, educators and therapists are reluctant to claim that participation in a perceptual-motor program can remediate learning deficiencies. Yet, they realize that such participation is beneficial to both normally developing children and exceptional children. Perceptual-motor programs at least provide valuable experience in performing skills based on key perceptual characteristics of a task. As such, they can contribute to a positive outlook on one's ability to perform. Perceptual-motor activities also can reinforce concepts needed for motor and cognitive tasks, such as shapes and directions. Most current physical education curricula for young children devote significant time to perceptual-motor activities. In addition, supplemental perceptual-motor programs frequently are offered to special groups.

Let's consider the nature of perceptual-motor programs first and then consider some contemporary views on the linkages among perception, cognition, and motor activity (action). Perceptual-motor programs can be comprehensive, or they can focus on certain aspects of perception. They also can be designed for young children at large, for groups with a characteristic deficiency, or for individuals based on their particular deficits. This variability among perceptual-motor programs is illustrated in table 10.1. Parents and educators alike must be "critical consumers" in assessing the value of any program and its claim for success. Until we understand more about the linkages among perception, cognition, and action, the most realistic claims are those focused on the development of motor skills; the best programs do not advocate a single approach to the exclusion of others.

Scanning techniques that allow imaging of the brain and its specific areas are giving rise to new viewpoints. Diamond (2000) reviewed newer evidence of brain function and development to suggest that motor development and cognitive development may

TABLE 10.1 Stated Features of Various Contemporary Perceptual-Motor Programs

Factor	Typical features
Purpose of the program	Develops the ability to remember patterns of movement, sequences of sounds, and the look and feel of objects via training of the nervous system
	Enhances brain development by stimulating the five senses through movement
	Helps children become efficient movers and enhances learning readiness
	Develops gross motor skills and fine motor skills
	Improves self-esteem through success at play
	Replicates early movement experiences required to establish "wiring" of the brain
Intended participants	Preschool and primary children
	Preschool children with speech and motor development delays
	Normally developing 2-, 3-, and 4-yr-olds
	Special needs students
	Children with neurodevelopmental delays (learning difficulties, attention disorders, behavior problems)
Instructors	Teachers
	Professional preparation students
	Physiotherapists
	Occupational and speech therapists
Context	Regular school offering
	Fee-based weekend programs
	Fee-based after-school programs
Location	Preschool
	Elementary school
	University
	Clinic
Activities	Gross motor skills
	Fine motor skills
	Swimming skills
	Rhythmic skills
	Visual-spatial skills (tracking objects, matching shapes)
	Ocular control activities (converging, tracking, fixating)
	Eye–hand coordination activities
	Eye–foot coordination activities
	Crossing the midline of the body
	Body awareness activities
	Spatial awareness activities
	Establishment of a preferred hand
	Balance activities
	Directionality activities
	Laterality activities
	Localizing touch
	Body concept activities
	Body image activities
	Clapping to rhythms
	Recognizing sound rhythms and patterns
	Locating a sound source
	Musical games
	Auditory discrimination and figure-and-ground activities

be more interrelated than previously thought, even to the extent of being fundamentally intertwined. She pointed to the following findings:

▲ The prolonged development of the prefrontal cortex (involved in complex cognitive operations) has been emphasized, but the development of the cerebellum (involved in motor functions), which is also prolonged, has not (see figure 4.11 on p. 60).

▲ Similarly, although many complex cognitive skills are recognized as developing into adolescence, it is overlooked that many complex motor skills also develop into adolescence.

▲ Functional neuroimaging has demonstrated that both the dorsolateral area of the prefrontal cortex and the neocerebellum in the contralateral hemisphere are coactivated during performance of cognitive tasks.

▲ Similar task characteristics activate both of these areas, such as difficult (rather than easy) cognitive tasks; a new task; or a task requiring a quick response, concentration, or greater memory demands.

▲ The prefrontal cortex may play a role in motor activity through connections with the cortical and subcortical areas important in motor control.

▲ The caudate nucleus in the basal ganglia (important in movement control) and dopamine, a neurotransmitter, are involved in neural circuits of both motor and cognitive functions.

▲ About half of the children with attention-deficit/hyperactivity disorder (ADHD) have motor coordination problems, and some studies report they have smaller cerebella.

▲ Children with dyslexia or specific language disorders frequently have motor deficits.

▲ Autistic children frequently have motor impairments.

All of these observations indicate greater interdependence of the brain in cognitive and motor tasks than previously emphasized. Ivry and Keele (Ivry, 1993; Ivry & Keele, 1989; Keele & Ivry, 1990) also proposed that the lateral hemispheres of the cerebellum are involved in critical timing functions key to sensory, cognitive, and motor tasks. It is interesting to note that dyslexic children have difficulty with bimanual tasks requiring timing precision (Wolff, Michel, Ovrut, & Drake, 1990). Several contemporary educators report success in promoting "active learning" for both normally developing and exceptional learners. Active learning is the notion that movement activates the brain and facilitates learning, as opposed to learning environments characterizing the learner as a passive absorber (Hannaford, 1995; Jackson, 1993, 1995, 2000). Finally, Sibley and Etnier (2003) conducted a meta-analysis of studies on the relationship between physical activity and cognition in children. These studies included a variety of physical activities and a variety of cognitive assessments. A significant positive relationship was found between physical activity and cognitive functioning, with the largest effects for cognitive assessment seen specifically with perceptual skills tests.

Motor development and cognitive development may be fundamentally intertwined.

It is important to recognize that motor development and cognitive development, even with their common link to perceptual development, have been studied separately for decades if not centuries. They have been treated as separate and distinct systems. Our thinking has been colored by this approach. Momentum is building to approach the study of the cognitive, perceptual, and motor systems in more integrated ways. Hopefully, this will allow us to one day better understand the nature of the linkages among them.

For now, the ecological view of development embraces the notion of a close link between perception and action (Kellman & Arterberry, 1998). Ecological developmentalists see the task of starting with very little perception and poor motor control and matching them through trial and error as too monumental for infants to achieve in a matter of months. Instead, the ecological view holds that the newborn infant perceives the environment and many of its properties before the onset of purposeful movements. Thus, the infant has a somewhat limited perception, this perception guides a movement, additional perceptions are generated, and the cycle is repeated with the infant eventually refining perception. This is termed a perception–action loop (Gibson, 1966, 1979). The difficulty with this view is that we don't observe behaviors among infants that appear to be perception–action loops. Whether we have not found a way to measure the behavior or these loops do not exist, developmentalists do not yet know.

Thinking back to our discussion of recent research in perceptual development, a slightly different view emerges. Perception develops ahead of movement skills. In infancy, new motor skills are acquired with guidance from the information obtained through perception. New actions in turn make new information available, and perceptual exploration is further refined (Kellman & Arterberry, 1998; von Hofsten, 1990). With this current perspective in mind, we now examine self-produced locomotion and its role in the refinement of perceptual abilities.

Self-Produced Locomotion

If action facilitates perceptual development, some types of perception would be evident only after an infant has begun performing the action. Researchers typically have observed perception in infants of the same age but with varying locomotor experience. As mentioned earlier, researchers must use research paradigms in which experience varies naturally or use animal studies in which they can control conditions. In 1963, Held and Hein studied early motor activity in kittens. These researchers deprived some newborn kittens of motor activity while permitting others to move. They kept the visual experience identical for all the kittens by placing them in pairs in a merry-go-round apparatus. One of the pair was harnessed but could walk around (active kitten) whereas the other was restricted to riding in a gondola (passive kitten; figure 10.1). The passive kittens later failed to accurately judge depth and failed to exhibit paw placing or eye blinking when an object approached. Evidently, in animals self-produced movement is related to the development of behavior requiring visual perception. There is also evidence of more brain growth and more efficient nervous system functioning in young animals when researchers provided them with extra perceptual-motor stimulation (Williams, 1986).

The visual cliff studies described in chapter 9 suggest that depth perception is present early in life. Other studies have suggested that avoidance of heights actually develops between 6 months and 1 year as a result of self-produced locomotor experience. Bertenthal, Campos, and Barrett (1984) found that prelocomotor infants given artificial locomotor experience by use of a baby walker (a seat in a frame on wheels) responded to heights, whereas other infants the same age but without this artificial locomotor experience did not. In addition, one infant whose locomotor skills were delayed as a result of a heavy cast did not respond to the visual cliff until self-produced locomotion began. Finally, many more infants who averaged 41 days of creeping experience avoided the visual cliff than infants with 11 days of experience, even at identical ages. Self-produced locomotion appears to facilitate development of depth perception.

Kermoian and Campos (1988) also investigated the link between infants' self-produced locomotion and their perception of spatial relationships by studying the infants' strategies in searching for objects. They gave infants a set of progressively more difficult searching tasks (called object permanence tasks), ranging from retrieving a half-hidden object to

----

Animal studies tend to support the notion that movement is necessary for normal perceptual development.

What might be the result for perceptual development if an infant with a disability could not walk? Could you design a way to compensate?

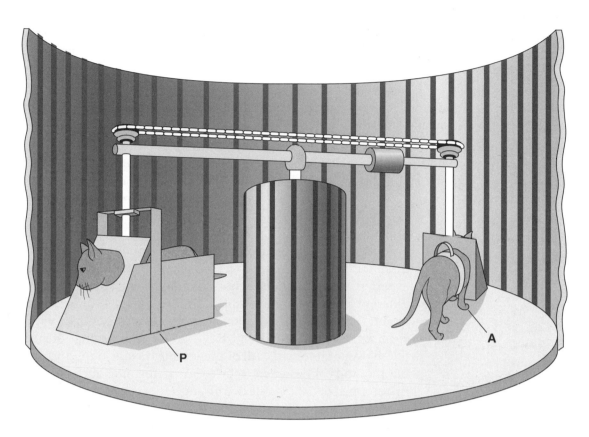

Figure 10.1 The apparatus Held and Hein used for equating motion and consequent visual feedback for an actively moving (**A**) and a passively moved (**P**) animal.

From R. Held and A. Hein, 1963, "Movement produced stimulation in the development of visually guided behavior," Journal of Comparative and Physiological Psychology 56: 872–876, fig. 1. Copyright © 1963 by the American Psychological Association. Reprinted with permission.

retrieving objects under one of several cloths after the passage of time. Three groups of 8.5-month-old infants performed the tasks:

1. Prelocomotor infants
2. Prelocomotor infants with walker experience
3. Locomotor (creeping) infants

The more locomotor experience infants had, the better they scored (figure 10.2). Other studies support the suggestion that locomotor experience facilitates development of **spatial perception.** Lockman (1984) found that a basic ability to detour around a barrier is present in 12-month-old infants. By testing infants longitudinally starting at age 8 months, Lockman identified a sequence of improvements in spatial perception:

▲ Infants first learn to retrieve an object hidden behind a cloth; they become aware that objects still exist even if they are hidden behind a barrier.

▲ Some weeks after developing this ability, infants can reach around a barrier to obtain their goal.

Spatial perception is the perception that enables one to deal effectively with spatial properties, dimensions, and distances of objects and object relations in the environment.

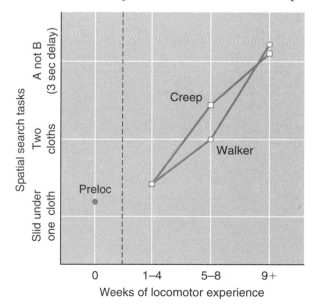

Figure 10.2 Performance on spatial search tasks improves with locomotor experience compared with no experience. No difference exists between infants whose locomotor experience comes from creeping (hands and knees) or from an infant walker. All infants, including the prelocomotor infants, were 8.5 months old.

Reprinted from Kermoian and Campos 1988.

▲ Infants can move themselves around a barrier to obtain their goal. On the average, several weeks pass between success in reaching around a barrier and success in traveling around it.

▲ Most infants can successfully detour around an opaque barrier before they can travel around a transparent barrier. Transparent barriers initially puzzle infants because visual and kinesthetic (tactile) cues conflict.

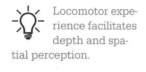 Locomotor experience facilitates depth and spatial perception.

Thus, infants are able to deal with spatial relationships at increasing distances from their bodies. McKenzie and Bigelow (1986) further demonstrated that infants become more efficient by taking the shortest path around a barrier (figure 10.3) and that they could better adapt to a relocated barrier by 14 months of age. Hence, with increasing movement experience in the environment, infants perceive spatial relationships even at a distance from their bodies.

Another line of research involves perception of surfaces. In these studies, researchers were interested in how locomotor experience influences the actions of infants when presented with different surfaces. For example, Gibson et al. (1987) presented infants with crawling experience and walking experience with a rigid surface (cloth over plywood) and a "deforming" surface (cloth over a waterbed). All of the infants traversed the surfaces, but the walkers hesitated to cross the deforming surface. They first stopped to explore the deforming surface, both by vision and touch, and eventually crossed the deforming surface by crawling. When presented the opportunity to cross either surface, rigid or deforming, the crawlers showed no preference, but the walkers chose the rigid surface.

Adolph, Eppler, and Gibson (1993) also noted that walkers were more sensitive than crawlers to surface slopes. Crawlers, with less locomotor experience, almost always attempted to crawl up and down slopes even if they were too steep for them. Walkers again tended to explore the surface by patting it with their hands or feet or by stepping onto the sloped surface and rocking back and forth over their ankles. All walked up slopes of 10, 20, 30, or 40 degrees. They often refused steep descending slopes or used another form of locomotion, such as crawling down backward. Thus, the walkers had enough experience with surface slopes

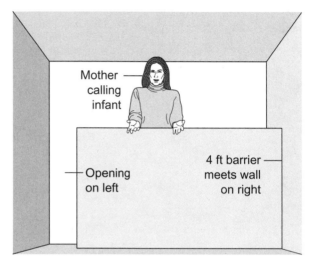

Infant's view

Figure 10.3 Room layout for a detour task. Infants can take the most efficient route around a barrier to their mothers (whom they can see over the barrier) by 14 months of age. By this age they also can adapt when the barrier is relocated against the left wall. Younger infants usually take less efficient routes, such as approaching the barrier, then traveling along it, sometimes turning the wrong way and backtracking, or going to where the opening was before barrier relocation.

 Locomotor experience facilitates surface texture and slope perception.

that they could immediately perceive which slopes did not afford walking. They quickly chose another form of locomotion appropriate for the surface slope.

Perception of Affordances

Recall that the ecological view of perception and action is based on direct perception of the environment rather than indirect perception. Indirect perception is derived from an assessment of environmental characteristics, cognitive calculations, and projections based on those characteristics. Consistent with the notion of direct perception, developmentalists with an ecological perspective (ecologists) believe that we directly perceive what the objects and surfaces in the environment permit us, given our own capabilities. That is, we perceive **affordances.**

Affordances are the actions or behaviors provided or permitted an actor by the places, objects, and events in and of an environment.

Stair climbing provides a good example of an affordance. A set of stairs with an 8 in. (20.3 cm) rise between steps does not afford an 18-month-old alternate-step climbing, as it does an adult. A 24 in. (61.0 cm) rise does not afford the average adult alternate-step climbing. As an individual grows and develops, her perception of affordances might change as her action capabilities change, even though an object's physical properties remain the same. Taking action, then, is a critically important aspect of development of the perception–action system. Interaction with the environment is valuable for the perception of affordances.

If we perceive affordances rather than object characteristics, as ecologists suggest, individuals must be sensitive to the scale of their bodies. In our stair-climbing example, perhaps individuals must be sensitive to their leg length to judge the "climbability" of any set of stairs. Warren (1984) tested this notion with adults and found that individuals perceived stairs with a riser height of more than 88 to 89% of their leg length to be "unclimbable" with alternate stepping. This model did not apply to older adults, whose affordances for stair climbing related more to strength and flexibility than to leg length (Konczak, Meuwssen, & Cress, 1988, cited in Konczak, 1990). Nor did the model apply to infants and toddlers. Infants in a study chose smaller step heights than toddlers (figure 10.4), but no anthropometric measurements related to the choice of step height (Ulrich, Thelen, & Niles, 1990).

 Think of the average home environment. What other objects or structures besides stairs do not afford infants certain actions? What about the elderly or those with a disability?

If we perceive affordances rather than object characteristics, the size of one's body in relation to environmental objects plays a role in that perception.

Figure 10.4 Infants might choose a set of steps depending on whether the step height affords them climbing. This in turn might depend on their body size; affordability is related to individual body scale. For example, the middle set of stairs might be too high to afford climbing by infants with short arms and legs. Either set of side stairs would afford infants climbing, and infants are as likely to choose one as the other. The researchers placed the same toys at the top of each set of steps as a motivation for climbing.

Photo provided by B.D. Ulrich of Indiana University.

Obviously, individuals may use many types of body scales, and the important scales may change throughout life. Perhaps changes in a person's various body systems influence which scale she or he uses. Our sensitivity to body scaling has implications for skill instruction. For example, if a child cannot swing a big, heavy adult-size tennis racket with one hand, the child cannot use adult technique in the sport. The large racket does not afford the adult style of movement. Either the racket must be scaled down to fit the child, or the child might need to use two hands to swing the racket. This helps us appreciate how important it is for those interested in motor development to understand the course of growth and aging. Continued research is necessary to determine the reference scales individuals use for particular tasks. This would help determine whether it is indeed the affordance that is perceived.

Affordances incorporate our body scale, our size relative to the environment.

Lockman (2000) suggested that infant tool use has its origins in perception–action routines repeatedly used by infants during the first year (figure 10.5). Through trial and error, infants gradually explore forms of tool use, relating objects to other objects and surfaces. In so doing, infants detect affordances. These are not affordances of individual tools, but affordances of the relationships between objects. This is in sharp contrast to the approach previously taken on infant tool use. In this prevailing perspective, tool use is assumed to be discontinuous, with the initial use of a tool reflecting a new level of representational thinking by the infant—an insight, so to speak. In the perception–action perspective, potential relationships between objects are detected from information directly perceived in the environment. Tool use depends on properties of both the tool and the surface or another object. So, trial-and-error tool use can be viewed as self-generated opportunity for perceptual learning (Lockman, 2000).

Figure 10.5 The ability to reach, grasp, and control objects such as blocks provides an infant the opportunity to explore relationships with and detect affordances of these objects.
© DigitalVisionOnline

 A neurological basis may exist for the necessity of movement experience to perceptual development.

Evidence indicates that movement facilitates continued perceptual development. Recall the earlier discussion of neurological development. Greenough, Black, and Wallace (1987) hypothesized that an excess number of synapses among neurons initially form. With continued development, some survive but others do not. Connections that are activated by sensory and motor experience survive; connections that are not used are lost. Synaptic proliferation prepares an organism for experiences, presumably the experiences common to all members of a species. Undergoing experiences during this sensitive period of development promotes survival of the synaptic connections.

These theories need more experimental verification, but they provide a plausible explanation for the role of action in perceptual development (Bertenthal & Campos, 1987). They also imply that deprivation of action experience puts an individual at risk of deficient perceptual development. Another way of looking at the interplay of perception and action is to examine the development of postural control and balance. Action must be coupled with perception so that individuals can deal with events or movements that disturb their posture and balance.

POSTURAL CONTROL AND BALANCE

Postural control and balance are perfect examples of perception and action as an ecosystem. To control our posture to sit, stand, or assume any desired position, we must continually change our motor response patterns according to the perceptual information that specifies the environment and our bodies' orientation in it. Several perceptual systems are involved in maintaining posture and balance. Vision tells us how our bodies are positioned relative to the environment. Kinesthetic input from our bodies' proprioceptors tells us how our limbs and body parts are positioned relative to each other. Kinesthetic input from the vestibular system provides information about our head position and movement. Even the auditory system can contribute information about balance (Horak & MacPherson, 1995).

We must maintain posture and balance in an almost infinite number of situations. Sometimes we balance when stationary (static balance) and sometimes when moving (dynamic balance). We must also sometimes balance on a variety of body parts, not just two feet. Think of all the body parts on which gymnasts must balance in their various events. Sometimes we need to balance on surfaces other than the ground, such as on a ladder. We might even have to balance without all the information we would like—for example, when we have to walk in the dark.

 The timing of developmental trends in balance is related to the type of balance task in consideration.

Given the number of perceptual systems involved in balance and the wide range of environmental and task constraints that are possible for any given balance task, the triangular model of constraints provides a good perspective on the development of balance. A developmental trend for a certain set of task and environmental constraints might differ from the trend for another set of constraints. In fact, movement scientists recognized some time ago that performance levels on various types of balancing tasks are specific to that task (Drowatzky & Zuccato, 1967). We discussed postural control and balance in infants earlier, in chapter 5. Now, let's consider the development of balance in childhood through older adulthood.

Balance in Childhood

Balance performance improves on a variety of balance tasks from 3 to 19 years of age (Bachman, 1961; DeOreo & Wade, 1971; Espenschade, 1947; Espenschade, Dable, & Schoendube, 1953; Seils, 1951; Winterhalter, 1974). The exact nature of the improvement trend depends on the task. For example, on some tasks we might see a plateau in performance for several years. This could reflect the way we measure improvement on that particular task. Perhaps the child is improving in a way not detected by our measurement. It is also possible that children begin to rely more on kinesthetic information and somewhat less on visual information for balance. Children 4 to 6 years old have been observed to regress on moving platform tests, and children 3 to 6 years have shown both adultlike and nonadultlike postural responses to a moving room (Schmuckler, 1997). They take longer to respond than younger children and vary greatly in the way they respond (i.e., in how the various muscles are activated to regain balance). Physical growth changes, such as changes in limb and trunk proportion and mass, do not seem to account for this, leading to the suspicion that shifts in reliance on different perceptual systems are involved (Woollacott, Debu, & Mowatt, 1987). By the time children reach the 7- to 10-year-old range, though, they show adultlike postural responses (Nougier, Bard, Fleury, & Teasdale, 1998; Woollacott, Shumway-Cook, & Williams, 1989; Shumway-Cook & Woollacott, 1985).

> As children grow, they rely more on kinesthetic information and less on visual information for balance.

Balancing during locomotion is a challenging task. When we walk or run, for example, we must maintain our stability yet propel the body forward in order to travel. To do so, we probably use two frames of reference. One is the supporting surface and the other is gravity. Another challenge is to control the degrees of freedom of movement at the various body joints. On the one hand, individuals might stabilize the head on the trunk to minimize the movement they must control. On the other hand, they might stabilize head position in space and use the orientation of the head and trunk to control their equilibrium.

Assaiante and Amblard (1995; Assaiante, 1998) proposed a model to explain the development of balance in locomotion over the life span. The model describes four important periods. The first covers birth to the onset of standing and is characterized by a cephalocaudal direction of muscle control. The second includes the achievement of upright stance to about 6 years of age. During this time, coordination of the lower and upper body must be mastered. The third period, from about age 7 to sometime in adolescence, is characterized by the refinement of head stabilization in balance control. The fourth and last period is reached in adulthood and is characterized by refined control of the degrees of freedom of movement in the neck. Thus, the task of childhood is to learn how the different frames of reference complement one another during movement. This is an intriguing model that may well stimulate future research on the development of dynamic balance.

> **?** Have you visited an amusement park attraction or "haunted house" that used visual displays to confuse your balance? How did the display do this?

Balance Changes With Aging

In adulthood, individuals standing on a force platform show a minimal amount of sway. If the platform is moved repetitively back and forth, adults use visual information to stabilize the head and upper body, the muscle response to movement occurring in the ankles (Buchanan & Horak, 1999). When adults stand on such a platform and it is moved slightly or slowly but unexpectedly, they use an ankle strategy to regain balance. That is, they use lower leg muscles that cross the ankle joint to bring themselves upright once again. When the movement is larger or faster, a hip strategy is used. Muscles crossing the hip and knee joints bring the center of gravity back over the base of support (Horak, Nashner, & Diener, 1990; Kuo & Zajac, 1993).

Older adults experience a decline in the ability to balance. Those over 60 sway more than younger adults when standing upright, especially if they are in a leaning position (Hasselkus & Shambes, 1975; Hellebrandt & Braun, 1939; Perrin, Jeandel, Perrin, & Bene, 1997; Sheldon, 1963). Age-related changes in balance also are seen with older adults on movable platform tests. Compared with young adults, slightly more time passes before an older adult's leg muscles respond after a perturbation to maintain balance, and sometimes the upper leg muscles respond first instead of the lower leg muscles, the opposite of the pattern in young adults. The strength of the muscles' response is more variable among repetitions in older adults (Perrin et al., 1997; Woollacott, Shumway-Cook, & Nashner, 1982, 1986).

Age-related changes in balance ability could be related to a variety of changes in the body's systems, especially in the nervous system. As mentioned previously, some older adults experience changes in the kinesthetic receptors, and these changes might be more extreme in the lower limbs than in the upper ones. Vision changes, as well as changes that occur in the vestibular receptors and nerves in adults over 75, might also place older adults at a disadvantage (Bergstrom, 1973; Johnsson & Hawkins, 1972; Rosenhall & Rubin, 1975). A decrease in fast-twitch muscle fibers or a loss of strength could hamper an older adult's quick response to changes in stability, as might arthritic conditions in the joints.

Perrin et al. (1997) recorded EMG activity in older adults during a backward tilt of a movable platform. They observed some of the reflexes in the lower legs that were not involved in balance control, as well as the responses necessary for regaining balance. By comparing the time from the balance perturbation with the onset of each of these muscle responses in young and older adults, the investigators determined that nerve conduction speed in both the peripheral and the central nervous system was slower in the older adults. Thus, the declines in balance performance with aging most likely are associated with age-related changes in a variety of systems.

Falls by older adults are a significant concern. In fact, falls are the leading cause of accidental death for people over 75 years old. A common result of falling, especially among older adults with osteoporosis, is fracture of the spine, hip (pelvis or femur), or wrist. Complications of such a fracture can result in death. Even when older adults recover, they experience heavy health care costs, a period of inactivity, and dependence on others. A fear of falling again can make them change their lifestyles or be overly cautious in subsequent activities.

Woollacott (1986) studied the reaction of older adults when a movable platform tipped forward or backward to perturb their balance unexpectedly. Half the older adults she observed lost their balance the first time, but these adults learned to keep their balance after a few more tries. Thus, older adults are more liable to fall on a slippery surface than young adults but are capable of improving their stability with practice. Campbell et al. (1997) compared the number of falls over a year in women over 80 years of age who participated in an individualized exercise program stressing strength and balance, and women over 80 who did not participate in an exercise program. The number of falls in the exercise group was significantly less: 88 falls versus 152 falls in the group that did not exercise. Prevention and rehabilitation programs, then, are useful in reducing the risk of falls in older adults.

▽☼— The difficulties older adults experience with balance probably reflect changes in a number of systems.

▽☼— Exercise programs focused on improving strength and balance can reduce the risk of falls in older adults.

? What types of surfaces and surface conditions could be riskier for an older adult than a young adult?

Summary and Synthesis

Perception and action are an ecosystem. Actions are coupled to perceptions, as shown by postural and balance responses. There is some disagreement about the exact role of action in the development of perception but little disagreement over its importance. Experience with movement has been shown to facilitate perception of space, including depth, surfaces, and slopes.

Perception–action coupling for posture and balance is evident in young infants. However, there does appear to be a developmental trend determining which perceptual system gets priority. Young infants depend more on visual information when it conflicts with kinesthetic information. With advancing development, this reverses. Older children, youths, and young adults, if placed in an environment in which vision and kinesthesis conflict, rarely fall. They have learned to rely more on kinesthetic information. Older adults show changes in their responses to balance perturbations. Although changes in the perceptual system could affect these responses, the changes seem to occur more in the timing and pattern of the muscle responses to perceptual information.

 ## Discussion Questions

1. What are some of the reasons that lead contemporary researchers to think that cognitive and motor development are more intertwined than previously thought?

2. What seems to be the role of experience in self-produced locomotion in the development of perception? Which aspects of perception are most affected?

3. Considering your answer to the preceding question, what would be the repercussions to perceptual and motor development of depriving an infant of locomotor experience?

4. How did views of perceptual-motor development change in the 20th century?

5. What changes in various body systems might lead to a higher frequency of falls in older adults?

 ## Learning Activities

Cognitive and Motor Deficits

Choose one of the following disorders: autism, dyslexia, or attention-deficit/hyperactivity disorder (ADHD). Research the characteristics of the disorder to determine whether both cognitive and motor deficits are common. Describe the specific characteristics of deficits in each area, cognitive and motor, if appropriate.

Functional Constraints to Motor Development

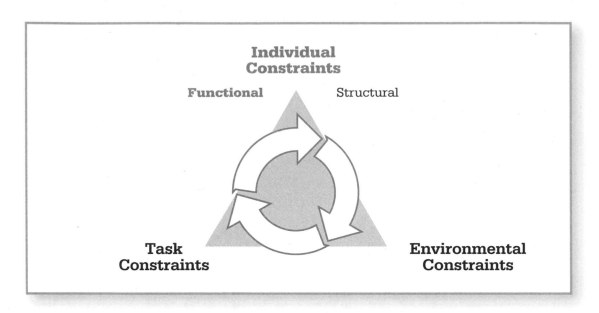

In this part, we focus on the effect of the sociocultural environment—for example, those constraints that exist as a function of family influences or cultural belief systems—on individual functional constraints. Functional constraints can include motivation, attitude, self-concept, perception of a gender role, and knowledge about a topic. Especially when working with children, we must wait for individual structural constraints to undergo change through growth and maturation. In contrast, the functional constraints can change more quickly. For example, a teacher could set a task goal that interacts with motivation to bring about a rather rapid change in motor behavior. Not all functional constraints change quickly, however. Self-concept is shaped over many years and is influenced by social interactions. Knowledge about a sport is often acquired over several years of experience in playing that sport.

There is a rich interaction of functional constraints and environmental constraints. For example, sociocultural norms strongly influence perceived gender roles, and one's perceived gender role in turn influences the types of physical activity one views as appropriate. Even the popularity of certain sports or dance forms in a culture can influence the knowledge someone living in that culture has about that sport or dance.

This part of the text examines functional constraints and the changes they undergo over the life span. Chapter 11 considers the role of society and culture in influencing individuals' choice of physical activities and play environments. Chapter 12 discusses how environmental constraints influence the functional constraints of self-esteem and motivation and how that interaction influences choices about physical activities. Chapter 13 explores how the amount of knowledge people acquire about a particular activity influences their play and participation in that activity.

Suggested Reading

Coakley, J. (2000). *Sport in society: Issues and controversies.* St. Louis: McGraw-Hill.

Giuliano, T., Popp, K., & Knight, J. (2000). Footballs versus Barbies: Childhood play activities as predictors of sport participation by women. *Sex Roles, 42,* 159–181.

Greendorfer, S.L. (1992). Sport socialization. In T.S. Horn (Ed.), *Advances in sport psychology* (pp. 201–218). Champaign, IL: Human Kinetics.

Heywood, L. (1998). *Pretty good for a girl.* New York: Free Press.

Lorber, J. (1994). Believing is seeing: Biology as ideology. *Gender & Society, 7,* 568–581.

Thomas, J.R., French, K.E., Thomas, K.T., & Gallagher, J.D. (1988). Children's knowledge development and sport performance. In F.L. Smoll, R.A. Magill, & M.J. Ash (Eds.), *Children in sport* (3rd ed., pp. 179–202). Champaign, IL: Human Kinetics.

Weiss, M.R., & Chamueton, N. (1992). Motivational orientations in sport. In T.S. Horn (Ed.), *Advances in sport psychology* (pp. 61–99). Champaign, IL: Human Kinetics.

chapter 11

Social and Cultural Constraints in Motor Development

The Effects of Environmental Constraints

EXTRA!!! The Times EXTRA!!!

GOING FOR THE TAKEDOWN!

Patricia Miranda: This Phi Beta Kappa from Stanford is heading for Yale Law School—after she goes for a gold medal in the first-ever women's Olympic wrestling competition.

"I am trying to do everything humanly possible an Olympic gold medallist could do to prepare"—including training on and off the mat up to eight hours a day. "In the end, all I can ask is, 'Did I hold myself accountable for my dream?'"

—*Newsweek, January 5, 2004*

For the first time in Olympic history, women have the opportunity to wrestle for gold, silver, or bronze medals. In 2004, women's wrestling became an official Olympic sport. The inclusion of wrestling in the 2004 Olympics in Athens, as well as women's ice hockey in 1998 and women's soccer in 1996, suggests a shift in social notions of what sports are acceptable for women (and men) to play. Society as a whole influences the activity choices individuals make; by officially sanctioning more sports for women, important institutions within our society inform us that the role of the female athlete is expanding. Girls and boys alike benefit from the addition of new athletic role models. When social or cultural factors influence the types of physical activities in which individuals get involved, those factors act as sociocultural constraints. You might not have considered sociocultural constraints as important to motor development. However, in this chapter, you will discover that these ever-present constraints can have a great influence on motor behavior throughout the life span. Just ask Patricia Miranda! She won a bronze medal in wrestling in the 2004 Olympic games.

The idea that social and cultural aspects can influence motor development may come as a surprise to a maturationist. If you believe that genetics determines development, then you would be hard pressed to think of society as a developmental agent. However, those who follow an ecological perspective believe that social and cultural influences (in the form of environmental constraints) may greatly influence and interact with individual and task constraints. Therefore, the influence of these types of constraints cannot be ignored. This means that the media coverage of events such as women's wrestling and ice hockey may encourage participation in these sports by women of all ages by changing some of the social and cultural stereotypes associated with females in sport.

 Chapter Objectives

This chapter will

- ▲ discuss the role of sociocultural constraints in motor development,
- ▲ define the role of specific social agents, such as parents and schools, on individual development, and
- ▲ explain the socialization process and how it differs for different groups.

SOCIAL AND CULTURAL INFLUENCES AS ENVIRONMENTAL CONSTRAINTS

In chapter 1, the idea of sociocultural influences as environmental constraints was introduced. That is, sociocultural attitudes of groups of people either encourage or discourage certain motor behaviors. These are considered environmental constraints because they reflect a general attitude or belief system present in society at large or within certain subcultures. If these attitudes are pervasive enough, they can modify someone's behavior. They may not be obvious at all, yet they may still exert a powerful influence on how individuals move. Just as temperature or ambient light can encompass a room, field, or community, so can attitudes, values, norms, or stereotypes. Even as late as the 1970s, girls were not expected to participate in some organized sports such as baseball and ice hockey. This attitude about girls in sport meant that the opportunity to play organized and even pickup sports was limited. In essence, this attitude discouraged sport participation for many girls, especially after puberty. However, the passage of Title IX (requiring equal opportunity for girls and women in sport) in 1972 drastically changed the face of sport in the United States, making it more possible and, in time, socially acceptable for girls and women to participate in sport.

Society and culture can have a profound effect on an individual's movement behaviors, particularly in the area of sport and physical activity (Clark, 1995). Sociocultural elements such as gender, race, religion, and national origin all can direct one's future movement behavior (Lindquist, Reynolds, & Goran, 1998). Even the media act to encourage and promote different types of physical activities (such as those that are gender specific) to mass audiences (Koivula, 2000; Wigmore, 1996; Messner, Duncan, & Jensen, 1993). A simple example will illustrate how sociocultural constraints work: Think of the American athlete you most admire. Most likely, you imagine a trim, muscular individual who plays a professional sport within the United States. However, if we asked this question of someone from Japan, he or she might picture Akebono, a popular Sumo wrestler born in Hawaii, who exemplifies superior physical ability in this 2,000-year-old sport (figure 11.1). Most Americans would not know Akebono. More important, within the context of motor development, most American children would not aspire to become Sumo wrestlers, and most American adults would not attempt to participate in Sumo wrestling, regardless of individual constraints such as body type (which may actually encourage participation in some cases). Sumo wrestling is not a socially or culturally encouraged sport within the United States. Thus, society and culture influence the choice of sport and physical activity in which one participates. The chances that a young boy or girl in America would pursue a career in Sumo wrestling are slim. As a result, an entire group of movements (those associated with Sumo wrestling) are discouraged and may never be performed; over time, this constraint interacts with individual constraints to limit or even eliminate these movements from emerging.

Societal and cultural beliefs, attitudes, and stereotypes can encourage or discourage motor behaviors. These are ever-present environmental constraints.

Figure 11.1 Akebono is considered one of the finest Sumo wrestlers in recent history.
© AP Photo/Chuck Stoody

SOCIETY AND SOCIALIZATION AS AN ENVIRONMENTAL CONSTRAINT

Participating in physical activities contributes to motor development. The benefits of experience in physical activity are well known, including improved physical and emotional health. In addition, sport may influence behavioral patterns of the participants (e.g., by

? What are some of the most important social and cultural elements (people, places, and so on) that have influenced you during your life? How have these changed from the time you were an infant to the present?

teaching leadership and other skills). Thus, it makes sense to provide opportunities for all people to participate in sport and physical activity from an early age throughout the life span. However, decisions to participate in sport or maintain a physically active lifestyle can have as much to do with social milieu as individual constraints. For example, most typically developing American children have individual constraints that allow them to participate in a wide variety of activities—yet many choose computer and video games and television over playing outdoors. Why?

An individual's early sport and physical activity socialization is a key factor in motor development and the likelihood of later participation. People and situations continue to influence individuals in their choice of activities throughout their lives. For example, your peers influence your recreational activities and lifestyle choices. These activities can be physical (pickup basketball vs. video game playing), academic (library vs. study group), and social (movies vs. bar hopping) among others. The **socialization process** as related to sport and physical activities, including the individuals who are influential in the process, deserves attention as a major environmental constraint on one's motor development.

The process by which one learns a social role within groups with certain values, morals, and rules is one's **socialization process**.

Three major elements of the socialization process lead an individual to learn a societal role, as shown in figure 11.2 (Greendorfer, 1992; Kenyon & McPherson, 1973):

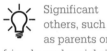

Significant others, such as parents or friends, and social situations, such as school or sports teams, contribute to an individual's socialization process.

1. **Significant others** (influential or important people, **socializing agents**)
2. **Social situations** (places socialization takes place—schools, home, playgrounds)
3. Individual constraints (personal attributes)

We examine the first two of these elements to see their influence and importance in the process of socialization into sport and physical activity. Of course, the third element, personal attributes, represents an interaction between environmental constraints (socializing agents and situations) and

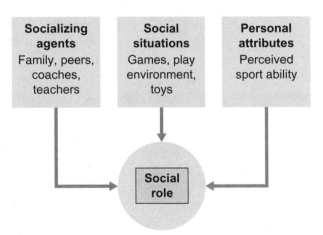

Figure 11.2 The three major elements of the socialization process that lead to the learning of a societal role for the participation in physical activity.
Based on Kenyon and McPherson 1973.

individual constraints. Among the socializing agents are family members, peers, teachers, and coaches. This section examines the different influences these people provide—and how they might encourage or discourage certain motor behaviors. First, however, we examine a cultural phenomenon that cuts across many contexts: gender typing in sport and physical activities.

Sociocultural Constraints in Action: Gender-Specific Stereotyped Behaviors

Sex refers to biological characteristics used to determine whether individuals are classified as male or female.

Gender refers to culturally defined sociological characteristics used to differentiate between males and females.

Significant others enter any context with socially and culturally prescribed notions of how they and others should act. Examination of one such notion, that of gender-specific stereotyping, can show how potent sociocultural constraints can be. In general, people are born physiologically either male or female; their biological characteristics determine their **sex**. In contrast, **gender** is a culturally determined sociological construct that differentiates between men ("masculine") and women ("feminine") (Eitzen & Sage, 1997).

Parents and other significant socializing agents often encourage children toward what they perceive as gender-appropriate behaviors, based on each child's biological characteristics (Lorber, 1994; Fagot & Leinbach, 1996; Fagot, Leinbach, & O'Boyle, 1992). In other words, significant others steer boys toward "masculine" and girls toward "feminine" activities. This practice is often termed **gender typing,** or gender-role stereotyping. In fact, children begin to learn these gender roles early, perhaps as early as their first year (Fagot & Leinbach, 1996).

Traditionally, Western societies gender-type participation in sport and physical activities. Certain sports are identified as masculine, such as football, baseball, and wrestling, and others are identified as feminine, such as figure skating, gymnastics, and field hockey. In addition, Westerners consider sport to be important and appropriate for boys; however, that attitude doesn't always carry through for girls. Therefore, adults often permit and encourage vigorous, outgoing, rough-and-tumble play for toddler boys, whereas they discourage girls from (or even punish them for) running, climbing, or venturing away from parents (McBride-Chang & Jacklin, 1993; Campbell & Eaton, 2000; DiPietro, 1981; Eaton & Enns, 1986; Eaton & Keats, 1982; Fagot & Leinbach, 1983; Lewis, 1972; Liss, 1983; Lloyd & Smith, 1985). Society reinforces constrained, sedentary types of play for girls, and thus many girls self-select away from vigorous play (Greendorfer, 1983). This leaves a comparatively small number of girls as active participants in vigorous, skilled play. Although the number of girls participating in high school sports has drastically increased since the inception of Title IX, only 63% as many girls participate as boys. Further, girls are more likely to drop out of sport and activity participation after high school.

Why is the issue of gender typing important for girls and boys? For girls, such limited involvement and practice may not allow them to develop their motor skills to their full potential. Even those girls who do participate may feel that all-out effort and skilled performance are gender inappropriate. This, in turn, could affect a girl's or woman's motivation for participating, for training, or for striving for high achievement standards that rival those of boys and men. At the same time, boys may be forced into participating in gender-appropriate sports they dislike. Worse yet, they may drop out of physical activity altogether rather than be subjected to participating in an undesired but gender-typed sport. Thus, this pervasive societal influence on boys' and girls' sport participation may factor into measurements of skill and fitness that compare the sexes. This is important to consider within the context of an integrated model of interacting constraints. What appear to be fitness or skill differences in boys and girls based on physiological makeup (sex) may in fact be related to a lifetime of stereotyped influences (gender) (Campbell & Eaton, 2000).

Despite a growing awareness during the 1970s and 1980s that these societal roles might limit girls' opportunities to enjoy the many benefits of sport participation, parents did not seem to change their contact patterns with their children. Research studies in the mid-1980s confirmed that parents still tend to interact differently with sons and daughters in play environments (Power, 1985; Power & Parke, 1983, 1986; see Williams, Goodman, & Green, 1985, on tomboys). For example, parents tend to direct their girls' play but allow boys more opportunities for independent, exploratory play (Power, 1985). Although many changes seemed to take place during the 1990s, research still indicates that boys and girls receive stereotypical messages about participation in physical activity (Eitzen & Sage, 1997; Coakly, 1998).

What happens to those girls who defy gender-role stereotypes? Giuliano, Popp, and Knight (2000) studied 84 Division III female college students, both athletes and nonathletes. They found that as children, the athletes tended to play with "masculine" toys and games, were considered tomboys, and played primarily with boys or mixed gender groups, whereas the nonathletes did not. This suggests that these early "masculine"

Gender typing, or gender-role stereotyping, occurs when a parent or significant other encourages activities that are deemed "gender appropriate."

experiences, rather than harm the females in any way, may have encouraged them to participate in athletics and physical activities throughout college—and perhaps beyond. Given the importance of a physically active lifestyle, this suggests that parents may wish to avoid rigid adherence to gender-typed behaviors for their daughters.

Significant Others: People's Values Acting As Constraints

Significant others, or **socializing agents,** are the people most likely to play a role in an individual's socialization process—family members, peers, teachers, and coaches (figure 11.3). People who act as socializing agents should be considered constraints because they will encourage or discourage certain motor behaviors. This section examines how each of these groups might influence participation in sport and physical activity.

The roles that parents, peers, teachers, or coaches play in the socialization of children can vary with the sex of a child. In addition, the gender of the person serving as a model for behavior may differentially influence the child's internalization of the behavior. The result of such socialization can constrain a child to very specific types of physical activities while virtually eliminating others.

> **Significant others,** or **socializing agents,** are family members, peers, teachers, coaches, and others who are involved in the socialization process of an individual.

Family Members

A person's family has a major influence in the process of socialization into physical activities as well as other pursuits in part because the family's influence begins so early in a child's life (Weiss & Barber, 1996; Kelly, 1974; Pargman, 1997; Snyder & Spreitzer, 1973, 1978). In fact, the family may be the only source of social interaction that an infant has—therefore the primary source of social constraints. From their very first interactions, family members expose their infants to certain experiences and attitudes. They reinforce the behaviors deemed appropriate through their gestures, praise, and rewards; at the same time, they punish inappropriate behaviors. The process is systematic, but at times it is so subtle that family members may hardly realize what and how they communicate to the infant.

Figure 11.3 Significant others such as parents have a strong influence on the socialization process in early childhood.

Parents When someone participates in physical activities after early childhood, he probably reflects his parents' interest and encouragement during the early years. Parents can encourage children to engage in either physical or sedentary activities. This may relate to the participation habits of the parent (DiLorenzo, Stucky-Ropp, VanderWal, & Gotham, 1998). As children become physically active, parents can encourage or discourage games and, eventually, specific sport or physical activities. Parents' early involvement could lead to a lifetime of participation in physical activities for a child (Weiss & Barber, 1996). About 75% of eventual sport participants become involved in sport by age 8 (Greendorfer, 1979; Snyder & Spreitzer, 1976). In fact, the best predictor of adult sport involvement is participation during childhood and adolescence (Greendorfer, 1979; Loy, McPherson, & Kenyon, 1978; Snyder & Spreitzer, 1976). It follows then that a parent's early bias toward or away from physical activities can have lasting consequences.

Each parent might play different roles in socializing children into physical activity. Snyder and Spreitzer (1973) proposed that a child's same-sex parent is most influential in the extent of that child's sport involvement. Further, McPherson (1978) suggested specifically that mothers serve as sport role models for their daughters. This notion was supported by DiLorenzo et al. (1998), who found that for eighth- and ninth-grade girls, their mothers' physical activity and support were predictors for physical activity. Some researchers believe that fathers more strictly reinforce gender-appropriate behavior, which would include sport participation for boys (Lewko & Greendorfer, 1988). Greendorfer and Lewko (1978) identified fathers rather than mothers as a major influence in the sport involvement of both boys and girls. In contrast, Lewko and Ewing (1980) found that fathers influenced boys between the ages of 9 and 11 who were highly involved in sport and that mothers influenced highly involved girls. A difference between girls and boys, however, was that to become involved, girls seemed to need a higher level of encouragement from their families than boys did, and they needed it from many members of the family. A similar pattern was found in Japanese children (Ebihara, Ikeda, & Miyashita, 1983). Although the research does not definitively indicate a differential role for mothers and fathers, parents clearly influence and affect the choices their children make in physical activities.

During the 1980s and 1990s, girls' and women's participation in sport and physical activity became more recognized and widespread. Furthermore, it has become far more socially acceptable for women to participate in sports that have been male gender typed in the past, such as soccer and ice hockey. Sport leagues for both genders have begun to include divisions for adults of different ages and skill levels, reflecting an increased interest in sport past high school and college. In addition, more opportunities exist for women and men to participate in nonsport physical activities ranging from spinning to step aerobics to cardio kickboxing. This increase in both types and opportunities of activities for parents will likely have a positive effect on the socialization of children into physical activity.

Siblings Siblings form an infant's first playgroup and thus may act as important socialization agents into physical activity. For example, both brothers (Weiss & Knoppers, 1982) and sisters (Lewko & Ewing, 1980) can influence girls' sport participation. Recent studies suggest that African-American boys see athletes as their role models and that their male siblings shape their idea of a role model (Assibey-Mensah, 1998). On the other hand, some children and teens report that older siblings were not important in their sport involvement (Greendorfer & Lewko, 1978; Patriksson, 1981). It is possible that for most children, siblings merely reinforce the socialization pattern into physical activity established by parents rather than act as a major socializing force (Lewko & Greendorfer, 1988).

How Do Race, Ethnicity, and Other Factors Affect the Role of the Family in Physical Activity Socialization? Various investigators reached different conclusions about the influence of family members on socialization into physical activity. Greendorfer and Lewko (1978) attempted to clarify these various conclusions by questioning children from a broad range of social backgrounds. They found some differences in the patterns of significant influences. The significant other who exerted the most influence on socialization into physical activity varied somewhat among children according to sex, social background, race, and geographic location. For example, fathers were influential in socializing Caucasian-American but not African-American boys into sport (Greendorfer & Ewing, 1981). In contrast, Lindquist et al. (1998) found few differences in children's physical activity based on ethnicity when they controlled for social class and family background. This suggests that the role of race, ethnicity, social background, and other factors in family socialization is more complex and difficult to characterize on a group basis. In fact, this complexity supports our notion of motor development: Socially and culturally specific agents constrain motor behaviors of individuals in different ways, leading to the emergence of different motor behaviors. We should not generalize about social agents but rather keep in mind that diverse patterns of influence may exist.

Peers

A child's peers have the potential to reinforce the sport socialization process begun in the family (Bigelow, Tesson, & Lewko, 1996; Weiss & Barber, 1996; Brown et al., 1990; Greendorfer & Lewko, 1978). If a peer group tends to participate in active play or sport, individual members are drawn to such activities. If the group prefers passive activities, individual members tend to follow that lead. Adult athletes typically report that peer groups or friends influenced the extent of their sport participation when they were in school, although the strength of this influence varies among sports. The first peer group a child encounters is typically a playgroup. Children become involved in such groups when they are about 3 to 4 years old and continue in them during their early school years.

Boys and girls from several countries, including the United States, Japan, and Canada, report that peers influenced their childhood sport participation (Ebihara et al., 1983; Greendorfer & Ewing, 1981; Greendorfer & Lewko, 1978; Yamaguchi, 1984). During preadolescence, children enter more formalized peer groups, such as cliques or gangs. These peers continue to be influential during adolescence (Patrick et al., 1999; Weiss & Barber, 1996; Brown et al., 1990; Brown, 1985; Butcher, 1983, 1985; Higginson, 1985; Patriksson, 1981; Schellenberger, 1981; Smith, 1979; Yamaguchi, 1984). In fact, among the women she questioned, Greendorfer (1976) found that the peer group was the only socializing agent that influenced sport involvement throughout all phases of the life cycle studied: childhood, adolescence, and young adulthood. Other socializing agents were important at some ages but not at others. For example, the family, so important to young children, probably is less influential to adolescents.

Peers often provide a stronger influence for participation in team sports than for participation in individual sports during childhood and adolescence (Kenyon & McPherson, 1973). Children's and adolescents' supportive peer groups are usually made up of others of the same sex as the participant. For adults, especially women, and particularly after marriage, spouses and friends of the opposite sex become more influential in either encouraging or discouraging involvement in certain activities (Loy et al., 1978). As individuals leave school and enter new social environments as members of the workforce, they often leave their peer groups. If a peer group was sport oriented, a reduction in sport involvement might follow. New peer groups at the workplace, on the other hand, could stimulate sport involvement; the individual may join a team in a recreational sport league or perhaps participate in company-sponsored exercise and recreational programs (Loy et al., 1978).

It is likely that the typical middle-aged adult, even one who was involved in sport as a young adult, reduces sport involvement. A recent study by Ebrahim and Rowland (1996) found that of the 704 women (ages 44–93 years) they studied, only 25% took part in vigorous activity during the week before the study. This trend might be due in part to a lack of programs aimed specifically at middle-aged and older adults, although this has been changing during the 1990s. The emphasis on fitness that began in the late 1970s has led to a greater availability of exercise and recreation programs for members of these age groups. In addition, adult participation in sport and exercise programs has become acceptable and even desirable in Western societies. With specific programs not available, peer groups might once again influence older adults' recreational involvement. Once involved, adults keep participating to be part of a peer group.

Despite the strong influence of peer groups on sport participation throughout life, it is still not clear that membership in a sport-oriented peer group always precedes participation—that is, that a person is drawn to an activity because of a desire to associate with peers. Possibly individuals first select groups that fit their interests, including an interest in sport (Loy et al., 1978). Although it is not clear which comes first, the interest in sport and the desire to be a part of a peer group make it likely that an individual will

An individual's peer group may either encourage or discourage physical activities. As socializing agents, peer groups can be as important as family.

continue to participate and to select membership in active groups. Peers apparently play just as important a role in sport socialization as the family plays (Lewko & Greendorfer, 1988).

Coaches and Teachers

Coaches and teachers can also influence an individual's sport and physical activity involvement (Greendorfer & Lewko, 1978). Male athletes consistently report that coaches and teachers influenced both their participation and their selection of sports, particularly when they were adolescents and young adults (Ebihara et al., 1983; Kenyon & McPherson, 1973). Female athletes report that teachers and coaches influenced them during childhood (Greendorfer & Ewing, 1981; Weiss & Knoppers, 1982) and adolescence (Greendorfer, 1976, 1977). In contrast, Yamaguchi (1984) found that schoolteachers and coaches were not influential. Participants rarely name teachers and coaches as the most influential agents in their sport involvement. Perhaps the role of teachers and coaches is to strengthen the sport socialization process begun earlier by family and friends.

Coaches As Socializing Agents

Assessing Youth Sport Coaching Behaviors

Participation in youth sport has grown steadily over the past several decades (Smoll & Smith, 2001). This growth has led to a demand for coaches who understand the needs of young participants. Remember, coaches can act as socializing agents for young children. Many of the feelings, values, and behaviors that people have about physical activity come from their experiences in youth sport. A good coach can facilitate a lifetime of positive experiences, just as a poor coach can drive young people away from sport and physical activity.

Frank Smoll and Ron Smith (2001) suggest that youth sport coaches adopt a four-part philosophy designed to enhance the enjoyment and benefits of children's participation in sport. They posit that the primary objective of youth sport is to have fun. Here are the four points:

1. Winning isn't everything, nor is it the only thing.
2. Failure is not the same thing as losing.
3. Success is not synonymous with winning.
4. Children should be taught that success is found in striving for victory (i.e., success is related to effort).

How do coaches evaluate their ability to make physical activity a fun, positive experience for kids? Coaches can understand their own coaching behaviors better through self-monitoring. To aid in this process, Smoll and Smith developed the Coaching Self-Report Form (right), which the coach should complete soon after each practice or game. This form helps coaches assess the frequency of desired behaviors in sport situations. This, along with feedback from knowledgeable sources such as other coaches or teachers, can facilitate a coach's ability to be a positive socializing agent for youth sport participants.

Coaching Self-Report Form

Complete this form as soon as possible after a practice or game.

For items 1, 2, and 3, think not only about what you did but also consider the kinds of situations in which the actions occurred and the kinds of athletes who were involved.

1. Approximately what percentage of the time did you respond to good players' actions with reinforcement? _____
2. Approximately what percentage of the time did you respond to players' mistakes/errors with each of the following communications?

   a. encouragement only _____

   b. corrective instructions given in an encouraging manner

   _____

   (sum of *a* and *b* should not exceed 100%)

3. About how many times did you reinforce athletes for showing effort, complying with team rules, encouraging teammates, showing team spirit, and exhibiting other good behaviors? _____
4. How well did your team play tonight? (Circle one.)

   very poorly   not very well   average   quite well   very well

5. How positive an experience *for the kids* was this practice/game?

   very negative   somewhat negative   neutral   somewhat positive   very positive

6. How positive an experience *for you* was this practice/game?

   very negative   somewhat negative   neutral   somewhat positive   very positive

7. Is there anything you might do differently if you had a chance to coach this practice/game again? (If so, briefly explain.)

Coaching Self-Report Form from *Applied sport psychology: Personal growth to peak performance,* 4th ed., by Jean M. Williams. Copyright © 2001 by Mayfield Publishing Company. Reprinted by permission of the publisher.

? Adults who dislike physical activity often report that they had poor movement experiences, particularly in physical education, when they were children. Many different constraints or factors may interact to cause this aversive socialization. What are some of these constraints that may discourage physical activity and movement?

It is essential that coaches and teachers understand that they have influence in promoting or deterring physical activity participation in their players and students.

Nevertheless, teachers and coaches should not overlook their potential to influence their students' sport involvement. They can introduce children and adolescents to exciting new activities and stimulate them to learn the skills and attitudes associated with sport. Conversely, teachers and coaches must also recognize the potential they have to turn their students away from sport and physical activity. Bad experiences in school can have lifelong consequences for a person's overall lifestyle (Snyder & Spreitzer, 1973). Such negative experiences, known as **aversive socialization,** can occur when teachers or coaches embarrass children in front of their peers, overemphasize performance criteria at the expense of learning and enjoyment, and plan class activities that result in overwhelming failure rather than success. Children who experience aversive socialization naturally avoid physical activities and fail to learn skills well; consequently, any attempts they make to participate frustrate and discourage them.

Social Situations

The situations in which children spend their formative years are a part of the socialization process. Play environments, games, and the toys children use can influence their later activities.

Play Environments and Games

An adequate environment for play, such as a backyard or playground, can provide the social situation and environment a child needs to begin involvement in sport and physical activity. Play spaces probably also influence activity selection. A child who lacks an adequate play space has a diminished opportunity to get involved in activities and practice skills. These environmental constraints thus discourage participation in sport and gross motor activities. Children who grow up in urban areas with limited play space are typically exposed to sports and activities that require little space and equipment, such as basketball. Colder climates provide children with an opportunity to learn ice skating; warmer climates encourage swimming.

Play environment may also act as a sociocultural constraint, especially if the play space has some gender-associated values. In turn, these could influence boys and girls to participate in gender-typed activities. For example, double-dutch rope jumping falls within the "feminine" domain; a boy might be labeled a "sissy" for rope jumping and thus may be discouraged from participating in that activity. A girl might be told that a certain sport (such as football) is inappropriate for girls or may be labeled as a tomboy if she does participate. Western society has traditionally considered certain types of games appropriate for boys but not for girls, and vice versa. This labeling is particularly apparent as children enter adolescence.

The pressure to participate in gender-appropriate games has implications for children's opportunities to practice skills. Traditional boys' games are typically complex and involve the use of strategy. They are encouraged to work hard toward specific goals and to use negotiation to settle disputes over rules. Traditional girls' games, on the other hand, are typically noncompetitive, and rather than encouraging interdependence among group members, they involve waiting for turns to perform simple repetitive tasks, such as jumping rope or playing hopscotch. Such games rarely give girls opportunities to increase game complexity or to develop increasingly more difficult skills. In fact, the games often end because the participants lose interest, not because they achieve a goal (Greendorfer, 1983).

More and more children now participate in activities that are not "gender appropriate" (Guiliano et al., 2000). Further, some sports and activities, such as soccer and aerobics, are losing their gender-specific associations. At the same time, gender typing of sports and activities still exists and acts as a strong constraint on movement activities. Although gender-role stereotyping through games has diminished in recent years, educators should keep in mind that a play environment that channels boys and girls into gender-typed games perpetuates a situation in which boys can better develop complex motor skills but girls cannot.

Play With Toys

Imagine walking into a toy store such as K-B toys or Toys-R-Us as a child. What do you experience? Bright colors and loud sounds beckon you toward toys that promise to enlighten, engage, and excite you. As a child (or even an adult), you may not realize that these toys act as part of the socialization process. That's right; even toys are constraints! Toys can encourage children to be active or inactive. For example, a Frisbee or koosh ball encourages a child to throw, catch, and develop an accurate shot. On the other hand, a board game or doll encourages sedentary play. Toys can also stimulate children to model sports figures. Among others, there are basketball, soccer, and cheerleader Barbies and World Wrestling Federation action figures. At the same time, video and computer games such as Nintendo or Sony PlayStation may simulate sports without promoting any physical activity at all. Obviously, each kind of toy has its advantages, but certain toys facilitate children's socialization into sport and physical activity more than others.

> **?** Consider a toy that is popular today. How does this toy encourage certain behaviors and discourage others?

Toys are also a means by which gender typing can occur in the socialization process. For example, toys marketed to boys tend to be more complex and encourage more vigorous activity than those marketed to girls. The typical girls' toy, such as a doll or kitchen set, promotes quiet indoor play (Greendorfer, 1983; Liss, 1983). Gender typing through toys is well entrenched in society, and even children under 2 years old may be aware of the gender associations of toys (Levy, 2000). Manufacturers often use gender-typed strategies to advertise their products. For example, commercials or packaging for sports equipment, racing-car sets, and action-oriented video games feature boys, and those for dolls picture girls (figure 11.4, a and b). Watch carefully for television advertisements during daytime television—most target either boys or girls but not both. These marketing ploys influence children as well as their parents.

Parents also enjoy giving their children the same kinds of toys they played with as children, thus tending to perpetuate traditional gender typing. For example, a father might buy a Lincoln Logs set for his son, remembering the hours he spent with one as a child—despite the more modern, complex toys on the market. Moreover, parents can promote gender typing by negatively reinforcing play with toys they judge to be gender inappropriate (Fagot, 1978), such as telling boys not to play with dolls. Raag and Rackliff (1998), in a study of gender typing, toys, and preschoolers, found that many of the boys thought their fathers would perceive cross-gender-typed toys as "bad." Raag (1999) also found that those children who had a parent or significant other who viewed gender-neutral toys as "bad" were somewhat influenced by gender-typed toy labels. Such gender typing through toys is slow to change, and there is little evidence of change over the past several decades (Marcon & Freeman, 1999; Campenni, 1999; Eisenberg, Welchick, Hernandez, & Pasternack, 1985; Lloyd & Smith, 1985). In a unique study, Pennell (1999), disguised as Santa's head elf, questioned 359 males and 417 females of various ages and ethnic backgrounds about their toy choices. Pennell found the girls and, to a greater extent, the boys had a strong gender-typed preference for toys.

In recent years, our society has become more aware of the many ways children are gender typed and the implications of this process. Yet there is little

a

b

Figure 11.4 Advertising for children's toys is often gender typed. Here we see advertisements directed toward *(a)* girls and *(b)* boys.

evidence of any substantial change away from gender typing (Banerjee & Lintern, 2000; Pennell, 1999; Turner & Gervai, 1995; Weisner, Garnier, & Loucky, 1994; Turner, Gervai, & Hinde, 1993). Teachers must realize that they influence this aspect of socialization (Fagot, 1984). Again, the evidence shows that teachers still behave differently toward the play of boys compared with that of girls (Fagot, 1984; Oettingen, 1985; Smith, 1985). They can reinforce early gender typing by continuing to label certain activities as more important or appropriate for one sex than for the other. They can choose different activities for boys' and girls' achievements. Or they can make every attempt possible to eliminate such distinctions and allow each individual to explore his or her full potential. It is likely that such day-to-day decisions and expectations accumulate over time to reduce differences in boys' and girls' motor development by channeling their practice opportunities (Giuliano et al., 2000; Brown et al., 1990; Brundage, 1983; Greendorfer & Brundage, 1984).

To determine for yourself the gender-role stereotypes present in games and toys, download Lab 11.1 Examining Gender Role Stereotyping from the Student Resources Section at www.HumanKinetics.com/LifeSpanMotorDevelopment.

OTHER SOCIOCULTURAL CONSTRAINTS: RACE, ETHNICITY, AND SOCIOECONOMIC STATUS

? Consider the different ways that low socioeconomic status might encourage certain behaviors and discourage others.

Earlier in this chapter, we described some constraints related to gender as socially constructed rather than biologically defined. In other words, the notion that girls are weaker than boys is firmly established within our culture, even though there is little biological evidence to back it up. (Recall that few physiological differences exist between boys and girl prior to puberty.) Socially constructed notions exist beyond gender differences, into the realms of race, ethnicity, and socioeconomic status (SES) as well. Oftentimes, it's difficult to distinguish between sociocultural constraints (e.g., prevailing cultural attitudes) and individual constraints (e.g., physiological functioning) because research may not be completely clearcut on how race, class, or ethnicity is defined. For example, race and ethnicity are often used together, but they are not equivalent. Racial characteristics are biologically based and relate to genetic similarities within groups. On the other hand, ethnic characteristics are culturally based and relate to cultural similarities that connect groups. Race and ethnicity do coincide (biologically similar individuals who live in a particular geographic locale likely share culture), which makes their independent study very difficult.

Furthermore, social class and SES have certain characteristics associated with them that may cut across race and ethnicity. Given that all of these factors interrelate, it is hard to identify constraints as strictly sociocultural or individual when considering socioeconomic status. It may be best to consider the relationship of SES to other factors when looking for the influence of constraints. For example, children who come from a lower SES background may have less access to organized sport and physical activity, particularly those that require expensive equipment (ice hockey) or lessons (figure skating, tennis) and extensive time commitments from at least one parent. As a result, these children may not gain experiences and practice related to these particular activities.

We should consider the research on race, ethnicity, and SES from a slightly different point of view—one that examines differences among groups without suggesting a priori that differences are biological in nature. This allows us to examine the potential influence of a variety of constraints without limiting our interpretation to "biological fact." Malina, Bouchard, and Bar-Or (2004) provide an extensive review of historical and contemporary research related to physical differences based on race, ethnicity, and socioeconomic status.

Summary and Synthesis

Humans are social beings. That is, individuals constantly interact with and depend on others as a part of everyday life. People form groups that can be small (family), medium (sports teams, town membership), or large (United States citizens). These groups often have distinct values, morals, rules, and other factors that create a social atmosphere under which group members live. Thus, different groups and group members act as socializing agents. Socializing agents, along with social situations, encourage socially and culturally "appropriate" motor development. As you might expect, these sociocultural constraints interact with functional individual constraints to influence motivation, self-esteem, and feelings of competence for a task. These types of constraint interactions are explored in the following chapter.

 ## Discussion Questions

1. Who are the socializing agents most likely to influence children's socialization into sport and physical activities?

2. How might gender-role stereotyping result in fewer women participating in sport and physical activities?

3. Describe how toys are part of the socialization process.

4. What is the difference between "sex" and "gender," and why does this distinction matter in the context of motor development?

5. Describe the changing roles of significant others across childhood and adolescence.

6. How do sociocultural constraints work in regard to our model of motor development? Provide some specific examples.

 ## Learning Activities

Observing Sociocultural Constraints on the World Wide Web

One of the benefits of the World Wide Web is that we have immediate access to information about many different societies and cultures. After a little Web browsing, it becomes clear that different societies and cultures promote different activities for their members. You will find different sports in which people participate, different ages at which certain activities are deemed appropriate, different roles for males and females, and so on. For this learning activity, you will use the Internet to explore several different countries and then determine their specific sociocultural constraints.

1. In this learning activity, you will discover what your motor development might be like if you had grown up in a different society and culture. To do this, you will assume the role of a college-aged individual from each of the six continents. First, select a country from each of the continents (Africa, Asia, Australia, Europe, North America, and South America). Do not choose the country in which you reside.

2. Next, visit at least two Web sites *from* each country as well as two Web sites *about* each country (e.g., from an encyclopedia or travel guide). Remember to record these Web sites for future reference. Also, the more Web sites you visit, the more information you will have to work with.

3. For each country, try to determine what sociocultural constraints exist.

4. Develop a biographical composite of yourself had you been born and raised in each of the different countries you chose. Focus on sociocultural constraints. What would you be like? How would your life and motor development differ from country to country? Would there be similarities between the countries? Finally, how would your different, hypothetical motor development compare with your actual motor development?

Psychosocial Constraints in Motor Development

Individual–Environmental Constraint Interaction

EXTRA!!! The Times EXTRA!!!

PROJECT ACES: THE WORLD'S LARGEST EXERCISE CLASS

Each May, on a designated date and time, millions of school children all over the globe exercise simultaneously in a symbolic gesture of fitness and unity to show the world that they do not fit into that negative stereotype of being "fat and weak." This noncompetitive program has proven to be educational, motivational, and fun. When Len Saunders created Project ACES back in 1989, he had no idea that it would reach the magnitude and success of today. The program has been praised by presidents of the United States, including Bill Clinton, George Bush, and Ronald Reagan. The program has also received praise from state governors, senators, and celebrities from sports and show business. Project ACES has reached millions of children, parents, and teachers all over the world, including participants from over 50 countries. (Project ACES Web site: www.projectaces.com)

Project ACES is designed to motivate children to participate in physical activity on a daily basis. The belief is that good experiences with physical activity in childhood will lead to continued participation throughout the life span, which in turn will result in a lifetime of improved health. Unfortunately, physical inactivity, associated with myriad health problems, permeates American society. The National Center for Chronic Disease Prevention and Health Promotion reports that the number of overweight children has doubled since 1980, and according to the Surgeon General, "physical inactivity is more prevalent among women than men, among blacks and Hispanics than whites, among older than younger adults and among the less affluent than the more affluent. More than 60% of U.S. women do not engage in the recommended amount of physical activity, and more than 25% are not active at all" (U.S. Department of Health and Human Services, 1996). This report suggests that it would serve all movement professionals well to understand why individuals do or do not participate in physical activities across the life span.

Why do some individuals participate in physical activities on a regular basis, while others avoid them? We have spent much of this book describing motor behaviors that most typically developing individuals exhibit; however, we have yet to discuss one type of constraint—an individual functional constraint—that can drastically alter the type and amount of personal physical activity and also affect the emergence of movement over time. An individual functional constraint is not a specific anatomical structure but a psychological construct, such as motivation, self-efficacy, or emotion. Often, socializing agents such as parents or peers play a strong role in developing an individual's functional constraints. Therefore, we consider the interaction between sociocultural constraints and individual functional constraints.

As noted in the previous chapter, the social or cultural environment can encourage or discourage different behaviors. Of course, these environmental constraints have different effects on different individuals. One person may not participate in an activity because of parental influences discouraging sport; another person may participate *because of* these same influences as an act of rebellion. This chapter explores the interaction between social factors and functional constraints such as emotions, perceived ability, motivation, and other personal attributes. One key functional constraint related to physical activity is self-esteem.

 ## *Chapter Objectives*

This chapter will

- ▲ explore the relationship between social influences and an individual's feeling of self-esteem,
- ▲ discuss the effect of self-esteem on motivation to participate in sport and physical activity,
- ▲ investigate why individuals continue participation or drop out of sport, and
- ▲ examine children's attributions for success or failure in physical activity.

Self-esteem is your personal judgment of your own capability, significance, success, and worthiness, and you convey it to others in words and actions (Coopersmith, 1967). It is your self-evaluation in general and in specific areas.

SELF-ESTEEM

All individuals evaluate themselves in different areas, such as physical ability, physical appearance, academic ability, and social skills. These self-judgments are called by many names, including self-esteem, self-concept, self-image, self-worth, and self-confidence. This chapter uses the term **self-esteem.** Self-esteem is your personal judgment of your own capability, significance, success, and worthiness; it is conveyed to others in words and actions (Coopersmith, 1967). Whether your self-evaluations are accurate is not as important to your self-esteem as your *belief* that they are accurate (Weiss, 1993). Others can identify your level of self-esteem through what you say to them as well as through your nonverbal behaviors in joining or avoiding certain activities. For example, someone with a high self-esteem for physical activity is not likely to avoid it. This is one of the reasons that self-esteem is so important. It influences one's motivation to join and sustain particular activities. In addition, researchers have found a high correlation between physical activity and self-esteem (McAuley, 1994; Sonstroem, 1997).

Self-esteem is not just a general sense. It is specific to **domains,** which are areas or situations. For example, a teenage boy may evaluate himself as high in the physical and social domains but low in the academic domain. Within each domain, individuals may differentiate their abilities at even more specific levels (Fox & Corbin, 1989). Academic ability may be perceived in terms of ability in mathematics, writing, foreign languages, and so on. This chapter focuses on self-evaluations in the physical domain related to physical skills.

Professionals interested in motivating people to be active must understand self-esteem and the factors that influence people's judgments of their capabilities. Those working with children should know how self-esteem develops. Those working with people of any age should be aware of the criteria people use as a basis for their evaluations and whether these criteria change as individuals grow older.

 Self-esteem influences participation in sport and physical activity as well as skill mastery. It becomes more accurate as a person ages. Over time, an individual's self-esteem in a domain matches his or her actual abilities.

A **domain** is an independent area or sphere of influence, such as social, physical, or academic.

Measuring Self-Esteem in Children

It would seem much easier for developmentalists to measure running and jumping or strength and flexibility than self-esteem in children. Susan Harter (1985) uses a question format ("Some kids … BUT other kids …") to measure children's self-perceptions. For example, one pair of statements is, "Some kids feel that they are better than other kids their age at sports BUT other kids don't feel they can play as well." Next to each statement are two boxes, one labeled *really true for me* and one labeled *sort of true for me.* Children check one of the boxes, indicating which kids they perceive as being like themselves and to what extent.

Harter's Self-Perception Profile for Children contains 36 different statements for five specific domains (scholastic competence, athletic competence, social acceptance, physical appearance, and behavioral conduct) and a global score for self-worth. This profile is appropriate for children ages 8 through early adolescence. For children under 8, Harter and Pike (1984) designed a pictorial scale. Instead of two statements, two pictures are presented: one shows a competent or accepted child and the other shows an unaccepted child or a child who is unable to do the accepted task. Children say whether they are a lot or a little like the child in the picture. Hence, the scale is made more concrete for young children and can be given to children who cannot read or understand written statements. The pictorial scale assesses four domains: cognitive competence, physical competence, peer acceptance, and maternal acceptance. Scales available for adolescents and adults typically cover many more domains.

Development of Self-Esteem

Children's self-esteem is greatly influenced by verbal and nonverbal communications from those who are significant to them, including parents, siblings, friends, teachers, and coaches (figure 12.1). Verbal comments such as, "Good," or, "Why can't you do better?" are sources of information, as are facial expressions and gestures (Weiss, 1993). Children are likely to compare themselves with other children, as well, and the results of this evaluation influence self-esteem. These appraisals and comparisons, though, do not have an equal influence throughout life. This section examines how the pattern of influence can change.

? Should improving patients' self-esteem be a primary concern for someone in the rehabilitation field? Why or why not?

Social interactions	Emotions
Parental appraisal Comparison with others Teacher or coach feedback	Enjoyment Pride, excitement with success Disappointment, stress with failure

Self-esteem

Figure 12.1 Social interactions and emotions influence the development of self-esteem for physical performance. Interactions are verbal and nonverbal.

Social Interactions

Children as young as age 5 can compare themselves with others (Scanlan, 1988), but under the age of 10 they depend more on parental appraisals and the outcomes of contests than on comparisons (Horn & Hasbrook, 1986, 1987; Horn & Weiss, 1991). Young children, too, are not as accurate as teenagers in their evaluations of their physical competence. The level of intrinsic motivation and the extent to which children believe they control their lives influence the accuracy of children's physical ability perceptions. Children older than 10 rely on comparisons to and appraisals given by their peers. Perceived competence is important; those with high perceptions of competence tend to have more positive reactions within sport and physical activities than those feeling less competence (Weiss & Ebbick, 1996).

Feedback and appraisal from teachers and coaches contribute to the development of self-esteem in the physical domain (Smoll & Smith, 1989). For example, male athletes 10 to 15 years old show high self-esteem when they play for coaches who give frequent encouragement and corrective feedback (figure 12.2), especially if the athletes begin with somewhat low self-esteem (Smith, Smoll, & Curtis, 1979). Coaches' appraisals and self-perceptions of improvement also influence teenage girls, but the pattern of coaches' influence is interesting: In a study by Horn (1985), self-esteem did not increase when girls received reinforcement from coaches after successful performances. Instead, an increase in perceived competence was associated with criticism. Apparently the coaches' positive comments were general and did not relate specifically to the girls' performance, whereas the criticisms were associated with a skill error and often included a suggestion for improvement. Therefore, teachers and coaches cannot expect global praise to automatically raise a child's self-esteem. Feedback should relate to performance (Horn, 1986, 1987).

Figure 12.2 Feedback from a teacher or coach can contribute to the development of an important individual constraint: self-esteem.
© Human Kinetics

Emotions

The development of self-esteem is also related to emotions associated with participation. The pride and excitement associated with success or the disappointment and stress associated with failure influence a person's self-esteem and motivation to sustain participation (Weiss, 1993). This, of course, relates not just to sport but to all physical activities in general. Enjoyment leads to higher levels of self-esteem and motivation to participate. In turn, perceptions of high ability and mastery, low parental pressure, and greater parent or coach satisfaction lead to enjoyment in preadolescents and young adolescents (Brustad, 1988; Scanlan & Lewthwaite, 1986; Scanlan, Stein, & Ravizza, 1988).

Relationship Between Causal Attributions and Self-Esteem

Self-esteem can influence behavior because people tend to act in ways that confirm their beliefs of themselves; that is, people tend to be self-consistent. If you have low perceived competency and low self-esteem surrounding your ability to perform a skill, then you tend to perform the skill with low competency. These beliefs often are evident in the reasons people give for their successes and failures. These reasons are called **causal attributions.** People of any age with high self-esteem tend to make attributions that are

1. *internal*, believing that they influence outcomes through their own behavior;
2. *stable*, believing that the factors influencing outcome are consistent from situation to situation; and
3. *controllable*, believing that they personally control the factors influencing outcome.

For example, competitors with high self-esteem attribute their success to their talent (internal), think they can win again (stable), and believe they are responsible for their successes, not merely lucky (controllable). They view their failures as temporary and meet them with renewed effort and continued practice to improve skills.

In contrast, people with low self-esteem attribute failure to factors that are

1. *external*, believing they could not change outcomes;
2. *unstable*, believing outcome is a product of fluctuating influences such as good and bad luck; and
3. *uncontrollable*, believing that nothing they do could result in a different outcome.

Competitors with low self-esteem often attribute losing to a lack of ability and attribute winning to luck or to a task so easy that anybody could win.

Examining causal attributions can help us understand adult behavior, but few researchers have studied the causal attributions of children in sport and physical activity. Because children are in the process of developing self-esteem, this information is important. We have seen that children use different factors in judging themselves as they develop. Therefore, we must be concerned with the accuracy of their self-estimates and the roles adults play in helping children make appropriate attributions.

Children's Attributions

The sparse information available on age-related changes in children's attributions indicates that children 7 to 9 years old attribute outcomes to effort and luck more than older children and teens do (Bird & Williams, 1980). These factors are unstable. The children in this study reacted to stories the researchers provided rather than to actual outcomes they experienced, however, and a more recent study failed to find age differences in attributions following actual participation (Weiss, McAuley, Ebbeck, & Wiese, 1990). Because young children might not be able to distinguish between ability and effort very well, more information is needed on age differences.

Differences do exist in the attributions made by children who differ in their perceived physical competence (Weiss et al., 1990). As expected, children with high physical self-esteem give internal, stable, and controllable reasons for their successes. Their attributions for success are more stable and their future expectations for success are higher than those of children with low physical self-esteem. As we mentioned previously, children vary in the accuracy of their physical estimates (Weiss & Horn, 1990). Girls who underestimate (rather than accurately estimate or overestimate) their physical abilities typically choose less challenging skills and attribute outcomes to external factors. Boys who underestimate their physical abilities report little understanding of what is responsible for their successes or failures. Children with low perceptions of their physical abilities who also tend to underestimate their abilities probably make inaccurate attributions about the outcomes of their efforts. Their behavior is characterized by the following:

Causal attributions are the reasons to which people credit their successes and failures. These differ for people with high and low self-esteem.

 Children who perceive their physical abilities as low are not likely to persist in physical activities and realize the associated health and psychosocial benefits (Weiss, 1993).

▲ An unwillingness to try challenging tasks

▲ A lack of effort to do well

▲ Avoidance of participation

Parents, teachers, and coaches can help children, especially those with low self-esteem, give proper credit to the reasons for success or failure. Adults can help children with low self-esteem retrain their attributions (Horn, 1987; figure 12.3). Rather than let children attribute failure to lack of ability and attribute success to luck, adults can emphasize improvement through effort and continued practice. They can also encourage children to set goals and can provide accurate feedback about the children's progress. Children who come to think their situations are hopeless (i.e., those with learned helplessness) need challenges that are accurately matched to their abilities and in which difficulty is increased in steps much smaller than those presented to other children. Children with high self-esteem for physical competence probably possess high levels of intrinsic motivation to participate in physical activities. If children with low self-esteem are ever to enjoy physical activities and ultimately realize the benefits of participation, adults must make special efforts to improve their self-esteem (Weiss, 1993).

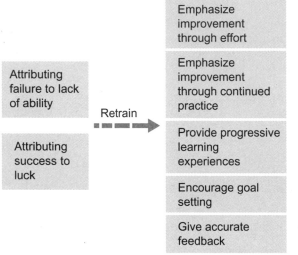

Figure 12.3 Adults must help children with low self-esteem for physical performance improve their self-esteem. Retraining can change causal attributions.
Based on Horn 1987.

☀ An adult's level of self-esteem affects motivation for physical activity. Just as with children, adults behave according to their beliefs about themselves, which are acquired from actual and vicarious experiences, others' opinions, and their physiological state.

Adults' Attributions

Self-esteem also influences the motivation of adults. Just as with children, adults tend to behave according to their beliefs about themselves. Recall that children obtain the information on which they base their self-judgments largely from their significant others and their own comparisons. Adults obtain information from four sources (Bandura, 1986):

1. Actual experiences (previous accomplishments or failures)

2. Vicarious experiences (observing a model)

3. Verbal persuasion from others

4. Their physiological state

An individual's actual experiences are particularly influential, and changing physiological status is a reality for most older adults. For example, failing eyesight lowers an older adult's confidence for participating in racket sports. In contrast, verbal persuasion is a much weaker influence. The models available to older adults vary considerably. Some older adults have opportunities to see others like themselves participating in a wide range of activities; others do not, especially on a personal basis rather than in a magazine or on television. Given these influences, it is obvious that a person's self-esteem can increase or decrease throughout life.

A few investigators have related adults' physical self-esteem and their motivation to maintain or improve their fitness. Ewart, Stewart, Gillilan, and Kelemen (1986) involved men with coronary artery disease, ages 35 to 70, in either a walk or jog plus a circuit weight training program or a walk or jog plus volleyball program for 10 weeks. They measured self-esteem before and after the program as well as arm and leg strength and treadmill running performance.

The researchers found that those with higher pretraining self-esteem improved more in arm strength than those with lower self-esteem, even when accounting for beginning strength level, type of training, and frequency of participation. Self-esteem did improve with training but only when participants received information indicating that their performance was improving. For example, the weight training group improved their self-esteem for lifting weights but not for jogging, even though they improved on both tests in a post-program assessment. They could monitor their improvements in weight training during the program, but their jogging distance remained constant, so they had no indication they were improving. Hogan and Santomeir (1984) also observed an increase in self-esteem for swimming in older adults after a 5-week swimming class. Thus, older adults' self-esteem can influence how much improvement they realize in a program, and participation can raise self-esteem when participants have information about their actual improvements.

To explore the causal attributions of players on a youth sports team, download Lab 12.1 Identifying Causal Attributions in Sport Participants from the Student Resources section at www.HumanKinetics.com/LifeSpanMotorDevelopment.

MOTIVATION

The **motivation** to participate in activities of a certain type involves many factors. One aspect of motivation is the factors that lead people to initiate or join an activity. Another aspect is factors that encourage people to persist in an activity and to exert effort to improve. Still another aspect concerns those factors that lead people to end their involvement. In the previous chapter, we discussed factors that encourage children's initial sport involvement, or the sport socialization process. Let's turn now to those factors that keep children in physical activity and sport or lead them to drop out. We also consider how the factors that motivate people to participate in physical activities change over the life span.

Persistence

Researchers have focused quite a bit of attention on the reasons children and teens continue to participate in sport (Weiss, 1993). In general, the reasons include the following:

- ▲ A desire to be competent by improving skills or attaining goals
- ▲ A desire to affiliate with or make new friends
- ▲ A desire to be part of a team
- ▲ A desire to undertake competition and be successful
- ▲ A desire to have fun
- ▲ A desire to increase fitness

McAuley (1994) and Sonstroem (1997) found that girls most often gave "fun," followed by health benefits, as the reason they participate in physical activity. Most individuals cite several of these reasons for participating rather than one or two. Harter (1978, 1981) proposed a competence motivation theory to explain this: Children are motivated to demonstrate their competency, and therefore they seek out mastery attempts, opportunities to learn and demonstrate skills. Those who perceive they are competent and believe they control situations have more intrinsic motivation to participate than others.

Membership in subgroups can also influence a person's motivation to persist in sport. Examples of subgroups include age groups, starters versus benchwarmers, elite athletes versus recreational participants, and so on. Consider age groups. Brodkin and Weiss (1990) studied varying age groups of competitive swimmers: ages 6 to 9, 10 to 14, 15 to 22, 23 to 39, 40 to 59, and 60 to 74. They found that children cited wanting to compete,

? Consider participation in sport from a coach's point of view rather than an athlete's. Why might a coach want an athlete to participate? What conflicts might arise?

liking the coaches, and pleasing family and friends as reasons to participate. The 15- to 22-year-olds gave social status reasons, as the young children did to an extent; fitness motives were important to the young and middle adults. Children and older adults did not consider fitness as important. Young children and older adults named "fun" as the most important reason to participate.

Another investigation of children involved in swimming found that children younger than 11 were motivated to participate by external factors: encouragement from family and friends, liking the coaches, social status, and activities that they enjoyed (Gould, Feltz, & Weiss, 1985). Teenagers in this study cited more internal factors: competence, fitness, and the excitement of swimming. Thus, different age groups have different reasons for participating, but more research is needed on other activities and with participants of varying skill levels (Weiss, 1993).

Dropping Out

Withdrawal from sport programs is a very real aspect of youth involvement in physical activity. Changing from one type of activity to another might be part of developing or might reflect a person's changing interests or desire to try something new, but withdrawing from all activity has serious repercussions for health at any point in life. It is often difficult for surveys and research studies to distinguish between participants who switch activities and those who withdraw from activity altogether. In addition, dropouts do not always quit by choice. Injuries or high monetary costs might force some to withdraw. The reasons participants give for quitting deserve further attention.

Some young dropouts cite very negative experiences as reasons for withdrawing from sport, including

- ▲ dislike for the coach,
- ▲ lack of playing time,
- ▲ too much pressure,
- ▲ too much time required,
- ▲ overemphasis on winning,
- ▲ lack of fun,
- ▲ lack of progress, and
- ▲ lack of success (McPherson, Marteniuk, Tihanyi, & Clark, 1980; Orlick, 1973, 1974).

Not all children and adolescents cite negative reasons for leaving sport and physical activity. Often, individuals simply want to pursue different activities, some of which may be physical.

Such negative reactions come from a small number of dropouts (Feltz & Petlichkoff, 1983; Gould, Feltz, Horn, & Weiss, 1982; Klint & Weiss, 1986; Sapp & Haubenstricker, 1978). The majority of dropouts withdraw to pursue other interests, to try different sport activities, or to participate at lower intensity levels. Teens often report dropping out to take jobs. Many plan to reenter their sports later. So, much of the attrition from youth sport reflects shifting interests and involvement levels rather than negative experiences. Professionals, however, should be concerned about negative experiences because they can be detrimental to a person's psychological development and can lead to a lifelong avoidance of healthful activities.

Adult Activity Levels

The amount and intensity level of physical activity decrease as adults grow older, especially among women (Ebrahim & Rowland, 1996; Boothby, Tungatt, & Townsend, 1981;

Curtis & White, 1984; McPherson, 1983; Rudman, 1986). In 1996, the U.S. Department of Health and Human Services reported that even when adding together all the different types of exercise in which individuals participate, two-thirds of adults ages 65 and older who did exercise did not achieve recommended levels (U.S. Department of Health and Human Services, 1996). This withdrawal from and reduction in physical activity are not the result of changes in physiological health alone (Spreitzer & Snyder, 1983). Psychosocial factors also influence adults' activity levels (McPherson, 1986). These factors include the following:

- ▲ Stereotypes of appropriate activity levels
- ▲ Limited access to facilities and programs
- ▲ Childhood experiences
- ▲ Concerns over personal limitations on exercise
- ▲ Lack of role models
- ▲ Lack of knowledge about appropriate exercise programs
- ▲ Belief that exercise is harmful or is ineffective in preventing disease (Duda & Tappe, 1989a)

However, indications exist that adults, especially older ones, are becoming more interested in health and the influence of physical activity on health status (Howze, DiGilio, Bennett, & Smith, 1986; Maloney, Fallon, & Wittenberg, 1984; Prohaska, Leventhal, Leventhal, & Keller, 1985). In fact, the number of women participating in the National Senior Games has increased by 110% from 1991 to 1998 (Women's Sports Foundation, 2000).

Duda and Tappe (1988, 1989a, 1989b) proposed that adult exercise participation reflects three interrelated factors (figure 12.4):

1. Personal incentives, such as a desire to demonstrate mastery, to compete, to be with others, to receive recognition, to maintain health, to cope with stress, and to improve physical fitness
2. A sense of self, particularly in regard to one's self-esteem for physical activity
3. Perceived options, or the opportunities a person has in a given situation, such as transportation to various sites where adult programs are offered

Personal incentive values and self-esteem can change throughout life. For example, the desire to compete can decrease and the desire to be with others can increase as an adult ages. Older adults can also come to perceive that their physical abilities have declined over time. Duda and Tappe surveyed 144 adults in three age groups (25–39, 40–60, and 61-plus years) who were participating in an exercise program. Personal incentives differed among the age groups and between men and women (figure 12.5). Middle-aged and older adults placed more value on the health benefits of exercise than did young adults. For example, figure 12.5 shows the extent to which men and women in each age group valued the stress-reducing benefits of exercise. Young adult men put little emphasis on this exercise benefit, as shown by their low average on the Personal Incentives for Exercise Questionnaire. Men also valued competitive activities more than women did. Exercise leaders, then, might help older adults stick to their exercise programs by emphasizing social interaction, health benefits, and stress reduction (Duda & Tappe, 1989b).

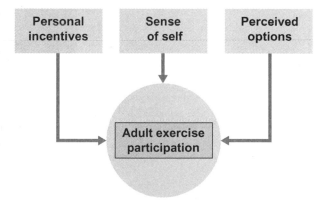

Figure 12.4 Three interrelated factors can influence the level of adults' exercise participation.
Based on Duda and Tappe 1989a, and Maehr 1984.

? If you were to design a physical activity program for older adults, what could you do to encourage your participants first to join, then to stay?

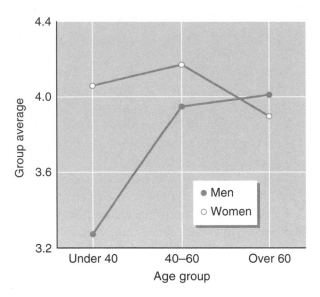

Figure 12.5 Personal incentives to exercise differ among adult age groups and between the sexes. Group averages on the Coping with Stress category of the Personal Incentives for Exercise Questionnaire (a five-point Likert-type scale) are plotted here.

Reprinted from Duda and Tappe 1989b.

No age group differences in self-esteem were apparent among these older adults, but differences did exist between men and women. The women had lower physical self-esteem and less feeling of control over their health status than the men did. These beliefs are typically associated with less involvement, but fortunately the women felt they had more social support for their involvement than the men, and they continued to participate.

Exercise leaders who adopt strategies targeted at those adults who might have low physical self-esteem can improve participants' self-esteem and exercise involvement (Duda & Tappe, 1989b). Another group of adults might not have the same characteristic incentives and perceptions as those Duda and Tappe surveyed. Yet exercise leaders can encourage older adults to persist in their exercise programs by being aware of the incentives and perceptions of their particular groups (figure 12.6). They can then emphasize the aspects and benefits of exercise most important to those participants.

Figure 12.6 Exercise leaders must be aware that older adults may have more individual structural constraints that discourage movement than younger adults, and also have different reasons for participation. In order to improve self-esteem and other individual functional constraints, exercise leaders should keep in mind the incentives and perceptions of physical activity that older adults have.

© Human Kinetics

 ## *Summary and Synthesis*

Across the life span, how individuals perceive their physical abilities can change dramatically. In turn, these perceptions can affect self-esteem. Maintaining high levels of self-esteem seems to enhance performance, as well as perceived competence—which motivates an individual to continue participation in physical activity. This is an example of how constraints can interact to encourage movement. For example, older adults may desire social interactions with friends as well as improved fitness levels, so they join an older adult exercise program. This program may involve activities that facilitate both socialization and fitness, which assist individuals in improving self-esteem. The higher levels of self-esteem and perceived competence help motivate the older adults to return to the program, which continues to foster self-esteem, and so on.

At the same time, these constraint interactions can discourage behavior. Consider children who begin participation in a sport such as soccer. They may have joined to be with friends and have fun. However, the coach wants to win and provides criticism and negative feedback to the players if they make a mistake. The players may begin to attribute losses to their lack of ability and believe they lack competence in that activity. In turn, their self-esteem begins to decrease. Eventually, they may drop out of the sport altogether.

These two examples demonstrate the powerful interplay between sociocultural and individual functional constraints. We all live in a social context and are subject to social opinions. These opinions help fashion and reinforce our beliefs about ourselves. Eventually, we act as we believe. Keeping this in mind, it is essential for those who work with others in physical activity and sport to look beyond the activity to the individuals themselves.

Discussion Questions

1. What is self-esteem? Is it general or specific? How is it developed?

2. People tend to attribute their successes and failures to various causes. What are the differences in the causal attributions made by those with high self-esteem and those with low self-esteem? To what do children tend to attribute their performance?

3. What factors are associated with persisting in sport and physical activity? With dropping out?

4. How does perceived competence change with children's causal attributions?

Learning Activities

Exploring Motivations for Physical Activity and Exercise

What motivates you and other students to be involved in sports and physical activities? If you evaluate a group of students, you will likely discover a diverse array of reasons to participate—or not to participate.

1. Determine your own motivations first.
   - Do you participate in sports and physical activity now? Look at the persistence list on page 213 and write down those that apply. Add new reasons.
   - Have you dropped out of physical activity? See if any of the reasons on page 214 apply.
   - Have you persisted in some activities and dropped out of others? What factors are related to these choices?

2. Compare motivation notes with a group of other students.
   - What are the most common factors associated with persistence?
   - What are the most common factors associated with dropping out?
   - Calculate percentages for easy interpretation ("Seventy percent of my group dropped out because of lack of time").
   - Reflect on these and try to make some generalizations about motivational factors and the students in your class.

Knowledge As a Functional Constraint in Motor Development

chapter 13

EXTRA!!! The Times EXTRA!!!

KURT WARNER FINISHES HISTORIC JOURNEY *(New York Post)*

KURT WARNER LIVES THE IMPOSSIBLE DREAM *(Chicago Tribune)*

WARNER HAS COME OUT OF NOWHERE, BUT HE'S NO PASSING FANCY *(New York Daily News)*

Media coverage of the 2000 National Football League Superbowl featured numerous stories about Kurt Warner, then quarterback for the St. Louis Rams. Warner had stepped into the starting role late in the preseason because of a season-ending injury to the team's experienced quarterback. News stories about Warner often expressed surprise that a player with almost no experience in the league could perform so well and lead a team to the Superbowl. So much was the value placed on quarterback experience at the professional level!

arner did have experience in other professional leagues that helped him in taking on the starting role. However, those who assess players, especially at the quarterback position, take into account not only athletic ability and physical attributes (individual structural constraints) but experience as well. They specifically acknowledge the experience of a quarterback in analyzing the opposing team's defensive patterns and quickly making adjustments to those patterns.

Great performers of skill bring not only their physical talents and conditioning but also their knowledge about a task to the physical performance of that task. Knowledge, then, is an individual constraint that interacts with other constraints to give rise to movement, specifically a functional individual constraint. Individuals and groups possess varying amounts of knowledge about a movement task. For example, children have had less time to acquire knowledge than adults. Older adults might have the advantage of far more experience than younger adults. This chapter examines how knowledge constrains movement over the life span.

Chapter Objectives

This chapter will

▲ discuss the benefits to motor performance of knowing about an activity,

▲ differentiate between the knowledge of novices and experts and recognize that children tend to be novices, and

▲ identify trends in the speed of cognitive processing over the life span.

KNOWLEDGE BASES

At any age, knowledge about an activity facilitates performance, and increased knowledge facilitates remembering information about that topic (Chi, 1981). Children undoubtedly possess a smaller base of knowledge than adults because they have had fewer experiences. Yet children who become experts on a particular topic can outperform adults in that area. Chi (1978) observed that child experts in chess recalled significantly more chess positions than adult novices in chess. Why would performance be related to size of the **knowledge base?** There are at least three reasons:

1. Increased knowledge reduces the need to remember a great deal of information in the short term (Chase & Simon, 1973).

2. Increased knowledge allows more effective use of the cognitive processes (Ornstein & Naus, 1984, cited in Thomas, French, Thomas, & Gallagher, 1988).

3. Increased knowledge reduces the amount of conscious attention needed to perform some tasks (Leavitt, 1979).

Thus, knowledge is a functional constraint that interacts with other constraints, especially with task constraints, to give rise to movement. Performance is facilitated not only by practice of physical skills but also by increased knowledge of the sport or activity.

Types of Knowledge

Before considering the development of knowledge about sport, we must identify the types of knowledge and the differences between experts and novices. Chi (1981) has defined three types of knowledge:

1. Declarative knowledge—knowing factual information

2. Procedural knowledge—knowing how to do something and doing it in accordance with specific rules

A **knowledge base** is the amount of information a person possesses on a specific topic, consisting of declarative knowledge and possibly procedural and strategic knowledge.

3. Strategic knowledge—knowing general rules or strategies that apply to many topics

Declarative and procedural knowledge are specific to a certain topic; strategic knowledge can be generalized. The "give-and-go" is an example of strategic knowledge that can be generalized. An athlete who understands how to execute a give-and-go (pass to a teammate, then advance toward the goal or basket for a return pass) in basketball can execute a give-and-go in hockey or soccer, provided she has the physical skills to do so. Experts have more declarative and procedural knowledge than do novices (Chi, 1978; Chi & Koeske, 1983; Chiesi, Spilich, & Voss, 1979; Spilich, Vesonder, Chiesi, & Voss, 1979). Experts independently organize the information they know in a similar way (Chiesi et al., 1979; Murphy & Wright, 1984)—that is, experts structure knowledge whereas novices do not. By organizing their information in a methodical **knowledge structure,** such as a hierarchy, experts facilitate their memory recall and, therefore, use of information.

Thomas and his colleagues (Thomas et al., 1988, adapted from Berliner, 1986) identified other sport-specific ways in which experts and novices differ. Those pertinent to our discussion follow:

▲ Experts make more inferences about objects and events. In sport, this helps experts predict upcoming events and anticipate the most likely occurrences.

▲ Experts analyze problems at a more advanced level. For example, expert athletes probably think of offensive plays as concepts rather than as lists of individual players' movements.

▲ Experts quickly recognize patterns. For example, expert sport participants quickly recognize defensive configurations.

▲ Experts preplan their responses for specific situations. Softball infielders, for example, do this before the batter hits, when they identify the base to which they will throw, considering the runners on base and the number of outs.

▲ Experts tend to organize knowledge in relation to the goal of the game. For example, an expert basketball player thinks of offensive strategies in terms of those that successfully attack a zone defense versus those that attack a player-to-player defense, not as a long list of individual offenses.

▲ Experts spend much time learning about their topics. Sport expertise, in particular, requires hours of practice and experience, especially if a player wants to develop procedural how-to knowledge.

Keep in mind that expertise is specific. For sport and dance, this means that individuals become experts in specific sports (tennis, basketball) or dance forms (modern, ballroom). In addition, expert performers in sport and dance possess a high level of physical skill. Both skill and the knowledge of how to use skills in specific situations are necessary for success (Thomas et al., 1988).

Development of a Knowledge Base

Let's consider how individuals, especially children, develop a knowledge base in a particular sport. They must acquire declarative knowledge first, to provide a foundation for procedural knowledge (Chi, 1981). Young children often lack declarative knowledge of a sport (figure 13.1). They typically are novices who must learn game rules, goals, and strategies before they can exhibit procedural knowledge and make appropriate decisions regarding which action to perform. Strategic knowledge is the last to develop. It requires

Experts possess more declarative and procedural knowledge, and they structure that knowledge differently than do novices.

A **knowledge structure** is the manner in which a person organizes information about a topic, typically expressed in hierarchical fashion. Experts structure information in ways similar to other experts.

Which athletes in particular positions (e.g., football quarterback) must have a great deal of knowledge about strategy to perform well?

Figure 13.1 Pass, dribble, or shoot? Knowledge helps players make more appropriate decisions.

With advancing knowledge, players tend to report their actions as dependent on opponents' actions.

experience with many different types of tasks, enabling children to generalize across topics.

French and Thomas (1987) conducted one of the first studies of knowledge development in sport with children. They proposed that children need both declarative knowledge of basketball and basketball skills to make appropriate decisions while playing basketball. Coaches classified the 8- to 12-year-old boys in a youth basketball program based on their skills, knowledge of the game, and ability to make good judgments in a game. The best third of the group was designated the expert group and the bottom third the novice group. The boys in these two groups then were tested on their basketball knowledge and skills. In individual interviews, they were asked to give the appropriate action for each of five basketball game situations described to them. The researchers also observed the players during games and graded their decisions as appropriate or inappropriate. The experts scored much better than the novices on both the knowledge and skill tests. More important, the experts chose the appropriate action in game situations more often than novices. During their situation interviews, experts were more likely to give answers dependent on the action of the opponents and gave more alternatives, indicating better memory of basketball knowledge.

French and Thomas observed some of the 8- to 10-year-old boys from their first study over the course of a season, along with a group of boys who did not play basketball. By the end of the season, both expert and novice players were making better decisions about actions and scored better on the knowledge test (figure 13.2). The control group made no significant progress. Interestingly, none of the children improved in physical skill over the season, either on skill tests or in game play. This initial study, then, indicates that basketball knowledge is related to children's skill performance and that children might acquire knowledge faster than they improve their physical skills.

French, Nevett, and colleagues (French et al., 1996; Nevett & French, 1997) also examined expertise in youth baseball players. In their first study, they hypothesized that players with more declarative and procedural knowledge solve game situation problems better, whereas those with less knowledge exhibit more errors in solving those game situation problems. They gave youth baseball players 7 to 8 years old and 9 to 10 years old five baseball situation problems to solve. The players' coaches categorized the players for skill level. In three of the problem situations, the players whom coaches categorized as more skilled solved the problem better, regardless of age. Overall, though, these 7- to 10-year-olds were still developing their knowledge base regarding baseball. They had difficulty quickly predicting base runners' actions and failed to monitor some critical game conditions.

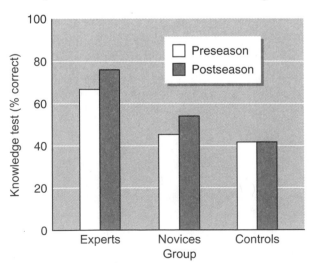

Figure 13.2 Both expert and novice boys scored better on a postseason basketball knowledge test than on a preseason test. A control group did not improve.

Data from French and Thomas 1987.

Nevett and French (1997) followed up this initial study with 8-, 10-, and 12-year-old and high school baseball shortstops. They trained players to use a talk-aloud procedure between pitches. Although players were told to verbalize any of their thoughts, information about possible plays that could be made if the batter hit the ball was of particular interest. Players 12 years of age and under did not develop advanced defensive plans, rehearsal plans, or update plans as well or as frequently as high school players. It is likely that frequent and repetitive responses to game situations through experience help in the development of procedural knowledge structures. Even though declarative knowledge can be acquired at young ages, experience in game situations is necessary to develop a knowledge structure beneficial to skilled performance.

McPherson (1999) expanded work on youth knowledge bases in sports to adults. She posed six tennis game situation problems to six novice tennis players and six college varsity experts, all women 18 to 22 years of age. Compared with youth experts in previous research, adult experts generated a greater number, variety, and level of sophistication of condition-and-action concepts. Adult novices were similar to youth novices in having weak representations of the game situation problems, with few solutions to the situations. The adult novices generated fewer tactical concepts than did youth tennis experts in previous studies. Thus, years of experience—from practicing, being coached, and playing—are influential in developing a knowledge base, and youths with more experience can have a more advanced knowledge base than adult novices (figure 13.3).

Experience in playing is important in developing a knowledge structure.

Figure 13.3 Youth experts can have more tactical concepts about their sports than do adult novices. Teaching children *about* sports as well as *doing* activities has great benefit. Knowledge can help older adults perform successfully even if physical abilities decline somewhat.

Assessing Cognitive Decision Making

The more knowledge an athlete has, the more quickly and accurately that athlete can decide on an action. So, in assessing decision making, the speed and accuracy of decisions in sport provide information about the size of an athlete's knowledge base.

In their study of knowledge development in sport, French and Thomas (1987) needed to assess the decisions that young basketball players actually made during games. The written

knowledge test and interview yielded useful information, but it was not certain that the players who gave good answers to questions away from the court would make good decisions in a fast-moving, demanding game situation.

To assess decision making in games, French and Thomas designed an observational instrument based on a typical offensive sequence in basketball: when a player catches the ball, he

(continued)

(continued)

or she must decide to hold the ball, pass, dribble, or shoot. They identified all the decisions a player could make, then categorized them as appropriate or inappropriate.

French and Thomas videotaped youth basketball games. A trained basketball expert watched each player in each game for one quarter of playing time and coded each decision the player made when he or she received a pass. A second expert watched independently and coded some of the players to ensure that an expert observer would code each decision the same way at least 90% of the time. The observer gave a player a score of 1 for an appropriate decision and a score of zero for an inappropriate decision. For example, a player received 1 point for passing to an open teammate but no points for passing to a closely guarded teammate. In this way the researchers could measure the players' decision making in actual games.

Observational instruments are an excellent means of measuring behavior. Performers can be observed in real situations rather than in artificial laboratory conditions. Note, though, that French and Thomas had to develop a coding system that included all of the decisions a player could make. They then had to locate experts and train them to use the assessment instrument. Two experts independently coded some of the trials so the experimenters could cross-check those trials and assure themselves that the coding system was reliable. Finally, the observers coded from videotape so that they could stop the tape to record their judgments, thereby not missing any action. This is obviously a tedious procedure, but it provides an interesting and accurate measure of decision-making behaviors in sport.

? Name some activities and sports in which an advanced knowledge base is advantageous for performance.

Teachers and coaches would benefit from continued study of knowledge development in sport. Educators may be able to improve children's skill acquisition in sport and dance by using appropriately timed instruction of and emphasis on rules, formations, strategies, and goals. Increased knowledge enhances memory.

Gender differences in sport performance might be attributable in part to differences between boys' and girls' knowledge of sport. Society makes it easier for boys to acquire sport knowledge by targeting sport-related merchandise to them—board and electronic games, books, collector cards, and so on. Girls' use of these items is viewed as less appropriate to their gender role, and as a result a performance gap between boys and girls persists. Also, children who practice more probably acquire more knowledge, so unequal opportunities to participate might widen the performance gap between most boys and at least some girls (Thomas et al., 1988).

Knowledge bases in older adults have not been widely studied. Langley and Knight (1996) conducted a case study of a single senior adult competitive tennis player, a man 58 years old. The investigators conducted interviews and observations, analyzing narrative information with coding techniques. They found that the senior player had a rich knowledge of tennis situations. This knowledge centered on performance capabilities and opponent limitations. The player knew how his opponent's actions in a particular setting affected his own capabilities in that setting. He realized that his physical conditioning had declined somewhat as he aged but felt that his better skill in executing a number of shots more than compensated. Langley and Knight used Gibson's (1979) notion of affordances to suggest that experienced players perceive the game play environment in terms of the actions that environment affords. Experience allows the player to perceive affordances that are opportunities for success against an opponent.

💡 Older adults can have a rich knowledge base in a sport or dance form through extensive experience, and this knowledge could compensate for slight declines in physical performance.

We can speculate that older adults with expertise in a sport have an advantage in performance. Superior knowledge might offset a loss of physical skill or speed. Also, older adults learning new sports can expect to improve as they acquire knowledge of the sport.

MEMORY

Knowledge and memory are inseparable topics. We remember what we understand. "Coming to understand" is related to our existing base of mental representations, representations that define our knowledge at that point in time. Sutherland, Pipe, Schick, Murray, & Gobbo (2003) found that providing children with prior information about an event improved their recall of the event and their knowledge acquisition about the event, both soon after the event and four months later. So, new experiences are integrated with our existing base of meaning.

The question asked most often about memory development is whether memory capacity changes with development. Yet, how much we remember, no matter what our age, depends on what we already know about a topic. Knowledge is organized or structured within specific content domains (Kuhn, 2000), such as chess, dinosaurs, or baseball. Memorizing, then, is a process of revising our knowledge of a topic. Although much research has been carried out on the topic of memory capacity, the answer to whether it increases with development has been elusive. This probably reflects researchers' approaching the study of memory without regard to one's knowledge context. That is, memory has been studied in isolation. The capacity answer awaits new research approaches that study memory in the broader context of the developing cognitive system.

People of all ages remember more when they have a reason to do so. Very young children first remember when adults engage them in recounting experiences. With advancing age, children internalize this remembering activity and carry it out on their own. Eventually they remember purposively, for their individual benefit or that of their social group. Again, laboratory research on memory often has involved memorizing items for no particular reason to participants other than completing the research task. Future researchers must study memory in the context of information that is important to people.

Young children typically do not employ strategies for remembering, but they can be taught to use strategies, such as rehearsal, labeling, and grouping. Thomas, Thomas, and Gallagher (1981) demonstrated that teaching children a rehearsal strategy along with a skill enhanced their skill acquisition. Gallagher and Thomas (1980) also found that grouping arm movements in an organized order helped children recall and duplicate movements. The difficulty is that children won't necessarily apply the strategies learned in one context to another context. Perhaps the use of memory strategies is related to a broader issue, the development of cognitive strategies such as inference and problem solving, and needs to be studied in that context.

Research on memory in adults and older adults tends to find a decline in performance on memory tasks. Yet, like the research with children, researchers have tended to study memory in isolation, without regard to adults' knowledge of a topic or motivation to remember. Moreover, a host of environmental factors might affect older adult performance on memory tasks. Diseases (e.g., hypertension) might impair memory performance. Highly fit older adults have been observed to perform better than unfit adults on memory tasks (Stones & Kozma, 1989), and memory performance has been linked to self-reported health status (Perlmutter & Nyquist, 1990). Improvements on memory tasks have also been noted after exercise interventions, so exercise probably has a small but positive effect on memory performance (Clarkson-Smith & Hartley, 1990).

Of course, Alzheimer's disease is one of the most devastating diseases of aging for individuals and their families. Late-onset Alzheimer's disease is the most common form and is characterized by confusion, memory loss, and behavioral problems. As the number of individuals living into older adulthood increases, so too will the number of older adults who develop Alzheimer's. The cause of late-onset Alzheimer's disease is probably both genetic and environmental, but researchers are investigating both genes that might trigger the disease, through production of a specific protein, and genes that might control the timing of onset. The hope is that drugs might be designed that could either block the protein or delay onset of the disease, perhaps past the natural life span.

Although performance on memory tests might show improvement through childhood and decline in older adulthood, it is most important to acknowledge that memory is related

Memories are knowledge structures resulting from our efforts to understand and know.

to current knowledge and understanding of information within a specific context, as well as to motivation to remember information.

SPEED OF COGNITIVE FUNCTIONS

Although there are general differences in the knowledge individuals have about specific sports and dance over the life span, there also are general differences in the speed with which individuals can access and use that knowledge. That is, a person can have considerable knowledge but not be able to recall and apply that knowledge as quickly as another person. This would be a more pertinent issue when participating in activities in which quick decisions and responses are needed. For example, slower cognitive function would not be an issue in deciding how to pick up a spare in bowling since there is sufficient time between deliveries. It would be an issue in the middle of a tennis point in deciding whether a lob is an appropriate shot for the situation. As such, let's consider age-related differences in the speed of cognitive functions.

Before we begin, let's acknowledge that most of the research on cognitive speed has been undertaken from an information processing perspective. From this viewpoint, short-term and long-term memory and information retrieval play a major role in movement responses. In contrast, ecological perspectives play down the role of knowledge and cognitive processes in movement responses. From this perspective, affordances in the environment are perceived. Experience might influence whether or not an affordance is perceived, but the affordance is always available in the environment. With this in mind, let's first consider cognitive speed in children.

Speed of Cognitive Processing in Children

Simple reaction time is the time between the onset of a stimulus (such as a light or buzzer) and the beginning of a movement response (such as lifting a finger from a button).

💡 Speed of initiating a response increases through childhood and youth and is faster when the response is compatible with the stimulus signal.

Children take longer than adults to process cognitive information to be remembered. As children get older, they can eventually process either the same amount of information faster or more information in the same amount of time. This is apparent in even the simplest of motor responses, **simple reaction time.** The maximum speed of this response increases from age 3 through adolescence (Wickens, 1974). An improvement with age also occurs in the time required to respond in continuous tracking (Pew & Rupp, 1971). In this type of task, children must continuously match their movement to a target. For example, a video game in which the player controls the image of a car with a joystick to keep the car on a curved road is a continuous tracking task. Factors considered to be central processes (processes of the central nervous system) rather than peripheral ones appear responsible for the slower processing speed that children exhibit (Elliott, 1972). Attention is one such central process, and speed of the memory processes is another.

The speed with which an individual can select motor responses is a function of age (Wickens, 1974). Clark (1982) demonstrated this by manipulating the spatial stimulus–response compatibility of a reaction-time task when testing 6-year-olds, 10-year-olds, and adults. In the compatible condition, participants pressed a key on the right if the right stimulus light came on and a key on the left if the left stimulus light came on. In the incompatible condition, participants pressed a key opposite the direction of the light. Spatial compatibility, then, affects the participant's response selection. Clark found that processing time decreased (performance improved) in the older groups tested in the incompatible condition.

Although these central factors of attention, memory, and response selection influence children's slower processing speeds, peripheral factors do not. For example, nerve impulse conduction speed in the peripheral nerves does not contribute substantially to the speed differences between children and adults. Young children are able to process information faster as they mature because of improvements in central factors such as response selection and speed of the memory process.

Speed of Cognitive Processing in Older Adults

Similar to young children, older adults exhibit limitations in the processing of information. These limitations are also apparently related to central rather than peripheral processes. However, researchers have found important differences between performers at opposite ends of the life span. For example, older adults do not exhibit declining performance in all types of skills. They undergo little change in their performance of single, discrete actions that can be planned in advance (Welford, 1977b) or of simple, continuous, and repetitive actions, such as alternately tapping two targets (Welford, Norris, & Shock, 1969). However, in actions requiring a series of different movements, especially when speed is important (Welford, 1977c), older adults show a large decrement in performance. The major limitations on older adults, then, seem to involve the decisions they base on perceptual information and the programming of movement sequences (Welford, 1980). These are central rather than peripheral factors. Let's consider in more detail some of the central components of information processing that are affected by aging.

Older adults apparently learn new tasks, whether cognitive or motor, more slowly than younger adults. For example, rote learning of cognitive material is slower in older adults because they need more repetitions to reach criterion—that is, to learn the material at a predesignated level. This may reflect the need for more time for the information to register in long-term memory. Similarly, older adults improve more slowly than younger adults in new motor skills, although they maintain well the skills they learned early in life (Szafran, 1951; Welford, 1980).

Attentional factors also play a role in the performance limitations of older adults. Older adults perform their fastest on a reaction-time task when a warning signal is given a consistent time before the stimulus; they perform their slowest when the warning signal interval varies from trial to trial. This suggests that a fixed interval minimizes distraction by irrelevant associations (Birren, 1964). Rabbitt (1965) also demonstrated that older adults are hampered more than younger adults by the presence of irrelevant stimuli in a card-sorting task. In this task, participants are challenged to sort a stack of cards based on information given on the card face, such as the shape of a symbol or its color. If information on the card face is not relevant to the sorting task, older adults' performance suffers compared with that of younger adults.

Many older adults are more easily distracted and do not attend to critical stimuli as well as they did when younger. The cause of this decline in performance might be a lowered signal-to-noise ratio in the central nervous system (CNS). The neural impulses of the CNS take place against a background of random neural noise such that the effectiveness of a neural signal depends on the ratio between the signal strength and the background noise—the signal-to-noise ratio. As a person ages, signal levels within the CNS decrease because of changes in the sense organs, loss of brain cells, and factors affecting brain cell functioning, while at the same time, noise level increases (Crossman & Szafran, 1956; Welford, 1977a). Older adults can compensate for this lower signal-to-noise ratio if they are given extra time to complete a task, but if they must perform a series of movements or make a series of decisions rapidly, they are at a disadvantage.

Central nervous system factors also influence the slower speed of processing in older adults. Researchers have consistently documented a slowing of reaction time with aging. Although a slight slowing of neural impulse conduction velocity is associated with aging, it is not great enough to account for the magnitude of lengthened reaction times.

> **?** What are the implications of slower cognitive processing for children in sports such as soccer, basketball, and tennis? How might you structure their tasks for increased success given this limitation?

> Older adults respond more slowly than young adults and are more susceptible to being distracted.

> Central nervous system factors play a much larger role in speed of cognitive processing than peripheral factors at any point in the life span.

Choice reaction time is a measure requiring the earliest possible response to more than one stimulus, usually with a different response matched to each of the possible stimuli.

Choice reaction time slows in older adults even more than simple reaction time. Making a task more complex by increasing the number of signals or designating responses that are less logical (e.g., pressing the left button in response to the right signal light) disproportionately increases older adults' reaction time compared with that of younger adults (Cerella, Poon, & Williams, 1980; Welford, 1977a, 1977b).

Older adults' movement time, too, shows a very slight slowing (Singleton, 1955), but they maintain the speed of planned, repetitive movements such as tapping (Earles & Salthouse, 1995; Fieandt, Huhtala, Kullberg, & Saari, 1956; Jagacinski, Liao, & Fayyad, 1995). Because almost all behaviors mediated by the central nervous system slow down as an adult ages, central factors are assumed to be largely responsible for slower information processing speed (Birren, 1964). However, the schemata of older adults can be particularly complete and refined for skills the adult has had a lifetime of experience with. This experience is particularly helpful when accuracy is more important than speed. When older adults are not pressed to perform as quickly as possible, they demonstrate very accurate performance on well-practiced tasks.

Several studies also document less dramatic slowing in older adults who maintain active lifestyles. When Spirduso (1975) tested active and inactive older men for simple reaction time, she found the active men were not much slower than younger men. The inactive older men were significantly slower than younger men. All of the older men had slower choice reaction times, but the gap between the younger men and the active older men was smaller than that between the younger men and the inactive older men. The same is true for older women (Rikli & Busch, 1986; Spirduso, 1980).

 Older adults with active lifestyles exhibit less slowing than do sedentary adults.

Because the nature of slowing in older adults implicates CNS functioning, maintaining an active lifestyle must have some effect on central processes. Two possibilities exist. Perhaps exercise enhances the production or functioning of neurotransmitters, which carry neural signals between neurons within the brain (Spirduso, Gilliam, & Wilcox, 1984). Or, exercise might increase oxygenation of the tissues, and oxygen plays a role in CNS energy metabolism (Birren, Woods, & Williams, 1980; Shephard & Kavanaugh, 1978). In either case, exercisers would maintain better cognitive and motor functioning than nonexercisers.

Dustman et al. (1989) found that aerobic exercisers better maintained cognitive and motor functioning. They placed sedentary 55- to 70-year-olds on a 4-month aerobic exercise program and compared them with strength-and-flexibility exercisers and nonexercisers on a battery of cognitive and motor tests. Among the tests were a culturally unbiased IQ test and a reaction-time test. Both exercise groups improved, but the aerobic exercisers improved significantly more (figure 13.4). Exercise, especially aerobic exercise, is associated with improved information processing for both cognitive and motor tasks in older adults.

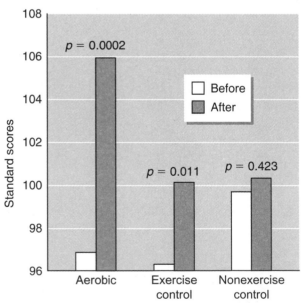

Figure 13.4 The standard scores (averaged over a battery of eight cognitive and motor tests) for three groups of older adults: aerobic exercisers, strength-and-flexibility exercisers, and nonexercisers. The exercise programs lasted 4 months. The *p* values indicate that the exercisers improved significantly, but the nonexercisers did not.

Reprinted from Dustman et al. 1989.

Summary and Synthesis

Knowledge acts as a constraint in performing skills. Those with more knowledge make more appropriate responses in settings requiring decisions. They anticipate situations and actions and think of global strategies more than specific, single occurrences. It takes time and experience to acquire knowledge.

Children need experience to develop an extensive knowledge base, yet expert children can bring more knowledge to a situation than a novice adult can. Older adults with long, extensive experience can make their knowledge base a great asset in the performance of skills.

There is a difference in the speed of cognitive processing over the life span, however. Although youth and older adult experts might surpass young adults with their knowledge, they might experience slower processing of that information. On the other hand, older adults with active lifestyles are less affected by this slowing. Older adults with active lifestyles who participate in an activity and acquire considerable experience can perform at a high level.

Discussion Questions

1. Name and define the types of knowledge and provide an example of each for one of your favorite sports or dance forms.
2. Describe four sport-specific ways that novices and experts differ in regard to their knowledge of a sport.
3. What can youth athletes do better as they increase their expertise in their sports?
4. What are some of the factors that can influence performance on memory tasks?
5. Describe the trend in cognitive processing speed over the life span.
6. How does maintaining an active lifestyle appear to affect speed of cognitive processing in older adults? What are the implications of this for automobile driving and sport participation?

Learning Activities

Teaching Strategies for Older Adult Learners

Older adults might learn new things more slowly than young adults. Given this possibility,

1. identify two strategies you would adopt to teach a new skill to an older adult, and
2. write a lesson plan for teaching a skill that demonstrates the use of each of the strategies.

Compensatory Strategies of Older Adults

Older adults who participate in sports sometimes compensate for limitations in their movement (due to changes in the skeletal system, muscle strength, flexibility, etc.) by anticipating their next movements based on experience playing the game. Interview an older adult who participates in a sport such as tennis, racquetball, or volleyball to find if they can describe making such adaptations. For example, Dodo Cheney, who won tennis championships into her 80s, recounts learning to position herself closer to the net (when in her younger days she would have positioned herself at the baseline) in order to reach drop shots or short balls.

PART VI

Interaction of Exercise and Structural Constraints

© Human Kinetics

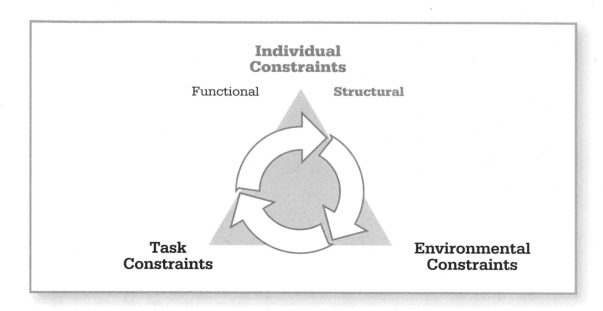

The theme of our study of motor development is that movement arises from the interaction of individual, environmental, and task constraints. We also note repeatedly that within each type of constraint, multiple systems interact. For example, chapter 4 examined many individual structural systems that interact with growth and aging, such as the skeletal, muscular, and neurological systems. Later chapters reviewed perceptual systems, their interaction, and how they constrained movement. In part VI, we explore the interaction of exercise and structural constraints.

Physical fitness has many systems or components, such as flexibility and strength. A person who is fit in one component is not necessarily fit in another. For example, an individual may be very strong but not very flexible. This part discusses in detail the following components of fitness:

1. Cardiorespiratory endurance (chapter 14)
2. Strength (chapter 15)
3. Flexibility (chapter 15)
4. Body composition (chapter 16)

Some writers describe additional components of fitness, such as agility and power, but the four mentioned here are the essential systems. Potentially, a person can improve physical fitness through a systematic program of exercise aimed at these four components. An individual's fitness level in each of the four systems and the interaction of these levels can either permit or restrain movements over the life span. We begin with endurance for vigorous activity.

Suggested Reading

Cahill, B.R., & A.J. Pearl (Eds.). (1993). *Intensive participation in children's sports.* Champaign, IL: Human Kinetics.

Feltz, D.L. (Ed.). (2004). The Academy papers: Obesity and physical activity. *Quest, 56,* iv–170.

Rowland, T.W. (Ed.). (1993). *Pediatric laboratory exercise testing.* Champaign, IL: Human Kinetics.

Rowland, T.W. (1996). *Developmental exercise physiology.* Champaign, IL: Human Kinetics.

Spirduso, W.W. (1995). *Physical dimensions of aging.* Champaign, IL: Human Kinetics.

Development of Cardiorespiratory Endurance

EXTRA!!! The Times EXTRA!!!

FOR HEALTH, DOCTORS TELL PATIENTS TO TAKE A HIKE

The next hot prescription might not come in a bottle from a major pharmaceutical company. Instead, it could be manufactured by the patient himself. More and more doctors are concluding that exercise is good medicine, and their patients are more likely to engage in physical activity if ordered to do so by prescription. Soon, many physicians may begin writing exercise prescriptions designed for patients suffering from heart disease, osteoporosis, arthritis, diabetes, and any number of other diseases and health problems. (Hellmich, 1999, May 18)

Of all the fitness components, cardiorespiratory endurance has the greatest implications for lifelong health, but its development in children is surrounded by many myths. For many years, experts thought that children's cardiovascular and respiratory systems limited their capacity for extended work. They thought so because measurements of children's blood vessel size were misinterpreted more than 60 years ago. Even though the mistake was soon discovered, the myth has persisted for decades (Karpovich, 1937/1991). In addition, many parents and teachers think that children automatically get enough exercise to become and remain fit. This belief serves as a social constraint to children's regular and systematic participation in exercise. Studies conducted in recent decades (Bailey, 1976; Gilliam, Katch, Thorland, & Weltman, 1977; Simons-Morton et al., 1990; Dollman, Olds, Norton, & Stuart, 1999) counter this view by showing that the sedentary lifestyle that many of today's adults have adopted has spilled over to the lives of their children. A high percentage of children and teens already exhibit one or more of the risk factors for coronary heart disease, and far too many are obese. Children in poor physical condition are likely to maintain that status throughout their adult lives. Educators and exercise leaders must thoroughly understand cardiorespiratory endurance development and potential so that they can challenge children to attain an appropriate level of fitness for vigorous activity.

 ## *Chapter Objectives*

This chapter will

▲ examine the body's response to short-term vigorous exercise and how this response changes over the life span,

▲ review the effects of short-term exercise over the life span,

▲ study the body's response to prolonged exercise and how this response changes over the life span, and

▲ review the effects of endurance training over the life span.

CARDIORESPIRATORY ENDURANCE

An individual's performance on endurance tests reflects a variety of factors. For example, people with good neuromuscular coordination can move more efficiently and are likely to perform longer than those less coordinated. Some tests require participants to maintain or match a cadence, and this might be difficult for young children. Cultural factors also influence performance because a person's culture sometimes dictates whether vigorous physical activity for endurance and all-out effort is socially acceptable.

Realizing that such factors play a role in the measurement of endurance, we now focus on those factors that directly influence endurance. We review the body's basic physiological responses to increased demand of vigorous activity and the changes in these responses that occur as a person grows. We also discuss the changes that tend to occur with aging and how they affect an older adult's capacity for prolonged activity.

PHYSIOLOGICAL RESPONSES TO SHORT-TERM EXERCISE

Vigorous physical activity can be a short burst of intense exercise, a long period of submaximal or maximal work, or a combination of these. Our bodies meet the demands of brief, intense activity and longer, more moderate activity with different physiological responses. During a brief period (10 s) of intense activity, the body responds by depleting local reserves of oxygen and phosphate compounds and by breaking down glycogen (energy reserves) to lactic acid, creating a deficit of oxygen that must eventually be replenished. These are **anaerobic** (without oxygen) systems. Anaerobic system performance can be reflected in measurements of anaerobic power and anaerobic capacity.

As the period of exercise demand grows longer, the anaerobic systems contribute less to the body's response. Respiration and circulation increase to bring oxygen to the muscles. Ninety seconds into an exercise bout, anaerobic and **aerobic** (with oxygen) energy systems contribute about equally. After 3 min, aerobic processes meet the demands of exercise. The types of exercise that promote anaerobic performance, then, are vigorous but of short duration, while those that promote aerobic performance are sustained and consequently less vigorous or intense.

> **Anaerobic power** is the rate at which a person's body can meet the demand for short-term, intense activity.
>
> **Anaerobic capacity** is the maximum oxygen deficit that a person can tolerate.

Developmental Changes in Anaerobic Performance

At any age, anaerobic performance is related to

▲ body size, particularly fat-free muscle mass and muscle size,

▲ the ability to resist acidosis as lactic acid accumulates in the muscles,

▲ the rate of phosphate compound resynthesis, and

▲ quick mobilization of oxygen delivery systems.

Some of these factors change as a person grows (Malina & Bouchard, 1991).

Childhood

Young children have smaller absolute quantities of energy reserves than adults because they have less muscle mass (Eriksson, 1978; Shephard, 1982). Therefore, children attain less absolute anaerobic power output than adults. As children grow, their muscle mass increases, as does the phosphate concentrations and glycogen content in their muscle tissue, and they develop a higher tolerance of lactic acid concentrations. Thus, mean and peak anaerobic power improve steadily as a person ages (Duche et al., 1992; Falgairette, Bedu, Fellmann, Van Praagh, & Coudert, 1991; Inbar & Bar-Or, 1986). Total work output scores improve over the entire adolescent period for boys but only until puberty in girls, perhaps reflecting the patterns of muscle growth in the sexes (figure 14.1, a and b) or sociocultural views of appropriate activities for girls.

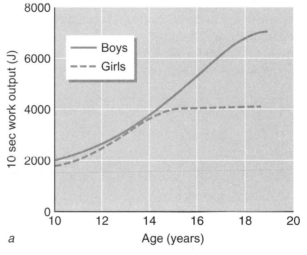

a

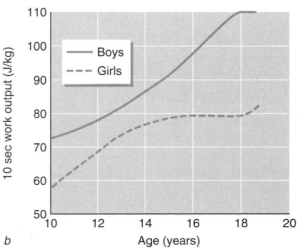

b

Figure 14.1 Anaerobic performance. *(a)* Change in total work output (measured in Joules) on a 10 s, all-out bicycle ergometer ride with advancing age. C. Bouchard and J.A. Simoneau (unpublished data) measured a cross-sectional group of French-Canadian youths on this task. When anaerobic performance scores are divided by body weight, as in *b*, scores still improve with age.

Reprinted from Malina and Bouchard 1991.

Accounting for differences in muscle mass, however, does not entirely eliminate the differences in anaerobic performance that favor boys (Van Praagh, Fellmann, Bedu, Falgairette, & Coudert, 1990). Not all of the differences between children and adults are attributable to difference in body size, either. When we divide anaerobic performance scores by body weight, scores still improve with age.

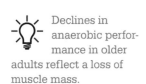
Anaerobic fitness improves with growth but at a faster rate than can be explained by growth alone.

Undoubtedly, better neuromuscular coordination and skill contribute to improved anaerobic performance as children grow older, and the capacity for energy production (rate of anaerobic glycolysis) improves with age (Rowland, 1996). Armstrong, Welsman, and Kirby (1997) found that advancing maturation independent of body mass was related to higher mean and peak anaerobic power. More mature children can be expected to show better anaerobic performance than other children even if they are similar in body size.

Adulthood

Once individuals attain adult body size, their anaerobic performance remains stable throughout young adulthood (Inbar & Bar-Or, 1986). Any improvement in anaerobic power and capacity is achieved through training alone. Because lactic acid production and removal decline with advancing age, older adults' anaerobic systems do not produce energy as quickly as those of younger adults. This likely is associated with loss of muscle mass, especially of fast-twitch fibers. At the same level of exercise, older adults accumulate lactic acid sooner than young adults do (Spirduso, 1995). The loss of anaerobic power was recorded as 50% by age 75 (Grassi, Cerretelli, Narici, & Marconi, 1991).

Declines in anaerobic performance in older adults reflect a loss of muscle mass.

It is not clear, however, whether anaerobic power and capacity necessarily decline as adults grow older. Those engaged in lifelong intense training showed no deterioration in anaerobic performance (Reaburn & Mackinnon, 1990). These master athletes likely maintained much of their muscle mass. Any loss of muscle mass in older adults is likely to affect their anaerobic performance, and a lack of training in anaerobic tasks to maintain conditioning logically would affect their performance.

Assessing Anaerobic Performance

No direct, noninvasive methods of measuring anaerobic fitness exist, so it is typically studied through short-duration tasks. The Quebec 10 s and the Wingate 30 s all-out rides on a bicycle ergometer and the Margaria step-running test are common laboratory tests that provide scores in total work output, mean power, or peak power. Total work output indicates how much work an individual can do in a 10 or 30 s time period. In contrast, power indicates the rate at which individuals can produce energy—that is, the work they can do within a specific time.

Mean power is the average power individuals achieve during the 10 or 30 s period, whereas peak power is the highest rate they achieve. The 50 yd dash and sprinting a flight of stairs are common field tests. Participants must be willing and able to give an all-out effort to provide an accurate measure of anaerobic performance. Anaerobic measurements can be difficult or even dangerous with older adults, especially those who have been inactive.

Anaerobic Training

Although the results of training studies are somewhat inconsistent, preadolescent and adolescent boys have demonstrated improved anaerobic power with anaerobic training (Grodjinovsky, Inbar, Dotan, & Bar-Or, 1980; Rotstein, Dotan, Bar-Or, & Tenenbaum, 1986). Improvements are not large, and some cross-sectional comparisons show no anaerobic differences between active and nonactive boys (Falgairette, Duche, Bedu, Fellmann, & Coudert, 1993; Mero, Kauhanen, Peltola, Vuorimaa, & Komi, 1990). Improvements with training might be associated with increased concentrations of phosphates and glycogen and improved rate of glycogen use, therefore improving anaerobic capacity (Eriksson,

1972). Less is known about girls, but McManus, Armstrong, and Williams (1997) found small improvements in prepubescent girls with both cycle and sprint running training.

Little is known about how untrained older adults respond to anaerobic training, although training programs that improve muscle mass are likely to bring about an improvement of anaerobic performance. Reaburn and Mackinnon (1990) studied master athletes over 46 years of age who were training for world swimming competition. After sprint swimming these athletes produced and removed lactic acid just as well as younger adults. Therefore, long-term training of sufficient intensity might maintain anaerobic performance.

Anaerobic training improves the anaerobic performance of preadolescent children and maintains that of master athletes.

PHYSIOLOGICAL RESPONSES TO PROLONGED EXERCISE

How do our bodies sustain submaximal physical activity for prolonged periods? Unlike in short-term exercise, the energy for prolonged exercise is derived from aerobic systems, the oxidative breakdown of food stores in addition to the local reserves depleted in the first few minutes of exercise. The success with which we meet the needs of prolonged activity can be indicated by measurements of **aerobic power** and **aerobic capacity.**

Sustained, prolonged activity depends on the transportation of sufficient oxygen to the working muscles for longer periods. Heart and respiratory rates, cardiac output, and oxygen uptake increase to deliver the oxygen needed for prolonged activity. An increased respiratory rate brings more oxygen to the lungs, making it available for diffusion into the bloodstream. Cardiac output (the amount of blood pumped into the circulatory system) increases to allow more oxygen to reach the muscles. The body achieves this increased cardiac output through increased heart rate or increased stroke volume. Changes in stroke volume during exercise are relatively small, but one of the long-term benefits of training is greater initial stroke volume.

Aerobic power is the rate at which long-term oxygen demand is met during prolonged activity.

Aerobic capacity is the total energy available to meet the demands of prolonged activity.

The limiting factor to continued vigorous activity is the heart's ability to pump enough blood to meet the working muscles' oxygen needs. When individuals engage in very heavy activity, their heart rate rises throughout the session until exhaustion ends the activity. When they stop vigorous activity, their heart rate drops quickly for 2 to 3 min, then more gradually for a time related to the duration and intensity of the activity. Fit individuals regain their resting heart rates more quickly than unfit individuals.

This description is only a brief summary of the physiological responses to exercise. A more detailed treatment is available in exercise physiology textbooks.

Changes in Aerobic Performance During Childhood

How do children respond physiologically to prolonged activity? Children tend to have hypokinetic circulation (Bar-Or, Shephard, & Allen, 1971); that is, their cardiac output is less than an adult's. Cardiac output is the product of stroke volume and heart rate. Children have a smaller stroke volume than adults, reflecting their smaller hearts. Children compensate in part with higher heart rates than adults at a given level of exercise, but their cardiac output is still somewhat lower than an adult's. Children also have lower blood **hemoglobin** concentrations than do adults. The hemoglobin concentration is related to the blood's ability to carry oxygen.

Hemoglobin is the protein in the blood that carries oxygen.

You might assume that these two factors, hypokinetic circulation and low hemoglobin concentration, result in an oxygen transport system that is less efficient in children than in adults. However, children's ability to extract relatively more of the oxygen circulating to the active muscles compared with adults (Malina & Bouchard, 1991; Shephard, 1982) seems to compensate for these factors. The result is a comparably effective oxygen transport system. Children also mobilize their aerobic systems faster than adults (Bar-Or, 1983).

Children's physiological response to endurance activity is very efficient, but children cannot exercise as long as adults can.

Children do have a lower tolerance than adults for extended periods of exercise, ostensibly because of smaller glycogen stores. When their glycogen stores are exhausted, performance is limited. As children grow, their hypokinetic circulation is gradually reduced as the following changes occur:

▲ Heart size increases.

▲ Hemoglobin concentration increases.

▲ Oxygen-extraction ability decreases to adult levels.

Longitudinal and cross-sectional studies demonstrate that absolute **maximal oxygen uptake** increases linearly in children from age 4 until late adolescence in boys and until age 12 or 13 in girls (Krahenbuhl, Skinner, & Kohrt, 1985; Mirwald & Bailey, 1986; Shuleva, Hunter, Hester, & Dunaway, 1990). Maximal oxygen uptake is the most common measure of fitness for endurance activities. Figure 14.2a pictures this trend between ages 6 and about 18 years. Boys and girls are similar in maximal oxygen uptake until about age 12, although boys have a slightly higher average. After this, maximal oxygen uptake plateaus in girls but continues to rise in boys. The increase with age is related to growth of the musculature, the lungs, and the heart.

A strong relationship exists between absolute maximal oxygen uptake and lean body mass. In fact, maximal oxygen uptake can be expressed in relative rather than absolute terms, dividing it by body weight, lean body weight, or another body dimension. As figure 14.2b shows, maximal oxygen uptake relative to body weight stays about the same through childhood and adolescence in boys. It declines in girls, probably because adipose tissue increases. When maximal oxygen uptake is related to fat-free mass, scores show a slight decline during and after puberty, and small gender differences remain.

Thus body weight appears to increase slightly faster than maximal oxygen uptake around puberty (Malina & Bouchard, 1991). Maximal oxygen uptake might depend somewhat on maturity in addition to body size; comparisons of maximal oxygen uptake to age show a relationship in adolescents who vary in age but are identical in size (Sprynarova & Reisenauer, 1978). Two adolescents identical in size could differ in maximal oxygen uptake if one is more physiologically mature than the other.

Even though maximal oxygen uptake is the best single measurement of endurance, it might not predict running performance in children as well as it does in adults. Running test performance relates more to anaerobic measures in children than in adults. In addition, children's ventilatory mechanisms, lower aerobic reserves,

Maximal oxygen uptake is the highest amount of oxygen the body can consume during aerobic work.

Absolute maximal oxygen uptake increases in boys through childhood and adolescence and in girls until age 12, after which it plateaus.

Maximal oxygen uptake per kilogram of body weight is stable in boys and declines slightly in girls throughout childhood and adolescence.

Maximal oxygen uptake is related to body size, especially lean body mass, as well as to maturity status.

Figure 14.2 The relationship between maximal oxygen uptake and age. (a) Absolute scores. (b) Maximal oxygen uptake values relative to kilograms of body weight. The boys' scores are centered in the shaded area, the girls' scores in the unshaded area.

Reprinted from Bar-Or 1983.

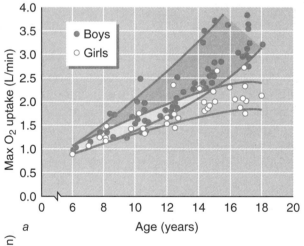

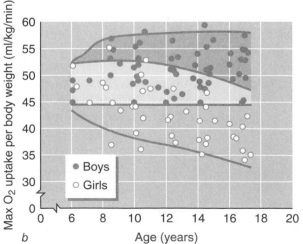

and mechanical inefficiencies affect their endurance fitness. Caution should be used when inferring maximal oxygen uptake levels from children's running performance.

It is important to recognize the relationship between children's increasing body size and their improving ability to sustain exercise during growth. With body growth come increases in lung volume, heart and stroke volume, total hemoglobin, and lean body mass. These factors foster improved cardiac output and, subsequently, improved exercise capacity and absolute maximal oxygen uptake. Because children vary in size despite their chronological age, evaluations of exercise capacity among children should relate to body size rather than chronological age alone. In the past, educators frequently based evaluation only on age.

To study the changes in endurance performance of five boys and five girls over 3 years, download Lab 14.1 Changes in Youth Endurance Performance from the Student Resources section at www.HumanKinetics.com/LifeSpanMotorDevelopment.

Average exercise capacity and average body size of groups of children and adolescents generally increase with age, but exercise capacity is also related to maturation rate. As noted in chapter 3, the relationship between chronological age and maturation status is imperfect. Therefore, each child's unique size and maturity level should be considered when establishing expectations for endurance performance (figure 14.3).

Figure 14.3 Structural constraints change rapidly in childhood and adolescence. Increasing size of the heart and lungs and increasing lean body mass foster improved exercise capacity. Also, a more advanced maturation status is associated with improved exercise capacity. Expectations for the exercise performance of children and youth should be based on growth and maturation status more than chronological age.

© Human Kinetics

In children, body size is also a far better predictor of endurance than the child's sex. After puberty, however, boys on average attain a considerable edge over girls in absolute maximal oxygen uptake and have the potential to retain this edge throughout life. Several factors contribute to this gender difference. One is body composition. The average man gains more lean body mass and less adipose tissue during adolescence than the average woman. Women are similar to men in maximal oxygen uptake per kilogram of fat-free body mass, but when adipose tissue is included, women have a lower maximal oxygen uptake. Another factor in gender differences in oxygen consumption is women's tendency to have lower hemoglobin concentrations than men do (Astrand, 1976).

By the time he reaches late adolescence, then, the average male has an edge over the average female in both oxygen consumption and working capacity (figure 14.4). It must be remembered that environmental factors, especially training, influence the endurance capacities of individual men and women throughout their lives. Thus it would not be surprising to find that an active woman has a higher maximal oxygen uptake than a sedentary man.

? If maximal oxygen uptake is related to body composition and physical maturity, what are the implications for youth sport programs?

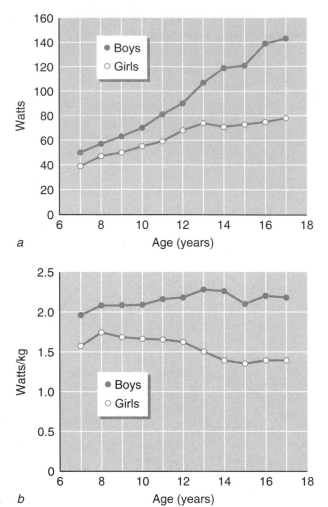

Figure 14.4 Physical working capacity with advancing age in childhood and adolescence. Measurements were made in school classrooms (without habituation of the Canadian subjects) at a heart rate of 170. Readings would probably be up to 10% higher given climatic control (20–22° C) and some familiarization with experimental procedures. Measurements are in watts (1 watt = 6 kg · m/min) and watts per kilogram of body weight.

Based on data of Howell and MacNab 1966. Adapted from Shephard 1982.

Assessing Aerobic Performance

Several methods can be used to assess a person's physiological responses to sustained activity requiring repetitive contraction of the large muscles. Cycling on an ergometer or walking or running on a treadmill are the most common activities used. The effort asked of the individual can be submaximal or maximal. Measurements of aerobic power and capacity tend to be specific to the task performed (e.g., cycling, running), so caution must be used in comparing scores on different tasks. Young children have difficulty keeping a cadence during bicycle ergometer tests. They are also more likely than adults to make unnecessary movements during testing. In addition, they may be at risk of falling on a treadmill.

Aerobic exercise tests are usually graded; that is, they increase workload in stages. There is no standard protocol for any age group, but intensity should always be appropriate for the fitness level and size of those tested.

A common measure of fitness for endurance activities is maximal oxygen uptake ($\dot{V}O_2$max), or maximal aerobic power,

the maximum volume of oxygen the body can consume per minute (Heyward, 1991; Zwiren, 1989). The more efficiently a person's body uses oxygen (i.e., consumes less oxygen for the same amount of work performed), the more fit the individual. Endurance exercise performance is too complex to be represented by any single measure, yet the relationship between maximal oxygen uptake and endurance activity performance is high.

In a test assessing maximal oxygen uptake, you can measure or estimate the actual amount of oxygen consumed during activity. This score is also expressed as oxygen consumed per minute per kilogram of body weight. Maximal oxygen uptake is a common measure of endurance in studies of children and older adults because it can be estimated from a submaximal test, thus avoiding the need for an exercise bout to exhaustion. Also, direct measures of oxygen use require more sophisticated and expensive equipment than is needed for estimates from submaximal tests.

Another measure of physiological response to prolonged exercise is that of maximal working capacity, which means

(continued)

the highest work, or exercise, load a person can tolerate before reaching exhaustion (Adams, 1973). Because this test requires maximal effort, it may be difficult to motivate individuals to work to exhaustion, and although it is unlikely, an individual may have a heart attack during such a test. For this reason this measure is not often used with children or older adults.

Other measures of endurance fitness are less common. For example, maximal cardiac output can be directly measured, but this test is difficult to administer because it requires intubation (inserting a tube into the body). Measuring an individual's electrocardiograph changes during exercise is of interest when studying adults (Heyward, 1991), but it does not apply very well to most children because its main purpose is to identify impaired heart function. Therefore, the preferred research measure of endurance fitness in children and older adults is maximal oxygen uptake for changes in aerobic power and adaptations to submaximal exercise efforts for changes in aerobic capacity.

Several research investigators attempted to identify field tests for children that estimate endurance nearly as reliably as when it is measured in a laboratory. Such field tests allow educators to measure aerobic performance without laboratory equipment. They compared maximal oxygen uptake scores from laboratory tests with performance in 800 m, 1,200 m, and 1,600 m runs for 83 children in the first, second, and third grades. Performance on the 1,600 m run was a better predictor of maximal oxygen uptake for boys and girls than performance on the 800 m or 1,200 m runs. An average velocity score on the 1,600 m run had a slightly higher correlation with maximal oxygen uptake than a total time score. We can conclude that a 1,600 m run is a better field test of endurance in children than shorter runs. This test proved to have a high test–retest reliability (Krahenbuhl, Pangrazi, Petersen, Burkett, & Schneider, 1978). In young trained runners the correlation between maximal oxygen uptake and race time is high (Cunningham, 1990; Unnithan, 1993).

Aerobic Performance in Adulthood

Average maximal oxygen uptake per kilogram of body weight peaks in the 20s then falls throughout the adult years. The loss is approximately 1% per year of life. The decline is found in both cross-sectional and longitudinal research and among athletic, active, and sedentary adults (Spirduso, 1995). Athletic and active adults, however, maintain a higher maximal oxygen uptake than sedentary adults. This section discusses the structural and functional changes in the cardiovascular and respiratory systems that contribute to this decline.

Cardiovascular Structure and Function

Cardiovascular function is related to the structure of the heart and blood vessels. The major structural changes in a nondiseased heart with aging include a progressive loss of cardiac muscle, a loss of elasticity in cardiac muscle fibers (Harrison, Dixon, Russell, Bidwai, & Coleman, 1964), a thickening of the left ventricular wall, and fibrotic changes in the valves (Pomerance, 1965). The major blood vessels also lose elasticity (Fleg, 1986). It remains unclear whether these changes are unavoidable in aging or reflect a chronic lack of oxygen. The consequences of these structural changes on cardiovascular function are numerous.

▲ **Maximum heart rate.** Whereas resting heart rate values of older adults are comparable to those of young adults, the maximum achievable heart rate with physical exertion gradually declines with aging (Lipsitz, 1989). The difference is about 188 beats per minute for persons in their 20s and 168 for persons in their 50s and 60s (Spirduso, 1995). Decreased maximum heart rate may be the major factor in reduced maximal oxygen uptake with aging (Hagburg et al., 1985).

▲ **Stroke volume.** The stroke volume of older adults may or may not decline with aging; research studies have yielded both results (see Stamford, 1988, for a review). Asymptomatic ischemic heart disease (affecting blood supply to the heart) may account for the equivocal results. Investigators using rigorous screening for heart disease may find no decrease in stroke volume, whereas researchers whose studies include participants with undetected disease may find a decrease (Safar, 1990).

▲ **Cardiac output.** Cardiac output is the product of heart rate and stroke volume. So, healthy older adults experience a decline in cardiac output during heavy activity with a decline in maximal oxygen uptake, while those with ischemic heart disease experience even greater decline as maximum heart rate and stroke volume decrease. Cardiac output at rest or with submaximal work is unchanged with aging, and cardiac output is much higher in adults who train aerobically than in sedentary adults.

▲ **Blood pressure.** Older adults reach their peak cardiac output at a lower intensity of work than do younger adults (Brandfonbrener, Landowne, & Shock, 1955; Shephard, 1978a). Older adults' more rigid arteries resist the volume of blood the heart pumps into them. This resistance is even greater if the person has atherosclerosis, the buildup of plaque on the artery walls. In turn, this resistance raises resting pulse pressure (the difference between systolic and diastolic blood pressure) and systolic blood pressure. Whether blood pressure increases or decreases during exercise also depends on the health of the cardiac muscle fibers and their ability to tolerate an increased workload. A lifestyle including regular physical activity is associated with lower systolic blood pressure (Reaven, Barrett-Connor, & Edelstein, 1991).

▲ **Blood flow and hemoglobin content.** For activity to be sustained, oxygen must be delivered to the working muscles by the blood. Peripheral blood flow is apparently well maintained in older adulthood. Hemoglobin is also maintained in older adulthood (Timiras & Brownstein, 1987). The incidence of anemia rises in older adulthood, however; this condition is associated with reduced hemoglobin values.

Respiratory Structure and Function

Elasticity of the lung tissue and chest walls declines with aging (Turner, Mead, & Wohl, 1968). Therefore, older adults expend more effort in breathing than young adults. Of interest is the lung volume, especially the volume termed **forced vital capacity.** A large vital capacity reflects a large inspiratory capacity of the lungs and results in better alveolar ventilation. Because the greatest part of oxygen diffusion to the capillaries takes place at the alveoli (figure 14.5), better alveolar ventilation contributes to increased amounts of oxygen circulating in the blood and reaching the working muscles.

A decreased vital capacity with aging is well established, the average decrease being 4 to 5% per decade (Norris, Shock, Landowne, & Falzone, 1956; Shephard, 1987). The loss is more dramatic in smokers than in nonsmokers, and well-trained persons in their 40s are known to maintain the vital capacity of their 20s (Shephard, 1987).

> **Forced vital capacity** is the maximum volume of air the lungs can expel following maximal inspiration.

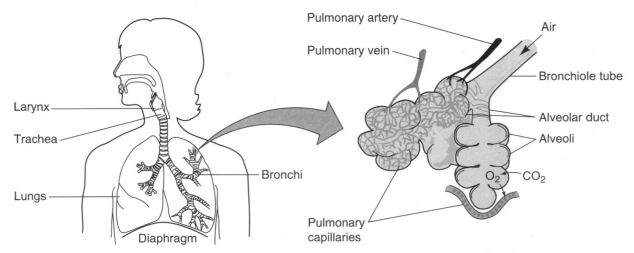

Figure 14.5 The respiratory system. Oxygen diffusion to the capillaries takes place at the alveoli, enlarged on the right.
Redrawn from Sharkey 1990.

The oxygen and carbon dioxide exchange in the lungs loses some efficiency with aging. This decline is not offset by training (Dempsey, Johnson, & Saupe, 1990). Generally, though, the pulmonary systems of older adults do well at rest and during moderate activity. Moreover, the pulmonary system is not the major limiting factor in exercise capacity.

The decline in maximal oxygen uptake is probably related to loss of muscle mass and the ability of muscles to use oxygen, as well as to cardiovascular and respiratory changes. Maximal oxygen uptake measures the amount of oxygen delivered to and used by the muscles. So, the more muscle mass, the more likely maximal oxygen uptake is greater. In fact, when maximal oxygen uptake is related to the kilograms of muscle (rather than kilograms of body weight) in older adults, declines shrink from 60 to 14% in men and 50 to 8% in women (Spirduso, 1995). A factor in minimizing the loss of endurance performance, then, is maintenance of muscle mass. The addition of adipose tissue with aging obviously would work against maintenance of maximal oxygen uptake.

The end result of cardiac and pulmonary changes and the loss of muscle mass is that maximum exercise capacity and maximal oxygen uptake (whether absolute or relative to body weight) decline as an adult ages, and the recovery period following vigorous activity lengthens. The results of both longitudinal and cross-sectional studies are plotted in figure 14.6. A decline with advancing age is evident. A lifetime of negative environmental factors such as smoking or poor nutrition can contribute to or accelerate the changes. Conversely, a lifetime of exposure to positive environmental factors such as healthful exercise can better maintain endurance levels.

Cardiovascular factors are a greater limitation to older adults' aerobic performance than pulmonary factors.

Maximal oxygen uptake declines throughout adulthood, related to a decrease in maximum heart rate and in muscle mass. Active older adults maintain an edge in maximal oxygen uptake over sedentary adults.

Changes with growth and aging dramatically affect endurance performance throughout the life span. Various systems can constrain the potential for vigorous, sustained activity. It is important for everyone to have some knowledge of how the various systems influence aerobic activity because of the health implications of regular participation in aerobic activity. Moreover, educators and therapists must understand these influences thoroughly in order to promote training that yields significant health benefits.

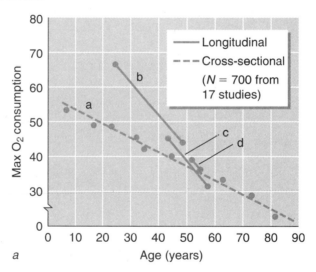

a

Endurance Training

The result of aerobic training is predictable in adults. An adult improves maximal oxygen uptake by training at least three times a week for at least 20 min at an intensity of 60 to 90% of maximum heart rate. Stroke volume increases, and maximal cardiac output subsequently increases. Oxygen is better extracted from the blood at muscle sites. Maximal ventilation per minute rises. Inactive adults who begin training typically increase maximal oxygen uptake by 25 to 50%

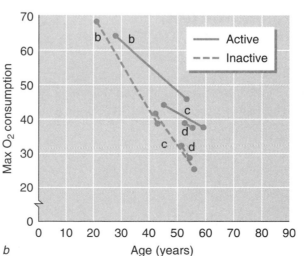

b

Figure 14.6 Maximal oxygen uptake declines as a person ages. *(a)* Cross-sectional studies and longitudinal studies show declines in adulthood. *(b)* The decline is not as rapid in active adults. The dotted lines represent the change in inactive adults and the solid lines the change in active adults.

Reprinted, by permission, from B.A. Stamford, 1986, Exercise and the elderly. In *Exercise and sport sciences reviews*, Vol. 16, edited by K.B. Pandolf (New York: Macmillan), 344. Reproduced with permission of The McGraw-Hill Companies.
Data plotted are from (a) Dehn and Bruce 1972; (b) Dill et al. 1967; (c) Hollman 1965, all cited in Dehn and Bruce 1972; and (d) Dehn and Bruce 1972.

(Hartley, 1992). Therefore, appropriate training yields benefits. Let's consider whether the same is true for children.

Training Effect in Children

The effect of growth and maturation on maximal oxygen uptake must be distinguished from the effect of training.

Children who begin an aerobic training program are continuing to grow, and as noted earlier, maximal oxygen uptake increases with growth. Therefore, to know the effect of training in children we must distinguish any increase in maximal oxygen uptake resulting from growth from that due to training. In research studies, this need for differentiation makes it absolutely necessary to include a control group that grows but does not train. Moreover, as noted in chapter 3, children mature at different rates. Comparing a group that contains many early maturers with a group that contains many late maturers can certainly bias an investigation of training effects. In fact, one research group noted that when they sought to compare "inactive" and "active" groups of children, late maturers more often fell into the inactive category (Mirwald, Bailey, Cameron, & Rasmussen, 1981). Maturation level must also be assessed in research studies.

Early studies of aerobic training in prepubescent children were equivocal. Consider the seven sample studies depicted in figure 14.7. Three found a significant increase in maximal oxygen uptake by the training group over the control group, and four found no significant difference after training. In a few longitudinal studies, training did not result in differences between active and inactive groups until the children reached peak height velocity (Kobayashi et al., 1978; Mirwald et al., 1981; Rutenfranz, 1986). In other words, activity was not associated with a higher maximal oxygen uptake in preadolescents

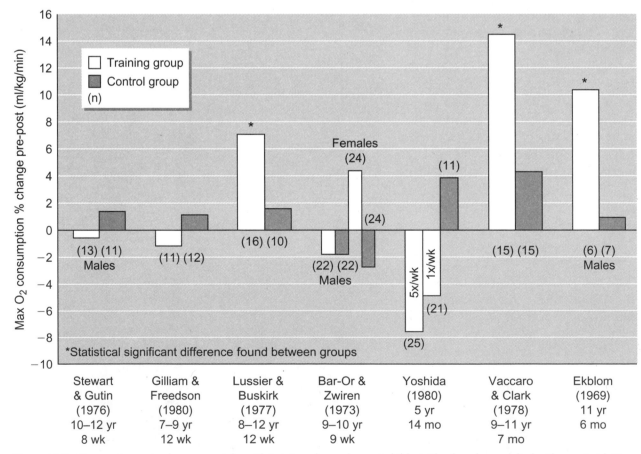

Figure 14.7 Changes in maximal oxygen uptake with training of prepubescent children. The three bars marked with an asterisk (*) indicate studies finding a significant improvement over the control group. The other four studies found no differences after training.

Graph data from Sady 1986; reprinted from Zwiren 1989.

(beyond the increase due to growth), but it was in adolescents. This led Katch (1983) to propose the "trigger" hypothesis, which states that until the results of the hormones that initiate puberty are realized, the effects of aerobic training on maximal oxygen uptake are minimal at best.

Several factors could account for the lack of a training effect:

▲ Training effects may be reliant on hormonal responses.

▲ High activity rates in children before training may minimize the training effect.

▲ Research studies may have included too few children or may have used flawed research methods.

▲ Training intensity may have been insufficient for children (Rowland, 1989b).

▲ Maximal oxygen uptake may not be as useful a measurement of aerobic fitness in children as anaerobic threshold (when lactic acid production in the blood exceeds its elimination) or ventilatory anaerobic threshold (when ventilation increases dramatically) (Rowland, 1989a; Washington, 1989).

Aware of these possibilities, investigators more recently based their reviews on studies meeting certain criteria for research method and training intensity. Pate and Ward (1990) screened and then analyzed 12 studies. Eight of the 12 found an increase in maximal oxygen uptake with training, although the mean increase was only 10.4% compared with the control group increase of 2.7%. Similar analyses led some to conclude that appropriate aerobic training can lead to maximal oxygen uptake increases of approximately 15% in children (Sady, 1986; Shephard, 1992; Vaccaro & Mahon, 1987).

Payne and Morrow (1993) reported from their meta-analysis of 23 studies that an average increase of less than 5% in fitness was found. Tolfrey, Campbell, and Batterham (1998) trained 26 children (boys and girls) matched to 19 control children for physiological maturation. They trained 30 min three times per week for 12 weeks at nearly 80% of maximum heart rate. Habitual physical activity level and percent body fat were considered in the analysis of results, but the exercise training group still did not improve in maximal oxygen uptake beyond the improvement also seen in the control group.

It is still possible that research studies on the whole have not used training intensity levels sufficient to yield a training effect in children. However, exercise programs must not be so demanding as to be harmful, nor should they involve a level of activity that results in children disliking exercise. The overload principle is useful to follow with children. This principle calls for training with increased intensity or duration beyond the individual's norm. Yet, the increase is incremental rather than drastic. The intensity or duration of each exercise bout is increased gradually over several weeks or months.

 Aerobic training yields small improvements at best in preadolescents but significant improvements after puberty.

In contrast, adolescents after puberty respond to aerobic training much as adults do. Heart size and volume, total blood volume, total hemoglobin, stroke volume, and maximal cardiac output all increase in adolescents who receive training (Ekblom, 1969; Eriksson & Koch, 1973; Koch & Rocker, 1977; Lengyel & Gyarfas, 1979), whereas submaximal heart rate for a given level of exercise decreases (Brown, Harrower, & Deeter, 1972). Kobayashi et al. (1978) found a 15.8% increase in aerobic power with training between ages 14 and 17. A longitudinal study of males and females over the 15 years between ages 13 and 27 showed that those who reported being physically active had a 2 to 5% increase in aerobic fitness over those who were not (Kemper, Twisk, Koppes, van Mechelen, & Post, 2001).

? If adolescents can improve aerobic performance with training, what would be the repercussions of not requiring physical education in the last 2 years of high school?

Training Programs in Adulthood

Earlier we reviewed the structural and functional changes that occur with aging in the cardiovascular and respiratory systems. We observed that maximal oxygen uptake declines with aging, even in those who train. However, we also noted that training and active adults had higher—even if declining with time—maximal oxygen uptakes compared with sedentary adults (figure 14.8). This provides a hint that training programs for adults yield benefits. Let's consider two groups: adults who maintain an active lifestyle and sedentary adults who take up training.

First, evidence exists (Dehn & Bruce, 1972; Drinkwater, Horvath, & Wells, 1975; Kasch, Boyer, Van Camp, Verity, & Wallace, 1990; Shephard, 1978b; Smith & Serfass, 1981) that declines are not as dramatic in older adults who remain active as in those who become sedentary. Figure 14.6b shows a steeper decline in maximal oxygen uptake in inactive (dotted line) than in active (solid line) adults with advancing age. Vigorous training can even keep maximal oxygen uptake steady for a time in older adults (figure 14.8; Kasch & Wallace, 1976). Over a long period of time, prolonged training can sharply reduce the decline in maximal oxygen uptake. Kasch et al. (1990) observed only a 13% decline in men 45 to 68 years of age who maintained exercise training, compared with an average loss in nonexercisers of about 40%.

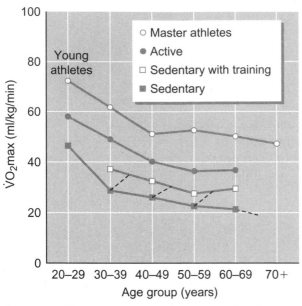

Figure 14.8 These average maximal oxygen uptake values for the adult years show that activity is associated with higher values, although all groups, active and inactive, experience decline. The dotted lines represent improvement in sedentary adults with training.

Reprinted from Spirduso 1995.

Second, older adults can significantly increase their maximal oxygen uptake with a good training program (Posner, Gorman, Klein, & Woldow, 1986; Shephard, 1978b), even if they have undertaken little training earlier in their lives and even into their 70s (Hagburg et al., 1989; Stamford, 1973). Improvements ranged from 10 to 25% (Blumenthal et al., 1991; Shephard, 1987). These gains are not as high in absolute terms as those in younger people who begin training but are similar to those in the young in relative terms. Even low training intensity can be very effective for older adults early in their exercise program.

💡 Adults can benefit from aerobic training, reducing the decline in performance that would otherwise accompany aging.

💻 To compare the aerobic performance of Senior Olympic competitors with anaerobic performance, download Lab 14.2 Aerobic and Anaerobic Performance in Older Adulthood from the Student Resources section at www.HumanKinetics.com/LifeSpanMotorDevelopment.

What mechanisms are involved in the improvements in older adults with training? Undoubtedly, training maintains or improves muscle mass. As mentioned previously, more muscle mass is associated with higher maximal oxygen uptake. Fit older adults also have larger vital capacity than sedentary older adults (Shephard, 1993). Information about the cardiovascular system is available from a case study of Clarence DeMar, who ran 12 miles a day throughout his life and competed in marathons at age 65. The autopsy performed after his death from cancer at age 70 showed well-developed cardiac muscle, normal valves, and coronary arteries two to three times the size normally seen (Brandfonbrener et al., 1955).

Although the benefits of endurance training even at low intensity are well established for the older adult, vigorous work can still overwhelm the diseased heart. Older adults with cardiovascular disease should participate in programs specifically designed for this population. The guiding principle in designing training programs for older adults as well as for children is a gradual increase in exercise intensity and duration.

Long-Term Training Effects

Despite the body's favorable response to training at any age, the question arises as to whether active youths have an advantage over their sedentary counterparts in maintaining endurance into older adulthood. Ideally, researchers would assess this aspect of fitness through long-term longitudinal studies; however, the difficulties involved in obtaining longitudinal data (expense and subject attrition) make such research nearly nonexistent.

In the absence of such research, consider a cross-sectional study conducted by Saltin and Grimby (1968) that measured the maximal oxygen uptake of three groups of men between ages 50 and 59. The men in the first group were nonathletes in their youth; those in the second group were former athletes but were now sedentary; and the men in the third group had been athletes in their youth and still maintained active lifestyles as older adults. The investigators had to rely on self-reports (rather than laboratory data) to determine the men's activity levels in youth. Even so, measures of maximal oxygen uptake yielded average values of 30, 38, and 53 ml/min/kg body weight for the nonathletes, sedentary former athletes, and active adults, respectively.

More recently, Trudeau, Laurencelle, Tremblay, Rajic, and Shephard (1998) followed up with participants 20 years after their participation in a semi-longitudinal study. The treatment group in the original study took a 1-hour specialized physical education class five times per week during their 6 years of elementary school. The control group received just 40 min of exercise per week during that time. As adults, women from the treatment group exercised three or more times per week more often than women from the control group. The men did not differ. Men and women from the treatment group more often self-reported their health to be very good to excellent. Telama, Yang, Laakso, and Viikari (1997) also followed up on participants 9 and 12 years after they initially answered a questionnaire about their leisure activities (at the ages of 9, 12, 15, and 18 years). The correlations between youth and adult activity were low but significant.

Despite the limitations of these studies, the evidence suggests that regular activity in childhood has positive lifelong benefits. Promoting an active lifestyle with children and youth could predispose them to be more active as adults (figure 14.9). Nevertheless, the most important factor for endurance is the individual's current activity level. At all ages, the capacity for prolonged, vigorous work tends to be transitory. People maintain (or

Figure 14.9 Endurance capacity is positively related to training, especially after puberty. Moreover, regular activity in childhood might predispose individuals to be more active in adulthood. Perhaps functional constraints such as a positive attitude toward exercise persist over the life span.

© Human Kinetics

improve) endurance if they are currently training for endurance; conversely, endurance capacity decreases when people discontinue their training programs.

Effects of Disease on Endurance Performance

Diseases and disabilities can constrain endurance performance at any point in the life span. A detailed discussion of diseases and working capacity is beyond the scope of this text, but it is important to realize that cardiovascular, pulmonary, infectious, and neuromuscular diseases affect performance. An individual with such a disease possesses a unique set of structural constraints that affect physical performance. Therapists and educators must prescribe initial levels of activity based on these constraints and then constantly adapt activities as a disease progresses or rehabilitation brings about improvements.

Short-term infectious diseases, such as influenza, mononucleosis, and chicken pox, generally reduce an individual's working capacity (Adams, 1973) to varying degrees. It is important for a teacher, coach, or exercise leader to keep this in mind when monitoring performance. Individuals who want to maintain their peak efficiency want to adhere to training schedules and performance levels even when they are ill, but this is an impractical goal.

Teachers, coaches, or exercise leaders; doctors, nurses, and therapists; and parents (when children are involved) should be a team, every member wanting to do his or her part to help the participant. Clearly, cooperation and communication are imperative. Activity may be beneficial in many cases, but it must never place the participant at increased risk. Those involved in the participant's exercise program, then, must plan the limits of activity carefully, set expectations accordingly, and monitor the participant closely.

Summary and Synthesis

Endurance for vigorous activities improves as the body grows. In addition, an individual can increase endurance after puberty by training, although the effects are transitory. A person must maintain training to preserve higher levels of endurance and to reap the benefits of high endurance levels.

After the adolescent growth spurt, gender differences in working capacity are apparent. Although the cause of these differences is still open to discussion, body size, body composition, and hemoglobin levels are at least partially responsible. Recall our discussion of individual functional constraints in part V. Earlier in this chapter we saw how a myth influenced attitudes about children's training. Functional constraints might also be responsible for some of the gender differences as well as some age group differences. Societal norms and expectations can constrain activity and training since some individuals are led to believe that such activity is inappropriate for their group. These attitudes are changing, but many people still do not undertake regular exercise. It remains to be seen whether the exercise and fitness movements of the 1980s and 1990s will have any effect on life span fitness in the 21st century.

Other components of physical fitness include muscular strength and flexibility. Performance of many sport activities as well as everyday living activities depends on a minimal level of strength and flexibility. The next chapter examines these two fitness components; they obviously interact with task and environmental constraints in giving rise to movements.

Discussion Questions

1. How do anaerobic endurance and aerobic endurance change with growth in childhood? How do they change with aging?

? Recall the last time you had an infection or flu. What was the effect on your energy and stamina? How long was it before you recovered your energy? Was there a time when you overextended yourself? Based on this, how would you react as an exercise leader or therapist when a student returns to class after an infection or flu?

2. Can prepubescent children improve anaerobic endurance with training? Aerobic endurance? Explain your answers.

3. What are the gender differences in anaerobic and aerobic endurance over the life span? To what factors might these differences be attributed?

4. Is it true that at any point in the life span individuals can improve aerobic endurance with training? Do those who build higher endurance in youth realize a lifelong benefit? How would you design a study to address this question?

 Learning Activities

Testing Children and Teens for Endurance

Locate five research articles on endurance or aerobic performance in children and teens. You can use articles referenced in your text, perform an electronic search, or check a journal such as *Pediatric Exercise Science*. Once you have located the articles, read about the methods the authors used to conduct their research. These are typically described in a section of the article subtitled "methods." Note the age and gender of the participants and summarize how endurance performance was tested. What was similar and what was different about how each set of researchers tested endurance? What accommodations, if any, were made for the age of the participants?

Development of Strength and Flexibility

chapter 15

SUPER ATHLETES TO SUPERMEN

USA Today (May 19, 1999) provided graphs showing the improvement in four different track events (long jump, high jump, 100 m run, and marathon) for men and women since 1900. This was done by plotting the world records in each event over time. The change was dramatic, especially in women's world records. Why have these world records improved so much? No doubt there are many reasons, but strength training would be on everyone's list. In the past and in some sports, athletes never trained with progressive resistance. Athletes today recognize the benefits of systematic strength training on performance. Top athletes in every sport accept strength training as part of their participation.

As well as performing increased weight training, athletes currently spend more time stretching. What used to be thought of as exercise just for gymnasts or dancers is now a part of most athletes' routines. In fact, today's coaches have come to realize that strength and flexibility are related. Athletes are at their best when they are strong and supple, and training that promotes increased muscle mass at the expense of flexibility puts athletes at risk of injury. Muscle balance is a goal of training today. Muscle strength should be built for all directions of joint movement, such as flexion and extension, and flexibility through the appropriate and full range of motion should be fostered.

High levels of strength and flexibility permit movements, whereas limited strength and flexibility limit movements. That is, strength and flexibility are individual structural constraints. A good illustration is the golf swing. The full swing and resulting long drives that professional golfers display are unattainable for most weekend golfers, who do not have comparable strength and flexibility. This chapter considers changes over the life span as well as the effects of training throughout the life span, first in strength and then in flexibility.

Chapter Objectives

This chapter will

▲ explore the relationship between muscle mass and strength and how these change in relation to each other over the life span,

▲ review the effects of strength training over the life span,

▲ describe changes in flexibility over the life span, and

▲ review the effects of flexibility training by individuals of any age.

DEVELOPMENT OF STRENGTH

As noted in chapter 3, muscle mass follows a sigmoid growth pattern, and this growth is largely the result of an increase in muscle fiber diameter. Gender differences are minimal until puberty, when boys add significantly more muscle mass than girls do, especially in the upper body. From young adulthood until the age of 50 there is a small loss of muscle, but thereafter the average loss can be pronounced. The loss is greater for sedentary individuals with poor nutrition.

What about muscle **strength?** Does it simply parallel the changes in muscle mass? Strength training programs are promoted for individuals of all ages. What effect does resistance training have on strength and muscle mass, especially before the adolescent growth spurt? What about in older adulthood, when muscle mass is typically lost?

These are important questions to answer because strength is related to motor performance and health. Many skills require a minimal level of strength, such as the gymnastics skills performed on parallel bars. Some skills can be performed better with more strength, such as baseball batting. Even activities of daily living can become difficult without sufficient strength. Older adults who have lost much of their strength have difficulty with everyday tasks, such as getting out of bathtubs and climbing the stairs, and are often at greater risk of falling.

The first step in answering these important questions about strength is to understand the relationship between muscle mass and strength. The patterns of change for the average individual are described first, followed by the effects of training.

Strength is the ability to exert force.

? What daily living activities are difficult or even risky when an individual loses a significant level of strength, either from disease, disability, or aging? What sport, exercise, and dance activities are better performed with increased strength?

Muscle Mass and Strength

The amount of force a muscle group exerts depends on the fibers (muscle cells) neurologically activated and on leverage (the mechanical advantage the muscle fibers gain by where the force is applied in relation to an axis of rotation). In turn, the fibers activated depend on the cross-sectional area of the muscle and the degree of coordination in activating the fibers—that is, the nervous system's pattern and timing in innervating the various motor units to bring about the desired movement. The cross-sectional area of muscle increases with growth; this means strength increases as muscles grow. However, muscle mass obviously is not the only factor in strength. Neurological factors are involved, and neurological changes over the life span influence muscle strength. Therefore, we cannot assume that strength changes simply as muscle mass changes. Keeping this in mind, let's see how strength changes over the life span.

Developmental Changes in Strength

Strength is certainly one of the individual structural constraints that change with growth and aging. As noted previously, multiple influences on strength and resistance training might bring about changes in strength, both in the long term and in the short term. Because an individual's strength level is a constraint that interacts with task and environmental constraints to permit or limit movements, strength levels change movements over the life span.

 Muscle strength is related to muscle size, but changes in strength do not always parallel changes in muscle size.

Isotonic strength is the exertion of force against constant resistance through the range of motion at a joint.

Isokinetic strength is the exertion of force at a constant limb velocity through the range of motion at a joint.

Isometric strength is the exertion of force without a change in muscle length, that is, without movement of a limb.

Assessing Strength

In strength assessments, individuals typically exert maximum force against resistance. They might actually move their limbs, as in an **isotonic** test (constant resistance, as in lifting a barbell) or **isokinetic** test (constant speed of movement, as with a Cybex machine), or they might exert force against an immovable resistance, as in an **isometric** test. For us to compare results among individuals, those conducting the assessment must report several things:

- The muscle group, such as knee flexors or elbow extensors
- The movement, such as knee flexion or elbow extension
- The speed of movement, usually in degrees per second

For isometric tests, the angle of the joint in degrees as force is exerted because a muscle group can exert different levels of force at different joint angles.

A common isotonic strength test is a one-repetition maximum (1RM) lift of a free weight such as a barbell. As a limb moves through a range of motion, there is one point where force production is maximal and subsequently submaximal at other points. The 1RM test therefore indicates strength at the weakest angle

in the joint's range of motion. If an isokinetic exercise machine is used, wherein the resistance is constant throughout the movement, the test reflects strength at the strongest joint angle. Because the 1RM test is difficult (and potentially dangerous) for novices, scales have been developed that estimate 1RM based on the maximum number of lifts at a given weight.

Several devices have been designed to assess isometric strength. The spring-loaded dynamometer requires individuals to compress a handle; their exertion is registered. Alternatively, the individual can pull on an anchored cable with a handle. A tensiometer is placed on the cable and registers the force of exertion. Dynamometers and tensiometers usually measure in Newtons, a measurement unit for force.

In school settings, functional tests of strength are often used with children. Among these are chin-ups, the flexed-arm hang, and rope climbing. Note that body weight is used as the resistance in these tasks, so body weight is a factor in performance levels. Some of these tasks also require skills, such as rope climbing, and the skill factor must be considered in interpreting test results.

Preadolescence

Strength increases steadily as children grow older (figure 15.1) (Blimkie, 1989; Pate & Shephard, 1989). Boys and girls have similar strength levels until they are about 13 years old, although boys are very slightly stronger than girls of the same height during childhood (Asmussen, 1973; Blimkie, 1989).

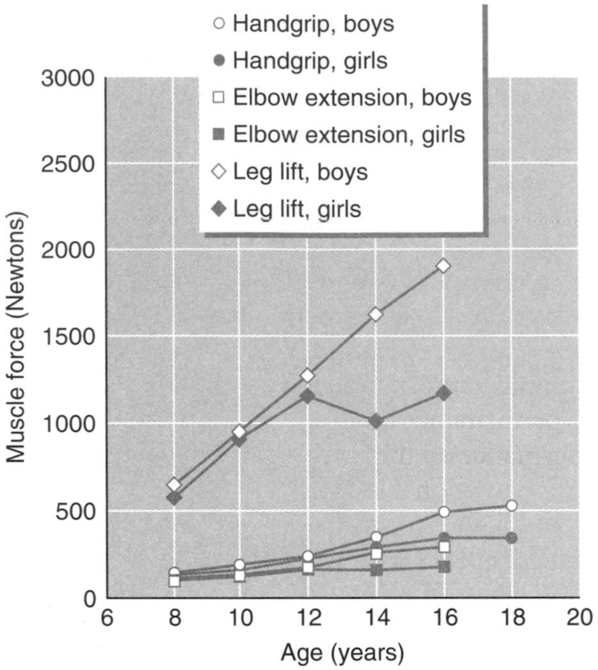

Figure 15.1 Development of isometric strength. Boys (open symbols) continue a steady improvement in isometric strength throughout adolescence, while girls (filled symbols) tend to plateau. Graph is based on data accumulated by Shephard (1978b) for handgrip and on unpublished results of Howell et al. (1968) for other measures.

Adapted from Shepard 1982.

We know that muscle mass also increases steadily as children grow older, so how is strength related to muscle mass in childhood? Davies (1990) addressed this question by determining whether gender differences in handgrip could be explained by lean arm mass. Boys and girls with an average age of 12 years took a handgrip strength test. Their lean forearm mass was then estimated from circumference, length, and skinfold measures. When grip strength was expressed relative to lean forearm mass, no gender differences were found. In children, then, strength is greatly related to muscle mass. In fact, Barrett and Harrison (2002) found that children matched adults in the functional ability of muscle per unit of muscle volume, implying that muscle size plays a large factor in child–adult strength differences.

On the other hand, there is evidence that other factors are involved in strength levels. Consider the age at which individuals reach peak gains in muscle mass and strength. As noted in chapter 3, peak gain (the peak in the velocity curve) indicates the point of the fastest increase. If strength development directly follows muscle mass development, the peak gain in strength would coincide with the peak gain in muscle mass. Teachers and coaches then could predict children's strength levels by measuring their muscle mass, which can be estimated from weight measurements or by subtracting a child's estimated fat weight from body weight.

However, several studies indicate that these peak gains do not coincide with each other in most adolescents (Carron & Bailey, 1974; Jones, 1947; Stolz & Stolz, 1951). For example, Rasmussen, Faulkner, Mirwald, and Bailey (1990) conducted a longitudinal study with boys. They found that peak muscle mass velocity occurred at an average of 14.3 years, but peak strength velocity occurred at 14.7 years. Tanner (1962) suggests that the typical sequence of peak muscle mass velocity followed by peak strength velocity probably results from the effects of adrenocortical and testicular hormones on the protein structure and enzyme systems of the muscle fibers. Thus, there is an endocrine influence on strength increase with growth.

Another method of examining muscle growth and strength development is to relate measures of muscle strength to various body sizes in children and determine whether strength increases at the same rate as body size. Asmussen and Heeboll-Nielsen (1955, 1956) took this approach in studying Danish children between ages 7 and 16. They assumed that body height could represent changes in body size, including body weight; the body weight is proportional to the body height raised to the third power in this age group. Asmussen and Heeboll-Nielsen showed this was approximately true for their sample of Danish boys and girls. Because height measures could represent body size, they grouped the children into height categories by 10 cm intervals and measured them for isometric strength. Successive height groups demonstrated increasing muscle strength but at a rate greater than that of their height increase.

Asmussen and Heeboll-Nielsen also divided boys of the same height into two age groups, one younger and one older by approximately 1.5 years. The older group showed greater arm and leg strength by about 5 to 10% per year of age. This experiment also demonstrates that strength is not related to muscle size alone. Rather, neural influences are likely. These influences might include myelination of nerve fibers, improved muscle coordination (movement requires a contraction of some muscles and a coordinated relaxation of the muscle on the opposite aspect of the body), and improved extent of motor unit activation (Blimkie, 1989; Sale, 1989; Kraemer, Fry, Frykman, Conroy, & Hoffman, 1989). Only one of these neural influences, improved motor unit activation, has been examined experimentally. Blimkie (1989) found some support for the suggestion that older children can activate a greater proportion of motor units to exert force.

The studies mentioned thus far typically measured isometric strength directly with a cable tensiometer or a dynamometer. The benefit of measuring strength with this equipment is that the effects of skill, practice, and experience are minimized. However, these factors do influence the performance of sport skills. For this reason, studies of functional muscle strength development are also interesting. Functional strength tasks have a skill component as well as a strength component.

Two skills that involve functional muscle strength are vertical jumping and sprinting. Practice and experience as well as leg strength influence children's performance on both tasks. Asmussen and Heeboll-Nielsen (1955, 1956) measured performance on these two skills in successive height groups of Danish children. They found that functional muscle strength, like isometric strength, increased at a faster rate than one would anticipate from muscle growth alone. Further, the rate of functional muscle strength gain was even greater than that of isometric strength, emphasizing again the role of neurological factors in improved muscle strength as children mature.

To examine Fitnessgram strength measures for trends with growth and gender differences, download Lab 15.1 Examining Trends in Strength Development from the Student Resources section at www.HumanKinetics.com/LifeSpanMotorDevelopment.

Adolescence and Young Adulthood

As noted in chapter 4, boys gain more muscle mass in adolescence than girls do, largely as a result of higher androgen secretion levels. It is no surprise, then, that boys undergo a spurt of increased strength at about age 13. Girls continue a steady increase in strength during adolescence before reaching a plateau.

As a result of differential growth of muscle mass during adolescence, then, the average adult man is stronger than the average adult woman. Women can produce only 60 to 80% of the force that men can exert, although most of these differences can be attributed to differences in arm and shoulder strength rather than in trunk or leg strength (Asmussen, 1973). As noted in chapter 4, gender differences in muscle mass are more pronounced in the arms and shoulders than the trunk and legs.

However, the average difference in body or muscle size accounts for only half of the difference in strength between men and women. Cultural norms probably play a role in the gender differences in strength. These norms, of course, begin their influence very early in life. For example, Shephard (1982) noted the effect of repeating strength measures on naive boys and girls (i.e., boys and girls who have never been tested for strength). Whereas the boys showed no tendency to improve over three visits, the girls improved on each subsequent visit in almost every case and improved significantly on two of the eight strength measures (figure 15.2). It is possible that the task gained acceptability to the girls as they became more familiar with it. The boys may have been more used to all-out

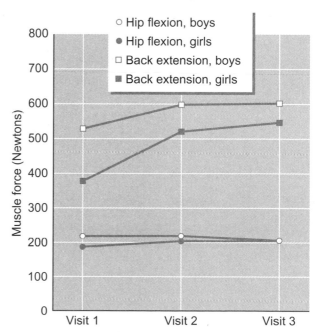

Figure 15.2 The effect of test repetition on muscle force measurement. With repeated visits to be measured, girls improved on these strength measures, while boys showed little or no change.

Adapted from Shephard 1982.

demonstrations of strength. Girls at that time were probably not encouraged to go all out, and might even have been discouraged from doing so. This would have limited their experience in exerting strength. Motivation should not be discounted as a major factor in strength measurement. Certainly, if Shephard had recorded only the first set of scores, he would have concluded that the gender differences in strength were much greater than he concluded after a comparison of the third set of scores.

Cultural norms can also influence strength differences between the genders through habitual physical activity. That is, the traditional physical activities promoted to growing boys tend to provide long-term resistance exercise. Those promoted to girls do not. Daily physical activities that promote strength have a cumulative effect over the growing years, resulting in significant gender differences that cannot be attributed to muscle size alone.

Some research has hinted that gender differences exist in muscle fiber composition; that is, men and women do not have the same proportions of type I (slow-twitch) and type II (fast-twitch) muscle fibers. If so, part of the gender differences in strength might be attributed to muscle fiber composition because indications from animal studies show that muscle composition is related to isometric strength (see Komi, 1984, for a review). On the other hand, Davies, White, and Young (1983) could find no relationship between strength and muscle fiber composition in boys and girls 11 to 14 years of age. Much more research on this topic is needed.

After the growth period, increases in muscle mass are associated with resistance training. Some drugs used in conjunction with training can increase muscle mass at a rate greater than training alone, but most have unhealthy side effects. Electromyographic measurements of muscle activation in strength tasks show that improved strength in adults engaged in resistance training is related to improved neurological activation and increased muscle size. In fact, in the early weeks of training most strength improvements are related to neurological factors since muscle has not yet increased in size (Moritani & DeVries, 1980).

Middle and Older Adulthood

Strength levels generally are maintained through the 20s and 30s. For the average adult, strength declines thereafter. The decline is somewhat gradual at first. Shephard (1978b) placed the loss in the 50s at 18 to 20%. Shock and Norris (1970) measured a significant loss in arm and shoulder strength after age 65. Murray, Gardner, Mollinger, and Sepic (1980) also reported a 45% loss of strength after age 65. Isometric strength, the ability to exert force against immovable resistance, and isotonic strength, the ability to exert force against movable resistance, both decline. The loss is particularly noticeable in the muscles of the upper leg.

Within the overall decline of strength with aging are several trends. Spirduso (1995) summarized these in table 15.1. On the left are the better maintained aspects of strength, and on the right are those aspects demonstrating more decline in the general population.

These losses are what we would expect from the loss of muscle mass in older adulthood. Yet the loss of strength might be larger than the loss of muscle mass. Young, Stokes, and Crowe (1985) found a 39% loss of strength but only a 25% loss in cross-sectional area in the quadriceps muscles of older men compared with younger men. Aniansson, Hedberg, Henning, and Grimby (1986) documented a 10 to 22%

💡 Strength increases gradually throughout childhood; boys experience a spurt of increased strength in adolescence, while girls continue their steady increase.

❓ Think back to your childhood activities. Did they promote strength by providing resistance exercise? Did they require lower body and upper body strength? Did boys and girls participate in these activities?

TABLE 15.1 **Summary of Strength Changes With Aging**

Better maintenance	Greater decline
Muscles used in daily activities	Muscles used infrequently in specialized activities
Isometric strength	Dynamic strength
Eccentric contractions	Concentric contractions
Slow velocity contractions	Rapid velocity contractions
Repeated low-level contractions	Power production
Strength using small joint angles	Strength using large joint angles
Males' strength	Females' strength

Reprinted from Spirduso 1995.

strength loss (figure 15.3) but a 6% muscle mass loss in the same muscle group over a 7-year span.

Thus, muscle mass loss does not parallel strength loss in older adulthood either. A greater loss of type II than type I muscle fibers could explain the discrepancy. However, it is not known whether the loss of muscle fibers is fiber-type specific (Green, 1986). Aging muscle also cannot develop as much tension as younger muscle in faster contractions (Laforest, St-Pierre, Cyr, & Gayton, 1990).

It is possible that the greater loss of strength is related to a reduction of motor neurons in the spinal cord with aging, resulting in a loss of motor units (Green, 1986; Grimby, 1988). Other units reinnervate some of the fibers of the lost motor neurons, such that the number of fibers per motor neuron increases (Campbell, McComas, & Petito, 1973; Fitts, 1981). The result would be a loss of muscular coordination. Hakkinen et al. (1998) recently compared 40- and 70-year-old men and women, finding that the older adults tended to increase coactivation of the opposing, or antagonist, muscle group in making dynamic, explosive movements. This has the effect of limiting force production.

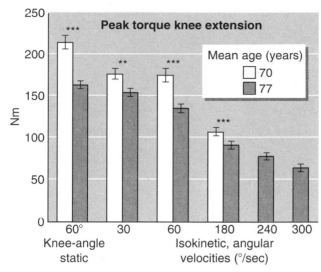

Figure 15.3 Changes in strength with aging. The average force (torque measured in Newton meters, Nm) exerted in a stationary knee position and at several speeds of knee extension decreased for 23 men over a 7-year interval. Changes are significant at the confidence levels of $p < .01$ (**) or $p < .001$ (***).

Reprinted from Aniansson et al. 1986.

As with so many other aspects of aging, it is difficult to distinguish whether older adults' loss of muscle mass and strength is related to aging of tissues or disuse. We know that frequently used muscles maintain their strength better than infrequently used muscles (Kauffman, 1985; Wilmore, 1991). Kallman, Plato, and Tobin (1990) demonstrated how variable the loss of strength is among older adults. They observed young, middle-aged, and older adults over a 10-year period. Many of the older adults lost *less* strength than middle-aged and young adults lost in the 10 years and some lost *no* strength at all. This variability most likely reflects extrinsic factors among these adults, especially exercise and activity levels, reminding us that significant loss of strength with aging is not a foregone conclusion.

Strength and muscle mass share the same five general phases of change over the life span. Yet, the timing of those changes can be distinct, as can the degree of change.

 Strength is maintained in adulthood, with gradual declines after the 30s and more notable declines beginning in the 50s; losses are extremely variable among older adults.

In the absence of training, adults lose strength at a greater rate than expected by the loss of muscle mass.

Strength Training

It's obvious that an adult can increase muscle strength with strength training. Strength training also results in a noticeable increase in muscle size. The effect is most noticeable in postpubescent men. Hence, circulating testosterone was considered the stimulus for such increases in muscle size. In the past this probably led many to think that resistance, or weight, training was of limited use to other groups. Thinking has changed dramatically. Numerous newspaper articles and television segments feature older adults who are taking up weight training. Resistance exercise has become a part of even elementary school physical education curricula (figure 15.4). Rehabilitation programs focus on regaining strength after injury, even when the patient is not a professional athlete.

Figure 15.4 Increasing muscle mass with growth, a structural constraint, leads to increased strength, but resistance training also increases strength over the life span.

© Human Kinetics

? Why might strength training be important for nonathletes and those not necessarily rehabilitating an injury?

Strength is often an individual constraint in the performance of motor tasks. The strength level of an individual interacts with the task and environment to either permit a task or not, or to influence how a movement is performed. If strength training can change an individual's level of strength in a relatively short time, then it obviously becomes a means to help individuals perform tasks. Educators and therapists can intervene to change motor performance over a matter of weeks. Hence we should have a great interest in how strength training can change strength at any point in the life span. This section considers how strength training affects various age groups.

Prepubescence

An early study (Vrijens, 1978) failed to show much strength improvement when prepubescent children received strength training. However, subsequent studies demonstrated decisively that boys and girls as young as 6 or 7 years old could increase their strength with a variety of resistance training methods, including weights, pneumatic machines, hydraulic machines, and isometrics (figure 15.5) (de Oliveira & Gallagher, 1994; Duda, 1986; Sadres, Eliakim, Constantini, Lidor, & Falk, 2001; Sale, 1989; Weltman, 1989).

For example, Pfeiffer and Francis (1986) compared the strength of 14 prepubescent boys with a control group before and after a 9-week, 3-day-a-week training program. The boys trained on a Universal machine and with free weights, completing three sets of 10 repetitions in each session. The young boys improved their strength significantly. In fact, they achieved a greater percentage of increase than the pubescent and postpubescent boys Pfeiffer and Francis also tested (figure 15.6). Others have confirmed that although postpubertal individuals gain more absolute strength with training, prepubertal individuals gain more strength expressed as a percentage change from their starting strength (Sale, 1989).

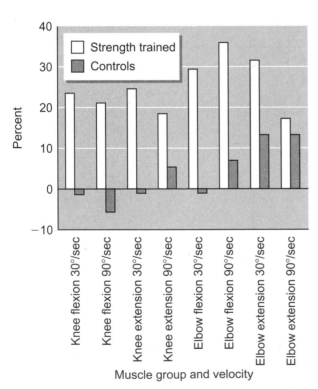

Figure 15.5 Muscle strength increases with training. Prepubescent boys achieved larger relative increases in strength of four muscle groups at two speeds of movement than their nontraining counterparts.

Reprinted from Malina and Bouchard 1991.

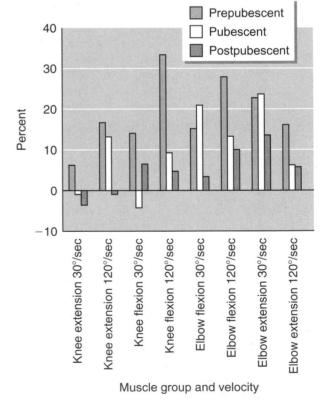

Figure 15.6 Percentage increases in strength with training. Prepubescent boys generally achieved larger relative increases in the strength of four muscle groups at two speeds of movement with 9 weeks of training than pubescent or postpubescent boys.

Reprinted from Malina and Bouchard 1991.

Several investigators found that increased muscle size did not accompany strength increase in prepubescents (Ramsay et al., 1990; Sale, 1989; Weltman et al., 1986). What accounts for the strength increase? As noted previously, strength is related to muscle size and the central nervous system's ability to fully activate muscles. Improvement in prepubescents likely results from their improved ability to exert force in the intended direction as they are better able to activate the agonist (contracting) muscles and coordinate the antagonist (lengthening) muscles (Sale, 1989). These neural factors probably account for much of the initial strength gain when any age group of males or females begins training.

Even if prepubescent children can improve their strength with training, are there negative effects of training? Children's bones are still growing and could be susceptible to injury at both traction and pressure epiphyses. Weight training could potentially cause a single traumatic injury or chronic injury from repeated lifts. Also, some professionals who work with children are concerned that a loss of flexibility or even stature may accompany strength training. Several studies found no damage to bones or muscles in training prepubescents and recorded no injuries (Rians et al., 1987; Servedio et al., 1985; Sewall & Micheli, 1986). In one study, 27 prepubescent boys, observed over 2 years of a twice-weekly resistance training program, had only one minor injury and were no different in height compared with a nontraining group (Sadres et al., 2001). Neither did researchers find loss of flexibility (Rians et al., 1987; Servedio et al., 1985; Sewall & Micheli, 1986; Siegel, Camaione, & Manfredi, 1989). However, all of the prepubescents in these studies were closely monitored. Educators should closely supervise weight training programs for young children and insist that participants adhere strictly to guidelines (Sale, 1989).

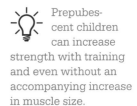
Prepubescent children can increase strength with training and even without an accompanying increase in muscle size.

? Aside from individual constraints, what are some other important constraints to consider when implementing a training program for children?

Adolescence

Developmentalists generally accept that strength training has beneficial effects for adolescents. Pfeiffer and Francis (1986) demonstrated that pubescent and postpubescent boys improved their strength with training, as previously described. Other training methods yield the same result, including isometric training (Nielsen, Nielsen, Hansen, & Asmussen, 1980) and plyometric training (Steben & Steben, 1981).

After puberty, muscle **hypertrophy** can accompany regular strength training. As noted previously, adolescent boys add far more muscle mass than do adolescent girls during the growth spurt. Do the sexes also differ in their response to training? Cureton, Collins, Hill, and McElhannon (1988) placed young adult men and women on a weight training program in which the resistance level was 70 to 90% of the individual's maximum. Men and women gained strength, the level being identical in terms of percentage increase but greater for the men in terms of absolute increase for two of four tests. For example, men and women might increase 5%, but if the men were stronger at the start, their increase was greater in absolute terms. Both men and women experienced muscle hypertrophy in their upper arms, again by an identical percentage increase, although one measure yielded a greater absolute increase in men. After puberty, then, both improved coordination in recruiting the muscle units needed to exert force and muscle hypertrophy response to strength training appear to be similar in men and women in relative terms. Muscle hypertrophy is more noticeable in men, in that a percentage increase of a larger muscle mass yields greater absolute dimensions.

Adolescents can increase strength and muscle mass with training.

Adolescents, like children, should be closely supervised when using weight training to improve strength. Their bones are still growing, and they are susceptible to a variety of musculoskeletal injuries (Risser & Preston, 1989). Performing Olympic-style lifts, in particular, can bring about back injuries (Jesse, 1977). Any activity that could possibly limit the ability to be active throughout life is of doubtful benefit to youth. Educators may want to take a cautious approach by starting adolescents with light resistance and scheduling progression in small increments. Close supervision is warranted because adolescents are susceptible to peer pressure; they can easily be drawn into games of trying to outperform each other.

Year-to-year comparisons of strength measurements taken between 7 and 17 years of age show that the strongest children are not necessarily the strongest adolescents (Rarick & Smoll, 1967). The weakest 7-year-olds might be late maturers who eventually catch up to or pass their peers. Researchers also have found that children and adolescents who participate regularly in sport are stronger than those who do not (Bailey, Malina, & Rasmussen, 1978). This could be seen as proof that the training provided by sport participation develops strength. It should be noted, though, that young athletes are often more mature than nonathletes. Hansen, Klausen, Bangsbo, and Muller (1999) noted that the elite 10- to 12-year-old soccer players selected for the best teams were taller, leaner, and more mature than those not selected.

Adults

Young and middle-aged adults can maintain or even increase their strength through resistance training. But what about older adulthood, when strength levels decline? Can older adults prevent or reverse losses in muscle mass and strength through training? It appears that older adults can benefit from specific resistance training programs. Frontera, Meredith, O'Reilly, Knuttgen, and Evans (1988) found strength gains as high as 227% after 12 weeks of high-resistance dynamic strength training in men 60 to 72 years of age. Willoughby and Pelsue (1998) found that moderate- and high-intensity training improved strength in men over 65. These results are consistent with many other research studies on a range of ages in older adulthood and on both men and women (Charette et al., 1991; Dupler & Cortes, 1993; Sipila & Suominen, 1995; Yarasheski, Zachwieja, & Bier, 1993). Absolute levels of strength increase are comparable with those in younger adults, while relative levels of increase depend on initial strength levels and the training regime.

Do older adults experience muscle hypertrophy with training as well as an increase in strength? Although Moritani and DeVries (1980) found that five older men (average age about 70) did not gain muscle mass along with their strength gain, most studies have observed muscle hypertrophy with training in the elderly (Aniansson & Gustafsson, 1981; Frontera et al., 1988; Larsson, 1982). Because early improvement in strength with training at any age reflects improved neurological coordination, training programs must be of sufficient length for individuals to realize a gain in muscle mass.

Some professionals are reluctant to recommend resistance training to older adults, especially weight training with high-intensity resistance or isometric exercises. Their fear is that high pressures in the chest during contractions could resist blood flow and trigger cardiovascular or cerebrovascular catastrophes. Lewis et al. (1983) actually found little pressure difference between isometric and dynamic exercises; however, older adults at high risk for cardiac catastrophe or with osteoporosis (skeletal atrophy) or arthritis should train with light resistance and under the supervision of a knowledgeable professional.

Older adults can increase strength and muscle mass with training.

? Consider the older adults you know. Do they participate in strength-promoting activities? Why or why not? On what constraints does their participation depend?

Resistance training is beneficial for increasing strength in preadolescence, adolescence, young adulthood, and older adulthood.

Development of Strength Summary

The typical pattern of strength change over the life span has five phases. In childhood there is a steady increase in strength. In adolescence, girls continue this steady increase, but boys have a spurt of strength. In the 20s and 30s strength levels are relatively stable. After this there is a gradual decline in strength until sometime in the 50s, when the loss becomes more dramatic.

This typical pattern can be changed by resistance training at any point in the life span. Hence, parents, teachers, and therapists can change the movement that arises from the interaction of person, task, and environment by introducing resistance training to those in their care. This changes an individual structural constraint.

Strength changes tend to parallel changes in muscle mass. However, muscle mass is not the only factor involved in increased strength. Neurological factors play a large role.

In fact, improvements in childhood with resistance training largely are related to neurological factors. Cultural norms probably play a role in strength levels by influencing the habitual physical activities undertaken by individuals.

Although muscle strength is important for the performance of skills, so is suppleness, or flexibility. Individuals must be able to move through full ranges of motion and position their limbs to undertake movements in sport and dance as well as in daily living.

DEVELOPMENT OF FLEXIBILITY

Flexibility often benefits maximal performance. Limited flexibility is a factor in sport injuries and restricted mobility. Despite this, young athletes sometimes overlook this important aspect of physical fitness, emphasizing endurance and strength at the expense of flexibility. Exceptions to this generalization are dancers and gymnasts, who have long realized the importance of flexibility in their activities. One reason for young athletes' indifference toward flexibility is their assumption that young people are naturally supple and need no further flexibility training. In addition, people typically view lack of flexibility as a problem only for older adults, whose movement limitations are more readily apparent. Many of these generalizations are misconceptions about flexibility. This section describes first the patterns of change in flexibility for the average individual, then the effects of training and how it alters the typical pattern.

Flexibility is the ability to move joints through a full range of motion.

Developmental Changes in Flexibility

The range of motion possible at any joint depends on that joint's bone structure and the soft tissues' resistance to movement. The soft tissues include muscles, tendons, joint capsules, ligaments, and skin. The belief that flexibility is related to limb length is incorrect. Habitual use and exercise preserve the elastic nature of the soft tissues, whereas disuse is associated with a loss of elasticity. To improve poor flexibility, a person must move the joint regularly and systematically through an increasingly larger range of motion to modify the soft tissues. Athletes, then, tend to increase the flexibility of joints they use in their sports, whereas laborers who spend much of their time in one posture may lose flexibility in some joints. It is likely that people who do not exercise fully lose flexibility because everyday activities rarely require movement through a full range of motion. Thus at any age, flexibility reflects the normal range of movement to which an individual subjects specific joints.

An important characteristic of flexibility is its specificity; that is, a certain degree of flexibility is specific to each particular joint. For example, an individual can be relatively flexible at one joint and inflexible at another.

Childhood

Most of us can recall seeing an infant lie on his back and bring his feet nearly to his head. Or, we remember a toddler who can sit on the floor with her bent legs out to the side. So, we know from experience that infants and toddlers are very flexible. Most observations of children show a decline in flexibility with advancing age.

After reviewing the information available in 1975, Clarke concluded that boys tend to lose flexibility after age 10 and girls after age 12. For example, Hupprich and Sigerseth (1950) administered 12 flexibility measures to 300 girls, ages 6, 9, 12, 15, and 18 years. Most of the flexibility measurements improved across the 6-, 9-, and 12-year-old groups but declined in the older groups (figure 15.7). Krahenbuhl and Martin (1977) found that flexibility in both boys and girls declined between ages 10 and 14, but Milne, Seefeldt, and Reuschlein (1976) reported that second graders in their study already had poorer flexibility than kindergartners.

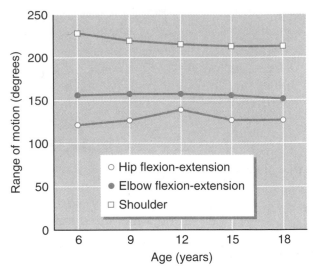

Figure 15.7 These three flexibility measures show that flexibility generally declines with advancing age, although some joints might increase in range of motion until approximately 12 years of age.

Adapted from Hupprich and Sigerseth 1950.

To examine Fitnessgram sit-and-reach measurements for trends with growth and gender differences, download Lab 15.2 Examining Trends in Sit-and-Reach Performance from the Student Resources section at www.HumanKinetics.com/LifeSpanMotorDevelopment.

Assessing Flexibility

Since flexibility is specific to a joint, one or two flexibility measures cannot accurately represent your overall flexibility. To know the flexibility in a specific joint in a particular individual, it must be measured. Most flexibility measures are made with a goniometer, a protractor with two long arms. The axis of the goniometer is centered over the joint to be measured. The limb is positioned at one end of the range of motion, and one arm of the goniometer is aligned with it. The limb is moved to the other end of the range, and the second arm is aligned with it. The degrees between the two arms on the goniometer represent the range of motion at the joint.

It is not quite as easy as it sounds to take accurate flexibility measurements. Starting and ending points are sometimes difficult to locate, and measurements often reflect the discomfort individuals are willing to endure to push themselves farther.

It is often impractical to give a battery of flexibility measures at various joints, especially if strength, endurance, and body composition are all being assessed at the same time. Fitness test batteries such as Physical Best (American Alliance for Health, Physical Education, Recreation and Dance, 1988), Fitnessgram (Meredith & Welk, 1999), and that used in the National Children and Youth Fitness Study II (Ross et al., 1987) employ a single representative flexibility measure. The sit-and-reach test (figure 15.8) was chosen because trunk and hip flexibility are thought to be important in the pre-

vention and care of low back pain in adults (Hoeger, Hopkins, Button, & Palmer, 1990).

Some researchers are concerned that the sit-and-reach test reflects body proportions as well as flexibility because it measures flexibility relative to a point even with the feet. A small number of individuals with unusually long legs, short arms, or both are at a disadvantage. A modified sit-and-reach test corrects for limb length bias by measuring flexibility relative to an individual's fingertips when sitting straight up (Hoeger et al., 1990).

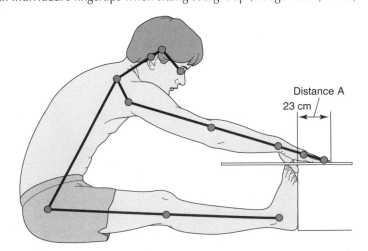

Figure 15.8 The sit-and-reach test. The individual sits with the feet against a box corresponding to the 23 cm point. Upon reaching forward as far as possible, the individual receives a score of 23 cm plus or minus the distance reached (distance A above).

Reprinted from Hoeger et al. 1990.

The sit-and-reach test has been used as the flexibility measure in several large studies of children and adolescents. Norms recently developed in the National Children and Youth Fitness Study II project (Ross, Pate, Delpy, Gold, & Svilar, 1987) for children ages 6 to 9 reflect generally stable sit-and-reach performance during childhood. In an extensive cross-sectional study of Flemish girls 6 to 18 years old, the sit-and-reach scores of girls in the *upper* percentiles were stable until age 12, then improved. The scores of girls in the *lower* percentiles declined from 6 to 12 years, improved somewhat in midadolescence, then declined again at 17 and 18 (figure 15.9). Thus, the range of scores was wider in successively older age groups (Simons et al., 1990). Belgian boys measured longitudinally improved their sit-and-reach performance from 12 to 18 years of age at a rate of about 1 cm per year (Beunen, Malina, Renson, & Van Gerven, 1988).

Generally, then, children maintain their sit-and-reach flexibility, whereas adolescents are able to improve their scores as they grow older. Some children and adolescents lose flexibility or improve very little. Abdominal strength might be a factor in sit-and-reach performance (Beunen et al., 1988). That is, individuals with strong abdominal muscles can pull the trunk forward to a greater degree of flexion. Performance might therefore be related to exercise and training, both for strength and range of motion.

Girls as a group are usually more flexible than boys (Beunen et al., 1988; DiNucci, 1976; Phillips et al., 1955; Simons et al., 1990). This probably reflects that stretching exercises are more socially acceptable for girls than vigorous exercises and that higher proportions of girls than boys participate in gymnastics and dance, activities that emphasize flexibility.

However, participation in exercise programs emphasizing flexibility is a far better predictor of flexibility than gender (figure 15.10).

Researchers, then, document both declines and improvements in flexibility during the growing years. It is possible that because the bones grow in length and then stimulate muscles to grow in length, a temporary loss of flexibility occurs during growth, especially in early adolescence (Micheli, 1984). It is not clear that the lag in muscle growth causes a measurable decline in flexibility.

Some changes might be particular to the joint or joints measured, but overall it is apparent that children and adolescents can lose their flexibility if they do not train to maintain or improve it. Flexibility becomes more variable within groups of adolescents because some adolescents train and others abandon exercise programs and physical activities.

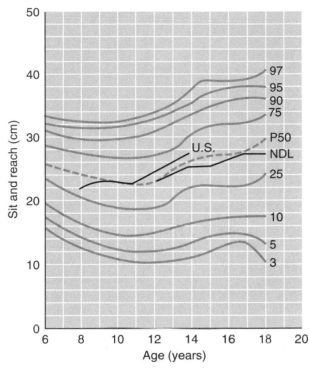

Figure 15.9 Changes in sit-and-reach test performance over age. Flemish girls at the upper percentiles maintained their flexibility during childhood, then improved in adolescence. Girls at the lower percentiles declined, with only slight improvement in midadolescence. The median scores of girls from the United States (U.S.) and Netherlands (NDL) are superimposed on the graph.

Redrawn from Bovend'eerdt et al. 1980, and Branta et al. 1984; reprinted from Simons et al. 1990.

Figure 15.10 It is not very clear as to how the changing structural constraints of skeletal system growth and muscle system growth influence flexibility, but flexibility becomes more variable in adolescence as some individuals exercise and others become sedentary.

© Human Kinetics

In adolescence, flexibility becomes more variable with advancing age, some individuals losing a significant degree of flexibility.

Adulthood

? Do you participate in activities or exercises that help you maintain your flexibility as you age? Which joints or body areas are exercised and which are not?

Unfortunately, adolescence does not mark the end of a person's trend toward reduced flexibility. Holland, Tanaka, Shigematsu, and Nakagaichi (2002) reviewed the research literature on flexibility and older adults. From the mid- to late 20s, maximum range of motion declines, faster in some joints than in others (Bell & Hoshizaki, 1981). For example, the decreases in spinal extension and shoulder flexion are relatively large compared with smaller decreases in hip extension and knee flexion (Einkauf, Gohdes, Jensen, & Jewell, 1987; Germain & Blair, 1983; Roach & Miles, 1991). Both upper and lower extremities showed decline (Rikli & Jones, 1999).

Osteoarthritis is a degenerative, chronic disease of the joints.

A variety of factors contribute to decreases in flexibility, including degeneration of musculoskeletal and soft tissues as well as diseases, especially **osteoarthritis** and **osteoporosis.** Collagen increases and elastin degenerates with advancing age, both increasing joint stiffness (Alnaqeeb, Al-Zaid, & Goldspink, 1984; Gosline, 1976). Disuse magnifies all these changes, although we do not know how disuse influences the rate of decline. The research studies of range of motion in adulthood have used the cross-sectional research design. Longitudinal studies would be needed to determine how much of the decline is due to age-related tissue change and how much is due to disuse. The learning activity at the end of this chapter gives you an opportunity to observe flexibility in some older adults.

Flexibility declines in adulthood, especially in little-used joints.

Flexibility Training

An individual's flexibility decreases without training at any point in the life span, but specific training can reverse a loss of flexibility at any age.

Researchers generally agree that both specialized stretch training and general exercise interventions moderately improve range of motion in older adults, including frail elderly. Munns (1981) formed two groups of 65- to 88-year-olds. One group served as a control, and the other participated in a 1-hour program of exercise and dance three times a week for 12 weeks. The exercising group improved significantly over the control group in all six of the flexibility measures taken. Germain and Blair (1983) also documented improved shoulder flexibility in adults ages 20 to 60 who participated in a stretching program for shoulder flexion, and Brown and Holloszy (1991) even found a 35% improvement in hip flexion with 5 days of slow stretch and calisthenic training per week over 3 months. Low-impact aerobics, Tai Chi, rhythmic stretching, and general fitness interventions all have yielded improvements (Hubley-Kozey, Wall, & Hogan, 1995; Lan, Lai, Chen, & Wong, 1998; McMurdo & Rennie, 1993; Rikli & Edwards, 1991).

Development of Flexibility Summary

The range of motion possible in a joint reflects a person's activity and training more than age per se. Flexibility declines in the average adolescent and adult as a result of limited daily activity and lack of exercise. Flexibility training can bring about an improvement in the range of motion at any age. For many individuals, then, if flexibility limits a desired movement, appropriate training can change this structural constraint.

 Summary and Synthesis

Muscle strength and flexibility have been discussed separately in this chapter, but their interrelationship as individual structural constraints should be noted. Individuals can improve strength and flexibility at any time in the life span with an appropriate training program. Ideally, though, individuals train for both. Having strong muscles to move a joint in one direction such that it cannot move through its appropriate range in the opposite direction can limit movement just as much as a lack of strength. Training for strength and flexibility is not just for athletes. Many movements needed for daily living can be difficult if not impossible if reasonable levels of strength and flexibility are lost. Therapists routinely help individuals regain lost strength and flexibility after accidents, injuries, and surgery.

Body composition is a component of fitness. A body composition high in lean muscle mass and low in fat tissue enhances cardiorespiratory endurance, is associated with increased strength, and permits flexibility as long as the muscles are balanced. Individuals who participate in endurance activities and resistance training programs can better maintain that body composition profile. The next chapter examines body composition more closely.

 ## Discussion Questions

1. How does the rate of increase in strength with growth compare with the rate of increase in muscle mass? How does the rate of decrease in strength and muscle mass compare in aging?

2. Can strength and flexibility improve with training? How?

3. How does flexibility change with growth and with aging?

4. What are the gender differences in the development of strength and flexibility in children and adolescents?

5. Consider the older adults in your society. Can you think of different types of constraints (individual, environmental, and task) that might lead to a loss of strength in the older years?

 ## Learning Activities

Older Adult Flexibility

Observe the following in two or three older adults and report your findings:

1. From a sitting position with back against a wall, can the individual keep the knee of the extended leg flat on the floor as he draws the other lower leg up against his thigh?

2. Can she raise her arms overhead, fingers pointing to the ceiling, to be even with or behind the ears?

3. When standing facing you, can he keep his elbows tucked in and turn his palms to face you?

4. In a standing position, can she link her hands behind her back and raise them up away from her back to a level even with her waist?

Did the individuals pass or fail all four items? Ask individuals about their favorite activities and see if you can account for the maintenance of flexibility by matching body areas to those activities.

Development of Body Composition

chapter 16

EXTRA!!! The Times EXTRA!!!

HEADLINES TELL THE STORY

Consider the following headlines that appeared in a single newspaper, *USA Today*, within 8 months:

▲ Name of This Game is Healthier Kids: Schools Face a Struggle to Change Food, Activity Habits (May 20, 2003)

▲ A Plan to "Get Kids in Action": Is Your Child at Risk of Becoming Overweight? (July 21, 2003)

▲ Dr. Phil Talks the Talk on Controlling Weight (September 9, 2003)

▲ Effects of TV on Kids Becoming Less Remote: Study Points to Way Too Much "Screen Time" (November 11, 2003)

▲ Shedding Unwanted Pounds: Teen Replaced Bad Habits With Exercise, Healthy Food (December 16, 2003)

▲ Ten Ways to Make It a Habit to Eat Less, Eat Better, and Exercise More (January 6, 2004)

It is clear there is concern today about fitness and fatness. Alarming rates of obesity have prompted more attention to the roles of diet and exercise in body composition and maintaining a healthy ratio of lean weight to fat weight at all points of the life span. But just what is the relationship of diet and exercise to body composition as one moves through the life span? It is valuable for everyone to know, both for any professional role that involves diet and exercise and for one's personal well-being.

Body mass can be divided into two types of tissue: **lean tissue**—which includes muscle, bone, and organs—and fat, or **adipose tissue.** The relative percentages of fat-free and fat tissue that make up the body mass give a measure of body composition. Many people care about body composition because it is related to appearance, but it also can influence individuals' feelings about themselves. Many societies value a lean body appearance. Obesity may contribute to a negative body concept and negative self-concept, thus making it difficult for an obese person to relate to others.

Aside from appearance, body composition is important in a variety of health issues:

▲ Higher proportions of lean body mass show a positive link to working capacity, and higher proportions of fat tissue show a negative link.

▲ Excess fat weight adds to the workload whenever the body is moved.

▲ Excess fat can limit an individual's range of motion.

▲ Obesity places a person at risk of suffering coronary heart and artery disease, stroke, diabetes, and hypertension.

Body composition is often related to success in executing motor skills. A body composition high in muscle mass and low in adipose tissue contributes to optimal performance. The muscle mass can be used to exert force, and low adipose tissue means a performer does not have extra weight to move, advantages in many physical activities.

As noted in chapter 4, everyone has some fat tissue. Fat tissue is needed for insulation, protection, and energy storage. Women need a minimal level of fat tissue (approximately 12% of body weight) to support functions of reproduction. Only *excess* fat weight is negatively related to fitness and health.

 Chapter Objectives

This chapter will

▲ review the effects of exercise on the body composition of children and youths through longitudinal research studies,

▲ note any gender differences in the effects of exercise on body composition,

▲ examine the effects of exercise on body composition in middle and older adulthood, and

▲ discuss the recent increase of obesity in Western societies.

BODY COMPOSITION AND EXERCISE IN CHILDREN AND YOUTHS

Genetic and environmental factors affect body composition. People can manipulate two major environmental factors—diet and exercise—to manage the relative amounts of lean and adipose tissue in their bodies. Maintaining body composition is in part a matter of balancing the calories consumed against the metabolic rate and amount of physical exertion (figure 16.1). The metabolic rate is the amount of energy an individual uses in a given amount of time to keep the body functioning. Individuals vary; some use more calories than others do just to keep the body running. The metabolic rate is under the control of various hormones, and it cannot be easily altered in the short term. In contrast, an individual can control exercise level on a daily basis. The relationship between body composition and exercise is the focus of this discussion.

Because children are not biochemically identical to adults, dividing the body into fat and fat-free mass oversimplifies body composition changes with growth. A more extensive breakdown, however, is beyond the scope of this text. This chapter considers what is known about the influence of exercise on fat and fat-free tissues in children and youths. This section considers the research of Jana Parizkova, much of which was published in the 1970s but which remains some of the little longitudinal work on this topic. More recent cross-sectional, or short-term, studies are also considered.

Figure 16.1 Diet and exercise are constraints that interact with the typical pattern of adipose tissue development.
© Human Kinetics

Assessing Amounts of Body Fat

There are numerous ways of measuring the amount of adipose tissue in the body. These measurements can be used directly to track changes with growth and aging, or they can be used to estimate the percent of the body's weight that is fat. Several methods allow us to measure lean body mass as well, also allowing an estimation of body fat:

- Measuring the thickness of the skin and underlying (subcutaneous) fat with skinfold calipers. The amount of total body fat can be estimated from skinfold measurements taken at specified sites. This is one of the most common ways of estimating fat weight, especially in children.

- Weighing an individual underwater and contrasting that value with normal body weight. This method estimates body density and subsequently the proportion of lean versus fat weight. It is difficult to take this measurement on young children and adults who are afraid of being underwater.

- Analyzing the intensity of reemitted infrared light emitted by a probe into the biceps brachii muscle with a near-infrared interactance device (NIR). This is an easy measurement method to use with children but may not be as accurate as other methods, especially underwater weighing (Smith et al., 1997).

The Parizkova Studies

Fat tissue increases rapidly during two periods: the first 6 months after birth and again in early adolescence. In girls, this increase continues throughout adolescence, whereas in boys the gain stops and may even reverse for a time. Muscle tissue also grows rapidly in infants, followed by a steady period of increase during childhood; it again increases rapidly during the adolescent growth spurt, more dramatically in boys than in girls. Either diet or exercise may alter this typical pattern. Overeating results in excess fat weight, and starvation can lead to levels of fat so low that the body obtains energy by muscle wasting (breaking down muscle tissue to use as energy). Exercise burns calories, potentially altering a person's body composition. Resistance training can increase muscle mass, especially after puberty.

In cross-sectional and longitudinal studies, researchers have examined the relationship between exercise and body composition. Cross-sectional studies generally show that young athletes have lower proportions of body fat than more sedentary children (Parizkova, 1973). However, it is impossible to determine from a cross-sectional study whether an active lifestyle results in leanness. (It may be that leaner children find activity easier and adopt active lifestyles.) Longitudinal studies, then, are more valuable in the study of the interrelationships between activity levels and body composition.

Parizkova conducted a series of studies on body composition and activity levels of boys and girls in Czechoslovakia. The first study was cross-scctional and was one of the few studies to examine very young children; the remainder of the studies were longitudinal. In the cross-sectional study, Wolanski and Parizkova (1976; cited in Parizkova, 1977) compared skinfold measures in two groups of children ages 2 to 5 years. One group of children attended special physical education classes with their parents, whereas the other group did not participate in any type of physical training program. Even at this young age, children in the physical education group had lower levels of subcutaneous fat.

Teenage Boys

In extensive longitudinal study of teenage boys, Parizkova (1968, 1977) divided nearly 100 boys into four groups by their activity level. The most active group of boys (group I) were involved in basketball or track at least 6 hours a week. The least active group (group IV) participated only in unorganized and unsystematic activity. The boys in the other two groups had intermediate activity levels.

Parizkova first tested the boys at an average age of 10.7 years and followed them in successive years until they were 14.7 years old. Over the 4 years, the children in the most active group significantly increased in body mass while their absolute level of fat weight remained the same; hence, the fat proportion of their total weight decreased. In contrast, the boys in the inactive group increased significantly in absolute fat weight. The two groups did not differ in initial amount of fat weight, but they differed at the end of the 4 years. In the active group, the increase in lean body mass *alone* accounted for the increase of body weight with growth (figure 16.2, a and b). Physical activity had a beneficial effect on body composition in these boys.

Parizkova (1972) followed 41 of these boys for another 3 years. The body composition trends of the first 4 years continued. The most active and least active groups differed in total weight by the time they reached age 16.7. The active group was heavier in total body weight because of the boys' greater lean body mass. The active boys had less total fat weight than the inactive boys, and their fat weight actually declined in some years. Parizkova determined that the groups did not differ in average skeletal age, so the body composition differences noted cannot be attributed to maturational differences. He also noted that the boys maintained their relative position within the group in both distribution and absolute amount of subcutaneous fat. This means that the relative amount of fat weight and its pattern of distribution in the body were relatively stable over the years of the study.

Parizkova followed 16 of these 41 young men for another 6 years. Although this number was too small for a reliable analy-

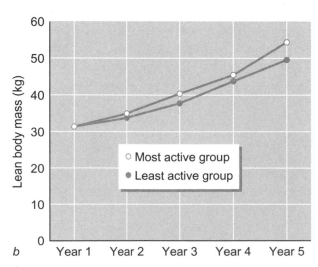

Figure 16.2 *(a)* Relative percent body fat in the most and least active groups of boys followed by Parizkova from an average age of 10.7 years to 14.7 years. *(b)* Lean body mass of the same groups in Parizkova's study.

Data from Parizkova 1968a, 1968b, published in Parizkova 1977.

sis by activity level, Parizkova (1977) noted that percent body fat declined in the group until age 21.7 years, then varied widely among individuals, probably reflecting changes in lifestyle. The Parizkova studies, then, indicate that physical activity has a favorable influence on boys' body composition during the growing years.

Physical activity has a favorable effect on boys during the growing years by increasing lean body mass and minimizing addition of fat weight.

Teenage Girls

The growth of adipose and lean muscle tissue differs dramatically between the sexes during adolescence. Girls gain proportionately more fat than muscle compared with boys. Even so, the beneficial effect activity has on body composition found in boys also occurs in active girls. Over a span of 5 years, Parizkova (1963, 1977) studied 32 girls who belonged to a gymnastics school and 45 girls who were not engaged in any type of training. The girls were first measured at the age of 12 or 13. The gymnasts followed a regular yearly cycle of training in which they attended a rigorous camp in the summer, stopped training in the fall, and resumed a heavy training schedule from October to December.

These cycles are shown (for 11 of the gymnasts) in figure 16.3 as black-outlined bars; the higher the bar, the more intense the training. Measurements of the girls' fat weight paralleled Parizkova's findings with boys. The gymnasts remained at the same level of subcutaneous fat during the 5 years, and the total skinfold thickness showed no trend, even though it rose or fell for short periods. In contrast, the control group gained a significant amount of fat weight. Height and body weight trends in the two groups were similar throughout the 5 years, so the differences were truly in body composition.

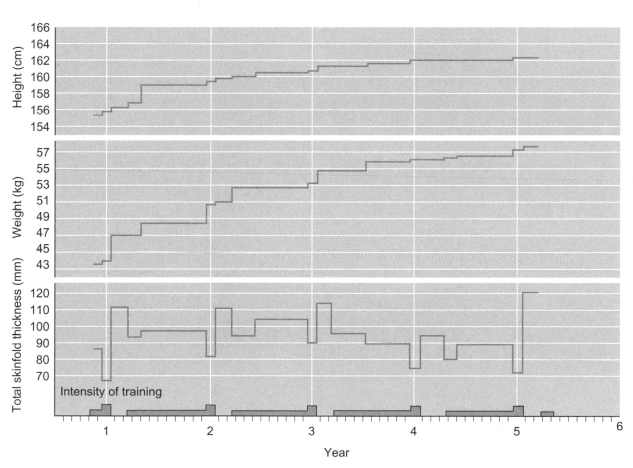

Figure 16.3 Changes in height, weight, and subcutaneous fat (sum of 10 skinfold measurements) in a group of regularly training female gymnasts (N = 11) during a 5-year period of varying intensity of training (see bottom scale).

Data from Parizkova 1963, 1965; reprinted from Parizkova 1977.

The cyclic nature of the gymnasts' training schedule provided information about their weight and skinfold thicknesses as they progressed through the various training cycles. During periods of inactivity, the gymnasts gained in both total body weight and skinfold thickness (including subcutaneous fat tissue), but during training, the gymnasts increased in total body weight while their skinfold thicknesses declined. (Note that in figure 16.3, total skinfold thickness goes down when the intensity of training bar goes up, and total skinfold thickness goes up when training stops for a time.) Total height and weight keep increasing with age. Therefore, their weight increases during the various activity periods resulted from changing ratios of fat and lean body weight. Parizkova also recorded the gymnasts' caloric intake and found that they consumed more calories during periods of intense training, but fat deposits declined and lean body mass increased.

Teenage girls in training can increase lean body mass and decrease subcutaneous fat, even when they eat more calories in response to training.

Comparing Adolescent Boys and Girls

Parizkova's longitudinal studies show the same general relationship between body composition and activity in both boys and girls, but they do not allow direct comparison of the sexes. So Parizkova (1973, 1977) simultaneously followed 12 boys and 12 girls engaged in swimming training from ages 12 to 16. At 12, the average height, weight, lean body mass, and fat weight of the two groups were about the same. Lean body mass values were higher for the swimmers than the average levels for teens not in training, probably reflecting the swimmers' previous training. By age 15, the boys were significantly taller, heavier, and leaner than the girls, but both sexes showed an increased proportion of lean body mass at the expense of fat weight over the 3 years of training. Although higher in percent fat than the boys, the girls did not gain as much fat as the typical nontraining adolescent girl. More research on this topic is necessary, especially to determine the length and intensity of training programs that have favorable results with girls. Tremblay, Despres, and Bouchard (1988) did not find a decline in fatness or a gain in lean body mass in girls after 15 weeks of intense training, although boys experienced significant changes in this length of time.

? How has your body composition changed throughout your life span? Can you think of a relative or friend who has experienced great change? In what direction? To what would you attribute these changes?

Short-Term Studies

Dollman, Olds, Norton, and Stuart (1999) compared more than 1,400 Australian children who were 10 and 11 in 1997 with a group measured in 1985. The 1997 children as a group were heavier and fatter, although slightly taller, than the 1985 group. They were also slower in the 1.6 km walk/run and 50 m sprint. These differences did not occur in the leaner and fitter children but rather in the one-fourth of the children who were fatter and less fit. Although it's not clear whether one decline caused the other decline (or something else caused both), being fatter coincided with poorer fitness performance.

The Muscatine study is a longitudinal investigation of cardiovascular disease risk factors among the residents of Muscatine, Iowa. Measurements of the participants included those of fitness, body composition, blood pressure, heart mass, and maturation level in youths. Janz, Burns, and Mahoney (1995) reported on a 2-year follow-up of more than 120 children, age 10 at the first set of measurements. They found that increased systolic blood pressure was associated with increased body fatness and decreased physical fitness. Again, the two factors coincided in a group approximately the same age as that observed by Dollman et al. (1999).

In summary, these investigations show that involvement in training programs affects adolescents' body composition favorably. Limited information suggests that the body composition of preschool children also benefits from activity. Although children and adolescents who engage in active training exhibit the general growth trend of increased weight, this increase represents the addition of relatively more lean body mass and less fat weight than in their nontraining peers. A person's higher caloric intake during training evidently increases lean body mass rather than fat stores.

It is possible for a person to carry training to an extreme so that the body cannot meet the energy required for continued growth. This condition mimics starvation and can lead to loss of lean body mass and detrimental effects on growth (Lemon, 1989).

Appropriate levels of exercise in youth are associated with a healthier body composition.

BODY COMPOSITION AND EXERCISE IN ADULTS

In middle age, the average adult loses fat-free body mass and gains fat such that body weight increases and the portion of body weight that is fat increases. Of particular concern is an accumulation of trunk fat, which is associated with increasingly poor cardiovascular health. In old age, fat-free body mass and fat mass decline. It is important to remember that this is the typical profile and individuals are extremely variable. Also, obese individuals often die before reaching older adulthood, and this can change average measurements taken on groups of older adults.

Exercise might favorably influence body composition in two ways: it could increase fat-free mass or decrease fat. The increase in fat-free mass could be an increase in muscle mass, an increase in bone density, or obviously both. Some studies, discussed in this section, have tracked these changes in exercising adults.

Middle-aged and older adult athletes and regular exercisers tend to maintain their muscle and fat masses, many comparing favorably with younger adult populations (Asano, Ogawa, & Furuta, 1978; Kavanagh & Shephard, 1977; Pollock, 1974; Saltin & Grimby, 1968; Shephard, 1978b). However, we cannot assume from these observations that the same would be true of the population at large or of sedentary older adults who begin training. It is possible that healthier older adults are more able to be active so that what is being observed is good health status rather than the benefits of exercise. For this reason, it is important to longitudinally study older adults for exercise effects. The number of longitudinal studies is almost nonexistent, though, so short-term studies must often be relied on for information.

Recent studies of changes in muscle mass with exercise have used computed tomography (CT) to document changes in muscle area. A study of men ages 60 to 72 (Frontera, Meredith, O'Reilly, Knuttgen, & Evans, 1988) and a study of men ages 86 to 96 (Fiatarone et al., 1990) reported increases in muscle area in the range of 4.8 to 11.4% after 12 and 8 weeks of training, respectively. Both type I and type II fibers increased. Other studies have found smaller changes (Forbes, 1992). It is clear that individuals are extremely variable. Fiatarone et al. (1990) reported individual subjects who lost 8% of muscle area with training and subjects who gained 30% in the same number of weeks. This makes it difficult to predict whether every older adult would see an increase in muscle mass with training.

Studies of young athletes have concluded that regular exercise promotes bone growth, but the few studies of older adults reached conflicting conclusions. This might be due in part to weak research methods. For example, in some studies the exercise program undertaken by the adults did not stress the body locations that were measured for bone density (Going, Williams, Lohman, & Hewitt, 1994). Several studies of change in the bone mineral density of lumbar (lower back) vertebrae have shown improvements with weight training in premenopausal (Going et al., 1991; Lohman et al., 1992) and postmenopausal women (Dalsky et al., 1988; Pruitt, Jackson, Bartels, & Lehnhard, 1992). Another study, however, reported a decline in bone mineral density (Rockwell et al., 1990). Researchers need to do much more work, especially on a wide range of older adults, and they need to determine the type, duration, and frequency of exercise that is helpful.

Adults can increase muscle mass and bone density with resistance training and lose fat weight with endurance training, but individuals are variable in their amount of change.

Schwartz et al. (1991) placed 15 men between 60 and 82 years of age on a 6-month endurance training program. Their training intensity gradually increased so that eventually they were walking or jogging 45 min 5 days per week at 85% of heart rate reserve. Over the 6 months, their body fat decreased 2.3% and their waist circumferences decreased 3.4%. Although the loss of body fat overall was small, the loss of fat in specific trunk locations was more dramatic. This is significant because of the association between trunk fat and increased cardiovascular risk.

Although more longitudinal research in the area of body composition and exercise is needed, there are clear indications that exercise has a favorable effect on body composition. Observation of those engaged in vigorous activity over their life spans demonstrates at the very least that a decline of fat-free mass and increase of fat mass is not a foregone conclusion for everyone.

OBESITY

Obesity is most commonly defined as a body mass index (BMI) over 30.0.

The prevalence of **obesity** is increasing around the world and in all age categories. Rates of obesity vary among countries, with a higher prevalence in industrialized nations. Increasing rates among upper classes in developing countries, however, demonstrate the strong universal trend toward obesity (Kotz, Billington, & Levine, 1999; Rudloff & Feldmann, 1999). Various organizations and researchers use slightly different criteria to determine who is considered obese. The most common definition for adults is a **body mass index** (BMI) over 30.0 (Kotz et al., 1999). BMI is the ratio of body weight (kg) to height squared (m), with normal being 18.5 to 24.9. It is more challenging to define obesity for children because of ongoing growth, but a weight-for-height measurement over the 95th percentile or a triceps skinfold over the 95th percentile are frequently used criteria (Rudloff & Feldmann, 1999).

Body mass index (BMI) is the ratio of body weight to height squared, with a "normal" index being 18.5 to 24.9.

To observe BMI measurements for a group of children as they advanced from 5.5 years to 9.5 years of age, download Lab 16.1 Body Composition in Childhood from the Student Resources section at www.HumanKinetics.com/LifeSpanMotorDevelopment.

Obesity is a concern at any point in the life span. Yet, chances are great that obese children will remain obese into adulthood, and obesity tends to be stable over young, middle, and older adulthood. Hence, it is important to address obesity in children even while recognizing its medical and social repercussions at any age.

In the United States about one-fourth of children and adolescents are obese, an increase of 54% in children and 39% in adolescents over 20 years (Rudloff & Feldmann, 1999). Parents often believe that their child's obesity is caused by a metabolic or thyroid disorder. In fact, these disorders account for less than 1% of obesity in children (Dietz & Robinson, 1993). What is the cause of obesity, then?

Basal metabolic rate is the amount of energy needed to sustain the body's vital functions in the waking state.

Obesity is a good example of the interaction between genetic and extrinsic factors. Certainly genetic factors are related to obesity. Body mass index is highly correlated in twins, even if they are raised apart, but is poorly correlated in parents and adopted children. However, there is no single genetic factor that is related to obesity in all individuals. **Basal metabolic rate,** dietary **thermogenesis,** appetite control and satiety, and lipid metabolism and storage are various factors under genetic influence (Rudloff & Feldmann, 1999).

Thermogenesis is the production of heat in the body.

The increase in obesity over the last several decades demonstrates the strong influence of extrinsic factors on obesity since genetic influences could not change the incidence rate so rapidly (Rosenbaum & Leibel, 1998). Increasing modernization lessens energy expenditure as laborious tasks are taken over by machines (figure 16.4). A Westernized diet, high in fat and sugar, also is a major factor in obesity (Kotz et al., 1999). Because genetic predispositions are fixed, manipulation of energy intake and expenditure is the most available means to alter body fatness during the life span.

Restricting caloric intake in children is challenging because sufficient energy must be provided to support growth. Overweight children typically do not eat large quantities. Rather, they have a small but daily caloric imbalance (Dietz & Robinson, 1993). A relatively modest adjustment of calories with good nutritional balance in diet can be very effective. However, reduced motor activity is a common characteristic of obese children (Roberts, Savage, Coward, Chew, & Lucas, 1988). Increasing calorie expenditure through exercise has multiple benefits in altering body fat. First, it can offset the decrease in basal metabolic rate that accompanies caloric restriction. Second, it can promote the growth of muscle tissue, which requires more calories for maintenance than fat tissue requires (Bar-Or, 1993). This is significant because without exercise, 30 to 40% of the weight loss with caloric restriction in adults is from lean body mass (Harris, 1999), and this is likely the trend with children, too.

Figure 16.4 Television, especially in the form of home theater systems, and Internet surfing are becoming increasingly attractive forms of entertainment for individuals of all ages. As a result more people are tempted to be sedentary rather than active. These environmental and task constraints interact with body systems to create a downward health spiral: lean body mass decreases, fat tissue increases, and the cardiovascular system develops increased risk for disease.

It is well established that obese children do not perform as well as lean children on a variety of physical fitness and motor skills tests. Malina et al. (1995) selected a group of Belgian girls between 7 and 17 years of age. At each age the leanest 5% outperformed the fattest 5% on arm strength and endurance tasks, trunk strength tasks, the vertical jump, an agility shuttle run, and a balance task. Adolescent boys show the same performance differences (Beunen et al., 1983). On the other hand, participation in regular physical activity reduces fatness in obese children. Sasaki, Shindo, Tanaka, Ando, and Arakawa (1987) found that a 2-year program of daily aerobic activity significantly decreased skinfold thicknesses. Even short-term training programs of 10 weeks and 4 months yield decreased body fat percentages in obese children between 7 and 11 years of age (Gutin, Cucuzzo, Islam, Smith, & Stachura, 1996; Gutin, Owens, Slavens, Riggs, & Treiber, 1997). These findings imply that activity programs might be relatively difficult for obese children, yet the benefits of regular activity can be significant. Well-designed programs that set the workload appropriately for obese children are needed.

 Exercise is an important strategy in altering obesity because it expends calories and offsets a decrease in basal metabolic rate that accompanies caloric restriction.

The incidence of obesity increases in men and women from age 20 to age 50 (Kotz et al., 1999; figure 16.5). Obesity puts individuals at risk for hypertension, cardiovascular disease, diabetes, gallstones, osteoarthritis, and some forms of cancer; hence, the obese are at greater risk of early mortality. In fact, a decrease in the prevalence of obesity in the 70s and 80s might reflect the shortened life span of the obese. The association of obesity and mortality is stronger among those whose increased fatness is particularly concentrated in the abdomen (Kotz et al., 1999).

To gain experience taking and comparing two types of measurements on a small group of individuals, download Lab 16.2 Comparing Body Composition Measures from the Student Resources section at www.HumanKinetics.com/LifeSpanMotorDevelopment.

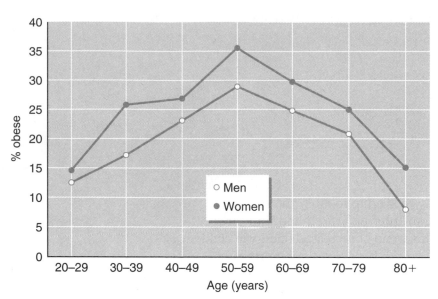

Figure 16.5 The prevalence of obesity with advancing age in adults. Declines in prevalence in later decades reflect the greater risk of early mortality in the obese; that is, declines reflect that many obese individuals died at younger ages than their nonobese counterparts.

Drawn from data contained in the National Health and Nutrition Examination Survey III, as modified in Kotz, Billington, and Levine 1999 from Flegal et al. 1998.

As at younger ages, genetic and extrinsic influences play a role in adult obesity, although the relative contributions of each can vary within an individual over the life span (Rosenbaum & Leibel, 1998). It is well known that activity levels are low among adults in Westernized countries. In the United States less than one-fourth of adults regularly exercise at least 30 min per day, and 24% are sedentary. Of overweight adults, 41% of women and 33% of men are completely sedentary (Cowburn, Hillsdon, & Hankey, 1997). As with children and teens, a combination of caloric restriction and increased activity is the most effective strategy in altering body fatness among adults. Research studies show that progress is greater with a combination than with exercise alone or caloric restriction alone. The difference is not great, but even a modest 10% loss of body weight can have a substantial benefit for cholesterol (LDL) levels, fasting blood glucose levels, and blood pressure (Harris, 1999).

 ## Summary and Synthesis

Body composition is an important component of physical fitness and is related to physical performance. Although body composition is related to genetic factors, the extrinsic factors of diet and exercise can greatly affect an individual's relative levels of fat and lean body mass. A person of any age who wishes to change his or her body fatness can manipulate both diet and exercise. Regular exercise can play a large and favorable role in altering body composition because it promotes muscle mass and an increase in basal metabolic rate. In turn, a body composition higher in lean mass and lower in fat mass makes exercise and physical performance easier.

This highlights the interactive nature of the body's structural constraints and movement. Physical activity can alter the constraints over time and thus permit movements requiring fitness. A lack of activity can alter the structural constraints over time such that the eventual effect is to constrain and restrict the possible activities and movements that require a certain level of fitness. Individuals can change their fitness levels with training, but there are age-related differences in the impact of training. Teachers, parents, coaches, therapists, and movers themselves must consider how the individual constraints related to the fitness systems interact with environment and task.

Discussion Questions

1. How does participation in regular physical activity affect body composition in children and adolescents?

2. What are the gender differences in body composition? Does exercise affect the body composition of males and females similarly or differently? How?

3. What are the best weight-management strategies for obese children?

4. What are the favorable effects of exercise on the body composition of older adults?

 ### Learning Activities

Children and Obesity

The increase in the number of children in countries around the world who are obese is of great concern to all of us. In the past few years, this topic has received much attention in the popular press, and many people have tried to identify the causes and suggest interventions to reverse the trend. Conduct an Internet search and find three different solutions that have been proposed to reverse the trend of increased obesity in children. Do the writers present evidence that would lead you to believe the solutions would work?

Interactions Among Constraints

Applications to Movement

chapter 17

EXTRA!!! The Times EXTRA!!!

ATHENS 2004 PARALYMPIC GAMES: PURSUIT, STRENGTH, INSPIRATION, CELEBRATION

"The Paralympic Games is the top sports event in the life of every Paralympic athlete. In Athens, about four thousand athletes will engage in noble competition to achieve ever higher results, performances and goals. The challenge to break records and the striving for distinction and victory mark the athletes' presence at the Paralympic Games of Athens, in 2004.... In the Paralympic Games, athletes engage in obstinate, noble and sustained competition to achieve the highest sports distinction. Their efforts are guided and shaped by a unique strength and determination. Their strength and ability to overcome hardship becomes a shining flame, a pole of attraction for everyone who values sports as the highest expression of humanity."

—*Official Web site of the 2004 Athens Paralympic Games*

What does this mean to you now that you have finished reading this text on life span motor development? We hope that you view Paralympians as people who have unique sets of constraints along with many others that are common to all humans. The structural and functional individual constraints of these Paralympians do not stop them from participating in physical activity at the highest levels. Their constraints allow them to move in activities of daily living, as well as compete at a high level of athletics. These interacting constraints include high levels of strength (structural), motivation (functional), a supportive environment (sociocultural), and high-tech equipment (task), among others. Put these into the context of a sporting event and the results are elite record-breaking athletes.

Not everyone can be, or wants to be, an elite athlete, but everyone moves constantly, every day. All movement occurs in a context and results from an interaction of constraints. Certain constraints may influence movement behavior more at a particular time than others do. Other constraints can change drastically over the course of the life span. But all exist and interact, allowing movement to emerge. Why have we spent so much time emphasizing this point?

During the course of this text, we utilized a developmental perspective in discussing the different types of constraints that affect motor development across the life span. To conceptualize how constraints work, we separated them into individual, environmental, and task constraints. It is important to realize, however, that although one type of constraint may be more influential at any given time, all are present and constantly interacting. In fact, something can only act as a constraint when it interacts with an individual in a movement context. That means that you must understand how constraints affect each other. At first glance, this may seem somewhat confusing. However, assessing the influence of constraints on each other is what we have been doing all along. Remember the example about a young man being recruited as early as his freshman year to play football or basketball? The significance of the story is related to his individual constraints (height, strength), environmental constraints (availability of courts, sociocultural expectation of playing basketball), and task constraints (rules of basketball, size of the ball) all acting together. If any of the constraints are changed, his motor development will change. For example, what if he grew up in Sweden, where basketball is not as popular a sport?

Looking at the interaction of constraints is helpful in understanding life span motor development. The most important message of this text is that manipulating different constraints can be useful in influencing movement and motor development (figure 17.1). We would like to emphasize this point: If a change in a constraint leads to a change in the interaction between constraints, then it can lead to a change in motor behavior. In other words, we can influence our own motor behavior and that of others by manipulating constraints to make them more developmentally appropriate. Isn't that the point of teaching and rehabilitation?

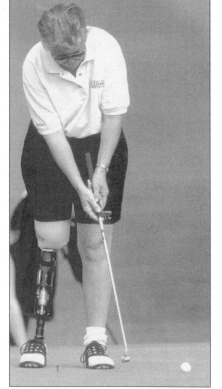

Figure 17.1 By manipulating task constraints—in this case, providing a prosthetic limb—a person with unique individual constraints can participate in many different physical activities in the same capacity as a person with typical individual constraints.

USING CONSTRAINTS TO ENHANCE LEARNING IN PHYSICAL ACTIVITY SETTINGS

In everyday life, people frequently modify constraints in order to change movements. These adjustments can make movements possible that otherwise may have been difficult. For example, individuals in wheelchairs can perform activities of daily living more easily if their household appliances such as sinks, stoves, and countertops are scaled to their relative (seated) height. Sometimes without even thinking, individuals alter something in the relationships between themselves, their environment, and the task at hand. We would probably slide a heavy book across the table and closer to us before picking it up, rather than attempt to lift it an arm's length away. Further, children have small hands and arms; to help them succeed in learning to play a violin, music teachers often provide them with smaller instruments scaled to their body size. These examples illustrate how modifying a task or environmental constraint allows for a more developmentally appropriate, functional motor skill. For movement educators, it is important to consider all types of constraints and how they interact. As you might expect, interaction is a dynamic process and may result in a change in one or all of the interacting constraints. Movement educators, therefore, must attempt to manipulate constraints to allow their students or clients to perform skills more proficiently or to achieve a goal (Gagen & Getchell, 2004).

Physical educators often manipulate constraints when designing play experiences for students in their classes. Using the notion of constraints, movement educators can adjust play experiences by altering the environment or the task. Theoretically, one can manipulate individual constraints as well; practically speaking and on a day-to-day basis, educators cannot change children's structural constraints. Over the course of a semester, individual constraints such as height and weight may change very little. Changing functional constraints such as fear or motivation may require longer time periods as well. So, teachers must accept that individual constraints cannot be easily manipulated on a given day within the gym. However, by modifying environmental or task constraints, movement educators manipulate the *interactions* between the constraints and facilitate change to encourage more proficient or desired movements. For example, distances can be shortened for shorter students or softer balls can be used with timid students. Ultimately, if done in a developmentally appropriate way, adjusting the relationships between constraints will lead to more permanent changes in the individual constraints and more proficient movement patterns.

Structuring the Learning Environment

In this textbook, you have read about many developmental changes that occur across the life span. Movement educators should keep these in mind as they structure their learning environments. For example, it's easy to consider a gymnasium a static environment. However, factors such as wall color can influence how proficiently a child catches a ball. Remember, younger children will have greater difficulty discriminating objects from the environment and will benefit from more salient visual cues. To provide these cues, a physical educator can purchase equipment that is multicolored or distinct from the wall color. What could an instructor do if new equipment is not an option? Why not tape white paper to the wall as a backdrop? In a rehabilitation setting, the environment can be structured to be more "ecologically valid," or "real world." The setting could be restructured to resemble a home or work environment, which would facilitate movement within that context.

When young children run at play, the running surface dictates how fast they run and how well they can remain on their feet. Long, clumpy grass presents different problems to running children than blacktop playground surfaces or slippery tile gym floors. Weather is another environmental aspect that may influence activities. Running a mile on a hot, humid day when breathing is difficult for most will be nearly impossible for others. Planning more strenuous activities for days when the temperature is cooler, the humidity is lower, and the air is clearer of pollen or pollutants (such as after a rain) will allow students to be more successful (Gagen & Getchell, 2004).

Let's not forget the sociocultural environment. When selecting activities and games, teachers can choose games that do not promote success based on gender, race, ethnicity, or socioeconomic status. For example, when activities are gender neutral, both boys and girls feel comfortable playing and succeeding. Some new games promote the same movement skills in traditional games but do not have particular sociocultural associations—team handball or sepak (a sport in which players kick a ball over a volleyball-type net) are examples. This approach opens opportunities to children who might otherwise not participate in a more traditional American sport. Different types of environmental constraints influence the structure of the learning environment. Manipulating the environment—or at the very least, being mindful of its influence—will allow movement educators in many different fields to create a setting that promotes movement proficiency.

Designing the Learning Task

No matter what the setting, movement educators *design* learning tasks. Consider how the interaction of relevant constraints encourages particular movement skills, keeping in mind that making changes can make skills easier or more difficult to achieve. How do the goals and rules of the task, as well as the equipment used in a task, interact with students' unique individual constraints within the class environment to allow the children to perform a desired, successful movement?

Task goals are the behavioral outcomes of the lesson. Teachers choose the goal of the task to encourage certain desired movements. Consider the task of throwing a ball. How a child throws depends on the goal of the task: to throw the ball as far as possible, as high as possible, as accurately as possible, or as quickly as possible. The throwing movements that result from each of these different task goals will differ substantially.

If children are young, small, or not very strong, some task goals are developmentally inappropriate and will not result in the practice of good throwing technique. For example, competitive games such as "pickle" (a game that simulates a baseball runner caught between two bases while two throwers attempt to get the runner "out") encourage children to throw quickly but may inhibit the use of appropriate throwing technique. When children focus on competition, they may simply pick up the throwing objects and use any method to propel them in the interest of speed. This does not encourage children to set their feet and use an appropriate backswing or aiming technique, nor does it promote correct use of all the body parts that should be sequentially involved in applying force and direction to the throw. In this example, if the task goal is proficient throwing technique, competitive games should be avoided with young children. Movement educators can carefully manipulate the task goals so that children achieve an intended skill without being conscious of the intent. If a teacher places large pieces of paper against a wall and tells her students to "make the biggest noise possible," the students will throw harder without any potentially negative comparisons with their classmates for not throwing as far as another child. In this case, throwing harder without throwing farther will often encourage children to use better technique; throwers will get feedback from the noise of the paper targets as the balls hit them, but the students need to control the throw in order to hit the target.

Teachers can also modify the rules of a task to elicit a desired movement behavior. Often teachers modify games (change the rules) to encourage different movements or levels of participation. Playing three-on-three soccer on small fields is a game modification that allows shorter, more controlled kicking and receiving of the soccer ball and more participation by each child, thus changing the focus of the game from running and chasing to movement technique. Playing volleyball with rules that allow the ball to bounce once will often give children the time to move into a better striking position, thus allowing them to use more appropriate striking technique. Requiring three passes before a shot in basketball promotes team play and cooperation.

Body scaling is a relatively easy way to manipulate task constraints by modifying the equipment and play spaces in proportion to the physical size or strength of the movers. Movement educators and rehabilitation specialists often scale equipment and play spaces to assist movers who have a smaller stature or lesser strength. Bats, rackets, golf clubs, and balls designed for women are often smaller and lighter than those designed for men, and those designed for children are smaller and lighter still. Soccer fields and base paths for children's leagues are often shortened to more closely "match" the shorter legs of younger children. Shorter volleyball nets and 6- and 8-foot basketball standards are thought to promote more effective ball skills in younger performers (Chase, Ewing, Lirgg, & George, 1994; Davis, 1991). When teaching, coaching, or rehabilitating people, movement educators should think through the process of choosing equipment to match physical size and strength very carefully. Smaller balls that fit into smaller hands are easier to throw, *but* larger balls are easier to catch (Payne & Koslow, 1981). Therefore, the overall goal of the task (e.g., throwing or catching) must always be kept in mind.

Let's consider the example of a striking task for children, that of batting a ball. A range of bat characteristics must be considered relative to the child: the weight of the bat (the child's strength interacting with gravity to allow her to swing this bat using correct technique), the length of the bat (the child's ability to judge where the barrel of the bat will be relative to the ball and his own body), the grip size of the bat (so that the child's hands can fit around the grip to hold it well), and perhaps the size of the barrel of the bat (a wider barrel provides more surface area and perhaps a higher chance of contacting the ball). Certain choices can allow the child to swing the bat easily, while other choices can lead to difficulty in swinging it. A good bat choice for very young children might be lightweight with a small grip, short but with a wider barrel. When educators work with a group of children, they should expect a wide range of size, strength, and maturation level. Providing bats with a wide range of characteristics gives a child the opportunity to select his or her own bat, one he or she can succeed with (Gagen & Getchell, 2004).

Constraints-Based Task Analyses: Charting Constraints to Enhance Developmentally Appropriate Teaching

Imagine that you are coaching a volleyball team made up of 10-year-olds for the first time. Heights, weights, and skill levels vary widely within the group. How do you approach coaching this team? You could simply teach the skills they need to learn by showing them the "correct" form, then make them practice over and over again.

This approach may or may not provide results over the long run, but it will probably prove to be frustrating or boring for all involved. Is there a better way to teach motor skills? By using constraints-based task analyses (referred to as developmental [Herkowitz, 1978] or ecological [Burton & Davis, 1996] task analyses), you can create developmentally appropriate lesson plans as well as assess movement ability.

When someone uses traditional task analysis to teach or coach, he compares the movement pattern of an individual with the "correct" form; in that way, traditional task analysis provides an error model. Each person moves somewhere on the continuum of incorrect to correct. The instructor teaches skills by interceding in the production of the skill wherever it deviates from the ideal performance and correcting that portion of the movement.

What could be improved in this approach to teaching movement skills? For one thing, the traditional task analysis doesn't account for the different individual constraints each person might have. Second, there is no real accounting for the environmental and task constraints and the ways they might act in conjunction with individual constraints. Constraints-based task analysis does both of these things. This method acknowledges the interaction of different types of constraints and uses these to the advantage of the teacher or coach so that a developmentally appropriate or skill-level appropriate challenge can be provided to students. Further, each person moves on a developmental continuum, which enhances the current ability of the performer rather than labels it as correct or incorrect.

Creating a Developmentally Appropriate Constraints-Based Task Analysis

Burton and Davis (1996) outline four steps involved in creating a constraints-based task analysis (what they call an ecological task analysis). The initial step involves establishing the task goal through structuring the environmental constraints. Next the movement educator should allow the mover to solve the movement task in a variety of ways. In other words, don't provide one "solution" to the movement task (e.g., "Throw like this"); instead, let the mover pick from a variety of available movements. The next step comes into play after the individual moves: manipulate the mover, environment, or task in a way that allows more proficient movement to emerge. Finally, the movement educator should provide instruction to assist a more proficient performance.

What does a movement educator do as a first-time teacher who has never attempted to make a constraints-based task analysis? Here is a practical method of working through the process using a constraints perspective. Essentially, there are three steps for any given skill to be taught. Begin by considering the most important individual constraints related to that skill. Of course, there may be many, but try to narrow the list to the two or three that seem most important or influential. Consider the skill of kicking a ball. Three important individual constraints include balance (an individual must balance on one foot while striking the ball with the other), coordination (an individual must sequence and time the action within and between legs), and strength (an individual must strike the ball with sufficient power). Here is where the interaction of constraints comes in: now consider ways to change the environment or task to make the skill easier or harder in relation to the individual constraints. This is the basis of the constraints-based task analysis. If coordination is an important individual constraint to kicking, what changes can be made to the task to make it easier or harder? How about changing the speed of the ball? A stationary ball is easier to kick, and a moving ball is harder. This change in task constraint is also related to balance. To account for strength, changing the distance to be kicked changes the individual–task constraint interaction.

To develop a task analysis, systematically scale environmental and task constraints to accommodate individual constraints in a developmentally appropriate manner. To summarize, the process is as follows:

▲ Pick out a skill or task to teach.

▲ Determine the individual constraints that are most important for this skill.

▲ Pick several environmental or task constraints for this particular task that can be manipulated in relation to each individual constraint.

▲ For each environmental or task constraint, determine a practical range for the learner, from easy to hard. Keep in mind when scaling that small changes in a constraint can lead to large changes in performance.

The finished product is a constraints-based task analysis for a particular skill (figures 17.2 and 17.3). There are two ways to use your task analysis. First, use the task analysis to structure lesson plans or teaching progressions. If an individual or group has difficulty with the task as initially designed, the task analysis suggests changes in task and environmental constraints to make the challenge more appropriate. As individuals progress in skill level within a particular profile, the task analysis suggests ways to make the task harder, by scaling up one or more of the constraints. This keeps the task interesting, rewarding, and challenging for learners. Success is more likely when a new challenge is slightly more difficult than what one can achieve easily. Building success on success through small steps in difficulty contributes to confidence.

The constraints-based task analysis also provides a way to standardize a test environment so performers can easily be compared with each other (or themselves on different

Factors	Size of the object being thrown	Distance object must be thrown	Weight of the object being thrown	Accuracy required of the throw	Speed at which target being thrown at is moving	Acceleration and deceleration characteristics of the target being thrown at	Direction in which target being thrown at is moving
Simple	Small	Short	Light	None	Stationary	No movement	No movement
			Moderately light	Little	Slow	Steady speed	Left to right of thrower
							Right to left of thrower
	Medium	Medium					
Complex				Moderate	Moderate	Decelerating	Toward thrower
	Large	Long	Heavy	Much	Fast	Accelerating	Away from thrower

(Levels)

Figure 17.2 General task analysis for throwing behavior.

Reprinted from Herkowitz 1978.

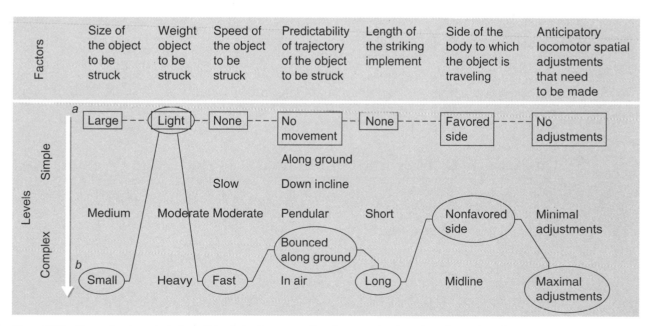

Figure 17.3 General task analysis for striking behavior. *(a)* Profile of a general task analysis for a relatively simple striking task (dotted line). *(b)* Profile of a general task analysis for a relatively complex striking task (solid line).

Reprinted from Herkowitz 1978.

Figure 17.4 A simple device such as a Jolly Jumper provides postural support and reduces the need for strength. By manipulating these rate controllers, the infant can enjoy moving upright on his own.

occasions). In this case, select a particular profile and set up an assessment environment accordingly. Using these standard task and environmental constraints, assess students' developmental levels for that skill within that profile. This will allow for more systematic assessment between students and over a set period of time.

INTERACTING CONSTRAINTS: CASE STUDIES

By manipulating different constraints, we can make immediate, short-term, and long-term changes in motor development and behavior. Often, knowing what changes to make is simply an issue of understanding the varying degrees of influence exerted by different constraints. Sometimes, even small changes in one constraint will allow a wide variety of behaviors to emerge. For example, providing an infant with support can account for both strength and posture, allowing for many different upright movements (figure 17.4). With this in mind, read the following case studies; try to determine the most important constraints and what you can change to allow certain motor behaviors to appear. After identifying the constraints to be changed, analyze how these constraints interact with one another, if they do, and whether the interaction helps achieve the goal or works against it.

Case Study A: Gender Typing of Physical Activities

You are the movement educator for a class of 25 fourth graders. During your first class, you attempt to teach gymnastics skills. The boys in your class show an obvious dislike for the activities, and one exclaims, "Gymnastics is for girls!" What can you do to modify the task so that the children learn the skills you want but are not put off by gender typing?

Case Study B: Older Adults

Abe is a 76-year-old Caucasian man who recently lost his spouse of 45 years. He lives in a suburb of a large metropolitan area. Since the death of his spouse, Abe has not gone on the daily strolls they used to take together. He is losing strength and flexibility, and his arthritis is flaring up. How can you reintroduce physical activity into Abe's life?

Case Study C: Teaching Fundamental Motor Skills

You are coaching an under-10 soccer team. You've noticed a wide diversity of individual constraints (height, weight, skill level) among the players. How can you make practices challenging for all the different players?

Case Study D: Cerebral Palsy

You are teaching an 11th-grade physical education class. In your class is an individual with cerebral palsy. He can walk, but he has some muscle spasticity and rigidity. You would like your class to participate in an activity or game where everyone can be equally involved, without having to change or modify the rules. What kind of activity could you play?

Summary and Synthesis

The challenge confronting motor developmentalists, teachers, coaches, and parents is to tailor goals and expectations to individual capabilities and characteristics. Optimal motor development is likely related to the degree that practice opportunities and insightful instruction are matched to individual constraints. Although it is complex and time consuming to individualize motor development goals and instruction in most institutional settings, findings from motor development research at various stages of the life span point in this direction. Continued research and observation of motor development will undoubtedly yield a better understanding of developmental processes, but our task remains to find ways of using our knowledge to foster optimal motor development in every individual.

Appendixes

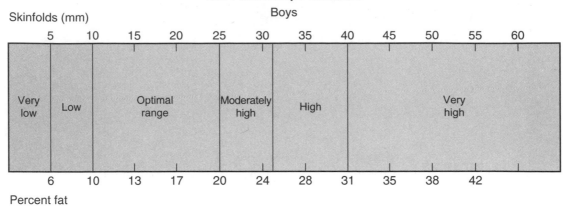

Figure A.1 Calf Plus Triceps Skinfolds: Boys

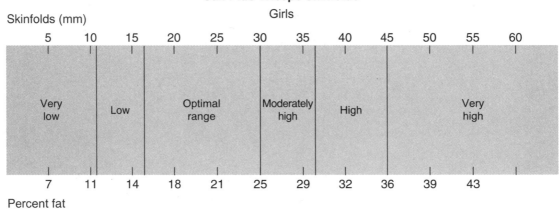

Figure A.2 Calf Plus Triceps Skinfolds: Girls

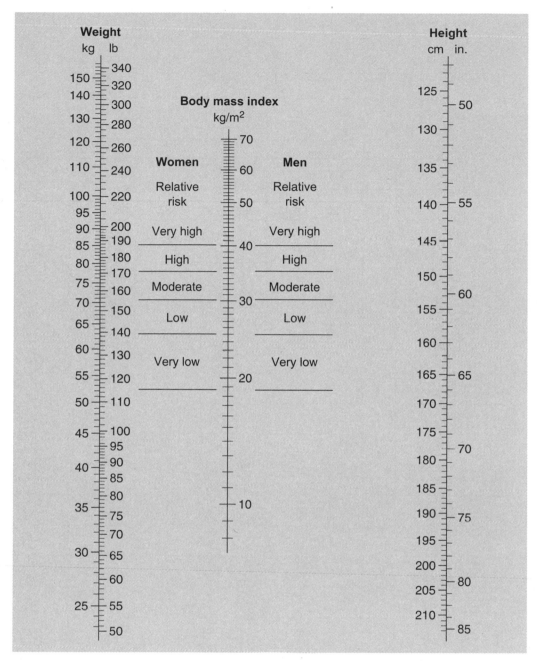

Figure B.1 Body mass index chart. Instructions for use: 1) Determine person's height and weight; 2) Connect person's height on chart with person's weight using a ruler or straight edge; 3) Find body mass index at point where ruler or straight edge intersects BMI line; 4) Also, determine appropriate cardiovascular risk from chart (very high, high, moderate, low, very low).

Reprinted, by permission, from G.A. Bray, 1992, "Pathophysiology of obesity," *American Journal of Clinical Nutrition* 55 (2 Suppl), 488S-499S.

TABLE B.1 **Interpreting Body Mass Index**

Weight class category	Body mass index
Underweight	20
Normal weight	21-24
Overweight	25-29
Obese (very overweight)	30

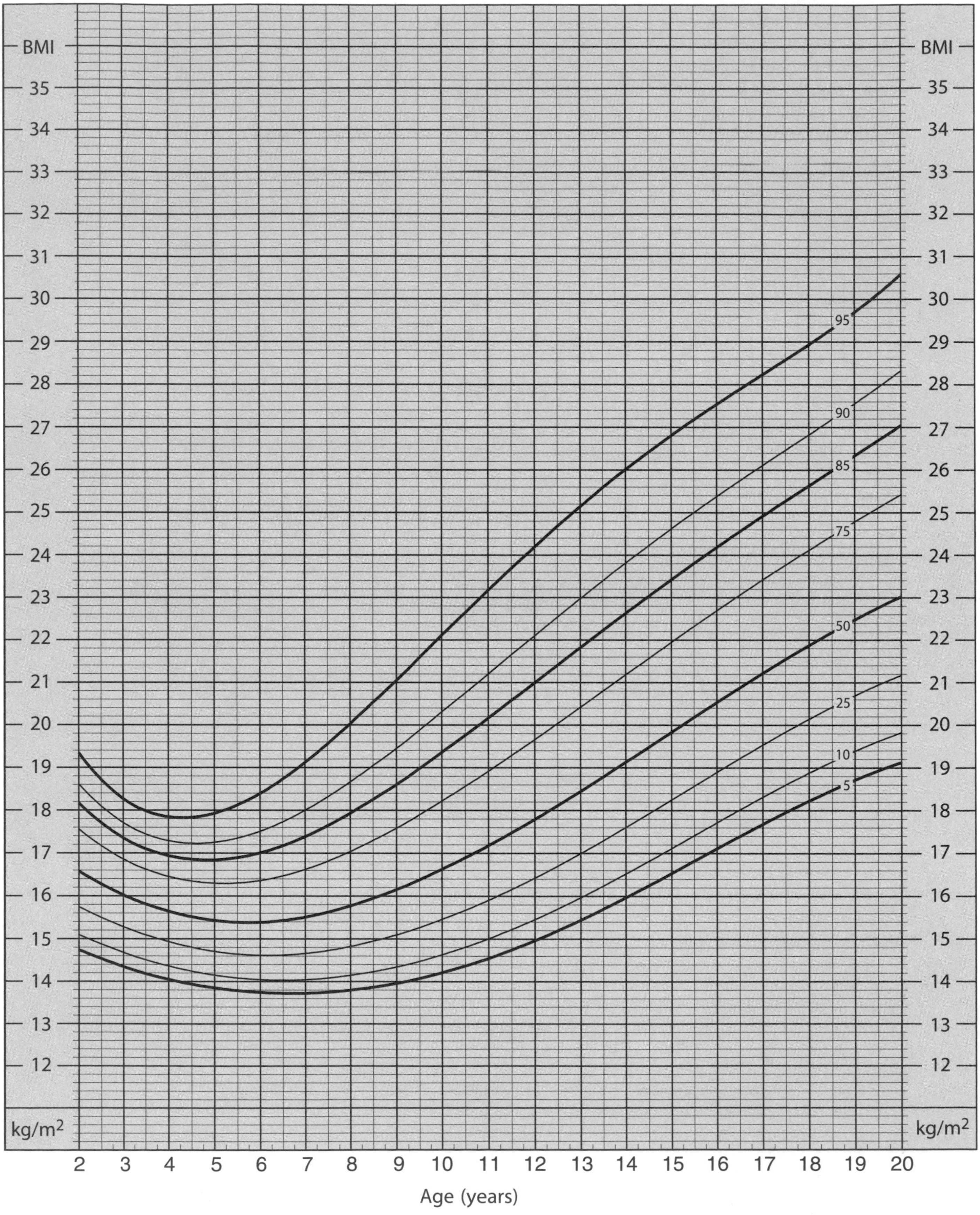

Figure B.2a Body mass index-for-age percentiles for boys, ages 2 to 20 years.

Adapted from www.cdc.gov/nchs/about/major/nhanes/growthcharts/clinical_charts.htm.
Developed by the National Center for Health Statistics in collaboration with the National Center for Chronic Disease Prevention and Health Promotion (2000).

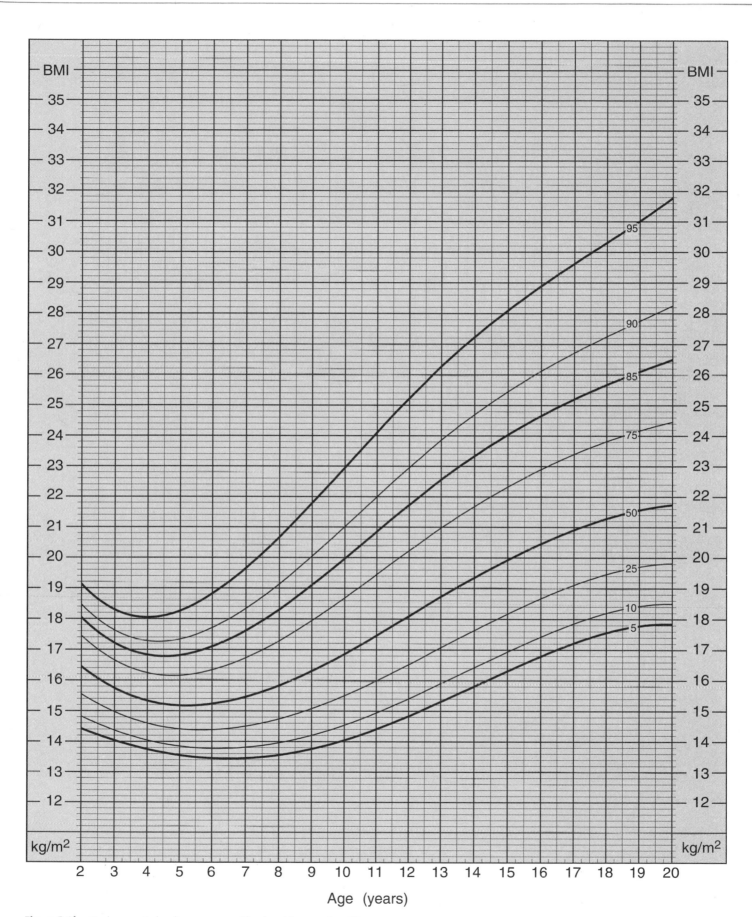

Figure B.2b Body mass index-for-age percentiles for girls, ages 2 to 20 years.

Adapted from www.cdc.gov/nchs/about/major/nhanes/growthcharts/clinical_charts.htm.
Developed by the National Center for Health Statistics in collaboration with the National Center for Chronic Disease Prevention and Health Promotion (2000).

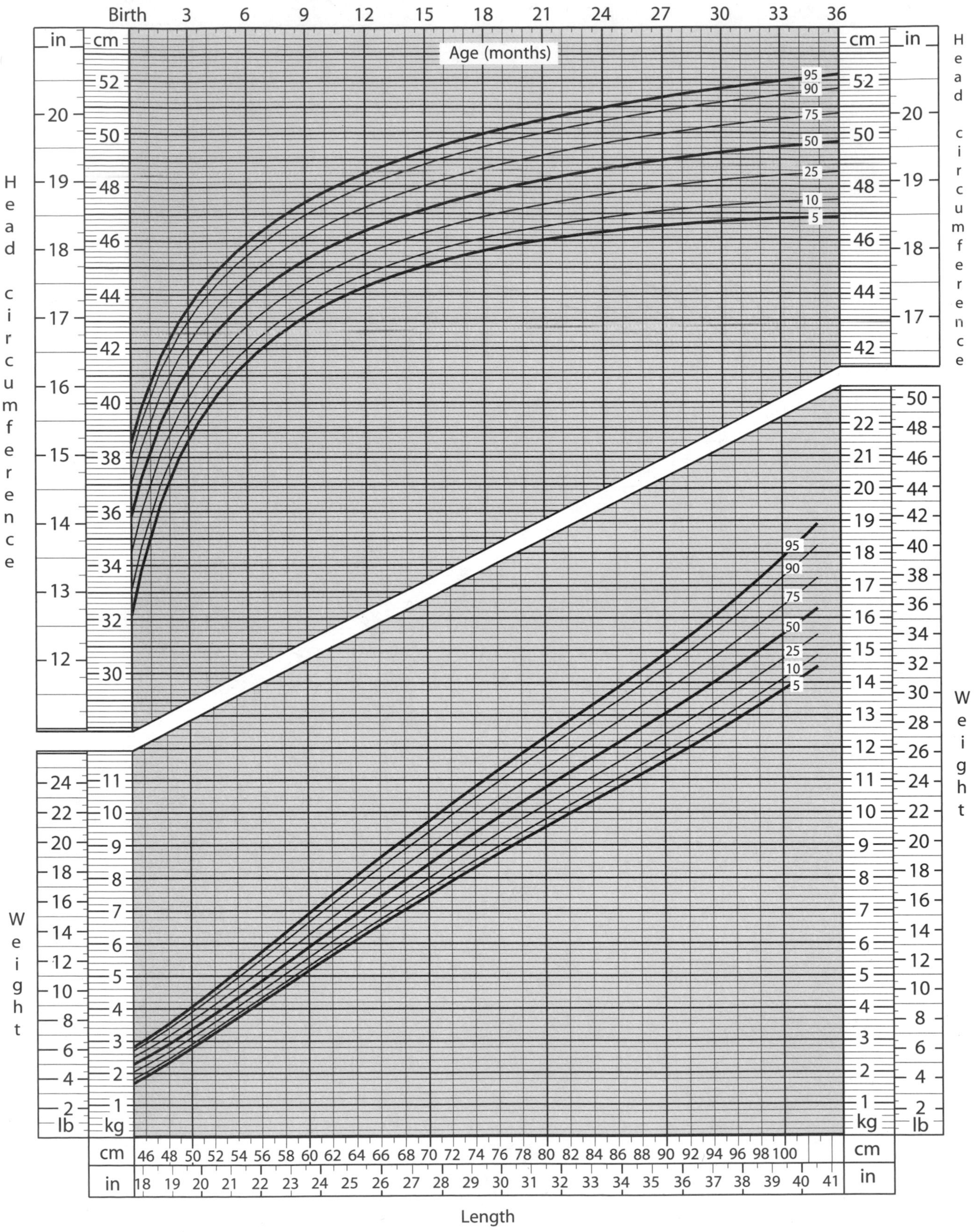

Figure C.1a Head circumference-for-age and weight-for-length percentiles for boys, birth to 36 months.

Reprinted from www.cdc.gov/nchs/about/major/nhanes/growthcharts/clinical_charts.htm.
Developed by the National Center for Health Statistics in collaboration with the National Center for Chronic Disease Prevention and Health Promotion (2000).

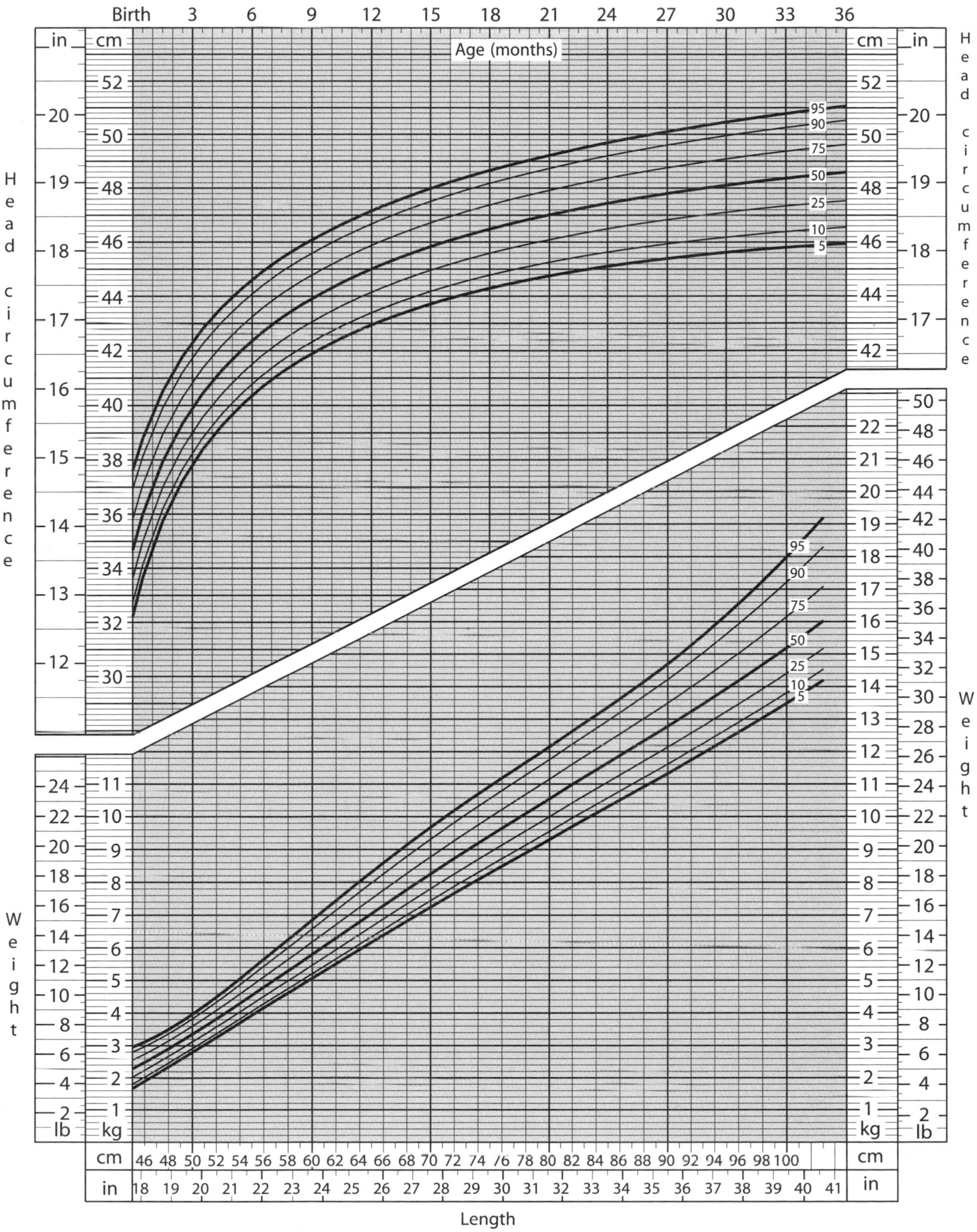

Figure C.1b Head circumference-for-age and weight-for-length percentiles for girls, birth to 36 months.

Reprinted from www.cdc.gov/nchs/about/major/nhanes/growthcharts/clinical_charts.htm.

Developed by the National Center for Health Statistics in collaboration with the National Center for Chronic Disease Prevention and Health Promotion (2000).

References

Abernethy, B., Wood, J.M., & Parks, S. (1999). Can the anticipatory skills of experts be learned by novices? *Research Quarterly for Exercise and Sport, 70,* 313–318.

Adams, F.H. (1973). Factors affecting the working capacity of children and adolescents. In G.L. Rarick (Ed.), *Physical activity: Human growth and development* (pp. 80–96). New York: Academic Press.

Adolph, K. (1997). Learning in the development of infant locomotion. *Monographs of the Society for Research in Child Development, 62* (3): 1–162.

Adolph, K., Vereijken, B., & Denny, M. (1998). Learning to crawl. *Child Development, 69,* 1299–1312.

Adolph, K., Vereijken, B., & Shrout, P.E. (2003). What changes in infant walking and why. *Child Development, 74*(2), 475–497.

Adolph, K.E., Eppler, M.A., & Gibson, E.J. (1993). Crawling versus walking in infants' perception of affordances for locomotion over sloping surfaces. *Child Development, 64,* 1158–1174.

Adrian, M.J. (1982, April). *Maintaining movement capabilities in advanced years.* Paper presented at the American Alliance for Health, Physical Education, Recreation and Dance, Houston, TX.

Advancing Indiana. (2004). Ground-breaking baby research. January. http://advancing.indiana.edu/discoveries/baby.shtml (accessed September 16, 2004).

Allen, M., & Alexander, G. (1994). Screening for cerebral palsy in preterm infants: Delay criteria for motor milestone attainment. *Journal of Perinatology, 14,* 190–193.

Allen, M., & Alexander, G. (1997). Using motor milestones as a multistep process to screen preterm infants for cerebral palsy. *Developmental Medicine and Child Neurology, 39,* 12–16.

Alnaqeeb, M.A., Al-Zaid, N.S., & Goldspink, G. (1984). Connective tissue changes and physical properties of developing and aging skeletal muscle. *Journal of Anatomy, 189*(4), 677–689.

American Alliance for Health, Physical Education, Recreation and Dance. (1988). *Physical best.* Reston, VA: Author.

American Heritage Dictionary of the English Language, 4th ed. (2000). Boston: Houghton Mifflin.

Aniansson, A., & Gustafsson, E. (1981). Physical training in elderly men with special reference to quadriceps muscle strength and morphology. *Clinical Physiology, 1,* 87–98.

Aniansson, A., Hedberg, M., Henning, G.B., & Grimby, G. (1986). Muscle morphology, enzymatic activity and muscle strength in elderly men: A follow-up study. *Muscle Nerve, 9,* 585–591.

Arabadjis, P.G., Heffner, R.R., & Pendergast, D.R. (1990). Morphologic and functional alterations in aging rat muscle. *Journal of Neuropathology and Experimental Neurology, 49,* 600–609.

Armstrong, N., Welsman, J.R., & Kirby, B.J. (1997). Performance on the Wingate Anaerobic Test and maturation. *Pediatric Exercise Science, 9,* 253–261.

Asano, K., Ogawa, S., & Furuta, Y. (1978). Aerobic work capacity in middle- and old-aged runners. In F. Landry & W.A.R. Orban (Eds.), *Proceedings of the International Congress of Physical Activity Sciences: Vol. 4. Exercise physiology.* Quebec: Symposia Specialists.

Ashmead, D.H., Clifton, R.K., & Perris, E.E. (1987). Precision of audi- tory localization in human infants. *Developmental Psychology, 23*(5), 641–647.

Aslin, R.N., & Shea, S.L. (1990). Velocity thresholds in human infants: Implications for the perception of motion. *Developmental Psychology, 26*(4), 589–598.

Asmussen, E. (1973). Growth in muscular strength and power. In G.L. Rarick (Ed.), *Physical activity: Human growth and development* (pp. 60–79). New York: Academic Press.

Asmussen, E., & Heeboll-Nielsen, K. (1955). A dimensional analysis of physical performance and growth in boys. *Journal of Applied Physiology, 7,* 593–603.

Asmussen, E., & Heeboll-Nielsen, K. (1956). Physical performance and growth in children: Influence of sex, age, and intelligence. *Journal of Applied Physiology, 8,* 371–380.

Assaiante, C. (1998). Development of locomotor balance control in healthy children. *Neuroscience and Biobehavioral Reviews, 22*(4), 527–532.

Assaiante, C., & Amblard, B. (1995). An ontogenetic model for the sensorimotor organization of balance control in humans. *Human Movement Science, 14,* 13–43.

Assibey-Mensah, G. (1998). Role models and youth development: Evidence and lessons from the perceptions of African-American male youth. *Western Journal of Black Studies, 21,* 242–252.

Astrand, P. (1976). The child in sport and physical activity: Physiology. In J.G. Albinson & G.M. Andrew (Eds.), *Child in sport and physical activity* (pp. 19–33). Baltimore: University Park Press.

Astrand, P.O., & Rodahl, K. (1986). *Textbook of work physiology.* New York: McGraw-Hill.

Atkinson, J., & Braddick, O. (1981). Acuity, contrast sensitivity, and accommodation in infancy. In R. Aslin, J. Alberts, & M. Peterson (Eds.), *Development of perception* (pp. 245–277). New York: Academic Press.

Ayres, A.J. (1966). *Southern California sensory-motor integration tests.* Los Angeles: Western Psychological Corporation.

Ayres, A.J. (1969). *Southern California perceptual-motor tests.* Los Angeles: Western Psychological Services.

Ayres, A.J. (1972). *Southern California sensory-motor integration tests manual.* Los Angeles: Western Psychological Services.

Bachman, J.C. (1961). Motor learning and performance as related to age and sex in two measures of balance coordination. *Research Quarterly, 32,* 123–137.

Bailey, D.A. (1976). The growing child and the need for physical activity. In J.G. Albinson & G.M. Andrew (Eds.), *Child in sport and physical activity* (pp. 81–93). Baltimore: University Park Press.

Bailey, D.A., Malina, R.M., & Rasmussen, R.L. (1978). The influence of exercise, physical activity, and athletic performance on the dynamics of human growth. In F. Falkner & J.M. Tanner (Eds.), *Human growth* (Vol. 2, pp. 475–505). New York: Plenum Press.

Baldwin, K.M. (1984). Muscle development: Neonatal to adult. In R.L. Terjung (Ed.), *Exercise and sport science reviews* (Vol. 12, pp. 1–19). Lexington, MA: Collamore.

Bandura, A. (1986). *Social foundations of thought and action: A social cognitive theory.* Englewood Cliffs, NJ: Prentice Hall.

Banerjee, R., & Lintern, V. (2000). Boys will be boys: The effect of social evaluation concerns on gender-typing. *Social Development, 9*(3), 397–408.

Bar-Or, O. (1983). *Pediatric sports medicine for the practitioner.* New York: Springer-Verlag.

Bar-Or, O. (1993). Physical activity and physical training in childhood obesity. *Journal of Sports Medicine and Physical Fitness, 33*(4), 323–329.

Bar-Or, O., Shephard, R.J., & Allen, C.L. (1971). Cardiac output of 10- to 13-year-old boys and girls during submaximal exercise. *Journal of Applied Physiology, 30,* 219–223.

Bard, C., Fleury, M., Carriere, L., & Bellec, J. (1981). Components of the coincidence-anticipation behavior of children aged 6 to 11 years. *Perceptual and Motor Skills, 52,* 547–556.

Bard, C., Fleury, M., & Gagnon, M. (1990). Coincidence-anticipation timing: An age-related perspective. In C. Bard, M. Fleury, & L. Hay (Eds.), *Development of eye-hand coordination across the life span* (pp. 283–305). Columbia, SC: University of South Carolina Press.

Barela, J.A., Jeka, J.J., & Clark, J.E. (1999). The use of somatosensory information during the acquisition of independent upright stance. *Infant Behavior & Development, 22*(1), 87–102.

Barrett, K.R. (1979). Observation for teaching and coaching. *Journal of Physical Education and Recreation, 50,* 23–25.

Barrett, U., & Harrison, D. (2002). Comparing muscle function of children and adults: Effects of scaling for muscle size. *Pediatric Exercise Science, 14,* 369–376.

Barsch, R.H. (1965). *Achieving perceptual-motor efficiency.* Seattle: Special Child Publications.

Bartlett, D. (1997). Primitive reflexes and early motor development. *Journal of Developmental and Behavioral Pediatrics, 18,* 151–157.

Bayley, N. (1935). The development of motor abilities during the first three years. *Society for Research in Child Development, 1*(1).

Bayley, N. (1969). *Manual for the Bayley scales of infant development.* New York: The Psychological Corporation.

Beck, M. (1966). *The path of the center of gravity during running in boys grades one to six.* Unpublished doctoral dissertation, University of Wisconsin, Madison.

Bell, R., & Hoshizaki, T. (1981). Relationships of age and sex with joint range of motion of seventeen joint actions in humans. *Canadian Journal of Applied Sport Sciences, 6,* 202–206.

Bennett, S., Button, C., Kingsbury, D., & Davids, K. (1999). Manipulating visual informational constraints during practice enhances the acquisition of catching skill in children. *Research Quarterly for Exercise and Sport, 70*(3), 220–232.

Bergstrom, B. (1973). Morphology of the vestibular nerve: II. The number of myelinated vestibular nerve fibers in man at various ages. *Acta Oto-Laryngologica, 76,* 173–179.

Berliner, D.C. (1986). In pursuit of the expert pedagogue. *Educational Researcher, 15,* 5–13.

Bertenthal, B., Campos, J., & Barrett, K. (1984). Self-produced locomotion: An organizer of emotional, cognitive and social development in infancy. In R. Emde & R. Harmon (Eds.), *Continuities and discontinuities in development* (pp. 175–210). New York: Plenum Press.

Bertenthal, B., & von Hofsten, C. (1998). Eye, head, and trunk control: The foundation for manual development. *Neuroscience and Biobehavioral Reviews, 22*(4), 515–520.

Bertenthal, B.I., & Bai, D.L. (1989). Infants' sensitivity to optical flow for controlling posture. *Developmental Psychology, 25,* 936–945.

Bertenthal, B.I., & Campos, J.J. (1987). New directions in the study of early experience. *Child Development, 58,* 560–567.

Bertenthal, B.I., Rose, J.L., & Bai, D.L. (1997). Perception-action coupling in the development of visual control of posture. *Journal of Experimental Psychology: Human Perception and Performance, 23*(6), 1631–1643.

Beunen, G., & Malina, R.M. (1988). Growth and physical performance relative to the timing of the adolescent spurt. *Exercise and Sport Sciences Reviews, 16,* 503–540.

Beunen, G., Malina, R.M., Ostyn, M., Renson, R., Simons, J., & Van Gerven, D. (1983). Fatness, growth and motor fitness of Belgian boys 12 through 17 years of age. *American Journal of Physical Anthropology, 59,* 387–392.

Beunen, G., Malina, R.M., Renson, R., & Van Gerven, D. (1988). *Adolescent growth and motor performance: A longitudinal analysis of Belgian boys.* Champaign, IL: Human Kinetics.

Bigelow, B., Tesson, G., & Lewko, J. (1996). *Learning the rules: The anatomy of children's relationships. The Guilford Series on Personal Relationships.* New York: Guilford Press.

Birch, L.L. (1976). Age trends in children's timesharing performance. *Journal of Experimental Child Psychology, 22,* 331–345.

Bird, A.M., & Williams, J.M. (1980). A developmental-attributional analysis of sex-role stereotypes for sport performance. *Developmental Psychology, 16,* 319–322.

Birren, J.E. (1964). The psychology of aging in relation to development. In J.E. Birren (Ed.), *Relationships of development and aging* (pp. 99–120). Springfield, IL: Charles C Thomas.

Birren, J.E., Woods, A.M., & Williams, M.V. (1980). Behavioral slowing with age: Causes, organization, and consequences. In L.W. Poon (Ed.), *Aging in the 1980s.* Washington, DC: American Psychological Association.

Blimkie, C.J.R. (1989). Age- and sex-associated variation in strength during childhood: Anthropometric, morphological, neurologic, biomechanical, endocrinologic, genetic, and physical activity correlates. In C.V. Gisolfi & D.R. Lamb (Eds.), *Youth, exercise, and sport* (Vol. 2, pp. 99–164). Indianapolis: Benchmark Press.

Blumenthal, J.A., Emergy, C.F., Madden, D.J., Coleman, R.E., Riddle, M.W., Schniebolk, S., Cobb, F.R., Sullivan, M.J., & Higginbotham, M.B. (1991). Effects of exercise training on cardiorespiratory function in men and women > 60 years of age. *American Journal of Cardiology, 67,* 633–639.

Boff, K.R., Kaufman, L., & Thomas, J.P. (Eds.). (1986). *Handbook of perception and human performance.* New York: Wiley.

Boothby, J., Tungatt, M., & Townsend, A. (1981). Ceasing participation in sports activity: Reported reasons and their implication. *Journal of Leisure Research, 13,* 1–14.

Borkan, G.A., Hunts, D.E., Gerzof, S.G., Robbins, A.H., & Silbert, C.K. (1983). Age changes in body composition revealed by computed tomography. *Journal of Gerontology, 38,* 673–677.

Bornstein, M.H. (1985). Habituation of attention as a measure of visual information processing in human infants: Summary, systematization, and synthesis. In G. Gottlieb & N.A. Krasnegor (Eds.), *Measurement of audition and vision in the first year of postnatal life: A methodological overview* (pp. 253–300). Norwood, NJ: Ablex Publishing.

Bovend'eerdt, J.H.F., Bermink, M.J.E., van Hijfte, T., Ritmeester, J.W., Kemper, H.C.G., & Verschuur, R. (1980). *De MOPER fitness test: Onderzoeksverlag.* Haarlem: De Vrieseborch.

Bower, T.G.R. (1972). Object perception in infants. *Perception, 1,* 15–30.

Bower, T.G.R. (1977). *A primer of infant development.* San Francisco: W.H. Freeman.

Bower, T.G.R., Broughton, J.M., & Moore, M.K. (1970a). The coordination of visual and tactual input in infants. *Perception and Psychophysics, 8,* 51–53.

Bower, T.G.R., Broughton, J.M., & Moore, M.K. (1970b). Demonstration of intention in the reaching behavior of neonate humans. *Nature, 228*(5272), 679–681.

Bower, T.G.R., Broughton, J.M., & Moore, M.K. (1970c). Infant responses to approaching objects: An indicator of response to distal variables. *Perception and Psychophysics, 9*, 193–196.

Brandfonbrener, M., Landowne, M., & Shock, N.W. (1955). Changes in cardiac output with age. *Circulation, 12*, 557–566.

Branta, C., Haubenstricker, J., & Seefeldt, V. (1984). Age changes in motor skill during childhood and adolescence. In R.L. Terjung (Ed.), *Exercise and sport science reviews* (Vol. 12, pp. 467–520). Lexington, MA: Collamore.

Brodkin, P., & Weiss, M.R. (1990). Developmental differences in motivation for participation in competitive swimming. *Journal of Sport and Exercise Psychology, 12*, 248–263.

Brouwer, W.H., Waterink, W., Van Wolffelaar, P.C., & Rothengartter, T. (1991). Divided attention in experienced young and older drivers: Land tracking and visual analysis in a dynamic driving simulator. *Human Factors, 33*, 573–582.

Brown, B., Frankel, G., & Fennell, M. (1990). Hugs or shrugs: Parental and peer influences on continuation of involvement in sport by female adolescents. *Sex Roles, 20*, 397–412.

Brown, B.A. (1985). Factors influencing the process of withdrawal by female adolescents from the role of competitive age group swimmers. *Sociology of Sport Journal, 2*, 111–129.

Brown, C.H., Harrower, J.R., & Deeter, M.F. (1972). The effects of cross-country running on pre-adolescent girls. *Medicine and Science in Sports, 4*, 1–5.

Brown, M., & Holloszy, J.O. (1991). Effects of a low-intensity exercise program on selected physical performance characteristics of 60- to 71-year-olds. *Aging—Clinical and Experimental Research, 3*(2), 129–139.

Brundage, C.L. (1983). *Parent/child play behaviors as they relate to children's later socialization into sport.* Unpublished master's thesis, University of Illinois, Urbana.

Bruner, J.S. (1970). The growth and structure of skill. In K.J. Connolly (Ed.), *Mechanisms of motor skill development* (pp. 63–94). London: Academic Press.

Brustad, R.J. (1988). Affective outcomes in competitive youth sport: The influence of intrapersonal and socialization factors. *Journal of Sport and Exercise Psychology, 10*, 307–321.

Buchanan, J.J., & Horak, F.B. (1999). Emergence of postural patterns as a function of vision and translation frequency. *Journal of Neurophysiology, 81*(5), 2325–2339.

Bull, D., Eilers, R., & Oller, K. (1984). Infants' discrimination of intensity variation in multisyllabic stimuli. *Journal of the Acoustical Society of America, 76*, 13–17.

Burnett, C.N., & Johnson, E.W. (1971). Development of gait in childhood, part II. *Developmental Medicine and Child Neurology, 13*, 207–215.

Burton, A.W. (1999). Hrdlicka (1931) revisited: Children who run on all fours. *Research Quarterly for Exercise and Sport, 70*, 84–90.

Burton, A.W., & Davis, W.E. (1996). Ecological task analysis: Utilizing intrinsic measures in research and practice. *Human Movement Science, 15*, 285–314.

Bushnell, E.W. (1982). The ontogeny of intermodal relations: Vision and touch in infancy. In R. Walk & H. Pick (Eds.), *Intersensory perception and sensory integration* (pp. 5–36). New York: Plenum Press.

Bushnell, E.W. (1985). The decline of visually guided reaching during infancy. *Infant Behavior and Development, 8*, 139–155.

Bushnell, I.W.R. (1998). The origins of face perception. In F. Simion & G. Butterworth (Eds.), *The development of sensory, motor and cognitive capacities in early infancy: From perception to cognition* (pp. 69–86). Hove, England: Psychology Press/Erlbaum (UK) Taylor & Francis.

Bushnell, I.W.R., Sai, F., & Mullin, J.T. (1989). Neonatal recognition of the mother's face. *British Journal of Developmental Psychology, 7*, 3–15.

Butcher, J. (1983). Socialization of adolescent girls into physical activity. *Adolescence, 18*, 753–766.

Butcher, J. (1985). Longitudinal analysis of adolescent girls' participation in physical activity. *Sociology of Sport Journal, 2*, 130–143.

Butterworth, G., & Hicks, L. (1977). Visual proprioception and postural stability in infancy. *Perception, 6*, 255–262.

Butterworth, G., Verweij, E., & Hopkins, B. (1997). The development of prehension in infants: Halverson revisited. *British Journal of Developmental Psychology, 15*(2), 223–236.

Campbell, A.J., Robertson, M.C., Gardner, M.M., Norton, R.N., Tilyard, M.W., & Buchner, D.M. (1997). Randomised controlled trial of a general practice programme of home based exercise to prevent falls in elderly women. *British Medical Journal, 315*, 1065–1069.

Campbell, D., & Eaton, W. (2000). Sex differences in the activity level of infants. *Infant and Child Development, 8*, 1–17.

Campbell, M.J., McComas, A.J., & Petito, F. (1973). Physiological changes in aging muscles. *Journal of Neurology, Neurosurgery, and Psychiatry, 36*, 174–182.

Campenni, C.E. (1999). Gender stereotyping of children's toys: A comparison of parents and nonparents. *Sex Roles, 40*, 121–138.

Carnahan, H., Vandervoort, A.A., & Swanson, L.R. (1998). The influence of aging and target motion on the control of prehension. *Experimental Aging Research, 24*(3), 289–306.

Carron, A.V., & Bailey, D.A. (1974). Strength development in boys from 10 through 16 years. *Monographs of the Society for Research in Child Development, 39*, 4.

Cerella, J. (1990). Aging and information-processing rate. In J.E. Birren & K.W. Schaie (Eds.), *Handbook of the psychology of aging* (3rd ed., pp. 201–221). New York: Academic Press.

Cerella, J., Poon, L.W., & Williams, D.M. (1980). Age and the complexity hypothesis. In L.W. Poon (Ed.), *Aging in the 1980s*. Washington, DC: American Psychological Association.

Charette, S., McEvoy, L., Pyka, G., Snow-Harter, C., Guido, D., Wiswell, R., & Marcus, R. (1991). Muscle hypertrophy response to resistance training in older women. *Journal of Applied Physiology, 70*, 1912–1916.

Chase, M.A., Ewing, M.E., Lirgg, C.D., & George, T.R. (1994). The effects of equipment modification on children's self-efficacy and basketball shooting performance. *Research Quarterly for Exercise and Sport 65*(2), 159–168.

Chase, W.G., & Simon, H.A. (1973). Perception in chess. *Cognitive Psychology, 4*, 55–81.

Chi, M.T.H. (1978). Knowledge structures and memory development. In R.S. Siegler (Ed.), *Children's thinking: What develops?* (pp. 73–105). Hillsdale, NJ: Erlbaum.

Chi, M.T.H. (1981). Knowledge development and memory performance. In M.P. Friedman, J.P. Das, & N. O'Connor (Eds.), *Intelligence and learning* (pp. 221–229). New York: Plenum Press.

Chi, M.T.H., & Koeske, R.D. (1983). Network representation of a child's dinosaur knowledge. *Developmental Psychology, 19*, 29–39.

Chiesi, H.L., Spilich, G.J., & Voss, J.F. (1979). Acquisition of domain related information in relation to high and low domain knowledge. *Journal of Verbal Learning and Verbal Behavior, 18*, 257–273.

Chugani, H.T., & Phelps, M.E. (1986). Maturational changes in cerebral function in infants determined by 18FDG positron emission tomography. *Science, 231*, 840–843.

Clark, J.E. (1982). Developmental differences in response processing. *Journal of Motor Behavior, 14*, 247–254.

Clark, J.E. (1995). On becoming skillful: Patterns and constraints. *Research Quarterly, 66*, 173–183.

Clark, J.E., & Phillips, S.J. (1985). A developmental sequence of the standing long jump. In J. Clark & J. Humphrey (Eds.), *Motor development: Vol. 1. Current selected research* (pp. 73–85). Princeton, NJ: Princeton Book.

Clark, J.E., & Phillips, S.J. (1993). A longitudinal study of the intra-limb coordination in the first year of independent walking. *Child Development, 64,* 1143–1157.

Clark, J.E., Phillips, S.J., & Petersen, R. (1989). Developmental stability in jumping. *Developmental Psychology, 25,* 929–935.

Clark, J.E., & Whitall, J. (1989a). What is motor development? *Quest, 41,* 183–202.

Clark, J.E., & Whitall, J. (1989b). Changing patterns of locomotion: From walking to skipping. In M.H. Woollacott & A. Shumway-Cook (Eds.), *Development of posture and gait across the life span* (pp. 128–151). Columbia, SC: University of South Carolina Press.

Clark, J.E., Whitall, J., & Phillips, S.J. (1988). Human interlimb coordination: The first 6 months of independent walking. *Developmental Psychobiology, 21,* 445–456.

Clarke, H.H. (Ed.). (1975). Joint and body range of movement. *Physical Fitness Research Digest, 5,* 16–18.

Clarkson-Smith, L., & Hartley, A.A. (1990). Structural equation models of relationships between exercise and cognitive abilities. *Psychology and Aging, 5,* 437–446.

Clifton, R.K., Perris, E.E., & Bullinger, A. (1991). Infants' perception of auditory space. *Developmental Psychology, 27*(2), 187–197.

Clouse, F. (1959). *A kinematic analysis of the development of the running pattern of preschool boys.* Unpublished doctoral dissertation, University of Wisconsin, Madison.

Coakly, J. (1998). *Sport in society: Issues and controversies.* Madison, WI: WCB McGraw-Hill.

Cobb, K., Goodwin, R., & Saelens, E. (1966). Spontaneous hand positions of newborn infants. *Journal of Genetic Psychology, 108,* 225–237.

Colling-Saltin, A.S. (1980). Skeletal muscle development in the human fetus and during childhood. In K. Berg & B.O. Eriksson (Eds.), *International congress on pediatric work physiology: Children and exercise IX* (pp. 193–207). Baltimore: University Park Press.

Comery, T.A., Shah, R., & Greenough, W.T. (1995). Differential rearing alters spine density on medium-sized spiny neurons in the rat corpus striatum: Evidence for association of morphological plasticity with early response gene expression. *Neurobiology of Learning & Memory, 63*(3), 217–219.

Comery, T.A., Stamoudis, C.X., Irwin, S.A., & Greenough, W.T. (1996). Increased density of multiple-head dendritic spines on medium-sized spiny neurons of the striatum in rats reared in a complex environment. *Neurobiology of Learning & Memory, 66*(2), 93–96.

Connolly, K.J., & Elliott, J.M. (1972). The evolution and ontogeny of hand function. In N. Blurton-Jones (Ed.), *Ethological studies of child behavior* (pp. 329–383). Cambridge, England: Cambridge University Press.

Contreras-Vidal, J.L., Teulings, H.L., & Stelmach, G.E. (1998). Elderly subjects are impaired in spatial coordination in fine motor control. *Acta Psychologica, 100,* 25–35.

Coopersmith, S. (1967). *The antecedents of self-esteem.* San Francisco: Freeman. (Reprinted in 1981 by Consulting Psychologists Press, Palo Alto, CA.)

Corbetta, D., & Bojczyk, K.E. (2002). Infants return to two-handed reaching when they are learning to walk. *Journal of Motor Behavior, 34*(1), 83–95.

Corbetta, D., & Mounoud, P. (1990). Early development of grasping and manipulation. In C. Bard, M. Fleury, & L. Hay (Eds.), *Development of eye-hand coordination across the life span* (pp. 188–216). Columbia, SC: University of South Carolina Press.

Corso, J.F. (1977). Auditory perception and communication. In J.E. Birren & K.W. Schaie (Eds.), *Handbook of the psychology of aging* (pp. 535–553). New York: Van Nostrand Reinhold.

Cowburn, G., Hillsdon, M., & Hankey, C.R. (1997). Obesity management by lifestyle strategies. *British Medical Bulletin, 53*(2), 389–408.

Craig, C.H., Kim, B., Rhyner, P.M.P., & Chirillo, T.K.B. (1993). Effects of word predictability, child development, and aging on time-gated speech recognition performance. *Journal of Speech and Hearing Research, 36,* 832–841.

Craik, R. (1989). Changes in locomotion in the aging adult. In M.H. Woollacott & A. Shumway-Cook (Eds.), *Development of posture and gait across the life span* (pp. 176–201). Columbia, SC: University of South Carolina Press.

Cratty, B.J. (1979). *Perception and motor development in infants and children* (2nd ed.). Englewood Cliffs, NJ: Prentice Hall.

Crossman, E.R.F.W., & Szafran, J. (1956). Changes with age in the speed of information intake and discrimination. *Experientia (Suppl.), 4,* 128–135.

Crowell, J.A., & Banks, M.S. (1993). Perceiving heading with different retinal regions and types of optic flow. *Perception and Psychophysics, 53,* 325–337.

Cumming, R.G. (1990). Calcium intake and bone mass: A quantitative review of the evidence. *Calcified Tissue International, 47,* 194–201.

Cunningham, L.N. (1990). Relationship of running economy, ventilatory threshold, and maximum oxygen consumption to running performance in high school females. *Research Quarterly for Exercise and Sport, 61,* 369–374.

Cureton, K.J., Collins, M.A., Hill, D.W., & McElhannon, F.M. (1988). Muscle hypertrophy in men and women. *Medicine and Science in Sports and Exercise, 20,* 338–344.

Curtis, J.E., & White, P.G. (1984). Age and sport participation: Decline in participation with age or increased specialization with age? In N. Theberge & P. Donnelly (Eds.), *Sport and the sociological imagination* (pp. 273–293). Fort Worth, TX: Texas Christian University Press.

Dalsky, G.P. (1989). The role of exercise in the prevention of osteoporosis. *Comprehensive Therapy, 15,* 30–37.

Dalsky, G.P., Stocke, K.S., Eshani, A.A., Slatopolsky, E., Lee, W.C., & Birge, S.J. (1988). Weight-bearing exercise training and lumbar bone mineral content in postmenopausal women. *Annals of Internal Medicine, 108,* 824–828.

Davies, B.N. (1990). The relationship of lean limb volume to performance in the handgrip and standing long jump tests in boys and girls, aged 11.6–13.2 years. *European Journal of Applied Physiology, 60,* 139–143.

Davies, C.T.M., White, M.J., & Young, K. (1983). Muscle function in children. *European Journal of Applied Physiology, 52,* 111–114.

Davis, C.I. (1991). The effects of game modification on opportunities to respond in elementary volleyball classes. *Dissertation Abstracts International, 52*(2), 465.

Davis, W.E., & Burton, A.W. (1991). Ecological task analysis: Translating movement behavior theory into practice. *Adapted Physical Activity Quarterly, 8,* 154–177.

Dehn, M.M., & Bruce, R.A. (1972). Longitudinal variations in maximum oxygen intake with age and activity. *Journal of Applied Physiology, 33,* 805–807.

Dekaban, A. (1970). *Neurology of early childhood.* Baltimore: Williams & Wilkins.

Delacato, C.H. (1959). *Treatment and prevention of reading problems.* Springfield, IL: Charles C Thomas.

Delacato, C.H. (1966). *Neurological organization and reading.* Springfield, IL: Charles C Thomas.

Demany, L., McKenzie, B., & Vurpillot, E. (1977). Rhythmic perception in early infancy. *Nature, 266,* 718–719.

Dempsey, J.A., Johnson, B.D., & Saupe, K.W. (1990). Adaptations and limitations in the pulmonary system during exercise. *Chest, 97 (Supplement)* (3), 81S–87S.

Dent-Read, C., & Zukow-Goldring, P. (1997). Introduction: Ecological realism, dynamic systems, and epigenetic systems approaches to development. In C. Dent-Read & P. Zukow-Goldring (Eds.), *Evolving explanations of development* (pp. 1–22). Washington, DC: American Psychological Association.

de Oliveira, A.R., & Gallagher, J.D. (1994). *Strength training in children: A meta-analysis.* Paper presented at the North American Society for Pediatric Exercise Medicine, Pittsburgh, PA.

DeOreo, K., & Keogh, J. (1980). Performance of fundamental motor tasks. In C.B. Corbin (Ed.), *A textbook of motor development* (2nd ed., pp. 76–91). Dubuque, IA: Brown.

DeOreo, K., & Wade, M.G. (1971). Dynamic and static balancing ability of preschool children. *Journal of Motor Behavior, 3,* 326–335.

DeOreo, K.L., & Williams, H.G. (1980). Characteristics of kinesthetic perception. In C.B. Corbin (Ed.), *A textbook of motor development* (2nd ed., pp. 174–196). Dubuque, IA: Brown.

Diamond, A. (2000). Close interrelation of motor development and cognitive development and of the cerebellum and prefrontal cortex. *Child Development, 71,* 44–56.

Dietz, W.H., & Robinson, T.N. (1993). Assessment and treatment of childhood obesity. *Pediatric Review, 14,* 337–343.

DiLorenzo, T., Stucky-Ropp, R., Vander Wal, J., & Gotham, H. (1998). Determinants of exercise among children: II. A longitudinal analysis. *Preventive Medicine, 27,* 470–477.

DiNucci, J.M. (1976). Gross motor performance: A comprehensive analysis of age and sex differences between boys and girls ages six to nine years. In J. Broekhoff (Ed.), *Physical education, sports, and the sciences.* Eugene, OR: Microform.

DiPietro, J.A. (1981). Rough and tumble play: A function of gender. *Developmental Psychology, 17,* 50–58.

DiSimoni, F.G. (1975). Perceptual and perceptual-motor characteristics of phonemic development. *Child Development, 46,* 243–246.

Dittmer, J. (1962). *A kinematic analysis of the development of the running pattern of grade school girls and certain factors which distinguish good from poor performance at the observed ages.* Unpublished master's thesis, University of Wisconsin, Madison.

Dodwell, P.C., Muir, D.W., & DiFranco, D. (1976). Responses of infants to visually presented objects. *Science, 194,* 209–211.

Dollman, J., Olds, T., Norton, K., & Stuart, D. (1999). The evolution of fitness and fatness in 10–11-year-old Australian schoolchildren: Changes in distribution characteristics between 1985 and 1997. *Pediatric Exercise Science, 11,* 108–121.

Dorfman, P.W. (1977). Timing and anticipation: A developmental perspective. *Journal of Motor Behavior, 9,* 67–80.

Doty, D. (1974). Infant speech perception. *Human Development, 17,* 74–80.

Drillis, R. (1961). The influence of aging on the kinematics of gait. *The Geriatric Amputee,* Publication 919. National Academy of Science, National Research Council.

Drinkwater, B.L., Horvath, S.M., & Wells, C.L. (1975). Aerobic power of females, age 10–68. *Journal of Gerontology, 30,* 385–394.

Drowatzky, J.N., & Zuccato, F.C. (1967). Interrelationship between static and dynamic balance. *Research Quarterly, 38,* 509–510.

Duche, P., Falgairette, G., Bedu, M., Fellmann, N., Lac, G., Robert, A., & Coudert, J. (1992). Longitudinal approach of bioenergetic profile in boys before and during puberty. In J. Coudert & E. Van Praagh (Eds.), *Pediatric work physiology: Methodological, physiological and pathological aspects* (pp. 43–45). Paris: Masson.

Duda, J.L., & Tappe, M.K. (1988). Predictors of personal investment in physical activity among middle-aged and older adults. *Perception and Motor Skills, 66,* 543–549.

Duda, J.L., & Tappe, M.K. (1989a). Personal investment in exercise among middle-aged and older adults. In A.C. Ostrow (Ed.), *Aging and motor behavior* (pp. 219–238). Indianapolis: Benchmark Press.

Duda, J.L., & Tappe, M.K. (1989b). Personal investment in exercise among adults: The examination of age and gender-related differences in motivational orientation. In A.C. Ostrow (Ed.), *Aging and motor behavior* (pp. 239–256). Indianapolis: Benchmark Press.

Duda, M. (1986). Prepubescent strength training gains support. *The Physician and Sportsmedicine, 14,* 157–161.

Dunham, P. (1977). Age, sex, speed and practice in coincidence-anticipation performance of children. *Perceptual and Motor Skills, 45,* 187–193.

Dupler, T., & Cortes, C. (1993). Effects of a whole-body resistive training regimen in the elderly. *Gerontology, 39,* 314–319.

DuRandt, R. (1985). Ball catching proficiency among 4-, 6-, and 8-year-olds. In J.E. Clark & J.H. Humphrey (Eds.), *Motor development: Current selected research* (pp. 35–44). Princeton, NJ: Princeton Book.

Dustman, R.E., Ruhling, R.O., Russell, E.M., Shearer, D.E., Bonekat, H.W., Shigeoka, J.W., Wood, J.S., & Bradford, D.C. (1989). Aerobic exercise training and improved neuropsychological function of older individuals. In A.C. Ostrow (Ed.), *Aging and motor behavior* (pp. 67–83). Indianapolis: Benchmark Press.

Earles, J.L., & Salthouse, T.A. (1995). Interrelations of age, health, and speed. *Journal of Gerontology: Psychological Sciences, 50B,* P33–P41.

Eaton, W.O., & Enns, L.R. (1986). Sex differences in human motor activity level. *Psychological Bulletin, 100,* 19–28.

Eaton, W.O., & Keats, J.G. (1982). Peer presence, stress, and sex differences in the motor activity levels of preschoolers. *Developmental Psychology, 18,* 534–540.

Ebihara, O., Ikeda, M., & Miyashita, M. (1983). Birth order and children's socialization into sport. *International Review of Sport Sociology, 18,* 69–89.

Ebrahim, S., & Rowland, L. (1996). Towards a new strategy for health promotion for older women: Determinants of physical activity. *Psychology, Health & Medicine, 1*(1), 29–40.

Einkauf, D.K., Gohdes, M.L., Jensen, G.M., & Jewell, M.J. (1987). Changes in spinal mobility with increasing age in women. *Physical Therapy, 67,* 370–375.

Eisenberg, N., Welchick, S.A., Hernandez, R., & Pasternack, J.F. (1985). Parental socialization of young children's play: A short-term longitudinal study. *Child Development, 56,* 1506–1513.

Eitzen, D.S., & Sage, G.H. (1997). *Sociology of North American sport* (6th ed.). Madison, WI: WCB McGraw-Hill.

Ekblom, B. (1969). Effect of physical training on oxygen transport system in man. *Acta Physiologica Scandinavica Supplementum, 328,* 1–76.

Elkind, D. (1975). Perceptual development in children. *American Scientist, 63,* 533–541.

Elkind, D., Koegler, R., & Go, E. (1964). Studies in perceptual development: Whole-part perception. *Child Development, 35,* 81–90.

Elliott, R. (1972). Simple reaction time in children: Effects of incentive, incentive shift, and other training variables. *Journal of Experimental Child Psychology, 13,* 540–557.

Elliott, C.B., Whitaker, D., & Thompson, P. (1989). Use of displacement threshold hyperacuity to isolate the neural component of senile vision loss. *Applied Optics, 28,* 1914–1918.

Eriksson, B., & Koch, G. (1973). Effect of physical training on hemodynamic response during submaximal exercise in 11–13 year old boys. *Acta Physiologica Scandinavica, 87,* 27–39.

Eriksson, B.O. (1972). Physical training, oxygen supply and muscle metabolism in 11 to 15 year old boys. *Acta Physiologica Scandinavica Supplementum, 384,* 1–48.

Eriksson, B.O. (1978). Physical activity from childhood to maturity: Medical and pediatric considerations. In G. Landry & W.A.R. Orban (Eds.), *Physical activity and human well-being.* Miami, FL: Symposia Specialists.

Espenschade, A.S., Dable, R.R., & Schoendube, R. (1953). Dynamic balance in adolescent boys. *Research Quarterly, 24,* 270–274.

Espenschade, A.S. (1947). Development of motor coordination in boys and girls. *Research Quarterly, 18,* 30–44.

Ewart, C.K., Stewart, K.J., Gillilan, R.E., & Kelemen, M.H. (1986). Self-efficacy mediates strength gains during circuit weight training in men with coronary artery disease. *Medicine and Science in Sports and Exercise, 18,* 531–540.

Exton-Smith, A.N. (1985). Mineral metabolism. In C.E. Finch & E.L. Schneider (Eds.), *Handbook of the biology of aging* (2nd ed., pp. 511–539). New York: Van Nostrand Reinhold.

Fagard, J. (1990). The development of bimanual coordination. In C. Bard, M. Fleury, & L. Hay (Eds.), *Development of eye-hand coordination across the life span* (pp. 262–282). Columbia, SC: University of South Carolina Press.

Fagot, B., & Leinbach, M. (1996). Gender knowledge in egalitarian and traditional families. *Sex Roles, 32,* 513–526.

Fagot, B., Leinbach, M., & O'Boyle, C. (1992). Gender labeling, gender stereotyping, and parenting behaviors. *Developmental Psychology, 28*(2), 225–230.

Fagot, B.I. (1978). The influence of sex of child on parental reactions to toddler children. *Child Development, 49,* 459–465.

Fagot, B.I. (1984). Teacher and peer reactions to boys' and girls' play styles. *Sex Roles, 11,* 691–702.

Fagot, B.I., & Leinbach, M.D. (1983). Play styles in early childhood: Social consequences for boys and girls. In M.B. Liss (Ed.), *Social and cognitive skills: Sex roles and children's play* (pp. 93–116). New York: Academic Press.

Falgairette, G., Bedu, M., Fellmann, N., Van Praagh, E., & Coudert, J. (1991). Bio-energetic profile in 144 boys aged from 6 to 15 years. *European Journal of Applied Physiology, 62,* 151–156.

Falgairette, G., Duche, P., Bedu, M., Fellmann, N., & Coudert, J. (1993). Bioenergetic characteristics in prepubertal swimmers. *International Journal of Sports Medicine, 14,* 444–448.

Farley, C. (1997). Just skip it. *Nature, 394,* 721–723.

Feltz, D.L., & Petlichkoff, L. (1983). Perceived competence among interscholastic sport participants and dropouts. *Canadian Journal of Applied Sport Sciences, 8,* 231–235.

Fiatarone, M.A., Marks, E.C., Ryan, N.D., Meredith, C.N., Lipsitz, L.A., & Evans, W.J. (1990). High-intensity strength training in nonagenarians. *Journal of the American Medical Association, 263,* 3029–3034.

Fieandt, K.V., Huhtala, A., Kullberg, P., & Saari, K. (1956). *Personal tempo and phenomenal time at different age levels (Report No. 2).* Helsinki, Finland: Psychological Institute, University of Helsinki.

Fitts, R.H. (1981). Aging and skeletal muscle. In E.L. Smith & R.C. Serfass (Eds.), *Exercise and aging: The scientific basis* (pp. 31–44). Hillside, NJ: Enslow.

Fleg, J.L. (1986). Alterations in cardiovascular structure and function with advancing age. *American Journal of Cardiology, 57,* 33C–44C.

Flegal, K.M., Carroll, M.D., Kuczmarski, R.J., & Johnson, C.L. (1998). Overweight and obesity in the United States: Prevalence and trends, 1960–1994. *International Journal of Obesity, 22,* 39–47.

Forbes, G.B. (1992). Exercise and lean weight: The influence of body weight. *Nutrition Reviews, 50,* 157–161.

Forssberg, H., & Nashner, L. (1982). Ontogenetic development of postural control in man: Adaptation to altered support and visual conditions during stance. *Journal of Neuroscience, 2,* 545–552.

Fox, K.R., & Corbin, C.B. (1989). The physical self-perception profile: Development and preliminary validation. *Journal of Sport and Exercise Psychology, 11,* 408–430.

Franck, H., Beuker, F., & Gurk, S. (1991). The effect of physical activity on bone turnover in young adults. *Experimental and Clinical Endocrinology, 98,* 42–46.

Frankenburg, W.K., & Dodds, J.B. (1967). The Denver Developmental Screening Test. *Journal of Pediatrics, 71,* 181–191.

French, K.E., Nevett, M.E., Spurgeon, J.H., Graham, K.C., Rink, J.E., & McPherson, S.L. (1996). Knowledge representation and problem solution in expert and novice youth baseball players. *Research Quarterly for Exercise and Sport, 67*(4), 386–395.

French, K.E., & Thomas, J.R. (1987). The relation of knowledge development to children's basketball performance. *Journal of Sport Psychology, 9,* 15–32.

Frontera, W.R., Meredith, C.N., O'Reilly, K.P., Knuttgen, H.G., & Evans, W.J. (1988). Strength conditioning in older men: Skeletal muscle hypertrophy and improved function. *Journal of Applied Physiology, 64,* 1038–1044.

Frostig, M., Lefever, W., & Whittlesey, J. (1966). *Administration and scoring manual for the Marianne Frostig Developmental Test of Visual Perception.* Palo Alto, CA: Consulting Psychologists Press.

Gabel, R.H., Johnston, R.C., & Crowinshield, R.D. (1979). A gait analyzer/trainer instrumentation system. *Journal of Biomedical Engineering, 12,* 543–549.

Gabell, A., & Nayak, U.S.L. (1984). The effect of age on variability of gait. *Journal of Gerontology, 39,* 662–666.

Gagen, L., & Getchell, N. (2004). Combining theory and practice in the gymnasium: "Constraints" within an ecological perspective. *Journal of Physical Education, Recreation, and Dance, 75,* 25–30.

Gallagher, J.D., & Thomas, J.R. (1980, April). *Adult-child differences in movement reproduction: Effects of kinesthetic sensory store and organization of memory.* Paper presented at the annual convention of the American Alliance for Health, Physical Education, Recreation and Dance, Detroit.

Geerdink, J.J., Hopkins, B., Beek, W.J., & Heriza, C.B. (1996). The organization of leg movements in preterm and full-term infants after term age. *Developmental Psychobiology, 29,* 335–351.

Germain, N.W., & Blair, S.N. (1983). Variability of shoulder flexion with age, activity, and sex. *American Corrective Therapy Journal, 37,* 156–160.

Gesell, A. (1928). *Infancy and human growth.* New York: Macmillan.

Gesell, A. (1954). The ontogenesis of infant behavior. In L. Carmichael (Ed.), *Manual of child psychology* (2nd ed.). New York: Wiley.

Gesell, A., & Amatruda, C.S. (1949). *Gesell developmental schedules.* New York: Psychological Company.

Getchell, N., & Roberton, M.A. (1989). Whole body stiffness as a function of developmental level in children's hopping. *Developmental Psychology, 25,* 920–928.

Getman, G.N. (1952). *How to develop your child's intelligence: A research publication.* Lucerne, MN: Author.

Getman, G.N. (1963). *The physiology of readiness experiment.* Minneapolis: P.A.S.S.

Gibson, E.J., Riccio, G., Schmuckler, M.A., Stoffregen, T.A., Rosenberg, D., & Taormina, J. (1987). Detection of the traversability of surfaces by crawling and walking infants. Special issue: The ontogenesis of perception. *Journal of Experimental Psychology: Human Perception & Performance, 13*(4), 533–544.

Gibson, E.J., & Walk, R.D. (1960). The "visual cliff." *Scientific American, 202*(4), 64–71.

Gibson, J.J. (1966). *The senses considered as perceptual systems.* Boston: Houghton Mifflin.

Gibson, J.J. (1979). *An ecological approach to visual perception.* Boston: Houghton Mifflin.

Gilliam, T.B., Katch, V.L., Thorland, W., & Weltman, A. (1977). Prevalence of coronary heart disease risk factors in active children, 7 to 12 years of age. *Medicine and Science in Sports, 9,* 21–25.

Giuliano, T., Popp, K., & Knight, J. (2000). Football vs. Barbies: Childhood play activities as predictors of sport participation by women. *Sex Roles, 42,* 159–181.

Goggin, N.L., & Keller, M.J. (1996). Older drivers: A closer look. *Educational Gerontology, 22,* 245–256.

Goggin, N.L., & Stelmach, G.E. (1990). A kinematic analysis of precued movements in young and elderly participants. *Canadian Journal on Aging, 9,* 371–385.

Going, S.B., Lohman, T., Pamenter, R., Boyden, T., Houtkooper, L., Ritenbaugh, C., Hall, M., Barc, L., Bunt, J., & Aickin, M. (1991). Effects of weight training on bone mineral density in premenopausal females. *Journal of Bone and Mineral Research, 6,* S104.

Going, S.B., Williams, D.P., Lohman, T.G., & Hewitt, M.J. (1994). Aging, body composition, and physical activity: A review. *Journal of Aging and Physical Activity, 2,* 38–66.

Goldfield, E.C., & Michel, G.F. (1986a). Spatiotemporal linkage in infant interlimb coordination. *Developmental Psychology, 19,* 259–264.

Goldfield, E.C., & Michel, G.F. (1986b). The ontogeny of infant bimanual reaching during the first year. *Infant Behavior and Development, 9,* 81–89.

Goodale, M.A. (1988). Modularity in visuomotor control: From input to output. In Z. Pylyshyn (Ed.), *Computational processes in human vision: An interdisciplinary perspective* (pp. 262–285). Norwood, NJ: Ablex.

Goodman, L., & Hamill, D. (1973). The effectiveness of the Kephart Getman activities in developing perceptualmotor and cognitive skills. *Focus on Exceptional Children, 4,* 1–9.

Goodnow, J.J. (1971a). Eye and hand: Differential memory and its effect on matching. *Neuropsychologica, 9,* 89–95.

Goodnow, J.J. (1971b). Matching auditory and visual series: Modality problem or translation problem? *Child Development, 42,* 1187–1201.

Gosline, J.M. (1976). The physical properties of elastic tissue. In D.A. Hull & D.S. Jackson (Eds.), *International review of connective tissue research* (Vol. 7, pp. 184–210). New York: Academic Press.

Gould, D., Feltz, D., Horn, T., & Weiss, M.R. (1982). Reasons for attrition in competitive youth swimming. *Journal of Sport Behavior, 5,* 155–165.

Gould, D., Feltz, D., & Weiss, M.R. (1985). Motives for participating in competitive youth swimming. *International Journal of Sport Psychology, 6,* 126–140.

Granrud, C.E., Yonas, A., Smith, I.M., Arterberry, M.E., Glicksman, M.L., & Sorknes, A.C. (1984). Infants' sensitivity to accretion and deletion of texture as information for depth at an edge. *Child Development, 55,* 1630–1636.

Grassi, B., Cerretelli, P., Narici, M.V., & Marconi, C. (1991). Peak anaerobic power in master athletes. *European Journal of Physiology, 62,* 394–399.

Green, H.J. (1986). Characteristics of aging human skeletal muscles. In J.R. Sutton & R.M. Brock (Eds.), *Sports medicine for the mature athlete* (pp. 17–26). Indianapolis: Benchmark Press.

Greendorfer, S.L. (1976, September). *A social learning approach to female sport involvement.* Paper presented at the American Psychological Association, Washington, DC.

Greendorfer, S.L. (1977). Role of socializing agents in female sport involvement. *Research Quarterly, 48,* 304–310.

Greendorfer, S.L. (1979). Childhood sport socialization influences of male and female track athletes. *Arena Review, 3,* 39–53.

Greendorfer, S.L. (1983). Shaping the female athlete: The impact of the family. In M.A. Boutilier & L. Sangiovanni (Eds.), *The sport woman* (pp. 135–155). Champaign, IL: Human Kinetics.

Greendorfer, S.L. (1992). Sport socialization. In Thelma S. Horn (Ed.), *Advances in sport psychology* (pp. 201–218). Champaign, IL: Human Kinetics.

Greendorfer, S.L., & Brundage, C.L. (1984, July). *Sex differences in children's motor skills: Toward a cross-disciplinary perspective.* Paper presented at the 1984 Olympic Scientific Congress, Eugene, OR.

Greendorfer, S.L., & Ewing, M.E. (1981). Race and gender differences in children's socialization into sport. *Research Quarterly for Exercise and Sport, 52,* 301–310.

Greendorfer, S.L., & Lewko, J.H. (1978). Role of family members in sport socialization of children. *Research Quarterly, 49,* 146–152.

Greenough, W.T., Black, J.E., & Wallace, C.S. (1987). Experience and brain development. *Child Development, 58,* 539–559.

Greenough, W.T., Wallace, C.S., Alcantara, A.A., Anderson, B.J., Hawrylak, N., Sirevaag, A.M., & Weiler, I.J. (1993). Development of the brain: Experience affects the structure of neurons, glia, and blood vessels. In N.J. Anatasiow & S. Harel (Eds.), *At-risk infants: Interventions, families, and research* (pp. 173–185). Baltimore, MD: Paul H. Brookes.

Grimby, G. (1988). Physical activity and effects of muscle training in the elderly. *Annals of Clinical Research, 20,* 62–66.

Grodjinovsky, A., Inbar, O., Dotan, R., & Bar-Or, O. (1980). Training effect on the anaerobic performance of children as measured by the Wingate anaerobic test. In K. Berg & B.O. Eriksson (Eds.), *Children and exercise IX* (pp. 139–145). Baltimore: University Park Press.

Gutin, B., Cucuzzo, N., Islam, S., Smith, C., & Stachura, M.E. (1996). Physical training, lifestyle education, and coronary risk factors in obese girls. *Medicine and Science in Sports and Exercise, 28,* 19–23.

Gutin, B., Owens, S., Slavens, G., Riggs, S., & Treiber, F. (1997). Effects of physical training on heart period variability in obese children. *Journal of Pediatrics, 130,* 938–943.

Gutteridge, M. (1939). A study of motor achievements of young children. *Archives of Psychology, 244,* 1–178.

Hagburg, J.M., Allen, W.K., Seals, D.R., Hurley, B.F., Ehsani, A.A., & Holloszy, J.O. (1985). A hemodynamic comparison of young and older endurance athletes during exercise. *Journal of Applied Physiology, 58,* 2041–2046.

Hagburg, J.M., Graves, J.E., Limacher, M., Woods, D.R., Leggett, S.H., Cononie, C., Gruber, J.J., & Pollock, M.L. (1989). Cardiovascular responses of 70- to 79-year-old men and women to exercise training. *Journal of Applied Physiology, 66,* 2589–2594.

Hakkinen, K., Alen, M., Kallinen, M., Izquierdo, M., Jokelainen, K., Lassila, H., Malkia, E., Kraemer, W.J., & Newton, R.U. (1998). Muscle CSA, force production, and activation of leg extensors during isometric and dynamic actions in middle-aged and elderly men and women. *Journal of Aging and Physical Activity, 6,* 232–247.

Halverson, H.M. (1931). An experimental study of prehension in infants by means of systematic cinema records. *Genetic Psychology Monographs, 10,* 107–286.

Halverson, L.E. (1983). *Observing children's motor development in action.* Paper presented at the American Alliance for Health, Physical Education, Recreation and Dance, Eugene, OR.

Halverson, L.E., Roberton, M.A., & Langendorfer, S. (1982). Development of the overarm throw: Movement and ball velocity changes by seventh grade. *Research Quarterly for Exercise and Sport, 53,* 198–205.

Halverson, L.E., & Williams, K. (1985). Developmental sequences for hopping over distance: A prelongitudinal screening. *Research Quarterly for Exercise and Sport, 56,* 37–44.

Handfuls of Happiness (2000). [Online]. Available: www.abcnews.com.

Hannaford, C. (1995). *Smart moves: Why learning is not all in your head.* Arlington, VA: Great Ocean Publishers.

Hansen, L., Klausen, K., Bangsbo, J., & Muller, J. (1999). Short longitudinal study of boys playing soccer: Parental height, birth weight and length, anthropometry, and pubertal maturation in elite and non-elite players. *Pediatric Exercise Science, 11,* 199–207.

Hansman, C.F. (1962). Appearance and fusion of ossification centers in the human skeleton. *American Journal of Roentgenology, 88,* 476–482.

Harris, J.E. (1999). The role of physical activity in the management of obesity. *Journal of the American Osteopathic Association, 99*(4), S15–S19.

Harrison, T.R., Dixon, K., Russell, R.A., Bidwai, P.S., & Coleman, H.N. (1964). The relation of age to the duration of contraction, ejection, and relaxation of the normal human heart. *American Heart Journal, 67,* 189–199.

Harter, S. (1978). Effectance motivation reconsidered: Towards a developmental model. *Human Development, 21,* 34–64.

Harter, S. (1981). A model of intrinsic mastery motivation in children: Individual differences and developmental change. In W.A. Collins (Ed.), *Minnesota Symposium on Child Psychology* (Vol. 14, pp. 215–225). Hillsdale, NJ: Erlbaum.

Harter, S. (1985). *Manual for the self-perception profile for children.* Denver: University of Denver.

Harter, S., & Pike, R. (1984). The pictorial scale of perceived competence and social acceptance for young children. *Child Development, 55,* 1969–1982.

Hartley, A.A. (1992). Attention. In F.I.M. Craig & T.A. Salthouse, (Eds.), *The handbook of aging and cognition* (pp. 3–49). Hillsdale, NJ: Erlbaum.

Hasselkus, B.R., & Shambes, G.M. (1975). Aging and postural sway in women. *Journal of Gerontology, 30,* 661–667.

Haubenstricker, J.L., Branta, C.F., & Seefeldt, V.D. (1983). *Standards of performance for throwing and catching.* Paper presented at the Annual Conference of the North American Society for Psychology of Sport and Physical Activity, Asilomar, CA.

Haubenstricker, J.L., Seefeldt, V.D., & Branta, C.F. (1983, April). *Preliminary validation of a developmental sequence for the standing long jump.* Paper presented at the American Alliance for Health, Physical Education, Recreation and Dance, Houston, TX.

Hausler, R., Colburn, S., & Marr, E. (1983). Sound localization in subjects with impaired hearing: Spatial discrimination and discrimination tests. *Acta Oto-Laryngologica, Supplement, 40C,* 6–62.

Hawn, P.R., & Harris, L.J. (1983). Hand differences in grasp duration and reaching in two- and five-month old infants. In G. Young, S. Segalowitz, C.M. Carter, & S.E. Trehub (Eds.), *Manual specialization and the developing brain* (pp. 331–348). New York: Academic Press.

Haywood, K., & Trick, L. (1990). Changes in visual functioning and perception with advancing age. *Missouri Journal of Health, Physical Education, Recreation and Dance,* 51–73.

Haywood, K.M. (1977). Eye movements during coincidence-anticipation performance. *Journal of Motor Behavior, 9,* 313–318.

Haywood, K.M. (1980). Coincidence-anticipation accuracy across the life span. *Experimental Aging Research, 6*(3), 451–462.

Haywood, K.M. (1982). Eye movement pattern and accuracy during perceptual-motor performance in young and old adults. *Experimental Aging Research, 8,* 153–157.

Haywood, K.M. (1989). A longitudinal analysis of anticipatory judgment in older adult motor performance. In A.C. Ostrow (Ed.), *Aging and motor behavior* (pp. 325–335). Indianapolis: Benchmark Press.

Haywood, K.M., Greenwald, G., & Lewis, C. (1981). Contextual factors and age group differences in coincidence-anticipation performance. *Research Quarterly for Exercise and Sport, 52,* 458–464.

Haywood, K.M., & Williams, K. (1995). Age, gender, and flexibility differences in tennis serving among experienced older adults. *Journal of Aging and Physical Activity, 3,* 54–66.

Haywood, K.M., Williams, K., & VanSant, A. (1991). Qualitative assessment of the backswing in older adult throwing. *Research Quarterly for Exercise and Sport, 62,* 340–343.

Heaney, R.P. (1986). Calcium, bone health, and osteoporosis. *Journal of Bone and Mineral Research, 4,* 255–301.

Hecaen, H., & de Ajuriaguerra, J. (1964). *Left-handedness: Manual superiority and cerebral dominance.* New York: Grune & Stratton.

Hecox, K. (1975). Electro-physiological correlates of human auditory development. In L.B. Cohen & P. Salapatek (Eds.), *Infant perception: Vol. 2. From sensation to cognition* (pp. 151–191). New York: Academic Press.

Held, R. (1985). Binocular vision: Behavioral and neuronal development. In J. Mehler & R. Fox (Eds.), *Neonate cognition: Beyond the blooming buzzing confusion* (pp. 37–44). Hillsdale, NJ: Erlbaum.

Held, R. (1988). Normal visual development and its deviations. In G. Lennerstrand, G. Von Noorden, & E. Campos (Eds.), *Strabismus and amblyopia* (pp. 247–257). London: Macmillan.

Held, R., & Hein, A. (1963). Movement-produced stimulation in the development of visually guided behavior. *Journal of Comparative and Physiological Psychology, 56,* 872–876.

Helfer, K.S. (1992). Aging and the binaural advantage in reverberation and noise. *Journal of Speech and Hearing Research, 35,* 1394–1401.

Hellebrandt, F.A., & Braun, G.L. (1939). The influence of sex and age on the postural sway of man. *American Journal of Physical Anthropology, 24*(Series 1), 347–360.

Hellmich, N. (1999, May 18). For health, doctors tell patients to take a hike. *USA Today,* 6D.

Hellmich, N. (1999, November 15). Aging Americans settle up in size. *USA Today,* 6D.

Heriza, C.B. (1986). *A kinematic analysis of leg movements in premature and fullterm infants.* Unpublished doctoral dissertation, University of Southern Illinois, Edwardsville.

Herkowitz, J. (1978). Developmental task analysis: The design of movement experiences and evaluation of motor development status. In M.V. Ridenour (Ed.), *Motor development* (pp. 139–164). Princeton, NJ: Princeton Book.

Heyward, V.H. (1991). *Advanced fitness assessment and exercise prescription* (2nd ed.). Champaign, IL: Human Kinetics.

Hickey, T.L., & Peduzzi, J.D. (1987). Structure and development of the visual system. In P. Salapatek & L.B. Cohen (Eds.), *Handbook of infant perception: From sensation to perception* (pp. 1–42). New York: Academic Press.

Higginson, D.C. (1985). The influence of socializing agents in the female sport-participation process. *Adolescence, 20,* 73–82.

Hoeger, W.W.K., Hopkins, D.R., Button, S., & Palmer, T.A. (1990). Comparing the sit and reach with the modified sit and reach in measuring flexibility in adolescents. *Pediatric Exercise Science, 2,* 155–162.

Hogan, P.I., & Santomeir, J.P. (1984). Effect of mastering swim skills on older adults' self-efficacy. *Research Quarterly for Exercise and Sport, 55,* 294–296.

Hohlstein, R.E. (1982). The development of prehension in normal infants. *American Journal of Occupational Therapy, 36*, 170–176.

Holland, G.J., Tanaka, K., Shigematsu, R., & Nakagaichi, M. (2002). Flexibility and physical functions of older adults: A review. *Journal of Aging and Physical Activity, 10*, 169–206.

Holtzman, R.E., Familant, M.E., Deptula, P., & Hoyer, W.J. (1986). Aging and the use of sentential structure to facilitate word recognition. *Experimental Aging Research, 12*, 85–88.

Hopkins, B., & Ronnqvist, L. (1998). Human handedness: Developmental and evolutionary perspectives. In F. Simion & G. Butterworth (Eds.), *The development of sensory, motor and cognitive capacities in early infancy: From perception to cognition* (pp. 191–236). Hove, England: Psychology Press/Erlbaum (UK) Taylor & Francis.

Horak, F.B., & MacPherson, J.M. (1995). Postural orientation and equilibrium. In J. Shepard & L. Rowell (Eds.), *Handbook of physiology* (pp. 252–292). New York: Oxford University Press.

Horak, F.B., Nashner, L.M., & Diener, H.C. (1990). Postural strategies associated with somatosensory and vestibular loss. *Experimental Brain Research, 82*, 167–177.

Horn, T.S. (1985). Coaches' feedback and changes in children's perceptions of their physical competence. *Journal of Educational Psychology, 77*, 174–186.

Horn, T.S. (1986). The self-fulfilling prophecy theory: When coaches' expectations become reality. In J.M. Williams (Ed.), *Applied sport psychology: Personal growth to peak performance* (pp. 59–73). Palo Alto, CA: Mayfield.

Horn, T.S. (1987). The influence of teacher–coach behavior on the psychological development of children. In D. Gould & M.R. Weiss (Eds.), *Advances in pediatric sport science: Vol. 2. Behavioral issues* (pp. 121–142). Champaign, IL: Human Kinetics.

Horn, T.S., & Hasbrook, C.A. (1986). Information components influencing children's perceptions of their physical competence. In M.R. Weiss & D. Gould (Eds.), *Sport for children and youths* (pp. 81–88). Champaign, IL: Human Kinetics.

Horn, T.S., & Hasbrook, C.A. (1987). Psychological characteristics and the criteria children use for self-evaluation. *Journal of Sport Psychology, 9*, 208–221.

Horn, T.S., & Weiss, M.R. (1991). A developmental analysis of children's self-ability judgments in the physical domain. *Pediatric Exercise Science, 3*, 310–326.

Howell, M.L., & MacNab, R. (1966). *The physical work capacity of Canadian children.* Ottawa: Canadian Association for Physical Health Education and Recreation.

Howze, E.H., DiGilio, D.A., Bennett, J.P., & Smith, M.L. (1986). Health education and physical fitness for older adults. In B. McPherson (Ed.), *Sport and aging* (pp. 153–156). Champaign, IL: Human Kinetics.

Hrdlicka, A. (1931). *Children who run on all fours: And other animal-like behaviors in the human child.* New York: Whittlesey House.

Hubley-Kozey, C.L., Wall, J.C., & Hogan, D.B. (1995). Effects of a general exercise program on passive hip, knee, and ankle range of motion of older women. *Topics in Geriatric Rehabilitation, 10*, 33–44.

Hughes, S., Gibbs, J., Dunlop, D., Edelman, P., Singer, R., & Chang, R.W. (1997). Predictors of decline in manual performance in older adults. *Journal of the American Geriatrics Society, 45*, 905–910.

Hupprich, F.L., & Sigerseth, P.O. (1950). The specificity of flexibility in girls. *Research Quarterly, 21*, 25–33.

Inbar, O., & Bar-Or, O. (1986). Anaerobic characteristics in male children and adolescents. *Medicine and Science in Sports and Exercise, 18*, 264–269.

Isaacs, L.D. (1980). Effects of ball size, ball color, and preferred color on catching by young children. *Perceptual and Motor Skills, 51*, 583–586.

Isaacs, L.D. (1983). Coincidence-anticipation in simple catching. *Journal of Human Movement Studies, 9*, 195–201.

Ivry, R.B. (1993). Cerebellar involvement in the explicit representation of temporal information. In P. Tallal, A.M. Galaburda, R.R. Llinas, & C. von Euler (Eds.), *Temporal information processing in the nervous system: Special reference to dyslexia and dysphasia* (pp. 214–230). New York: New York Academy of Sciences.

Ivry, R.B., & Keele, S.W. (1989). Timing functions of the cerebellum. *Journal of Cognitive Neuroscience, 1*, 136–152.

Jackson, T. (1993). *Activities that teach.* Cedar City, UT: Red Rock Publishing.

Jackson, T. (1995). *More activities that teach.* Cedar City, UT: Red Rock Publishing.

Jackson, T. (2000). *Still more activities that teach.* Cedar City, UT: Red Rock Publishing.

Jagacinski, R.J., Greenberg, N., & Liao, M. (1997). Tempo, rhythm, and aging in golf. *Journal of Motor Behavior, 29*(2), 159–173.

Jagacinski, R.J., Liao, M.J., & Fayyad, E.A. (1995). Generalized slowing in sinusoidal tracking in older adults. *Psychology and Aging, 10*, 8–19.

Janz, K.F., Burns, T.L., & Mahoney, L.T. (1995). Predictors of left ventricular mass and resting blood pressure in children: The Muscatine study. *Medicine and Science in Sports and Exercise, 27*(6), 818–825.

Jeka, J.J. (1998). Touching surfaces for control, not support. In D.A. Rosenbaum & C.E. Collyer (Eds.), *Timing of behavior: Neural, psychological, and computational perspectives* (pp. 89–105). Cambridge, MA: MIT Press.

Jeka, J.J., & Lackner, J.R. (1994). Fingertip contact influences human postural control. *Experimental Brain Research, 100*, 495–502.

Jeka, J.J., & Lackner, J.R. (1995). The role of haptic cues from rough and slippery surfaces in human postural control. *Experimental Brain Research, 103*, 267–276.

Jensen, J.L., Thelen, E., Ulrich, B.B., Schneider, K., & Zernicke, R.F. (1995). Adaptive dynamics of the leg movement patterns of human infants: III. Age-related differences in limb control. *Journal of Motor Behavior, 27*, 366–374.

Jesse, J.P. (1977). Olympic lifting movements endanger adolescents. *The Physician and Sportsmedicine, 5*, 60–67.

Johansson, G., von Hofsten, C., & Jansson, G. (1980). Event perception. *Annual Review of Psychology, 31*, 27–63.

Johnsson, L.G., & Hawkins, J.E., Jr. (1972). Sensory and neural degeneration with aging, as seen in micro-dissections of the inner ear. *Annals of Otology, Rhinology, and Laryngology, 81*, 179–193.

Jones, H.E. (1947). Sex differences in physical abilities. *Human Biology, 19*, 12–25.

Jouen, F. (1990). Early visual-vestibular interactions and postural development. In H. Bloch & B.I. Bertenthal (Eds.), *Sensory-motor organization and development in infancy and early childhood* (pp. 199–215). Dordrecht, the Netherlands: Kluwer.

Jouen, F., Lepecq, J.C., Gapenne, O., & Bertenthal, B.I. (2000). Optical flow sensitivity in neonates. *Infant Behavior and Development, 23* (3-4), 271–284.

Kallman, D.A., Plato, C.C., & Tobin, J.D. (1990). The role of muscle loss in the age-related decline of grip strength: Cross-sectional and longitudinal perspectives. *Journal of Gerontology: Medical Sciences, 45*, M82–M88.

Karpovich, P.V. (1937). Textbook fallacies regarding the development of the child's heart. *Research Quarterly, 8*, 33–37. (Reprinted in 1991 in *Pediatric Exercise Science, 3*, 278–282.)

Kasch, F.W., Boyer, J.L., Van Camp, S.P., Verity, L.S., & Wallace, J.P. (1990). The effects of physical activity and inactivity on aerobic power in older men (a longitudinal study). *The Physician and Sportsmedicine, 18*, 73–83.

Kasch, F.W., & Wallace, J.P. (1976). Physiological variables during 10 years of endurance exercise. *Medicine and Science in Sports, 8,* 5–8.

Katch, V.L. (1983). Physical conditioning of children. *Journal of Adolescent Health Care, 3,* 241–246.

Kauffman, T.L. (1985). Strength-training effect in young and aged women. *Archives of Physical Medicine and Rehabilitation, 65,* 223–226.

Kauranen, K., & Vanharanta, H. (1996). Influences of aging, gender, and handedness on motor performance of upper and lower extremities. *Perceptual and Motor Skills, 82,* 515–525.

Kavanagh, T., & Shephard, R.J. (1977). The effect of continued training on the aging process. *Annals of the New York Academy of Sciences, 301,* 656–670.

Kawai, K., Savelsbergh, G.J.P., & Wimmers, R.H. (1999). Newborns and spontaneous arm movements are influenced by the environment. *Early Human Development, 54*(1), 15–27.

Keele, S.W., & Ivry, R. (1990). Does the cerebellum provide a common computation for diverse tasks? A timing hypothesis. *Annals of the New York Academy of Sciences, 608,* 179–211.

Kellman, P.J., & Arterberry, M.E. (1998). *The cradle of knowledge: Development of perception in infancy.* Cambridge, MA: MIT Press.

Kelly, J.R. (1974). Socialization toward leisure: A developmental approach. *Journal of Leisure Research, 6,* 181–193.

Kemper, H.C.G., Twisk, J.W.R., Koppes, L.L.J., van Mechelen, W., & Post, G.B. (2001). A 15-year physical activity pattern is positively related to aerobic fitness in young males and females (13–27 years). *European Journal of Applied Physiology, 84,* 395–402.

Kenshalo, D.R. (1977). Age changes in touch, vibration, temperature, kinesthesis, and pain sensitivity. In J.E. Birren & K.W. Schaie (Eds.), *Handbook of the psychology of aging* (pp. 562–579). New York: Van Nostrand Reinhold.

Kenyon, G.S., & McPherson, B.D. (1973). Becoming involved in physical activity and sport: A process of socialization. In G.L. Rarick (Ed.), *Physical activity: Human growth and development* (pp. 301–332). New York: Academic Press.

Kephart, N.C. (1964). Perceptual-motor aspects of learning disabilities. *Exceptional Children, 31,* 201–206.

Kephart, N.C. (1971). *The slow learner in the classroom* (2nd ed.). Columbus, OH: Merrill.

Kermoian, R., & Campos, J.J. (1988). Locomotor experience: A facilitator of spatial cognitive development. *Child Development, 59,* 908–917.

Kidd, A.H., & Kidd, R.M. (1966). The development of auditory perception in children. In A.H. Kidd & J.L. Rivoire (Eds.), *Perceptual development in children* (pp. 113–142). New York: International Universities Press.

Kinsbourne, M. (1988). Sinistrality, brain organization and cognitive deficits. In D.L. Molfese & S.J. Segalowitz (Eds.), *Brain lateralization in children: Brain implications* (pp. 259–280). New York: Guilford.

Kinsbourne, M. (1997). The development of lateralization. In H.W. Reese & M.D. Franzen (Eds.), *Biological and neuropsychological mechanisms: Life span developmental psychology.* Mahwah, NJ: Lawrence Erlbaum Associates.

Kisilevsky, B.S., Stach, D.M., & Muir, D.W. (1991). Fetal and infant response to tactile stimulation. In M.J.S. Weiss & P.R. Zelazo (Eds.), *Newborn attention: Biological constraints and the influence of experience* (pp. 63–98). Norwood, NJ: Ablex.

Klausner, S.C., & Schwartz, A.B. (1985). The aging heart. *Clinical Geriatric Medicine, 1,* 119–141.

Kline, D.W., Culham, J., Bartel, P., & Lynk, L. (1994). Aging and hyperacuity thresholds as a function of contrast and oscillation rate. *Canadian Psychology, 35,* 14.

Klint, K.A., & Weiss, M.R. (1986). Dropping in and dropping out: Participation motives of current and former youth gymnasts. *Canadian Journal of Applied Sport Sciences, 11,* 106–114.

Kobayashi, K., Kitamura, K., Miura, M., Sodeyama, H., Murase, Y., Miyashita, M., & Matsui, H. (1978). Aerobic power as related to body growth and training in Japanese boys: A longitudinal study. *Journal of Applied Physiology, 44,* 666–672.

Koch, G., & Rocker, L. (1977). Plasma volume and intravascular protein masses in trained boys and fit young men. *Journal of Applied Physiology, 43,* 1085–1088.

Koivula, N. (2000). Gender stereotyping in televised media sport coverage. *Sex Roles, 41,* 589–604.

Komi, P.V. (1984). Physiological and biomechanical correlates of muscle function: Effects of muscle structure and stretch-shortening cycle on force and speed. In R.L. Terjung (Ed.), *Exercise and sport science reviews* (Vol. 12, pp. 81–121). Lexington, MA: Collamore.

Konczak, J. (1990). Toward an ecological theory of motor development: The relevance of the Gibsonian approach to vision for motor development research. In J.E. Clark & J.H. Humphrey (Eds.), *Advances in motor development research* (Vol. 3, pp. 201–224). New York: AMS Press.

Kotz, C.M., Billington, C.J., & Levine, A.S. (1999). Obesity and aging. *Clinics in Geriatric Medicine, 15*(2), 391–412.

Kraemer, W.J., Fry, A.C., Frykman, P.N., Conroy, B., & Hoffman, J. (1989). Resistance training and youth. *Pediatric Exercise Science, 1,* 336–350.

Krahenbuhl, G.S., & Martin, S.L. (1977). Adolescent body size and flexibility. *Research Quarterly, 48,* 797–799.

Krahenbuhl, G.S., Pangrazi, R.P., Petersen, G.W., Burkett, L.N., & Schneider, M.J. (1978). Field testing of cardiorespiratory fitness in primary school children. *Medicine and Science in Sports, 10,* 208–213.

Krahenbuhl, G.S., Skinner, J.S., & Kohrt, W.M. (1985). Developmental aspects of maximal aerobic power in children. *Medicine and Science in Sports and Exercise, 13,* 503–538.

Kuczaj, S.A., II, & Maratsos, M.P. (1975). On the acquisition of front, back, and side. *Child Development, 46,* 202–210.

Kuffler, S.W., Nicholls, J.G., & Martin, A.R. (1984). *From neuron to brain* (2nd ed.). Sunderland, MA: Sinauer.

Kugler, P.N., Kelso, J.A.S., & Turvey, M.T. (1980). On the concept of coordinative structures as dissipative structures. I. Theoretical lines of convergence. In G.E. Stelmach & J. Requin (Eds.), *Tutorials in motor behavior* (pp. 3–47). New York: North-Holland.

Kugler, P.N., Kelso, J.A.S., & Turvey, M.T. (1982). On the control and coordination of naturally developing systems. In J.A.S. Kelso & J.E. Clark (Eds.), *The development of movement control and coordination* (pp. 5–78). New York: Wiley.

Kuhn, D. (2000). Does memory development belong on an endangered topic list? *Child Development, 71,* 21–25.

Kuhtz-Buschbeck, J.P., Stolze, H., Boczek-Funcke, A., Joehnk, K., Heinrichs, H., & Illert, M. (1998). Kinematic analysis of prehension movements in children. *Behavioural Brain Research, 93,* 131–141.

Kuo, A.D., & Zajac, F.E. (1993). Human standing posture: Multi-joint movement strategies based on biomechanical constraints. *Progress in Brain Research, 97,* 349–358.

Laforest, S., St-Pierre, D.M.M., Cyr, J., & Gayton, D. (1990). Effects of age and regular exercise on muscle strength and endurance. *European Journal of Applied Physiology, 60,* 104–111.

Laidlaw, R.W., & Hamilton, M.A. (1937). A study of thresholds in appreciation of passive movement among normal control subjects. *Bulletin of the Neurological Institute, 6,* 268–273.

Lan, C., Lai, J.S., Chen, S.U., & Wong, M.K. (1998). 12-month tai chi training in the elderly: Its effects on health fitness. *Medicine and Science in Sports and Exercise, 30*(3), 345–351.

Landahl, H.D., & Birren, J.E. (1959). Effects of age on the discrimination of lifted weights. *Journal of Gerontology, 14*, 48–55.

Langendorfer, S. (1980). *Longitudinal evidence for developmental changes in the preparatory phase of the overarm throw for force.* Paper presented at the American Alliance for Health, Physical Education, Recreation and Dance, Detroit, MI.

Langendorfer, S. (1982). *Developmental relationships between throwing and striking: A prelongitudinal test of motor stage theory.* Unpublished doctoral dissertation, University of Wisconsin, Madison.

Langendorfer, S. (1987). Prelongitudinal screening of overarm striking development performed under two environmental conditions. In J.E. Clark & J.H. Humphrey (Eds.), *Advances in motor development research* (Vol. 1, pp. 17–47). New York: AMS Press.

Langendorfer, S. (1990). Motor-task goal as a constraint on developmental status. In J.E. Clark & J.H. Humphrey (Eds.), *Advances in motor development research* (Vol. 3, pp. 16–28). New York: AMS Press.

Langendorfer, S., & Roberton, M.A. (2002). Individual pathways in the development of forceful throwing. *Research Quarterly for Exercise and Sport, 73*, 245–256.

Langley, D.J., & Knight, S.M. (1996). Exploring practical knowledge: A case study of an experienced senior tennis performer. *Research Quarterly for Exercise and Sport, 67*(4), 433–447.

Larsson, L. (1982). Physical training effects on muscle morphology in sedentary males at different ages. *Medicine and Science in Sports and Exercise, 14*, 203–206.

Lasky, R.E. (1977). The effect of visual feedback of the hand on the reaching and retrieval behavior of young infants. *Child Development, 48*, 112–117.

Leavitt, J. (1979). Cognitive demands of skating and stickhandling in ice hockey. *Canadian Journal of Applied Sport Science, 4*, 46–55.

Lee, D.N., & Aronson, E. (1974). Visual proprioceptive control of standing in human infants. *Perception & Psychophysics, 15*, 529–532.

Lefebvre, C., & Reid, G. (1998). Prediction in ball catching by children with and without a developmental coordination disorder. *Adapted Physical Activity Quarterly, 15*(4), 299–315.

Leme, S., & Shambes, G. (1978). Immature throwing patterns in normal adult women. *Journal of Human Movement Studies, 4*, 85–93.

Lemon, P.W.R. (1989). Nutrition for muscular development of young athletes. In C.V. Gisolfi & D.R. Lamb (Eds.), *Perspectives in exercise science and sports medicine: Vol. 2. Youth, exercise, and sport* (pp. 369–400). Indianapolis: Benchmark Press.

Lengyel, M., & Gyarfas, I. (1979). The importance of echocardiography in the assessment of left ventricular hypertrophy in trained and untrained school children. *Acta Cardiologica, 34*, 63–69.

Lenoir, M., Musch, E., Janssens, M., Thiery, E., & Uyttenhove, J. (1999). Intercepting moving objects during self motion. *Journal of Motor Behavior, 31*(1), 55–67.

Levy, G.D. (2000). Gender-typed and non-gender-typed category awareness in toddlers. *Sex Roles, 41*, 851–873.

Lew, A.R., & Butterworth, G. (1997). The development of hand–mouth coordination in 2- to 5-month-old infants: Similarities with reaching and grasping. *Infant Behavior and Development, 20*(1), 59–69.

Lewis, M. (1972). Culture and gender roles: There is no unisex in the nursery. *Psychology Today, 5*, 54–57.

Lewis, S.F., Taylor, W.F., Bastian, B.C., Graham, R.M., Pettinger, W.A., & Blomqvist, C.G. (1983). Haemodynamic responses to static and dynamic handgrip before and after autonomic blockage. *Clinical Science, 64*, 593–599.

Lewko, J.H., & Ewing, M.E. (1980). Sex differences and parental influences in sport involvement of children. *Journal of Sport Psychology, 2*, 62–68.

Lewko, J.H., & Greendorfer, S.L. (1988). Family influences in sport socialization of children and adolescents. In F.L. Smoll, R.A. Magill, & M.J. Ash (Eds.), *Children in sport* (3rd ed., pp. 287–300). Champaign, IL: Human Kinetics.

Lexell, J., Henriksson-Larsen, K., Wimblad, B., & Sjostrom, M. (1983). Distribution of different fiber types in human skeletal muscles: Effects of aging studies in whole muscle cross-sections. *Muscle and Nerve, 6*, 588–595.

Lexell, J., Taylor, C., & Sjostrom, M. (1988). What is the cause of ageing atrophy? Total number, size, and proportion of different fiber types studied in whole vastus lateralis muscle from 15- to 83-year-old men. *Journal of Neurological Sciences, 84*, 275–294.

Lindquist, C., Reynolds, K., & Goran, M. (1998). Sociocultural determinants of physical activity among children. *Preventive Medicine, 29*, 305–312.

Lipsitz, L.A. (1989). Altered blood pressure homeostasis in advanced age: Clinical and research implications. *Journal of Gerontology: Medical Sciences, 44*, M179–M183.

Liss, M.B. (1983). Learning gender-related skills through play. In M.B. Liss (Ed.), *Social and cognitive skills: Sex roles and children's play* (pp. 147–166). New York: Academic Press.

Lloyd, B., & Smith, C. (1985). The social representation of gender and young children's play. *British Journal of Developmental Psychology, 3*, 65–73.

Lockman, J.J. (1984). The development of detour ability during infancy. *Child Development, 55*, 482–491.

Lockman, J.J. (2000). A perception-action perspective on tool use development. *Child Development, 71*, 137–144.

Lohman, T.G., Going, S.B., Pamenter, R.W., Boyden, T., Houtkooper, L.B., Ritenbaugh, C., Hall, M., Bare, L.A., Hill, A., & Aickin, M. (1992). Effects of weight training on lumbar spine and femur bone mineral density in premenopausal females. *Medicine and Science in Sports and Exercise, 24*, S188.

Lohman, T.G., Roche, A.F., & Martorell, R. (Eds.). (1988). *Anthropometric standardization reference manual.* Champaign, IL: Human Kinetics.

Long, A.B., & Looft, W.R. (1972). Development of directionality in children: Ages six through twelve. *Developmental Psychology, 6*, 375–380.

Lorber, J. (1994). Believing is seeing: Biology as ideology. *Gender and Society, 7*, 568–581.

Lowrey, G.H. (1986). *Growth and development of children* (8th ed.). Chicago: Year Book Medical.

Loy, J.W., McPherson, B.D., & Kenyon, G. (1978). *Sport and social systems.* Reading, MA: Addison-Wesley.

Lutman, M.E. (1991). Degradations in frequency and temporal resolution with age and their impact on speech identification. *Acta Oto-Laryngologica, Supplement, 476*, 120–126.

Lyons, J., Fontaine, R., & Elliott, D. (1997). I lost it in the lights: The effects of predictable and variable intermittent vision on unimanual catching. *Journal of Motor Behavior, 29*(2), 113–118.

Maehr, M.L. (1984). Meaning and motivation. In R. Ames and C. Ames (Eds.), *Research on motivation in education* (Vol. 1, pp. 115–144). New York: Academic Press.

Malina, R.M. (1978). Growth of muscle tissue and muscle mass. In F. Falkner & J.M. Tanner (Eds.), *Human growth: Vol. 2. Postnatal growth* (pp. 273–294). New York: Plenum Press.

Malina, R.M., Beunen, G.P., Claessens, A.L., Lefevre, J., Vanden Eynde, B., Renson, R., Vanreusel, B., & Simons, J. (1995). Fatness and fitness of girls 7 to 17 years. *Obesity Research, 3*, 221–231.

Malina, R.M., & Bouchard, C. (1991). *Growth, maturation, and physical activity.* Champaign, IL: Human Kinetics.

Malina, R.M., Bouchard, C., & Bar-Or, O. (2004). *Growth, maturation, and physical activity* (2nd ed.). Champaign, IL: Human Kinetics.

Maloney, S.K., Fallon, B., & Wittenberg, C.K. (1984). *Aging and health promotion: Market research for public education, executive summary* (Contract No. 282-83-0105). Washington, DC: Public Health Service, Office of Disease Prevention and Health Promotion.

Marcon, R., & Freeman, G. (1999). Linking gender-related toy preferences to social structure: Changes in children's letters to Santa since 1978. *Journal of Psychological Practice, 2,* 1–10.

Marques-Bruna, P., & Grimshaw, P.N. (1997). 3-Dimensional kinematics of overarm throwing action of children age 15 to 30 months. *Perceptual and Motor Skills, 84,* 1267–1283.

Marshall, W.A., & Tanner, J.M. (1969). Variations in pattern of pubertal changes in girls. *Archives of Disease in Childhood, 44,* 291–303.

Marshall, W.A., & Tanner, J.M. (1970). Variations in the pattern of pubertal changes in boys. *Archives of Disease in Childhood, 45,* 13–23.

Martorell, R., Malina, R.M., Castillo, R.O., Mendoza, F.S., & Pawson, I.G. (1988). Body proportions in three ethnic groups: Children and youth 2–17 years in NHANES II and HHANES. *Human Biology, 60,* 205–222.

McAuley, E. (1994). Physical activity and psychosocial outcomes. In C. Bouchard and R. Shephard (Eds.), *Physical activity, fitness, and health: International proceeding and consensus statement* (pp. 551–568). Champaign, IL: Human Kinetics.

McBride-Chang, C., & Jacklin, C. (1993). Early play arousal, sex-typed play and activity level as precursors to later rough-and-tumble play. *Early Education and Development, 4,* 99–108.

McCaskill, C.L., & Wellman, B.L. (1938). A study of common motor achievements at the preschool ages. *Child Development, 9,* 141–150.

McClenaghan, B.A., & Gallahue, D.L. (1978). *Fundamental movement: A developmental and remedial approach.* Philadelphia: W.B. Saunders.

McConnell, A., & Wade, G. (1990). Effects of lateral ball location, grade, and sex on catching. *Perceptual and Motor Skills, 70,* 59–66.

McDonnell, P.M. (1975). The development of visually guided reaching. *Perception and Psychophysics, 18,* 181–185.

McDonnell, P.M. (1979). Patterns of eye-hand coordination in the first year of life. *Canadian Journal of Psychology, 33,* 253–267.

McGraw, M.B. (1943). *The neuromuscular maturation of the human infant.* New York: Columbia University Press. (Reprinted by Hafner, 1963.)

McKenzie, B.E., & Bigelow, E. (1986). Detour behavior in young human infants. *British Journal of Developmental Psychology, 4,* 139–148.

McLeod, P., & Dienes, Z. (1993). Running to catch the ball. *Nature, 362,* 23.

McLeod, P., & Dienes, Z. (1996). Do fielders know where to go to catch the ball or only how to get there? *Journal of Experimental Psychology: Human Perception and Performance, 22*(3), 531–543.

McManus, A.M., Armstrong, N., & Williams, C.A. (1997). Effect of training on the aerobic power and anaerobic performance of prepubertal girls. *Acta Paediatrica, 86,* 456–459.

McMurdo, M.E., & Rennie, L. (1993). A controlled trial of exercise by residents of old people's homes. *Age and Ageing, 22,* 11–15.

McPherson, B.D., Marteniuk, R., Tihanyi, J., & Clark, W. (1980). The social system of age group swimmers: The perception of swimmers, parents, and coaches. *Canadian Journal of Applied Sciences, 5,* 143–145.

McPherson, B.D. (1978). The child in competitive sport: Influence of the social milieu. In R.A. Magill, M.J. Ash, & F.L. Smoll (Eds.), *Children in sport: A contemporary anthology* (pp. 219–249). Champaign, IL: Human Kinetics.

McPherson, B.D. (1983). *Aging as a social process: An introduction to individual and population aging.* Toronto: Butterworths.

McPherson, B.D. (1986). Sport, health, well-being and aging: Some conceptual and methodological issues and questions for sport scientists. In B. McPherson (Ed.), *Sport and aging* (pp. 3–23). Champaign, IL: Human Kinetics.

McPherson, S.L. (1999). Tactical differences in problem representations and solutions in collegiate varsity and beginner female tennis players. *Research Quarterly for Exercise and Sport, 70*(4), 369–384.

Meltzoff, A.N., & Borton, R.W. (1979). Intermodal matching by human neonates. *Nature, 282,* 403–404.

Meredith, M.D., & Welk, G.J. (1999). *Fitnessgram test administration manual* (2nd ed.). Champaign, IL: Human Kinetics.

Mero, A., Kauhanen, H., Peltola, E., Vuorimaa, T., & Komi, P.V. (1990). Physiological performance capacity in different prepubescent athletic groups. *Journal of Sports Medicine and Physical Fitness, 30,* 57–66.

Messick, J.A. (1991). Prelongitudinal screening of hypothesized developmental sequences for the overhead tennis serve in experienced tennis players 9–19 years of age. *Research Quarterly for Exercise and Sport, 62,* 249–256.

Messner, M., Duncan, M., & Jensen, K. (1993). Separating the men from the girls: The gendered language of televised sports. *Gender and Society, 7,* 121–137.

Michaels, C.F., & Oudejans, R.R.D. (1992). The optics and actions of catching fly balls: Zeroing out optical acceleration. *Ecological Psychology, 4,* 199–222.

Michel, G.F. (1983). Development of hand-use preference during infancy. In G. Young, S. Segalowitz, C.M. Carter, & S.E. Trehub (Eds.), *Manual specialization and the developing brain* (pp. 33–70). New York: Academic Press.

Michel, G.F. (1988). A neuropsychological perspective on infant sensorimotor development. In C. Rovee-Collier & L.P. Lipsitt (Eds.), *Advances in infancy research* (Vol. 5, pp. 1–37). Norwood, NJ: Ablex.

Michel, G.F., & Goodwin, R.A. (1979). Intrauterine birth position predicts newborn supine head position preferences. *Infant Behavior and Development, 2,* 29–38.

Michel, G.F., & Harkins, D.A. (1986). Postural and lateral asymmetries in the ontogeny of handedness during infancy. *Developmental Psychobiology, 19,* 247–258.

Micheli, L.J. (1984). Sport injuries in the young athlete: Questions and controversies. In L.J. Micheli (Ed.), *Pediatric and adolescent sports medicine* (pp. 1–9). Boston: Little, Brown.

Milani-Comparetti, A. (1981). The neurophysiologic and clinical implications of studies on fetal motor behavior. *Seminars in Perinatology, 5,* 183–189.

Milani-Comparetti, A., & Gidoni, E.A. (1967). Routine developmental examination in normal and retarded children. *Developmental Medicine and Child Neurology, 9,* 631–638.

Milne, C., Seefeldt, V., & Reuschlein, P. (1976). Relationship between grade, sex, race, and motor performance in young children. *Research Quarterly, 47,* 726–730.

Milner, A.D., & Goodale, M.A. (1995). *The visual brain in action.* New York: Oxford University Press.

Mirwald, R.L., & Bailey, D.A. (1986). *Maximal aerobic power: A longitudinal analysis.* London, Ontario: Sports Dynamics.

Mirwald, R.L., Bailey, D.A., Cameron, N., & Rasmussen, R.L. (1981). Longitudinal comparison of aerobic power in active and inactive boys aged 7.0 to 17.0 years. *Annals of Human Biology, 8,* 405–414.

Molen, H.H. (1973). *Problems on the evaluation of gait.* Unpublished doctoral dissertation, Free University, Amsterdam.

Moritani, T., & DeVries, H.A. (1980). Potential for gross muscle hypertrophy in older men. *Journal of Gerontology, 35,* 672–682.

Morris, G.S.D. (1976). Effects ball and background color have upon the catching performance of elementary school children. *Research Quarterly, 47,* 409–416.

Morrongiello, B.A. (1984). Auditory temporal pattern perception in 6- and 12-month-old infants. *Developmental Psychology, 20,* 441–448.

Morrongiello, B.A. (1986). Infants' perception of multiple-group auditory patterns. *Infant Behavior and Development, 9,* 307–320.

Morrongiello, B.A. (1988a). The development of auditory pattern perception skills. In C. Rovee-Collier & L.P. Lipsitt (Eds.), *Advances in infancy research* (Vol. 6, pp. 135–172). Norwood, NJ: Ablex.

Morrongiello, B.A. (1988b). Infants' localization of sounds along the horizontal axis: Estimates of minimum audible angle. *Developmental Psychology, 24*(1), 8–13.

Morrongiello, B.A., & Clifton, R.K. (1984). Effects of sound frequency on behavioral and cardiac orienting in newborn and five-month-old infants. *Journal of Experimental Child Psychology, 38,* 429–446.

Morrongiello, B.A., Fenwick, K.D., Hillier, L., & Chance, G. (1994). Sound localization in newborn human infants. *Developmental Psychology, 27*(8), 519–538.

Morrongiello, B.A., Trehub, S.E., Thorpe, L.A., & Capodilupo, S. (1985). Children's perceptions of melodies: The role of contour, frequency, and rate of presentation. *Journal of Experimental Child Psychology, 40,* 279–292.

Morrow, D., & Leirer, V. (1997). Aging, pilot performance, and expertise. In A.D. Fisk & W.A. Rogers (Eds.), *Handbook of human factors and the older adult* (pp. 199–230). San Diego: Academic Press.

Munns, K. (1981). Effects of exercise on the range of joint motion in elderly subjects. In E.L. Smith & R.C. Serfass (Eds.), *Exercise and aging: The scientific basis* (pp. 149–166). Hillside, NJ: Enslow.

Murphy, G.L., & Wright, J.C. (1984). Changes in conceptual structure with expertise: Differences between real-world experts and novices. *Journal of Experimental Psychology: Learning, Memory, and Cognition, 10,* 144–155.

Murray, M.P., Drought, A.B., & Kory, R.C. (1964). Walking patterns of normal men. *Journal of Bone and Joint Surgery, 46-A,* 335–360.

Murray, M.P., Gardner, G.M., Mollinger, L.A., & Sepic, S.B. (1980). Strength of isometric and isokinetic contractions. *Physical Therapy, 60,* 412–419.

Murray, M.P., Kory, R.C., Clarkson, B.H., & Sepic, S.B. (1966). Comparison of free and fast speed walking patterns of normal men. *American Journal of Physical Medicine, 45,* 8–24.

Murray, M.P., Kory, R.C., & Sepic, S.B. (1970). Walking patterns of normal women. *Archives of Physical Medicine and Rehabilitation, 51,* 637–650.

Nanez, J., & Yonas, A. (1994). Effects of luminance and texture motion on infant defensive reactions to optical collision. *Infant Behavior and Development, 17,* 165–174.

Napier, J. (1956). The prehensile movements of the human hand. *Journal of Bone and Joint Surgery, 38B,* 902–913.

Naus, M., & Shillman, R. (1976). Why a Y is not a V: A new look at the distinctive features of letters. *Journal of Experimental Psychology: Human Perception and Performance, 2,* 394–400.

Nelson, C.J. (1981). *Locomotor patterns of women over 57.* Unpublished master's thesis, Washington State University, Pullman.

Nevett, M.E., & French, K.E. (1997). The development of sport-specific planning, rehearsal, and updating of plans during defensive youth baseball game performance. *Research Quarterly for Exercise and Sport, 68*(3), 203–214.

Newell, K.M. (1986). Constraints on the development of coordination. In M.G. Wade & H.T.A. Whiting (Eds.), *Motor development in children: Aspects of coordination and control* (pp. 341–361). Amsterdam: Martin Nijhoff.

Newell, K.M., Scully, D.M., McDonald, P.V., & Baillargeon, R. (1989). Task constraints and infant grip configurations. *Developmental Psychobiology, 22,* 817–832.

Newell, K.M., Scully, D.M., Tenenbaum, F., & Hardiman, S. (1989). Body scale and the development of prehension. *Developmental Psychobiology, 22,* 11–13.

Nielsen, B., Nielsen, K., Hansen, M.B., & Asmussen, E. (1980). Training of "functional muscle strength" in girls 7–19 years old. In K. Berg & B.O. Eriksson (Eds.), *Children and exercise IX* (pp. 69–78). Baltimore: University Park Press.

Nilsson, L. (1990). *A child is born.* New York: Delacorte Press/Seymour Lawrence.

Nordlund, B. (1964). Directional audiometry. *Acta Oto-Laryngologica, 57,* 1–18.

Norris, A.H., Shock, N.W., Landowne, M., & Falzone, J.A. (1956). Pulmonary function studies: Age differences in lung volume and bellows function. *Journal of Gerontology, 11,* 379–387.

Northman, J.E., & Black, K.N. (1976). An examination of errors in children's visual and haptic-tactual memory for random forms. *Journal of Genetic Psychology, 129,* 161–165.

Nougier, V., Bard, C., Fleury, M., & Teasdale, N. (1998). Contribution of central and peripheral vision to the regulation of stance: Developmental aspects. *Journal of Experimental Child Psychology, 68,* 202–215.

Nyhan, N.L. (1990). Structural abnormalities. *Clinical Symposia, 42*(2), 1–32.

Oettingen, G. (1985). The influence of the kindergarten teacher on sex differences in behavior. *International Journal of Behavioral Development, 8,* 3–13.

Olson, P.L., & Sivak, M. (1986). Perception-response time to unexpected roadway hazards. *Human Factors, 28,* 91–96.

Orlick, T.D. (1973, January/February). Children's sport: A revolution is coming. *Canadian Association for Health, Physical Education, and Recreation Journal,* 12–14.

Orlick, T.D. (1974, November/December). The athletic drop-out: A high price for inefficiency. *Canadian Association for Health, Physical Education, and Recreation Journal,* 21–27.

Ornstein, P.A., & Naus, M.J. (1978). Rehearsal processes in children's memory. In P.A. Ornstein (Ed.), *Memory development in children* (pp. 69–99). Hillsdale, NJ: Erlbaum.

Oudejans, R.R.D., Michaels, C.F., Bakker, F.C., & Dolne, M.A. (1996). The relevance of action in perceiving affordances: Perception of catchableness of fly balls. *Journal of Experimental Psychology, 22*(4), 879–891.

Parfitt, A.M., & Kleerkoper, M. (1984). Diagnostic value of bone histomorphometry and comparison of histologic measurements and biochemical indices of bone remodeling. In C. Christiansen, C.D. Arnaud, & B.E.C. Nordin (Eds.), *Osteoporosis* (pp. 111–120). Copenhagen: Glostrupt Hospital.

Pargman, D. (1997). *Understanding sport behavior.* Upper Saddle River, NJ: Prentice Hall.

Parizkova, J. (1963). Impact of age, diet, and exercise on man's body composition. *Annals of the New York Academy of Sciences, 110,* 661–674.

Parizkova, J. (1968). Longitudinal study of the development of body composition and body build in boys of various physical activity. *Human Biology, 40,* 212–225.

Parizkova, J. (1972). Somatic development and body composition changes in adolescent boys differing in physical activity and fitness: A longitudinal study. *Anthropologie, 10,* 3–36.

Parizkova, J. (1973). Body composition and exercise during growth and development. In G.L. Rarick (Ed.), *Physical activity: Human growth and development* (pp. 97–124). New York: Academic Press.

Parizkova, J. (1977). *Body fat and physical fitness.* The Hague, the Netherlands: Martinus Nijhoff B.V.

Pate, R.R., & Shephard, R.J. (1989). Characteristics of physical fitness in youth. In C.V. Gisolfi & D.R. Lamb (Eds.), *Youth, exercise, and sport* (Vol. 2, pp. 1–46). Indianapolis: Benchmark Press.

Pate, R.R., & Ward, D.S. (1990). Endurance exercise trainability in children and youth. In W.A. Grana, J.A. Lombardo, B.J. Sharkey, & J.A. Stone (Eds.), *Advances in sports medicine and fitness* (Vol. 3, pp. 37–55). Chicago: Year Book Medical.

Patrick, H., Ryan, A.M., Alfeld-Liro, C., Fredricks, J., Hruda, L., & Eccles, J. (1999). Adolescents' commitment to developing talent: The role of peers in continuing motivation for sports and the arts. *Journal of Youth and Adolescence, 28,* 741–763.

Patriksson, G. (1981). Socialization to sports involvement. *Scandinavian Journal of Sports Sciences, 3,* 27–32.

Payne, V.G. (1982). Simultaneous investigation of effects of distance of projection and object size on object reception by children in grade 1. *Perceptual and Motor Skills, 54,* 1183–1187.

Payne, V.G., & Koslow, R. (1981). Effects of varying ball diameters on catching ability of young children. *Perceptual and Motor Skills, 53,* 739–744.

Payne, V.G., & Morrow, J.R. (1993). Exercise and $\dot{V}O_2$max in children: A meta-analysis. *Research Quarterly for Exercise and Sport, 64,* 305–131.

Peiper, A. (1963). *Cerebral function in infancy and childhood.* New York: Consultants Bureau.

Pennell, G. (1999). Doing gender with Santa: Gender-typing in children's toy preferences. *Dissertation Abstracts International, 59-8*(B), 4541.

Perlmutter, M., & Nyquist, L. (1990). Relationships between self-reported physical and mental health and intelligence performance across adulthood. *Journal of Gerontology: Psychological Sciences, 45,* P145–P155.

Perrin, P.P., Jeandel, C., Perrin, C.A., & Bene, M.C. (1997). Influence of visual control, conduction, and central integration on static and dynamic balance in healthy older adults. *Gerontology, 43,* 223–231.

Pew, R.W., & Rupp, G. (1971). Two quantitative measures of skill development. *Journal of Experimental Psychology, 90,* 1–7.

Pfeiffer, R., & Francis, R.S. (1986). Effects of strength training on muscle development in prepubescent, pubescent, and postpubescent males. *The Physician and Sportsmedicine, 14,* 134–143.

Phillips, M., Bookwalter, C., Denman, C., McAuley, J., Sherwin, H., Summers, D., & Yeakel, H. (1955). Analysis of results from the Kraus-Weber test of minimum muscular fitness in children. *Research Quarterly, 26,* 314–323.

Piaget, J. (1952). *The origins of intelligence in children.* New York: International Universities Press.

Pick, A.D. (Ed.). (1979). *Perception and its development: A tribute to Eleanor J. Gibson.* Hillsdale, NJ: Erlbaum.

Pick, H.L. (1989). Motor development: The control of action. *Developmental Psychology, 25,* 867–870.

Piek, J.P. (2001). Is a quantitative approach useful in the comparison of spontaneous movements in full term and preterm infants? *Human Movement Science, 20,* 717–736.

Piek, J.P., & Gasson, N. (1999). Spontaneous kicking in full term and preterm infants: Are there leg asymmetries? *Human Movement Science, 18,* 377–395.

Piek, J.P., Gasson, N., Barrett, N., & Case, I. (2002). Limb and gender differences in the development of coordination in early infancy. *Human Movement Science, 21,* 621–639.

Pollock, M.L. (1974). Physiological characteristics of older champion track athletes. *Research Quarterly, 45,* 363–373.

Pomerance, A. (1965). Pathology of the heart with and without failure in the aged. *British Heart Journal, 27,* 697–710.

Ponds, R.W., Brouwer, W.H., & Van Wolffelaar, P.C. (1988). Age differences in divided attention in a simulated driving task. *Journal of Gerontology: Psychological Sciences, 43,* P151–P156.

Pope, M.J. (1984). *Visual proprioception in infant postural development.* Unpublished doctoral dissertation, University of Southampton, Highfield, Southampton, United Kingdom.

Posner, J.D., Gorman, K.M., Klein, H.S., & Woldow, A. (1986). Exercise capacity in the elderly. *American Journal of Cardiology, 57,* 52C–58C.

Power, T.G. (1985). Mother- and father-infant play: A developmental analysis. *Child Development, 56,* 1514–1524.

Power, T.G., & Parke, R.D. (1983). Patterns of mother and father play with their 8-month-old infant: A multiple analyses approach. *Infant Behavior and Development, 6,* 453–459.

Power, T.G., & Parke, R.D. (1986). Patterns of early socialization: Mother- and father-infant interactions in the home. *International Journal of Behavioral Development, 9,* 331–341.

Prader, A., Tanner, J.M., & von Harnack, G.A. (1963). Catch-up growth following illness or starvation: An example of developmental canalization in man. *Journal of Pediatrics, 62,* 646–659.

Prohaska, T.R., Leventhal, E.A., Leventhal, H., & Keller, M.L. (1985). Health practices and illness cognition in young, middle aged, and elderly adults. *Journal of Gerontology, 40,* 569–578.

Pruitt, L.A., Jackson, R.D., Bartels, R.L., & Lehnhard, H.J. (1992). Weight-training effects on bone mineral density in early postmenopausal women. *Journal of Bone and Mineral Research, 7,* 179–185.

Pryde, K.M., Roy, E.A., & Campbell, K. (1998). Prehension in children and adults: The effects of size. *Human Movement Science, 17*(6), 743–752.

Purdue News. (2000). Researchers look at brain and behavior development in infants. August. www.purdue.edu/UNS/html4ever/0007. Corbetta.babybrain.html (accessed September 16, 2004).

Raag, T. (1999). Influences of social expectations of gender, gender stereotypes, and situational constraints on children's toy choices. *Sex Roles, 41*(11/12), 809–831.

Raag, T., & Rackliff, C.L. (1998). Preschoolers' awareness of social expectations of gender: Relationships to toy choices. *Sex Roles, 38*(9/10), 685–700.

Rabbitt, P. (1965). An age decrement in the ability to ignore irrelevant information. *Journal of Gerontology, 20,* 233–238.

Ramsay, D.S. (1980). Onset of unimanual handedness in infants. *Infant Behavior and Development, 3,* 377–386.

Ramsay, D.S., Campos, J.J., & Fenson, L. (1979). Onset of bimanual handedness in infants. *Infant Behavior and Development, 2,* 69–76.

Ramsay, D.S. (1985). Infants' block banging at midline: Evidence for Gesell's principal of "reciprocal interweaving" in development. *British Journal of Developmental Psychology, 3,* 335–343.

Ramsay, D.S., & Willis, M.P. (1984). Organization and lateralization of reaching in infants: An extension of Bresson et al. *Neuropsychologia, 22,* 639–641.

Ramsay, J.A., Blimkie, C.J.R., Smith, K., Garner, S., MacDougall, J.D., & Sale, D.G. (1990). Strength training effects in prepubescent boys. *Medicine and Science in Sports and Exercise, 22,* 605–614.

Rarick, G.L., & Smoll, F.L. (1967). Stability of growth in strength and motor performance from childhood to adolescence. *Human Biology, 39,* 295–306.

Rasmussen, R.L., Faulkner, R.A., Mirwald, R.L., & Bailey, D.A. (1990). A longitudinal analysis of structure/function related variables in

10–16 year old boys. In G. Beunen, J. Ghesquiere, T. Reybrouck, & A.L. Claesseus (Eds.), *Children and exercise* (pp. 27–33). Stuttgart: Ferdinand Enke Verlag.

Reaburn, P.R.J., & Mackinnon, L.T. (1990). Blood lactate response in older swimmers during active and passive recovery following maximal sprint swimming. *European Journal of Applied Physiology, 61*, 246–250.

Reaven, P.D., Barrett-Connor, E., & Edelstein, S. (1991). Relation between leisure-time physical activity and blood pressure in older women. *Circulation, 83*, 559–565.

Rians, C.B., Weltman, A., Cahill, B.R., Janney, C.A., Tippett, S.R., & Katch, F.I. (1987). Strength training for prepubescent males: Is it safe? *American Journal of Sports Medicine, 15*, 483–489.

Rikli, R.E., & Busch, S. (1986). Motor performance of women as a function of age and physical activity level. *Journal of Gerontology, 41*, 645–649.

Rikli, R.E., & Edwards, D.J. (1991). Effects of a 3 year exercise program on motor function and cognitive speed in older women. *Research Quarterly for Exercise and Sport, 62*(1), 61–67.

Rikli, R.E., & Jones, C.J. (1999). Functional fitness normative scores for community-residing older adults, ages 60–94. *Journal of Aging and Physical Activity, 7*, 162–181.

Risser, W.L., & Preston, D. (1989). Incidence and causes of musculoskeletal injuries in adolescents training with weights. *Pediatric Exercise Science, 1*, 84 (abstract).

Roach, K.E., & Miles, T.P. (1991). Normal hip and knee active range of motion: The relationship to age. *Physical Therapy, 70*, 656–665.

Roberton, M.A. (1977). Stability of stage categorizations across trials: Implications for the "stage theory" of overarm throw development. *Journal of Human Movement Studies, 3*, 49–59.

Roberton, M.A. (1978a). Longitudinal evidence for developmental stages in the forceful overarm throw. *Journal of Human Movement Studies, 4*, 167–175.

Roberton, M.A. (1978b). Stages in motor development. In M.V. Ridenour (Ed.), *Motor development: Issues and applications* (pp. 63–81). Princeton, NJ: Princeton Book.

Roberton, M.A. (1984). Changing motor patterns during childhood. In J.R. Thomas (Ed.), *Motor development during childhood and adolescence* (pp. 48–90). Minneapolis: Burgess.

Roberton, M.A. (1988). The weaver's loom: A developmental metaphor. In J.E. Clark & J.H. Humphrey (Eds.), *Advances in motor development research* (Vol. 2, pp. 129–141). New York: AMS Press.

Roberton, M.A. (1989). Motor development: Recognizing our roots, charting our future. *Quest, 41*, 213–223.

Roberton, M.A., & DiRocco, P. (1981). Validating a motor skill sequence for mentally retarded children. *American Corrective Therapy Journal, 35*, 148–154.

Roberton, M.A., & Halverson, L.E. (1984). *Developing children: Their changing movement*. Philadelphia: Lea & Febiger.

Roberton, M.A., & Halverson, L.E. (1988). The development of locomotor coordination: Longitudinal change and invariance. *Journal of Motor Behavior, 20*, 197–241.

Roberton, M.A., & Konczak, J. (2001). Predicting children's overarm throw ball velocities from their developmental levels in throwing. *Research Quarterly for Exercise and Sport, 72*, 91–103.

Roberton, M.A., & Langendorfer, S. (1980). Testing motor development sequences across 9–14 years. In D. Nadeau, W. Halliwell, K. Newell, & G. Roberts (Eds.), *Psychology of motor behavior and sport—1979* (pp. 269–279). Champaign, IL: Human Kinetics.

Roberts, S.B., Savage, J., Coward, W.A., Chew, B., & Lucas, A. (1988). Energy expenditure and intake in infants born to lean and overweight mothers. *New England Journal of Medicine, 318*, 461–466.

Rockwell, J.C., Sorensen, A.M., Baker, S., Leahey, D., Stock, J.L., Michaels, J., & Baran, D.T. (1990). Weight training decreases vertebral bone density in premenopausal women: A prospective study. *Journal of Clinical Endocrinology and Metabolism, 71*, 988–992.

Rosenbaum, M., & Leibel, R.L. (1998). The physiology of body weight regulation: Relevance to the etiology of obesity in children. *Pediatrics, 101*(3S), 525–539.

Rosenhall, V., & Rubin, W. (1975). Degenerative changes in the human sensory epithelia. *Acta Oto-Laryngologica, 79*, 67–81.

Ross, J.G., Pate, R.R., Delpy, L.A., Gold, R.S., & Svilar, M. (1987). New health-related fitness norms. *Journal of Physical Education, Recreation and Dance, 58*, 66–70.

Rotstein, A., Dotan, R., Bar-Or, O., & Tenenbaum, G. (1986). Effect of training on anaerobic threshold, maximal power, and anaerobic performance of preadolescent boys. *International Journal of Sports Medicine, 7*, 281–286.

Rowland, T.W. (1989a). Oxygen uptake and endurance fitness in children: A developmental perspective. *Pediatric Exercise Science, 1*, 313–328.

Rowland, T.W. (1989b). On trainability and heart rates. *Pediatric Exercise Science, 1*, 187–188.

Rowland, T.W. (1996). *Developmental exercise physiology*. Champaign, IL: Human Kinetics.

Roy, E.A., Winchester, T., Weir, P., & Black, S. (1993). Age differences in the control of visually aimed movements. *Journal of Human Movement Studies, 24*, 71–81.

Rudel, R., & Teuber, H. (1971). Pattern recognition within and across sensory modalities in normal and brain injured children. *Neuropsychologia, 9*, 389–400.

Rudloff, L.M., & Feldmann, E. (1999). Childhood obesity: Addressing the issue. *Journal of the American Osteopathic Association, 99*(4), S1–S6.

Rudman, W. (1986). Life course socioeconomic transitions and sport involvement: A theory of restricted opportunity. In B. McPherson (Ed.), *Sport and aging* (pp. 25–35). Champaign, IL: Human Kinetics.

Ruff, H.A. (1984). Infants' manipulative exploration of objects: Effects of age and objects' characteristics. *Developmental Psychology, 29*, 9–20.

Ruff, H.A., & Halton, A. (1978). Is there directed reaching in the human neonate? *Developmental Psychology, 4*, 425–426.

Rutenfranz, J. (1986). Longitudinal approach to assessing maximal aerobic power during growth: The European experience. *Medicine and Science in Sports and Exercise, 15*, 486–490.

Sadres, E., Eliakim, A., Constantini, N., Lidor, R., & Falk, B. (2001). The effect of long-term resistance training on anthropometric measures, muscle strength, and self-concept in pre-pubertal boys. *Pediatric Exercise Science, 13*, 357–372.

Sady, S.P. (1986). Cardiorespiratory exercise in children. In F. Katch & P.F. Freedson (Eds.), *Clinics in sports medicine* (pp. 493–513). Philadelphia: Saunders.

Safar, M. (1990). Aging and its effects on the cardiovascular system. *Drugs, 39* (Supplement 1), 1–18.

Sale, D.G. (1989). Strength training in children. In G.V. Gisolfi & D.R. Lamb (Eds.), *Perspectives in exercise science and sports medicine. Vol 2: Youth, exercise and sport* (pp. 165–222). Indianapolis: Benchmark Press.

Salkind, N.J. (1981). *Theories of human development*. New York: D. Van Nostrand.

Salthouse, T.A. (1984). Effects of age and skill in typing. *Journal of Experimental Psychology, 113*, 343–371.

Saltin, B., & Grimby, G. (1968). Physiological analysis of middle-aged and old former athletes: Comparison with still active athletes of the same ages. *Circulation, 38*, 1104–1115.

Sapp, M., & Haubenstricker, J. (1978). *Motivation for joining and reasons for not continuing in youth sport programs in Michigan.* Paper presented at the American Alliance for Health, Physical Education, Recreation and Dance, Kansas City, MO.

Sasaki, J., Shindo, M., Tanaka, H., Ando, M., & Arakawa, K. (1987). A long-term aerobic exercise program decreases the obesity index and increases the high density lipoprotein cholesterol concentration in obese children. *International Journal of Obesity, 11,* 339–345.

Scanlan, T.K. (1988). Social evaluation and the competition process: A developmental perspective. In F.L. Smoll, R.A. Magill, & M.J. Ash (Eds.), *Children in sport* (3rd ed., pp. 135–148). Champaign, IL: Human Kinetics.

Scanlan, T.K., & Lewthwaite, R. (1986). Social psychological aspects of competition for male youth sport participants: IV. Predictors of enjoyment. *Journal of Sport Psychology, 8,* 25–35.

Scanlan, T.K., Stein, G.L., & Ravizza, K. (1988). An in-depth study of former elite figure skaters: II. Sources of enjoyment. *Journal of Sport and Exercise Psychology, 11,* 65–83.

Schellenberger, B. (1981). The significance of social relations in sport activity. *International Review of Sport Sociology, 16,* 69–77.

Schmidt, R., & Lee, T. (1999). *Motor control and learning: A behavioral emphasis* (3rd ed.). Champaign, IL: Human Kinetics.

Schmidt, R., & Wrisberg, C. (2000). *Motor learning and performance* (2nd ed.). Champaign, IL: Human Kinetics.

Schmuckler, M.A. (1997). Children's postural sway in response to low- and high-frequency visual information for oscillation. *Journal of Experimental Psychology: Human Perception and Performance, 23*(2), 528–545.

Schwanda, N.A. (1978). *A biomechanical study of the walking gait of active and inactive middle-age and elderly men.* Unpublished doctoral dissertation, Springfield College, Springfield, MA.

Schwartz, R.S., Shuman, W.P., Bradbury, V.L., Cain, K.C., Fellingham, G.W., Beard, J.C., Kahn, S.E., Stratton, J.R., Cerqueira, M.D., & Abrass, I.B. (1990). Body fat distribution in healthy young and older men. *Journal of Gerontology: Medical Sciences, 45,* M181–M185.

Schwartz, R.S., Shuman, W.P., Larson, V., Cain, K.C., Fellingham, G.W., Beard, J.C., Kahn, S.E., Stratton, J.R., Cerqueira, M.D., & Abrass, I.B. (1991). The effect of intensive endurance exercise training on body fat distribution in young and older men. *Metabolism, 40,* 545–551.

Seefeldt, V., Reuschlein, S., & Vogel, P. (1972). *Sequencing motor skills within the physical education curriculum.* Paper presented at the American Association for Health, Physical Education, and Recreation, Houston, TX.

Seils, L.G. (1951). The relationship between measures of physical growth and gross motor performance of primary grade school children. *Research Quarterly, 22,* 244–260.

Servedio, F.J., Barels, R.L., Hamlin, R.L., Teske, D., Shaffer, T., & Servedio, A. (1985). The effects of weight training using Olympic style lifts on various physiological variables in prepubescent boys. *Medicine and Science in Sports and Exercise, 17,* 288 (abstract).

Sewall, L., & Micheli, L.J. (1986). Strength training for children. *Journal of Pediatric Orthopedics, 6,* 143–146.

Sheldon, J.H. (1963). The effect of age on the control of sway. *Gerontologia Clinica, 5,* 129–138.

Shephard, R.J. (1978a). *IBP Human Adaptability Project Synthesis: Vol. 4. Human physiological work capacity.* New York: Cambridge University Press.

Shephard, R.J. (1978b). *Physical activity and aging.* Chicago: Year Book Medical.

Shephard, R.J. (1981). Cardiovascular limitations in the aged. In E.L. Smith & R.C. Serfass (Eds.), *Exercise and aging: The scientific basis* (pp. 19–29). Hillsdale, NJ: Enslow.

Shephard, R.J. (1982). *Physical activity and growth.* Chicago: Year Book Medical.

Shephard, R.J. (1987). *Physical activity and aging.* Rockville, MD: Aspen Publishers.

Shephard, R.J. (1992). Effectiveness of training programs for prepubescent children. *Sports Medicine, 13,* 194–213.

Shephard, R.J. (1993). Aging, respiratory function, and exercise. *Journal of Aging and Physical Activity, 1,* 59–83.

Shephard, R.J., & Kavanagh, T. (1978). The effects of training on the aging process. *The Physician and Sportsmedicine, 6,* 33–40.

Shirley, M.M. (1963). The motor sequence. In D. Wayne (Ed.), *Readings in child psychology.* Englewood Cliffs, NJ: Prentice Hall.

Shock, N.W., & Norris, A.H. (1970). Neuromuscular coordination as a factor in age changes in muscular exercise. In D. Brunner & E. Jokl (Eds.), *Physical activity and aging.* Baltimore: University Park Press.

Shuleva, K.M., Hunter, G.R., Hester, D.J., & Dunaway, D.L. (1990). Exercise oxygen uptake in 3- through 6-year-old children. *Pediatric Exercise Science, 2,* 130–139.

Shumway-Cook, A., & Woollacott, M. (1985). The growth of stability: Postural control from a developmental perspective. *Journal of Motor Behavior, 17,* 131–147.

Sibley, B.A., & Etnier, J.L. (2003). The relationship between physical activity and cognition in children: A meta-analysis. *Pediatric Exercise Science, 15,* 243–256.

Siegel, J.A., Camaione, D.N., & Manfredi, T.G. (1989). The effects of upper body resistance training on pre-pubescent children. *Pediatric Exercise Science, 1,* 145–154.

Siegler, R.S., & Jenkins, E.A. (1989). *How children discover new strategies.* Hillsdale, NJ: Erlbaum.

Simons, J., Beunen, G.P., Renson, R., Claessens, A.L.M., Vanreusel, B., & Lefevre, J.A.V. (1990). *Growth and fitness of Flemish girls: The Leuven growth study.* Champaign, IL: Human Kinetics.

Simons-Morton, B.G., Baranowski, T., O'Hara, N.M., Parcel, G.S., Huang, I.W., & Wilson, B. (1990). Children's frequency of participation in moderate to vigorous physical activities. *Research Quarterly for Exercise and Sport, 61,* 307–314.

Sinclair, C. (1971). Dominance pattern of young children, a follow-up study. *Perceptual and Motor Skills, 32,* 142.

Sinclair, C.B. (1973). *Movement of the young child: Ages two to six.* Columbus, OH: Merrill.

Singleton, W.T. (1955). *Age and performance timing on simple skills: Old age and the modern world* (Report of the Third Congress of the International Association of Gerontology). London: E. & S. Livingstone.

Sipila, S., & Suominen, H. (1995). Effects of strength and endurance training on thigh and leg muscle mass and composition in elderly women. *Journal of Applied Physiology, 78,* 334–340.

Skrobak-Kaczynski, J., & Andersen, K.L. (1975). The effect of a high level of habitual physical activity in the regulation of fatness during aging. *International Archives of Occupational and Environmental Health, 36,* 41–46.

Slater, A., Mattock, A., & Brown, E. (1990). Size constancy at birth: Newborn infants' responses to retinal and real size. *Journal of Experimental Child Psychology, 49*(2), 314–322.

Smith, A.B. (1985). Teacher modeling and sex-types play preferences. *New Zealand Journal of Educational Studies, 20,* 39–47.

Smith, D.B., Johnson, G.O., Stout, J.R., Housh, T.J., Housh, D.J., & Evetovich, T.K. (1997). Validity of near-infrared interactance for estimating relative body fat in female high school gymnasts. *International Journal of Sports Medicine, 18,* 531–537.

Smith, E.L. (1982). Exercise for the prevention of osteoporosis: A review. *The Physician and Sportsmedicine, 3,* 72–80.

Smith, E.L., Sempos, C.T., & Purvis, R.W. (1981). Bone mass and strength decline with age. In E.L. Smith & R.C. Serfass (Eds.), *Exercise and aging: The scientific basis* (pp. 59–87). Hillside, NJ: Enslow.

Smith, E.L., & Serfass, R.C. (Eds.). (1981). *Exercise and aging: The scientific basis.* Hillside, NJ: Enslow.

Smith, M.D. (1979). Getting involved in sport: Sex differences. *International Review of Sport Sociology, 14,* 93–99.

Smith, R.E., Smoll, F.L., & Curtis, B. (1979). Coach effectiveness training: A cognitive-behavioral approach to enhancing relationship skills in youth sport coaches. *Journal of Sport Psychology, 1,* 59–75.

Smoll, F.L., & Smith, R.E. (1989). Leadership behaviors in sport: A theoretical model and research paradigm. *Journal of Applied Social Psychology, 19,* 1522–1551.

Smoll, F.L., & Smith, R.E. (2001). Conducting sport psychology training programs for coaches: Cognitive-behavioral principles and techniques. In J.M. Williams (Ed.), *Applied sport psychology* (4th ed., pp. 378–400).

Snyder, E.E., & Spreitzer, E. (1973). Family influences and involvement in sports. *Research Quarterly, 44,* 249–255.

Snyder, E.E., & Spreitzer, E. (1976). Correlates of sport participation among adolescent girls. *Research Quarterly, 47,* 804–809.

Snyder, E.E., & Spreitzer, E. (1978). Socialization comparisons of adolescent female athletes and musicians. *Research Quarterly, 79,* 342–350.

Sonstroem, R. (1997). Physical activity and self-esteem. In W. Morgan (Ed.), *Physical activity and mental health.* Series in health psychology and behavioral medicine (pp. 127–143). Washington, DC: Taylor and Francis.

Spetner, N.B., & Olsho, L.W. (1990). Auditory frequency resolution in human infancy. *Child Development, 61,* 632–652.

Spilich, G.J., Vesonder, G.T., Chiesi, H.L., & Voss, J.F. (1979). Text processing of individuals with high and low domain knowledge. *Journal of Verbal Learning and Verbal Behavior, 18,* 275–290.

Spirduso, W.W. (1975). Reaction and movement time as a function of age and physical activity level. *Journal of Gerontology, 30,* 435–440.

Spirduso, W.W. (1980). Physical fitness and psychomotor speed: A review. *Journal of Gerontology, 35,* 850–865.

Spirduso, W.W. (1995). *Physical dimensions of aging.* Champaign, IL: Human Kinetics.

Spirduso, W.W., Gilliam, P., & Wilcox, R.E. (1984). Speed of movement initiation performance predicts differences in [3H] spiroperidol receptor binding in normal rats. *Psychopharmacology, 83,* 205–209.

Spreitzer, E., & Snyder, E. (1983). Correlates of participation in adult recreational sports. *Journal of Leisure Research, 15,* 28–38.

Sprynarova, S., & Reisenauer, R. (1978). Body dimensions and physiological indications of physical fitness during adolescence. In R.J. Shephard & H. Lavallee (Eds.), *Physical fitness assessment* (pp. 32–37). Springfield, IL: Charles C Thomas.

Stadulis, R.I. (1971). *Coincidence-anticipation behavior of children.* Unpublished doctoral dissertation, Columbia University, New York.

Stamford, B.A. (1973). Effects of chronic institutionalization on the physical working capacity and trainability of geriatric men. *Journal of Gerontology, 28,* 441–446.

Stamford, B.A. (1988). Exercise and the elderly. In K.B. Pandolf (Ed.), *Exercise and sport sciences reviews* (Vol. 16, pp. 341–379). New York: Macmillan.

Steben, R.E., & Steben, A.H. (1981). The validity of the strength shortening cycle in selected jumping events. *Journal of Sports Medicine and Physical Fitness, 21,* 1–7.

Stein, B.E., Meredith, M.A., & Wallace, M.T. (1994). Development and neural basis of multisensory integration. In D.J. Lewkowicz & R. Lickliter (Eds.), *The development of intersensory perception: Comparative perspectives* (pp. 81–105). Hillsdale, NJ: Erlbaum.

Sterritt, G., Martin, V., & Rudnick, M. (1971). Auditory-visual and temporal-spatial integration as determinants of test difficulty. *Psychonomic Science, 23,* 289–291.

Stine, E.L., Wingfield, A., & Poon, L.W. (1989). Speech comprehension and memory through adulthood: The roles of time and strategy. In L.W. Poon, D.S. Rubin, & B.A. Wilson (Eds.), *Everyday cognition in adulthood and later years* (pp. 195–221). Cambridge, UK: Cambridge University Press.

Stolz, H.R., & Stolz, L.M. (1951). *Somatic development of adolescent boys.* New York: Macmillan.

Stones, M.J., & Kozma, A. (1989). Age, exercise, and coding performance. *Psychology & Aging, 4,* 190–194.

Strohmeyer, H.S., Williams, K., & Schaub-George, D. (1991). Developmental sequences for catching a small ball: A prelongitudinal screening. *Research Quarterly for Exercise and Sport, 62,* 257–266.

Sutherland, D. (1997). The development of mature gait. *Gait and Posture, 6*(2), 162–170.

Sutherland, D.H., Olshen, R., Cooper, L., & Woo, S. (1980). The development of mature gait. *Journal of Bone and Joint Surgery, 62-A,* 336–353.

Sutherland, R., Pipe, M., Schick, K., Murray, J., & Gobbo, C. (2003). Knowing in advance: The impact of prior event information on memory and event knowledge. *Journal of Experimental Child Psychology, 84,* 244–263.

Swanson, R., & Benton, A.L. (1955). Some aspects of the genetic development of right-left discrimination. *Child Development, 26,* 123–133.

Szafran, J. (1951). Changes with age and with exclusion of vision in performance at an aiming task. *Quarterly Journal of Experimental Psychology, 3,* 111–118.

Tanner, J.M. (1962). *Growth at adolescence* (2nd ed.). Oxford: Blackwell Scientific.

Tanner, J.M. (1975). Growth and endocrinology of the adolescent. In L.I. Gardner (Ed.), *Endocrine and genetic disease of childhood and adolescence* (2nd ed., pp. 14–63). Philadelphia: Saunders.

Teeple, J.B. (1978). Physical growth and maturation. In M.F. Ridenour (Ed.), *Motor development: Issues and applications* (pp. 3–27). Princeton, NJ: Princeton Book.

Telama, R., Yang, X., Laakso, L., & Viikari, J. (1997). Physical activity in childhood and adolescence as predictor of physical activity in young adulthood. *American Journal of Preventive Medicine, 13,* 317–323.

Temple, I.G., Williams, H.G., & Bateman, N.J. (1979). A test battery to assess intrasensory and intersensory development of young children. *Perceptual and Motor Skills, 48,* 643–659.

Thelen, E. (1981). Kicking, rocking, and waving: Contextual analysis of rhythmical stereotypes in normal human infants. *Animal Behaviour, 29,* 3–11.

Thelen, E. (1983). Learning to walk is still an "old" problem: A reply to Zelazo. *Journal of Motor Behavior, 15,* 139–161.

Thelen, E. (1985). Developmental origins of motor coordination: Leg movements in human infants. *Developmental Psychobiology, 18,* 1–22.

Thelen, E. (1995). Motor development: A new synthesis. *American Psychologist, 50,* 79–95.

Thelen, E. (1998). Bernstein's legacy for motor development: How infants learn to reach. In M. Latash (Ed.), *Progress in motor control* (pp. 267–288). Champaign, IL: Human Kinetics.

Thelen, E., Bradshaw, G., & Ward, J.A. (1981). Spontaneous kicking in month-old infants: Manifestations of a human central locomotor program. *Behavioral and Neural Biology, 32,* 45–53.

Thelen, E., & Fisher, D.M. (1983). The organization of spontaneous leg movements in newborn infants. *Journal of Motor Behavior, 15,* 353–377.

Thelen, E., Kelso, J.A.S., & Fogel, A. (1987). Self-organizing systems and infant motor development. *Developmental Review, 7,* 37–65.

Thelen, E., Ridley-Johnson, R., & Fisher, D.M. (1983). Shifting patterns of bilateral coordination and lateral dominance in the leg movements of young infants. *Developmental Psychobiology, 16,* 29–46.

Thelen, E., & Ulrich, B.D. (1991). Hidden skills. *Monographs of the Society for Research in Child Development, 56* (Serial No. 233).

Thelen, E., Ulrich, B.D., & Jensen, J.L. (1989). The developmental origins of locomotion. In M.H. Woollacott & A. Shumway-Cook (Eds.), *Development of posture and gait across the life span* (pp. 25–47). Columbia, SC: University of South Carolina Press.

Thomas, J.R. (1984). *Motor development during childhood and adolescence.* Minneapolis, MN: Burgess.

Thomas, J.R., French, K.E., Thomas, K.T., & Gallagher, J.D. (1988). Children's knowledge development and sport performance. In F.L. Smoll, R.A. Magill, & M.J. Ash (Eds.), *Children in sport* (3rd ed., pp. 179–202). Champaign, IL: Human Kinetics.

Thomas, J.R., Gallagher, J.D., & Purvis, G.J. (1981). Reaction time and anticipation time: Effects of development. *Research Quarterly, 52,* 359–367.

Thomas, J.R., Thomas, K.T., & Gallagher, J.D. (1981). Children's processing of information in physical activity and sport. *Motor Skills: Theory into Practice Monographs, 3,* 1–8.

Timiras, M.L., & Brownstein, H. (1987). Prevalence of anemia and correlation of hemoglobin with age in a geriatric screening clinic population. *Journal of the American Geriatrics Society, 35,* 639–643.

Timiras, P.S. (1972). *Developmental physiology and aging.* New York: Macmillan.

Tolfrey, K., Campbell, I.G., & Batterham, A.M. (1998). Aerobic trainability of prepubertal boys and girls. *Pediatric Exercise Science, 10,* 248–263.

Trehub, S.E., Bull, D., & Thorpe, L.A. (1984). Infants' perception of melodies: The role of melodic contour. *Child Development, 55,* 821–830.

Tremblay, A., Despres, J.-P., & Bouchard, C. (1988). Alternation in body fat and fat distribution with exercise. In C. Bouchard & F.E. Johnston (Eds.), *Fat distribution during growth and later health outcomes.* New York: Liss.

Trevarthan, C. (1984). How control of movement develops. In H.T.A. Whiting (Ed.), *Human motor actions: Bernstein reassessed* (pp. 223–261). Amsterdam: North-Holland.

Trudeau, F., Laurencelle, L., Tremblay, J., Rajic, M., & Shephard, R.J. (1998). A long-term follow-up of participants in the Trois-Rivieres semi-longitudinal study of growth and development. *Pediatric Exercise Science, 10*(4), 366–377.

Tun, P.A., & Wingfield, A. (1993). Is speech special? Perception and recall of spoken language in complex environments. In J. Cerella, J. Rybash, W. Hover, & M.L. Commons (Eds.), *Adult information processing: Limits on loss* (pp. 425–457). San Diego: Academic Press.

Turner, J.M., Mead, J., & Wohl, M.E. (1968). Elasticity of human lungs in relation to age. *Journal of Applied Physiology, 35,* 664–671.

Turner, P., & Gervai, J. (1995). A multidimensional study of gender typing in preschool children and their parents: Personality, attitudes, preferences, behavior, and cultural differences. *Developmental Psychology, 31*(5), 759–779.

Turner, P., Gervai, J., & Hinde, R.A. (1993). Gender-typing in young children: Preferences, behaviour and cultural differences. *British Journal of Developmental Psychology, 11*(4), 323–342.

Ulrich, B.D., Thelen, E., & Niles, D. (1990). Perceptual determinants of action: Stair-climbing choices of infants and toddlers. In J.E. Clark & J.H. Humphrey (Eds.), *Advances in motor development research* (Vol. 3, pp. 1–15). New York: AMS Press.

U.S. Department of Health and Human Services, Centers for Disease Control and Prevention, National Center for Chronic Disease Prevention and Health Promotion (1996). *Physical activity and health: A report of the Surgeon General.* Atlanta: Author.

Unnithan, V.B. (1993). *Factors affecting submaximal running economy in children.* Unpublished doctoral dissertation, University of Glasgow, Glasgow, Scotland.

Vaccaro, P., & Mahon, A. (1987). Cardiorespiratory responses to endurance training in children. *Sports Medicine, 4,* 352–363.

Van der Fits, I.B.M., & Hadders-Algra, M. (1998). The development of postural response patterns during reaching in healthy infants. *Neuroscience and Biobehavioral Reviews, 22*(4), 521–525.

van der Kamp, J., Savelsbergh, G.J.P., & Davis, W.E. (1998). Body-scaled ratio as a control parameter for prehension in 5- to 9-year-old children. *Developmental Psychology, 33*(4), 351–361.

Van Duyne, H.J. (1973). Foundations of tactical perception in three to seven year olds. *Journal of the Association for the Study of Perception, 8,* 1–9.

Van Praagh, E., Fellmann, N., Bedu, M., Falgairette, G., & Coudert, J. (1990). Gender difference in the relationship of anaerobic power output to body composition in children. *Pediatric Exercise Science, 2,* 336–348.

van Rooij, J.C.G.M., & Plomp, R. (1992). Auditive and cognitive factors in speech perception by elderly listeners. III: Additional data and final discussion. *Journal of the Acoustical Society of America, 91,* 1028–1033.

Vercruyssen, M. (1997). Movement control and speed of behavior. In A.D. Fisk & W.A. Rogers (Eds.), *Handbook of human factors and the older adult* (pp. 55–86). San Diego: Academic Press.

Vereijken, B., & Thelen, E. (1997). Training infant treadmill stepping: The role of individual pattern stability. *Developmental Psychobiology, 30,* 89–102.

Victors, E. (1961). *A cinematographical analysis of catching behavior of a selected group of seven and nine year old boys.* Unpublished doctoral dissertation, University of Wisconsin, Madison.

von Hofsten, C. (1979). Development of visually directed reaching: The approach phase. *Journal of Human Movement Studies, 5,* 160–178.

von Hofsten, C. (1982). Eye–hand coordination in the newborn. *Developmental Psychology, 18,* 450–461.

von Hofsten, C. (1984). Developmental changes in the organization of pre-reaching movements. *Developmental Psychology, 3,* 378–388.

von Hofsten, C. (1990). Early development of grasping an object in space-time. In M.A. Goodale (Ed.), *Vision and action: The control of grasping* (pp. 65–79). Norwood, NJ: Ablex.

von Hofsten, C., Kellman, P., & Putaansuu, J. (1992). Young infants' sensitivity to motion parallax. *Infant Behavior and Development, 15*(2), 245–264.

von Hofsten, C., & Spelke, E.S. (1985). Object perception and object-directed reaching in infancy. *Journal of Experimental Psychology: General, 114*(2), 198–212.

Vrijens, J. (1978). Muscle strength development in the pre- and post-pubescent age. *Medicine and Sport, 11,* 152–158.

Wade, M.G. (1980). Coincidence-anticipation of young normal and handicapped children. *Journal of Motor Behavior, 12,* 103–112.

Walk, R.D. (1969). Two types of depth discrimination by the human infant. *Psychonomic Science, 14,* 253–254.

Walk, R.D., & Gibson, E.J. (1961). A comparative and analytical study of visual depth perception. *Psychological Monographs, 75*(519).

Wallace, C.S., Kilman, V.L., Withers, G.S., & Greenough, W.T. (1992). Increases in dendritic length in occipital cortex after 4 days of differential housing in weanling rats. *Behavioral & Neural Biology, 58*(1), 64–68.

Warren, R., & Wertheim, A.H. (1990). *Perception and control of self-motion.* Hillsdale, NJ: Erlbaum.

Warren, W.H. (1984). Perceiving affordances: Visual guidance of stair-climbing. *Journal of Experimental Psychology: Human Perception and Performance, 10,* 683–703.

Washington, R.L. (1989). Anaerobic threshold in children. *Pediatric Exercise Science, 1,* 244–256.

Wattam-Bell, J. (1996a). Visual motion processing in one-month-old infants: Preferential looking experiments. *Vision Research, 36*(11), 1671–1677.

Wattam-Bell, J. (1996b). Visual motion processing in one-month-old infants: Habituation experiments. *Vision Research, 36*(11), 1679–1685.

Weisner, T., Garnier, H., & Loucky, J. (1994). Domestic tasks, gender egalitarian values and children's gender typing in conventional and nonconventional families. *Sex Roles, 30*(1/2), 23–54.

Weiss, M.R., & Barber, H. (1996). Socialization influences of collegiate male athletes: A tale of two decades. *Sex Role, 33,* 129–140.

Weiss, M.R., & Ebbick, V. (1996). Self-esteem and perceptions of competence in youth sports: Theory, research and enhancement strategies. In O. Bar-Or (Ed.), *Encyclopedia of sports medicine: Vol. 6. The child and adolescent athlete* (pp. 3364–3382). Oxford, UK: Blackwell Scientific.

Weiss, M.R. (1993). Psychological effects of intensive sport participation on children and youth: Self-esteem and motivation. In B.R. Cahill & A.J. Pearl (Eds.), *Intensive participation in children's sports* (pp. 39–69). Champaign, IL: Human Kinetics.

Weiss, M.R., & Horn, T.S. (1990). The relation between children's accuracy estimates of their physical competence and achievement-related characteristics. *Research Quarterly for Exercise and Sport, 61,* 250–258.

Weiss, M.R., & Knoppers, A. (1982). The influence of socializing agents on female collegiate volleyball players. *Journal of Sport Psychology, 4,* 267–279.

Weiss, M.R., McAuley, E., Ebbeck, V., & Wiese, D.M. (1990). Self-esteem and causal attributions for children's physical and social competence in sport. *Journal of Sport and Exercise Psychology, 12,* 21–36.

Welford, A.T. (1977a). Causes of slowing of performance with age. *Interdisciplinary Topics in Gerontology, 11,* 23–51.

Welford, A.T. (1977b). Motor performance. In J.E. Birren & K.W. Schaie (Eds.), *Handbook of the psychology of aging* (pp. 450–496). New York: Van Nostrand Reinhold.

Welford, A.T. (1977c). Serial reaction times, continuity of task, single-channel effects, and age. In S. Dornic (Ed.), *Attention and performance VI* (pp. 79–97). Hillside, NJ: Erlbaum.

Welford, A.T. (1980). Motor skill and aging. In C.H. Nadeau, W.R. Halliwell, K.M. Newell, & G.C. Roberts (Eds.), *Psychology of motor behavior and sport—1979* (pp. 253–268). Champaign, IL: Human Kinetics.

Welford, A.T., Norris, A.H., & Shock, N.W. (1969). Speed and accuracy of movement and their changes with age. *Acta Psychologica, 30,* 3–15.

Weltman, A. (1989). Weight training in prepubertal children: Physiological benefit and potential damage. In O. Bar-Or (Ed.), *Biological issues* (Vol. 3, pp. 101–130). Champaign, IL: Human Kinetics.

Weltman, A., Janney, C., Rians, C.B., Strand, K., Berg, B., Tippitt, S., Wise, J., Cahill, B.R., & Katch, F.I. (1986). The effects of hydraulic resistance strength training in prepubertal males. *Medicine and Science in Sports and Exercise, 18,* 629–638.

Whitall, J. (1988a). The development of visual directed reaching: From description to explanation. In J.E. Clark & J.H. Humphrey (Eds.), *Advances in motor development research* (Vol. 2, pp. 143–163). New York: AMS Press.

Whitall, J. (1988b). *A developmental study of interlimb coordination in running and galloping.* Unpublished doctoral dissertation, University of Maryland, College Park.

Whitall, J., & Getchell, N. (1995). From walking to running: Using a dynamical systems approach to the development of locomotor skills. *Child Development, 66,* 1541–1553.

White, B.L., Castle, P., & Held, R. (1964). Observations on the development of visually directed reaching. *Child Development, 35,* 349–364.

Wickens, C.D. (1974). Temporal limits of human information processing: A developmental study. *Psychological Bulletin, 81,* 739–755.

Wickstrom, R.L. (1983). *Fundamental motor patterns* (3rd ed.). Philadelphia: Lea & Febiger.

Wickstrom, R.L. (1987). Observations on motor pattern development in skipping. In J.E. Clark & J.H. Humphrey (Eds.), *Advances in motor development research* (Vol. 1, pp. 49–60). New York: AMS Press.

Wiegand, R.L., & Ramella, R. (1983). The effect of practice and temporal location of knowledge of results on the motor performance of older adults. *Journal of Gerontology, 38,* 701–706.

Wigmore, S. (1996). Gender and sport: The last 5 years. *Sport Science Reviews, 5*(2), 53–71.

Wild, M. (1937). *The behavior pattern of throwing and some observations concerning its course of development in children.* Unpublished doctoral dissertation, University of Wisconsin, Madison.

Wild, M. (1938). The behavior pattern of throwing and some observations concerning its course of development in children. *Research Quarterly, 9,* 20–24.

Williams, H. (1968). *Effects of systematic variation of speed and direction of object flight and of age and skill classification on visuo-perceptual judgments of moving objects.* Unpublished doctoral dissertation, University of Wisconsin, Madison.

Williams, H. (1973). Perceptual-motor development in children. In C. Corbin (Ed.), *A textbook of motor development* (pp. 111–148). Dubuque, IA: Brown.

Williams, H. (1983). *Perceptual and motor development.* Englewood Cliffs, NJ: Prentice Hall.

Williams, H. (1986). The development of sensory-motor function in young children. In V. Seefeldt (Ed.), *Physical activity and well-being* (pp. 104–122). Reston, VA: American Alliance for Health, Physical Education, Recreation and Dance.

Williams, K., Goodman, M., & Green, R. (1985). Parent–child factors in gender role socialization in girls. *Journal of the American Academy of Child Psychiatry, 24,* 720–731.

Williams, K., Haywood, K., & VanSant, A. (1990). Movement characteristics of older adult throwers. In J.E. Clark & J.H. Humphrey (Eds.), *Advances in motor development research* (Vol. 3, pp. 29–44). New York: AMS Press.

Williams, K., Haywood, K., & VanSant, A. (1991). Throwing patterns of older adults: A follow-up investigation. *International Journal of Aging and Human Development, 33,* 279–294.

Williams, K., Haywood, K., & VanSant, A. (1993). Force and accuracy throws by older adult performers. *Journal of Aging and Physical Activity, 1,* 2–12.

Williams, K., Haywood, K., & VanSant, A. (1996). Force and accuracy throws by older adults: II. *Journal of Aging and Physical Activity, 4*(2), 194–202.

Williams, K., Haywood, K., & VanSant, A. (1998). Changes in throwing by older adults: A longitudinal investigation. *Research Quarterly for Exercise and Sport, 69*(1), 1–10.

Willoughby, D.S., & Pelsue, S.C. (1998). Muscle strength and qualitative myosin heavy chain isoform mRNA expression in the elderly after moderate- and high-intensity weight training. *Journal of Aging and Physical Activity, 6,* 327–339.

Wilmore, J.H. (1991). The aging of bones and muscle. In R.K. Kerlan (Ed.), *Sports medicine in the older adult* (pp. 231–244). Philadelphia: Saunders.

Winter, D.A. (1983). Biomechanical motor patterns in normal walking. *Journal of Motor Behavior, 15,* 302–330.

Winterhalter, C. (1974). *Age and sex trends in the development of selected balancing skills.* Unpublished master's thesis, University of Toledo, Toledo.

Witelson, S.F. (1987). Neurobiological aspects of language in children. *Child Development, 58,* 653–688.

Wolff, P.H., Michel, G.F., Ovrut, M., & Drake, C. (1990). Rate and timing precision of motor coordination in developmental dyslexia. *Developmental Psychology, 26,* 349–359.

Women's Sports Foundation (WSF). (2000). [Online]. Available: www.womenssportsfoundation.org.

Wood, J.M., & Abernethy, B. (1997). An assessment of the efficacy of sports vision training programs. *Optometry and Vision Science, 74,* 646–659.

Woollacott, M., Debu, B., & Mowatt, M. (1987). Neuromuscular control of posture in the infant and child. *Journal of Motor Behavior, 19,* 167–186.

Woollacott, M., Shumway-Cook, A.T., & Nashner, L.M. (1982). Postural reflexes and aging. In J.A. Mortimer (Ed.), *The aging motor system* (pp. 98–119). New York: Praeger.

Woollacott, M., Shumway-Cook, A.T., & Nashner, L.M. (1986). Aging and posture control: Changes in sensory organization and muscular coordination. *International Journal of Aging and Human Development, 23,* 97–114.

Woollacott, M.H. (1986). Gait and postural control in the aging adult. In W. Bles & T. Brandt (Eds.), *Disorders of posture and gait* (pp. 326–336). New York: Elsevier.

Woollacott, M.H., Shumway-Cook, A., & Williams, H. (1989). The development of posture and balance control in children. In M.H. Woollacott & A. Shumway-Cook (Eds.), *Development of posture and gait across the life span* (pp. 77–96). Columbia, SC: University of South Carolina Press.

Woollacott, M.H., & Sveistrup, H. (1994). The development of sensorimotor integration underlying posture control in infants during the transition to independent stance. In S.P. Swinnen, J. Massion, & H. Heuer (Eds.), *Interlimb coordination: Neural, dynamical and cognitive constraints* (pp. 371–389). San Diego: Academic Press.

Wright, C.E., & Wormald, R.P. (1992). Stereopsis and aging. *Eye, 6,* 473–476.

Yamaguchi, Y. (1984). A comparative study of adolescent socialization into sport: The case of Japan and Canada. *International Review for Sociology of Sport, 19*(1), 63–82.

Yarasheski, K., Zachwieja, J., & Bier, D. (1993). Acute effects of resistance training on muscle protein synthesis rate in young and elderly men and women. *American Journal of Physiology, 265,* E210–E214.

Yekta, A.A., Pickwell, L.D., & Jenkins, T.C.A. (1989). Binocular vision, age and symptoms. *Ophthalmic and Physiological Optics, 9,* 115–120.

Young, A., Stokes, M., & Crowe, M. (1985). The size and strength of the quadriceps muscles of old and young men. *Clinical Physiology, 5,* 145–154.

Zaichkowsky, L.D., Zaichkowsky, L.B., & Martinek, T.J. (1980). *Growth and development: The child and physical activity.* St. Louis: Mosby.

Zelazo, P.R. (1983). The development of walking: New findings and old assumptions. *Journal of Motor Behavior, 15,* 99–137.

Zelazo, P.R., Zelazo, N.A., & Kolb, S. (1972a). "Walking" in the newborn. *Science, 176,* 314–315.

Zelazo, P.R., Zelazo, N.A., & Kolb, S. (1972b). Newborn walking. *Science, 177,* 1058–1059.

Zimmerman, H.M. (1956). Characteristic likenesses and differences between skilled and non-skilled performance of the standing broad jump. *Research Quarterly, 27,* 352.

Zwiren, L.D. (1989). Anaerobic and aerobic capacities of children. *Pediatric Exercise Science, 1,* 31–44.

Index

Note: Page numbers followed by an italicized *f* or *t* refer to the figure or table on that page, respectively.

About the Authors

Kathleen M. Haywood, PhD, is professor and associate dean for graduate education at the University of Missouri at St. Louis, where she has taught courses in motor behavior and development, sport psychology, and biomechanics. She has served as secretary and treasurer and president of the North American Society for Psychology of Sport and Physical Activity and as chairperson of the Motor Development Academy of the American Alliance for Health, Physical Education, Recreation and Dance. She also is a recipient of the Alliance's Mabel Lee Award.

Dr. Haywood is also the coauthor of the first and second editions of *Archery: Steps to Success* and *Teaching Archery: Steps to Success*. She earned her PhD in motor behavior from the University of Illinois at Urbana-Champaign in 1976.

Nancy Getchell, PhD, an assistant professor at the University of Delaware, has been a contributor to the study of motor development for nearly 20 years. Previously, she was an assistant professor at the University of Missouri at St. Louis. She has taught courses in motor development, motor control and learning, biomechanics, research methods, and women in sport. She is a member of the North American Society for Psychology of Sport and Physical Activity, the International Society of Motor Control, and the American Alliance for Health, Physical Education, Recreation and Dance. She is currently the chair of the Motor Development Academy of the National Association for Sport and Physical Education. In 2001, Dr. Getchell was the recipient of the Lolas E. Halverson Young Investigators Award in motor development. She earned a PhD in kinesiology from the University of Wisconsin at Madison in 1996.

CD-ROM Instructions

Minimum System Requirements

Windows
- Windows® 95/98/NT 4.0/2000/ME/XP
- Macromedia Flash Player Plug-In 7
- At least 16 MB RAM with 32 MB recommended
- 4x CD-ROM drive

Macintosh
- System 7.x/8.x/9.x/10.x
- Macromedia Flash Player 7
- At least 16 MB RAM with 32 MB recommended

Getting Started

Windows
1. Insert the *Life Span Motor Development* CD-ROM. (Note: the CD-ROM must be present in the drive at all times.)
2. The program will launch automatically if auto insert notification is turned on. If not, proceed to the next step.
3. Use Windows® Explorer to locate the CD-ROM drive and double-click on the "start.exe" file in the root directory.
4. Once the program is started, select the Begin button from the Title screen.
5. Close your browser when you wish to exit the program.

Macintosh
1. Insert the *Life Span Motor Development* CD-ROM. (Note: the CD-ROM must be present in the drive at all times.)
2. Double-click on the "LSMD" CD icon on the desktop.
3. Double-click on the "MacStart" icon. Note Mac 8.x users: Open your browser then open the "MacStart" file.
4. Once the program is started, select the Begin button from the Title screen.
5. Close your browser when you wish to exit the program.

Video Clip Navigation

- Use the expandable tree-view directory on the right side of the screen to navigate from clip to clip.
- When you select a video clip, the title will be highlighted yellow in the tree-view directory.
- The video clips are organized into two sections under the Lab-Specific tab and Auxiliary tab. Video clips under the Lab-Specific tab relate to content in the online student labs. Lab-specific videos grouped under Set A: Guided Assessments include questions related to the video clips. Clips grouped under Set B: Practice Assessments do not include questions but provide additional assessment practice. Video clips under the Auxiliary tab relate to content in the *Life Span Motor Development, Fourth Edition,* textbook.
- For lab-specific video clips in Set A: Guided Assessments, select your answer from the choices at the bottom of the page and click the Submit button. Feedback will appear to the right of the question.
- If a video clip includes multiple questions, the Next Question button will appear. Click the Next Question button to proceed to the next question. When the question set is complete, the Next Question button will disappear and you will need to use the tree-view directory to navigate to the next video clip you wish to view.

Using the Video Player

- Click the Play button to start the clip.
- You can control the play speed of the video by moving the Speed control and then clicking and holding down on the either the forward motion Step button or the backward motion Step button. The Play button will always play the video clip at 100 percent, even if you've moved the Speed control. If you wish to reduce the speed, be sure to click on one of the Step buttons instead.
- You can view the video frame-by-frame by clicking on the forward or back motion Step buttons.
- Click the Pause button to pause the video image.
- Check the Loop box if you want the video clip to play repeatedly.

Screen Resolution

Note: The program is designed for a 1024 x 768 minimum screen area. If your monitor is set to a smaller screen area, use the following instructions to adjust it. This will allow you to see the complete screen content.

Windows
1. Right-click anywhere on your desktop.
2. Select "Display Properties" or "Properties" from the pop-up menu.
3. Select the "Settings" tab and adjust the screen area to 1024 x 768.
4. Click OK.

MACs: OS 8 and 9
1. Click on the Apple in the upper left hand corner of the screen.
2. Select Control Panels.
3. Select Monitors.
4. Select Display and highlight the resolution you need.

OSX
1. Select System Preferences from the Dock at the bottom of the desktop.
2. Select Displays.
3. Select the Display tab.
4. Highlight the resolution you need and click Confirm.

Customer Support
E-mail: support@hkusa.com
Phone: 217-351-5076 (ext. 2970)
Fax: 217-351-2674
Web site: www.HumanKinetics.com